DEATHS AND OBITUARY NOTICES

FROM THE

SOUTHERN CHRISTIAN ADVOCATE

1867–1878

BY

Brent Howard Holcomb
Certified Genealogist

HERITAGE BOOKS
2024

HERITAGE BOOKS

AN IMPRINT OF HERITAGE BOOKS, INC.

Books, CDs, and more—Worldwide

For our listing of thousands of titles see our website
at
www.HeritageBooks.com

Published 2024 by
HERITAGE BOOKS, INC.
Publishing Division
5810 Ruatan Street
Berwyn Heights, MD 20740

International Standard Book Number
Paperbound: 978-0-7884-2758-9

INTRODUCTION

The *Southern Christian Advocate* was the publication for the Methodist Conferences of South Carolina, Georgia, and Florida, for the period covered in this volume. It was published in Macon, Georgia, through the issue of May 28, 1878. After a brief hiatus the *Southern Christian Advocate* was re-established in Columbia, South Carolina, as the publication for the South Carolina Conference. Publication continued in Macon for the Georgia and Florida conferences, but the title of the newspaper was changed to the *Wesleyan Christian Advocate* with the issue of June 4, 1878.

This volume includes only death and obituary notices. There are many marriage notices contained in the issues 1867-1878, but to include those notices as well would have doubled the size of this volume and thereby would have made it too expensive. The marriage notices alone for this period would make a sizeable volume. The obituary notices are consistently placed on the last page of each issue. The column headed "Died" was usually on the third page, and usually a rather brief column, as the notices published herein indicate.

The death notices are quite important for this period, not only because of the details of the lives of the individuals including the places of birth and former residences, but because during the difficult years of reconstruction, many persons could not afford tombstones or erected only wooden markers which have not survived. The abstracts included herein are, of necessity, brief. If any notice appears to pertain, I strongly suggest obtaining a copy of the entire notice from the microfilm or from the original newspaper. Copies of such notices can be ordered from the South Caroliniana Library, USC, Columbia, SC 29208.

Brent H. Holcomb
January 25, 1993

DEATH AND OBITUARY NOTICES FROM THE SOUTHERN CHRISTIAN ADVOCATE 1867-1878

Issue of January 25, 1867

William Mackie was born in Scotland, but in 1804 he became a citizen of Augusta, Ga., where he lived -- with a short interval of residence at Sparta -- until the past Summer, when he came to Macon with the family of his son-in-law, the writer, at whose house he died, on 9th December 1866, in his 82nd year. He became a member of the Methodist Church in 1836, and lived a quiet, unobtrusive, simple Christian life.... The companion of many years of joy and trial, Mrs. Sarah Mackie, had preceded him a few months, aged about 76 years. She was a daughter of Mr. Isaac Herbert-- for years known as one of the patriarchal citizens of Augusta-- who with his sainted wife were friends of the earliest Methodist preachers-- of Hope Hull, of Bishop Asbury, and many others.... E. H. Myers.

Capt. F. W. Bailey, of Savannah, died of Cholera, the last of October in the 60th year of his age [eulogy].

Mrs. Roxey Ramsey, wife of S. A. Ramsey, was born May 30th 1820, and died near Gainsville, Fla., Oct. 26th 1866. She joined the M. E. Church, South, in 1848... She and her very king hearted husband then lived in Tampa, in whose house the writer found at all times, a very hospitable reception... She leaves a husband and seven children. W. K. Turner.

Joseph Lawrence died near Lawrenceville, Ala., on the 21st October 1866 at about 66 years of age. He removed from Georgia to this State upwards of twenty years ago and settled in Henry Co., where he has lived ever since.... It may be said with emphasis, that he was the father of the community in which he lived, of the village which bears his name, and the Church of which h was a member.... W. K. Norton.

Issue of February 1, 1867

Died.

December 20, 1866, Little Willie Bartow, infant son of Dr. Willoughby and Anna Bartlow, of Burke Co., Ga.

Obituary.

James Shackelford died in Early co., Ga., on the 28th Dec. 1866, in the 81st year of his age. He was born in Georgetown, S. C., married and settled in Abbeville Dist., and removed to Georgia in 1840. He was rom his early manhood, a member of the Methodist E. Church. [eulogy]

Rev. William V. Burney, of the M. E. Church, died on 8th October 1866 in Tuskegee, Ala., after a long and protracted illness. He was born in Green co., Ga., Sept. 14th 1805, and at the age of twenty-one he commenced the practice of law.... He leaves a bereaved widow and six children.

Willie M., elder son of Dr. Wm. and Arabella Hafer, of Marshallville, Ga., died on the 18th January 1867, aged nearly thirteen years. [eulogy]

Mrs. Sarah Dunwody, daughter of Benjamin and Susannah Sutton, was born in Edgefield District, S. C., January 30th 1798, and died in Houston co., Ga., Jan. 2nd, 1867, in the 69th year of her age. She joined the M. E. Church, in Twiggs co., Ga., in 1822, and was married to the Rev. Jas. Dunwody, of the Georgia Conference 6th May 1823. [eulogy]

Mrs. Sarah A. wife of Dr. John H. Thomas, died on Chunnenuggee Ridge, Jan. 9th 1867. She was the daughter of Samuel and Elizabeth Hunter and was born in Clarke co., Ga., Dec. 10th 1813. At

1

a very early age she joined the Methodist Church.... She lived to see all of her children members of the Church. W. M. Motley.

Mrs. Mollie E. Bentley, eldest daughter of Milton M. and Miriam M. Bentley, aged 15 years, died in Henry co., Ga., Dec. 27, 1866. She joined the Church in Sept. 1865....

Tribute of Respect on the death of Miss Julia Whitten, teacher in Mt. Zion S. School, Crawford ct., Montgomery Conference.

Issue of February 8, 1867

Mrs. Virginia A. Braden, widow of Dr. James A. Braden, was born near Fredericksburg, Va., and died in Jacksonville, Fla., Jan. 4th, 1867, in the 53d year of her age. She was the sister of the late lamented Col. George T. Ward of Virginia, who settled near Tallahassee when she was quite young... About 1846, she was confirmed in the Episcopal Church, of which she continued a consistent and exemplary member for about eight years. On 5th of March [1854] she and her husband joined the M. E. Church, South... F. A. Branch.

Mary B. Golsan, wife of Col. J. H. Golsan, and daughter of Mage H. P. Brodnax, was born in Georgia, Oct. 29th 1821, and died in Autaugaville, Ala., Oct. 28th 1866. Sister G. professed religion in 1838 and joined the Methodist Church... [eulogy] A. J. Briggs.

Died, Oct. 18th 1866, Mrs. Harriet P. Wood, wife of Benj. J. Wood, of Johnson Co., Ga., in her 25th year. She was a devoted wife, a kind and tender mother and a good neighbor. [eulogy]

Dr. J. G. Jenkins, son of Rev. James Jenkins, formerly of the South Carolina Conference, was born March 2d, 1805, and died in peace and hope at Orangeburg, Aug. 10, 1866. For 25 years he labored as a practitioner of medicine in St. Matthews Parish.... In '62 and '63 he represented Orange Parish in the State Legislature.

Issue of February 15, 1867

James P. Hockenhull was born in Forsyth co., Ga., Dec. 4th 1842, and died at New Market, Tenn., on the 5th Dec., 1863, the 7th day after he had received his mortal wound, aged twenty years and one day. [eulogy] Goodman Hughes.

Mr. Charles B. Stone, died near Adairsville, Ga., on 2d January, 1867, aged about 35 years. He was formerly and for several years a resident of Macon... He had been for a number of years a member of the Presbyterian Church. [eulogy]

Miss Ella Virginia Crawford, died on 7th January, at her brother's in Davis co., Texas, of typhoid pneumonia, in the 18th year of her age. She left Monroe co., Ga., about 1st of Nov. last to see a home in the West, and was taken sick on her journey....

Amanda Josephine Jinkins, died in Shelby, N. C., Dec. 5, 1866, aged 13 years. She was the daughter of Olive and Matilda Jinkins. Her mother dying when she was an infant, her training devolved upon her grandmother... Jno. W. North.

John Boring Smith, son of Rev. Sidney M. Smith, late of Forsyth, Ga., died with consumption at the residence of his widowed mother, in Jefferson co., Ga., on 14th Dec 1866 in his 20th year. [eulogy]

Issue of February 22, 1867

Died

Of cholera infantum, on the 2nd day of Feb 1867, in Jackson co., Ga., Charley O. Whitehead, only child of sister Jane and brother Marcus J. Whitehead, aged four months and 15 days.

In Burke co., Ga., Dec. 20th 1867, Floyd Willoughby De Gilsie, only child of Dr. Willoughby and Anna E. Barton, aged 9 months and 18 days.

Little Charlie Gordon, infant son of W. P. and Lee Graham, aged 9 months and 6 days was left along on 10th January for a few minutes, was heard to scream; his mother and father ran to him and found his clothing in a blaze of flame. In about two short hours the spirit had fled.

Obituary.

Major Joseph Koger. Extract from the proceedings of the Senate of the State of Mississippi, Tuesday, Jan. 11, 1867.... Mississippi whose interested he served so long and faithfully was not his native State, but the home of his adoption. He was born in Colleton District, South Carolina, Oct. 27th 1779... for twenty years he was a member of the Senate and House of Representatives of South Carolina. He came to our State in 1838. Major Koger was for more than fifty-five years a member of the Methodist Church. He died on Saturday, Aug 25, 1866, and on the next day his remains were removed to Soule Chapel, where as funeral discourse was delivered by Rev. E. Callaway, who had been his pastor more than forty years ago.

Major Augustus G. Nagel was born in Anhalt, Germany, and died in Macon, Ga., Dec. 26th 1866, aged about 80 years. His father and two brothers were ministers of the gospel in the Presbyterian Church... In early manhood he made a tour of the United States, and having married a lady in Edgefield Dist., S. C., settled permanently there, where he raised a large family. He was the last surviving member of the old Savannah Guards of 1812. [eulogy]

Mrs. E. M. Pharr was born in Baldwin county, Ga., 1842, and died at her mother's residence, Mrs. Winiford West, Feb. 1st, 1867. She joined the Baptist Church in 1859, was married to Rev. T. A. Pharr, of the Georgia Conference, Oct. 28th 1862, and joined the Methodist Church in Clinton in 1863.

Peter Vaught, Sr., died in Horry District, S. C., Jan 19th 1867, in his 80th year. He was one of the oldest, perhaps the oldest citizen of the District. For many years he held offices of trust and honor in his Parish, of which he was representative in the Legislature until the exhaustion of his vigorous body by age.... G. H. Wells.

Mrs. Ann Rahn died the 6th February, aged 50 years. [eulogy]

Rev. Thomas Cliffs, who emigrated from Colleton District, S. C., about forty years ago and settled in Lowndes co., Ga., died 13 Nov 1865 [sic], after a short illness.... William Smith.

Leveret A. Osborne of Anderson C. H., S. C., was born in 1813, and died Jan. 20th 1867. He was converted and joined the M. E. Church in 1842. [eulogy] John M. Carlisle

Tribute of Respect to the Memory of Robert H. Vickers, First Quarterly Conference, Washington Station, Ga., Jan. 12th 1867. On the 16th Dec. last, at about 8 o'clock in the afternoon he was stricken with paralysis and died at 10 1/2 o'clock.

Issue of March 1, 1867

Mrs. Mary Lemle, died of paralysis at the residence of her son-in-law, Dr. Roger K. Dixon, in Jefferson county, on the 15th of January in the eightieth year of her age. [eulogy]

Theodore A. Beall, son of John H. and Martha A. Beall, was born January 1845 and died of spinal affection January 14, 1867, in Taliaferro county, Ga. He was converted September 1866 and joined the church....

Issue of March 8, 1867

Major David Meriwether died in Monticello, Jasper co., Ga., on Friday, the 18th of January, 1867, in the 67th year of his age, leaving a wife and nine children, together with a large family connexion and numerous friends to mourn his death. He was a native of Oglethorpe co., Ga., but in early manhood removed to Jasper co., where he has resided for about 42 years....

Mrs. Mary V. Adams, wife of B. B. Adams, and daughter of sister Little, of Milledgeville, died at the residence of her mother on 2d February, 1867. At the age of twelve she embraced religion and joined the Methodist church. [eulogy]

Conway Mayson, Esq., died in Edgefield District, S. C., on 4th February, aged 63 years. The deceased was a consistent member of the Methodist Episcopal Church for about 37 years... He leaves a companion and several children to mourn their irreparable loss.

Miss Laura Julia, daughter of Job and Julia Thompson, was born in Macon co., Ala., April 25th 1846, and died at Union Springs, Jan. 24th, 1867. [eulogy]

Mrs. Elizabeth Graham, wife of Martin Graham, died in Forsyth county, Ga., on the 8th February 1867, in the 57th year of her age... Wm. A. Simmons.

Sister Catherine Cox, wife of B. R. Cox, died Dec. 25, 1866, in the 64th year of her age. She had for over thirty years been a member of the M. E. Church, South. W. B. McH.

My father, Thomas McHan, died in Christ on the 16th of August 1866, aged over four-score years. W. B. McHan.

Issue of March 15, 1867

Miss Mary S. Whitaker, daughter of Samuel S. Whitaker, died in Baldwin county, Ga., Jan. 18th 1867, in the 20th year of her age.

William Warwick, eldest son of the late Rev. Wiley Warwick, died in Dahlonega, Ga., February 7, 1867, in his 74th year. G. Hughes

Mrs. Rachel Smith, wife of Mr. W. R. Smith and daughter of Rev. Jordan Flanders, died in Emanuel county, Georgia, February 18th 1867. She left a husband and a large family of children.... S. S. Bouchelle.

Issue of March 22, 1867

George Penney was born in Newberry Dist., S. C., Feb. 22d, 1785, and died in Ellaville, Ga., Jan. 21st, 1867. ...his 46th year he joined the M. E. Church. He reared eight children by his first marriage; four survive him, and are living in the faith. He was happily married the second time to Mrs. Nancy McKallar, who still survives him.... Susie M. S. Berry.

James Nicholas Taylor died in Sumter co., Ga., Nov. 5, 1866, in the 62nd year of her age. In 1834 he embraced religion and joined the Methodist Church under the ministry of Rev. Sam'l Anthony....

Mrs. Lucretia Ballough died in Savannah, 25th Feb., in the 66th year of her age. She was born in Bridgeport, Conn., but had been a resident of Savannah, mostly, for 46 years....

George W. Funches, only son of Jacob S. and Sarah A. Funches, was born in Orangeburg Dist., S. C., Sept. 29th 1846, and died Feb. 8, 1867. He joined the M. E. Church in Oct. 1865 and realized peace with God the 2d of Feb. 1867.... W. W. Jones

Issue of March 29, 1867

Sister Martha A. Rushing was born in Colleton District, S. C., April 11th 1813, and married the Rev. R. R. Rushing, December 9th, 1829. Her religious life dates from her eleventh year, when she was converted and joined the M. E. Church... killed on the night of 28th of February last....

Issue of April 5, 1867

Mrs. Susannah Williams was born in Scriven co., Ga., Jan. 24th, 1803, and died in Madison co., Fla., Dec. 22nd, 1866. Her maiden named was Lewis. She was married to Roland Williams in Bulloch county, Ga., April 24.

Mrs. Harriet Shackelford, wife of Jas. Shackelford, died in Early co., Ga., January 20, in the 67th year of her age. Only a few weeks intervened between the death of this excellent lady and that of her husband. [eulogy]

Mrs. M. E. Bullock, wife of James Bullock, was born 8th May 1827, professed religion and joined the M. E. Church South in 1850, and died in Monroe, Walton co., Ga., March 8th, 1867. [eulogy]

Solomon Laney, (or uncle Solomon, as he was more familiarly known) was born in Edgefield District, S. C., January 17th 1807, and died in Carroll co., Ga., February 11th, 1867, of cancerous affection. He joined the M .E. Church in his twenty-first year....

Mary A. Latimer, wife of W. T. Latimer, died in Abbeville District, S. C., on the 3d March 1867, in her 26th year of age. She had been a consistent member of the M. E. Church for near 13 years....

Tribute of Respect from Second Q. C. Glennville Station, Montgomery Conference, to Mrs. Elizabeth Glenn, relict of Rev. Jas. E. Glenn.

Mrs. Mary Powel, my grandmother, died near Darien, Ga., March 6th, 1867, in the 77th year of her age. Susie M. S. Berry.

Issue of April 12, 1867

Wm. T. West was born July 17th ,1840, and died Jan 29th, 1867. The disease of which he died was contracted in the army... Bro. West has left a wife and two children....

Capt. Wm. H. Dorsey was born in Franklin county, Georgia, on the 7th of August 1810. In his youth his parents removed to Habersham county, where he lived until about twenty one years ago, since which time he has been in Athens, Ga., where he died March 27th, 1867. He joined the Methodist Church when he was about fourteen years of age.... As a citizen, he has filled several important offices-- Justices of the Peace, Marshal of the town, Public Auctioneer, Clerk of Council, Town Treasurer and Justices of the Inferior Court.... H. H. Parks.

Richardson Hancock died in Madison County, Georgia, on 20th of February 1867. He was born in Franklin county, North Carolina, 27th Oct 1789, moved to George in the year 1811, was married in 1812, and joined the M. E. Church soon thereafter.... C. A. Mitchell

Mrs. Mary Smith died on 14th March 1867, in Abbeville District, S. C. She was born in Newberry District, 25th March 1805, and was for about 35 years a faithful and consistent member of the Methodist Church. She was twice married, in 1823, to George Cameron, and in 1855 to William Cutlino Smith, who survives her.

Issue of April 19, 1867

Henry Tate was born Jan. 16, 1801, and died Dec. 8, 1866. His death was very sudden. Old age found him a class leader, and now he is missed by the band of Christians who worship at Gethsemane. An official member, and a man of true worth is lost to Pacolet ct. He reared a large and pious family, of which two are now stewards of the Church.... J. E. Watson.

Rev. Jno. C. Wright, a local preacher of the Coweta circuit was born in Clarke co., Ga., 31st Dec. 1803, educated at Salem in the same county, licensed to exhort while at school by Rev. Whitman C. Hill in 1823 and at the close of the same year was licensed to preach by the District Conference, Rev. Samuel K. Hodges, P. E. He immediately joined the South Carolina Conference. He was employed at the time of his death by the P. E. of the LaGrange District to serve the Houston

Mission. On the 27th Feb. last while at the supper table of a brother Turner, he was struck with paralysis... He lived after the stroke four days.... R. F. Jones.

Martha Ann Jennette Gowan was born 16th June 1838, and died in Morgan co., on 30th March 1867, aged 28 years, 7 months and 14 days. She was married to Dr. R. A. Gowan 22d July 1858.... Her mother came to see her the next day and remained till her death. R. A. Gowan.

Tribute of Respect to Rev. Jno G. Wright, who died March 4, 1867, by the Lodge of F. & A. Masons at Haralson.

Issue of April 26, 1867

Mrs. Kate Senter was born in Monroe co., Tenn., Feb. 9th 1832, was married to Mr. A. N. Senter in 1853 and died in Dalton Ga., Jan. 27th 1867, aged 35 years.

Mrs. Rachel S. Coxwell, wife of Mr. John D. Coxwell, and daughter of Joel and Rebecca English, was born in Glasscock co., Ga., Aug. 10, 1854, and died April 1, 1867. W. Lane.

Hon. Willard Boynton died in Lumpkin, Stewart co., Ga., on the 30th September 1866. He was a native of Vermont, removed when a young man to the county of Twiggs, Ga., where he intermarried with a Miss Bryan....

Mrs. A. S. Hollinshead, relict of William Hollinshead, was born in Richland District, S. C., April 17th 1787, moved to Houston co., Ga., Feb. 15th, 1831, and died at the house of her son-in-law, W. J. Anderson in Fort Valley, March 7th 1867, where she had come on a visit. She had been a member of the Baptist church.

Dr. James Thweatt died in Monroe co., Ga., APril 4th, 1867. He was a native of Hancock co., Ga. he died in the 74th year of his age. [eulogy] W. G. Allen

Issue of May 3, 1867

Mrs. Mary L. Johnson, wife of Calvin E. Johnson, and daughter of James K. Redd, died in Columbus, Ga., April 1, 1867, in the 30th year of her age, having been about fourteen years a faithful member of the M. E. Church, South. [eulogy] L. Pierce.

Margaret W. Will, wife of the late Robert W. Will, of Charleston, S. C., died January 17th, 1867, in her 75th year. In 1809, she gave herself to the Church... Her body sleeps near the altar of Bethel Church, in Charleston, where she was converted....

Mrs. Mary E. Hawkins, only child of Jno. and Ann S. Finn, and wife of Col. Willis A. Hawkins, was born in Augusta, Ga., Sept. 17, 1832, and died in Americus, Ga., March 26th, 1867. She was a graduate of the Wesleyan Female College, although she did not join the Church until after her marriage in 1856.... Geo. G. N. MacDoneld.

Mrs. Mary Redding, widow of Rev. Arthur Redding, died at the residence of her son-in-law, in Chattahoochee county, Ga., March 20th, 1867. She was born in North Carolina, Feb. 12th, 1780, and was there married to Peyton R. Clemmons, removed to Georgia and settled in Putnam co., where both herself and husband were converted and joined the M. E. Church... W. G. Hanson.

Olin B. Davis, son-in-law of R. W. Burnham, of Charleston, S. C., died at Columbia, S. C., Dec. 9th, 1865, aged twenty-five years. He was a native of Beaufort District, S. C., where he spent his life in agricultural pursuits... leaves his smitten wife and his bereaved mother and family.

Charles S. Sorrells was born in Madison co., Ga., on 14th October 1802, and died 20th December 1866, at Monroe, Walton co,. aged 64 years. He embraced religion in 1859, and became a member of the M. E. Church, South....

Mrs. Susan H. Lowman, wife of W. G. Lowman, formerly of Macon co., Ga., and daughter of L. R. and M. E. Brewer, died in Griffin, Ga., 16th March 1867, aged 22 years...

Martha Rebecca, daughter of J. S. and Mary Chipley was born 31st Dec 1853 and died 10 Feb. 1867, of acute rheumatism.

William T. King, was born in Green co., Ga., and died suddenly in Muscogee co., in his 62nd year. He joined the Methodist Church when but a boy... In 1829, he moved to Morgan co., and held his membership in Madison until 1838, where he removed to Harris, and remained a member in Hamilton until his death.

Miss Mary Jane Wood, daughter of Rev. Isham J. Wood, of Clay co., died on 19th Jan. 1867, at the residence of Mr. Robt. B. Livingston, in Covington, Ga. She was, at the time of her death, a member of the Senior class of the Southern Masonic Female College. Gustavus J. Orr, President S. M. F. College.

Mrs. Nancy H. Allen, the daughter of Hardy B. Stanley, was born in Laurens co., Ga., July 25th, 1821,; married Bryan Allen of the same place in 1838; moved to Floyd co., Ga., in 1841; lost her husband in August 1851, since which time she lived a widow, and died April 13, 1867. For the last ten years she lived a consistent member of the M. E. Church.

Tribute of Respect by Oxford Lodge, Knight of Jericho, to Rev. Dabney P. Jones, so long and favorably known in Georgia.

Tribute of Respect. Trinity Church, Greenville Circuit, Georgia Conference. Sister Amy Parham, was born October 20, 1787, and died July 17th 1866, in her 79th year.

Issue of May 10, 1867

Rev. William J. Gantrell, son of Col. H. Gantrell, was born in Columbia co., Ga., Aug. 5th, 1827, embraced religion in 1844; received license to exhort in 1848, license to preach in 1852, and was ordained in 1858, and died 13th April 1867. He emigrated from near Resaca, Ga., to Marion co., Fla. in 1864.

Rev. Fielding Pope, was born in Goochland co., Va., Nov. 24th, 1800, and died at Lumpkin, Ga., March 23rd, 1867. In early life his parents removed from Virginia to Kentucky, where he resided until he entered the Theological College at Maryville, Tenn., where he completed his literary and theological course. He was afterwards called to the pastorate of the Presbyterian Church at Athens, Tenn.... [account] ...removed to Lumpkin, Ga., and served the Presbyterian Church until his useful life was terminated. L. J. Davies

Hon. Joseph Day, died on ___ April, in Vineville. He had reached the ordinary limit of life.

Mrs. Mary H. Parrish, wife of Henry C. Parrish, was born May 8th, 1820, and died in Oglethorpe co., Ga., March 25, 1867. D. J. Myrick

Tribute of Respect from quarterly conference of Union ct., Montgomery Conference, April 18, 1867, to Brother Samuel C. Rutland.

Tribute of Respect to E. Moses Brundage, who was for several years a Steward of this circuit... J. B. Cottrell, P. E.

Issue of May 17, 1867

The Rev. Barnett Smith was born in Union Dist., S. C., July 1790, and died at the residence of his son-in-law, W. H. Martin, in Laurence District, April 2nd 1867. [account] F. Auld.

Dr. Henry F. Solomon, third son of John and Rebecca Solomon, was born inTalcot co., Ga., Feb. 28, 1830, and died in Dale co., Ala., April 13th 1867. He was married to Bethenia Steward, Nov. 24th 1852. John W. Solomon.

Sister Mary Edwards died in Vineville, Ga., on 30th of March, aged 81 years. Her maiden name was Hill. She was first married to James Daniel in 1805, who died in 1816. In the year 1827 she was married to Rev. Robert L. Edwards of the Georgia conference. J. S. Key.

Miss Martha Rebecca Branda died February 10th 1867....

Issue of May 24, 1867

Children

Another little Sabbath-school scholar has passed from "Time to Eternity." Little Charlie Hudson, died near Ellaville, Ga., April 3d, aged 8 years 10 months and 13 days. [eulogy] Susie M. S. Berry

Milton Cloud, only son of J. F. and Sarah Cloud, died in Fairfield Dist., March 13th 1867. D. W. Seale.

Obituary

Judge James Woodruff died at the residence of his son-in-law, Mr. A. Nabors, near Montevallo, Shelby co., Ala., Feb. 14th, 1867, in the 79th year of his age. He was a native of Southern Georgia, and was educated at Athens. He commenced the practice of law in Monticello, Ga., when quite a young man, where he was united in marriage to Miss Agatha Medlock. By an unfortunate suit at law he lost his property. He then (about 1826) removed to Shelby Co., Ala. In 1834 he was elected Judge of Probate.... He had been spending some time with his son in Mississippi, and was on his returned to Ala., to spend the remnant of his days with Mrs. A. Nabors, when by a rail road accident, he received injuries which terminated in his death. R. S. Woodward

Mrs. Anna Edens, died near Clio, S. C., Feb. 19th, 1867. She was the daughter of Nathan Thomas and was first married to James McDaniel. Her first husband being suddenly taken from her, she, after the lapse of several years, was married to Rev. Allen Edens, who about twelve years ago passed away to the better land.... Her first husband, herself and their only child, were riding out when suddenly their horse dashed into the woods, and the husband and darling boy were killed. By the death of her second husband she was again left a widow with all the responsibilities of raising three daughters. Lewis M. Hamer

Maj. John Hodnett was born in Prince Edward co., Va., March 10th 1786, and died in Merriwether co., Ga., March 14th, 1867, aged 81 years and 4 days. During his boyhood his parents removed to Oglethorpe co., Ga. He performed two terms of service during the war of 1812-1815, in the latter of which he served as captain of a company. Wm. Park.

Miss Fannie Louse Graham, formerly of Newton co., Ga., died at heart disease in Egpyt, Miss., April 12th, 1867. She was left an orphan at a tender age in the hands of her uncle, the late Yverson L. Graves.

Mrs. Rhoda Maria Rea, wife of William T. Rea, was born in 1818, and died in Subligan, Chattooga co., Ga., on 15th April 1867. J. D. Anthony.

Mrs. Elizabeth A. Black, wife of John B. Black, died 16th March 1867. She was born in Newberry, S. C., 21st February 1817, and when only twelve years old, became a member of the M. E. Church. W. Martin

Mrs. C. A. Treadwell, wife of Hardy Treadwell, and daughter of Rev. Hiram and Cynthia Pendergrass, died January 10, 1867, in Atlanta, in her 40th year. W. H. Evans

Sister Eliza Ann Morris, was born in Jackson co., Ga., May 11th 1815, and died March 2nd, 1867. She joined the M. E. church in her youth.

Dr. Wm. H. Clark, son of the lamented Dr. Samuel B. Clark, of Brotherville, Ga., was born May 14th, 1840, graduated at Emory College in 1859, at the Augusta Medical College in 1861, served as a soldier, and died at the home of his pious mother, March 29th, 1867.

Mrs. Martha Sumpter, died in White co., Ga., March 24, in the 83d year of her age....

Tribute of Respect from the second Quarterly Conference to Eatonton station, to Wm. B. Carter.

Tribute of Respect by the Quarterly Conference, Ft. Valley Ct., S. Ga. Conference, to Lewis Avant, who died on Wednesday last, the 17th inst.

Tribute of Respect to Rev. William J. Gartrell, a local deacon of the Ocala circuit, who died April 13th, 1867, by the Ocala Quarterly Conference, at Flemington, East Fla.

Issue of May 31, 1867

Judge Turner H. Trippe died suddenly in Bartow co., Ga., on Sabbath morning, January 20th, 1867.

Mrs. Margaret Searcy, died near Griffin, Ga., March 23d, in the 75th year of her age. A few days before she died, after joyously testifying to her husband, Rev. B. R. Searcy, and some relatives present, of her deathless faith. R. W. Bigham

Sister Catharine Beach was born in Delaware, Nov. 22nd, 1772, and died in Talbot co., Ga., April 15th, 1867, in her 95th year.

Mrs. Sicily Coke Wilson, wife of Thomas Wilson, and daughter of Rev. Wm. M. Menefee, was born in Chambers co., Ala., Jan. 26, 1836, and died in Cotton Valley, Macon co,. March 31, 1867.

Mrs. Anna McDaniels was born in Abbeville District, in 1793, professed religion in Alabama, and joined the Presbyterian Church at Robison's Cross Roads, and died 25th March 1867, at her son's, Dr. Jas. McDaniels, in Pike co., Ala.

Mrs. Mary Treadwell, relict of Mr. Samuel Treadwell, was born in Newark, N. J.. January 29th, 1777, and died of pneumonia, at the residence of her son-in-law, Rev. John P. Margart, in Barbour co., Ala., September 26th, 1866. [eulogy] Southern Lutheran and Camden Journal, S. C., will please copy. J. P. Margart

John M. Pearson was born near Raleigh, N. C., in 1802, in 1825 came to Ga., and in 1849 removed to Tallapoosa co., Ala., where he died April 5th, 1867. L. R. Bell

Azariah Bostick, died in Monroe co., Ga., March 18th.

Mrs. Sarah K. Bridges, wife of Thomas Bridges of Schley co., Ga., was born July 4th, 1804, in Marion District, S. C., was married Dec. 28th 1826, and died May 2nd, 1867, while on a visit to her daughter Mrs. John E. Cox., Macon co., Ga.

Tribute of Respect from Quarterly Conference of Hamilton Circuit, S. Ga., to William G. King.

Tribute of Respect from Quarterly Conference for Buena Vista Ct., S. Ga., to Brother Seaborn McMichael, who died on the night of the 19th March.

Issue of June 7, 1867

Samuel Goodwin died March 21st, 1867, in Colleton District, S. C., aged 32 years... T. J. Clyde.

Eliza Jane Castleberry, wife of Mr. S. G. Castleberry and daughter of Mr. M. and Mrs. C. Bell, was born in Haywood co., N. C., May 5th, 1825, and died in White co., near Nacoochee, Ga., March 5th, 1867. H. H. Walker

Mr. Samuel Pearse, of Columbia, S. C., died at the residence of his son-in-law, A. W. Lewis, in Augusta, Ga., March 10th, 1867, in the 73d year of his age. He was a native of Charleston, S., C., where in 1812, he joined the M. E. Church under the ministry of Rev. W. M. Kennedy. In 1817, he moved to Columbia, S. C.... He has left a widow and one daughter with several grand children.

Mrs. M. A. M. Heidle, daughter of Pelatiah and Sarah Whitehurst, died in Leon co., Fla., April 15th, 1867, in the 51st year of her age.

Eugenius S. Thompson, aged 14 years, died near Salem, Clarke co,. Ga., 9th April 1867....

Mrs. Annie W. Pooser, wife of Mr. Edward Pooser, late of Newnansville, Fla., was born in Beaufort, S. C., in 1845, and died in Waldo, Fla., on 2d April, 1867. She removed to Newnansville in 1863.

Mrs. Catharine Louisa Oeland, died at the residence of her daughter Mrs. Dr. Vernon in Spartanburg, S. C., on 5th May 1867, aged 80 years, 4 months and 1 day... five children... Mrs. Oeland was a native of Charleston, and her maiden name was Clark. She was married first to Mr. William Faber and then to Mr. John Oeland. In early life she claimed her place in the Lutheran Church, but in after years, when separated from early associations by her removed to Spartanburg District, she became a member of the Methodist Church.

Mrs. Mary Jane McGehee, wife of Mr. A. C. McGehee, of Columbus, Ga., and daughter of Mr. B. Watkins, of Monroe co,. Ga., died 23d April in her 28th year. J. E. Evans

Seaborn McMichael was born August 8th 1805, and died near Buena Vista, Ga., March 20, 1867. The companion of his youth had passed on before him only a few months. J. E. Evans

Mrs. Sarah R. Shivers, died in Griffin Ga., May 17th 1807, at the residence of Dr. J. H. Connally, in the fifty-seventh year of her age. In 1859 she removed with her husband to Texas to better the fortunes of their children. Not long after, she lost her husband and one son soon after. When the South called upon her sons to defend their rights, she gave her only two surviving sons to the cause.

John E. Flournoy, oldest son of Rev. Robt. W. Flournoy, of the South Georgia Conference, died in Thomas co., Ga., 26th May 1867, aged 15 years, 3 months and 12 days. N. S. Bousley

Tribute of Respect from 2nd quarterly conference of the Bethel circuit, S. Ga., Conference, to Rev. Peyton L. Wade.

Tribute of Respect from 2nd quarterly conference of the Vienna circuit, S. Ga., Conference, to Brother S. N. Lasseter, who died in Vienna, Dooly co., on March 11th, 1867. Brother Lassiter was born in Abbeville District, S. C., in 1812, removed to Georgia in early life.

Tribute of Respect from the M. E. Church at Thomson to Brother A. L. Massengale, who died May 19th.

Issue of June 14, 1867

Miss Elender Trader, died May 5th 1867 at Richmond Factory, Richmond co., Ga., in the 28th year of her age. She was born in S. C., Dec. 25th 1839. When she was about 12, her parents moved to Ga.

Sarah Adella, second daughter of Mr. S. M. and Mrs. Ellen Moorer, died in Orangeburg Dist., S., C., on 19th May, after an illness of one week, in her 14th year. William Hutto

Mrs. Christian Mood, one of the eldest and best members of our church, Columbia, S. C., was born at St. James Goose Creek, 6 Oct 1800, married to William Morgan in 1818, soon left a widow, again

1827 married to Rev. Christian Mood, whose relict she remained... her death on 12th May. She leaves the rich inheritance of her faith to her only child and to her children, who are all communicants of the same church.... By her influence, Bethel church was formed. M. Martin

Mr. Thomas Wayland, was born in Frome, Somersetshire, England. He left England in 1832 and commenced a long and useful career as a teacher of youth in this country, at Pendleton, S. C. He subsequently taught in Sparta, Warrenton and Marietta, Ga. He died in Marietta, Ga., 5th of Feb. 1867.

Mrs. Mary Ann Ballew, wife of Major John G. Ballew, died in Lenoir, N. C., May 25, 1867, aged 34 years, 4 months and 29 days.

D. T. B. Holland, youngest son of Dr. W. T. and Mrs. J. E. Holland, died April 24th, 1867, aged 14 years, 3 months and 3 days.

Tribute of Respect to John C. Stubblefield by Mulberry Street Sunday School in Macon.

Tribute of Respect by Quarterly Conference, Little River Circuit, North Georgia Conference, to Rev. G. G. Norman.

Issue of June 21, 1867

Died

Lee Hampton, son of Rev. O. L. and Mrs. Amanda N. Smith, aged 1 year, four months and four days in Quitman, Brooks county, Ga., on the 14th of June 1867.

Obituary

George Thomas was born in Richmond County, North Carolina, February 27, 1797, and died at Lowndesboro, Ala., March 16, 1867, aged 70 years. He served 3 or 4 years in the Legislature of North Carolina. In 1840 he moved to Montgomery county, Ala. B. F. Perry

Barnard C. Wagner, only remaining son of John Wagner deceased, and step-son of Robt McIntire of Savannah, died January 12 in his 25th year.

Mrs. Mary A. Davies, wife of C. H. Davies and daughter of L. C. Coppedge, was born in Randolph co., Ga., January 9, 1837, died at Hawkinsville, Ga., May 30, 1867. J. J. Morgan

Mrs. Carrie M. Stewart, wife of W. H. Stewart and daughter of Charles and Agnes Morris, was born in Pendleton, S. C. She spent 8 years of her childhood in Atlanta, and at the age of 12 moved to Sparta, where she died May 21, aged 25 years. A. J. Jarrell

Mrs. Amanda B. Webb, wife of John Webb of Thomaston, Ga., was killed in a buggy accident June 3, in the 47th year of her age. John W. Reynolds

Mrs. E. Eugenia Crews, wife of T. B. Crews of Laurensville, S. C., died of consumption, 25th May 1867 in her 34th year. She was the daughter of Mr. and Mrs. William Hance.

Tribute of Respect by Bennettsville circuit, S. C. Conference to James C. Thomas.

Tribute of Respect by Bennettsville circuit, S. C. Conference to John McCollum, a citizen of Marlboro District, who died 11 May 1867.

<u>Issue of June 28, 1867</u>

Died

in Monticello, Ga., April 6th, Susan Elizabeth, only child of Samuel and George R. Fulton, aged 4 months and 11 days.

Obituary

Died, in Columbus, Ga., on the 5th inst., Leonora, daughter of Frank A. and Arabella C. Nisbet, of Russell co., Ala., aged 17 years and 2 months.

Lewis Smith Avant was born in Washington co., Ga., Sept 5th 1802, and died of bronchitis in Crawford Co., Ga., April 17, 1867. I. L. Avant

Mrs. Aurelia Kenan, relict of Hon. Thos H. Kenan, a resident of Baldwin co., Ga., died at the residence of Col. Horne in Griffin, Ga., June 2, 1867, aged about 95 years. R. W. Bigham

<u>Issue of July 5, 1867</u>

Died

on April 20th, Mrs. Sallie E. Harrison, daughter of Dr. J. M. Sullivan, of Greenville Dist., S. C.

Obituary

My friend Thos. Eison and his wife Mary J. Eison, with several of the younger members of their family, left Union Dist., S. C., last fall for East Tennessee. Beatty Hughes, a son of Mrs. Eison by a former husband, was the oldest of the children who left thus. He was born January 23, 1850, and was drowned after their arrival in Tennessee, in the French Broad, March 17, 1867. J. W. Kelly

Mrs. Mary Jane Greer, wife of William H. Greer and daughter of Richard and Serena Rucker, died in Taylor Co., Ga., May 8th 1867.

Mrs. Martha A. B. Venable, wife of Captain John M. Venable, was born January 13, 1824, and died June 14, 1867.

William M. Varnum was born in Amherst co., Va., March 9, 1811. Early in life removed with his parents to Georgia. He joined the M. E. Church at Dahlonega and married Miss Susan L. Saxon, of Twiggs co., and died there May 27, 1867.

Mrs. Mary Ann Strickland was born Feb. 1794 and died 21 May 1867. Reidsville, June 12, 1867.

<u>Issue of July 12, 1867</u>

Moses Chappel Heath died at his residence near Waxhaw, Lancaster District, S. C., 30 May 1867, aged 61 years, 3 months, and 10 days.... L. Wood

Mrs. Hester Hemmingway died in Conwayboro, S. C., June 11, 1867, aged about 55 years. J. H. C. McKinney

Georgie, infant son of Dr. Joseph F. and Mrs. Lottie C. Harrell, died March 5, 1867, in Conwayboro.

Mrs. Mary Ann Day, wife of Joseph Day, was born Nov. 22, 1811, in Washington co,. Tenn., and died June 1, 1867, at Oak Bowery, Ga. Joe H. C.

Rev. Lewis Ledbetter, pastor of Broad River ct., was a native of Greene Co., and died June 10, aged 49. W. R. Branham

Col. John L. Woodward was born in Brunswick co., Va., 1804. His parents moved to Hancock co., Ga., in 1805. In 1822 he moved to Monroe co., Ga., where he lived many years. In 1866 he moved to Indian Springs, where he died 18 June 1867.

Issue of July 19, 1867

James R. DuBose, Sr., was born in Sumter Dist., S. C., spent most of his life in Washington, Ga., and died in Abbeville Dist., S. C., in his 60th year.

Rev. Mahlon Bedell was born in Burke co,. N. C., Oct. 8th 1806, licensed to preach in 1826.... in the Ga. Conference and the Florida Conference.

Sarah C. Spencer, wife of Capt. John B. Spencer, died at White Springs, Fla., 31 May 1867. She was a daughter of Mrs. Thos. E. Hardee, born in Camden Co., Ga., May 17, 1834.

Rev. G. G. Norman, a native of Wilkes co., Ga., and a local minister, died in Washington, Ga., May 1867 in his 59th year.

William Rowland was born Nov. 26, 1797, and died in Greene co,. May 21, 1867.

Willie M. Lanham, of Spartanburg Dist., S. C., died in March last, in the 13th year of his age.

Elvin E. Funches was born in Orangeburgh Dist., S. C., Feb. 2, 1823, and died near Rowe's Pump, S. C. R. R., May 24, 1867. Wm. W. Jones

Tribute of Respect from the Ebenezer church, Cumming ct., N. G. Conf, to Elizabeth Graham, formerly Elizabeth Ryler, born Dec 19, 1811, married Martin Graham, Oct. 5, 1830, died Feb. 8, 1867.

Issue of July 26, 1867

Died

near Rose Hill, Covington Co., Ala., Oct. 5, 1866, John R., infant son of John R. and Lavonia A. Baisden, aged 13 months and 13 days.

Obituary

Mrs. Susan Magruder, wife of George Magruder, deceased, of Richmond co., Ga., died at the residence of Dr. Thomas K. Slaughter, Randolph co., Ga., April 23, 1867, in the 86th year of her age. Thos K. Slaughter. Christian Index please copy.

Rev. Wm. M Breedlove was born March 4, 1795, and died March 9, 1867, having just closed his 72d year. Born in Virginia, his father moved to Hancock co., when he was quite young. In 1821 he married the widow Warren, moved to Tallapoosa co., Ga., in 1843. In 1852 sister B. Preceded him to the grave. Later in that year, he married Miss M. A. Rape. Wm. B. Neal

Mrs. Hannah Miller, relict of Francis Miller of Henry co., Ga., was born April 24, 1802, and died June 25, 1867. F. E. M.

A. B. Slaughter died at the residence of his father, Dr. Thomas K. Slaughter, in Randolph co., Ga., 8 June, in his 35th year... 20th May. Thos K. Slaughter

Sylvanus Gibson, an old citizen of Upson co., Ga., fell from his wagon June 14 and was instantly killed... left widow and nine children.

SOUTHERN CHRISTIAN ADVOCATE NOTICES 1867-1878

Issue of August 2, 1867

Miss Eliza Ellen Walker, youngest daughter of Wm. H. and Mary A. Walker, died in Culloden, June 18, 1867, aged 23 years.

William G. Crawford, son of Elisha G. and Nancy Crawford, was born in Lincoln co., Ga., Feb. 13, 1810, and died at Cotton Valley, Ala., June 27, 1867. His father removed to Jasper co., Ga., while he was an infant. In 1837 he removed to Macon co., Ala., and in 1840 was married to Miss Sarah Tatom of Monroe co., Ga., who survives him. B. B. Ross

Mr. Anthony Brantley died in Madison co., Fla., March 29.... R. H. Howren

Mrs. Sallie J. Miller, wife of John F. Miller and eldest daughter of H. J. and I. K. Wilson, died in Augusta, 31st of May 1867, aged 23 years and 2 days.

Agnes, wife of Jas. Littlejohn, was born Sept. 12, 1812, and died June 1, 1867. J. E. Watson

Miss Martha Stringfellow died in Chattahoochee co,. Ga., May 15, 1867, in the 22d year of her age.

Tribute of Respect from New River Lodge, No. 94, at Corinth, Heard co., Ga., to Rev. Jas. McKinzie who died 10 June 1867.

Rev. Thomas M. Lynch died 19 last April at Nixburg, Coosa co., Ala. He was born in Wilkinson co., Miss. 1 August 1824.

Issue of August 9, 1867

William W. D. Weaver died in Greensboro, Ga., July 19, 1867.

Mrs. Rachel Wright, wife of John L. Wright, and youngest child of Wm. Bradford, Sr., died in Lowndes co., Ga., 13 July 1867, in the 22d year of her age. L. Pierce

Albon Chase died in Athens, Ga., July 9, 1867, in the 60th year of his age. J. S. Key

William H. Parker was born in Elbert county, Ga., 1797, and died in Campbell co., Ga., July 9th 1867, being in the 70th year of his age.

Mrs. Rebecca Sapp, wife of Theophilus Sapp, died in Chattahoochee co., Ga., July 26, 1867, in the 37th year of her age... married 5 January 1867. L. Pierce

Mrs. Caroline J. Goodwin was born in Burke co., Ga., March 25, 1815, died in Monroe co,. Ga., July 2, 1867. W. G. Allen. Christian Index please copy.

Robert W. Flournoy, only son of Rev. Robert W. Flournoy, Spring Hill ct., S. Ga. Conference, died in Thomas co., 26 July in his 14th year. N. B. Ousley

The Rev. Elisha Brown (colored) was born in Columbia co., Va., 1778... tribute of respect 17 June 1867.

Mrs. Rachel A. Clonts, wife of Rev. M. A. Clonts and daughter of Mr. Jeremiah & Mrs. Anna Stover, was born in Habersham co., Ga., Sept. 23d 1830, and died in Ocala, East Fla., July 13, 1867.

Mary Ammons, wife of Richard Ammons and daughter of Asa and Mahala Alsabrook, aged 50 years, died June 7, 1867.

Mrs. Sarah Simms died in Tallahassee, Fla., July 6, 1867, at the residence of her daughter, Mrs. Lydia E. Grant, at the advanced age of nearly 90 years. She was born in Worcestershire, England, 22d July 1777, and came to the U. S. in 1843-- to Florida in 1857.

Mrs. S. A. Cleaton, wife of M. Cleaton, decd., was born in Walton co., Ga., August 28, 1829, and died 19 July 1867 in Monroe, Walton co., Ga.

Tribute of Respect to Anna Kate McNair by Cuthbert Sabbath School.

Issue of August 16, 1867

Died

Thursday morning, 8th inst., Lipscomb, son of Rev. Atticus G. and Mrs. Mary Y. Haygood of the North Georgia Conference.

Obituary

Rev. Stephen S. Sykes was born near Montgomery, Ala., Nov 30th 1830 and died in that city June 25th 1867. The marriage of Mr. Sykes to Miss A. F. Lane in 1849... mother and six orphan children survive. B. F. Perry

Archibald Brydie, a native of Fayetteville, N. C., emigrated to Georgia in 1826 and resided in Athens till 1851, removed to Macon where he died 25 July in his 76th year.

William W. McNeil died 18 July in the 61st year of his age. J. O. A. Cook

Rev. Stephen Fagan was born in Washington co,. N. C., 13 January 1817. Having removed to Florida and finally to Newnansville... died 4 June 1867.

Lilla Gertrude, daughter of Jno. A. and Mrs. Rosa Felkel, aged 11 years, 8 months and 22 days, died in Orangeburg Dist., S. C., on the 22d ult.

Issue of August 23, 1867

Wm. C. Smith, Jr., died at Athens, Ga., 8 July 1867. He was a native of Sumter co., Ga., born 11 October 1845. His parents removed with him, their only child, to Alabama in 1853 and settled in Barbour county.

Samuel McClurken was born in Laurens Dist., S. C., 14th June 1813, removed to Ala. in 1833 and died near Oxford, Calhoun co., July 11, 1867. R. B. Crawford

Mrs. Sarah Rebecca, wife of Mr. J. M. Wood and daughter of F. J. and Martha O'Hara, was born May 12, 1843, and died July 11, 1867. E. B. Norton

Pascal D. Klugh died in Abbeville District, S. C., June 2d, 1867 in his 75th year. Jas. T. Kilgo

Henry H. Bowles was born in Morgan co., Ga., 1801, and died in Maury co., Tenn., in his 66th year. He was an orphan boy. S. M. B.

Mrs. Milly Thompson, wife of Rev. Robt. Thompson, died in Emanuel co., Ga., June 8, 1867, aged 60 years. Louis B. Bouchelle

Tribute of Respect to Wm. A. Cole who died 23d May in 1867 in his 19th year... Assistant Librarian of the Trinity Sunday School, Savannah, Ga.

Issue of August 30, 1867

Died

In Savannah, on the 16th of July 1867, Anna Josephine; and on the 23d July 1867, Mary Harriet, children of Ely and Anna G. Otto.

Obituary

Hardy H. Hodges was born May 28th 1808 in Bulloch co., Ga. He died in Bulloch co. on 23d July 1867. W. Knox

Mary C. Olive, wife of Thos. W. Olive and daughter of Aquila and Catharine Mathews died in Columbia co., Ga., July 4th in her 39th year. R. A. Conner

Mrs. Sarah Head died in Putnam co., Ga., July 27th 1867, aged 75 years and six months. In early life she joined the Primitive Baptist church in which she lived and died.

Mrs. Nancy McGlaun, the wife of John McGlaun, of Henry co., Ala., and daughter of Thomas and Elizabeth Covington, was born in Lincoln county, Ga., March 1813 and died July 3, 1867. When she was quite young, she was left an orphan and was raised by an uncle, who settled in Pike county, Ga., while she was yet young. In 1831 she was married to Mr. McGlaun. John W. Solomon

Mrs. Bethena Blythe, wife of the Rev. Wm. H. Blythe, daughter of Jonathan and Bethena Ward, died in Greene county Ga., July 25th 1867 in her 50th year. Wm. Bryan

Lewis Kaminer was born in Orangeburg District, S. C., February 27th 1801 and died July 22d 1867.

Susan Victoria, daughter of C. C. and Julia Ragin, died on the 24th July 1867, aged 9 years, 5 months and 2 days.

Tribute of Respect from Quarterly Conference of the Marion (S. C.) Station, to Major Samuel Ferdinand Gibson. Though born and receiving his early education in Darlington, yet had his home for the larger part of his life in Marion District, and for about twenty years resided in Marion village.

Issue of September 6, 1867

Mrs. Sarah Varn, relict of Aaron Varn, Sr., was born Nov. 1st 1790 and died August 11th 1867. T. J. Clyde

Mrs. Fannie T. Boylston, wife of Mr. G. W. Boylston, of Barnwell Dist., S. C., daughter of Rev. Lewis J. and M. M. Crum, of Orangeburg, S. C., died in Barnwell Dist., 16th August, in the 24th year of her age.

Mary Z. E. Freeman was born in Wilkinson co,. Ga., July 22d, 1852, and died 5th August. Wm. H. Freeman also died 5th August, aged 17 years. N. D. Morehouse

Rev. Warren Summerhill died in Paulding co., Ga. His father, Jas. Summerhill, was born of the early settlers of Cobb county, Ga., and was mysteriously murdered near his own residence. His mother was a pious member of the Baptist Church. Brother S. was born in Spartanburg District, S. C., April 23d 1816. J. B. C. Quillian

Benjamin Prescott, Sr., died in Scriven co., Ga., July 31st 1867, in the 67th year of his age. For several years he represented his county in the Georgia Legislature. He leaves and wife and many children. J. M. Stokes

Mrs. Emily J. Hunt, wife of Thomas Hunt, died on 20th July in Jones county, in her 53d year. She leaves an only son by a prior marriage.

John Freeman was born in Scriven county, Ga., March 30th 1796, and died 6th of August, aged 71 years. He came to Wilkinson county, Ga., in 1818, and was married to Miss Cauly in 1822. He leaves a wife and several children and grandchildren. N. D. Morehouse

Miss Mary E. Ozmer, daughter of Robert Ozmer, was born July 20, 1839 and died on 4th August 1867. She was a member of the Sabbath-school at Wesley Chapel, Dekalb county, Ga.

16

Mrs. Lethe A. B., wife of Thos. H. Phillips, died 11th July, aged 44 years and 10 months. She was born in Jasper county, Ga., September 1822, was married in 1836, moved with her husband to Troup county, and from thence in 1844 to Macon co., Ala., where she died.

Jessie Alexander, daughter of Mr. Hugh A. and Mrs. S. A. Hall, was born in Chambers county, Ala., Oct. 8th 1861, and died July 23d 1867. Lula Lee, daughter of Mr. Hugh A. and Mrs. S. A. Hall, was born in Chambers county, Ala., Jan. 9, 1859, and died Aug. 4, 1867.
Mrs. Fannie E. Brown died near Augusta on the 30th July 1867, aged 27 years.

Issue of September 13, 1867

Died

At Alpharetta, Ga., on 23d August, Margaret Josephine, infant daughter of Rev. John R. and Sarah E. Gaines, aged 2 months and 9 days.

Martha Emily, infant daughter of Wm. G. and Mary A. F. England, died in Oglethorpe co., Ga., July 18, 1687, aged 3 years, 10 months and 21 days.

In Salem, N. C,. July 28th, Willie Capers, fifth son of H. D. and E. J. Lott, aged 6 months and 5 days.

Obituary

Peter G. Bessent was born in St. Mary's., Ga., January 1, 1803, and died in Atlanta, July 12th 1867. He leaves and widow and children.

Nancy Ann Carlton, wife of John Carlton, was born in Duplin co., N. C., on 17th November 1775 and died in Madison co., Fla., on 4th June 1867, in her 93d year. Her son, Rev. John W. Carlton.... J. M. Hendry

Thomas H. Everett, son of Thomas and Rebecca Everett, was born Oct. 19th, 1847, and was killed near Lumpkin, Stewart co., Ga., August 10, 1867.

Mrs. Susannah Edwards was born Feb. 24, 1804, and died in Madison co., Fla., July 31, 1807. Her maiden name was Bennett. She was married to Samuel Edwards in Marlboro Dist., S. C., Nov. 23, 1820. She was left a widow in 1850 with a large family of children.

Sister Mary A. E. Cook, only surviving daughter of Rev. John W. and Mary A. Cook, was born in Jasper co., Nov. 25th 1850, and died in Dooly co., August 22, 1867.

Fannie Hook, daughter of Dr. L. M. and E. W. Hook, died Aug. 2, 1687, aged 11 years, a d 20 days. She was a member of the Sunday school at Big Spring, Canton Circuit, Ga. Conference. J. R. Parker

Mrs. Margaret Johnson, wife of Rev. C. G Johnson, of Twiggs co., Ga., died on 1st inst. She has left a mother, brother, husband, and six small children. Wm. Griffin. September 4th 1867.

Mrs. Sally Littlejohn, relict of Abraham Littlejohn, died at Nacoochee, Ga., on 21st June 1867, in her 71st year. She was born in N. C., July 18, 1796, was the daughter of Rev. Jesse Richardson. N. H. Palmer

Issue of September 20, 1867

W. W. D. Weaver was born in Halifax, N. C., on 5th December 1798. His parents moved to Greensboro, Ga., when he was about six years of age. He was married in 1824. He died 18th July 1867. W. C. Bass

Mrs. Nancy Wadsworth, formerly Nancy Johnson, was born in Newberry, S. C., in 1795, and died in Decatur, Ga., July 9th 1867, aged 72 years. She was married to Walter Wadsworth, August 1830. W. A. Dodge

Mrs. Elizabeth, wife of James S. Alexander, died in Bold Spring, Franklin co., Ga., on 14th August 1867, aged 61 years. She married brother James S. Alexander in 1829 and joined the Presbyterian Church, the church of her husband. A. G. Worley

Malcolm K. McCaskill was born August 22nd 1799 in the Isle of Skye, Scotland, and died in Chesterfield District, S. C., July 18th 1867. He came to America when about two years old with his parents. He married the daughter of Rev. Wm. Hudson, a local preacher, and settled near Fork Creek Church. O. Eaddy

Ella E. Houser, daughter of W. and Margaret Houser of Fort Valley, Ga., died 9th August, in her 19th year.

Issue of September 27, 1867

Died

In Conwayboro, S. C., Sept. 9, 1867, Willie Murdock, infant son of G. C. and M. E. Richwood, aged 4 months and 25 days.

On 8th Sept. 1867, in Jefferson co., Ga., Sarah F., daughter of James F. and Amanda Walker, aged five years.

Obituary

James H. Middlebrooks in the month of June last, departed this life. G. F. Pierce

The Rev. Peyton L. Wade has passed away. G. F. Pierce

Hugh Allen, one of the oldest citizens of Houston co., died on the 4th September at his residence, near Fort Valley, at the advanced age of 71 years. He leaves five children. Just five years since, their mother bid adieu to the earth.

Thomas S. White was born in Elbert co., on 19th February 1808 and died in Coweta co., 15th August 1867.

Mrs. Nancy Hill Freeman was born 20th Nov 1821, in Stanly co., N. C., and died 12th June 1867. J. W. Puett

Norman McRae was born in Marion District, S. C., January 1st 1789, and died at the residence of Duncan McRae, his brother, in Telfair county, Ga. He moved early in life to Georgia where he spent the greater portion of it. He represented Montgomery county in the State Legislature, and served as Justice of the Peace in Lumpkin county, Ga. He moved to Putnam county, East Florida, and then to Georgia where he died. He was a member of the Presbyterian Church.

Issue of October 4, 1867

Rev. Wm. Brockington was born Sept 3, 1795 in Darlington District, S. C., where he died July 13, 1867. Tribute of Respect.

Mrs. Charlotte Veal, wife of William Veal, Sen., of Wilkinson co., Ga., was born in Washington co., Ga., December 25th 1796, and died Sept. 25, 1867. She was married to Mr. Veal in 1812, who settled in Twiggs co., Ga., the following year-- in 1846, moved to Wilkinson. She left an aged husband and three children.

James E. Cotton, son of the late Rev. J. G. and A. E. Cotton, of Harris co., Ga., was drowned July 11th in attempting to swim from Hargetts Island to the Georgia side of the Chattahoochee. W. J. Cotter

Mrs. Nancy E. Hudgins, daughter of Mr. and Mrs. John B. Knowles, died at the residence of her father, Chattooga co., Ga., August 25, 1867, aged 19 years and 23 days. J. T. Lowe

Rabun Shivers Hartson was born in Madison, Fla., Aug. 14, 1850, and died Aug. 8, 1687. He was left an orphan at the age of two years, and his subsequent life was spent at Macon, Ga., under the care of his grandfather, Wm. Shivers, and his aunts Maria E. and Sarah W. Shivers. J. R. Danforth

Miss Ellenor Louisa Brown died in Macon, Aug. 23, in the 35th year of her age. The only daughter, and for some years the only child of a widowed Christian mother. J. S. Key

Stephen Bassett was born Nov. 27, 1788, and died in Houston co., August 1867.

Mrs. Amanda Vickers, wife of Matthew Vickers and daughter of Wm. Bradford, Sr., died in Lowndes co., Ga., August 7th 1867, in her 37th year, leaving a husband and four children, aged parents. A. Stephens

Tribute of Respect to Wm. C. Davis from Quarterly Conference of Covington and Oxford circuit.

Issue of October 11, 1867

Died

Little Eddie, youngest child of Rev. W. J. and Mary Wardlaw, died in Harris co., Ga., Sept. 23d, aged 3 years, 1 month and 8 days.

Obituary

Mrs. Martha J. Edmonson was born in Georgia, June 27th 1826 and died near Louisville, Ala., Sept. 13, 1867. This lady was the daughter of the Rev. Richard Q. Lane.

Mrs. Mary P. Booth, daughter of Thomas R. and Deborah Smith, was born in Gadsden co., Fla,. on 12th March 1845 and died in Attapulgus, Ga., 18th July 1867. Thomas William Booth, infant son of Dr. Robert and Mary P. Booth, was born 31st October 1866 and died at the residence of his grandfather, Thos. R. Smith, in Attapulgus on 19th August 1867, aged nine months and 19 days.

William Thomas Riggins, only son of Mr. E. L. D. and A. Riggins, died in Bibb county, Sept. 20, aged 14 years 9 months and 4 days.

Miss Caroline M. Lester, daughter of Jno. Lester, died in Monroe county, Ga., on 7th Sept 1867. M. H. White

Mrs. Lucy W. Beaty, wife of Rev. John H. Beaty, was born in Horry Dist. S., C., Nov. 29, 1801, and died near Conwayboro, S. C., Sept. 11, 167. She leaves a husband and children. J. H. C. McKinney

Mrs. Josephine E. Story, wife of Geo. C. Story and daughter of T. L. and H. Nobles, was born January 15, 1848, and died July 20, 1867, in Macon co., Ala. She had been married about eight months. J. A. Green

Mr. Abraham Willis died in Colleton Dist. S. C., July 17, 1867, aged about 70 years. John W. McRoy.

Cynthia L. Christopher, daughter of Jas. and Frances C. Christopher, died in Monroe, Walton co., Ga., 10th August 1867, in her 13th year. W. H. Evans

Tribute of Respect from church in Graniteville, S. C., to William Gregg.

Died

Lula, youngest daughter of James and Mary Holmes, died in Bibb co., Ga., Sept. 29, 1867, aged 6 years and 1 day.

Obituary

Gideon Thomason, Sr., died in Greenville District, So. Ca., July 24th 1867, in his 85th year. He was born about the year 1804. R. C. Oliver

John Dorsey was born in Oglethorpe co., Ga., on 10th Feb. 1792. He moved to Greene co., at an early age, and died 18th Sept 1687.

Miss Lizzie Love, daughter of J. M. Lowe, died in Chattahoochie co., Ga., on the 22d September.

Mrs. Sarah R. Shelton, wife of Dr. V. H. Shelton, died in Micanopy, Alachua co., Fla., August 19, 1867. She was born in Clarke co,. Ga., June 29th 1826. W. K. Turner

Mrs. Eliza Harriet Passmore, daughter of Abner Legette, was born in Marion Dist., S. C., and died in Macon co., Ga., September 17th 1867. She was married to Miley Passmore in March 1838 and in Dec. of that year moved with her husband to Georgia. R. W. Dixon

David Mortimer Varner, son of David M. and L. Isabella Varner, died in Bullock co., Ala., August 8th 1867, being six years, six months and seven days old. J. W. Shores

Mrs. Mary B. Thomas, wife of Spencer T. Thomas was born in Baldwin co., Ga., Oct. 20, 1818 and died in Florida 11th August 1867.

Mrs. Mary DeJarnette, wife of Mr. R. R. DeJarnetet, formerly of Putnam co., Ga., died in Lee co., Ga., Aug. 22d, 1867, and was buried in the cemetery at Eatonton, Ga., on the following Sabbath. J. T. Norris

Mary Ann, daughter of Benj. C. and Nancy Jackson, was born in Chester Dist., S. C., on 19th Dec. 1848 and died in Hamilton co., Fla., on 23d of July 1867. Geo. S. Johnston

Died

In Orangeburgh District, S. C., Oct. 16th 1867, Charles Williams, son of Rev. A. M. and Anna E. Chrietzberg, aged seven years, nine months and eight days.

Susan P., infant daughter of H. L. R. and Sarah J. Roberts, on Oct. 1, 1867, in Columbia county, Fla., aged nine months.

Obituary

Mrs. Esperann Reese, wife of Rev. Jere. Reese, died near Eufaula, Ala., on 13th Sept., in her 47th year.

Ellen Victoria, wife of Donald McLaughlin, and eldest daughter of John H. and R. S. A. Heise, of Columbia, S. C., was born Nov. 26th 1838, and died Oct. 6th 1867.

Mr. Nathanael G. H. Griner was born in Bullock co., Ga., June 23d 1844 and died in Marion co., E. Fla., Sept. 5th 1867.

Mrs. Sebbiah Morrison was born in Scriven co., Ga., 1806, died in Marion co,. E. Fla., Oct. 2d 1867.

On 4th August 1867, my sister, Mrs. Margaret Ann Davis, wife of Lieut. B. Washington Davis died. She had just completed her thirty-second year. In early life she connected herself with the Presbyterian church. She resided in the vicinity of Broxton's Bridge, Prince William's Parish. Whiteefoord Smith

Alexander Joseph Ferree died on 26th Sept. 1867 in his 15th year. he was the only son of his mother, and she is a widow. P. G. Bowman

Mrs. Othella J. Boyd, wife of C. w. Boyd, and daughter of Dr. L. and P. Watkins was born in Laurens Dist., S. C., May 29th 1831; was married Oct. 5, 1851, and died in Franklin, Heard co., Ga., July 28th 1867, leaving parents, one brother, husband, and four children.
T. J. Embry

Susan Turner, youngest daughter of Mr. B. T. and Mrs. Susan Moore, of Marshallville, Ga., was born April 6, 1856, and died Aug. 5, 1867.

Mrs. Mary A. Scott, wife of Nathanael Scott, died in Scriven co., Ga., August 26, 1687, aged 71 years. J. M. Stokes

Memoir of Rev. James Stripling from Quarterly Conference, Carrolton ct., N. Ga. Conf. Brother S. was born in Jones co., Ga., 1808, and died in Carroll co., Ga., August 7, 1687.

Issue of November 1, 1867

Died

Near Indiantown, Williamsburg Dist., S. C., David Edward, son of Mr. R. Harvey and Jane B. Wilson, aged 8 years.

In Manning, S. C., Martha Eliza, infant daughter of the late Rev. Wm. A. Hemingway, aged 14 months and 5 days.

Near Fort Browder, Barbour co,. Ala,. Oct. 21, 1867, Edward Dantzler, son of Col. E. S. Ott, aged 4 years, 1 month and 3 days.

In Clopton, Dale co., Ala., on 24th Sept., Eluda, infant daughter of William S. and Ann J. Powell, aged 18 months and 16 days.

In Macon, Ga., on 29th Oct., Carrie Young, youngest child of Rev. John W. Burke, aged 11 months and 13 days.

Obituary

Mrs. Mary C. Poole, daughter of Charles S. and Mary D. G. Sibley, and wife of Maj. W. G. Poole, of Tallahassee, Fla., was born in Gadsden co,. Fla., Sept. 15th 1846; was married Jan. 16, 1687, and died in Quincy, Fla., at the residence of her step-father, Mr. J. R. Harris, Oct. 4th, 1867. A. J. Woldridge

Emily Olivia Cox was born in Harris co., January 5th 1835, but was reared in Columbus, Ga. She was married to the Rev. D. D. Cox, of the Georgia Conference, 20th Feb. 1856, and died in Baldwin co., 23d Aug 1867, leaving a husband and two children. W. M. Crumley

William C. Davis was born in Virginia, Aug. 25th 1776. At about 20 years of age, the family came to Elbert co,. Ga. He died 27th July 1867. About 42 years of the latter portion of his days he was a citizen of Newton co., Ga. W. J. Parks

Mrs. Mary E. McAfee, wife of Rev. W. H. McAfee, was born March 3d, 1843, in Dahlonega, Ga., where she died Oct. 11th 1867. G. Hughes

21

Mrs. Jane Wallace Davis of Atlanta, Ga., a daughter of the late Rev. Wm. Holmes, of S. C., died on the 4th Oct. at the residence of Major W. D. Martin, in Lauderdale co,. Tenn., in her 53d year.

Wiley R. Garrison died in Jackson co,. Ga., August 24th 1867, in his 38th year.

James Shanks died in Jackson co., Ga., Sept. 14, 1867, aged 20 years and 22 days. His Sister

E. Smith Walkly was born in Haddom, Conn., in the year 1804 and died near Central Institute, Ala., Aug. 7, 1867, aged 64 years. He leaves a large family and many friends. Wm. A. Edwards

Tribute of Respect by Quarterly Conference of the Gainesville Circuit, N. Georgia Conference, to Jones W. Roark.

Issue of November 8, 1867

Mrs. Caroline E. Walker, wife of Edward B. Walker, and third daughter of the late Rev. John Howard, died on 10th Sept 1867 in her 48th year.

Robert Hayes was born in King and Queen co., Va., and died at Columbus, Ga., in his 69th year. Richmond, Va., Advocate, please copy

Ambrose W. Gray was born May 13, 1805 and died in Fayette co., Ga., September 18th 1867. Wm. Park

Mary Catharine Padget, second daughter of Mahlon M. and Mary Padget, was born 3d July 1853, and died in Edgefield District, at the residence of her uncle, Russell Eidson, Oct. 2d, 1867. R. C. Oliver

Mrs. Sarah Evans (relict of Martin Evans) died 1st August 1867 in Cherokee co., Ga., in her 78th year.

Permelia Burns, wife of Wm. Burns, died on 20th Sept 1867 in Columbia co., Fla., aged 75 years. She was born in Scriven co., Ga., and removed to Decatur co., where she lived until last winter, since which time she had resided in Florida. She left a companion and children.

James T. Hightower, son of Asbury W. and Sarah F. Hightower, was born in Russell co., Ala,. Jan. 28, 1842, and died in Montgomery co., Ala., Oct. 12, 1867. A. Dowling

Lucius W. Kendrick, son of Rev. G. M. and C. Kendrick, was born in Wilkes co,. Ga., 10th August 1852 and died in Warren co., Ga., 23d Sept. in his 16th year.

Mrs. Elizabeth Jacobs, died 5th Aug. 1867 in the 76th year of her age.

Mrs. Elizabeth Summers died Oct. 16th 1867 in Newberry District, S. C., aged 74 years, 10 months and 16 days. She was a member at Capers' Chapel, Newberry circuit.

Miss Prudence Persons died in Russell co., Ala,. August 1, 1867.

Tribute of Respect from Autauga Lodge, No. 31, to Edwin Stoudemire, M. W. M. Lewis Stoudemire, S. W., who died a few days after his brother.

Issue of November 15, 1867

Mrs. Harriet C. Plowden, wife of E. Ruthvine Plowden, of Clarendon district, S. C., and daughter of Wm. Rogers of Bishopville, S. C., died Sept. 19th 1867, aged 28 years.

Mrs. Susan L. Smith, wife of W. T. Smith, Esq., died in Wadesboro, N. C., Aug. 14, 1857 [sic] in her 23rd year

James Arthur McCrea died in Williamsburg dist., S. C., on the 23d Sept 1867, aged 22 years.

Bro. Hiram Yarbrough of the Protestant M. Church died in his 66th year in Spartanburg dist., S. C., on 25th Sept 1867. Left widow and children. J. S. Ervin

Mrs. Jane Nicholson, wife of William R. Nicholson, was born in Pendleton dist., S. C., March 11, 1797, and died in DeKalb co., Ala., Sept. 23, 1867. J. G. Gurley

Sister Jane V. Budd was born Feb. 10th 1793 in S. C., was married to William Budd of Charleston in early life, removed with her family to Florida many years ago, and died in Monticello, Oct. 5th 1867. Josephus Anderson

Mrs. Mary Mickler was born May 11th 1798 and died in Lexington dist. S., C., Sept. 14th 1867, at the residence of her son-in-law, Mr. John Smith. She lived to see all her children and many of her grandchildren members of the Church. J. R. Mobley

Osborne Smart, about 70 years of age, died October 26th in Centreville. She was the only remaining member of the family. A. Richards

Mrs. E. P. Cobb, wife of J. N. B. Cobb, died in Dalton, Georgia, Sept. 19th 1867, in her 46th year. She leaves a husband and seven children.

Mrs. Sarah Foster, wife of Joseph W. Foster, died near Creek Stand, Macon co., Ala,. September 1, 1867. Sister Foster's maiden name was Lloyd. She was born, I believe, in Georgia.

William T. Westberry was born in Colleton dist., S. C., Dec. 8th 1809 and died in St. George's Parish, Oct. 9th 1867.

William Franklin Peach, in his 36th year, died in Perote, Bulloch co., Ala., June 17, 1867. He left a wife and two children.

Bro. Francis Baxter, an exhorter of long standing in the Branchville ct., S. C. Conference, died 18th Sept., in his 81st year.

Issue of November 22, 1867

Died

Sarah Florence, third daughter of Rev. Chas. W. and Mily J. Thomas, born at the United States Navy Yard, Pensacola, Fla., Oct. 27th 1850, died in Atlanta, Ga., October 19th 1867.

In Crenshaw co., Ala,. on 1st September ult., James Franklin, son of Capt. W. N. and Elizabeth Brandon, in the third year of his age.

Obituary

Sister Nancy Ethridge, wife of David Ethridge and daughter of Thos. Hunter, died on 22d Sept. 1867, in her 41st year in Gwinnett co,. Ga. W. H. Evans

Mary E. Tarver, daughter of Caswell and S. A. Black, was born Feb. 21, 1843, in Harris co., Ga., was married to Chas. H. Tarver, March 20th 1862, and died 29th Sept 1867. Wm. B. Neal

Rev. Spencer Moore was born in Pitt co., N. C., in 1800 and died in Levy co., Fla., Oct. 14, 1867. He joined the M. E. Church in Tatnall co., Ga., in 1827. He has left an aged widow and six children. E. J. Knight.

Mr. Aaron Odom was born in Ga., Feb. 3d, 1804 and died in Henry co., Ala., Sept. 27, 1867. He leaves a wife and seven children. B. F. Blow

Sister Eliza Johnson died in Smithville, Ga., on 1st Sept. 1867 in the 24th year of her age. She left a husband and one little daughter. S. Anthony

Dr. William M. Harris, son of Edward and Mary Harris, was born in Montgomery co., Ala., July 12, 1823 and was married to Miss Harriet C. Walker, Jan. 27th 1848, with whom he lived till called to his reward, August 1, 1867. He leaves a wife and six children. A. Dowling

Miss Lizzie Rebecca, a daughter of John and Sandab B. Nash, died in Dekalb co., Ga., Oct. 21st 1867 in the 27th year of her life. W. A. Dodge

Bro. Green Montgomery died in Crenshaw co., Ala., on 17th Sept. last, aged 50 years.

Mrs. Mary M. Leitner died in Henry co., Ga., in her 76th year.

Issue of November 29, 1867

Died

Richard Turnbull, only son of Capt. W. R. and Emma Reid, was born Feb. 8th, and died Oct. 20th 1867.

Susan P., infant daughter of H. S. R. and S. A. Roberts, on the 2nd of October.

Charlie A. F., infant son of Col. Arthur and A. M. L. Roberts, on the __ Nov., both of Columbia co., Fla.

Children

Mary Lula Logan, eldest daughter of Jas. H. and Sophia W. Logan, was born 15th Jan 1852, and died Oct. 24th, 1867.... among pupils of Griffin Female College in 1865. W. A. Rogers.

Obituary

John W. Hanson, was born March 2d, 1794, in Columbia co., Ga., and died Oct. 20, 1867, in Morgan Co. For more than half a century he had been a member of the M. E. Church. W. R. Foote

Thomas H. Everett, was born in Chowan co., N. C., Feb. 23d, 1805, died in Lumpkin, Stewart co., Ga., Nov. 14, 1867. Brother E. lived a number of years in West Florida, but for many years past, in Lumpkin. Last year he went to Texas and remained a month or two, and on his way home at Columbus, heard that his dear wife was dead and buried. A few months before his death, his son Thomas died by violent hands. Carrie, one of his daughters, asked him if he felt that God was sustaining him, to press her hand.... J. C. Simmons.

Mrs. Mary C. Billingslea, wife of Cyrus Billingslea, and daughter of George and Mary Chatfield, died near Oak Bowery, Ala., Aug. 7, 1867, aged about sixty years. There is left to mourn her loss a devoted husband and a little step grand-daughter.

Capt. Daniel Bird was born in Edgefield, S. C., in September 1784, became a member of the Methodist Church in 1805, removed to Florida more than thirty years ago, and died near Monticello, Fla., Nov. the 6th, of the present year.... J. Anderson.

Mrs. Harriet Elizabeth Birdsong, daughter of Thomas and Elizabeth Clarke, was born in Nottaway co., Va., on the 8th Dec., 1818, moved to Ga. in 1836, was married to E. F. Birdsong, Nov. 21, 1837, and died the 14th of Oct. 1867. When a child, her parents died.... A good wife, a good mother.... J. Lewis

SOUTHERN CHRISTIAN ADVOCATE NOTICES 1867-1878

Issue of December 6, 1867

Mrs. Harriet F. Florence exchanged her toils on earth for her rest in Heaven, on the 19th Nov. 1867. She was the wife of Rev. William A. Florence of the No. Ga. Conference. She was born at Sandy Hook, Washington co., N. Y., on the 16th of March 1802. She removed to the South in 1830, and settled in Greensboro, Ga., where her uncle, the Rev. Adid Sherwood, a preacher of distinction in the Baptist denomination, then resided; and on the 19th of July, 1832, was married to Rev. W. A. Florence. She lived long enough to raise and train an interesting family. Two noble sons fell martyrs to the cause of their country; a third, lost his right arm.... A. Means.

James W. Simmons, of Hancock co., Ga., Died Nov. 11th 1867. I preached his funeral sermon on the following day.... G. F. Pierce.

Miss Susan R. Frasier was born in Schley county, Ga., Oct. 5, 1843, and died October 18, 1867.... S. M. S. Berry.

Dr. N. M. Holton was born in Concord, N. C., November 17th ,1810, and died in Tazewell, Ga., October 28, 1867. He professed religion July, 1831, in Charlotte, No Ca., at a union meeting held by Rev. Mr. Barnes of the Presbyterian Church and Rev. Mr. Furman of the Baptist Church, and joined the Presbyterian Church... became dissatisfied and removed to Lincoln co., Ga., where he joined the M. E. Church, under Rev. J. C. Simmons, at New Hope, 1834, moved to Talbotton, Ga., 1835.... He leaves a wife and three children to mourn his loss.

Miss Elizabeth Coppedge, wife of Rev. J. W. Coppedge, died on 5th Sept, in her 43d year, after an illness of 8 days. She was born and raised in Dooly co., Ga. She has left a husband and five children to mourn their loss.

Issue of December 13, 1867

Died

Little Ellen Blum, daughter of Wm. A. and Martha C. Bessent, died at Little River, S. C., Sept 24th 1867, aged five years and six months.

Jimmie, son of Wesley and Eleanor R. Leak, died suddenly in Madison co., Fla., Nov. 13th, in his 15th year.

Obituary

Miss Mary Ann McLennan died near Louisville, Ala., Oct. 1, 1867. She was the daughter of Rev. Alexander McLennan....

Bryant Stripling died in Tattnall co., Ga., on the 15th Nov. in his 74th year. L. B. Payne

Roscius F. Attwood died at his residence near Mt. Elba, Bradley co., Arkansas, on Saturday morning, 2nd Nov 1867, in his 52nd year. He leaves a family and aged mother. M. T. McGehee

Mrs. Elizabeth Muse, wife of Dr. Geo. W. Muse, died near Midway, Barnwell Dist., S. c., 19th October last, at the age of 30 years, 4 months, and 7 days. Charles Wilson.

Mrs. Achsah Duke, aged 65 years, 1 month and 23 days, died near Savannah, Ga., Aug. 2, 1867. She was born in West Dennis, Mass., June 10, 1802, moved to Savannah in November 1820....

Issue of December 20, 1867

Rev. Thos. McMillan, was born May 10, 1786, and passed peacefully into his eternal rest at Aiken, S. C., Nov. 8, 1867. A. J. Stokes.

Sister Adeline Varn, wife of Mr. Gabriel Varn, was born Feb. 3, 1813, and died in Colleton Dist., S. C., Nov. 4, 1867. T. J. Clyde

Mrs. S. C. Morgan, wife of W. H. W. Morgan, and daughter of Rev. George Watts, and sister of Rev. R. M. Watts, of South Georgia Conference, died Dec. 3, 1867, in Marion co., Ga., in her 38th year. She has left an affectionate husband and four little children, one an infant. W. G. Booth.

Dr. James W. Yarbrough, died on the 23d Oct. 1867, at the residence of his brother, J. F. Yarbrough, in Lee co., Ala., aged 43 years, 8 months and 11 days. For a number of years, he practiced his profession with ability and success at Gordon, Henry co., Ala. J. F. Dowdell

James Johnson, of Randolph co., died very suddenly in Mitchell co., Oct. 7, 1867, in his 79th year.... S. R. Weaver.

Tribute of Respect from the Quarterly Conference for Bennettsville Circuit, to Rev. Tracy R. Walsh.

Issue of January 3, 1868

Mrs. Annie A. Hunter, daughter of Alexander Pope, Sr., and wife of Commander Thos. T. Hunter, of the Confederate States Navy, died in Washington, Ga., Aug. 20, 1867. One year ago, she stood before the marriage altar....

W. W. Seals died at his son's, Cornelius Seals, in St. John's co., Fla., 29th Sept., in the 80th year of his age. He died away from home. He was taken to Florida a few months before to improve his health....

Mrs. Margaret Seals, wife of the above, died on 3d Oct., in St. Marys, in the 80th year of her age.

Miss Adele E. Seals, a daughter of the above, also departed this life, only ten days after the death of her mother.

Richard Shelton Gill, son of Maj. Josiah Gill, was born Oct. 23, 1845, and died Oct. 19, 1867. About a month before his death he made a visit to his father's house in Cave Spring, Ga., on the eve of going to Homer, La., where he hoped to enter business with his brother. W. P. R.

Mr. Charles J. Fletcher died in Tattnall co., Nov. 1867, in his fifty-eighth year. He was an elegant citizen, and had the honor of a place in the senate of Georgia.... L. B. Payne

Mrs. C. S. Deloach, daughter of Mr. C. J. Fletcher, died in Tattnall co., Oct. 1867, in her 19th year. She was married to brother David Deloach about one year since... L. B. Payne

Issue of January 10, 1868

Mrs. Mary Elizabeth, wife of Rev. J. P. Jones, of the Montgomery Conf., and daughter of Rev. A. B. and Lucinda Elliott, was born Sept. 27, 1845, and died Dec. 1, 1867 at her father's residence in Elmore co., Ala. She was dedicated to God by baptism in early infancy by Rev. Jesse Ellis. In Nov. 1865 she was married to Rev. J. P. Jones... leaves a boy of 16 months. A. B. E.

Miss Sallie, youngest daughter of Henry and Ann Key, died in Harris co., Oct. 15th, 1867, of pulmonary disease.... L. M. M.

Susan Eufaula, wife of Edwin J. Burch, and eldest daughter of Rev. W. D. Bussey, died at the residence of Dr. Wm. Burch, Telfair co., Ga., Nov. 18, 1867, aged 22 years and 23 days.... E. J. B.

Mary E. Coleman, wife of W. S. Coleman, daughter of Rev. Wm. Littlejohn, died in Harrison co., Texas, Nov. 10th 1867-- seven months from the date of her marriage. Many pupils of the Wesleyan Female College remember the sweet-spirited Mollie Littlejohn and her amiable elder sisters.

Francis Baxter, was born 26th Dec 1796 in Orangeburg District, S. C., and died Sept. 18, 1867.

Mrs. Antoinette Eugenia, wife of Matthew J. Goodin, daughter of Henry and Sarah Butts, of Upson county, Ga., died in Crawford county on 6th Nov., in the 19th year of her age, leaving infant twins only a few days old.... Evie G.

Issue of January 17, 1868

Caroline Burrett, wife of John C. McTyeire, died in Crenshaw co., Ala., Oct. 191, 1867, in the 29th year of her age.

Martha Burrett, her mother, and wife of Alexander Burrett, died there, as only the Christian dies, in April, aged 70 years. H. N. M.

Mrs. Ruth McMillan, wife of Col. Robert McMillan, of Clarksville, Ga., died suddenly at her residence on the 23d of Dec.

Dr. Thomas O. Heard died in Griffin, Ga., Dec. 2, 1867 k,in the 38th year of his age... was preparing to locate near Hardstown, Kentucky. He was converted and joined the Methodist Church in his native city, Augusta Ga. R. W. Bigham.

Miss Bella M. Smith, daughter of the late Rev. Sidney M. Smith, died at her mother's in Jefferson co., Ga., on 6th Dec., of typhoid dysentery.

Tribute of Respect by the Methodist S. S. at Cuthburt, Ga., on the death of Willie Harris, son of West and Martha W. Harris.

Issue of January 24, 1868

Albert Crawford Hornady died at the residence of Mr. F. P. Green in Schley co., Ga., on 22d October 1867 in the 43d year of his age. When about 18 years old, he joined the M. E. Church, but did not profess religion until he was about 28, at Buena Vista, Ga. In September, 1855, he was married to Miss Sallie E. Green, and soon afterwards settled in Americus where he remained until the beginning of the late war, when the volunteer company to which he belonged (Sumter Light Guards) was summoned to the field....

Jesse Sample, was born Dec. 25, 1808 and died Dec. 25, 1867. He was born, lived and died in Georgia. he has been a prominent citizen of Forsyth county for the last thirty-five years.... J. D. Anthony.

Issue of January 31, 1868

John W. Porter died in Madison, Ga., after a brief illness of only four days on the 7th Jan., 1868, aged 70 years.

Rev. Thos. C. Norton was born in Barbour co., Ala., 11th Sept. 1845, and died in Brundidge, Pike co., Ala., Sept. 24th, 1867. He was the youngest son of the venerable John Norton, who died in Barbour co., in 1862. He was the brother of Revs. W. K. and Ethelbert Norton, of the Montgomery Conference. Joseph B. Cottrell

Mrs. Georgia Alma Cheeseborough, wife of Mr. Charles Cheeseborough, of Augusta, Ga., died 12th January 1867. In childhood left an orphan, her home with her brother General Doles, of Milledgeville, a noble and gallant Confederate soldier. She was a cousin of Bishop G. F. Pierce. She has left a kind and affectionate husband and many friends to mourn.

Dr. Lewis Myers died near Ocala, Florida, on the 4th November 1867. He was the only son of the well known Rev. Lewis Myers of the Methodist Church. he was a native of Charleston, S. C., was educated at Oxford, Ga., attended Medical lectures at the S. C. College and there received the degree of M. D. in 1854, and commenced the profession in the surrounding country of Lawtonville, S. C.

Mr. James Sanderford died in St. Marys, Ga., Jan. 2nd, 1868, in the 74th year of his age. He was a native of Beaufort District, S. C.. His youth and early manhood were spent in that State, the latter portion of his life in Savannah, and Camden co., Ga. He raised a large family....

Mrs. Martha Faulkner, wife of Mr. P. Faulkner and daughter of Martin Fowler, was born Nov. 25, 1825, and died at Graniteville, S. C., Dec. 2d, 1867. She leaves a husband and five children to mourn her loss. T. F.

Issue of February 7, 1868

[on page 2:] Death of Rev J. W. McIver. The Memphis Advocate states that this brother, a member of the Memphis Conference, died on the 17th January....

Died

Little Johnny, infant daughter of Mr. Alfred L. and Mrs. Florida C. Willis, of Calhoun co., Ga.

Obituary

Augustus Berrien Redding, eldest son of Col. Anderson W. Redding was born in Monroe co., Ga., December 27th, 1827, and died of cholera at his residence, Wesson, Mississippi, Jan. 15, 1868. He moved last December to Wesson, a manufacturing town on the N. O. J. & G. N. Railroad.... His Brother.

Chapman F. Maddux, whose name is precious in the memory of many itinerant preachers is not more. He was born in Warren co., Ga., Nov. 27, 1804, and died in Rusk co., Texas, Nov. 29, 1867. He was a brother of Rev. Patrick N. Maddux of Pike co. J. B. S.

John Ira Huff was born at Red Clay, Ga., March 20th, 1845, joined the M. E. Church, South, when about 9 years, old, and died in Dalton, Ga., Nov. 24th, 1867, from a gunshot wound received a few hours before. J. T. Norris

Mrs. Louisa E. Nichols, wife of Alonzo Nichols and daughter of John S. Jackson, died in Clark co., Ga., January 10th, 1868, aged 18 years.... A year wanting a few days only, had rolled round since she became the wife of Bro. Nichols.... I. M. Kenney

Our sister, Ada M. Jackson, wife of Hon. James Jackson of Macon, Ga., entered into rest on 7th January in her 33d year... J. S. Key

Mollie Wilburn Ward, only daughter of Rev. Richard J. and Hattie I. Harwell, was born Nov. 24, 1862, and died Nov. 25, 1867.

Tribute of Respect to John W. Porter who died on Tuesday night, the 7th of January, 1868, aged 70 years. From Board of Stewards, Methodist Church, Madison.

Issue of February 14, 1868

Mrs. Martha Malinda P. Golson died in Union Springs, Ala., Nov. 28, 1867. Her maiden name was Harden. She was born in Putnam co., Ga., 1817 and was married to Mr. W. C. M. Golson in 1840. W. M. M.

Mrs. Mary H. Birdsong was born Nov 3, 1807 and died Jan 16, 1868 in Macon, Ga. H. H. Parks. Athens, Ga., Feb. 4, 1868.

Dr. Wm. L. Felder was born in Sumter Dist., S. C., in 1807 and died in Hamburg, S. C., Dec. 10, 1867. He moved to Augusta, Ga., in 1853. G. H. Pattillo

SOUTHERN CHRISTIAN ADVOCATE NOTICES 1867-1878

William V. Samples, son of Jesse and Phoebe Samples, was born in Forsyth co., Ga., Feb. 7, 1836, and died in Vanzant co., Texas, Oct. 25, 1867. J. D. S.

Miss Mollie C. Stillwell, daughter of Richard and Sarah A. Stillwell, was born Oct. 31, 1834, and died Jan. 14, 1868.

Charles D. Bagby was born July 14, 1867, and died in Union Springs, Ala., Jan. 3, 1868. W. M. M.

Issue of February 21, 1868

Mrs. S. J. Miller, eldest daughter of Rev. J. J. Little, died suddenly, in Harris co., Ga., on 27th Jan. 1868, in her 27th year. In 1860, she was married to N. W. Miller, Esq,. who died at Petersburg of wounds received there. W. J. Cotter

Mrs. Harriet Pegues Gillespie, widow of the late General Samuel Wilds Gillespie, died on 23d Nov 1867, at the residence of Rev. R. R. Pegues, in Marlboro District, S. C., in the 74th year of her age. She reared seven children, six of whom survive. A. M. Shipp

Miss Susan Jane McDonell, wife of Col. T. A. McDonell, died at Gainesville, East Florida, Nov. 2d, 1867, in the 36th year of her age. Geo. G. N. MacD.

Minor Gladden was born in Fairfield District, S. C., 16th Nov 1878, and died Dec. 16, 1867, one month over eighty years of age. In my boyhood he was my neighbor and his children were my school fellows. Amongst them was one who linked his name to the history of his country-- Gen. A. W. Gladden, who commanded the South Carolina Regiment after the fall of his superior officers in Mexico, under Gen. Scott; and who fell by a wound received on the battle-field of Shiloh. He left several children and grand-children.

Mrs. Mary Virginia Stanaland, wife of S. T. Stanaland, and daughter of Rev. James Woody, formerly of the Florida Conference, died in Savannah, Ga., Jan. 25th, 1868, in the 28th year of her age. Geo. G. N. MacD.

Tribute of Respect from the M. E. Church, South at Aiken, to Rev. J. P. Morris....

Issue of February 28, 1868

Ada Jane Mitchell, my wife--dropping after our marriage the Jane, and calling herself Ada Mitchell Jackson, was born in Putnam County on 25th September 1835, and died in Macon on 7th January 1868. She was the daughter and only child of Walter H. and Camilla D. Mitchell, until recently, of Milledgeville, Georgia. James Jackson

Mrs. Martha Sewell, wife of Nicholas Sewell, died in Meriwether co., Ga., Dec 28th 1867. J. B. S.

Mrs. Barbary A. Conn died on the 4th of Feb. 1868 in the 76th year of her age. Reared in Virginia... She removed with her husband to Milledgeville, Ga., 50 years ago.

Issue of March 6, 1868

Mrs. Margaret Miller Sale, wife of Col. W. W. Sale, and daughter of Rev. Robert Walker, late of Edgefield District, S. C., died in Charleston, S. C., on the 19th February in the 44th year of her age. C. W. Key

Lewis M. Dickey was born in Rutherford county, N. C., April 29, 1785, removed to Greenville District about forty years since. While on a visit to her daughter, Sister A. Cannon, Spartanburg District, on February 4th, he was taken by a severe chill, that completely prostrated him, from which he never recovered. Having lived 82 years, 9 months, and 10 days, on the 9th of February 1868. J. A. Wood

29

Mrs. Mary C., wife of Henry B. Ware, and daughter of Capt. Robert H. Waring, deceased, of Columbia, S. C., aged 58 years, died at her residence in Wilcox county, Ala. [verse] F. W. C.

Bro. David L. Wicher was born 6th Feb. 1822 in Newberry District, S. C., and died in Macon county, Ga., 31st December 1867. He was converted at Ebenezer C. M., S. C.... his removal to Georgia in 1859. He was married 15th December 1842 to Nannie J. Lane.... S. Anthony

Rev. John Pendergrass of Jackson county died on 20th Of January 1868, at nearly ninety years of age.

Martha Jane Shields, wife of Mr. John Shields of Sumter county, Ga., died in the 36th year of her age. She was the daughter of Gen. Smith, formerly of Morgan county, Ga., and was married in 1858. S. Anthony

Mrs. Sarah Clements died in Marion County, Ga., on 13th December in her 80th year. W. L. Booth.

George W. Shepherd died in Griffin, Ga., on 18th February in the 23d year of his age. H. J. A.

Tribute of Respect to James B. Jackson, President Elder of the Jacksonville District.

Tribute of Respect to Rev. John P. Morris who died at Darlington, S. C.

Issue of March 13, 1868

Mrs. Henrietta M. Williams, daughter of the Rev. George Stewart, was born August 19, 1836, and died Dec. 31st, 1867, at Summerville, Lee co., Ala. She was married to the Rev. B. S. Williams, of the Alabama Conference, March 24th, 1859. Bro. W. died in 1863. She has left two little children. Wm. M. Motley

Marcus A. Grady died of rheumatism in Anson co., N. C., Dec. 2d, 1867, in the 26th year of his age.

Mrs. Virginia A., wife of John P. Smith, M. D., and daughter of Lyman and Esther Smith was born April 30th 1845, and died January 22d, 1868, at Miccosukee, Leon co., Fla. Her mother died May 20th, 1863, leaving on her hands the care of her younger brothers and sisters. In November 1865, she was married to Dr. Smith.

Bro. Hardy Duncan, died Dec. 29, 1867, aged about 78 years.... J. H. C. McKinney.

James Martin Brooks was born in Spartanburg District, S. C., Nov. 23, 1821, joined the M. E. Church, South, at 18; emigrated to Florida in December, 1845, and died January 13, 1868. He was a kind husband and a loving father.

Miss Corinne Hughes, daughter of Capt. Wm. Hughes, Sr., of Liberty co., died in Burke co,. Jan. 23, 1868, in the 27th year of his age.

Tribute of Respect from the Lake City, Fla., Lodge to Rev. James B. Jackson.

Tribute of Respect to Aaron H. Jones from the Quarterly Conference of St. James Methodist Episcopal Church, South. Augusta, Ga.

Tribute of Respect to Samuel Presson, who died in Union Co., N. C., 13th Feb 1868, aged 84 years, 11 months and 24 days.

Issue of March 20, 1868

Wade Turner, R. Harper, Susannah Harper, and Father and Mother McMullin. They were members of the same class at Turner's Chapel. Wade Turner was a brother of the late Rev. Allen Turner of the Georgia Conference. He was one of the first settlers of this (Henry) county.

Father and Mother McMullin commenced life's journey near the same time and were companions in joy for nearly sixty years and their earthly pilgrimage terminated in the same month and in the same year, in August 1867.

R. Harper was born March 5th, 1782, and died 30th July 1866. Susannah Harper was born August 12th 1785 and died 23d December 1867.

Mrs. Sarah E. Marcus died in Troup co., Ga., Dec. 2, 1867, in her 70th year. ...we carried her to the family burying ground and laid her by the side of her husband.... T. S. L. Harwell.

Maj. Thos. H. Holmes died in Conwayboro, S. C., Feb. 19, 1868, aged about 55 years and 6 months. J. H. C. McKinney.

Mr. Geo. C. Richwood died in Conwayboro, S. C., Dec. 15, 1867, aged about 29 years. From the time of the death of his father-- J. J. Richwood, which occurred in Conwayboro, S. C., Nov. 7, 1866, George's mind is thought to have been more seriously impressed with the realities of religion.... J. H. C. McKinney.

Sister Ann M. Foster was born Jan. 18, 1810, and died in Ringgold, Ga., Nov. 2nd, 1867, in the 58th year of her age. She professed religion and joined the church in Barnwell ct., S. C., in 1840. She leaves no children, only her husband, Bro. A. H. Foster, and one sister to mourn her absence.

Miss Elizabeth Beatey, of Georgetown, S. C., died on Santee, at the residence of H. J. Bailey, Dec. 1st, 1867, aged 81 years and 20 months. She joined the Methodist Church in 1810.... J. A. P.

Sarah Paul, wife of Abraham Paul, was born Dec. 11, 1819, and died near Drayton, Dooly co., Dec. 11, 1867. She joined the M. E. Church, South, in 1834... Enos Young

Bro. Samuel Smith was born Jan. 6, 1802, and died Jan. 21, 1868. His remains slumber in the grave-yard at Smith's Chapel. W. A. Hodges

Issue of March 27, 1868

My mother in law, Mrs. Anna Jane Rogers, was born in Roberson co,. N. C., Feb. 28th, 1810, and died in Bishopville, S. C., Jan. 25th, 1868. Her parents, Daniel and Jane McCallum, were of Scotch descent and of the Presbyterian faith. When she was but eight years old, her pious mother died, and she and her young brothers were deprived of her care. After she grew up, several of her brothers settled in South Carolina, and her time was mostly spent among them. It was in Marlboro District, S. C., in 1832, that she first met Wm. Rogers, who one year after became her husband. She lived to see all of her children educated. Two of her grown children, Dr. D. M. Rogers and Mrs. H. C. Plowden, with a little daughter who died in childhood, were called before her, to their reward on high.... One week after, we were hastily summoned by the message that not only Mrs. R., but also her deal little grand-children and namesake, daughter of Mr. and Mrs. H. G. Scarborough, were both alarmingly ill.

My wife, Carolina B. Jobson, daughter of Washington and Harriet Spier, was born in Baldwin Co., Oct. 14th, 1839, and died in Perry, Ga., February 16th, 1868. John S. Jobson

Sister Mary Murph died at Midway, near Milledgeville, Ga., Feb. 5th, 1868, aged 83 years and a few days. She was born in South Carolina Feb. 1, 1785, joined the M. E. Church when 18 years old. She had buried two husbands, the last George Murph, in 1856.... These venerable female members of our Church at Milledgeville died in February-- Sister Conn aged 75; Sister Murph, aged 83, and Sister Fitzgerald, aged 93 years.

Rev. Hinton Crawford, was born Dec. 27th, 1798, in Greene co., Ga., and died Feb. 22d, 1868, in the Asylum, Milledgeville, Ga. W. R. Foote

Sister Mary E. Edwards, wife of Mr. R. D. Edwards and daughter of Rev. William H. and Gabriella E. Evans, was born in Covington, Ga., July 7th, 1842, and died near Oxford, Ga., Jan. 20th, 1868. J. J. Singelton

Mrs. Susan K. Frierson was born in Williamsburg District, Nov. 18th, 1807, married Feb. 22, 1827, was the mother of seven children, three daughters and four sons (two of the daughters and one of the sons having preceded her to the grave), and died at the house of her son-in-law, E. R. Goodman, Jan. 20th, 1868, in Sumter District, S. C. D. J. McMillan

Elsberry Robison was born Dec. 25, 1800 and died at his son-in-law's in Pike co., Ga., February 13, 1868. He was left an orphan when quite young and was raised in Washington co., Ga., by his grand mother, a Presbyterian lady.... In 1824, he joined the Church at Rock Spring C. M. He has had seven children-- five of whom and his wife had gone before him. M. Bellah

Mrs. Julia Morton, wife of Judge John F. Morton, of Chattooga co., Ga., died on 17th February 1868, aged 84 years and 9 months.

Issue of April 3, 1868

Sister Caledonia Brooks was born Dec. 2nd, 1823, in Newnan, Ga., was married to Mr. E. A. Brooks in 1852.... E. P. Birch

Wm. I. Morgan (my father) was born in Effingham co., Ga., Feb. 5, 1796, and died Feb. 1, 1868, within three miles of his birth place. He was married to Miss Christiana E. Heidt in 1822 (who still survives), joined the M. E. Church under the ministry of Rev. Joseph Edwards... member at Turkey Branch Church. He left our mother and six children. J. J. Morgan

Mrs. Sally P. Reneau, wife of Norris Reneau, died in Savannah, Ga., March 7th, 1868, in the 23d year of her age. She was born and reared in Eatonton, Ga. In May, 1867, she was married to Mr. N. Reneau and removed to Savannah. Geo. G. N. MacD.

Daniel Weaver, died in Marion co., Fla., Feb. 20, 1868, aged 60 years. Rowena Weaver, his wife, preceded him on 7th Nov. 1867, aged 50 years. Jackson Weaver, their son, died May 20, 1865, aged 20 years. Temperance E., their grand-child, and daughter of Wm. J. and Cartha Buchanan, died Aug. 16, 1867, aged 6 months. Brother Weaver and his family removed from Montgomery co., Ala., to Marion co., Fla., in 1862, where they have lived ever since. They are all buried together the Cabbage Hammock church, Marion Co., Fla. There remained seven children... D. L. Browning

Mrs. Rebecca Callaway (whose maiden name was Cockrell) was born March 4th, 1803, in Chester Dist., S. C., and died March 11th, 1868, in Noxubee co., Miss., at the residence of her son-in-law, Judge J. J. Beauchamp. She was married to the Rev. Elisha Callaway, now a member of the Mobile Conference, Jan. 27th, 1825. In 1839 she became a resident of Macon... J. Bancroft

Miss Sarah Virginia Mulkey, daughter of Rev. Homer V. and Sarah A. Mulkey, died on 19th March, at Dover, Terrell co., Ga., aged 23 years.

Asenath C. Mabry, died in peace on 19th Dec 1867, aged 61 years and 1 day... D. Whisnant

Issue of April 10, 1868

Bro. M. B. Clark was born in Mecklenburg co., Va., in 1801, and died in Newnan, Ga., January 1st, 1868. E. P. Birch

Mrs. Electra Fancena Leonard, wife of R. H. Leonard, of Talbot co, Ga., died in Talbotton, Ga., March 26th, 1868, in her 36th year. R. W. Dixon

Miss Julia A. Evans, daughter of Edward and Martha B. Evans, died in Savannah, Ga., March 15, 1868, in the 17th year of her age. Geo. G. N. MacD.

Tribute of Respect to Elder J. B. Jackson by Quarterly Meeting, Columbia ct., Florida Conference.

Tribute of Respect to Rev. Thos. J. Embry who died March 1, 1868, by Corinth Church, Franklin ct., North Georgia Conference.

Tribute of Respect to Rev. F. W. Pate by Quarterly Conference for the Marion Street Church, Columbia, S. C.

Issue of April 17, 1868

Benjamin J. Smith was born in Greenville co., Va., and died in Lowndes co., Ala., aged about 64 years. he settled in Alabama, near the line of Lowndes and Montgomery counties, 15 miles from the city of Montgomery in 1828, and pursue the life of an active, intelligent and successful planter for a score of years. B. F. Perry

Mrs. Margaret M. Wilson, wife of E. A. Wilson, and daughter of the late Wm. Eaken of Putnam co., Ga., died in Sumter co., 3d Feb. 1868, in the 32d year of her age. W. A. W.

Sister Mary J. Bayne, wife of Adolphus F. Bayne, died after an illness of only about 24 hours, near Milledgeville, Ga., on the 20th of March, in the 39th year of her age. She was formerly Mary J. Jenkins.

Campbell Raiford, son of Morris Raiford, born in Jefferson co., Ga., April 11th, 1809, died at Auburn, Ala., March 29th 1868, being nearly 59 years old. In 1836 he was married to Elizabeth Bostick and moved to Culloden; thence, in 1851, to Auburn, Ala. He married his second wife, Mrs. Henrietta A. Wimberly, in Auburn. She survives him and, wife her four children, mourns his loss. Jesse Wood

Mrs. Sarah A. Flinn, died in Brunswick, Ga., on March 24th, 1868, aged 63 years and 19 days. She was a member of the Methodist Church for about forty years... R. J. Corley

Col. Dennis Hills was born in Leominster, Mass., 6th May 1800, became a citizen of Floyd co., Ga., in 1834, and died near Rome, on the eleventh of March 1868.

William Hardin died in Chester District, S. C., December 19, 1867, aged 45 years, 8 months and 8 days. He was converted in 1840 and joined the M. E. Church under the ministry of the Rev. W. C. Patterson. Saml Leard

Mrs. Eliza Perkins, widow of William E. Perkins, and daughter of Horace and Maria Holtzclaw, died at the residence of her son-in-law, in Stewart co., Ga., aged 41 years, 8 months and 14 days. Her husband was killed at the battle of Griswoldville in 1864.... She left a mother, one brother and three children.

Jesse T. McLeran died in Suwannee co., Fla., on 27th March 1868, in the 36th year of his age. He has life a wife, four children and numerous relatives.

Tribute of Respect by the Board of Stewards of Unionville station, S. C. Conference, to A. W. Thomson, Esq., and Judge D. Goudelock.

Issue of April 24, 1868

Died

In Athens, Ga., Little Carrie, daughter of Rev. H. H. and S. A. Parks, 2 months and 2 weeks old.

Obituary

Mrs. Narcissa Stephens, wife of Captain Reuben Stephens of Colleton Dist., S. C., and mother of Rev. A. B. Stephens of the S. C. Conference was born 16th April 1805 and died 14th of March 1868. L. Wood

Rev. Henry Merk was born in Edgefield Dist., S. C., Dec. 8th, 1799. When of age he removed to Abbeville District, where at age 23, he embraced religion and joined the M. E. Church. In 1827 he removed to Athens, Ga. In 1828, to Jackson Co., Ga. In 1857, he removed to Carroll co., Ga., where he ended his labors. Father Merk leaves an aged companion and five children to mourn over their irreparable loss. W. C. Dunlap

Lewis Pou, of Lexington S. C., died April 3d, 1868, in the 78th year of his age. For more than fifty years he was a consistent member of the Methodist Church.

Andrew O. Houser of St. Mathews, S. C., died of consumption, April 6th 1868, in the 26th year of his age. [account of military service] He has left a loving wife and little daughter, some two years old. Besides, an aged father laments a Benjamin gone.

Miss Sarah Warren Shivers, daughter of Wm. Shivers Jr., and Susan F. Shivers was born in Hancock co., Ga., June 15th, 1828. Bereaved of her mother in early womanhood, she never entered into married life.... J. R. Danforth

John Buchan died in Pulaski co., Ga., in peace on 23d March, aged 87 years. Wm. F. Robison

Tribute of Respect by the Board of Trustees of East Alabama College, Auburn, to Campbell Raiford.

Issue of May 1, 1868

James M. Norwood was born Aug. 25, 1850, in Chambers co., Ala., and died Apl. 1, 1868. E. B. Norton

James Baker, died on 23d December 1867, at the residence of his son, Russell, of Fulton co., Ga., in the 86th year of his age. He was born in Albert co., removed to his parents to Franklin. In 1834 he removed to the place on which he resided as long as he was able to attend to his business. He was an associate of the late Rev. J. M. Smith.

Mrs. Ann, wife of Thos S. Glass, formerly Miss Porter, died near Newborn Ga., April 10th 1868, aged about 25 years. Before her marriage, Jan. 1861, she made a public profession of religion and joined the M. E. Church, South... left children. J. F. Mixon

Sarah A. Hill was born in Rutherford co., N. C., March 10, 1812. She was one of a family of eight sisters. Only two of these sisters now lives... she died 20th February last in the present of husband, children and friends. In the family burial ground near by, we lower her mortality into the tomb....

Mrs. Permelia F. Jackson, wife of Judge L. B. Jackson, died in Greene co., Ga., on 25th March 1868, in the 45th year of her age. She was baptized by the Rev. Charles D. Mallory.

Issue of May 8, 1868

Mrs. Clara Columbia Wiggins, widow of Dr. N. H. Wiggins, and youngest daughter of Rev. L. and A. M. Pierce, was born in Greensboro, Ga., November 8th, 1829, and died in Hancock, at the house of her brother, Bishop G. F. Pierce, April 14, 186, after three years of suffering from a diseased heart. Her Father

Rev. Williamson Smith, M. D., was born in Stanly co., N. C., and died in Clarendon District, S. C., April 2, 1868. James B. Campbell

Mrs. J. T. Wilson, relict of Wm. Wilson, Esq., and mother-in-law of the late Rev. J. Wesley Miller, of the S. C. Conference, was born April, 4th 1811, and died in Georgetown, S. C., March 27th, 1868, nearly 57 years of age.

Mrs. Aleatha P. Smith, wife of E. B. Smith, died in Talbotton, Ga., April 10th, 1868, in the 56th year of her age. R. W. Dixon

William Edward Fisher was born in Fauquier co., Va., September 13th, 1821, came to Florida with his parents in 1827, joined the M. E. Church in 1842. In January 1868, he removed from Leon co., Fla., to Cartersville Ga., and died Feb. 20th near that place.

Mr. Jas. H. Dumas was born in Monroe co., Ga., March 6th 1812, and died April 2nd, 1868-- aged 56 years.

Mrs. Nancy Wilson, daughter of Penuel and Sarah Wilson, was born Sept. 11th, 1795, in S. C. When she was quite young her parents moved to Jackson co., Ga. In Feb. 1822, she was married to Ansel B. Wilson of Oglethorpe co., Ga. They settled in Jackson co., where they lived until she died. About the last of Feb., she was taken worse and continue to grow worse until 7th March when she fell asleep in Jesus. M. F. Malsby

The latter part of the year 1867 was a period of the severest affliction in the family of Rev. Thos. Friday, of Richland District, S. C. Typhoid fever, of a malignant type, commence its deadly work, by claiming as its first victim Thomas L., a promising and pious son. He was born May 17, 1857, and died Sept. 8th, 1867. John D. was taken ill a short time after his brother was buried, and after seven days went to his reward. He was born June 27th, and died Sept. 16th 1867. The next was Nannie F., the only daughter, sick only 5 days, born July 22d, 1861, and died Sept. 16th, 1867.

Hiram Traywick was born in Twiggs co., Ga., and died near Natasulga, Macon co., Ala., April 13, 1868, aged 54 years and 10 months. He leaves a wife and three children.

Reuben H. Newton was born in South Carolina, Oct. 31, 1807, embraced religion and joined the M. E. Church in his 18th year... J. W. Parks

Bro. Seaborn Godall was born in Burke co., Ga., and died in Savannah, Ga., April 12th 1868, in the 73d year of his age.

Issue of May 15, 1868

Hiram Adolphus Troutman, third son of Mr. H. B. Troutman, of Vineville, Ga., was born in Crawford co., Ga., April 9th 1832; was a graduate of the South Carolina College in the class of 1852; was united in marriage 7th Feb. 1855 to Miss T. E. Napier, daughter of the late Mr. Skelton Napier. In the late Confederate war, he served his country.... Late in the afternoon of 21st April 1868, he visited the store of Messrs. Seymour, Johnson & Co., on 2nd Street, Macon, Ga., with view to perfect a purchase... died there.

John Kelly was drowned in the Oconee river while fishing, April 6th, 1868, in the 89th year of his age. He was born in Maryland and emigrated to Georgia in his 18th year and settled in the vicinity of Salem church, a few years after. Wm. Bryan

Dr. David A. Telfair, died in Quincy, Fla., Feb. 2d, 1868, of injuries received by being thrown from his buggy. He was born in Washington, N. C., Nov. 12th, 1823, and was a son of the late Dr. Thomas Telfair of that place. Early in life, he entered upon the practice of medicine, in his native town, and there continued until the year 1851, when he removed to Florida. A. J. W.

Mrs. Caroline Allen, wife of B. L. Allen, was born i Jasper co., Ga., and died in Davis City, Texas, March 2d, 1868, of pulmonary consumption. R. Lane

Mrs. Francis Harvill, daughter of Wm. and Elizabeth Vanlandingham, was born Dec. 1, 1834, and died in Wilkinson co., Ga., April 29, 1868. W. Lane

Mrs. Ada R., wife of Jas. E. Baugh, and daughter of W. W. and Mary W. Smith, was born near Opelika, Ala., Nov. 16, 1848, married May 9, 1865, and died March 30, 1868. She left two children, the youngest four days old. J. Lewis

Sister Sarah Bregan, daughter of Rev. Jacob Ozier, died in Cuthbert, Ga., on 26th April in the 37th year of her age. J. O. A. Cook

Mrs. Martha A. Maddux, wife of J. T. Maddux, was born in Henry co., Ga., Feb. 13th, 1838, and died of consumption ,near Midway, Ala., on 1st March 1868. She leaves a husband and two little girls to mourn her loss. W. K. Norton

Mrs. Elizabeth H., wife of Rev. G. W. Epps, died in Harris co., Ga., aged about 74 years. A husband and two surviving sons and many friends mourn her loss. W. A. Parks. Texas Advocate please copy.

Mrs. Ann Banks Smith, wife of John H. Smith, died in Culloden, April 23d, in the 48th year of her age.

Judy Harkey, died in Stanly co., N. C., on Friday 13th April 1868, aged 71 years. J. W. Puett

Marshall Everette Kendle, died on Sunday, 19th April, in Stanly co., N. C., aged 7 years and 4 months. He came to his death by the kick of a horse.... leaves his mother, Mrs. Francis Kendle, and numerous friends. J. W. Puett

Tribute of Respect by W. A. Graham Council, U. D., Fort Gaines, Ga., to Rev. James B. Jackson.

Tribute of Respect from the quarterly conference for Santee circuit, held at St. Paul's Church, to Rev. Williamson Smith, M. D.

Issue of May 22, 1868

Mrs. Celestia M. Rose, grand daughter of Mrs. M. J. Waterman, of Marietta, Ga., and wife of Samuel P. Rose, Esq., of Memphis Tenn., died at the former place April 8th, 1868, aged 22 years... She was in the care of her aunt, Mrs. Wm. Phillips.

Mrs. Mary Ann Dwight, daughter of Dr. V. D. V. Jamison, formerly, and until his decease, a resident of Orangeburg District, S. C., and widow of Samuel B. Dwight, died suddenly at Hopedale, Murray co., Ga., April 12th, in the 69th year of her age. She was a native of Orangeburg, and spent far the larger part of her life there, being one of the original founders of the Orangeburg Presbyterian Church. Cartersville Express please copy.

Mary Eliza Turner, died in Greenville, Ga., May 4th, 1868, aged 13 years, 10 months and 22 days. W. P. Kramer

Mrs. Mary Moorer, widow of Henry Moorer, died in Orangeburg Dist., S. C., on 1st April, in her 84th year. Wm. Hutto

Mrs. Milly Glenn, wife of Rev. Wm. Glenn, was born 31st August 1798, and died the 10th April 186. W. A. Hodges

Mr. William Maurice Raiford, eldest son of Rev. Capel and Ann Rebecca Raiford, was born in Jefferson co., Ga., May 2nd 1847, and died of consumption in Thomas, Ga., May 7, 1868.

Sarah Huckabee, relict of Rev. Allen Huckabee, formerly of South Carolina Conference, died in Stanly co., N. C., on 22d of January 1868. J. W. Puett

SOUTHERN CHRISTIAN ADVOCATE NOTICES 1867-1878

Issue of May 29, 1868

Col. Robert McMillan was born on 7th January 1805 near the city of Belfast, Ireland, and died in Clarksville, Ga., on 6th May 1868. From the son of the deceased I learn that he came to America about the year 1832, and engaged in mercantile pursuits in Augusta, Ga. In 1836 he was married to Miss Ruth A. Banks, of Elbert co., where he settled and continue his mercantile pursuits until 1839, when he abandoned this for the profession of the law. F. G. Hughes

Prof. J. W. Stacy was born in Burke co., N., C., Nov. 8, 1830. In his 17th year he entered Emory and Henry College, where he graduated. He began to teach in 1850 and during that year was married to Miss Margaret L. Allen of North Carolina... W. M. Patterson

B. F. Bradford, Esq., of Walterboro, S. C., was brutally murdered on 26th Feb. 1868. John W. McRoy

Walter Raleigh Pearson, son of Thos. G. and Susan H. Pearson, was born in Heard co., Ga., Dec. 25th, 1845, and died of pulmonary disease, in Tallapoosa co., Ala., April 5th, 1868. L. R. Bell

James M. Richardson died in Gainsville, Fla., April 13th 1868, in the 58th year of his age. He was born in Lancaster, S. C., where he devoted himself to God in early life and became a humble but earnest member of the Methodist Church. Removing to Florida in after years.... Jas. O. A. S.

Mrs. Mary B. Persons, wife of Augustus A. Persons, and daughter of John Quigly, was born at Fort Valley, Ga., Jan. 2, 1820, and died near Enon, Ala., on the 11th April 1868.... W. K. Norton

Rev. R. McHan died in Waldo, Fla., March 2nd, 1868, in the 44th year of his age. He has left a disconsolate widow and three little ones.

Tribute of Respect by Newnansville, Fla., Quarterly Conference to Bro. James B. Jackson.

Issue of June 5, 1868

Died

In Athens Ga., on 28th May, Albon Chase, infant son of Rev. W. P. and Sallie E. Pattillo, aged one month, two weeks, and two days.

Obituary

Mrs. Caroline M, widow of the late W. W. D. Weaver, was born in Washington, Ga., Jan 4th, 1800 and died in Greensboro', Ga., April 29th, 1868. W. C. Bass

Capt. Joseph M. Kennedy was born May 19th, 1833, and died at Cedar Shoals, in Newton co., Ga., 18th May 1868. He entered the service of the Confederate States, in the late was, in the 9th Texas Infantry.... After the close of the war he was united in marriage with Miss Foster, a daughter of Dr. Edward Foster, of Louisville, Mississippi. Gustavus J. Orr

Ida F. Wright, wife of Dr. C. C. Wright, and daughter of Silas D. and Frances Allen, died in Wakulla, Fla., on 16th Feb. 1868, aged 18 years.

Hattie A. Garrison, daughter of R. S. and S. E. Garrison, formerly of Bowdon, Ga., died at San Marcos, Texas, on 19th of April 1868, in her 5th year. M. A. Texas Christian Advocate please copy.

Miss Fannie H. Crawford, daughter of John L. Crawford, of Wakulla co., Fla., died Feb. 28th, 1868, in the 19th year of her age.

Tribute of Respect to Rev. James B. Jackson, by Florida Conference, M. E. C. S.

Tribute of Respect to J. Morton Watts, eldest son of Mrs. W. W. Jackson, born September 12, 1853, and died 21st April 1868, by Culloden Sabbath School.

Tribute of Respect to Obadiah Foster, who was killed by falling from the wall of a house, May 11, 1868, in the 83d year of his age.

Issue of June 12, 1868

Sister Arrilla H. Tennyson died on 17th Feb., near Society Hill, Macon co., Ala., in the 65th year of her age. She was born in Lincoln co., Ga., and was united in marriage to Maj. Samuel Tennyson, Jan. 26th 1826. She leaves an aged husband and six children-- one in Mississippi.

Sister Mary Corley, daughter of John and Sarah Renehart, was born in Edgefield Dist., S. C., Nov. 13th, 1822, professed religion and joined the Methodist Church in her 18th year. She was married to the Rev. John Corley, Aug. 4, 1842, and died near Harpersville, Shelby co., Ala., April 23, 1868. N. H. Self

Willie Fouche, son of George W. and L. Fouche, died near Culloden, May 8th, aged 18 years.

Mrs. Elizabeth Bird, was born 14th Sept 1799, in Maryland, and died at the residence of her daughter, Mrs. Upton in Abbeville Dist., S. C., on April 25th, 1868. Mother Bird was in the little town of Greenwood where she had long resided, a proverb of piety.

Mary Catharine Davis, daughter of N. S. and Margaret Duke, was born in Macon co., Ala., Oct. 18, 1840, and died in Bullock co., Ala., April 30, 1868. In Dec. 1865 she was married to Geo. F. Davis.... J. W. Shores

William M. Chipley was born Feb. 27, 1839 in Abbeville Dist., S. C., and died in Madison co., Fla., March 2, 1868.

Brother C. G. Welborn was born Oct. 1839 and died in Columbia co., Ga., April 29th, 1868. He has left a devoted wife and two small children.

Herbert Murray Gaddy, youngest son of Samuel Y. and C. E. Gaddy, was born in Marion District, S. C., July 29th, 1864 and died April 13th 1868. J. B. Platt

Tribute of Respect by St. Paul's and Summerton churches, Santee ct., S. C. Conference, to Rev. Hartwell Spain.

Tribute of Respect by McDonough ct., N. G. Conference, to J. C. Simmons.

Tribute of Respect from Upper St. Matthews ct., Orangeburg, S. C., to Lewis Pou.

Issue of June 19, 1868

Died

On the 11th inst., at the residence of Mr. David H. Dougherty of Atlanta, Ga., Mrs. Sarah A. Wilson, wife of W. A. Wilson, of Fulton co., Ga., and daughter of Mason and Minerva Gloss, of Newton Co.

Obituary

A Trio of Worthies Gone. 1st Mrs. Elizabeth Hargroves died near Harmony Grove in Jackson co., Ga., April 15th, 1868, aged 84 years 4 months and 8 days. 2d. Mrs. Permelia A. Pharr, aged about 67 years, died in Newton co., Ga., near the "Circle," April 17, 1868. 3d. More than two years before sister Pharr's death, her husband Alexander Pharr, died at the same place and about the same age. They were both raised in Oglethorpe co. W. J. Parks

Mrs. Abraham S. Harris was born in Hancock co., Ga., 10th Sept. 1818, married 31st Oct 1833, joined the M. E. Church in 1838 and died at LaGrange, Ga., 10th May 1868. Nashville Advocate please copy.

My dear wife, Mrs. Louisa O. Turner, fell asleep in Jesus on 7th May 1868, in her 34th year.... A. M. Turner

Mrs. Cynthia Cotton, wife of Wm. G. Cotton, was born Oct. 5th 1791 and died in Troup co., Ga., April 23d 1868. In the 12th year of her age, she embraced religion and joined the Baptist Church. After her marriage she joined the M. E. Church of which her husband had been a member... Her husband, who is quite old, still lingers on the shores of time. P. M. Ryburn

Tribute of Respect adopted at Old Church, Waynesboro ct., South Georgia Conference to John Devine Carswell, who was born in Richmond co., Ga., July 16th 1841 and died of pneumonia in Burke co., Feb. 28, 1868.

Issue of June 26, 1868

Died

in Savannah, Ga., on the evening of the 5th June 1868, Alexander Wellington, aged only nine hours; and on the evening of the 13th June 1868, Eddie Wynn, aged only eight days and five and a half hours, infant and twin children of Ely and Anna C. Otto.

Obituary

Sister Elizabeth Rumph was born 29th Nov 1788 and died May 20th 1868 in her 80th year. Her birth-place was Orangeburg Dist., S. C. Here she grew to womanhood and was married to John Rumph. She died at the residence of Rev. C. A. Crowell in Dawson, Ga., who married her daughter. Sister Crowell of Dawson and sister Pooser of Jackson co., Fla. are the only children that survived her.... T. T. Christian

Mrs. Mary J. Sherman died in Macon, Ga., at the residence of her son-in-law, Mr. William Wilder, April 14, 1868. She was born in Charleston, S. C., July 9, 1794. Her parents removed to Camden when she was quite young, where she was reared and lived until her marriage with my father, Samuel Sherman in 1814. She came to Georgia in 1821, where she resided until her death. She leaves five children to mourn her loss. Her husband and eight children preceded her to the tomb. M. K. Sherman

Jarvis Seale was born in Prince William co., Va., June 19, 1785. His mother having died when he was a few days old, he was reared until his 7th year by a devout aunt.... He held membership for many years with the church at Independence, Wilkes co., Ga. The last two or three years of his life were spent at Zebulon, Ga., where he died April 15, 1868, being with a few weeks of 83 years old. In a note, his son, Rev. R. A. Seale, says: "His illness was of short but painful duration...." R. W. Bigham

Sister Sarah M. G, Parker died in Spaulding co., on the 16th May 1868, In her 72nd year, making only a brief tarry behind her husband with whom she had journeyed up and down the hill of life for half a century. They were among the early settlers of Georgia.... W. M. Crumly

Miss Miranda Woody died in Thomasville 20th May at the residence of her brother in law, Bro. Bottoms, aged 21 years. She was the daughter of Rev. James Woody, deceased, of the Florida Conference. Death is fast gathering Bro. Woody's children to him, as this is the second one this year... N. S. Ousley

Mrs. Catharine A. Fears, daughter of Jas. and Mary E. Ramsey, was born in Henry co., Ga., April 21st 1821, moved with her parents to Harris co., Ga., and was married to Rev. Thos J. Fears, M. D., December 23d, 1840, and died in Salem, Ala., May 18th, 1868. J. H. Lockhart

George McMillan was born on 2d April 1847 and died on 28th May 1868. This is the third member of the family who has died within the last six months--the father, mother and son. F. G. Hughes

Rev. West Williams was born in April 1792 and died in St. James Goose Creek, S. C., May 2d 1868. He was admitted in the itinerant minister of the Methodist Church in South Carolina, Jan. 1814. For about fifty years he had regularly preached at Spring Hill Church the first Sabbath of each month.

Sister H. Wheeler died in Monroe co., on 2d June 1868. She had been a consistent member of the M. E. Church, South, for forty-three years. F. B. Davies

Tribute of Respect by Conyers ct., N. Ga. Conference, to Joseph M. Kennedy.

Issue of July 3, 1868

Rev. George Watson, Jr., a local elder of the Newnansville Station, Florida Conference, was born in Maine, Dec. 24th, 1811. A graduate of West Point, he served six years in the U. S. service. He moved to this country over thirty years ago. He was one of the chief surveyors in this "Land of flowers." On Sunday evening March 22d, 1868, he was transferred to that "Land of pure delight." E. S. Tyner

Mrs. Martha E. Goode, relict of Dr. S. W. Goode, died in Stewart co., March 7th, 1868, having reached almost the close of her 44th year of life.

Henry R. Barr was born May 24th 1838 and died in Lexington Dist., S. C., Feb. 13th, 1868. He was for a number of years a consistent member of the M. E. Church, South. he had been for several years laboring under epilepsy, which towards the close of his mortal career, was protracted and severe. Bro. Barr has left a widow, five children, and numerous relatives. This affliction not only rests heavily upon his disconsolate widow, but also on his aged parents. he and his family resided with them. And he was the son of their old age.

Rev. John P. Moate was born March 6th 1793 in S. Ca., and died in Dooly co., Sept 4, 1867, with paralysis. He was licensed to preached in 1813 and for seven years was a member of the Georgia Conference. Bro. Moate for the last ten years lived in Dooly Co.... E. J. Rentz

Mrs. Leah E. White, wife of W. T. White, was born Nov. 10th 1846 and died May 29th 1868, in Houston co., Ga.... W. W. Stewart

Daniel Davis died in Lumpkin co., Ga., June 10th 1868 in the 83d year of his age. He was one of the first settlers of this county and was a good citizen, an obliging neighbor, an affectionate husband, a kind father, and a humane master. G. Hughes

Miss Sarah F. Golden died in Roanoke, Randolph co., Ala., April 28th 1868. She was an acceptable member of the Methodist Church... T. J. G.

James Marshall, second son of Samuel and Sarah Ellis, died in Jasper co., Ga., May 12th 1868, in his 15th year. W. W. Oslin

Dr. J. D. Smith was born near Charlotte, N. C., Sept. 11th 1816, and died in Baker co,. Ga., May 28th 1868 of consumption. H. D. Moore

Florella Singleton Ingram, daughter of Wm. R. A. and Martha Ingram, of Schley co., Ga., was born Feb. 26th 1855, died 5th May 1868.

Tribute of Respect by 2nd quarterly conference of Mt. Hilliard Circuit, Montgomery Conference, also the Magnolia Methodist Church, Bullock county, Ala., to Brother Samuel C. Watkins who was born in North Carolina, Feb. 1, 1811.

Issue of July 10, 1868

My Mother, Mrs. Sarah Kibble McGehee, daughter of Marshall and Jane McMartin, was born in Wilkes co.,Ga., Nov. 28th 1804, was married to Thos F. McGehee, Dec. 29th 1826, and died in Meriwether co., June 20, 1868, of chronic diarrhoea. Her husband, son, and her brother, the late W. D. Martin were ministers. J. W. McGehee.

Rev. Thomas Cook was born Oct. 20th, 1802, and died May 22d, 1868. His father, James Cook, was one among the first Methodists of Marlborough Dist.,S. C., and was for many years a class leader at Beauty Spot Church. L. M. Hamer

Mrs. Martha E. Hargrove, wife of Col. J. P. Hargrove, was born in Lunenburg co., Va., June 25, 1819, and died near Quincy, Fla., March 4, 1868.... A. J. Woldridge

Mr Mother, Mary Kensall, was born in Wilkes co., Ga., 24th July 1780, and died near Flatshoals, Meriwether co., 24th April 1868, after an illness of but a few days.... She was married twice, and her last husband the late Maj. E. Kendall she survived over twenty five years. She was the mother of eleven children, all of whom she survived but three.

Mrs. Sarah A. Wilson, wife of Judge Wm. A. Wilson, of Fulton co., Ga., and daughter of Manson and Minerva Glass, of Newton co., Ga., was born March 16, 1840, graduated with honor at the S. M. F. College, Covington, Ga., June 1858, married Dec. 1859, and died in perfect peace, June 14th 1868. F. A. Kimbell

Mrs. H. H. Dodge, wife of Rev. W. A. Dodge of the N. G. Conference, and daughter of Robert L. and A. L. Williams was born in Oxford, Ga., Jan 25th, 1844, and died in DeKalb co., Ga., April 12th, 1868, in the 25th year of her life.

James E. Bustin, only son of Edward C. and Caroline T. Bustin, of Fayette co., Ga., was thrown from a mule and instantly killed May 23d, 1868.... Robert Stripling

Samuel P. Walker was born in So. Ca., May 15, 1807, was left an orphan at an early age, was brought to DeKalb co., Ga., where he grew up to manhood. He was married in Elbert co., Ga., Jan 21st, 1841, joined the M. E. Church in 1840, and died in Cobb co., Ga., May 17th, 1868, aged 61 years and 2 days.... James N. Myers, Pastor.

Issue of July 17, 1868

Bro. John Harper died in Pike co., Ga., on 20th June 1868, in the 85th year of his age. He was one of the first settlers in this county. The mother of his children died many years since. He married a second wife with whom he lived until separate from her and his children and grand children and many relatives and friends by death.... R. A. Seale

Mrs. Rebecca Williamson died April 17th 1868, in the 59th year of her age. In her 20th year she became a member of the M. E. Church. She was probably the first person that joined the infant society at Old Sandy Spring, Laurens Dist., S. C.,... She subsequently removed to Spartanburg District, where she spent the greater portion of her life as a teacher.

Mrs. Hattie Brown, wife of the late Mr. J. W. Brown, and daughter of Rev. D. N. and A. E. Burkhalter of Marion co., Ga., died near Columbus, Ga., June 10th 1868, in her 34th year. She graduated in the Wesleyan Female College in 1852. She called out the name of her sister Fannie and children, sometime since deceased.

Henry W. Ackerman died June 13th 1868, aged ___ years. A widow, a son and two daughters are left to mourn. John W. McRoy

Mrs. Mary M. Wyly, wife of James A. Wyly and daughter of E. P. and Elizabeth Williams, died in Nacoochee Valley, on 28th June, in her 26th year... F. H. Hughes

Mr. John M. Tatom, son of Isaac and James Tatom, was born in Lincoln co., Ga., on 30th Nov 1804, removed to Monroe co. and married Miss Francis D. hicks in 1827, from thence removed to Upson, then to Troup co., then to Union co., Arkansas, where he died of typhoid pneumonia in peace on 4th May 1868. His wife still survives him... Abel Tatom

Judge Burrel Thomas Pope died May 8, 1868, in Gadsden, Ala., after an illness of six weeks. He was born in Oglethorpe co., Ga., Jan. 7, 1813, was the son of Wiley and Sarah Pope, joined the M. E. Church in Athens, Ga., in 1827. he studied law with Judge Clayton of Athens. In 1837 he removed to Wetumpka, Ala., until he removed to Ashville, St. Clair co., Ala in 1844. He married Miss Joanna Lester, January 8, 1838. He removed to Gadsden, Ala., in 1867. He leaves a widow and eight children. W. L. Clifton

Mrs. Mary Wright died on Cypress ct., S. C., 28th May 1868, in her 83d year She has left two children... A. R. Danner

Mrs. Lucretia Brown, wife of Mr. D. P. Brown, died in Baldwin co., on the 19th of June 1868, in the 54th year of her age, leaving a husband and nine children.

William Marcellus Nolan, son of Q. R. Nolan, of McDonough, Ga., was toying with a small repeater, while engaged in pleasant conversation, when the pistol was accidentally discharged. He lived but one hour and died thus on the 15th June 1868, aged 17 years.

Tribute of Respect by White Sulphur Springs S. School to Rev. Richard S. Marks.

Tribute of Respect to Bro. John C. Simmons by quarterly conference of Griffin Station....

Issue of July 24, 1868

Died

Clarence Lee, first son of f. L. and W. L. Stanton, was born on 14th Feb. 1866 and died 17th June 1868, near Spring Place, Georgia.

Obituary

Mrs. Elizabeth Hameter, widow of the excellent Joel Hameter, the memory of whose virtues is cherish in the churches of Ala., died March 10th, in Barbour co., Ala. She was the daughter of Andrew and Nancy Bates, born in Edgefield Dist., S., C., Jan. 15, 1808. Nov. 14, 1833, she was happily married to him who for more than thirty years was her earthly stay and comfort, until God took him and left her with two affectionate daughters. Her daughter Julia died in 1857 while at College in Tuskegee.... A. J. Hamill

Mrs. Idia Thornton was born Aug 13th 1843 and died at her uncle's Captain Thomas Prather's in Quitman co., June 27th, 1868. She was greatly afflicted in the loss of her husband and two lovely children in less than one year... S. R. Weaver

Sister Anna E. Jones, wife of Geo. H. Jones, and daughter of A. W. and Exer A. Martin, formerly of Americus Ga., was born Sept 29th 1837, and died in Gwinnett co., Ga., June 7, 1868. J. M. Lowrey

Mrs. Keziah Ford, relict of Hezekiah Ford, was born in Fairfield Dist., S. C., and died in Talbotton, Ga., July 3, 1868, in her 75th year. R. W. Dixon

Miss Josie E., daughter of L. C. and S. A. Mims, was born at Lumpkin, Stewart co., Ga., May 6, 1848, and died at Whitesville, Harris co., Ga., June 26, 1868. She was a pupil at Oak Bowery Female College, Ala.... W. J. Cotter

Issue of July 31, 1868

Mrs. Kitty Hamer, wife of Daniel H. Hamer, died June 11th 1868... L. M. Hamer

Mrs. Martha R. Gore, wife of Mr. James W. Gore, who removed to Florida last January from South Carolina, died in Marion co., Fla., on 15th June 1868, in the 40th year of her age. She was the mother of a large family of children.

Irbin Collins was born Nov. 28th, 1808, and died with disease of the heart in Butts co., Ga., July 4th, 1868. The family has lost a devoted and affectionate husband and parent.... Texas, Arkansas, and N. O. Christian Advocate please copy.

Frances T. Reid, wife of Alexander Reid, of Putnam co., Ga., was born in Green co., Ga., Nov. 20th, 1810, died on 13th June 1868.

Mr. Joseph Swicord of Sumter co., Fla., was born in Decatur co., Ga., July 22nd 1826, and died at the residence of his brother-in-law's, Dr. T. P. McHenry, of Newnansville, Fla., June 23d, 1868. E. S. Tyner

Tribute of Respect by the Quarterly Conference of Zebulon circuit, N. Ga. Conference, to Thos. F. McCarty who died on the 25th inst [June].

Issue of August 7, 1868

Died

Willie Harris, son of Rev. W. B. and Mrs. M. A. Turner, died of Cholera Infantum in Dadeville, Ala., on Sunday morning, July 26th 1868--aged 11 months, 22 days, and 3 hours.

Obituary

Daniel Wesley Morse, son of Oliver and Anna Morse, was born in Forsyth, Ga., Jan 1st 1854, and died of bilious remittent fever, July 18th 1868, aged 14 years, six months and 18 days.... W. P. Pledger.

Mrs. Isabella J. Collins was born Nov. 11th 1810 and died of tumor, June 14th 1868 near Cade's Turnout, Williamsburg District, S.C. D. J. McMillan

Mrs. Frances L. Potter, wife of G. A. Potter, was born July 15th 1844 and died in Taylor co., Ga., July 10th 1868. G. L. W. Anthony

D. W. Holloway, of Abbeville Dist., S. C., died on the 15th May 1868, aged 24 years.

John Holly died in Barnwell Dist., S. C., on 15th July 1868, in the 77th year of his age. Joseph Holmes

William King, born in N. C., June 20, 1786, died near Hartsville, S. C., May 17th 1868.

Miss Mary C. Ferguson, second daughter of the late Rev. F. G. Ferguson of the Alabama Conference, was born in Tuscaloosa, Ala., May 5th 1849, and died in Tuskegee, Ala., July 2d 1868.

Miss Mattie E. Turnipseed was born in Richland Dist., S. C., her parents removed to Georgia in 1859, and she died in Meriwether co., Ga.... N. E. Turnipseed

Mrs. Hannah Conley died in Jackson co., Fla., June 10th 1868, aged 72 years. She leaves a husband 86 years of age, children and grand children. A. M. Gillespie

Mrs. Nancy A., wife of Allen Goodwin, and daughter of Seth and Martha Hamer, died very suddenly in Harris co., Ga., aged 27 years.

Tribute of Respect from Weston Lodge to Rev. J. G. M. Hall, P. M., who died on the 4th July.

Issue of August 14, 1868

Rev. James G. M. Ball was born July 31st 1809, joined the M. E. Church Feb. 22d, 1825, was licensed to preach Sept. 27, 1837, ordained Deacon by Bishop Soule, January 1844, Elder by Bishop Capers Feb. 1848, and fell asleep in Jesus July 4th, 1868. J. B. McGehee

Richard R. Richardson, a member of Mulberry Street Church, Macon, Ga., died July 26th, in the 29th year of his age.

Miss Sue Crittenden, daughter of Judge Wm. Crittenden, of Griffin, Ga., died near Fort Valley, July 22.

Mrs. Elizabeth W. Hawkins (whose maiden name was Boon) was born July 13, 1794, and died in Americus, Ga., July 28, 186, in the 75th year of her age. She was converted in 1812 under the preaching of Rev. Hope Hull, and married to Willis A Hawkins, Sr., in 1816. S. Anthony

Rev. Phillip Dell, of Sumter Co., Ga., has been bereaved of two lovely and amiable sons. Maxey B. Dell was born in 1847. Also John H. Dell, his brother, in the 24th year of his age. S. Anthony

Nicholas Eugene Arnold, son of E. B. and Susan Arnold of Henry co., Ga., was born Jan. 14, 1868, and died July 8, 1868. Hudson Wade Arnold, son of Hon. E. B. and Susan Arnold, was born June 1st, 1850, and died July 15, 1868. B. J. Johnson

Wesley Nix, son of Miles and Rachael Nix, died in Union Dist., S. C., July 5, 1868, in his 20th year.

James M. Brown died at the residence of his father in Telfair Co., Ga., May 20, 1868... The deceased leaves a father and mother, four sisters and a brother.

Issue of August 21, 1868

Died

Pringle, only son of Dr. J. R. and Lula P. Campbell, died at Catoora Springs, July 30, 1868, aged 5 months and 10 days.

In Houston co., Ga., on the 28th July 1868, I. J. M., son of Irvin H. and Joana English, aged 5 years.

Sarah Norman, youngest daughter of Wm. B. and M. V. Stewart, was born in Sumter co., Ga., Dec. 5, 1863, and died July 23, 1868.

Wistar Curtis, son of Rev. J. E. and Lavinia Watson, S. C. Conference, died Jun 31, 1868.

Obituary

Emily Celestie Carson, daughter of Wiley M. and Mary S. White, was born June 11, 1838, in Greensboro, Ga., and died in Fla., June 22, 1868. S. W. Carson

Miss Willie B. Aaron, daughter of J. C. and Bethire Aaron, was born in Jasper co., Ga., 24th July 1848, and died 25 July 1868.

Miss Josie C daughter of Rev. Dr. W. T. and Sarah A. Harrison was born in Jefferson co., Fla., Sept. 17th 1847, and died in Ocala, June 16th 1868.

Mrs. Elizabeth A. DuBose, died at the residence of her son, Jas. R. DuBose, in Abbeville Dist., S. C., on Friday 31st July in the 42nd year of her age.

Ira H. Harden, Esq., died on Lady Lake, Sumter co., Fla., aged 52 years and 2 months. He emigrated from Chester Dist., S. C., in 1846.

John W. Miller was born August 14, 1833 and died near West Point, Ga., June 25, 1868. He leaves a widow, a babe, an aged father, brothers and sisters. P. M. Ryburn

Tribute of Respect by Kimbrough Lodge, No 118, to Robt. W. Faulkenberry.

Issue of August 28, 1868

Thomas A. Lipsey was born June 22, 1836, and died Aug. 4, 1868. Wofford College is bereaved of a son... J. E. Watson

Miss Polkie Thomason, daughter of Rev. E. D. and Sarah Thomason, died in Carrollton, Ga., July 14th 1868. She was born May 7, 1845... W. C. Dunlap

Eliza A. W. Cain, daughter of James B. and Elizabeth Cain, was born May 8, 1812, married Judge Robert Walker, Feb. 15, 1828, and died in Spalding co,. Ga., Aug. 6, 1868.

Mrs. Rebecca Christian was born Aug 12, 1789, and died May 6, 1868. She, with her family, moved from Montgomery co., N. C., in 1835, and settled in Calhoun co., Ala. From thence they moved to Pike co.,Ala., where her husband William L. Christian died in Greenville, Ala. She lived with her great grandson Martin Teage, until her death.

Mrs. Jane McRae, wife of John C. McRae, was born Feb. 26, 1806, in Anson Co., N., C., married Sept. 21, 1826, joined the M. E. Church in 1843, and died in Barbour Co., Ala., June 17, 1868.

My Father, Zadock Blalock, died in peace, in Fayette co., Ga., on 31st May 1868, aged 84 years and 21 days. he was born, raised, and married to my mother Margaret Lewis, in Randolph co, N. C., where he has many friends and relatives. My mother preceded him to the good world nearly 20 years. He has left a wife and nine children. W. H. Blalock.

Mrs. Sarah Ann Crow was born in S. C., in 1836, and died in Greenville, Ala., June 1868.

Andrew J. Phipps, aged 39 years, was suddenly killed by a fall from his horse, on June 15th, and on 18th July following, his brother, William Henry Phipps, aged 27 years, died of brain fever. They were the sons of Mr. and Mrs. Elbert and Eliza Phipps, of Stewart co., Ga. B. J. Baldwin.

Sister Nancy Smith was born Dec. 25, 1792, and died June 5, 1868. In her youth she joined the Presbyterian Church. A few years afterward she joined the Methodist Church. She reared a pious family. J. E. Watson

Gadson W. Stephens, son of Mr. John K. and Mrs. Mary S. Stephens, died near Newnansville, Fla., on 29th June 1868, in his 18th year. Within three weeks of his death, his little sister, Laura, six years old, died.

Mrs. Nannie E. Shettles died at Woodbery, Merlwether Co., Ga., __ July 1868, in the 20th year of her age.

Issue of September 4, 1868

Mrs. Sarah M. Willisson died at the residence of her son-in-law, Major Chas. L. Scott, in Camden, Wilcox co., Ala., July 26, 1868, aged 71 years. She was born in Columbia, S. C., in 1797.

Mrs. Frances A. Black, wife of Capt. C. B. Black, and daughter of Thomas and Mary Johnson, of Putnam co,. Ga., died in Russell co., Ala., July 20, 1868. She was married to her now bereaved husband Oct. 28, 1852. She leaves a husband and five small children. Wm. B. Neal

Miss Emma F. Osier, daughter of Perry and Clarissa Osier, was born in Pike co,. Ala., June 11, 1851, and died in Montgomery co., Ala., Aug. 6, 1868, aged 17 years, 1 month and 25 days. A. Dowling

Mrs. Mary Jane Harper, wife of Rev. Robert L. Harper, of the S. C. Conference, and only daughter of Dr. Sam'l D. and Mrs. Martha J. Sanders, formerly of Cheraw, S. C., but now of Jackson, Tenn., was born Oct. 29, 1848, and died in Greenville, S. C., at the residence of Mr. J. A. David, on 22d July 1868. In her 18th year while attending a meeting at the church of her grandmother, Mrs. Jane Pegues in Marlborough Dist., she was soundly converted to God. Eleven months before her death she was happily married to Rev. Robert L. Harper.... Sam'l D. Sanders

Miss Margaret V. Mulling, daughter of Bro. J. T. and sister Mulling, died in Jefferson co., Ga., Aug. 2, 1868, aged 14 years and 6 days. Tribute of respect from Oak Grove Sunday School.

John S. Murray was born in Burke co., Ga., Nov. 3, 1808. His parents were Stephen and Mary Murray. In 1829 or 1830 he came to Houston co., Ga., married Miss Julia Ann Royal, Dec. 1831; removed to Marion, now Taylor Co., until called to his reward on the 16th August. Wyatt Brooks.

Miss Mary J. Miller died at the residence of her grandmother near Micanopy, May 27, 1868, aged 27 years and 10 months. John C. Ley

Nathaniel Scott of Scriven co., Died Aug 5, 1868, aged 74 years. W. B. Jarrell

Mrs. Elizabeth Bethea, relict of Parker Bethea, Esq., was born in Marion dist., S. C., April 23, 1794, and died in her native district, April 27, 1868.

Annie F. Pitner was born April 13, 1845-- the daughter of Rev. Jno. L. Richardson and Susan W. Richardson. She was married to Jno. C. Pitner of Athens, Ga., Nov 1856, and died at Nocoochee, Ga., Aug. 11, 1868. H. H. Parks

J. D. Slater died with disease of the heart in Barnwell dist., S. C., July 30, 1868.

Willis Bulloch was born about the year 1800 and died in Wilkinson co., Ga., Aug. 5, 1868. W. Lane.

Issue of September 11, 1868

Died

In Buenta Vista, Ga., Little "Sallie," daughter of Elamn Johnson, Esqr., and his wife Permelia S. Johnson, born Sept. 21st 1807, died August 1, 1868.

Obituary

Mrs. Caroline C. S. Weaver, wife of Judge T. A. D. Weaver, was born April 2, 1805, and died in Thomaston, Ga., August 8, 1868. In 1829 she was married to her surviving husband. She is missed by two sons, a daughter and granddaughter. D. Kelsey

Mrs. Anna Maria Seale, wife of Rev. D. W. Seale, of the S. C. Conference, died at the residence of her father, James Graham, Esq., near Marion, S. C., Aug. 25, in her 34th year. She did not make a profession of conversion until 1860, when at Bethel camp ground, Sumter Dist., S. C., she experienced a change. She was married to Rev. D. W. Seale May 8, 1866. G. H. Wells

Miss Mary Ann Dickert was born near Pomaria, Newberry Dist., S., C., May 19, 1821, and died Aug. 1, 1868. W. H. D.

Alonzo W. Jones was a citizen of Bibb co., and died in Macon, whither he had gone for medical treatment, June 14.... He left and wife and three children. John M. Marshall

Samuel Elvah, eldest son of Rev. Wm. E. Jones of West Point Ga., died Aug 23, aged 9 years and 6 months.

Issue of September 18, 1868

Died

in Cokesbury, S., C., Aug 19, Manning Austin, infant of Rev. W. H. and Mrs. E. Carrie Fleming, aged 14 months and 8 days.

Obituary

Oliver Moore died in Forsyth, Ga., Aug. 7, 1868, in the 65th year of his life. J. T. Lin

John Robert Zitrouer fell asleep in Jesus at his residence near Paine's Prairie, Alachua co., Fla., Aug. 7th 1868. He was born in Effingham co., Ga., April 11, 1802. March 13th 1828 he was happily married to Miss Eliza Remshart of Savannah, by whom he had thirteen children. In 1834 he removed to Florida, where he has since lived respected by the community. John A. Kennedy

Henry J. Slappey died in 2d August in Baker co., Ga., aged the age of 41. When quite a young man, he removed from Twiggs in Baker co., and engaged in the business of agriculture....

Miss N. A. St. John was born April 24th 1847 and died of typhoid fever in Troup co., Ga., July 19th 1868.

Susan Elizabeth, daughter of J. E. and Sarah Groce, was born in Talladega co., Ala., July 30th 1849 and died Aug 10th 1868. W. B. Kirk

Mrs. Elizabeth Aldred was born in 1780 and died in Warren co., Ga., Sept. 4, 1868. She was a member of the Methodist Church 65 years... Amos Johnson

Mrs. Sarah H. Lunsford died on 2nd June in the 57th year of her age.

Issue of September 25, 1868

Died

Mrs. Nannie Amelia, wife of Rev. Charles J. Oliver, aged 21 years, died in Atlanta, Ga., Sept 16, 1868, at the residence of Mr. J. B. D. Ogburn, of congestion of the brain.

Obituary

Bro. William Morel was born in Savannah, Ga., in 1796, and died in that city, Aug 6, 1868, in the 73d year of his age. His early life was devoted to the study and practice of law. Geo. G. N. MacD.

Rev. Gabriel Toombs Spearman, son of John and Ann Dawson Spearman, was born in Wilkes co., Ga., Sept. 26, 1798, and died in Jasper co., Ga., 17th August 1868. 1. F. Mixon

Mrs. Mary Buff, wife of Daniel W. Buff, of Houston co., Ga., Died Aug. 11, 1868, aged about 57 years... Samuel N. Dunwody

Riley J. Johnson, a prominent and faithful member of our Church in Rome, Ga., died Aug. 28, 1868, in the 53d year of his age.

Col. Robert Mitchell was born in Franklin co., Ga., Jan. 4, 1801, and died in Rome, Ga., June 30, 1868. In early life he was in the legal profession, and practiced with success in Hall and the adjoining counties of Georgia. In 1840 he moved to Lafayette, Chambers co., Ala.... later to Tuskegee where his family now resides.

Harriet Boyd, wife of the Rev. J. M. Boyd, a local preacher of the Newberry ct., S. C., died Sept. 4, 1868. She was born in Columbia, Oct. 22, 1839, and was left without a mother and two and a half years of age; was raised and educated by her aunt, Mrs. S. Cromer, who is now a member of the family. married in 1854. She gave her father-in-law, Rev. M. M. Boyd, to understand that all was peace and calm.

Wm. McKendree Littlejohn, son of John Littlejohn, of Polk co., N. C., was born Aug. 22, 1842, and died 18th August 1868. J. A. Wood

William H. G., son of Philip H. and Jane E. Delane, was born in Sumter co., Ga., Feb. 1, 1851, and died in Macon, Ga., Aug. 17, 1868.

Issue of October 2, 1868

Died

in Fort Valley, Ga., on Saturday evening, the 19th Sept., James Charles, only child of George W. and Ella E. Maddox, aged one year and five days.

In Sandersville, Ga., Sept. 19th, Tallula, youngest daughter of Rev. J. M. and Orellie S. Austin, aged two years, one month and 25 days.

Obituary

Capt. Thomas Surtis died at the residence of his son-in-law, John D. Doig, in Gainsville, Fla., June 19, 1868, in his 68th year. he became a citizen of Charleston, S. C., in 1817. His business was on the sea-- being a pilot of the bar and harbor of Charleston for 49 years. His aged companion still lingers with the children he has left.... S. L. S.

Mrs. Mary Brown, wife of Judge B. B. Brown, died in Fort Valley, August 16. She was a member of the Presbyterian Church. She was a resident of Staunton, Virginia, and her home was in her native State until the removal of the family to Georgia during the recent war.

Mrs. Mary Pattillo died in the 72nd year of her age, at Whitesville, Harris co., Ga., on 11th Sept 1868. She was a daughter of Nathan Winfield and was married to John Pattillo, who survives her, in Feb. 1815. Converted in Greene co., Ga., in 1820. W. J. Cotter

Mrs. Susan Walker Shaw, wife of Mr. Alfred Shaw, died in Madison, Ga., on 6th July last. She was born March 26th, 1808, in Greenville, S. C., and several years afterward removed to the city in which she breathed her last. She became identified with the Methodist E. Church in 1826, and four years from that time she united with Mr. Alfred Shaw of that place. A. Means

Wm. W. Palmer, son of Amasa Palmer, born in Greene co., Ga., Sept. 19, 1810, and died near South Butler, Butler co., Ala., July 29th 1868.

Mrs. Elizabeth B. Hall, daughter of Mr. J. B. Mabrey, was born in Covington, Newton co,. Ga., June 15, 1840, graduated at the college in Covington, Ga., and taught school in Claiborne Parish, La. in 1860 and 1861. April 6th 1865 she was married to Mr. B. F. Hall went with him to Mississippi. They settled in Leon co., Fla. in 1867 where she departed this life on 26th July 1868.

Sister Martha J. Clawson died in Yorkville, S. C., on 16th June. She was the daughter of Col. Thomas Williams, formerly of York District. Subsequently he removed to Montgomery, Ala.

Philip D. Wightman was born in Jacksonville, Fla., August 16, 1845, and died at Tallahassee, Fla., May 26th, 1868... Wm. Davies

Robert Birdsong born Dec. 25, 1796, died in Macon, Ga., Aug. 28, 1868.

Died

in Atlanta, Ga., Oct. 1, 1868, of pneumonia Mary Nelle, infant daughter of Mr. and Mrs. Mark W. Johnson, aged 13 months.

Obituary

Thomas S. Gunn, son of William S. and Harriet Gunn, was born in Gadsden co., Fla., May 28th 1846, and died of typhoid fever, at the residence of Mr. Wm. D. Silva, in New York city, July 13th 1868. A. J. Woldridge

Mrs. Jane E. Thompson was born in Elbert co., Ga., and died in Savannah, Ga., July 18th 1868, in the 73d year of her age. Mr. T. was the relict of Capt. Drury Thompson, who was for many years a resident of the city of Macon, and who removed to Savannah in 1850 and died in 1855. She was the youngest and last surviving sister of Gen. Wylly Thompson, deceased. She leaves a numerous kindred among the families of the Thompsons, Watkins, Wynns, Olivers, Burtons, Lamars, Napiers and Mannings, the nearest of whom is her only daughter, Mrs. Amanda E. Palmer. Mrs. A. E. Palmer.

Wylly Cobb Adams, Esq., my eldest brother, died at Petersburg, Indiana, on the 10th of September, in the 46th year of his age.

Casiner Carilla, son of Dr. Wm. R. and Mrs. G. A. Joiner, was born Feb'y 29th 1856 and died April 3 1868, by a fall from a loaded wagon and the wheels passing over him. James Perry Joiner, his brother, was born July 27th 1857, and died Sept. 14, 1868. S. G. Chiles

Mrs. Hattie G. Sullivan, wife of Mr. W. D. Sullivan, and daughter of the late Rev. John G. Humbert, died in peace at Tumbling Shoals, S. C., Aug. 27th 1868, in the 27th year of her age.

Mrs. Alsy S. Mauldin, wife of Benj. F. Mauldin, was born June 17th 1838, and died in Fulton co., Ga., August 31st 1868.

Capt. R. H. L. Buchanan was born in Hancock co,. Ga., 13th August 1799 and died in Spring Place, Ga., 22d August 1868.

Mrs. Hettie Maples, wife of Israel Maples, Esq., died in Mitchell co., Ga., June 17th 1868. She was form many years a member of the Baptist Church.

Lucy J. Barrow, daughter of Rev. William and Mary A. F. Barrow, was born Oct. 25, 1845 and joined the Church in 1857 in Macon co., Ala., and died Aug 31, 1868.

Tribute of Respect of the 3d Q. Conference, Lanier ct., S. Ga. Conference, to Bro. John S. Murray who died Aug 16, 1868, aged 59 years 9 months and 13 days.

Tribute of Respect from Walterboro circuit, S. C., to Henry W. Ackerman.

Tribute of Respect by Kimbrough Lodge, for Rev. Ben. W. Clark, who died 13th Sept 1868.

Died

Mary, infant daughter of Rev. W. T. and Mrs. Parazade Pinkerton, in Summerville, Ga., Sept. 29, 1868.

On the 12th Sept., at residence of Mr. Wm. Peek, in Polk co., Ga., Hattie, the second daughter of John O. and Ella Peek Waddell, aged one year, nine months and thirteen days.

Obituary

Rev. William McKay was born in Fifeshire, Scotland, Feb. 10, 1842. When about twelve years of age, he was brought to America, and the family settled in Rome, Ga., During the late war between the States, he became a soldier in the Southern army.... died on 3d of August. Josephus Anderson

Mrs. Florida Caroline Willis, my dear daughter, passed away August 23, in Calhoun co., Ga. She was born in Macon in 1840. Her sister, Virginia my darling first-born, Mrs. Robt. W. Hubert, sleeps on the banks of the Trinity in Texas. Her two brothers left for the eternal world amidst the tempest of war. J. P. Duncan

Sister Mary Jane Page, relict of Alexander Page, and daughter of Brother and Sister E. B. Black, was born Feb. 9, 1844, and died in Warrenton, Ga., on 23d September 1868. In December 1866 she was married to Mr. A. Page. R. W. Hubert

Mrs. Mary E. Bass, wife of Capt. John Bass of Newton co., Ga., is no more. She was a native of Nottoway co., Va., and in her 20th year, as the lovely Miss Winfree, was led to the altar on 21st January 1821, not her surviving husband.... A. Means

L. I. Hansford was born in Elbert co., Ga., and died in Macon, Ga., Sept. 21, 1868, in his 59th year. He left a wife and nine children. J. Jones

Mary Robinson, a daughter of William Forbes, a Revolutionary soldier, was born near Cambridge, in Ninety Six, now Abbeville Dist., S. C., Nov. 3, 1779;. She was married to Ephraim Robinson in 1804. She died June 15, 1868, at the residence of her son-in-law, A. O. Norris, Esq., in Anderson District. Samuel A. Weber

C. L. Morgan, of Effingham co., Ga., died on 17th July 1868, in his 68th year. W. M. Watts.

Issue of October 23, 1868

Died

Near Wisdom's Store, Ga., July 16, 1868, Byron Henry, infant son of Heslam C. and Laura Watson, aged 1 month and 29 days.

Obituary

Mrs. Fanny Kennon, wife of Warren L. Kennon, died at the residence of her step-father, Randal Folsom, Esq., in Lowndes co,. Ga., on the 30th Sept 1868, in the 25th year of her age. She has left a husband and one little child.... H. W. Sharpe

Elizabeth Haralson, wife of Rev. Herndon Haralson, was born Nov. 29th 1794, on the eastern shore of Maryland, was married to her first husband Isaac L. Patterson, in the 20th year of her age, with whom she lived only 18 days, when he died. After the lapse of eight years she was married on Herndon Haralson on the 21st May 1821, in New Market, Eastern Shore of Maryland; in 1824, they moved to Green co., Ga., where they lived 10 years; then removed to Troup co., Ga., where they lived about 20 years; then to Tallapoosa co., Ala., Jan. 1857 where they lived until her death on 21st August 1868. L. R. Bell

Mrs. Winifred W. Camp, wife of Col. B. Camp of Campbell co., Ga., was born in Laurens District, S. C., Nov. 20, 1802, and died July 20, 1868. J. J. Davis

Miss Mattie M. Mullins, third daughter of Mr. R. and Mrs. C. Mullins, died on 20th Sept in the 20th year of her age. C. A. Fulwood

Rebecca Bailie Barlow, wife of Dennis Barlow and daughter of Eli S. Hill was born Feb. 4, 1830, in Walton co,. Ga., and died of consumption September 23, 1868, in Arkadelphia, Arkansas. Three of her children had gone before to glory. She leaves a husband and daughter... John H. Riggin.

Mrs. Caroline C. Davis died August 14th in Rome, Ga. (whither she had gone on a visit) in the 65th year of her age. Born in Jones county, where she spent a large portion of her life. There, she was united in marriage to her first husband, Mr. Green Gray, the result of which union was a large family of children. her second husband was William Davis of Arkansas.... John M. Marshall

Mrs. Jennie G. Gordon, daughter of Dr. P. G. and Mrs. J. M. A. McGregor of Columbia, S. C., and wife of Mr. Benj. F. Gordon, of Greene Co., Ala., died near Union, Ala., in the 29th year of her age. She was married to Mr. B. F. Gordon, Dec. 22, 1864, and soon after removed to Green co., Ala.... leaves a tender child of two years.

Rev. Benjamin W. Clark, formerly a member of the Georgia Conference, and for a number of years a local elder in Muscogee co., Ga., died 11th Sept 1868. J. E. Evans

Abraham Smith was born in Hancock co., Ga., Dec. 29th 1807, moved thence to Jasper co., and finally settled in Monroe co., Ga., where he died on the 21st Sept 1868.

Issue of October 30, 1868

Died

Little Leslie, child of Mr. W. F. and Mrs. K. Whittle, died in Madison co., Fla., Sept 29th 1868, aged 1 years and 9 months.

At Brown's Station, Ga., Little "Sallie," daughter of Elamn Johnson, Esqr., and his wife Permelia S. Johnson, born Sept. 21st 1867, died August 1, 1868.

Obituary

Miss Mandane Allen Glenn, daughter of the Rev. John B. Glenn, deceased, who was a member of the S. C. Conference more than fifty years ago, died Aug. 13, 1868, in her 50th year. New Orleans Advocate, please copy.

Bro. David Mediman, aged 67 years, died Sept. 5, 1868. He was one of the leaders at Hopewell church, formerly of Newberry circuit, now Clinton.

Mrs. Sarah Meddows, wife of Pascal Meddows, died Sept. 8, 1868, aged 54 years... left husband and seven children.

Mrs. Elizabeth A. Dubose was born in Charleston, S. C., Feb. 4, 1827; married Mr. J. R. DuBose in 1849. In the fall of 1866, she left Washington, Ga., to reside in Abbeville District, S. C.... left four orphan children.

Jonathan Chunn was born Feb. 15, 1809, in Charles co., Md., moved to Georgia in December 1816, died in Meriwether co., Ga., Aug. 2, 1868. W. P. Kramer

Perry Patton died Oct. 11, and his wife Jane Patton, Oct 12, in Laurens district, S. C.

Elizabeth East died in Laurens district, S. C., April 29, 1868, aged about 83 years.

Tribute of Respect to Miss Lizzie Chamberlin, who died 30th Sept. in the 15th year of her age, from the Sabbath-school at Weston, Ga.

Issue of November 6, 1868

Died

Sept 29 in Alachua co., Fla., Sallie Maxwell, daughter of C. P. and M. Crawford, aged 4 years, 10 months and 13 days.

Obituary

Mrs. Ann A. Waller, wife of T. T. Waller, and daughter of W. G. and N. Tatom, was born in Lincoln co., Ga., 25th November 1836, removed to Macon co., Ala., 1857.

Mrs. Judith Findley, wife of Dempsy Findley of Gordon co., Ga., was born 3d June 1808 and died 3d Oct 1868. She leaves a husband and seven children. B. J. Johnson

Mrs. M. H. Huff died in August in Jackson co., Fla., aged about 25 years. She leaves a husband and three small children.

Sister Nancy C. Young died in Jefferson co., Ga., in her 46th year... D. R. McW.

Mrs. Martha Salina Robinson, wife of Jacob E. Robinson, was born 19th May 1824 in Orangeburg Dist., S. C., and died September 28th 1868 in Alachua co., Fla. J. E. Dodd

Joseph K. Risher, Esq., of Colleton Dist., S. C., was born 31st March 1807 and died 9th October 1868. He leaves four daughters and two sons. L. Wood

Mrs. Mary A. Oliver, relict of James M. Oliver, Esq., died in Quitman co., Ga., on 7th inst., in her forty-third year. She leaves a husband and a large family of affectionate children.

Tribute of Respect by Newton Sabbath-school (Newton, Baker co., Ga.) to henry J. Slappey, who died Aug 2d, 1868.

Tribute of Respect to Bro. Lewis Lawshe by Evans Chapel Sabbath-school.

Issue of November 13, 1868

Died

Sept 24th, Lily Dell, an interesting daughter and only child of Rev. D. H. and Mrs. Amelia A. Starr, of Clayton co., Ga., aged two years and twenty days.

Obituary

Thomas G. Lyle was born in Jackson co., Ga., June 12, 1808 and died Aug 22, 1868, near Cusseta, Ala. E. B. Norton

Miss Sarah E. Conley, eldest daughter of Bro. Jason Conley of Walker co., Ga., was born May 13, 1849 and died of consumption Oct. 25, 1868.

My Aunt, Ann W. Dougherty, was born in Columbia co., Ga., about the first of 1800 and died in Decatur, ga., on 12th October 1868. S. P. Hutchingson

Mrs. Martha Ann Hightower, wife of James W. Hightower, died in Upson co., Ga., on 8th October in the 40th year of her age. She was one of eight daughters of William and Jane Trice, dec'd. She leaves a husband, six children.

Issue of November 20, 1868

Died

Nov. 8th, Charles Green, youngest child of Judge J. J. and Mrs. Martha C. Sparrow of Hawkinsville, Ga., aged 17 months and 16 days.

Obituary

Daniel Smith was born in Montgomery co., Ga., in 1816, moved thence to Dooly co., where he joined the M. E. Church, South, at Friendship, in 1838. He finally married and settled on Swift Creek in Dooly co., where he died Oct. the 2d 1856 of congestion of the brain. He leaves a wife and ten children. J. T. Johnson, P. C.

Mrs. Arminda Stipe, wife of the Rev. J. W. Stipe of Campbell co., Ga., and daughter of the late Wm. H. Parker, died Oct. 9th 1868, aged 29 years.

Mrs. Mary E. E. Hunter died Oct. 27, 1868, aged 24 years.

Lawson H. Kistler, brother to Rev. R. F. Kistler, of the S. C. Conference, was born in Lincolnton, N. C., March 28, 1819, and died there, Sept. 22, 1868, in the 50th year of his age. A. W. W.

Mrs. Emily Dunbar, daughter of E. E. and Sarah Pugh, was born Jan. 6, 1840, and died in Thomas co., Ga., Oct. 31, 1868. She was married to Mr. Thomas Dunbar in December 1858, who was last heard of at Camp Chase, a prisoner of war. Two beloved sisters had preceded her-- Mary A. Pugh, who died Nov. 9, 1867, in the 22d year of her age, and Thomas Jane Pugh who died Nov. 11, 1867, in the 19th year of her age. J. W. Talley

Mrs. Catharine J. Cochran, wife of John Cochran, died in Upson county, Ga., August 24, 1868....

Tribute of Respect from 4th Quarterly Conference, Monticello ct., No. Ga. Conference to Rev. Gabriel T. Spearman

Issue of November 27, 1868

Died

Nov. 17 at her residence in Athens, Ga., Mrs. Caroline M. Oliver, wife of C. S. Oliver, in the 62d year of her age.

Obituary

Mrs. D. A. Gordon, daughter of Jonathan and Dorothy Palmer, of Richmond co., Ga., was born 30th March 1835-- was married to Col. Thomas Gordon in the year 1853, and died at Opelika, Ala., August 20th 1868.

Mrs. Annie M. Chapman, wife of Mr. John Chapman, and eldest child of Elliot and Lucy A. Carleton, died at Twiggs co., Ga., in her 34th year.

John Lawrence Wyche, son of George and Margarette his wife, was born June 20, 1828, died September 20, 1868.

Wm. H. Kennedy was born in Effingham co., Ga., Jan. 1, 1816, in Jan 1854 he moved to Florida and on 9th July he died at his home in Alachua co.

Mrs. Mary McLean (widow of Allan McLean, deceased) died in Telfair co., Ga., on the 31st Oct. 1868, in the 82d year of her age. She left two sons (one of them a Methodist minister in Jacksonville, Fla., brother Wm. McLean) and three daughters and many grand-children.

Mrs. Ann E. Traxler died in Columbia co., E. Florida, Sept. 16th, 1868. She was born in St. Paul's Parish, Charleston Dist., S. C., 1st January 1825. In 1848 she was married... She leaves a devoted husband and ten children.

Mrs. Mary Ann Welchel, daughter of Francis and Mary Waters, deceased, died at Porter Springs, Lumpkin co., Ga., Sept. 28th 1868, in her 83d year. She leaves four children and many relations. G. Hughes

Charles Louis Meyers was born in Wurtemberg, Germany, Dec. 21st, 1829 and died in Anderson C. H., S. C., Nov. 2, 1868. He came to the United States in early manhood. He was brought up in the Lutheran Church. he leaves a wife. Samuel A. Weber

Mrs. Martha, wife of Bro. Thos Lane, of houston co., Ga., Died Oct. 11th 1868.

Mrs. Nancy A. Duke, daughter of Jeremiah and Margaret Payne, was born Feb. 17, 1836, and died in Dahlonega, Ga., Sept. 2, 1868. G. Hughes

Miss Martha Tooke, daughter of Bro. Joseph Tooke, of Houston co., Ga., died Sept. 29, 1868.

Tribute of Respect to Dr. G. M. T. Brockman by Oak Bowery Lodge, Ala.

Tribute of Respect to Miss Susan Ann Eliza Fletcher, who died Oct. 8, 1868, by Asbury M. E. Sunday School at Augusta, Ga.

Issue of December 4, 1868

Obituary

Arthur T. Camp was born June 20, 1800 and died Nov. 5, 1868. J. Chambers.

Jonathan Lindley died at Powder Springs, Ga., Sept 5. 1868. He was born in Pendleton Dist., S. C., Feb. 23, 1803, married November 15, 1827. J. N. Myers.

Joseph Evans was born in Union Dist., S. C., July 21, 1803, and died in Marion co., Fla., March, 1868. Isaac Munden

Mrs. Sarah R. Hutchinson, wife of Mr. Henry Hutchinson, died in Berrien co., Ga., Oct. 22, 1868, in the 62d year of her age. She spoke of her departed children, six in number. She called all her surviving children to her bedside. H. W. Sharpe

Mrs. Nancy Manship, widow of Travis Manship. and daughter of Wm. Hamer, Esq., of Marlborough Dist., S. C., was born 20th June 1818, and died Nov. 9, 1868. L. M. Hamer

Mrs. S. S. Gamble, wife of John Gamble, daughter of Mr. James Ravens, of Sumter co., Ga., dec'd, died at the residence of her brother-in-law, Mr. E. Johnson, in Terrell co., in the 27th year of her age.

Miss Sallie J. Linton was born Dec. 25, 1848, and died Oct 11, 1868. She was the youngest daughter of Bro. Thomas J. Linton, formerly of Monticello, Fla., now of Madison co. Fla.... J. A.

Mrs. Amanda C. Wilson, wife of Alfred G. Wilson, died Nov. 5, 1868, aged about 30 years. She has left a babe five days old.

Issue of December 11, 1868

Miss Mittie Latimer died in Hancock co., Ga., on 15th October 1868 in the 23d year of her age.

Mrs. Nancy Penny, relict of George Penny, was born in Abbeville District, S. C., 2d January 1789, and died of pneumonia at the residence of her son, Dr. J. W. McKellar, Ellaville, Ga., on 12th November 1868. In her 18th year she was married to Mr. John McKellar, in 1819 joined the Presbyterian Church and the same year was left a widow. In 1820 she joined the M. E. Church. In 1837 she married Mr. Geo. Penny who died in 1867. R. J. Redding

Mrs. Malinda B. Freeman, widow of the late Jeremiah Freeman, formerly an itinerant preacher of the Georgia Conference, was born October 26, 1797, and died in Meriwether co., Ga., Nov. 21st 1868, aged 71 years and 26 days. W. P. Kramer

Simon Wootten died in Telfair co., Ga., Nov. 15, 1868, in the 64th year of his age... leaving a wife and children.

Capt. Henry H. Smith died in Valdosta, Ga., Oct 27th 1868, in the 39th year of his age. For many years he had held the office of Clerk of the Superior Court of Lowndes co.... He leaves a wife and four children. J. J. Giles

Mrs. Sarah Grace was born and reared in N. C., came with her husband early in the settlement of the county to Houston co., Ga., where she died, Nov. 15th, in her 64th year... S. N. Dunwody

Sister Elizabeth Beacham of Cokesbury ct., S. C., was born in Cumberland co., Va., in 1798, moved to S. C. in her sixth or seventh year; was married to D. S. Beacham in 1814. She and her husband, who still survives her, joined the Methodist E. Church between thirty-seven and forty years ago. She died on the 17th November. She was the mother of eight children--three only of whom survive her. Joel W. Townsend

Mrs. Isabella McCall died Aug 6, 1868, in the 50th year of her age--long a member of Taylor's Creek Church, Liberty co., Ga. W. M. Watts

Issue of December 18, 1868

Died

At Cave Spring, on the 16th October last, Sue Ada, infant daughter of C. H. and Eva Wood...

Mary Seila Lane, daughter of Josiah J. and Elisabeth Lane, was born in Lowndes co., Ga., and died in Columbia co., East Florida, Nov. 20th, being about 6 years old.

Obituary

Rev. Joseph Law, son of Samuel and Rebecca Law, was born in Sunberry, Liberty co., Ga., Aug. 22d, 1815, and died of bronchial consumption, near Bainbridge, Ga., Nov. 30th 1868, in his 53d year. In 1850 he was married to Miss A. C. Green, of Upson co., Ga., who, with four children, survives him. A. J. Dean

Dr. Robert Henry Howard, eldest son of James and Tabitha Howard, was born in Washington co., Ga., Jan 13, 1812, and died in Butler co., Ala., Oct. 24, 1868. In 1817 his parents removed to Autauga co., Ala., and after some years, to Lowndes co., and in 1833 settled near Tuskegee, Ala., where he resided at his death. Soon after attaining his majority he was married to Miss Rebecca Hurt, who became the mother of two children. After her death, he was married to Miss Cornelia Lamar, who survives him. He, with his sister, Mrs. Bascom, was converted at Dutch Bend, Autauga co., Ala., in 1832. B. B. Ross

Mrs. Jane Matthews, relict of the late Josiah Matthews, of Talbot co., Ga., died 9th November 1868 at the residence of her son-in-law, Mr. John H. McCoy. She passed the anniversary of her 74th year the day before her death. Her maiden name was Brown. She was born in Abbeville District, S. C. When she was about ten years of age her parents removed to Ga., and located in Baldwin co. She was married in 1811. Her husband died in 1863. They raised a family of 13 children, 7 of whom still survive. Charles A. Fulwood

Mary, daughter of Rev. ___ and Rosanna Thurmond, and wife of Rev. John Watts of the S. C. Conference, was born Aug. 18, 1806, and died at the parsonage of the South Fork circuit, Catawba co., N. C., Nov. 20, 1868, in the 63d year of her age. In 1831, she became the wife of Bro. Watts. A. W. W.

My sister, Mrs. M. Galenia Caldwell, wife of M. J. Caldwell, and daughter of James B. and Jane R. Banks, died at Enon, Ala., on 10th Nov. 1868, aged 22 years. In 1867 she was married to M. J. Caldwell. Sallie.

Tabitha Abney was born May 12, 1789, and died Oct. 10, 1868. Her children and grandchildren will miss her kindness to them. W. A. Clarke

Mrs. Ann Eliza Veal, of Clark co., Ga., died Oct. 25, 1868. Henry J. Ellis

Mrs. Mary A. E. Stokes, wife of John A. Stokes of St. George's Parish, S. C., was Born Dec. 1st, 1841, and died Nov. 5th, 1868. She was the eldest daughter of Col. John Rumph... W. M. Shuler

Issue of January 1, 1869

Mr. Newman Bradley, my father-in-law, died in Liberty co., Ga., on 29th Nov. 1868, of hemorrhage of the bowels in his 71st year. He was a native of South Carolina, and one of the first settlers on Taylor's Creek. Wm. T. McMichael

Miss Julia V. Palmer died in Burke co., Ga., in 11th September 1868. She was a daughter of Edward and Laura W. Palmer, and a granddaughter of Dr. Anthony, the eminent physician in Augusta. Henry W. Hillard

Mr. James F. Gray, a native of Charleston, S. C., died on 1st Oct., at the residence of Dr. Harley in Colleton District.

Issue of January 8, 1869

Memoir of Rev. L. Q. Allen. He was born in Habersham county, Ga., June 1st 1826, and died in Dawson co., Ga., August 11th 1868. In the autumn of 1858 he was united in marriage with Miss Margaret M. Mills of Jackson co., Ala., whom his death leaves a widow with four children, Joshua Soule, Luella, Julian, and Clarence, aged respectively 9, 7, 5, and 3 years. H. P. Bell. Cumming, Ga., Dec. 27th, 1868.

Dr. James M. Eppes died in Newberry District, South Carolina, Nov. 23d, 1868, in the 53d year of his age. He was the son of Daniel and Mary Eppes. The father died at R. M. College, Va., in 1834 while on a visit to his two sons, James and Georgia. His body rests in the College Cemetery. The mother died about ten years ago. They raised but two children James and George. George died 23 years ago at Newberry C. H. In 1843 he married Miss Law, of Newberry. She with four sons and one daughter, survives him. Clough S. Beard. Glenn Springs, Dec. 26, 1868.

Mrs. Sarah M. Mason, wife of Edward Mason, died in Wetumpka, Ala., Dec. 5th, 1868 in the 38th year of her age. C. D. Oliver

James G. Wall died in Twiggs co., Ga., Dec. 28th, 1868, in the 74th year of his age... W. C. B.

Major Wiley J. Gibson died in Lee co., Ala., on the 7th Dec. 1868, in the 69th year of his age... L.

William Mikell, of Telfair co., was born 2nd March 1806 and died 25th Nov 1868.

Mrs. Lucy Jane Mood, daughter of Wm. and Anna Jane Rogers, was born at Clio, in Marlborough District, S. C., 19th Nov 1833; in Nov 1855 was married to Rev. W. W. Moody of the S. C. Conference, and died on the 18th Sept 1868, at the residence of Capt. Jas. T. Caraway, Williamsburg District, S. C.

Edward Peabody Powers came to his death by a very sad accident Dec. 6th, aged 19 years less a few days. He was the son of Mr. Chas. Peabody of Russell co., Ala., but having been adopted by Mr. Edward Powers, dec'd, his name was changed.

Sister Mary A. P. Green, wife of Fred J. Green, of Schley co., Ga., was born 20th August 1816, married to F. J. Green July 25th, 1838, and died on 8th Dec 1868. Her maiden name was Hill. He leaves a husband and a number of sons and daughters. S. Antony

Sister Sutton of Albany, Ga., was born June 17th 1816, married in 1838, and died 7th Nov 1868. She was left a widow a few years since, and now leaves three daughters and one son. S. Anthony.

John S. Smith, son of the Rev. H. F. and Sarah A. Smith, was born in Stewart co., Ga., and died suddenly in Ocala, Fla., Dec. 27th 1868, in the 20th year of his age.

Juliet Alice McClutchen was born Sept, 23, 1852, in Walker county, Ga., and died Oct 4th 1868.

Mrs. Fanizy Bloodworth, relict of the late Rev. Thomas Bloodworth died in Pike co., 3rd December at the advanced age of 93 years, two months and ten days. She had been a member of the Baptist church about seventy years, and leaves about 250 descendants.

Issue of January 15, 1869

Mrs. Emma T. Reid was born November 11th 1835--was united in marriage with Capt. Richard W. Reid, Feb. 12th 1861 and died in peace Dec. 27th 1868. J. Anderson

Rev. Andrew T. Green was born Nov 20th 1814 and died in St. George's Parish, S. C., Oct 2nd 1868. T. L. S.

Mrs. Leonora A. Conn, wife of Capt. W. T. Conn, died in Milledgeville, Ga., on the 27th of December in the 30th year of her age. F. L. Brantly

Mrs. Eleanor K. Tatom, daughter of Ignatius and Rebecca Stokes, was born in Spartanburg District, S. C., June 20, 1806. In 1812 her parents removed to Jasper co., Ga. On the 11th of May 1828 she was joined in marriage to Abel Tatom, and they removed to Monroe co., Ga., in November of that year... died October 20th 1868. J. E. Evans

Mr. John A. Cummings was born near Ridgeville, April 3, 1812, and died at Orangeburg C. H., on 2nd December 1868 in his 57th year. He leaves a widow and son and daughter.

John M. Gordon died in Augusta, Ga., Dec 4th aged 23 years...

Mrs. Ann E. Roberts, wife of George Roberts, fell asleep in Jesus, in Augusta, Ga., Dec. 21, 1868....

Mr. McW. Wimberly of Alexander, Burke co., died in Augusta, Ga., on 28th December last, aged 30 years.

Jethro Jackson died in Griffin, Ga., Dec. 6th. He leaves a wife and several daughters to mourn.

Nancy M. Little, daughter of the Rev. T. D. Oxford, was born in Jones co., April 16th 1818, married Willis Little, August 4th, 1835, and died in Schley co., Nov. 23d 1868. The estimable lady was raised in the Baptist faith. R. F. Williamson.

Tribute of Respect from Weston Lodge, No. 80, to John C. Byrd.

Issue of January 22, 1869

Mrs. Rebecca Russell, whose maiden name was Rebecca Furman, was born April 15th 1793 in Charleston, S. C. Her father was Captain Josiah Furman, who served under Gen. Marion in the American Revolution. He having died in 1800, she became a member of the family of Capt. Thos Baker, whose wife was her cousin, and the daughter of Dr. Richard Furman, who was for many years the pastor of a Baptist Church in Charleston. In 1816 she was married to Joseph A. Russel, who died in 1833. died on a visit with Bro. R. F. Baldwin at Marshallville, Macon Co., Ga., 19th December 1868. Thomas B. Russell

Col. Woodson L. Ligon died at Orange Springs, Fla., Oct. 6th, 1868. He was born in South Carolina, Oct. 29th 1820, and graduated at Randolph Macon College, Virginia. He had resided in Griffin, Ga., Newnan, Ga., and Auburn, Miss.

Beacham P. Ligon, son of Col. Ligon, died in Bartow co., Ga., Dec. 29th 1868. He was born in Mississippi, April 9th 1848.

Sister Martha C. Ligon, whose maiden name was Powell, was born Sept. 5th, 1830....

Rev. John Francis Ellison, son of Rev. Wm. H. Ellison, D. D., was born in Lagrange, Ala., June 1st 1833, and died at the parsonage of the Methodist Church in Clayton, Ala., Dec. 9th 1868. His mother was Anna W., eldest daughter of Bishop Capers.... Joseph B. Cottrell

John Venable was born in Prince Edward co., Va., June 2nd 1779. In early boyhood the family removed to Georgia... died 9th Nov 1868 in Jackson co., Ga. Wm. J. Parks

Tudie, wife of L. A. Caldwell, of Atlanta, and daughter of Samuel and Antoinete Pilsbury of Americus, died at the latter place on Tuesday, Dec. 22nd 1868.

William Burt, son of J. J. Tooke, aged 16 years and ten months, died in Geneva, Talbot co., Ga., on the 21st Dec 1868.

Mrs. Martha Stripling, wife of Rob't Stripling, was born in South Carolina, removed thence to Alabama, and afterwards to Georgia, where she died Dec. 24th, 1868, in her 43d year.... She leaves a husband and one little boy. I. L. Avant

Emma, second daughter of Mr. and Mrs. Marlin White, was born at Tuskegee, Ala., Nov. 11th, 1858, and died at Greenville, Ala., October 7th 1868. Chas. A. King

Mrs. Elizabeth Elliott was born in North Carolina, Nov. 1st 1806. Her only daughter married Dr. Bowden of South Carolina, with whom she ever after resided. She died on 4th Nov 1868. J. A. W.

In Memoriam. Mrs. Margaret E. Furlow, wife of Hon. T. N. Furlow, and daughter of the late Major Tarpley Hall, Sr., of Bibb County, Georgia, was born in Putnam County, January 4th 1820, was married November 2d 1839, and died in Americus, Georgia, December 22d 1868.

Issue of January 29, 1869

Died

In Charleston, S. C., Dec. 27th 1868, James Just Mood, son of Dr. James R. and Martha K. Mood, aged 8 years, 7 months and 3 days.

In Griffin, on Monday, Dec. 26th, Johnnie, infant son of Mr. and Mrs. John M. Williams, aged nearly 20 months.

Obituary

Rev. George L. Barry was born in Baltimore, Md., 20th Feby 1804 and died in Cuthbert, Ga., on 21st Dec 1868. He leaves and widow and four children.... J. O. A. Cook

My father, H. H. Geiger, raised by a Baptist mother, died when he had just entered his 72d year.... J. S. Geiger

Lucy Elizabeth Lovett, daughter of Dr. R. W. and Elizabeth M. Lovett and grand-daughter of Bishop Andrew, was born May 27th 1854 in Newton co., and died Dec. 6, 1868, in Scriven county, Ga. Her mother died when she was two years of age.... S. S. Sweet

Mrs. Eliza Ann Darsey died in Liberty co., Ga., Dec. 28th 1868, in the 58th year of her age. J. W. Turner.

Jas. G. McNabb died in Putnam ct., E. Fla., on Dec. 5th 1868. Born and reared in Bladen ct., N. C., when about grown moved with his parents to Ga., and then married Miss E. Pitman. He moved to Florida in 1852.... E. L. King.

Mrs. Margaret Chappel, relict of Rev. John Chappel, was born in Wilkes co., Ga., and died Dec. 30, 1868, in Oglethorpe co., in the 77th year of her age. She was married twice; first to Silas Griffin in 1814, who died in 1841; in 1845 she was married to Bro. Chappell. D. J. Myrick

Mrs. Margaret Kistler, wife of David Kistler, and daughter of the late Wm. and Margaret Allison, died in Charlotte, N. C., Dec. 19, 1868, in her 57th year. She has left a husband and three daughters.

Mrs. Elizabeth S. Walls, wife of Oliver Walls, and daughter of Thomas and Henrietta Ansley, formerly of Warren co., Ga., was born August 27th 1815, and died in Upson co., Ga., Dec. 21st 1868. She has left an affectionate husband and eight children. D. Kelsey

Joseph B. Smith, son of G. L. Smith, died in Dooly co., Ga., Oct. 6th 1868, aged 13 years and four days with typhoid fever. E. J. Rentz

Rev. John E. Fort died in St. James, Santee, on the 13th Dec 1868, in the 57th year of his age. E. J. Pennington

Sister Obedience Lovelace, wife of Lucius Lovelace, Sr., Died Dec. 17, 1868, in Troup co., Ga., in her 59th year... W. H. Evans

Tribute of Respect to Mrs. Margaret E. Furlow from Sunday school of Americus, Ga., who died 22d December 1868.

[No copy of the issue of February 5, 1869 has been located.]

Issue of February 12, 1869

William Overby was born in Brunswick co., Va., on the 10th of April 1813, was married in his native county in March 1833, a few years after, he removed to Ga., and died in Coweta co., 9th Jan 1869. He was twice happily married, his first wife died in 1851. His second wife and three children and three of the children of his first wife survive. Three sons and two daughters preceded him to the grave.

My father, George P. Holmes, was born in Oneida co., N. Y., Feb. 8th 1865, and died in Sevier co., Ark., Nov 15th 1868. He emigrated to Ga. in early life, marriage and settled in Green co. In 1861 he removed to Arkansas... D. T. Holmes.

Mrs. Louisa L. Hewett died in Valdosta, Ga., Jan. 15th 1869, in the 52nd year of her age.

Solomon Smith, Sr., was born in Effingham co., Ga., 1790, moved tin early life to Bryan co., where he died on the 12th Dec 1868, in his 79th year... W. M. Watts

William Stenbridge was born in Virginia, but was raised from a small boy in Hancock co., Ga. He joined the church more than 40 years ago and has been a member of Montepelier, in Baldwin co., where he died 14th Jan 1869, aged 72 years. J. V. M. Morris

Mary Stevens was born at Duloe, England, Aug 10th 1818, and died in Dec. 1839, having emigrated from the land of her birth, found a home with other members of the family in Greene co., Ga. This was her place of residence till Dec. 19th 1868 when she died. C. A. Mitchell

Sister Margaret E. Gilbert, daughter of Thomas and Marilah Mann, was born in Fairfield District, S. C., Feb. 27th 1847 and was married to W. B. Gilbert, Dec. 5th 1865, and died Jan 1st 1869, leaving an interesting little son and an affectionate husband.

William A. Curry was born in August 1813 and died 12 Dec 1868.... William R. Curry.

Issue of February 19, 1869

Died

In Macon, Ga., on the 10th inst., Fannie S., daughter of Rev. H. J. and Laura Harvey, aged 6 years.

Obituary

Mrs. Jane Davis Bennett was born in Franklin co., N. C., Sept. 17, 1799, and died at Acworth, Ga., Dec. 14th 1868 from the effect of an injury sustained some weeks previously. Two of her children, Mr. B. F. Bennettt of Atlanta and Mrs. Wester, the wife of Rev. W. V. Wester of Acworth.

Mrs. Harriet E. Ramsaur, wife of our Bro. L. R. Ramsaur, and daughter of J. S. and E. D. Erwin, was born May 2nd 1822, and died near Fairmount, Ga., Nov. 18, 1868.

Mrs. Milly Smith, wife of John Smith, died Dec. 19th 1868, in the 75th year of her age.... She has left an aged husband, children, and grandchildren.

Franklin C. Ross, son of Benj. F. and Martha A. Ross, of Macon, Ga., died January 18th aged 25 years. He was born and reared in Macon.

Mrs. Elizabeth B. Head, daughter of Richard and Elizabeth B. Harper, was born in Elbert co., Ga., Aug 24th 1812, married Willis R. Head, Nov 11th 1829, and died Nov 18th 1868 in Henry co., Ga. J. W. Turner

Dr. James Morgan Butler was born in Clarendon Dist., S. C., April 14th 1835, and died at Social Circle, Ga., Jan. 7th 1869. he graduated at the Charleston Medical College in 1858. M. F. Malsby.

Brother B. G. Hodges was born in Bullock co., Ga., May 6th 1816 and died at Worthington Spring, Bradford co,. Fla., Nov. 26th 1868. He moved to Madison co., Fla., about 1841 of '42. In 1854 he married Miss Mary Zeigler, and shortly afterwards moved to Worthington Spring. W. M. Kennedy

John T. Mobley died in Pulaski co, Ga., Jan. 12th 1869. He was 53 years old. L. B. Bouchelle

Mrs. Mary Kendrick died Jan. 14th 1869 at the residence of her son-in-law, Josiah Allen, of Meriwether co., Ga; born March 30th 1786 in Green co. R. F. Jones

Mrs. Susan Slaughter died Jan 1st 1860 in the 86th year of her age. Wm. Bryan

Died

On the 10th Jan 1869 in Clark co., Ga., William, infant son of John G. and Alice V. Tomlinson, aged eight months.

On Jan 20th 1869, Richard Theophilus, infant son of T. L. and C. H. McCall, aged six weeks.

Obituary

James Pollard died in Hurtville, Ala., Jan. 26th 1869, in the 82d year of his age. He was born in Wilkes co., Ga., removed from thence to Green co., Ga., afterwards to Harris co., where he resided twenty-five years--thence to Macon co. Ala. He leaves three children, two by a former marriage, James Pollard, Esq., of Hurtsville, Ala., and Mrs. Howard of Hamilton, Ga., and one by his last wife, Mrs. Col. Ramsey, of Columbus, Ga.

Mrs. Mary Ann Treadwell, whose maiden name was Bennett, was born in St. Mary's, Ga., Dec. 20th 1815, and died at the residence of her son-in-law, Rev. Wm. A. McLean, in Jacksonville, Fla., on 8th Dec. 1868. She was married to Bro. David Treadwell in Dec. 1834. F. A. Branch

Mrs. Annie Johnson died in Abbeville District, S. C., on the 20th January 1869, in her 81st year. She was born Nov 5th 1788 of pious parents-- Hugh and Nancy McLin, prominent members of the Presbyterian church. On the 5th day of June 1810, she was married to Jonathan Johnson, who died in 1865.

Miss Rossa Floyd, daughter of Edmund P. and Mrs. Cornelia Floyd, of Lee co., Ga., died in Albany, of typhoid pneumonia, Jan. 4th, in the 25th year of her age.

Lemuel Tennyson died in Lee co., Ala., 17th Nov 1868, was born in Lynchburg, Va., in June 1784. In 1826 he was married to my death mother, then Miss Aurilla Sale. Fanny C. T.

Mrs. Mary J. Talley, wife of Dr. James W. Talley, was born in Henry co., Ga., February 5th 1834, and died in Mill Town, Ga., February 9th 1869, aged 33 years and 4 days. She has let a husband and three daughters. Jas. D. Mauldin. Griffin Star please make a note.

James M. Hightower died at Valley Mills, Bosque co., Texas, on the 11th Oct 1868, aged about forty-four years. his daughter Mary Virginia died at Palistine, Texas, in August, aged nine years. Bro. H. was a native of Georgia, conveyed tin Marion co., in 1854. He married the daughter of Chapman Maddox (whose obituary appeared in the Advocate last year).... He had lived for some years in Rusk co., but spent some months in Bosque co. J. Blakely Smith. Texas advocate please copy.

Mrs. Mary M. McKay, daughter of Dr. William E. Collier-- present Presiding Elder of the Tampa District, and grand daughter of the late Rev. William Holmes of South Carolina. died in Tampa, Fla., aged 21 years. F. A. Holmes

Mrs. Susan A. Lever, wife of Stephen Lever, was born Dec. 27th 1827, and died in Richland District, S. C., January 15, 1869. A. J. Cauthen

Mrs. Dicy Winn, wife of John A. Winn, and daughter of James and Elizabeth Horton, was born in Orange co., N. C., June 8th 1797, and died in Tuskaloosa co., Ala., Nov. 13th 1868. E. Nicholson

Rev. William H. Campbell was born in Madison, Ga., Sept. 12, 1811, and died in Oxford, Ga., Jan. 17, 1869, after a painful and protracted illness. He was a son of Charter Campbell, favorably known to the early Methodists of Middle Georgia... Luther M. Smith

Rev. James Quillian, a superannuated preacher of the N. G. Conference, died at his son's residence in White co., Ga., at 1 o'clock P. M., Jan. 27th 1869. He was born May 10th 1793... Wm. J. Parks.

Belle, daughter of T. and N. Swearingen, was born in Ga., July 14th 1834; married Dr. Jno. B. Barnette, Oct. 28th 1859, died in Opelika, Ala., Jan. 20, 1869. New Orleans Advocate please copy.

William Henry Taylor began his life in Cuthbert, Ga., 29th June 1848, and closed its earthly period on 31st of December 1868. J. Anderson

Col. Giles Mitchell was born Oct. 5, 1805, and died in Athens, Feb. 15, 1869. He graduated at the University of Georgia in 1827.

Mrs. H. M. Parks, wife of Capt. Thos Parks, and daughter of James and Elizabeth Avery of Burke co., N. C., died Feb. 3d 1869, in her 35th year. She was happily marriage in Oct. 1867. She leaves a husband, parents, brothers and sister. R. P. Franks

Mrs. Celestia A. Griffith, daughter of Burton C. and Mary Thrasher, was born in Clarke co., Ga., married to Francis P. Griffith, Esqr., 10th Dec 1867, and died 1st Feb. 1869 in the 23d year of her age.

Issue of March 12, 1869

James Inglis Snider, son of Benjamin Snider, deceased, was born in Savannah, Ga., July 20th 1830, and died on February 5th 1869 in Macon, Ga., where he had resided since 1862. E. H. Myers

Tribute of Respect from quarterly conference of Mulberry St. Church, Macon, to James I. Snider.

Mrs. America Viola Snow was born in Walton co., Ga., in the summer of 1843, and died in Monroe, Dec. 11th 1868. She was married to Francis J. Snow, April 14th 1859... She leaves husband and three little children.

Jas. H. Carter was born 4th May 1804 in Wilkes co., Ga., and died 14 Jan 1869 of apoplexy. He joined the M. E. Church in 1821 or '22 and married Miss Ann Chappell the same year. He was a brother of John and George Carter, formerly of the Georgia Conference... W. R. Singleton.

Issue of March 19, 1869

Miss Ella C. Martin died near Eufaula, Ala., January 24th 1869, in the 18th year of her age. E. P. Birch

Mr. John Carraway died at Thomaston, Ga., January 30th 1869, in the 82nd year of his age. He was a native of North Carolina, but for many years resided in Thomaston. D. Kelsey

William L. Patrick died at Orangeburg C. H., S. C., on 28th Feb. of sequel of typhoid fever, in the 65th year of his age. He lived formerly in Barnwell and had recently moved to Orangeburg in the last state of the disease. J. C. Crisp

J. T. Moore was born in Clarke co., Ga., March 27th 1814, and died in Sumter co., Dec. 11th 1868.

Mrs. Jennette Hair, wife of Rev. Malcolm Hair, and daughter of John and Catharine Bledsoe, was born in Muscogee co., May 13th 1833, and died in Buena Vista, Marion co,. Ga., January 24th 1869. She joined the Primitive Baptist church in June 1852. W. G. Booth

Mrs. Vicy Banks, wife of James Banks, and daughter of Thomas and Mary Harman was born in Newberry Dist., S. C., 1804, and died in Abbeville Dist., Feb. 27th 1869. J. B. Traywick

SOUTHERN CHRISTIAN ADVOCATE NOTICES 1867-1878

Issue of March 26, 1869

Died

In Yorkville, So. Ca., March 4th 1869, Edward Sidney, eldest son of Dr. Alfred and Mrs. Cornelia Craven, aged 12 years.

Obituary

Mrs. Annie Tindall Crumley, wife of Dr. M. F. Crumley, and daughter of Mr. and Mrs. H. W. Tindall died on February 1st.

John Smith died suddenly at his residence, Feb. 27th 1869, in the 82nd year of his age. he joined the M. E. Church at Liberty Chapel, Sparta Circuit. Wm. Bryan

Mrs. Lucinda A. Echols, daughter of Rev. Jesse and Mary Pate, and wife of Mr. Thomas J. Echols died in Atlanta, Ga., on the 7th March in the 46th year of her age. F. A. Kimbell

Mrs. Martha Jones (familiarly known as Mother Jones) was born in Virginia in May, 1783, was brought to Anson co., N. C., when an infant, was married to Mr. J. K. Jones, April 1803, and died in Chesterfield, S. C., 4th March 1860, aged nearly 93. She died leaving a husband (about 100 years of age) and several children. J. C. Hartsell

James O'Hara was born in Edgefield Dist., S. C., Feb. 20th 1790, and died in Eufaula, Ala., March 1st 1869. A. J. Briggs

Sister Mary H. Stone, wife of Bro. Octavius Stone, died in Walton co., Ga., on 7th Feb. 1869, after an illness of only 4 days. J. W. Baker

Brother Alexander Harden died in Barnwell co., S. C., on 23rd Nov. 1868, and Sister Sarah Harden, his wife, on 4th March 1869. The former died in the 88th year of his age, an latter in her 79th year.

James Just Mood, the only son of Dr. James B. Mood, of Charleston, S. C., died on the 27th Dec. 1868, aged 8 years, 7 months and 3 days.

Mrs. Magdalen Zeigler, of Orangeburg, S. C., died suddenly, March 2nd 1869, aged 54 years.

Bro. A. Moon died in Jackson co., Ga., Dec. 6th 1868, aged 66 years. He was a Methodist circuit steward.

Mrs. A. Lampkins was born in Virginia, and died in Jackson co., Nov. 16th, 1868, aged 82 years. R. J. Harwell

Tribute of Respect by Louisville Circuit to James W. Clarke.

Tribute of Respect to James I. Snider from Trinity Sunday-school, Savannah.

Issue of April 2, 1869

Died

At Tampa, Fla., Feb. 17, Richard Nichols, infant son of C. R. and S. Mobley, aged 18 months.

At Stilesboro, Ga., Feb. 5, 1869, Mary Lou, daughter of Thomas K. and Willie Sproull, aged seven and a half months.

Obituary

Mrs. Martha Thomas, wife of our brother Lovick P. Thomas, Sen., was born in Clarke co., Ga., July 11, 1807, and died in Atlanta, February 16, 1869.

Sister Margarett Ann Philips was born Nov. 20, 1814, and died Jan. 31, 1869. J. Anderson

Mrs. Laura V. Saxon, daughter of Richard Johnson, was born Jan. 8, 1824, in Barnwell Dist., S. C., and died in Scriven co., Ga., March 6, 1869.

Mrs. Mary Eugenia, daughter of the late Rev. Alexander Speer, of the Georgia Conference, and wife of George Winship, Esq., of Atlanta, Ga., was born Nov 4, 1840, and died Feb. 18, 1869. T. B. Russell

Fielding Ellis, my grandfather, was born in Va., Oct. 1774, and died in Barbour co., Ala., 24th Feb. 1869... He removed from Va. to Baldwin co., Ga., in 1812, thence to Walton co., where he resided until the death of his wife, and which he passed his time with his children and grandchildren. He died a member of the Baptist church.

Tribute of Respect by St. Luke's quarterly conference, Columbus, Ga., to James M. Chambers....

Issue of April 9, 1869

Mrs. Octavia Goss, youngest daughter of the late A. W. Thomson, Esq., and wife of Mr. H. L. Goss, died in Unionville, S. C., March 17th 1869. O. A. Darby

Philip McLennan was born Oct. 16th 1829 in Chesterfield District, S. C., and died 22nd Dec 1868 near Louisville, Ala.

Mrs. Annie Jones, wife of Mr. Benj. Jones, of Louisville, Ala., was born Fe.b 12th 1843, was married Oct. 17, 1867, and died March 8th 1869.

Isaac Hall was born in Jackson co., Ga., Nov. 12th 1788, and died in Wilkinson co., March 5th, 1869, in his 71st year [sic]. W. S. Baker

Sister Eliza A. Hardy, wife of Aaron Hardy, of Lincoln co., Ga., was born May 10th 1813, and died Feb. 17th 1869. B. Sanders

Miss Julia E. Sears, daughter of Joseph G. and Mary J. Sears, died in Griffin, Ga., March 25th 1860, aged 13 years, 8 months and 24 days.

Mrs. Elizabeth W. Cannon was born Aug. 31st 1799, and died Dec. 20th 1868, in Terrell co., Ga. C. A. Crowell

Issue of April 16, 1869

Died

Byron Lee, son of B. D. and Virginia Bailey, died in Houston co., near Fort Valley, March 21, 1869, being six years, 10 months and 1 day old.

Obituary

Memorial of Mrs. Mary Jones. She was born in Sandersville, Ga., Jan. 13, 1788, and died in Columbua, Ga., Feb. 5, 1869, aged 81 years. Her maiden name was Howard. She came to this city with her husband Col. Seaborn Jones, in 1828. A. M. Wynn, Pastor.

Mahulda C. Davenport, wife of Dr. James T. Davenport, and daughter of John F. and Mary P. Wilson, was born March 23, 1835, and died Jan. 23, 1869.

Mary, second daughter of the late Dr. Joseph and Mrs. Nancy Hamilton, was born in Virginia, May 7th 1797, and died in Rutherfordton, N. C. Feb. 12th 1869. V. A. Sharpe. Nashville Christian Advocate please copy.

Mrs. A. L. Miller was born Oct. 16, 1806, and died in Orangeburg co,. Jan. 4, 1869. J. L. S.

Mr. Henry E. Solomons was born in Beaufort Dist., S. C., March 14, 1802, and died Feb. 1st 1869. L. C. Loyal.

Mrs. Martha Reynolds, wife of Lorenzo Dow Reynolds, died at her father's--Mr. Durden's-- in Terrell co., Ga. Feb. 14, 1869. Wm. N. Chaudoin.

Mrs. Mary E. Dillaberry, wife of F. J. Dillaberry, and daughter of Rev. H. F. Smith, late of the Florida Conference, was born in Blunt co,. Tenn, and died March 7th 1869, at the residence of her mother in Ocala, Fla.

Issue of April 23, 1869

Miss Synthelia V. Daniel, daughter of Berry and Isabella Daniel, formerly of Taylor's Creek, Liberty co., Ga., died of consumption, at the residence of her friends, Mr. and Mrs. J. M. Wilcox, Coffee co., Ga., on March 19th 1869 in her 22nd year. [account]

Mrs. Sarah Joanna Smith, eldest daughter of R. F. Ousley, Esq., and wife of the Rev. Geo. G. Smith, of the Baltimore Conference, was born in Culloden, Monroe co,. Ga., February 14th 1840, and died in Lewisburg, W. Va., March 25th 1869. Her childhood and early girlhood was spent in Vinevall. [long account] G. G. Smith

My mother, Mrs. Catherine Sheridan, wife of the late Dr. Hugo G. Sheridan, died in Colleton District, S. C., Feb. 16th 1869. Her maiden name was Spears, and she was born about the year 1786. Hugo G. Sheridan

Patrick J. Barnett died in Wilkes co., Ga., 4th March 1869, in the 77th year of his age. C. H. Ellis.

Mrs. Sarah Porter, wife of Benj. C. Porter and eldest daughter of Benj. Kennedy, died in Effingham co., Ga., 2nd March 1869 in her 60th year. R. H. Howren

Tribute of Respect from the First Quarterly Conference for Black Swamp Circuit to Bro. H. E. Solomons.

Issue of April 30, 1869

William Bessent, son of A. J. and Eliza Bessent, was born at St. Marys, Ga., on 15th November 1835, and died at Valdosta, Ga., 17th March 1869.

Mrs. Jane Franklin, wife of Benj. Franklin, died in Augusta, Ga., March 19 in the 42d year of her age.... Having been raised an orphan from early childhood. C. W. Key

Eliza Deborah, daughter of Richard W. and Mary R. Davis, of Beaufort Dist., S. C., was born June 14, 1846, and died March 5th 1809.

Miss Laura O. Dudley was born in Effingham co., Ga., February 11th 1833, and died in Savannah, Ga., Feb. 22nd 1869. D. D. Cox

Rev. Herndon Haralson was born in Greene co., Ga., 25th Dec 1796, embraced religion in his 25th year in Maryland, married there, thence moved to Greene co,. Ga., thence to Troup co., Ga., thence to Tallapoosa, Ala., where he died. K. L. H.

Mrs. Sarah Matilda Wright, wife of John W. Wright, and second daughter of John and Mary C. Wilkins, of Effingham co,. Ga., was born Sept. 23, 1846, and died in Green co., Ga., March 13, 1869.

Greene B. Turner died in Newton co., Ga., April 1st, 1869, lacking a few days of being 82 years. "Uncle Green" was the elder of four brothers. Bro. Jas. B. Turner, the younger perhaps of the brothers, was the first to die. Bro. Wade Turner succeeded him. Then Uncle Allen... God bless his two sons, the only children that survive him. A. Gray

Mrs. Mary Charlotte Burnley died in Augusta, Ga., March 5... left two children. C. W. Key.

Jane Harriet, daughter of John and Elizabeth McTyeire, and wife of Wm. C. Hart, was born in Barnwell Dist., S. C., Oct. 11, 1831, and died in Opelika, Ala., April 11, 1869. After her marriage, which was in 1851.

Mr. E. A. Center of Atlanta, died on 22d March 1869. He was born May 16, 1839; was married to Miss Frances P. Thorn, of Newton co., Ga., Oct. 23, 1867. F. A. Kimbell

Issue of May 7, 1869

Died

Georgia Virginia Curtis, daughter of W. T. and A. E. Mobly, of Troup co., Ga., was born March 18th 1866, and died April 11, 1869-- an invalid from her birth but very intelligent for one of her age.

Obituary

Rev. David K. Crenshaw was born Nov. 13, 1807, was licensed to preach in 1846, and died April 11, 1860. He was a native of Lunenburg co., Va., spent several months in Tennessee, and finally removed to Florida, where he died, near the city of Jacksonville. Josephus Anderson. Memphis and Richmond Advocates please copy.

Mrs. S. M. Roberts was born in Crawford co., Ga., May 22, 1822; married L. M. Roberts, Dec. 14, 1837, and died of consumption in Dawson, Ga., April 6th 1869. She joined the Presbyterian Church in Macon, Ga., in her 18th year, subsequently removed to Dawson, and there being no Presbyterian Church in the place, she joined the M. E. Church, South.

Mrs. Hannah Guthrie, wife of W. J. Guthrie was born in Wilkes co., Ga., March 3rd 1800, and died in Bullock co., Ala., near Mt. Hilliard, Jan. 13th 1869. A. Dowling

Mrs. Catharine Mashburn, wife of Rev. J. H. Mashburn, of N. G. Conference was born in Rutherford co., N. C., Feb. 15th 1799, and died in Forsyth co., Ga., April 20th 1869. J. D. Anthony.

Mrs. Caroline Houston, wife of John Houston, was born in Camden, S. C., and died in Savannah, Ga., April 13th 1860, in the 33rd year of her age. In 1853 she was married to Bro. John Houston.... Geo. G. N. MacD.

Mrs. Martha Walker died in Crawfordville, Wakulla co., Fla., in the 52nd year of her age. Soon after, her daughter, Mrs. Maria W. Nixon, followed her mother. She was born in Wakulla co., Fla. on the 30th August 1846, and died in San Pedro, Republic of Honduras, on 17th Feb 1869.

Mrs. Mary Hodge was born in Sumter Dist., S. C., May 24th 1786. Her husband, John R. Hodge, died in Charleston, a soldier during the British war. April 1831 she came to Alabama and settled in Montgomery co. ...died March 15th, she being aged 84 years. A. Dowling

Issue of May 14, 1869

Died

Sunday night, May 2, 1869, Mrs. Sarah E. Sanders, wife of Rev. B. Sanders, of Lincolnton ct., N. G. Conference. Her remains passed through Athens, May 4th for interment in the cemetery at Danielsville, Ga.

Obituary

Lewis E. Flemister, eldest son of Lewis and Hattie E. Flemister, died in Griffin, Ga., April 3, of cerebral meningitis. He was 14 years, 4 months and 12 days old.

Elizabeth Mitchell, whose maiden name was Mann, was born in Cumberland co., N. C., on Cape Fear River, 24th Feb 1806, came to Ga. in 1824, was married to Col. Daniel R. Mitchell, Dec. 10, 1828, and removed to Rome, Ga., in Oct. 1835. H. H. Parks

Mrs. Caroline Johnson, died in Augusta, Ga., March 22, 1860, aged nearly 53 years. One of her brothers was Rev. J. M. Marshall, being a worth member of the S. Ga. Conference....

Sampson T. Foy was born in Edgefield District, S. C., January 7th 1812; moved to Jones co., Ga., in 1834, and from Jones to Talbot in 1837, where he lived until his death, April 3d, 1869. In 1836 he was married to Frances S. Edwards, of Jones co., who died in 1857-- and again in 1861 with Harriet A. Hays, of Taylor co., Ga., who survives him. ...left wife and children.

Mrs. Parsha Ann Chapman, wife of Wm. T. Chapman and daughter of Benjamin Lifsey, deceased, was born in Pike co., Ga., March 1, 1835, and died April 20, 1860. T. J. Barret

Sarah L. McGowin died in Laurens co., Ga., 27th April 1869, aged 11 years, 7 months and 20 days.

Mrs. Martha H., daughter of Rev. Levi and Sarah Shankle, and wife of Mr. J. J. Misenhimer, was born Nov. 8, 1827, and died in Mt. Pleasant, N. C., April 4, 1860.

Tribute of Respect from M. E. Church at Aiken, S. C,. to Marion M. Kemme. He died in Aiken, S. C., April 16th, 1860, aged 18 years, 3 months and 20 days.

Issue of May 21, 1869

Mrs. Mary E. Wilburn, my beloved aunt, sister of my sainted father, Rev. John Mood, and wife of the late Wm. W. Wilburn, of Charleston, S. C., died in Columbia, 29th April, in her 81st year. Recently she had been visited by her daughter, the wife of Rev. John W. Kelley, of the So. C. Conference, and soon after her brother, uncle Peter Mood, from N. Y.... Wm. W. Mood.

Mrs. Mary Achsah Montgomery, wife of Rev. T. F. Montgomery, died in Auburn, Ala., on the 24th April 1869. She was the daughter of Dr. Thos. B. and Mrs. Ann Turner, of Talbotton, and was born Oct. 3rd 1829. T. T. Christian

Miss Sallie A. Blount of Chambers co., Ala., died in New York, 16th April 1860.

Ezekiel M. Park was born February 3rd, 1849, and died of meningitis, April 20th 1869, in Greene co., Ga., in his 21st year. He was at Emory College the Spring term of 1868....

Jas. W. Clark was born May 14th 1819 and died in Jefferson co., Ga., Jan. 29th, in the 50th year of his age. He left a wife and several children. old father Charles Clark, and his sons Charles, Samuel, James, and John, will from a bright constellation in that galaxy of redeemed spirits.

Mrs. Harriet C. West was born in Lawrenceville, Ga., on the 1st Dec. 1823, and died on 29th March 1860.

Mr. John Wesley Summers was born July 27th 1845 and died March 14th 1860. E. S. Tyner.

Issue of May 28, 1869

Sister Julia Ann Chitty was born in Charleston, S. C., and died in Savannah, Ga., February 20th 1860, in the 58th year of her age. Geo. G. N. MacD.

Sister C. Taylor, daughter of Isaac and Esther Kornegan, and wife of Rev. Wm. T. Taylor, died in Thomasville, Ga., 30th of April 1869, in the 36th year of her age.

Mrs. Caroline Belser was born Sept. 9th 1804, and died March 14th 1869, in Clarendon District, S. C. In early life she joined the Lutheran Church, was confirmed in Charleston by Dr. Bachman.... Wm. Thomas

Mrs. Sarah E. E. Matthias, daughter of Mr. and Mrs. H. S. Gardner, was born Feb. 7th 1848; was married to Mr. John A. Matthias in December 1866, and died May 3d 1860, at her father's house. She leaves a husband and a babe about nine months old, father and mother, sisters and brothers.

Mr. Augustus A. Massebeau died April 13th 1869 in Camden, S. C. Born of Catholic parents in France. Wm. Thomas

Mrs. L. A. Carlyle was born Nov. 4th 1849, married Mr. W. C. D. Carlyle Dec. 19th 1867, and died in Irwinton, Ga., March 20th 1869. She left two little daughters, only ten days old. In one month, one of them died and some ten days after the other was taken. W. S. Baker

Issue of June 4, 1869

Died

At Gainesville, Fla., April 20th 1869, Oscar A., infant son of O. A. and M. E. Myers, aged 1 year and 2 weeks.

Obituary

Sister Ann Elizabeth Tyler, long a devoted member of Mulberry St. Church, Macon, Ga., has passed away... on the 19th of April, aged about 77 years. J. S. Key

Mrs. Sophia Langston, widow of Jno. Langston, was born December 10th 1808, and died March 13th 1869.   Gilmer

William Eubanks Sen'r was born in Glynn co, Ga., A. D. 1785. When a young man, removed to Florida, then a Spanish province, and settled in Duval co. his daughter, Mrs. Miner.... R. R. Rushing

Mrs. A. E. Cheatham was born in Habersham co., May 3rd, 1833, married R. S. Cheatham June 17th 1852 and died of consumption at the residence of her father, Rev. E. B. Loyless, in Dawson, Ga. May 5th 1869.

Mrs. Sallie Edelen died April 13th 1860, aged 20 years and 10 days.

George Bennett died March 1869 in his 25th year. At the beginning of the late war, he was a student at the University of Georgia.

Rev. Ellis Stafford died at Grantville, Ga., on 17th April, in his 60th year. He was born near Greensboro, N. C., but when a lad he came to Upson co., Ga., where he grew to manhood, married, and lived till 1851, when he moved to the vicinity in which he breathed his last.... W. J. C.

Mrs. Elizabeth Parmore, wife of Nathan Parmore, Esq., of Harris co., Ga., died on the evening of the 20th May 1869, aged 59 years, 6 months 12 days. She was the daughter of the late John E. Lester, of Jones co., Ga.

J. W. Brown died March 6th, 1869 in the 50th year of his age. For many years he was a member of the Methodist Church at Hawkinsville.... He leaves a wife and three children. W. F. Robison

Zere Middlebrooks died at his residence in Newton co., Ga., April 17th 1860, in the 87th year of his age. He was born in Caswell co., N. C., moved to Georgia in 1817, was married in 1808, and in 1832, with four children, joined the M. E. Church.

Lillie C. Harris, a member of the Clinton, S. C. Sunday-school, died 2nd May in her 10th year.

Issue of June 11, 1869

The Rev. Levi Stansell died on Tuesday 11th May, near Oxford, Newton co., Ga., in the 75th year of his age. He was born in Abbeville, South Carolina, and removed to Stanley co., North Carolina, where, on 4th Nov 1819, he married Miss Charlotte Howell. There he remained for 12 years. About 1831 he removed to Georgia. A. Means

Mrs. Mary Elizabeth Bird died in Orangeburg Dist., S. C., April 19th 1869, in the 36th year of her age. T. J. Clyde

James H. Worley was born in Spartanburg, S. C., Sept 10th 1807 and died in Dahlonega, Ga., April 1st 1869, in the 62nd year of his age. He was one of the first settlers of the present Lumpkin co. He was sheriff of the county or Clerk of the Superior Court. J. T. Lin

Archibald M. Peurifoy went to his reward May 14th, having one month before completed the thirty second year of his age. He was a son of the late Rev. Archibald Peurifoy (local preacher) of Charleston. He was born in Sumter, but lived in Charleston from childhood until he came, early in 1863, to Buena Vista on the boundary line of Spartanburg and Greenville Districts.... leaves a young widow and three children. A. H. Lester

Rev. W. J. Duval was born in New York city in 1811, was converted at the age of 14... [account]... chaplin in 3d Florida Regiment in several States. D. L. Branning

Mr. Norman Terry died 19th March 1869, in the 51st year of his age, near Talbotton, Ga....

Mrs. Mary Belcher was born about the year 1778 in Green co., Ga., and died in Jasper co., Ga., Dec. 22d 1868. A. C. Mixon

Mr. J. J. Adams was born in Abbeville Dist., S. C., Feb. 25th 1818 and died in Columbia co., Fla., Feb. 10th 1869 in the 52nd year of his age... left a wife and five sons. J. W. Jackson. Abbeville Banner, S. C., please copy.

J. T. Carpenter was born 2d October 1833, married Miss Emily Hutchison 17th December 1854, died in Burk co., N. C., of typhoid fever the 5th May 1869. He left a mother, three brothers, one sister, a wife and seven children.... D. L. C.

Simon Slade, twin brother of the late Samuel Slade, was born in Virginia in 1792, and died in Pike co., Ga., 11th May 1869. He leaves a wife and eight children.

Tribute of Respect to Sister Catharine Mashburn, wife of Rev. J. H. Mashburn, of N. Ga. Conference.

Issue of June 18, 1869

Died

Lucy Eugenia, eldest daughter of Martin B. and Drucilla C. Maxwell of Hart Co., Ga., died June 9th 1869, aged 8 years, 8 months, and 10 days.

Lou Emma, daughter of Wm. S. and M. W. Battle of Polk Co., Ga., of diptheria, 21st May, 1869, in her 3rd year.

On the 4th April, near Whitesville, Ga., infant daughter of J. F. and N. C. Spear, aged 2 years and 24 days.

In Atlanta, Ga., on the 11th June, William Chase, infants on of W. P. and Sallie E. Pattillo, aged two months and six days.

Obituary

Mrs. Sarah Fambrough, wife of the late Judge William L. Fambrough, was born in Elbert co., Ga., and died in Monroe co., Ga., on 27th May, in the 71st year of her age. [long account]

Perry Dobbs was born Dec. 21st 1822, and died in Cherokee co., Ga., April 16th 1869. [eulogy] C. M. McClure

Mrs. Mary E. Ellison, eldest daughter of Henry Key, of Russell co., Ala., and wife of Dr. James E. Ellison, Creek Stand, Ala., died 10th April 1869. She was born in Monroe co., Ga., 31st July 1827. Subsequently her father removed to Talbot co., Ga. In November 20th 1849 she became the wife of Dr. Ellison.

Mrs. Ann Oliver died March 14th 1860, at the residence of her son, Rev. R. C. oliver, in Spartanburg, S. C. She was the daughter of Rev. James Dickerson (P. Episcopal) of Cumberland co., Va., and she was born in that state November 18th 1795. When about fifteen years of age, she became a resident of Augusta, Ga., where she afterwards married James L. Oliver, and they fixed their home in Edgefield Dist., S. C. A. H. Lester. The Richmond Advocate is requested to copy.

Mrs. Susannah Strickland, widow of the Rev. John Strickland, who died a few years ago, died in Gordon co., Ga., April 20th 1869, aged 70 years.

Mrs. Catherine Cook was born in Hartford, Conn., Dec. 20th 1796, removed South in 1827, and died in Augusta, Ga., April 25th 1860, aged 73 years. She joined the Presbyterian Church about the year 1841.

Mrs. Martha A., wife of John M. Lovelade died 1st June 1869, in Troup co., Ga., in the 39th year of her age. W. H. Evans

Jeremiah Morgan of Edgefield co., S. C., died May 30th 1869, in his 76th year. He was extensively known as Squire Morgan, having filled the office of magistrate for years... J. H. Zimmerman.

Issue of June 25, 1869

Died

In McDonough, Henry county, Ga., on the 18th instant, Little Lula, infant daughter of J. A. and M. E. McMullan, aged 1 year and nearly 5 months.

Obituary

The Rev. William T. Harrison was born in North Carolina Jan. 10th 1812. While quite young, his parents removed into South Carolina. In 1838 he was ordained by Bishop Morris. [long account] He died at the residence of his daughter Mrs. Lou F. Crowson, in Cala, April 22d 1869. S. W.

Rev. Charles Barino was born in Onslow co., N. C., A. D. 1790. He death occurred in Union co., N. C., March 28th 1869. Tribute of Respect. J. A. Mood

Miss Jullia A. Carpenter was born near Little Rock, Arkansas, and died on the 13th May 1869, at the residence of her uncle, Wm. T. Carpenter, in Bartow, Polk county, Fla.

Dr. John W. Quincey was born in Coniers (England) Jan 31st 1829, and died in Levy co., Florida, March 25th 1869. He came to this country when quite a young man.

Capt. John A. Summerlin died at Jacksonville, Fla., March 18th 1869, aged 47 years. His title was acquired in the 1st Florida regiment of cavalry in the Confederate army... D. L. Branning

Mrs. Mary Page, wife of Captain William Page, died in Marion Dist., S. C., 18th April 1860, having lived upwards of sixty years... J. B. Platt

Tribute of Respect from Richmond ct., N. Ga. Conference, to Col. L. D. Lallerstedt, a local minister.

Issue of July 2, 1869

Died

In Harris co., Ga., on the 17th June, Willbur Little Williams, infant son of John H. and Sallie A. Williams, aged 1 year, 6 months and 18 days.

Obituary

Mrs. Catharine A. Felder, wife of Hamlin R. Felder, of Houston co., Ga., and daughter of the late James E. and Mrs. Catharine Duncan, died in Atlanta, at the residence of the Hon. James M. Calhoun, on the 13th May 1869, in the thirty-third year of her age... J. Rufus Felder

Mr. Gilly Moore died at the residence of Green Moore, Esq., in Green co., Ga., on 27th May 1869, in the 93d year of his age. He was a native of Delaware, and early in life emigrated to Georgia, landing at Savannah, at the age of 12 years.

Mrs. Mary Ann Rebecca Lowry, widow of the late Isham Lowry, was born in Round O., Colleton Dist., S. C., in 1790, and died on the 17th of April 1769, at Hendersonville, Colleton co., S. C. [account]

Mrs. Matilda Elizabeth Futch, consort of John A. Futch, and daughter of Hope H. and Martha A. Colson, was born in Charlton co., Ga., February 16th 1845, and died at the residence of her father in Bradford co., Fla., April 11, 1869.

Andrew Pless was born in S. C., 25th Jan 1800. When but a child his parents moved to Morgan co., Ga. On 4th Jan. 1821, he married Miss Priscilla Brown and moved to Talbot co., and thence to Meriwether co., where he spent the remainder of his days. J. L. S., M. D.

Mrs. Harriet Amelia Williams, wife of James B. Williams, died in Effingham co., Ga., in the 39th year of her age.

Mrs. Mary Hogg was born in Burke co., Ga., May 20 1795, was married to John Hogg in Barnwell Dist., S. C., Feb. 12, 1812, and died in Augusta, GA., April 15, 1869.

James M. Lanham of Spartanburg co., S. C., died March 1869, in his 55th year... J. S. E.

Issue of July 9, 1869

Died

Fannie Levica, daughter of Rev. John W. and Mrs. Martha Ann Abernathy was born in Monroe, N. C., June 20th 1868 and died in the same place, June 15th 1869.

Obituary

Bro. John T. Boykin was born in Greene co., Ga., in 1799, and died in Troup co., Ga., April 13th 1869. E. P. Birch

Sister Patience Raiford died in Muscogee co., Ga., May 20th 1869, in her 65th year.

Brother Joshua Cannon was born June 10th 1795 and died June 6th 1869 in Terrell co., Ga. C. A. Crowell

Julia, daughter of J. A. and Harriett McCutchen, was born July 6, 1855, in Pickens co., Ga. Her death was by a sad accident. A. C. Carson

Mrs. Mary C. Felder, wife of Capt. Lewis Felder, of Orangeburg, died June 3d, in the 58th year of her age. William Hutto

James L. Hudson died in Levy co., Fla., April 17, 1869, aged 16 years. J. H. D. McRae

Tribute of Respect by Ocala and St. John's Circuit, Fla. Conference, to Rev. Dr. William T. Harrison.

Issue of July 16, 1869

Died

In Gainesville, Ga., on June 21, Little Olie, infant daughter of Lee M. and Roberta Lyle, aged six months and four days.

Obituary

Philip Coleman Pendleton was born in Eatonton, Ga., Nov. 17th 1812, and died near Valdosta, June 19th 1869. While residing in Savannah, he married Miss Catherine S. M. Tebeau, who survives. [long account]

Wm. H. Hammock was drowned on 26th June in his 30th year. Walter T. Byrd, aged 11 years, terminated his young life on the same day. He was a member of the Mt. Zion Sabbath-school, Lee co., Ala. Mr. John Byrd was the father of Walter. Jas. M. Wright.

James C. Branch of Clark co.,Ga., was born in Chesterfield co., Va., where he resided until 1818, when he with his excellent companions moved to Ga., and in Green and Clark cos., spent the balance of his long life, near 77 years, and died on the 8th June 1869. J. N. Glenn.

Mr. William F. Pemberton died in Charleston, S. C., June 24th 1869, in the 57th year of his age. He was a native of England, and came in early life to this county. For many years he was a citizen of Augusta, Ga., where he married.

Mrs. Ann Kolb died in Madison, Ga., June 8th 1869.

Mary G. Dismukes, daughter of Joseph and Sarah Wilson, of Jasper co., Ga., died 13th May 1869, in the 69th year of her age... She lived a widow for more than eight years. She sleeps by the side of her husband at Georgetown church.

Mrs. Jane Streater was born May 15th 1798, and died in Chesterfield co., S. C., 25th June 1869. Her daughter, Mrs. Mary E. McCrae passed on a few weeks before. J. C. Hartsell

Mr. Lewis Henry Mouzon, a native, and until recently a resident of Charleston, S. C., died in Clarendon District, S. C., in the 67th year of his age. W. P. M.

Issue of July 23, 1869

Died

May 17th, 1869, Lizzie, infant daughter of J. L. and A. V. Biggers, aged 4 months and 27 days.

Leta Elvira, daughter of Dr. L. B. and Mrs. S. S. Bouchelle, aged 15 months, died June 15th, 1869.

Obituary

My father, William Williams, was born Jan. 30th 1812, and died in Walton co., Ga., June 6, 1869, aged 57 years... joined the M. E. Church in Newton co., Ga., in 1824. Amicus W. Williams.

David Treadwell was born in Samson co., N. C., Dec. 4th 1797, married Dec. 4th 1834, moved to Georgia in 1842 and to Florida about 14 years ago; and died April 30th 1869. J. Anderson

James W. Rees, son of William L. and Harriet Rees, was born July 7th 1842, and died June 13th 1869 of consumption... joined M. E. Church in Green co., Ga., in 1858.

Mrs. Mary Isabella Farnell, daughter of Charles H. & Q. A. Johnson, was born in Jackson co., Ga., Feb. 1849, and died in Jefferson co., Ga., May 24th 1869. H. D. Murphy

Mrs. Mary Ann, wife of W. W. Giles, died in Wakulla co., Fla., June 4th 1869, of typhoid fever, aged 21 years. Her mother died and left her quite young, the eldest of three sisters... W. A. G.

Mrs. Julia A. Causey died in Griffin, Ga., June 18th, aged 63 years. She was the mother of Mrs. Joseph G. Sears of this city.

Miss Fannie A. Nixon was born May 6, 1861, in Horry Dist., S. C., and died in July 14th 1869 at her mother's in the same district. E. G. Gage

Issue of July 30, 1869

Died

in Monroe co., Ga., July 23d, Lizzie Ellen, infant daughter of Rev. Thomas G. and Emma L. Scott, aged nine months and two days.

Obituary

Gen. Henry Harrison Kinard was born 29th March 1806 and died June 17th 1869. He was a native of Newberry District, S. C., in which his parents and also his grand parents resided. On 20th Feb 1827, he was united in marriage to Miss Mary A. Counts. By this marriage he had four children, two sons and two daughters. The elder son, Dr. James Pinckney, and the younger Capt. Jno. Martin, were called from time to eternity in the freshness and bloom of manhood. The two daughters Mrs. F. E. Holman, and Mrs. M. M. Humbert, wife of Rev. J. W. Humbert of the So. Ca. Conference, survive the death of their father. In 1851 he sustained the loss of the companion of his youth, and in the following year was happily married to Miss Louisa C. Counts. By this marriage he had four children. The eldest, little Mamie, was at the early age of seven called by the Good Shepherd, and three are left.

John C. Miller died in Charleston, S. C., July 6th 1869, having attained 79 years. He was married in 1817. His devoted wife still lingers. Of ten children, two daughters survive, but among the happy dead is the Rev. J. W. Miller, late of the S. C. Conference. The funeral sermon was performed at Trinity and his remains were laid in the family cemetery at Magnolia, near the city of his birth.

Bro. John W. Hutchinson died in Brunswick on 9th June in the 60th year of his age. He was a native of St. James Parish, S. C., removed to Georgia in 1841-2. Chas. A. Fulwood

Mrs. Margaret Black, wife of Joseph S. Black and daughter of Elijah and Elizabeth Stillwell (the latter still living) was born in Mecklenburg co., N. C., on 18th Feb 1799 and died in McDonough, Ga., July 14th 1869. John Stilwell

Susan E., wife of Philip Wolf, and daughter of Peter and Elizabeth Rape, was born in Mecklenburg co., N. C., 25th August 1825 and died in Tallapoosa co., Ala., June 27th 1809. May God bless her five little children and her three step children, and the bereaved husband. The New Orleans Christian Advocate will please copy.

Sister M. A. Lovelace, wife of the late J. T. Lovelace, and daughter of Jacob Brooks, died in great peace in Troup co., Ga., 5th July, in her 28th year. W. H. Evans

Dr. C. W. Bedell, formerly of Georgia, was shot by one of his tenants on 22d June and died on 4th July at Lawrenceville, Ala.

Issue of August 6, 1869

Died

Lizzie Biggers, born Dec. 20th 1868, died May 17th 1869, infant daughter of J. L. and A. V. Biggers.

Obituary

Mrs. Ann E. Daniel was born Oct 2d 1807, married to the late Capt. E. Daniel of Liberty co., Ga., May 18th 1826, and died April 19th 1869. W. M. Watts

Mrs. Martha Williams was born in Washington co., Ga., and died in Macon, Ga., July 21st 1869, in her 77th year.

Mrs. Susan L. Bigby, relict of the Rev. John Bigby, died at the residence of her son in Newnan, Ga., on the 15th of May in her 69th year.

Mrs. Martha Ann Fergusson (maiden name Stormon) was born in Chester Dist., S. C., June 3d 1845, joined the M. E. Church, South, in Hamilton co., Fla., at the age of twelve years. She was married at about the age of 16 years to Thos. Fergusson and died June 25th 1869, aged 24 years.

John W. Weldon was born in Columbia co., Ga., May 13th 1810. When three years old, his parents moved to Jasper co., in which county he was married in 1824, to Miss Jane C. Phillips. In the fall of 1858 he came to Macon, and died in this city July 18th 1869.

Mrs. Elizabeth Ann Frith, daughter of Wallen and Martha Stone, was born in April 27, 1791, and died in Autauga co., Ala., April 22 1869, aged nearly 78 years. She was twice married, and outlived by a few years, both of her husbands. She moved to Alabama in 1818 with her first husband, Colonel Hester, who died in 1832, and she married Dr. Frith in 1823. Wm. A. Edwards

Bro. Jesse Stephens was born in S. C. April 11th 1802 and died in Walker co., Ga., April 16th 1869.

Arabella Wightman, youngest daughter of O. P. and E. A. Fannin, died July 18th 1869, at West Wynntos, Florida.

Issue of August 13, 1869

Died

In Floyd co,. John Francis, on 19th July, infant son of F. M. and M. A. Fuller.

In Charleston, S. C., on July 8, Powell Reed, infant son of Rev. Louis C. and Mrs. Ann F. Loyal, aged 1 year, 1 month and 4 days.

Obituary

Aquilla Cherry died near Russellville, Monroe co., Ga., on June 1st 1869 in the 84th year of his age. L. Moncrief

Mrs. Martha Johnson, widow of George Johnson, of Laurens co,. S. C., died at the residence of her brother Mr. Thomas Neill on the 6th July 1860, in the 69th year of her age. She was born in the vicinity of Hopewell church.

Mrs. Lucy A. Crowder, wife of brother Richard P. Crowder, died in Spalding co., Ga., July 13th, aged 44 years.

Charity Ann F. Causey, wife of Samuel H. Causey, died in Crawford co., Ga., on 10th of July 1869 in the 39th year of her age.

Joseph Shaw of Richmond co., N. C., died June 14th 1869, in his 38th year. He leaves a wife with two little daughters.

Mrs. Mary E. Cobb, daughter of Jeremiah Smith, and wife of George C. Cobb, was born in Macon, Ga., 29th May 1831 and died in Talbotton, Ga., 7th July 1869. Thos. T. Christian.

Issue of August 20, 1869

Mrs. Caroline Frederick died in Marshallville, Ga., on 4th July 1869, aged 70 years. She was a daughter of Jacob Rumph of Revolutionary memory, and was a native of Orangeburg District, S. C. She joined the Methodist Church in her twelfth year. She married Mr. Daniel Frederick, was the mother of six children, five daughters and one son; lived to see them grown and married.... T. B. Russell.

Mrs. Eliza Hunt, daughter of Dr. Thos. Henderson, of Charlotte, N. C., died 30th July 1869, at the residence of her son-in-law, Maj. T. A. Brown, in Talbotton, Ga., in her 89th year. She was first married to Burrell Smart, and he and brother John Hill, father of Hon. B. H. Hill, were among the first settlers of Jasper co., Ga. At the death of Mr. Smart she was married to Bro. Jno Hunt, who died in Macon in 1854. She has left loving daughters and kindred.

Mrs. Hannah Howren was born April 11th 1797 and died July 4th 1869. About two weeks before her death, she came on a visit to her sister, Mrs. Brantly, on Cherry Lake, Madison co., Fla. R. M. Tydings

Mrs. Louisa J. D. Myrick, wife of Dr. John W. Myrick, and daughter of James Dowdell of Chambers co., Ala., died on 22d July in her 29th year. J. F. Dowdell

Mrs. Mary A. E. Platt, wife of Geo. F. Platt, Esq., died at Lexington, Ga., August 11th 1869.

Mary Elizabeth, daughter of G. W. and Martha M. Sunday, died July 13th in Gadsden co., Fla., in her eighth year.

Issue of August 27, 1869

Mrs. Eliza Charlton, widow of Major John Charlton, late of Springfield, Effingham co., Ga., died in Savannah, Ga., July 11, 1869, in the 76th year of her age. She was born in Savannah, Ga., Feb. 13, 1793, of pious Lutheran parents.... removed to the vicinity of Goshen church where the remainder of their long life was spent and where Mrs. Charlton was married. In July 1822 she with her widowed and only sister, Mrs. H. Nolan, became identified with the Methodist Church. Their aged parents, Mr. David Gugle and his wife... Ann E. McD.

Dr. James Seaborn Moore was born at Millhaven, Scriven co., Ga., 13th February 1807, and died at Warrior Stand, Ala, July 23d 1869, aged 62 years. B. B. Ross

Mrs. Julia D. Hutchingson, wife of S. P. Hutchingson, and daughter of William and Elizabeth Skinner, dec'd, was born Oct. 1, 1827, and died in Columbia co., Ga., July 29, 1869. R. A. Conner

Tribute of Respect to Seth Dupois. Stillwood, S. C.

Miss Eliza T. Hill died on 5th Aug. 1860, aged about 19 years. John W. McRoy

Mrs. Sarah Pope, wife of Burrell Pope, and daughter of John and Tabitha Perkins, was born in Jones co., Ga., Sept 15, 1805, and died at John B. Pope's, on June 12, 1869. She moved from Jones to Talbot co., Ga., thence to Macon, Ala., thence to Tallapoosa co., Ala., then to Lee co., Miss., where she died. Henry Brooks

Mrs. Elvirah Comings, wife of Mr. Richard Comings, and daughter of William and Louisa Comings, of Cypress circuit, S. C., died on July 31, aged 42 years. A. R. Danner

Mrs. Frances V. Stuart, wife of W. D. Stuart and daughter of W. w. Palmer, was born in Chambers co., Ala., Dec. 8th 1844, and died on 6th August 1869, at the residence of her mother-in-law, in South Butler, Ala.

Allen Pope, third son of John B. and Sarah A. Pope, died 16th July 1869, in his 12th year. Henry Brooks

Issue of September 3, 1869

Died

William James Snipes, son of Dr. Wm. T. and Mrs. M. A. Snipes, in Centreville, Fla., July 23d, 1869, aged one year, six months and three days.

Annie Mary Smith, daughter of Bro. J. A. and Sister M. E. Smith, in Miscomukie, Fla,. July 8th, 1869, aged four months and ten days.

On the 21st July 1869, in Henry co,. Ga., Charlie Wesley, infant son of Bro. D. L. and Sister A. E. Coleman, aged 13 months and 10 days.

On the 18th Aug. 1869, infant son of Rev. J. B. and Mary Ann Johnson, of Appling co., aged 3 years.

On the 23rd of May 1869, in the city of Bahin, Brasil, Col. George Leitner, aged 87 years.

Obituary

Mrs. Jerusha King died on the 13th August, at the residence of William B. King in Gwinnett co., Ga., in the 80th year of her age.

Mrs. Tinie E. Fuller, wife of John E. Fuller and daughter of John W. and Martha M. Dozier, died in Geneva, Ga., July 30th 1869. B. B. Lester

Mrs. Sarah M. Wynn, wife of R. J. Wynn, of Putnam co., died in Morgan co., Ga., July 28th 1869, aged 48 years. Thos. F. Pierce

Seth Stafford Dupuis was born in Beaufort District, S. C., December 25th 1808, and died August 1st 1869. L. C. Loyal

Mrs. Margaret E., wife of Daniel Avinger, died in Orangeburg Co., S. C., July 14th 1869, in the 43d year of her age. J. C. S.

Wm. H. Nixon was born in Orangeburg Dist., S. C., January 7th 1796, and died in Talbot co., Ga., August 2d, 1869. Hugh A. Nixon

Edwin G. McCreight, youngest child of Samuel J. and Rebekah R. McCreight, was born in Fairfield Dist., S. C., August 31st 1839 and died in Marion co., Fla., August 12, 1869. H. W. Long

Tribute of Respect to Elizabeth W. and Julia W. Mitchell who died June 7th by Beulah Sabbath-School.

Issue of September 10, 1869

Mrs. Lucy Falconer of Montgomery, Ala., died July 14, 1869. She was a widow of more than three score and ten years. [long eulogy] H. M. McTyeire

Mrs. Eliza Martin Cato, wife of Dr. P. W. Cato, and daughter of Samuel and Tabitha Holland, was born at Forsyth, Ga., June 8, 1813, married Dr. Cato on 31st May 1838, in Russell co., Ala., removed to Florida, February 1848, and died in Houston, Fla., 15th August 1869. Lem'l G. R. Wiggins

Issue of September 17, 1869

Rev. Daniel Sikes, M. D., was born at Tatnall co., Ga., December 18th 1804, and died near the spot where he was born May 10th 1869. He was married about 1824 to Miss Elizabeth J. Eason, a daughter of the late Rev. Wm. Eason... David Crenshaw

Hon. Samuel Bell was born in Pitt co., N. C., October 7th 1823, married Miss Sarah Adaline Hartsfield, February 22d, 1844, and died in Conwayboro, S. C., August 21st 1869. E. G. Gage

Rev. Thomas Munnerlyn was born in Marion Dist., S. C., in 1794, of revolutionary ancestors. His father being one of several brothers who passed the struggle of the revolution under Gen. Marion. He has left a large family.

Mrs. Mary Allen was born in Louisa co., Va., Feb. 16th 1791, and died in Oak Bowery, Ala., July 29th 1869. At an early date she removed with her parents to Georgia, where she spent about 25 years of her life... Her son, William C. Allen, with whom she was living at the time was born August 3d, 1817, and died August 18th 1869, at Oak Bowery, Ala. E. B. Norton

Silas Brown was born in Cabarras co., N. C., May 17th 1795, was married to Miss Jane Ormand, Feb. 20th 1816, removed to Cobb co., Ga., in 1834, and died June 8th 1869, aged 73 years and 11 days. S. J. Bellah

Dr. H. T. Brown was born in Rutherford co,. Tenn., Dec 17th 1833, and died in Murfreesborough, May 28th 1869. In 1852 he married, removed to Florida.

Joseph T. Bond was born in Hall co., Ga., March 15th 1823. When a boy his father moved to DeKalb co., Ga., where he died. He married a Miss Corley... He married a second time a Miss Nall of Alabama... died about 5 o'clock, August 14th 1869.

Mrs. Caroline Arrington, wife of Willis Arrington, and daughter of Ursula and Dickson Atkinson, was born in Columbia co., and died in Jefferson co., Ga., on 20th July 1869, in her 65th year.

Sister Kesiah Hammock died 11th June at the residence of Silas Tootle, her brother-in-law, near Reidsville, Tatnall co., Georgia, in her 53d year. W. J. Jordan

Mrs. Elizabeth Kitchens died at Cave Spring, Ga., August 3d, 1869, in the 70th year of her age. She was the wife of old Brother Meredith Kitchens. B. B. Quillian

Mrs. Mollie T. Pickett, wife of John Pickett, was born Oct. 3d, 1841, and died in Girard, Ala., August 3d, 1855 [sic]. J. A. P.

Mary T. West, daughter of Rev. W. H. Clark, and Mrs. T. J. Clarke, died in Baker co., Ga., on 19th August, aged 16 months, 10 days. Matilda H., the only surviving daughter died on 21st August, aged 5 years, 8 months, 20 days.

Issue of September 24, 1869

Died

William Gordon Crawford was born in Cotton Valley, Macon co., Ala,. Dec. 31, 186, and died August 30, 1869.

Bettie Rhodes, daughter of Mr. W. R. and Mrs. Mary C. Swain, was born in Greenville co., N. C., Sept. 28, 1863 and died in Leon co., Fla., Sept. 2, 1869.

John R. Jeffcoat died in Leon co., August 21, aged ten years, two months and fourteen days.

Obituary

Mrs. Margaret Amanda Marshall was the daughter of Rev. Daniel F. and Catherine E. Wade, and was born in Orangeburg Dist., S. C., January 16th 1830. In December 1849 she became my wife... John M. Marshall

Sister Elizabeth H. S. Stearns wife of Rev. Zachariah Stearns, was born in Franklin co., N. C., and died in Talbot co., Ga., July 4th 1869, in the 80th year of her age. S. J. Corley

Mrs. Dorcas Leak was born in Laurens Dist., S. C., Feb. 1st 1793, and died at Cave Spring, Floyd co., Ga., July 19th 1869. She lost her mother at an early age. She was left a widow over 30 years ago. She was the mother of ten children, four of whom were living at her death.

Spencer Moore died in Lee co,. Ala., July 27, 1869, in the 89th year of his age. Father Moore married his first wife in Green co,. Ga., Miss Susannah Graham. From thence he moved to Baldwin and then to Monroe, to Macon co., Ala., in the year 1837 where he ended his life.... William B. Neal

Mrs. Mary A. Ponder, wife of John H. Ponder, of Walton co., Ga., and daughter of Lemuel Black, deceased was born in Covington, Ga., on the 9th of Dec 1833, married in 1860 and died August 18th 1869, in the 36th year of her age. A. Means

William C. Wisdom was born July 6th 1790, in E. Va., and died in Harris co., Ga., August 11th 1869, aged 70 years. During the late war his youngest son, Melville, was killed at Franklin, Tenn. Some 23 years since a beloved wife died... L. C. W. Richmond Christian Advocate, will please copy.

The Rev. Ephraim M. Penington was born in Newton co., Ga., July 29th 1829 and died at Social Circle, Ga., on 30th Aug 1869.

Dr. John W. L. Robarts was born at Beaufort, S. C., July 13, 1801, resided at different periods in S. C., Ga., Ala., and Florida, and died at Tustenuggee, Columbia co,. Fla., at the residence of his sister, Mrs. Collin, on 16th July 1869 of pneumonia. George O. E., son of William H. T. and Sarah A. Roberts, nephew of the above, was born May 17th 1858, and died at Ichtucknee, Columbia co., Fla.

Joseph Barber, marshal of the town of Covington and constable of this District, died Sept 1st of a wound received from a pistol in the hands of a freedman... Bro. B. was born in 1818 in Melbourne, Derby co., England, landed in America 2d April 1846, enlisted in the Confederate army.... P. A. Heard

Sister Olivia Godbold, wife of General Elly Godbold of Marion S. C., died on 2d August 1869, aged 67 years. G. H. Wells

John Eady died in West Point, Ga., Aug 26, 1869, aged about 74 years. He was a native of Lincoln co., Ga., but the greater part of his life was spent in Ala.

Harriet R. Van, wife of Edward Van, and daughter of Rev. A. Skinner died in Butler co., Ala., July 14, 1869, in her 34th year. H. J. Hunter

Mrs. S. E. M. Davis, wife of Mr. R. M. Davis and eldest daughter of Mr. L. B. and Mrs. H. E. Beckwith, was born near Charleston, Jefferson co., Va., July 21st 1814, married March 3d 1868, and died near Newnansville, Fla., August 2d, 1869, leaving a little babe five months old with a husband, widowed mother, a brother and four sisters. E. S. Tyner

Issue of October 1, 1869

Died

Willie Seals, daughter of Mr. Joseph and Mrs. Mattie Vann, in Cedar Town, Ga., Sept 19th 1869, aged 11 months.

Obituary

Dr. Jas. Bivings, was born in Edenton, N. C., and died near Crawfordsville, Spartanburg co., S. C., August 18th 1869, in the 83d year of his age. Early in life he located at Lincolnton, N. C. [long account] He leaves a wife, children, grandchildren and great grandchildren. W. Bowman

Sister Hollon Johnson, mother of W. P. Johnson, died in Troup co., Ga., in her 83d year on 13th August 1869. W. H. Evans

Jacob S. DePass died at the residence of his son, Wm. L. DePass, Camden, S. C., on 8th Sept 1869, in the 71st year of his age.

Mrs. Mary M. C. Saunders, wife of Capt. Z. F. Saunders, and daughter of E. B. and Nancy B. Loyless, was born in Richmond co., Ga,. Nov. 26th 1830, and died in Weston, Webster co., Ga., Sept. 12th 1869. C. R. Moore

Miss Sarah Williams Clark, daughter of James A. and Francis M. Clark of Elbert co., Ga., was born April 14, 1848, and died Sept. 5, 1869, at Franklin Spring, Franklin co,. Ga. A. G. Worley

Mrs. Martha Stephens, died at the residence of her son-in-law, Henry Stevens, in Baldwin co,. Ga., on 31st August 1869, aged about 80 years. C. W. Smith

Bro. E. J. M. Callaway was born in Baldwin co., Ga., April 12th 1819 and died in Sumter co,. Aug. 22d, 1869. He leaves a large family. J. M. Marshall

Mrs. Lucinda Pendergrass died in Clarke co., Ga., 13th August 1869. Born and reared in Virginia, she there joined the Baptist Church. Joined the M. E. Church at Salem, Clarke co., Ga., in 1840.

Mrs. Ellen Craps died at her brother's, Mr. William Jennings, in Terrell co., Ga., July 1st, aged 36 years. She joined the Evangelical Lutheran Church in S. C., in 1853, and continued until her removal to Ga... J. M. Marshall

Robert S. Holloway died in Upson co., Ga., Aug. 29th 1869, in the 43d year of her age.

Burroughs Peak, daughter of Rev. L. and Mrs. Julia Peak, was born 31st May 1861, and died 31st August 1869.

Issue of October 8, 1869

James Ellison was born in Fairfield Dist., S. C., June 1st 1788, and died in Talbot county, Ga., July 1st 1869. He entered life in the mercantile firm of his brother, John Ellison, in Charleston, with whom he remained until 1808, when he removed to Chester, S. C., where he married Miss Jane A. Patterson in 1812... Tribute of Respect from Sardis Church, Talbot ct., S. Ga.

Mrs. Lou J. Quillian, daughter of Lewis and Elizabeth Vanzant, and wife of Rev. B. B. Quillian, the present steward of the Deaf and Dumb institute at Cave Spring, Ga., was born Feb. 27th 1840, in Fannin co., Ga.... Thomas W. Craven

Robert Kendrick was born in Person co, N. C., Aug. 17th 1794. He moved to Clarke co., Ga., when about grown and joined the U. S. Army under Gen. Jackson in the Florida Indian war... died on August 4th 1869.

Mrs. Margaret E. Owen, wife of Mr. J. O. Owen, was born in Gwinnett co., Ga., June 16th, 1823, and died in Whitfield co,. Ga., on 12th August 1869. She has left a young husband and five children. T. J. Simmons

Miss Mollie McLarin died in Fairburn, Ga., in the 16th year of her age.

Mary Ann Lasater was born in Blount co, Tenn., in 1812, and died in Whitfield co,. Ga., Aug 25th 1869. T. M. Pledger, Pastor.

Tribute of Respect to Dr. Robert J. Boyd, late P. Elder of Marion Dist., S. C. Conference.

Issue of October 15, 1869

Died

Oct. 1st 1869, Minie Lee, youngest child of Dr. S. J. and S. V. Brabham, aged 1 year and 2 days.

In Monticello, Sept. 3d, Lucy Kate, only child of Saml and Georgia R. Fulton, aged 2 months and 2 days.

In Marietta, Ga,. on the 9th of Sept., Cattie, infant daughter of L. S. and Fannie J. Northcut, aged 8 months and 18 days.

Obituary

Mrs. Sarah E. Evans, the youngest child of the lamented Dr. Wm. Booth, dec'd, was born in Quincy, Fla., Nov. 9th 1836 and died on 29th August 1869 at the residence of her brother-in-law, Dr. C. A. Hentz. In Oct 1857 she was married to Capt. James C. Evans, who preceded her to ge five only a little more than five months, leaving her with three small children. F. A. Branch

Dr. James W. Stephens of Colleton, S. C., died on 23d August 1869, aged 44 years, 1 month and 29 days. L. Wood

Mrs. Sabra Durham, widow of Hardy Durham, late of Twiggs co., Ga., died July 14th 1869, aged about 72 years.

Joseph Black, Junior, was born in N. C., 11th October 1823, and died in Forsyth co., Ga., Sept. 14th 1869. J. D. Anthony

Seaborn J. Lawrence died in Hancock co., on 28th August 1869, in the 78th year of his age... J. Lewis

Alexander Crawford died in Upson co., Ga., July 21st 1869 in the 57th year of his age, after having suffered for two years from cancer.

Mrs. Martha Myrick was born in Jones co., Ga., May 21st 1818, and lived in Crawford co., until her death. Left a widow in 1857 with a large family.

Tribute of Respect by Muddy Creek S. School to Francis G. Hughes.

Issue of October 22, 1869

Mrs. Mary G. Montgomery, daughter of Dr. J. B. Cottrell of Tenn., was born in Miltonsville, Anson co., N. C., on 31st March 1837, moved with her parents to Tenn., in 1857 where she resided until her marriage with Maj. W. J. Montgomery on 19th July 1859, when she returned to her native State and died in Concord, N. C. 18th Sept 1869. [eulogy] R. R. Pegues. The Episcopal Methodist at Raleigh, N. C., will please copy.

Mrs. Martha Ann Stephens, formerly Rice, a native of Colleton District, S. C., died at Valdosta, Ga., on 13th Sept 1869, in the 62nd year of her age.

Mrs. Mary Rigsby, wife of Allen Rigsby of Marietta, Ga., was born in Wayne co., N. C., Aug. 3d 1801. She joined the Methodist Church at Prospect, Stewart co., Ga, with her husband in 1837.

Winifred Letitia Delilah Walker, daughter of Rev. Joseph and Sarah Camp, was born Jan. 25th 1845, married to Rev. Jno. G. Walker of the Montgomery Conference, Nov. 15th 1854, and died Sept. 18th, 1869. W. R. Kirk

Judge William O. Kendrick was born in Columbia co., Ga., Dec. 14th 1800, and died 12th August 1869.

Mrs. Martha Rast, wife of Wm. Rast of Orange Spring, Fla., died of typhoid fever, 19th September 1869, aged 29 years.

Dr. W. B. Taylor was born in Laurens co,. Ga., in 1807. He removed thence to Leon county, Fla., in the 19th year of his age. In his 30th year he was married to Miss Jane McCoy. God gave them sons and daughters... At the close of the late war, he removed to Thomas co., Ga., where he died 6th July 1869.

Miss Matthew Sawrie died in Rome, Ga., Oct. 5th, aged 22 years. She was the last one of a large family, left to cheer and comfort the mother. H. H. Parks

Alfred W. Davis, son of Robert and Jane Davis, was born in Union co., S. C., Nov. 23d, 1811, was married in 1832 to Miss Hannah R. Williams, daughter of Patrick and Lucy Williams, and died of cancer, Sept. 23d 1869. He leaves a wife and thirteen children. Chas. C. Davis, Smith's Ford, Union Co., S. C.

John Kea, son of Wesley Kea, was born in Emanuel co., Ga., and died 31st August.

Mrs. James Lamberth, daughter of Larkin Dunn, Esq., was born 12th Feb. 1812; was married to Rev. James Lamberth, 29th April 1828, and died in Rome, Ga., 22d Sept 1869. After their marriage, she and her husband resided in Fayette county, in 1834 when they moved to Rome.

Marshall Holsomback, Sr., was born in S. C., and died in Columbia co., Ga., 2d Oct 1869, aged 64 years.

Matilda Hansford was born March 1, 1818, and died Sept. 25, 1869 in Macon, Ga., the mother of 12 children. She joined the M. E. Church, South in Elbert co., in 1839. Her husband preceded her (L. E. Hansford) one year and four days. James Jones

Tribute of Respect by Longstreet Sabbath-school to Wilbur F. Mason.

Issue of October 29, 1869

Mrs. Marcia, daughter of the late Dr. John G. Slappey, and the list surviving child of a large family, was married on the 21st of Oct. 1868 to Mr. Robert Walthour, and died at the home of her mother in Baker co., Ga., on the 13th of July 1869, in her 19th year. Ann Lane

Richard Milner Lyon died in Polk co., Ga., Sept. 20th 1869, aged 27 years.

Mrs. Mary Donald, my dear mother, wife of Rev. John A. Donald, was born 26th of March 1806 in Abbeville District, S. C., and died Sept. 23d 1869 in Cherokee co., Ga. Malcom M. Donald

Col. R. T. Price died near Columbus, Ga., in the 42d year of his age.

Mrs. Ann Bryant died Oct. 4th 1869 in Thomasville, Ga., aged 79 years.

Catharine W. Busby died in Paulding co., Ga., Sept. 25th 1869.

Tribute of Respect to Bro. James Ellison by quarterly meeting for Talbot circuit.

Issue of November 5, 1869

Died

Near Albany, Ga., Sept 29, 1869, Bennson H. Edwards, son of Dr. D. B. and grandson of Rev. Robt. L. Edwards. He was born in Lumpkin co., Ga., August 1850.

Obituary

John Wesley Rhodes, eldest son of Col. Jno. F. and Temperance C. Rhodes, was born in Pike (now Bullock) co., Ala., on 10th Nov 1850, and died at Union Springs, Ala., on 27th August 1869. Joseph B. Cottrell.

Abraham McKinna Williams was born in Maryland on 29th July 1780 and died at the residence of his son, Abraham Williams, near Union Springs, Ala., on 5th Aug 1869. His parents moved from Maryland to Hancock co., Ga., and settled there when the deceased was 8 years old. He married Miss Sarah Culver, daughter of Geo. and Elizabeth Culbert. His wife died the 31st Aug 1861. Joseph B. Cottrell.

Mrs. Fannie H. Miller, wife of W. R. Miller died in Burke co., Ga., on 27th Sept, in her 19th year.

Mrs. Mary E. Clayton, daughter of John and Martha W. Redding was born in Baldwin co., Ga., Nov. 18th 1822, moved to Monroe co., Ga., with her parents when quite young, where she lived till married to John B. Clayton in Nov. 1837. She died 3d Oct 1869.

Maj. Jehu Trammell was born 25th April 1793 and died 17th September 1869 in Nacoochee Valley, White co., Ga. He was elected senator from Habersham co... His aged companion still lingers on... in Cartersville, Ga.

Mrs. Mary W. Facklin Dickson, wife of W. J. Dickson, daughter of Robert J. Gregg, died in Marion, S. C., August 1st 1869. G. H. Wells

George B. Tooley, son of R. H. Tooley, died in Barnesville, Ga., Oct. 17th, aged 17 years.

Mrs. Mary S. Adams died in Henry co., Ga., Sept. 25th 1869, aged 68 years. J. H. Harris

Mrs. Rebecca A. Bowdon (formerly Miss Brooks) wife of R. S. Bowdon, was born Jan. 2d 1817, was married May 2d 1869, and died Oct. 4th 1869 in Meriwether co., Ga. W. W. Oslin

Victoria Garrison, daughter of Levi and Nancy A. Garrison, died in Jackson co., Fla. on 22d July 1860, aged 14 years, 9 months and 24 days. L. Duncan

Issue of November 12, 1869

Died

Roiser Evans Christian, only child of J. B. and Lucy E. Christian, died in the city of Americus, Oct. 26th 1869, aged 4 months and 20 days.

Obituary

Mrs. Sarah T. Underwood, whose maiden name was Sarah Twiggs Blount, was born in Burke county, Ga., Oct. 15th 1807, and died in Rome, Ga., Oct. 24th 1860.

Dr. James T. Center died 6th Sept 1869, near Cokesbury, S. C., in the 50th year of his age. About the year 1853, he removed to Cass co., Ga., and practiced medicine near Stilesboro. He returned to Carolina and finally settled with Mr. Daniel Beacham, his father-in-law.

William Price Allen, only son of J. R. and M. M. Allen, was born July 27th 1860, and died suddenly near Cuthbert, Ga., Oct. 18th 1869. A. J. Dean

Mrs. Eliza A. S. Jordan, daughter of John L. and Mary H. Bootey, formerly of Monroe co., Ga., died in Panola co., Texas, 27th May 1869, in her 31st year.

Mrs. Mary Plunket, widow of James Plunket, deceased of Anson co., N. C., died at Wadesboro, N. C., July 29th 1869, aged about 55 years.

Mrs. Margaret McLeod, aged nearly 95 years, died on 16th July 1869, in Sumter District, S. C.

Issue of November 19, 1869

R. N. R. Bradwell died of dropsy of the heart in Columbus, Ga., Oct. 13th 1869, in the 61st year of his age. Bro. B. passed some ten years of his young manhood in Augusta, Ga... He removed to Columbus, Ga., in 1836 or 1837. J. E. Evans

Mrs. Arana Ethridge was born Sept. 14th 1811, and died in Houston co., Ga., Sept. 29th 1869... I. L. Avant

Mrs. John DeBow was born in Charleston, S. C., April 9th 1803, and died at the house of Mr. Geo. Whaley in Abbeville Dist., S. C., Sept. 12th 1869. Thos. G. Herbert

Mrs. Eliza Ann Marable, wife of George Marable of Monroe, Walton co.,Ga., and daughter of Col. Isaac and Elizabeth Craton of Rutherfordton, N. C., died on 13th Oct 1869, aged 44 years, five months and 23 days.

Miss Jennie Thomasson, daughter of the Rev. B. D. and Sarah Thomasson, Carrollton, Ga., died on 29th Oct 1869, aged 22 years.

Little George N. Sentell, son of Rev. J. E. and E. M. Sentell of S. Ga. Conference, was born Sept 9th 1857 and died Oct 16th 1869 at the Taylor's Creek camp meeting, Liberty co., Ga. L. B. Payne

Hattie E. McGehee, only child and daughter of Mr. L. and M. B. McGehee, died near Notasulga, Ala., on 20th Sept 1869, in her 15th year.

Dr. Henry Matterson Mitchell was born Sept. 13th 1835... married Miss Mary Butler of Decatur co., Ga., and removed to Cairo, in Thomas co., where he died August 13th 1869. P. C. Harris

Georgia Cyrena Sweat, daughter of Thomas Sweat, was born Dec. 13th 1869, and died Nov. 8th 1869. W. T. McMichael

Tribute of Respect to A. E. Paschall.

Issue of November 26, 1869

Robert Bowman died suddenly in Bibb co., on Friday night, Nov. 5th 1869, in the 57th year of his age. He was born in Rockingham co,. N. C., and emigrated with his father to Ga., in early life. W. C. Bass

Mrs. Elizabeth Scott was born in Liberty co., Ga., between 70 and 75 years ago. She died in Newnansville, East. Fla., Sept. 26th 1869. Her only son, W. W. Scott.... E. S. T.

Mrs. Lucy Harris, wife of John P. Harris, died in Covington, Ga., Oct. 25th, aged 27 years. P. A. Heard

Brother George Overstreet was born in S. C., and when about twelve years old his father moved to Tatnall co., Ga. There he grew up and afterwards married and moved to Florida. Robert L. Wiggins

Mrs. Mary A. Dyer, wife of Mr. Otis Dyer of New York, and daughter of Samuel and Rebecca Goodall, died in Fort Valley, on 15th October 1869.

Mr. James Henry Buff was born 24th April 1827, was married to Miss Susanna Newton Dunwody, April 8th 1852, and died 21st Oct 1869, in Calhoun co., Ga.... S. N. Dunwody

Mrs. Charilla J. Kemme died in Louisville, Ga., on 18th October 1869, in the 26th year of her age.

Sister Judith Mitchell died Oct. 17, 1869, near Greenville, Merriwether co., Ga., in the 94th year of her age. For a number of years she lived in the family of her nephew, Rev. J. M. C. Robertson.... P. M. Ryburn

Mrs. Emma Cato, wife of Mr. Tamerlane H. Cato, and daughter of Jacob and Eliza Bugg, died at Newnansville, East Florida, Nov. 3d, 1869. She was married to Mr. Cato on 5th March 1867.... Lem'l G. R. Wiggins

Issue of December 3, 1869

Died

in Charleston co., S. C., Nov. 15, 1869, Cora Hart, youngest child of Dr. J. L. B. Gilmore, in her sixth year.

Obituary

Mrs. Permelia, wife of Col. Levi Ezell, was born in Wilkins co., April 20th 1813, and died in Houston co., Ga., Nov. 13th 1869. She joined the Presbyterian Church in Milledgeville.... W. W. Stewart. Southern Presbyterian please copy.

Mrs. Ann Christian, for 62 years a member of St. John's Church, Augusta, Ga., died Oct 27th 1869, in the 88th year of her age. Arminius Wright

Sister Mary Young was born in Washington co., Ga., in March 1799. In her early childhood her parents removed to Greene co., Ga. Her husband, Bro. Myles Young, who died some five years since, removed from Greene to Houston co., Ga., in 1838, and thence to Brooks county in 1856 where she died Nov. 21, 1869.

Capt. W. J. Dickinson was born in Barnwell District, S. C., January 28th 1830, and died near Monticello, Fla., Aug. 30th 1869. W. L. Pegues

Mrs. Sarah Bradford died at the residence of her son, George Auld, on 13th Sept 1869, just at the close of her 58th year. Her maiden name was Frederick. She was born in Charleston, S. C., Sept. 16, 1811. She married first Mr. Auld, and with him moved to the village of Laurens, S. C., Afterwards they went to Mobile, Ala., but soon returned to this place, where her husband soon after died leaving her five young children. One of her two children by her last husband died a soldier during the late war-- the other, a daughter, resides at the North. One of her sons, Frederick Auld, has been a member of the S. C. Conference.

J. B. Wollard was born in Washington, N. C., Sept. 20th 1792, and died in Marlboro', S. C., Sept 7th 1869.He served in Fayetteville as class leader for ten years previous to his removal to Cheraw in 1835. W. L. Pegues

Mrs. Elizabeth B. Stanford was born in Maryland in 1784. Her maiden name was Freeney. She came with her father's family to Georgia at the age of about ten years. She married Herbert Reynolds with whom she lived until she became the mother of six children. She was afterwards married to Thomas Stanford and gave birth to five other children. Out of eleven children, three only survive, viz. Dr. Frank Stanford of Columbia, Ga., Mrs. Persons of Auburn, Ala., and Mrs. Wesson, of Wesson, Mississippi. B. Jones

Mrs. Mary Frances, wife of D. Homer Brown, and daughter of Mrs. Hafer, died Oct. 13th 1869, in Houston co., Ga. Dr. S. A. Riley, her uncle. W. W. Stewart

Mrs. Jemima Martin, whose maiden name was Hall, was born in Abbeville Dist., S. C., April 11th 1796, and died in Chambers co., Ala., Nov. 9th 1869... Thos. J. Williamson

Sister Mary Ann Rigsby was born in Mecklenburg county, N. C., Aug. 4th 1820, was married to J. T. Draffin, Aug 21st 1845, and again to W. T. Rigsby, March 10th 1868, and died in Decatur co., Ga., Nov. 1, 1869.

Tribute of Respect to Fletcher W. Nash, youngest son of Rev. Dr. Miles Nash, who died in Tallahassee, Fla,. in his 23d year. Jas. O. Branch

Memorial Resolution to the late Rev. W. Asbury Gamewell, by Methodist Church of Spartanburg Station.

Issue of December 10, 1869

Mr. Simeon Dell, who was familiarly known as "Uncle Simy," was born in Ga., May 15th 1796. his parents moved to Duval co., East Fla., in 1800. In 1824 he removed to Alachua co., where he died Oct. 3d, 1869. E. S. Tyner The Baltimore Episcopal Methodist please copy.

Absalom Gray was born Sept. 17th 1803 and died in Griffin, Ga., Nov. 24th 1869. His daughter, Frances A. Gray, survived him but four days, and died Nov. 28th 1869.

Sallie Margaret, youngest daughter of Dr. W. C. Norwood of Cokesbury, S. C., died October 29, 1869. The 13th of October was the day appointed for the marriage of Miss Norwood to Dr. James F. Furman.

Mrs. Martha Whitefield, eldest daughter of Maj. Jas. Griffin, was born near Pendleton, S. C., April 20th 1797, was married to Maj. J. T. Whitefield in 1819, and died in Anderson, S. C., Nov. 15, 1869. Samuel A. Weber

Death of Sister Anna B. Edmondson, wife of Joseph A. Edmondson, died 17th October last, aged 45 years. She was a native of Middleburg, Virginia, removed to Florida in 1836, and was married in 1838.

Three little children have been removed from the Perry Sunday-school: Bruce Bain, May Fordham, and Jennie Smith.

Tribute of Respect by third quarterly Conference of the Harpersville circuit to Rev. Benjamin Glover.

Tribute of Respect to Robert Bowman.

Tribute of Respect by Warrenton Sunday School to Little Johnny Pottle.

Issue of December 17, 1869

Mrs. Susan J. Williams, wife of Maj. E. D. Williams of Baker co., died on Nov. 23d, at the residence of her mother, Mrs. Nancy Myrick, in the 47th year of her age. W. C. Bass

Abner Shuttlesworth was born in lower Georgia, on 28th Dec 1792, was reared in Newberry, and Greenville Dist., S. C., and was married Feb. 4, 1827... died on the 19th Sept. D. D. Byars

Mrs. Rebecca S. Conly, wife of William Conly, of Trion Factory, Chattooga co., Ga., born in South Carolina, Nov. 4, 1793, died August 26th 1869. Also, on 11th Sept 1869, William Conly, born in North Carolina, Nov. 3d, 1789. They were among the Pioneers of Methodism in Cherokee, Ga. A. J. Leet

Miss Eva Lamar Harvey, daughter of Michael A. Harvey, dec'd, and Susan Kendall, was born in Talbotton, Ga., and died on 9th November 1869, at the residence of her step-father, Dr. O. F. Knox, Brundidge, Pike co., Ala.

Miss Elizabeth G., daughter of Rev. Sam'l Henry Smith, of North Carolina Synod, died on 17th Nov 1869, at the residence of Rev. T. W. Moore. When a child, she joined the Presbyterian Church. T. W. Moore. The North Carolina Methodist, the North Carolina Presbyterian, and Memphis Advocate please copy.

Virginia L. Rast, daughter of Elijah and Sarah Blitch, died at Ocala, Morgan co,. Fla., October 19th 1869, aged 28 years.

Tribute of Respect at the fourth quarterly Conference of Lawrenceville circuit, Eufaula District, to Brother Daniel E. Corbitt, who died at his residence in Henry county, Ala., 21st June 1869, at the close of an earthly pilgrimage of 47 years.

Issue of December 24, 1869

Mrs. Patsy McCoy, died 10th Nov 1869, at her son-in-law, Col. M. Horton's, in Holmes county, Miss., in the 98th year of her age. She was born in Savannah, Ga., Aug. 9th 1772.

Col. James M. Flowers was born in Hancock co., Ga., July 21st 1800, removed to Troup co., in 1827, and died at his residence near LaGrange, Ga., Dec. 4th 1869.

Mrs. Sarah A. Huckabee, wife of W. G. Huckabee of Kershaw District, S. C., was born Sept 18th 1823, and died of consumption, Nov. 12th 1869.... left a husband and three children. R. R. Dagnall

Joseph C. Putchier died September 28, 1869, near Houston, Sawannee county, East Florida. He was the son of William and Martha Pouchier, born in McIntosh county, Georgia, April 5th 1831; came with his parents to East Florida in 1839... Lem'l G. R. Wiggins

Mr. John W. Legg died in Milton co,. Ga., Oct. 8th 1869, aged about 60 years. He was a refugee from East Tennessee... He leaves an only daughter and several sons.

SOUTHERN CHRISTIAN ADVOCATE NOTICES 1867-1878

Issue of January 7, 1870

Died

At Fort Valley, Ga., on the 23d inst., Mrs. Mattie F., wife of Rev. Charles H. Jewett, aged 34 years.

Obituary

Rev. Elijah Byrd was born in Edgefield District, S. C,. Sept. 16th 1786. He settled in DeKalb co,. Ga., and lived there until 1853 when he moved to Polk co., Ga., and there passed the remaining years of his life. He died October 21st 1869.

Daniel Frederick died in Marshallville, Ga., on the 28th Nov., in the 74th year of his age. Born in South Carolina in 1795, of one of those old families distinguished in the revolution.... He joined the Methodist Church in Orangeburg Dist., S. C., about the year 1820.... S. H. J. Sistrunk

John J. M. Ray was born in Putnam county, Ga., Feb. 29th 1832 and died in Talbot county, Ga., Nov. 20th 1869. R. J. Corley

Miss Mary A. Tuton was born Aug 17th 1852, and died in Marion co., Fla., Nov. 6, 1869. Anna Tuton was born Nov. 29th 1857, and died Nov. 18th 1869.

Mrs. Sarah M. Carswell, wife of Judge John W. Carswell, died in Burke co., Ga., on 21st November in her 59th year. N. F. Ousley

Daniel Bolin born and raised in North Carolina, but for many years a citizen of Troup co., Ga., died Oct. 19th 1969, in the 72d year of his age. J. P. Howell

Wm Cassady was born in Chesterfield Dist., S. C., August 23d 1787, and died in Sumter circuit, Fla., Oct. 14th 1869. He leaves and wife and seven children. W. C. Williams

Hiram T. Gaines, son of James and Ann Gaines, was born in Monroe co., Ga., 11th February 1823, and died in Macon co., 6th December 1869.

Robert N. Milner died suddenly on 1st Dec. 1869 in Elmore co., Ala., at about 60 years of age.

Wylie Span DuBose, son of Jas. R. DuBose, of Washington, Ga., died Oct. 22d 1869, in his eighth year.

Tribute of Respect from Longstreet Sunday-school to Albert Jordan.

Issue of January 14, 1870

Died

Near Newnansville, Fla., October 29th 1860, Benjamin F., infant son of William B. and Anna Treadwell, aged 8 months and 23 days.

Obituary

Stephen Wesley Williams was born in Charleston co., S. C., July 7, 1822, and died in the same, Nov. 18 1869. James C. Stoll

Mrs. Harriet H. Glascock died at the residence of her daughter, Mrs. Barrett, in Augusta, Ga., on the 9th instant, in the 75th year of her age. During the life of her late husband, Hon. Thomas Glascock, she was known extensively. Henry W. Hilliard

Sister Elizabeth A. Betts, wife of A. B. Betts, died in Jackson co., Ga., Dec. 22, 1860, in her 51st year. Her body was interred at Concord church... Amicus W. Williams

Mrs. Mary L. Stovall, wife of Josiah Stovall died 28th Oct 1869 at the residence of her sister, Mrs. M. E. Magruder in Columbia co., Ga., in the 54th year of her age. She was a member of the Presbyterian church for many years.

Evangeline Augustine, daughter of Mary A. and Augustus C. Jones, formerly of Columbia co., Ga., died in Baker co., 1st Oct 1869, aged ten years.

Sister Anna R. Shown, wife of Stephen (Bear) Brown, and daughter of Lewis and Mary Coppage, died Nov 7, 1869, aged 62 years. H. Puckett, P. C.

Tribute of Respect to Abner Shettlesworth who was born 28 Dec 1792.... by Quarterly Conference of Seneca and Tugalo ct., S. C. Conference.

Tribute of Respect to John J. M. Ray, who died in Talbot co., Ga., Nov 20th 1869.

Issue of January 21, 1870

Died

On 28th Dec., in Macon, Ga., Susie Key, youngest child of Mrs. James I. Snider.

Obituary

Mrs. Elizabeth Gilbert was born in the city of New York, Dec. 23, 1803, and died in Florence, S. C., Dec. 21st 1869, and her mortal remains were interred in the Cemetery of Sumter, S. C., on her 66th birthday, by the side of John T. Gilbert, her youngest son, a victim of the war. She was married in 1822 to Mr. Amos A. Gilbert of New Haven, Conn. She joined the Presbyterian Church in early girlhood.

Lysander Morgan died Dec. 12th 1869. The Mt. Hilliard Sabbath school reported a suitable tribute of respect.

Charles Humphries was born in Union District, S. C., and died Nov. 8th 1869, in his 31st year, at Alston, S. C., of an injury receive two hours before, by being caught between the platform and a car on the S. & U. R. R. ...being persuaded that he could better his condition, and settle all his children around him by removing to Texas, he sold out all his earthly goods and started with his family for his distant home.

Mrs. Elizabeth Pierce, wife of Wm. A. Pierce, died in Jefferson co., Ga., on the 16th inst., in the 42d year of her age. W. A. Hayles

Miss Amelia L. Crawford, daughter of Mr. Augustus and Mrs. Eliza E. Crawford, died at Appling, Columbia co., Dec. 20th 1869. Southern Presbyterian, please copy.

Mr. James Perry died in Brooks co., Ga., on 21st December last, aged about fifty years. Left a wife and one child.

Miss Christianna R. Maley, youngest daughter of Johnson and Mary C. Maley, of Hart co., Ga., died on 1st Dec. 1869.

Mrs. M. F. Walton, wife of the late O. F. Walton, died in Fort Valley on 8th January.

Issue of January 28, 1870

Died

William Rieves, infant son of Rev. Irvin R. and Margarett L. Booth, of Clinch co., Ga., was born May 3d 1869, and died Jan. 10th 1870.

Obituary

William Pinckney Steward was born in Union co., N. C., and died in Monroe, N. C., Dec. 8th 1869. In 1860 he removed to Bainbridge, Ga.... A. J. Dean

Mrs. Lucy Donnan was born in Louisa co., Va., March 31st 1779, and died January 5th 1870, at the residence of her son-in-law, John M. Lumpkin, in Talbot co., Ga. Mother Donnan was the widow of Rev. Hanover Donnan, a travelling preacher in S. C. and Ga. many years ago. After marriage he located, but continued preaching until his death in 1822. D. Lumpkin

Lucy White, wife of Col. J. White, was born 21st October 1800, married 4th Dec 1817, and died in Anson co., N. C., 20th Nov 1869. Thomas A. Boone

Henry H. Fincher, son of Wm. and Cynthia Fincher, was born in Lancaster District, S. C., February 10th 1828, was killed by the accidental firing of a gun in Monroe, December 23d, 1869. John W. Abernathy

Olivia Rhymes Shropshire, eldest child of Dr. James W. and C. J. Shropshire, was born October 27th 1860, and died at the residence of her grandfather Henry Davenport, on 23d December 1869,. J. M. Marshall

Seaborn J. Hawk, aged 63 years, died in Jasper co., Ga., Dec. 26th 1869. The church at Calvary have lost three of their mother useful and beloved members: Rev. G. T. Spearman, Col. H. H. Geiger, and Seaborn J Hawk. W. W. Oslin

Issue of February 4, 1870

Mrs. Martha P. Jewett, wife of Rev. Charles E. Jewett, of the S. Ga. Conference, died in Fort Valley, Ga., Dec. 22d, 1869. She was the daughter of Bishop and E. J. Clements and was born in Meriwether co., Ga., Jan. 19th 1835.

Rev. William H. Wheeler, of the North Carolina Annual Conference, of the M. E. Church, South, was born in Darlington, S. C., 7th August 1837 and died in Leesburg, N. C., 25th December. [account] His Father.

Sister Martha Marshall was born August 22d 1810, and died in Eatonton, Ga., January 6th. W. P. Kramer

Mrs. Mary Ann Warren, wife of Judge B. H. Warren, died in Augusta, Ga., on 14th January in the 69th year of her age. She was a wife fifty-one years, and for forty years a member of the Presbyterian Church. J. H. W.

Mrs. Rebecca Lockett died January 6th, 1870, at the residence of her son, Capt. Abner Lockett. She had lived to a ripe old age, having entered her 70th year on 29th December 1869, and was the mother of six children, two of whom, with the father, James Lockett, had preceded her to the spirit world.

Mrs. Judith L. Russell died on pneumonia in Roane co., East Tenn., Nov. 6th 1869, in the 75th year of her age... J. M. R.

Miss Jesse Irene Browne, daughter of Mr. Augustus T. and Mrs. S. M. Browne, died in Griffin, 6th Dec. 1869.

Mr. J. T. Gregory died of dropsy of the chest in Monroe co., Miss., Nov. 6th 1860. He was born in Union Dist., S. C., Oct. 21st 1816. He leaves his companion, ten children.... J. T. M. Gregory

George W. Harden, son of Stephen S. and Surany Harden of Columbia co., Ga., died 8th January 1870 in his 30th year. S. P. Huchingson

Tribute of Respect by Quarterly Conference of Leon circuit, Fla. Conference, held at Concord church, to A. P. Gramling.

Issue of February 11, 1870

Mrs. Mary E. England, died in Clarke co., Ga., on 24th Jan 1870, at the age of 70 years. C. A. E.

Mrs. Sarah H. Harris was born Feb. 12th 1786, and died in Athens, Jan. 3d 1870, having lived on earth nearly 84 years. In 1822 the death of her husband Stephen W. Harris, devolved upon her, at the age of 36, years the care of nine little children, the eldest being only 13 years old. C. A. E.

Mrs. Fernanda Jacinto Oliver, wife of J. Percival Oliver, Esq., and daughter of T. Hatcher, Esq., was born 4th Oct 1843, and died at the residence of her father in Dadeville, Ala., January 20th 1870.

Mother Ragland died on 17th Jan 1870. A native of N. C., but more recently of Mississippi, she came as a refugee to Cuthbert, Ga., during the war. J. B. Wardlaw. Nashville Christian Advocate please copy.

Rev. Henry H. Spann, who for the last 35 years has been one of our most worthy, zealous and faithful local preachers, died in Lexington, S. C., Jan. 24th 1870, in the 63d year of his age. On 21st Feb 1869, he preached his last sermon at Providence Church. A. Nettles

James P. Belk was born in Mecklenburg, now Union co., N. C., August 16th 1812, and died December 8th 1869. John W. Abernethy

Miss Eliza Ann Dell, daughter of Simeon and Miner Dell, of Alachua co,. East Fla., was born 1st March 1855 and died 2 Jan 1870. J. E. Dodd

Sister Susannah D. Gantman was born in N. C., 21st June 1792, and died 24th August 1860. She was the daughter of Thos Pledger who moved to Elbert co., Ga., when she was some 6 or 7 years of age.

A. R. White was born in Pickens Dist., S., C., 4th Oct 1807, lived in Marietta and Atlanta, several years, and finally in Floyd co., Ga., where he died 8th Nov 1860, leaving an affection wife and five children, all of age. Thos. C. Williams

Judson Gray died in Burke co., Ga., in his 15th year. N. B. Ousley

Issue of February 18, 1870

Mrs. Martha J. Fraley died on 21st January in Sparta, Ga. G. F. Pierce

Mrs. Laura C. Hart, wife of Dr. B. C. Hart, and daughter of Gabriel and Phoebe Hodges of Cokesbury, S. C., died Jan. 19, 1870. W. T. Capers

Daniel S. Beacham died of Catarrhal fever, near Cokesbury, S. C., on 19th Dec 1869 in his 79th year.

Bro. Andrew P. Gramblin was born in Orangeburg Dist., South Carolina, January 29th 1808, joined the church at Shiloh, Greenville circuit, S. C. Conference, under the minister of his uncle, Rev. Andrew Gramblin, at the age of twelve years. In December 1845 he removed to Leon Co., Fla., where he died November 8th 1769.

Benjamin C. Alfriend was born August 28th 1814 and died at White Plains, Greene co., Ga., Dec. 3d 1870. Thos F. Pierce

Sister Cynthia Ballen died 21st January at the residence of her brother in Talbotton, Ga. J. O. A. Cook

Olin Coward Hook, only son of Dr. L. M. and E. W. Hook, was born in Cherokee co., Ga., Dec. 24th 1851, and died Jan. 5th 1870. C. M. McClure

Tribute of Respect from quarterly conference of Providence ct., S. C. Conference to Stephen Wesley Williams.

Issue of February 25, 1870

Died

Near Magnolia Springs, Ga., Ada C. Clarke, youngest daughter of G. E. and M. E. Clarke, aged 2 years, 11 months and 8 days.

Obituary

Rebecca Billing Shepperson, only daughter of Wm. K. and Cornelia C. Moore, was born in Columbus, Ga., Nov. 30th 1844, and died in the same city Nov. 28th 1869, and was buried on the 30th. She was married to Mr. C. C. Shepperson, Nov. 28th 1868, by Rev. J. B. Cottrell of the Montgomery Conference, and was the mother of a sweet little son.

Reason D. Jones, son of Mr. J. Madison and Mrs. A. E. Jones of Macon, Ga., was born 9th January 1854 and died 28th January 1870, at Oxford. Ga.

Col. Wm. M. Davis was born in Sumter Dist., S. C., Feb. 20th 1830--moved to Ga. in 1851, and died in Houston co, Ga., Jan. 6th 1870. H. R. Felder

Mrs. Carrie J. Ogletree, daughter of Dr. J. W. and Mrs. M. L. Stinson, and wife of Jas. F. Ogletree, died 19th Jan, in Meriwether co., Ga., in her 28th year.

Bro. Mark Turner of Mt. Carmel Church, McDonough ct., N. Ga. Conference was thrown from his cart on January 21st and died on the next day. J. H. Harris

Mrs. Martha M. Dozier, wife of Wilson Dozier of Talbot co., Ga., was born in Columbia co., Ga., July 28th 1799, and died at the residence of her son, Mr. Thos. H. Dozier, in Union Springs, Ala., January 14th 1870. Thos. H. Dawson

Mrs. Eliza C. Wilder, wife of Mr. Milton Wilder, and daughter of John R. and Alice Lowry of Twiggs co., Ga., was born April 14th 1807, and died December 16th 1869 in Forsyth, Ga. She was sister to the Rev. Frederic D. Lowry... J. E. Danforth

Richard H. Brady died at Long Cane, Troup co., Ga., January 13th 1870, aged 75 years. A. M. Thigpen

Jessee N. Graham died in Kershaw co., S. C., Dec. 17th 1860, aged 15 years and 7 months. J. S. Nelson

Issue of March 4, 1870

Died

Of pneumonia, on 24th Feb 1870 in Buena Vista, Ga., Louise Bond, daughter of Rev. Jas. O. and Caroline T. Branch, aged 8 months and 26 days. In Bainbridge, Ga., Jan. 19, 1870, James Albert, son of J. D. and H. E. Wooten, aged 8 years, 1 month and 20 days.

Obituary

James Stewart was born in Oglethorpe co., Ga., June 10th 1793, and died in Americus, Ga., Feb. 3d, 1870. [long account] R. W. Dixon

Samuel Stoudenmire, son of George and Magdalene Stoudenmire, was born in Orangeburg Dist., S. C., Nov. 20th 1794, and died Dec. 21, 1869, near Autaugaville, Ala,. in the far-famed Dutch Bend. He settled in Dutch Bend in 1822. William A. Edwards

Mrs. Jessie F. Oliver, wife of P. J. Oliver, Esq., and only child of Tolbert and Parthena T. Hatcher, of Dadeville, Ala., died Jan 10th 1870. She was born Oct. 4, 1843, and was married Dec. 10th 1862. Monroe Advertiser, please copy.

Mrs. Parthenia A. Paris of Americus, Ga., died at her daughter's Mrs. E. G. Hill, in Terrell co., Ga., on Feb. 3d 1870, in her 79th year. Left a widow in early life with six small children.... R. W. Dixon

Mrs. Amanda Jones, wife of Seaborn Jones and daughter of Beverly and Sally Allen, was born in Jackson co., Ga., Oct. 24th 1821, was married Oct. 2d, 1845, and died in Forsyth co., Jan. 16th 1870.

Mrs. E. A. Ball was born Dec. 7th 1815 in Green co., N. C., married Rev. J. G. Ball, Dec. 28th 1838, and died in Weston, Ga., Dec. 7th 1869.

John B. Royal, a son of Ezekiel and Mary A. Royal was born Jan 9, 1849, and died at Fort Gaines, Ga., Nov. 18th 1869.

Miss Mattie K. Roberts died of measles in Anderson co., S. C., Jan. 1st 1870... W. A. Hodges

Gosper Sistrunk was born in Barnwell Dist., S. C., 11th Feb 1807. In his 12th year he moved to Georgia-- where he resided several years-- and then to Florida, where he died 7th December 1869, leaving a widow, thirty six children and grand-children.... John Penny

Issue of March 11, 1870

Died

Suddenly, near Selma, Ark., 20th January 1870, Rev. Jesse Peacock, in the 78th year of his age.

Obituary

Dr. Joseph H. Dogan was born at Mt. Bethel, Newberry Dist., S. C., Feb. 22nd 1793. Feb 8th 1825, he was happily married to Miss Sarah Ann Rice. [account] A. J. Stokes

Hon. Benj. R. McCutchen was born 8th April 1797 and died near LaFayette, Ga., on 21st Jan 1870. He was at the time of his death a member of the Legislature from this Senatorial District. B. F. Fariss

George Augusta Carlton died in Athens, Ga., on the 28th of Jan 1870.

Mrs. Mary Saxon, widow of Benjamin A. Saxon, and daughter of Robert and Mary Dunwody, died in Twiggs co,. on Jan. 21st 1870, aged 77 years. She joined the M. E. Church at Tarversville, Sept. 1815.

Mrs. Clara A. E. Matthews, wife of John S. Matthews of Oak Bowery, Ala., died 20th Jan. 1870, aged nearly 55 years. Thos. J. Williamson

Polly Horton, widow of Hardy Horton, died in Shelby co., Ala., on the 12th day February 1870, aged 82 years, 2 months and 18 days, being one month and ten days older than her husband when he departed from the earth. She was the mother of eleven children, ten of whom she raised to be grown. She had seventy grand-children and sixty great-grandchildren. D. S. McDonald

Mrs. Elizabeth W. Wood, daughter of Wm. P. and Sarah A. Hicklin, died at the residence of her father on 5th January 1870. C. J. Toole

Issue of March 18, 1870

Died

In Monroe co., Ga., Mr. John R. Smith, of said county.

On Friday morning, Feb. 4, 1870, at the residence of Mrs. M. M. Appleby, Colleton District, S. C., Mariana Caroline Mildred, daughter of John E. and Janie C. Larisey, aged 2 years, 8 months and 3 days.

Obituary

Mrs. Sallie A. Park, wife of John W. Park, Esq., of Greenville, Ga., and daughter of Col. Robert White, late of Sumter co., died on 26 Jan 1870, in the 31st year of her age. [account]

Mrs. Pauline M. Osborne, wife of Wm. A. Osborne, of Paris, Ky., died Dec. 23, 1869. She was a native of Bourbon co., Ky., but joined the church near Columbus, Ga., some 16 years since.

Julia Ann Colding, wife of Samuel B. Colding, and daughter of Capt. R. D. Bradley, died Jan. 26th, 1870, in her 31st year, in Hernando co., Fla. Isaac Munden

Hon. Wm. D. Luckie died in Montgomery co., Ala., on 3d Jan 1870, in the 70th year of his age. Holding for a long period the station of elder in the Presbyterian Church.

Bro. Ephraim David Waters was born in Scriven co., Ga., Jan. 8th 1815, and died in Bainbridge, Ga., Jan. 30th 1870. A. J. Dean

Sister Elizabeth Dutton was born in Effingham co., Ga., Dec. 17th 1792, and died at the residence of her son-in-law, R. R. Tennell, in Bainbridge, Ga., Jan. 24th 1870. In 1828 she was married to Rev. Mann Dutton, of the Virginia Conference. After marriage they settled first in Scriven co., Ga., then in Bulloch, and finally in Decator where she resided until her death. A. J. Dean

Mrs. Hallie L. Hurt died on 25th December 1869, and on 5th February 1870, Mrs. M. Clementina Hurt, both of Oglethorpe co., Ga., daughters of J. B. and Harriot N. Smith, the former 23 years old and the latter 26... T. Alonzo Harris

John Henry Sanders, son of J. B. Sanders, Esq., was born in Pickens Dist., S. C., July 4, 1849-- married to Amanda Mason 17 Nov 1854, and died Feb 2, 1870. D. D. Byars

Lewis Shephard was born in Lexington Dist., S., C., Aug 6th 1797, married to Elizabeth Pitts in Edgefield Dist., Feb. 14th 1819, and was instantly killed by the cars at Station 4 in Jefferson co., Fla., Feb. 14th 1870. C. R. Murdock

Eugenie Marian McLeod, daughter of Angus and Annie McLeod, was born in Hamilton co,. Fla,. in May 1855 and died on 7th January last.

Tribute of Respect from Montgomery Lodge, F. A. M., Zebulon, Ga., to John C. Allen.

James H. Blackston was born March 15th 1817, died near Cumming, Ga., 24th Jan 1870.

Issue of March 25, 1870

Died

G. W. Slaughter of Laurens co., Ga., Nov. 22d 1869, aged 55 years.

Near Bethel, Schley co., Ga,. on the 10th inst., at 3 o'clock, A. M., Reuben Tooke Walker, infant son of W. B. and M. J. Walker, aged 1 year, 1 month and 27 days.

Ida J. Frink, daughter of Sam'l J. and Martha E. Frink, died Jan. 10th 1870, Madison co., Fla., in her 13th year.

Obituary

Rachael Ellanor Cottrell, daughter of Rev. Z. D. Cottrell, was born at Spartanburg, S. C., and died in Chattooga, Co., Ga., near Rome, on 13th January 1870, at about 24 years of age. Joseph B. Cottrell.

Mrs. Eliza H. Trammell was born January 1st 1832, was married to Col. W. T. Trammell, April 6th 1850, and died in Griffin, Ga., February 27th 1870, leaving a husband and eight children. Arminius Wright

Mrs. H. E. Fryer was born Nov. 27, 1831, and died in Blakely, Ga., Feb. 19th 1870. She was married to Bro. H. C. Fryer, Oct. 5th, 1853. D. O'Driscoll

Morton Hackett was born in Virginia in 1787 and died in Greenwood, S. C., Dec. 7th 1869. All of his children went before him to the spirit world.

Mrs. E. L. Daniel, wife of E. B. Daniel, and daughter of the late Hardy Hodges of Bulloch co., Ga., Died Feb. 29th 1870. W. M. Watts.

Rev. Aaron Johnson was born Jan. 1784 and died in Warren co., Ga., March 1st 1870. He raised eleven children, three sons and eight daughters, all living but one daughter. Amos Johnson.

Sister Wealthy Ann Richards was born Oct. 18th 1809, and died in Talbot co., Ga., Dec. 16th 1869. R. J. Corley

Tribute of Respect from Culloden circuit, N. Ga. Conference to John W. Reynolds.

Issue of April 1, 1870

Mrs. Lizzie Simmons, wife of Dr. J. N. Simmons, of Atlanta, died 14th February 1870. G. B. S.

My father, Rev. J. H. Breedlove, died in Drew co., Ark., Jan. 7th 1870, aged 64 years. His father died when he was quite young, leaving him with for brothers and four sisters to the care of a mother. B. F. B.

Mrs. Mary Anderson Hemphill was born in Hamburg, S. C., Dec. 29th 1847, and died in Atlanta, March 4th 1870. Her childhood was spent in Augusta and her girlhood in Macon.

John Tripps was born in North Carolina, June 29th 1775, and died in Eatonton, Ga., March 11 1870, in the 95th year of his age. H. P. Kramer.

Mrs. Eliza Winslow, wife of Mr. James Winslow, and daughter of the late David Zoucks, Esq., of Liberty county, Ga., died in Savannah, Ga., Jan. 17th 1870, in the 28th year of his age. Geo. G. N. MacD.

Sister Frances Braddy was born Sept. 23d 1815 and died Feb. 20th 1870. Her remains quietly repose by those of her husband at Anderson C. H., South Carolina. She leaves several children.... W. A. Hodges.

Mrs. R. C. Jones, daughter of Mrs. E. McIntire, and wife of Dr. J. H. Jones, died in Hard co., Ga., March 6th 1870, aged 29 years. She was the child of Presbyterian parents.... A. M. T.

Capt. John Collinsworth Allen of Pike county, Ga., was born July 1838 and died 2d of March 1870. John P. Duncan, Pastor.

Walter B. Bessent, son of P. G. and V. F. Bessent, died of meningitis at the residence of his uncle Prof. J. H. Mayson, in DeKalb co., Ga., Jan 12th 1870, aged 12 years.

Mrs. Rebecca Ann Marshall was born in Camden, S. C., and died in Atlanta, Ga., Feb. 13th 1870, aged 53 years. R. W. B.

Ella V. Evans, daughter of Maj. T. D. and Mrs. Martha Evans, of Cherokee co,. Ga., was born Jan 1st 1856, and died Jan. 6, 1870. M. Puckett

Miss Lizzie S. Mitchell, daughter of Mrs. E. R. Mitchell, died in Griffin, Ga., on 20th Feb, aged 13 years and 11 months.

Rhoda Harwell, widow of Jackson Harwell, died in Newton county, Ga., Jan. 7th 1870... J. M. H.

Issue of April 8, 1870

Mrs. Julia M. Fuller, daughter of the late Jas. B. Nickelson, of Greensboro', Ga., died in Macon, Ga., on 10th March 1870. For a number of years she had been a communicant in the Presbyterian Church.

Capt. Reuben Stephens of Colleton co., S. C., died at the residence of his son-in-law, on 5th Feb 1870, in the 76th year of his age. He was born and brought up in Columbus co,. N. C., came to Colleton, S. C., when quite a young man... married Miss Narcissa Rutledge, with whom he lived for nearly fifty years--she preceding him to the spirit land not quite two years. They reared a large family, eight sons and a daughter. Two sons have died in manhood, six sons still and a daughter are left.... A. B. Stephens

John R. Smith of Monroe co., Ga., was born May 6th 1844 and died March 8th 1870. F. B. Davies.

Mrs. Sarah Matilda Wright, wife of John W. Wright and second daughter of John and Mary C. Wilkins of Effingham co,. was born 23d September 1846, and died in Green co., Ga., on 13th March 1869.

Mrs. Zilpha Hall was born in North Carolina, Jan 8th 1797, died Jan 31st 1870 in Thomas co., Ga. W. Lane

Mrs. Catharine Avery, wife of William Avery and daughter of Rev. Aaron Knight, was born 8th of May 1801, and married Wm. Avery 16th January 1823, and died 27th December 1869. S. G. P.

Elizabeth McMichael, daughter of T. J. and M. J. McMichael, was born in Marion co., Ga., Sep. 3d 1857, and died in Randolph co., Ga., Feb. 14th 1870. G. T. Embry

Tribute of Respect by Clinton circuit, North Ga. Conference to Rev. Wesley P. Arnold.

Tribute of Respect by Jacksonville circuit, South Georgia Conference to Bro. Jas Pittman.

Issue of April 15, 1870

Died

Died in Butler, Ga., Feb. 1870, Cola, infant daughter of John and Fanny Pilcher, of congestive chill.

Obituary

David Gray was born in Rutherford co., N. C., Jan. 18th 1783, and died there Jan. 29th 1870, aged 87 years and 11 days. When about seventeen years of age, he joined the Presbyterian Church... later joined the Methodist Church. In 1804, he was married to Mary Dickey, with whom he lived happily till his death. V. A. Sharp

James F. Fleming, son of Perry H. and Samantha J. Fleming, of Red River co., Texas., died at his Uncle Wiley Fleming's, in Monroe co., Ga., March 19th 1870, aged 23 years. F. M. Hunt

Mrs. Mary Ella Anderson, wife of Robert A. Anderson, died at the residence of her father Judge Ezzard, in Atlanta, Ga., on 14th February 1870, aged 24 years and 20 days. W. E.

Sister Ann Carroll, wife of Rev. Jesse W. Carroll, was born in Oglethorpe co., July 14th 1798 and died March 15, 1870, near Conyers, Newton co., Ga. She was the daughter of Rev. James Hodge, deceased. She was married to Bro. Carroll Dec 8th 1819. Wm. J. Parks

Mrs. Ann Jones, wife of Maj. Abram Jones, died in Edgefield Dist., S. C., March 25th 1870 in her 61st year. J. T. Kilgo

Robert Martin, Sr., died in Columbia co., Ga., on 16th January 1870, in the 85th year of his age. J. P. W.

Brother Joseph S. E. Spear was born in Sumter District, S. C., 1784 and died in Talbot co., Ga., Feb. 4th 1870 in his 86th year. In his 22nd year he was married to Elizabeth Brasington.

Mrs. Elizabeth I. Skinner, daughter of Rev. Abner and Massie Alexander, was born in Sumter Dist., S. C., Feb. 27th 1826, and died Feb. 23d 1870, aged 43 years, near Montgomery city, Mo., where she moved a year ago. H. H. Craig

Lauchlin McKinnon was born 1802 and was brought up in Telfair co., Ga., died at Nashville, Berrien co., Ga., Jan. 31st 1870. In 1840 he was married to Miss Mary, eldest daughter of Rev. Dr. Reddick Pierce, late of South Carolina. I. C. Peek.

Sister Elizabeth Evans was born Dec 3d, 1820, died in Decatur, DeKalb co., Ga., on 14th March 1870.

Minnie Mary Eugenia, daughter of J. N. and M. E. Wilson, died in Decatur, DeKalb co., Ga., February 28th 1870, in her 8th year.

G. M. Feanell died in Jones county, March 10th 1870, aged 63 years.

Tribute of Respect to Rev. John R. Pickett, late pastor of Spring Street Church.

Issue of April 22, 1870

The Rev. John W. Starr was born in Wilkes co., Ga., Aug. 7th 1806 and died in Bibb co., Ala., Feb. 24th 1870, in the 64th year of his age. [account] A. H. Mitchell

Mrs. M. J. Arnold, wife of Rev. M. W. Arnold, and daughter of Rev. James and Mrs. Henrietta Baskin, died in Oxford, Ga., 16th February. She was born Jan. 22d 1835 and married Sept. 19th 1854. Luther M. Smith

Our much esteemed mother, Mrs. Lessesne, died at her son-in-law's, Rev. L. Rush, in Thompson, Ga., on __ Feb last, in the 80th year of her age. Shew was a native of Charleston, S. C., but for the last 20 years a resident of Ga., the largest portion of which she resided in Talbotton. She was raised, educated, and confirmed in the Episcopal Church. C. W. Key

Mrs. Elizabeth Harris, wife of Mr. Matthew J. Harris, was born July 6th 1822, and died in LaFayette, Ala., March 14th 1870. Jas. T. Curry

William Logan was born near Broughshane parish, Antrim co., Ireland, Feb. 23, 1798; came to this county in 1812; was married in S. Carolina, Nov. 29th 1838; shortly after he removed to Alabama, till his death near LaFayette, March 16th 1870. Jas. T. Curry

Mrs. Sarah C. F. Carr, wife of Herbert Carr and eldest daughter of Dr. W. M. and Mrs. Martha Shuler, died on 2d April at her father's residence in Colleton Dist., S. C., in her 18th year. William Hutto

James David Buff, eldest son of James H. and S. N. Buff, was born 28th July 1853, and died April 4th 1870. S. N. Dunwody. The "Dawson Journal," please copy.

Miss Isabella E. , daughter of Mr. and Mrs. Jonathan Jordan, died 19th January 1870. M. W. McC.

Thomas F. M. Bowie, son of Asa and Arabella Bowie, was born June 17th 1846, and died 31st of March 1870. J. F. M.

Mrs. Fanny Heath, wife of Mr. Henry Heath of Warren co., was born Dec. 14th 1844, and died Feb. 23d 1870. T. A. S.

Sister Hester Ann Brown was born June 3d 1795, and died in Bulloch co., March 1st 1870, in her 75th year.

Miss Rebekah Jane Bell, daughter of Rev. Dr. W. R. Bell of Banks co., Ga., died 16th March 1870, in her 15th year, near Smyrna, Cobb co., Ga., to which please her father had just moved his children. W. T. Davenport.

William Alexander Carnley was born December 18th 1853, in Covington co., Ala., and died in Santa Rosa co., Fla., Feb. 24th 1870.

Mrs. Mary Shehee died at the residence of her son-in-law, Capt. A. J. Lea, Madison co., Fla., on 14th March, at 71 years of age. E. B. Duncan.

Tribute of Respect to David R. Blackmon who died Dec. 6th 1869.

Issue of April 29, 1870

The Rev. John F. Dickinson, son of Rev. John P. and Elvira E. Dickinson, was born in Henry co., Ga., Aug. 8th 1828. In Nov 1852 he was married to Miss Martha J., daughter of the Rev. John W. Norton, of Barbour co. He died on March 31st. [account]

Mrs. Mary C. Williams, wife of Ebenezer Williams and daughter of Robert Martin, both deceased died in Columbia co., Ga., March 1st, in the 60th year of her age. R. A. Conner

Mrs. Mary Hayes died March 23d in Thomas co., Ga., where she had lived for more than thirty years. She was born January 17, 1788. L. Pierce

Mrs. Mary A. Mann, wife of Dr. A. V. Mann of Forsyth, Ga., died April 9th. F. A. Kimbell

Horace T. Shaw, son of Alfred and Susan Shaw, was born Oct. 11th 1840. He June 1862 he married Miss Sallie R. Rogers, daughter of Dr. C. Rogers of Thomaston, Ga. He died in Madison, Morgan co., Ga., March 10th 1870, leaving a wife and three children.

Sarah C. Huffman, wife of Capt. A. W. Huffman and daughter of Andrew and Elizabeth Morrison, was born June 19th 1840 and died 19th January 1870 in Jasper, Pickens co., Ga. W. H. S.

Sister Georgia C. Hughs, wife of Rev. Andrew Hughs and sister of Rev. C. C. Hines, of the S. Ga. Conference, was born in Bryan co., Ga., and died in Liberty co., Ga., Feb. 10th 1870, in her 38th year. L. B. Payne

Miss Rebecca P. Gilliam, daughter of T. T. and M. J. Gilliam, died 4th Feb 1870, in her 18th year. A Odom

Mary Jane Kirby, a beloved pupil of the Summerville (Ga.) Sunday-school, died recently.

Tribute of Respect from Talbotton Station to Bro. J. D. Cottingham.

Issue of May 6, 1870

Dr. John Hughes Thomas, son of Edward and Hannah Thomas, was born in Va., on 2d November 1797. His mother's maiden name was Hughes. His brothers, William, Edward, Jesse, James, Moses, Reuben and Nelson, and his sisters, Elizabeth, Jane Nancy, and Mary all settled in Washington con, Missouri-- to which State the parents moved with the family in 1819. Dr. Thomas left Va., in early manhood, and settled in North Georgia. He closed his days at the residence of Dr. J. K. Rushing, his son-in-law, at Tallassee, Ala. Joseph B. Cottrell. N. Orleans, St. Louis and Richmond Advocates, please copy.

Henry Trammell, eldest son of Col. W. T. Trammell, was born in Rome, Ga., Feb. 5th 1851 and died in Griffin, Ga., March 29th 1870. Arminius Wright

Thomas B. Bilbro born in Greensboro, Ga., died Feb. 24th 1870 in Macon co., Ala., nearly 52 years of age. He moved to Ala., while young, was married to Miss Irene Trammel, Sept 29th 1842, and who died in 1854, leaving him with five children; was married again to Miss M. J. Hervy of Louisville, Ky, on 3d April 1856... William B. Neal

Mrs. Elizabeth A. Alexander, wife of Wm. E. Alexander, Esq., of Griffin, daughter of Bro. Isaac and Sarah B. Williamson, of Pike co., Ga., and sister of Rev. Robt F. Williamson, died in Hayneville, Lowndes co., Ala., 4th Feb. in the 33d year of her age. J. P. Duncan.

Elisha R. Reddick, son of Jonathan and Jane Reddick, was born in Gates co., N. C., April 29th 1835. While quite a boy his parents moved to Ga., and thence to Alabama. In 1861 he was married to Miss Elizabeth M. McCarty. Angus Dowling

Samuel Pitts died April 18th 1870, aged 86 years. Born in N. C., his family moved to Warren co., Ga., while a boy and from there to Harris co,. 35 or 40 years ago. H. P. Pitchford

Ephraim Rogers was born in the State of Delaware in 1782 and died in Walton co., Ga., April 7, 1870. He moved to Ga. in his 17th year.

Dr. John H. Colquitt was born in Hancock co., Ga., August 10th 1800 and died 13th Feb 1870 at the residence of his son-in-law (William Arnold). He had lived in Alabama but in 1865 came from LaGrange Ga., to Bossier Parish, La., where he died. E. W. B.

Mrs. Mattie Jemison, wife of S. M. Jemison, daughter of J. E. and Sarah Groce, was born in Lincoln co., Ga., 7th April 1834, and died in Talladega co., Ala., 19th April 1870.

Sister Hannah Peters, daughter of Thomas and Rebecca Vincent, and wife of W. B. Peters, was born in Darlington Dist., S. C., June 23d 1809, removed to Twiggs co., Ga., in 1827, married in 1834 and died in Henry co., Ga., April 10th 1870. W. P. H. Connerly, Pastor.

Sister Catherine Harden, wife of Bro. Neely Harden, was born Sept 2d 1813, and died April 8, 1870. J. B. Nelson

Issue of May 13, 1870

Died

In Americus, Ga., April 13th 1870, Joseph Asbury, son of William H. and Sallie Smith, aged 4 years and 6 months.

Obituary

Mrs. Rebecca S. Gregg, daughter of Richard and Ruth White, was born in Sumter Dist., July 5th 1811 and died at Lynchburg, Sumter co,. S. C., Feb. 9th 1870. Her parents were members of the

Presbyterian Church. She joined with her first husband (Mr. Keeffe) the M. E. Church, South. D. J. McMillan

Rev. Edward T. McGehee, M. D., died at Henderson, Ga., April 18th in the 62d year of his age. He was born in Jasper co., Ga., and lived in Jones, Baldwin, and Putnam cos. He was early left an orphan... married to Miss Owen.... A. Anthony

Mrs. Elizabeth Mitchell was born in Bullock co., Ga., Dec. 12th 1800, in her 17th year she married William Johnson and emigrated to Gadsden co., Fla. She died Feb. 13th 1870.

Mrs. Louisa M. Sims, wife of Major John F. Sims, died April 17th 1870, aged nearly 47 years. John W. McRoy

William Williams died at the residence of his grandmother (Mrs. Allen) in Elbert county, Ga., on the 2d April 1870, aged 30 years and 7 months. On the 17th November 1868, Mr. Williams married Miss Jessie Arnold, daughter of the late Rev. Wesley P. Arnold of the North Ga. Conference. A. G. Worley

Mrs. Eliza P., wife of Samuel Gray, was born Dec. 30th 1821 and died in Clay co., Ga., March 30th 1870. J. F. McKennie

Irby Singleton Thomas, son of Dr. J. R. and Arlena L. Thomas, was born in Oxford, Ga., Aug 22d 1863 and died in Vacaville, California, April 11th 1870. J. C. Simmons

Miss Arah Frances Turnipseed, daughter of Marthew and Barbara Turnipseed, was born Sept 8th 1854 and died Jan. 28th 1870, at her home in Coweta co., Ga.

Charles Westley Wolfe was born in Orangeburg Dist., S. C., and died at the residence of Capt. J. E. Scott, in Williamsburg Dist., S. C., on 25th Feb 1870, aged 40 years.

Issue of May 20, 1870

Died

Sterling, infant son of Rev. G. A. and M. A. Gardner, on 13th April 1870, in Tilton, Whitfield co., Ga., aged one year and eight days.

Obituary

Rev. William Rogers died on the 12th ult., at his home in Milton co., Ga., in the 65th year of his age. H. P. Bell

The church and whole community of Columbus, Ga., are afflicted in the loss of Dr. M. Woodruff who died April 27th, aged 59 years. He was a native of Newark, N. J. When 21 he moved to Augusta, Ga.

Miss Louisa Bennie Thompson died in Thomaston, April 2, 1870, aged 17 years and 26 days

William Derrick West was born August 23d, 1840 in Newberry District, S. C., and died February 23d 1870 near Graniteville, S. C. E. G. Gage

Mrs. M. E. Aford died in LaGrange, Ga., April 6, 1870, in the 60th year of her age. She was born near Burk's meeting house in Green county. The earlier years of her married life as Mrs. Cox and Mrs. Finney were lived in Putnam and Morgan counties. R. W. Bigham

Mrs. Elizabeth Ann Clarke, wife of the late Jesse Clarke and daughter of Thomas and Unity Mathews, was born January 1st 1816 and died March 24th 1870. Mollie E. Arnold

Oscar, son of P. W. and M. A. Merritt was born Feb. 1858 and died in Jonesboro, Ga., May 3d 1870.

Brother Hugh Archer was born in Beaufort District, South Carolina, May 9th 1829 and died at the residence of his cousin, Hugh A. Corley, Esq., on Lake Harris, Sumter co, Fla., March 30th 1870. E. L. T. Blake

Issue of May 27, 1870

Sister Jane Merritt was born October 12th 1808 and died April 6, 1870, aged 63 years. In 1823 she was married to Mickleberry Merritt who preceded her to glory some four years. H. Phinazer

Mrs. Mattie Eugenia Sampey, wife of the Rev. William A. Sampey of the Montgomery Conference, died at the parsonage, Westville, Dale co., Ala., April 28, 1870, aged 33 years, 3 months and 27 days. She was the daughter of Dr. C. H. Wilson, a native of South Carolina, who afterwards removed to Georgia, where she was born January 1st 1837. The family subsequently removed to Clarke co., Ala., where her aged father still resides. She was married to the Rev. William A. Sampey, February 2d, 1858. Wesley B. Dennis

Mrs. Mary H., wife of Thos. J. Hunt, died near Marshalville, Ga., April 26, 1780, aged about 33 years. J. B. S.

Sister E. A. Maxwell died at her residence near Talbotton, Ga., on the 20th April last. J. O. A. Cook

Sister Sarah E. Munroe, wife of Dr. Thomas Munroe and daughter of Rev. Freeman Fitzgerald, deceased, was born in Virginia in the year 1816 and died in Quincy, Fla., on the 5th May 1870. Robert L. Wiggins. Richmond Advocate please copy.

Mrs. Permelia Frances Senter, daughter of Ephraim and Letitia Thorn, was born in Newton co., Ga., May 18th 1845, and died at her father's residence in Conyers, April 8th 1870. S. P. Marbut

Jesse Smith died in Edgefield District, S. C., April 17th 1870. J. T. Kilgo

Jno. J. Wilkinson of Henry co., Ga., died 27th April 1870, aged about forty-six years. Jno. H. Harris

Issue of June 3, 1870

Roxie E. Payne, wife of J. T. Payne, was born in Stewart co., Ga., Sept 21st 1842, and died at her father's residence in Dawson, Ga., May 15, 1870.

Margaret Minerva, daughter of Stephen and Lavinia Cowart, and wife of William D. Richbourg, was born in Newton co., Ga., Jan. 24th 1826. When six years old her parents moved to Pike co., Ala., in which county she lived till April 6th 1843, when she and Mr. Richbourg were married. She died in peace May 13th 1870, aged 44 years, 4 months and 20 days. A. Dowling

Mrs. Florence P. Adams was born in Morgan co., on the 11th April 1846. She died at her mother's, Mrs. Nancy Shepherd on the morning of the 20th April. Her husband, W. Edgar Adams. Index and Baptist please copy.

Mrs. Nancy L. Fogle, wife of Dr. Jacob Fogle and daughter of the late Jacob P. and Mary Turner, was born in Sparta, Ga., June 22d, 1816, married in Putnam co., by Rev. Miles Greene, July 10th 1832. She departed this life in Columbus, Ga., April 4th 1870, leaving a husband and six children.

Mrs. E. E. Reynolds, wife of Rev. Freeman F. Reynolds, of the S. Ga. Conference is dead. The daughter of Benjamin Andrews of Elbert co., Ga. She was born on the 10th of Jan 1820 and died on 26th May 1870. Wm. Hauser, M. D.

Mrs. Florence M. Reeves, wife of J. T. Reeves, daughter of Henry and Mrs. Sarah Chanee, died May 2, in Burke co., Ga., in her 23d year. John N. Wilcox

Rev. John Baker, a local preacher, died in Polk co., Ga., May 1st 1870 He was born in Abbeville Dist., S. C., Nov. 28th 1796. Jno. A. Reynolds

Sarah Lizzie Hemphill, daughter of Wm. A. Hemphill, of the Atlanta Constitute, was accidentally drowned at Saye's mill-pond, near Athens on Friday May 6th 1870, aged a little more than four years.

Issue of June 10, 1870

Died

Moultrie S., son of the late Philip J. McCants, died in Orangeburg co., S. C., May 27th 1870, in the 10th year of his age.

Obituary

Mrs. Rebecca B. Nash, daughter of Eli B. and Martha Branch Witaker, was born Oct. 27th 1803, and joined the M. E. Church near Enfield, N. C., October 1819, was married to Rev. Miles Nash, May 1824, and died in Tallahassee, Fla., March 28th 1870. Jas. O. Branch. Richmond Advocate please copy.

Almira Smith Burtz, wife of M. T. Burtz and daughter of Rev. S. J. and Sarah Bellah, was born Dec. 24th 1845, was married in 1864 and died in Fulton co., Ga., May 5th 1870.

Mary Ann Bass, whose maiden name was Gibson, was born May 8th 1788 and died in Chattooga co., Ga., April 18th 1870. Her son, the Rev. David F. Bass.

Mr. Wm. H. Myers, son of James and Isabella Myers, of Glynn co., Ga., was born 12th Oct 1827. At Emory College he met with and afterwards married a daughter of the Rev. Stephen Potter and sister of Rev. W. H. Potter, of the N. Ga. Conference.

Samuel Madison Smith was born April 15th 1813 in Kershaw Dist., S. C., when grown he moved with his parents to Pike co., Ala., where he died May 20th 1870. A. Dowling

Sister Susannah N. Crump, wife of Dr. E. I. Crump, died at Herndon, Burke co., Ga., Apr. 25, 1870, aged 27 years. She was the daughter of Mr. and Mrs. Lewis Sample of Edgefield Dist., S. C. I. B. Bouchelle

Stephen Hawkins was born in North Carolina, March 20th 1799, was married to Frances Taylor in Washington, Georgia, Nov. 19th 1822; after which he moved to Ala., where he lived until his death in Geneva, May 9th 1870. J. Z. T. Morris

Lemuel Ragland of Henry co., Ga., died in 1870, aged 63 years. John H. Harris

Issue of June 17, 1870

Died

In Orangeburg, S. C., May 30th 1870, Charles Thornwell, son of Rev. T. E. and S. A. Wannamaker, aged nine years and six months.

Obituary

Sister Elizabeth Trammell was born 6th July 1791... died May 6th 1870. Major Trammell, her husband, was one of the early settlers in Nacoochee Valley. [long account]

William Rogers was born at Lebanon ct., 6th May 1810, and died 3d May 1870. He came South and opened a mercantile establishment at Clio, in Marlboro' District, S. C., but in 1841, removed to Bishopville, Sumter District, where he died. His first wife, Miss Anna Jane McCallum, died in January 1868. To his second, Mary A. B. Watson, Sumterville, he had been united only six weeks on the day of his death. Landy Wood

Mrs. Susan A. Murphy, wife of W. D. Murphy, and daughter of Rev. W. B. and Elizabeth Smith, died on May 17th near Grantville, Ga. Henry J. Ellis

Charles H. B. Collins, son of Captain William H. B. and Susan E. A. Collins of Colleton Dist., S. C., was born Jan 1832 and died at Lake City, Fla., April 6th 1870.

Sister Harriet N. Carson died May 29th 1870 in Lenoir, N. C.

Mrs. Clara Walker, youngest daughter of Mr. and Mrs. D. Frederick, late of Marshallville, Ga., died in that place April 13, 1870.

Rev. R. S. McCall was born in Liberty co., Ga., Sept. 18th 1846, and died May 8th 1870, near Taylor's Creek, Liberty co., Ga., W. M. Watts

Mrs. Jane Bassett, daughter of Elisha and Rachel Morris, was born in Barnwell District, S. C., April 17th 1799, and died at her residence in Houston co., Ga., April 4th 1870. J. B. S.

Mrs. Ann M. Green, wife of Wm. A. M. Green and daughter of John Chambless of Monroe co., Ga., died near Loachapoke, Ala., April 24th 1870, in the 42nd year of her age. She was married Nov 1843, and moved to Ala in 1859. Wm. B. Neal

Rev. Daniel Gartman was born in S. C., some 40 miles from Charleston, August 20th 1798, and died near Cave Spring, Ga., March 20th 1870. B. B. Quillian

Benjamin F. Godwin was born in Putnam co, Ga., May 4th 1825, was married to Sarah Caver, July 23d 1846, and died in Lee co., Ala., March 29th 1870.

Mrs. Elizabeth Sheppard, maiden name Pitts, was born in Edgefield Dist., S. C., January 4, 1802, married to Lewis Sheppard in 1819, and died in Jefferson co., Fla., May 17th 1870. Her husband was killed by the cares in February last. C. P. Murdock

Tribute of Respect to Rev. E. G. Gage by St. Johns' M. E. Church, South.

Issue of June 24, 1870

Died

In Jones co., Ga., June 5th 1870, Mattie Udora, only child of Mr. and Mrs. Joseph Haddock, aged 1 year, 4 months and 23 days.

Obituary

One Short Month. On my return, after an absence of one short month, in attendance upon the late General Conference at Memphis, I learned with deep sorrow of the ravages of death upon my work-- the Louisville circuit. The first victim was the estimable wife of Rev. F. F. Reynolds of the South Ga. Conference. The next was Sister Cheatham, wife of Bro. John T. Cheatham, near Mt. Moriah. The next was Sister Fleming, wife of Samuel Fleming, Esq. The next was Sister Thompson, daughter of Bro. S. Ingram and wife of Bro. A. Thompson, near Louisville. The next was young McDaniel, son of Abner McDaniel, near Bethany. Another was Jessie Sinquefield, of Louisville. S. S. Sweet

Mrs. Polly E. Hardaway, wife of G. W. Hardaway, and daughter of Thos. and M. E. Dooly was born in Columbia co., Ga., Feb. 12th 1849, and died in Lincoln co., Ga., April 10th 1870. W. F. Q.

Mrs. Martha E. J. Parker, wife of Rev. James A. Parker, of the Montgomery Conference, and daughter of Edward and Patsey Cullifer, was born in Muscogee co., Ga, July 30th 1840, and died in Milton, Fla., May 31st 1870. in 1854 she moved to Coffee co., Ala., and was married to Brother Parker Oct. 2, 1856. James W. Shores

Dr. John W. Strother was born in St. Mary's, Ga., May 9th 1802, and died in Barnesville, Ga., May 28th 1870. In infancy he lost his father and his mother returned with her little orphans to South Carolina, the land of their fathers.

Mrs. Mary Harden Wiggins was born Sept. 26th 1846-- married to Rev. R. L. Wiggins, Dec. 17th 1865, and died in Quincy, Fla., May 24th 1870.

William, only son of Joseph and Melinda Donaldson, was born near Canton, Cherokee co., Ga., Sep. 17th 1845, and on 4th May, while assisting his father in constructing a bridge across the Etowah river, near Cartersville, Ga., he fell from the bridge about 20 feet and died on 10th May. P. H. Brewster

James V. Culver, son of Dr. E. V. and S. E. Culver, was born in Hancock county, Ga., Dec. 22d 1845. On 27th April 1870, between Fort Deposit and Greenville, on the Mobile and Montgomery R. R., he fell and was killed.

Nathan V. Colclasure was born Aug. 5, 1834, and died May 7, 1870. His father was a local preacher. J. E. Watson.

Mrs. Mary S. Houser, wife of R. P. Houser, was born in Orangeburg Dist., S. C., 10th Oct 1813. Her father Rev. Henry Whetstone moved to Ala., when she was quite young, and she died in Autauga co., Ala., 28th April 1870.

Miss Romalie Bascom Dyer was born in Greenville, S. C., Aug 16th 1850 and died there of consumption, May 31st 1870. Samuel A. Weber

Mrs. Mary L. Johnson, daughter of James and Mary Ashmore, died in Greenville co., S. C., March 8th 1870, in her 67th year.

L. D. Harris died in Forsyth co., Ga., 30th May in his 67th year. About 35 years ago he moved from Gwinnett co., and was among the first settlers in the Cherokee region. He lost his wife in 1866. In 1868 he married again, whom he leaves with an infant daughter.

Mrs. Eliza J. McKinney died in Hernando co., Fla., March 23d 1870, in her 29th year. Isaac Munden

Mr. John Cooper died of a congestive chill at Palmetto, Ga., June 9th 1870, in the 42nd year of his age. He was a native of Pennsylvania, came into our midst a stranger in December 1869.

William Rush Tracy, only son of Dr. Tracy, of Cleveland co., N. C., died in March 1870, in his 23d year.

Issue of July 1, 1870

Died

Near Buford's Bridge, S. C., of gastritis, on the evening of the 11th inst., Little Lucy, infant daughter of J. H. and Mrs. Mary A. Barker.

Frank Perry, infant son of Dr. J. J. and Mrs. Zillah Subers, was born November 18th 1869 and died in Quincy, Fla., May 28th 1870.

Charles D., infant son of Mr. and Mrs. Wm. Munroe, was born November 12th 1869, and died in Quincy, Fla., June 9th 1870.

In Lancaster co., S. C., June 17th 1870, Milton Kennedy, infant son of T. C. and Miley Horton, aged eleven months and twenty days.

Obituary

Mrs. Harriet Howell, relict of the late Joseph Howell, local minister of the M. E. Church, South, died on the 10th May 1870 near Valdosta, Lowndes co., Ga., aged 73 years. She was a native of Barnwell District, S. C., had been twice married, and removed with her late husband to this county. In 1847, he having shortly thereafter departed this life, leaving her with several small children. A. J. B.

Benjamin Franklin Petty, son of B. F. Petty, was born in Clayton, Ala., Sept 1st 1841 and died April 15th 1870. W. B. Ellison

Rev. Richard H. Scruggs joined the Methodist E. Church in Oct. 1839 at Old Church Camp Ground... Jos. A. Shewmake

Mrs. Nancy Black was born in Surry co., N. C. In 1823 her parents moved to Ga., where in 1841 she married W. H. Black, who survives with six daughters and on son, who is a local preacher in the M. E. Church, South. J. W. Craig

Andesia F. Wyatt, daughter of J. M. C. and Nancy F. Montgomery and relict of Elijah Wyatt, was born in Jackson co., Ga., April 4th 1799 and died in Chattooga co., Ga., May 31st 1870. She was twice married, first to Samuel Priett, Sept. 10th 1816, again to Elijah Wyatt, June 9th 1831. W. D. Heath

Mrs. Rebecca Ellis, wife of Mr. John Ellis and daughter of Mr. Jas. and Mrs. Nancy Johnson, died May 2d in Gordon co., Ga., in the 56th year of her age. T. M. P.

Mrs. Ann A. Koger, relict of John Koger, was born 23d June 1788... her death in Colleton co., S. C., May 12th 1870. She leaves two daughters and many friends. A. E. Williams

Mrs. Ann B. Beard, relict of John Beard, was born in Anson co., N. C., and died at Brownsville, Prairie co., Ark., April 13th 1870, in the 68th year of her age. My mother was rather inclined to shrink from than to court notoriety. E. L. Beard. Memphis Christian Advocate please copy.

Edward D. Alfriend was born Aug 27th 1884, and died at White Plains, Green co., April 24th 1870. He came to this State from Virginia in the days of his youth. Thos. F. Pierce

Mrs. Elizabeth J. McCown died in Hogansville, Ga., on 6th June in the 34th year of her age. She was converted at a protracted meeting at Mt. Zion Church in Jasper co. Henry J. Ellis.

Albert Merritt was born April 11th 1861 and died May 25th 1870. W. A. M.

Mrs. Frances C. Keils, relict of George M. Keils, was born Dec. 9th 1812. In her youth she joined the Methodist E. Church under the ministry of Bishop Andrew, who was then stationed in Charleston, S.C. W. P. M.

Issue of July 8, 1870

Mr. Thomas Neill died in Laurens co., S. C., 20th May 1870, in the 73d hear of his age. His life was lived in the vicinity of Hopewell, S. C., the place of his nativity. He was three times married.

Rev. John C. W. Lindsay was born in Wilkes co., Ga., Nov 26th 1795, was married to Miss Nancy Horton of Green co., Ga., Nov. 26, 1817, and died in Upson co., Ga., May 22d, 1870. W. W. Oslin

Mrs. Eliza Wood, daughter of Abel and Tabitha Dixon and widow of Rev. Igdaliah Wood, was born April 1, 1802, and died at the residence of her son-in-law, H. J. Davis, at Mount Pleasant, Gadsden co., Fla. Out of twelve children she lived to see eleven professors of religion. The death of her husband, about six months before her own.... S. Woodbery

Peter Dorn died in Edgefield Dist., S. C., June 8th in his 65th year. For many years he served the church at McKendree's Chapel, Edgefield circuit, as class leader... J. T. Kilgo

Sister Elizabeth Ogilvie, formerly of Edgefield Dist., S. C., died June 20th at the residence of her son-in-law, Bro. R. B. Fortson in Walker co., Ga., in the 93d year of her age.

Mrs. Ann Clyett died in Houston co., May 30th 1870...

Mrs. Mary A. McClendon wife of Dr. J. C. McClendon, was born March 27th 1841... died near Youngville, Tallapoosa co., Ala., aged 29 years. L. R. Bell

Brother Joel Rivers died in Fayette co., Ga., May 23d 1870. She was born in Hancock co., February 13th 1804. E. Stripling

Mrs. Martha W. Redding, widow of John Redding, late of Monroe co., Ga., died on 20th June 1870, in Stewart co., Ga., at the residence of her son-in-law, Dr. J. N. Gilbert. She had lived three score years and more.

Mr. Absolom Whetstone was born on 11th Dec 1790 and died on 4th June 1870. R. B. Tarrant.

Tribute of Respect from Quarterly Conference for Bishopville circuit, held at Wells' Church, June 18, 1870, to William Rogers.

Issue of July 15, 1870

Died

In Brunswick, Ga., July 2d 1870, R. G. Davis, son of Dr. L. B. and S. A. E. Davis, aged 1 year, 9 months, and 22 days.

Obituary

Mr. David Brooks died in Hopewell, S. C., on 18th April 1870, in the 78th year of his age. He was married on 4th of Jan. 1821 to Miss Winniford Wilson with whom he lived nearly 50 years.

Rev. John W. McAfee died in Forsyth co., Ga., June 19th 1870, aged 71 years. He left a widow near his own age. H. F. Bell

Mrs. Susan B. Porcher, daughter of Emma Capers and Rev. S. B. Jones, and wife of Julian H. Porcher of St. John's Berkley, died at St. Stephen's, S. C., April 13, 1870. Twenty year of age, but two months married.... P. F. B.

John Shull died in Lexington, S. C., June 21st in his 71st year. A. Nettles

Brother James D. Callier, the oldest citizen in Talbotton, died on 13th June last, 74 years of age. He died away from wife and children... J. O. A. Cook, Pastor.

Mrs. Orpha Judson Lamb, daughter of Rev. Arfax Whitten was born in Chambers co., Ala., March 7th 1842, married to Mr. Alex Lamb, July 24th 1857, and died in Russell co., Ala., May 23d 1870. When quite young she was, by the death of her mother, left to the care of her eldest sister... She has left a husband and two little boys. Jno. H. Lockhart

W. E. Sloan was born in Darlington Dist., S. C., Dec. 16, 1831, and died in Fort Valley, Ga., May 6, 1870.

Mrs. Maria Saunders Reese, wife of Bro. Jordan Reese, died near Trinity Church in Meriwether co., Ga., on 2d June 1870.

Mrs. Hattie P. Bozeman, daughter of Judge Nathan Yarborough of Rome, Ga., and wife of C. M. Bozeman, Jr., died at Hawkinsville, 23d April 1870, in her 23d year. F. A. Branch. Christian Index please copy.

Mrs. Carrie K. White, wife of James T. White died near Thomson, Upson co., Ga., June 18th 1870, aged 27 years. J. M. White

Mr. Oliver McClendon died near Greenville, Ga., on Sunday, June 26th 1870. A. M. T.

Sister Ann Lee Campbell of Edgefield Dist., S. C., died 20th June, aged twenty six years. W. C. Patterson

Mrs. Flora C. Lester died on 17th June in Upson co., Ga., in the 36th year of her age.

Issue of July 22, 1870

Bro. James Pool died in Houston co., 29th June in the 63d year of his age. Edward W. Jones.

Elliott Cromwell Hannon, son of John and Elizabeth Hannon, was born in Warren co., Ga., August 18th 1800 and died at Montgomery Ala., June 21st 1870. He was married in September 1835 to Mary Ann Stubbs, daughter of the late Thos. B. Stubbs of Milledgeville, Ga., and the same month came to Montgomery. O. R. B.

Mrs. Ann Elizabeth Snead, wife of Younger Snead and daughter of Alexander P. and Sarah J. Newton, was born Oct. 8th 1844 in Marlboro Dist., S. C., and died June 15th 1870 in Richmond co., N. C. She was married in Oct 1862... H. H. Newton

William H. Stafford was born in Wayne co., Ga., Jan. 16th 1809 and died May 5th 1870, near Tuskegee, Ala. He was among the first settlers of the place. E. S. Smith

Bro. Thomas McClesky was born near Edgefield, S. C., 9th August 1796. he had lived in Washington, Greensboro, Macon, Savannah, and Augusta, where he died on 4th July. R. H. Parks

Richard B. Golightly was born Dec. 19th 1802 and died 31st May 1870. He was married in his 32d year. The widow and four children remain. R. P. Franks

Sister Wilmeth McManus of Talbot county, after a pilgrimage of four score and eight years, died on Sabbath evening June 26th 1870. M. P. M.

Sister Matilda H. Venable of Oothealoga Valley was a native of N. Carolina, was born Oct. 21st 1812, was married to Bro. J. L. Venable, July 5, 1831, and died on 25th April 1870. R. H. Jones

William Richardson, Sen., died near Dalton, Ga., on 31st May 1870, in his 89th year. He was born in North Carolina and was at one time a member of the Legislature from Rutherford county, N. C., moved to Georgia in 1848. Levi Brotherton

Mrs. Elizabeth Tunnel, wife of John Tunnel, and daughter of George and Nancy Anderson was born in Clark co., Ga., Aug. 23d 1843 and died June 26th 1870, aged 27 years. E. F. A.

Sarah Susannah Jeffords, relict of S. K. Jeffords, died in Darlington co., S. C., June 24th 1870, in her 69th year.

Sister Ann M. Collins, daughter of A. J. and Ann Roberts, niece of Bishop James O. Andrew and wife of C. H. B. Collins, died 18th June 1870. South Carolina was her native State, but as early as 1822, her husband adopted Florida as their home. She was in the 76th year of her age. Thos K. Leonard

Sister Susan Robertson died 17th June 1870. J. A. Wood

Wm. W. Williams was born in Tenn, near Clinch river, Feb. 2d 1808, and died near Wacoochee, Lee co., Ala., May 29th 1870. In his youth his parents moved to Morgan co., Ga., thence to Henry co., Ga. He was married to Miss Ann E. Jones, daughter of Allen and Nancy Jones of Va., May 26th 1839-- they having several children whom he lived to raise. Nashville Advocate please copy.

James T. Davenport, Sen., was born in Virginia, Oct. 12th 1899, and died in Cobb co., Ga., April 30th 1870.

Issue of July 29, 1870

Died

In Cheraw, S. C., on the morning of the 11th inst., William Douglas, son of John and Sallie M. Sundy, aged 11 months and 22 days.

On June 29th 1870, near Green Cove Springs, East Fla., Howard McKendree, infant son of Dr. A. and Mrs. S. Peeler, aged one year and five days.

On July 13th 1870 in Brooks co., Ga., Horace Eugenius, infant son of Flavius Eugenius and Lucretia Young, aged 10 months and 11 days.

Obituary

Mrs. Lucy G. Henry, wife of Wm. R. Henry of Campbell co., and sister of Bishop Andrew was born in Elbert co., Aug. 25th 1799, and died July 8th 1870. J. J. D.

Mrs. Civility McWilliams, wife of Rev. D. R. McWilliams of the South Georgia Conference, died at the parsonage in Lumpkin, Ga., on the 10th inst. She was born in North Carolina, Oct. 29th 1824, bur removed with her parents to Troup co., Ga. She was married to Bro. McWilliams Dec. 17th 1848. D. S. T. Douglas.

Mrs. Martha Frost (nee Witter), wife of Mr. Samuel Frost, died in Augusta, Ga., on the 23d of May 1870, in the 61st year of her age. She was born at Charleston, S. C., October 1st 1809, and moved with her parents to Athens, Ga., in 1826.

Mrs. Sarah W. Cox, wife of Rev. Cary Cox of Monroe co., Ga., was born the 19th Oct 1795, and died at four o'clock P. M., June 21st 1870. She was a niece of Rev. Jesse Lee. J. J. Singleton. Texas Christian Advocate will please copy.

Mary Antoinette, daughter of Alfred and Mary Drake and wife of W. M. Carter, died in Barnesville, Ga., May 29th 1870, in her thirty-sixth year.

Mrs. Elizabeth G. Williams, wife of Alfred W. Williams and daughter of Thomas and Ann Muckinfuss, was born in Colleton District, S. C., Oct. 23d 1818, and died in Colleton co., June 2d 1870. B. E. W.

Miss Dorothea Jane Anderson died in Bibb co., Ga., on 18th June in the 29th year of her age. W. C. Bass

Mrs. Margaret L., wife of Capt. C. W. Slaten, died at Hernando, DeSoto co., Miss., June 19th 1870. She was born in Walton co., Ga., 7th August 1837. In her early childhood, her father J. E. B. Loyons (who died in 1860) moved to Butts co., Ga., where she continued to reside up to late December, when with her husband she removed to Hernando, Miss. She left and husband and three little daughters.

Mrs. Virginia Hays, daughter of Robert P. and Elizabeth Hays, and wife of George J. McCants, was born December 17th 1846, and died in Taylor co., Ga., July 5th 1870. R. F. W.

Mrs. Henson J. Robertson, wife of John J. Robertson, was born March 22d 1817, and died June 24th 1870. She has left a husband, children and many friends.... W. L. Davenport.

Issue of August 5, 1870

Died

Of cholera infantum, July 3, 1870, at the residence of Mr. John Rush, Floyd co., the infant daughter of C. W. and A. B. Rush, aged eight months and thirteen days.

In LaGrange, Ga., on the 20th July, Edward Chesterfield, son of Dr. C. M. and S. M. Smith, aged 5 months and 20 days.

Obituary

Eliza Ansley Whedbee, oldest daughter of the late Mrs. Susan Whedbee, of Marietta, Ga., died at the residence of her sister, Mrs. Mary J. Heath, in Newton co., May 29th 1870. She was for many years a member of the Presbyterian Church.

Mrs. Mary Legwin, wife of Mr. Lot M. Legwin, of Watkinsville, Clarke co., Ga., died at Sulphur Springs, Hall co., on 9th June 1870, aged 73 years. She lived and died a Presbyterian. J. C. J. Southern Presbyterian please copy.

Lewis Redwine was born in Montgomery co., N. C., Sept. 27th 1791, and died in Coweta co., Ga., Feb. 28th 1870. His wife, Mary Redwine, was born in Elbert co., Ga., Sept 30th 1799 and died in Coweta co., Ga., May 28th 1870. D. D. Cox

John Caldwell was born in Newberry Dist., S. C., 31st May 1801, and died in Columbia, S. C., 15th May 1870. He was president of the S. C. R. R. Wm. Martin

Rev. Robt Newton Rowell was born in Pike co., Ala., January 23d 1838 and died in Bullock co., Ala., April 17th 1870. Tribute of Respect from Mt. Hilliard circuit, Ala. Conference.

W. J. Gutherie was born in Wilkes co., Ga., in 1805, and died in Bullock co., Ala., April 12th 1870. Tribute of Respect from Mt. Hilliard circuit, Ala. Conference.

Mrs. Mary Crews, wife of the late Thos M. Crews, died in Laurensville, S. C., June 3, 1870. He maiden name was Mary Patterson. She was born in Albemarle co., Va., in 1791. In early life she removed to Rutherfordton, N. C., and joined the M. E. Church at Irvin's meeting house. From thence she removed with her husband and family to Murray co., Ga. P. F. Kistler

Andrew Paxton, son of Rev. Thomas M. and Nancy A. Hughes, was born Nov. 14, 1852 and died in Blairsville, Ga., June 26, 1870. W. T. Caldwell

Mrs. A. M. Seawright, wife of C. R. Seawright and daughter of Major David and Mrs. Barbara Kaigler, died near Dawson, Terrell co., Ga., July 7th 1870. She moved with her husband from S. C. and settled in Randolph co., Ga., some thirty years ago. C. A. Cheatham.

Willis H. McCreight, twin son of Samuel J. and Rebekah R. McCreight, was born in Richland Dist., S. C., August 21st 1852 and died in Marion co., E. Fla., July 15th 1870. H. W. Long.

Mrs. Emily Blackwell, wife of Linsay Blackwell, Esq., was born and raised in Elbert co., Ga., by the late Joseph Blackwell and emigrated with the writer to Arkansas in 1857, and died in Jefferson co., Ark., on 11th July 1870. S. M. McGehee

Sallie Law, daughter of Hon. J. W. and Sarah E. Greene, in her 12th year, died in Thomaston, Ga., on 3d July.

Mrs. Listy L. Sellers, wife of Jessee W. Sellers and daughter of John and Sarah Ridgill, died in Barnwell, S. C., in the 48th year of her age. Chas. Wilson

Mrs. Marrah P. Hawthorn was born in Fairfield District, S. C., daughter of Mr. and Mrs. Furman, died in LaGrange, Ga., July 20, 1870, in her 55th year. F. M. T. Brannon

Tribute of Respect from church in Decatur, DeKalb county, Ga., to Rev. W. H. Evans, who died July 29th....

Issue of August 12, 1870

Died

In Buena Vista, on the 18th of July 1870, Lizzie, infant daughter of James M. and Eva M. Lowe.

Obituary

Rev. Patrick Neal Maddox was born in Warren co., Ga., Jan. 25th 1801, and died in Pike co., Ga., July 11, 1870. His father was a native of Virginia-- his mother of South Carolina. He was the eldest son. He married Miss Martha Neville in Charleston, S. C., who survives him.

Rev. B. O. Striplin was born 15th August 1788 in York Dist., S. C., and died 19th June 1870 in Cleberne co., Ala. He returned to his native State where he was married to a Miss Elizabeth R. Steward, who preceded him to the glory world many years ago. R. G. Ragan

Sister Martha J. Green, wife of Brother Thomas Green and daughter of Eli J. and Martha J. Carter, was born in Henry co., Nov 22d 1832, and died in Paulding co., Ga., May 6, 1870. W. D. Norton, Pastor

Mrs. Jennie G. Fuller was born in Montgomery co., N. C., in 1804, married to George C. Fuller in 1823, and moved to Georgia in 1831... died 21st April 1870.

Sister Louisa M. O'Cain was born in Sumter co., S. C., October 59 [sic], 1837 and died July 22, 1870. In 1857 her parents removed to Columbia county, Florida. W. H. H.

Tribute of Respect to Rev. Wm. H. Evans of the North Georgia Conference.

Tribute or Respect from Union Springs, Meriwether co., Ga., to J. T. McLaughlin.

Resolution of Respect to Mamie Hood and Rosella Spence, killed by lightning on Wednesday, the 22d inst.

Issue of August 19, 1870

Died

in Athens, Ga., July 29, 1870, Philie Allen, infant daughter of Jno. W. and Martha M. Nicholson, aged 3 months and 5 days.

Near Hogansville, Ga., on the 29th of May, Joseph F. son of R. J. And L. F. McDonall, nearly 4 years old.

Obituary

Mrs. Mary C. Dasher, daughter of Jonathan Norton, died 24th May at the residence of her daughter, Mr. Martha McGregor, of Montgomery co., Ga., in her 83d year. Born on 12th August 1787, she resided for the first thirty years of her life in Savannah, Ga., under the care of her aunt, Mrs. Dorcas McGarvin. In 1828 she was married to Caleb Harrison, who died in 1813, leaving one child (the writer) a little over two years old. Eight years afterwards, she was married to Joshua

Dash, of Tattnal co., who died several years ago, leaving four children, a son and three daughters. W. Harrison

James Monroe Adams, son of James M. and Sarah A. Adams, decd., grandson of Mr. and Mrs. Henry M. Trippe, and Col. Wm. E. Adams, of Eatonton, Ga., died at the residence of his father-in-law, Wm. Hunt, in Hancock co., Ga., on 30th July in his 24th year.

Mrs. A. E. Frederick, wife of D. B. Frederick, was born in Lexington Dist., S. C., and died near Marshallville, Macon co., Ga., June 13th 1870, in her 42nd year. B. F. B.

Mrs. Mattie A. Cofer, wife of M. J. Cofer and daughter of Thomas and Elizabeth McKibben, was born in Butts co., Ga., Feb. 8th 1838, and died in Atlanta, May 5th 1870. Mrs. Cofer was a member of the Presbyterian church.

Mrs. Cynthia G. Jepson, wife of William Jepson, was born in Green co., Ala., on 15th __ 1818....

Mrs. Annie A. Johnston, died in Corinth, Ga., July 8, 1870, in the 27th year of her age. She left a husband and three children. L. C. W.

Mrs. Roxana M. Smith, widow of Wm. H. Smith, was born May 6th 1841, and died July 5th 1870 in Walker co., Ga. She was left a widow during the war with one little boy. Samuel Brice.

John Ross was born Sep. 22d 1795 and died in Monroe county, Ga., May 28th 1870. W. G. H.

Issue of August 26, 1870

Mrs. Mary C. D. Bigby, wife of Judge John S. Bigby, of Newnan, Ga., was born in 1835, and died July 23 1870. Her sister, Mrs. Berry... L. J. Davies

Sister Elizabeth Payne, relict of Rev. James T. Payne, died July 21, 1870, at the age of 60 years. W. C. Dunlap

Mrs. Mary B. Studstill, daughter of Alex Graham dec'd, of Telfair co., wife of H. Studstill of Brooks co., Ga., born Feb. 3d, 1813, m. Oct. 21, 1836-- died 2d August. F. E. Young. Texas Christian Advocate please copy.

Mrs. Mary Rheney, widow of the late Charles Rheney, was born in Richmond co., Ga., 15th August 1792 and died in Burke co., Ga., 19th July 1870.

William Mizelle Edwards, son of Leroy M. and Martha Edwards, died in Dale co., Ala., on 28th July 1870, in his 18th year. H. J. M. Kennon

Mr. Thomas S. Parham, aged 85 years, died near Trinity, Merriwether co., Ga., July 26, 1870. A. M. T.

George W. Scott, son of Mary J. and Wm. W. Scott, of Madison co., Ga., was born 28th August 1854 in Jefferson co., Ga.... died on 27th July.

Mrs. Elizabeth Hatton Rosser, aged about 50 years, died near Greenville, Ga., July 27th 1870.

Tribute of Respect to Absalom Whetstone, aged 70 years, from upper Orange circuit.

Tribute of Respect from Hayneville ct., S. Ga. Conference, to Rev. Dr. E. T. McGehee.

Died

On August 10th, near Glennville, Ala., little Helen Louise, only daughter of Abram H. and Lizzie Persons Mitchell, aged 17 months and 16 days.

In LaGrange, Ga., August 20, 1870, Pearl, infant daughter of D. N. and A. R. Speer, aged 10 months.

In Warren co., July 31st 1870, Elizabeth Caroline, infant daughter of Henry W. and E. F. Heath, aged 18 months and 9 days.

Obituary

Columbus C. Clarke, third son of David Clarke, dec'd, was born in Houston co., Ga., Sept. 11th 1833, and died at Hawkinsville, June 29th 1870. F. A. Branch

Mrs. Lavinia A. Cottrell died at Mt. Hilliard, Bullock co., on 15th June 1870. She was married at Spring Hill, Marengo co., Ala., by the writer, on 30th of Sept 1860 to Rev. Hugh B. Cottrell. She was the daughter of Mr. Thos. Blunt, of Surry co., Va., where she was born June 25th 1828. Joseph B. Cottrell

Sister Anna D. Gains born Feb. 2d, 1804, died in Cartersville, Ga., July 17th 1870, in her 67th year. She was a native of Laurens Dist., S. C., but removed to Cass co., Ga., with her husband over 30 years since. W. W. L.

Mrs. Elizabeth Virden (whose maiden name was Gordon) was born June 9th 1793, was married to William Virden, Jan 3d, 1809, and settled in Warren co., Ga. They moved to Upson co., Ga., several years afterwards where he husband died Nov. 18th 1841,leaving her with a large family of children. From 1866 till her death she lived with her youngest daughter, Mrs. Elliott. She has left nine children and many grand children....

Mrs. Hannah Starr, relict of the late Elijah Starr, of Habersham co., Ga., was born in Charlotte co., Va., May 3d 1780, and died at the residence of her eldest son, John H. Starr, in Gordon co., Ga., June 19th 1870, aged 90 years, 1 month and 17 days.

Mrs. Julia E. Thomson died in Union Springs, Ala., on 19th July 1870. She was the wife of Mr. Job Thomson to whom she was married on 12 Feb 1835. She was born on 15th May 1811. Joseph B. Cottrell

Dr. Wm. Drain was born in Columbia co., Ga., on 30th of Jan. 1800, and died at the residence of his son-in-law, Thos. Mathews, in Marino co., on 15th July 1870. He joined the Presbyterian Church in 1852. Jas. O. Branch.

Oswald Miconius, second son of Rev. A. G. and C. R. Harmon, was born in Abbeville co., S. C., Nov. 20, 1854, and died June 30, 1870. G. T. Harmon

Mrs. Elizabeth Williamson, wife of Mr. Benjamin Williams, was born in Scriven co., Ga., Oct. 28th 1790, and died July 5, 1870, near Doctortown. W. M. Kennedy

Mary Sharp, wife of Rev. John D. Sharp, of South Carolina, died 6th August in DeKalb co., Georgia. She lived to the age of 82 years and 24 days... W. H. Clarke

Issue of September 9, 1870

Died

in Thomaston, Aug. 3d, George Emory, youngest son of Rev. D. Kelsey, of the North Georgia Conference, aged 10 years and 10 months.

In LaGrange, Ga., Aug. 20th, Pearl Amoss; and on August 29th, Aurelia Moreland, twin sisters, children of D. N. and A. R. Speer-- aged about 10 months.

On July 15, Martha Ann L. Barwick, infant daughter of Wm. J. and Sarah A. M. Barwick, of Johnson county, Ga., aged nearly three years.

Obituary

Mrs. Sarah Johnstone, wife of A. W. Johnstone, Esq., was born in N. C., Jan. 10th 1818, married 27th Oct. 1836, embraced religion in Mississippi in 1844, and died in Cumming, Ga., June 25th 1870. H. P. Bell

Mrs. Mary Barnes, in the 59th year of her age, died in Barnwell co., S. C., Aug. 17th 1870. She leaves four children.

Dr. William Garmany, a native of Columbia co., Ga., died in Wakulla co., Fla., July 14th in his 62d year. T. W. M.

Mrs. Rebecca Felkel, daughter of Gaspar and Nancy Houck, was born about 6th Sept. 1811, in Orangeburg Dist., S. C., was twice married; first to Mr. James J. Barnes, and last to Mr. Jacob L. Felkel, and died June 22d, 1870, near Centreville, Fla.

Tribute of Respect to Col. Jas. R. Lyons was born and raised in Newton co. He married Miss M. L. Walthall in 1859... from St. John's Lodge at Jackson.

Issue of September 16, 1870

Died

near Tuskegee, Ala., August 29, 1870, Sallie Albert, daughter of Rev. John A. and Laura W. Green, aged 7 years, 2 months.

Obituary

Mrs. Sarah F. Bryce, relict of John Bryce, Esq., late of Columbia, S. C., died on 30th May last, thus closing a pilgrimage of more than seventy-five years. Whitefoord Smith

Sister Milly Chapman, the oldest inhabitant of Chesterfield C. H., died July 3d 1870, 75 years old.

Also, Eliza Jane, daughter of John Swenny, aged about 20 years. J. Sandford.

Mother Herran, after a long pilgrimage of one hundred years, died on 18th June 1870. Her age is estimated between one hundred and one hundred and four years. She was born in N. C., married in S. C., and moved to Ga. in 1829 and died in Harris co. She left children to the 4th generation. S. D. C.

Mrs. Susannah P. Alston, relict of the late Col. William J. Alston and daughter of Mr. and Mrs. Phillip Cook, of Fairfield Dist., S. C., died May 31, 1870. She had removed to Spartanburg last autumn for the education of her children and the orphan children of a deceased sister.... W. S.

Henry C. Merritt was born Oct. 29th 1796, died in Henry co., July 18th 1870, in his 74th year, having been one of the first settlers of said county. L. P. Neese

Rev. Wm. Harris Evans was born August 11th 1814, and died in Oxford, Ga., July 20th 1870. W. R. Branham

Florence M. Smith, only child of Alfred F. and Martha C. Smith, and grandson of the late Rev. Noah Smith, was born July 16th 1854 and died in Newton co., Ga., July 20th 1870.

Mrs. Mary J. Bright died on 29th July 1870, in the 39th year of her life....

Mrs. Elizabeth W. Hays was born in Mecklenburg co., Va., Nov. 6, 1795, and died in Athens, Ga., July 9, 1870.

Mrs. Mary Jane, wife of John H. Houser and daughter of Emanuel T. and Frances W. Pooser, was born in Orangeburg Dist., S. C., Aug. 23d 1835 and died in Perry, Ga., July 25th 1870. Her infant child, John Hamlin, followed her on the 20th of August, being a little more than seven months old. W. Knox

Miss Mary Harriet Davis, daughter of Mr. J. A. Davis, died in Decatur co., Ga., August 28th, aged 13 years and 20 months. I. W. C. Critchett

Miss Indiana Mills died at the residence of her brother-in-law, S. B. W. Stephens, in Levy co., Fla., June 3d 1870, in the 25th year of his age. E. J. Knight

Mary A. Leviner, wife of E. J. Leviner and daughter of Samuel Goodwin, died in Randolph co., Ga., on 28th August. E. J. Leviner

Miss Ella Trussell, daughter of L. A. and Lottie Trussell, was born August 19th 1858 and died 7th August 1870.

Tribute of Respect by Palmetto ct., N. Ga. Conference, at Jones Chapel, to Wm. B. Shell who died 28 July 1870.

Tribute of Respect from Barnesville ct., N. Ga. Conference, to Rev. J. C. W. Lindsay, a veteran local preacher.

Issue of September 23, 1870

Died

Little Harry Bascom Renfroe, son of H. A. and Tinnie Renfroe, in Elyton, Ala., on the morning of the 9th Sept 1870, aged 28 months and 15 days.

At Perry, Ga., Sept. 7, 1870, John Mason, infant son of Andrew S. and Sue Giles, aged two years and one month lacking one day.

Obituary

Mrs. Louisa P. Trippe, relict of Col. John B. Trippe, died at Eatonton, July 20, in the 59th year of her age. She was born and eared in Edgefield, South Carolina, and moved to Georgia in 1833, soon after her marriage. She moved to Milledgeville in 1855, where she resided until her death. P. A. Heard

Mrs. Rebekah S. S. Rogers, wife of Col. Russel Rogers, was born in Mecklenburg co., N. C., Feb. 8th 1795, and died suddenly in Union co., N. C., May 16th 1870. J. W. Abernethy

Alexander Noble, youngest child of Dr. Theodore and C. A. Turnbull, died at Monticello, Fla., on the 10th August 1870. Alick's father having died when he was two years old, his training devolved upon his mother. U. S. Bird

Mrs. Lorena F. McDowal, wife of R. J. McDowal, died in Troup co., on the 13th of August 1870 in her 41st year. She was born in Newton County. Her maiden name was Duke. After her marriage she resided several years in the vicinity of Beech Creek, Floyd county. Her husband and three children out of sic are members of the church. W. J. Cotter

Mrs. R. M. Avery, widow of E. H. Avery and daughter of Philip and Mary Ward, was born in Georgia and died in Chambers co., Ala., June 14th 1870 in her 56th year. M. A. Spratling

Mary Susan White, daughter of Edward and Elvira White, died in Monroe co., Ga., 19th August 1870, in the 28th year of her age. F. M. Hunt

Elizabeth Loflin was born Dec. 25th 1803 in Lincoln co., Ga., and died in the same county, July 17th 1870. Her husband, James T. Loflin died Jan 15th 1870 in his 67th year. She leaves two sons and two daughters.

Mrs. Jane Barefield, wife of Frederick Barefield was born in Burke co., Ga., 12th April 1812, and died in Randolph co., Ga., 5th August 1870, in her 59th year. She leaves an aged companion.

Mrs. Sarah Brandon, widow of John Brandon, was born in August 1818 and died August 18th 1870. L. D. D.

Mrs. Dorcas Megee, relict of Wm. Megee, died in Troup county, Georgia, on the 2d June 1870, aged about 75 years. She was born in Morgan co., her maiden name was Evans. W. J. Cotter

Sister Mary W. Cook, the widow of John J. Cook, died at the residence of her son-in-law, Dr. M. W. Bogan, in Jasper co., Aug. 25th 1870, in the 68th year of her age. F. B. Davies

Rev. Wm. Bramlett, a local minister of the M. E. Church, South, departed this life at his own residence in Greenville co., S. C., on the 29th July 1870. Brother Bramlett was born July 2d, 1786. J. C. Crisp. The Christian Neighbor will please copy.

David James Burns died in Charleston, S. C., August 24th 1870, aged 16 years and 10 months.

Mrs. Susan E. Langston, wife of brother E. B. Langston and daughter of Richard and Leah Winters, was born in Claiborne co., Miss. Jan 18th 1816 and died at Jonesboro, Ga., Aug. 12th 1870, aged 54 years. L. P. Neese

Issue of September 30, 1870

Twenty years ago, the 4th day of December last, Mary Jane Bozeman and I were united in marriage by Rev. J. P. Duncan... eight children now survive. W. B. Merritt. Home, in Marion co., Ga., Aug. 10, 1870.

Martha C. McGehee, widow of Abraham McGehee, Esqr., died at the residence of Jos. B. Mason, Lowndes co., Ala., July 7th 1870 in her 80th year. Her maiden name was Smith. She was a native of Granville co., Va. [sic] Her family moved to Ala. in 1833. S. A. Pilley

Mrs. Grace Garrett died in Muscogee co., Ga., August 2 1870 in her 69th year. An orphan, she was raised by her brother-in-law, the Rev. Jno. Ardis of Putnam co., Ga. She was married to Mr. Byrd Garrett and removed with him to Muscogee. S. D. C.

Eugenia daughter of Edwin and Susan Lamberth, died in Tallapoosa co., Ala., August 24th 1870 in the 22d year of her age. She was born Jan. 31, 1849. T. B. F.

Ella C. Black was born January 5, 1850 and died in Newton co., Ga., July 13, 1870. A. G.

Rev. James Quantock, recently of Savannah, died on 15th June at the house of his youngest daughter, Mrs. Brandon, of Polk co., Ga. He was born at East Lambrook, Somersetshire, England on 9th Feb. 1795. Jno. A. Reynolds

Miss Mary Jane Boyd, daughter of C. W. Boyd, was born in Franklin, Heard co., Ga., 24th May 1853, and died 16th August 1870. J. M. Bowden

Mrs. Mary Justice was born in S. C., April 20th 1792 and died in Dooly co., Ga., Aug. 24th 1870.

Sister Martha V. Rogers, wife of Drury W. Rogers of Warren co., died July 20, 1870, aged 48 years.

David Gausey died July 5th 1870, aged 64 years. He lived in Fort Valley for many years. He married a daughter of old Father Fulwood. His mantle fell upon the shoulders of his son, Rev. Chas. Fulwood, of the So. Ga. Conference.

Joicy Sorrell of Monroe, Walton co., died Sept. 2, 1870.

Johnnie Manning Brown, youngest son of J. L. and Nancy Tiller, died near Cheraw, S. C., August 31st, 1870, aged 11 years, 6 months and 3 days. J. E. L.

Tribute of Respect from Crawford Q. Conference, Alabama Conference to Rev. Charles L. Hayes of the South Ga. Conference.

Issue of October 7, 1870

Death has been greedy of my flock on the Bishopville ct., S. C. Conference. On 9th January, Middleton DuBose, aged 73, having been 30 years a class leader, fell asleep in Jesus.
On 12th February John Folsom, an steward and class leader, died, lacking only two days of being 60 years of age.
You have before been told of Brother Rogers, aged 62, who died on 6th May.
On 31st May, Dennis McLendon, nearly 60.
On 30th June, Mrs. Matilda Wilson, formerly Mrs. Durant, mother of several sons of the latter name.
On 9th July, Mrs. Eliza C. Murchison, nearly 73 years old.
On 9th August, Josiah Luckey, nearly 73.
And, now, Mrs. Mary Alexander, wife of Rev. Abner Alexander. She was born April 4th 1804, married in 1819, died half past 5 o'clock p. m., Sunday the 18th Sept 1870. L. Wood

Father Edwin Payne was born in Dinwiddie co., Va., March 24th 1796, and died August 7th 1870. He emigrated to Georgia when a young man and located for a time in Morgan county. Here he was married to his first wife, Miss Theresa N. Barnes. From Morgan, he removed to Newton co., where he was married to his second wife, Mrs. Mary Cureton. He was left a widower the second time in 1852, and was married for the third time to Mrs. Hoyt, widow of Rev. Dr. Hoyt, a minister of the Presbyterian Church and she lives to mourn the loss of her second husband. He came to Atlanta, then Marthasville, in 1843. [account] W. C. Dunlap.

Irene Garnett, daughter of Dr. George D. and Mrs. M. G. Connor of Glenville, Ala., died August 20th, aged 9 years; and four days afterwards her sister, Mollie Hunter, aged 12, followed her. R. B. Crawford.

Mrs. Adaline F. Kennon, wife of the Rev. H. J. M. Kennon, M. D., died at Westville, Dale co., Ala., August 13th 1870, in the 48th year of her age. She was the daughter of the venerable Rev. William Mizel, deceased, and was born in Jones co., Ga., Oct. 24, 1834. With the family in 1835 she emigrated to Russell co., Ala; in 1855 removed to Dale co., and in 1864 was married to Dr. Kennon. Wesley B. Dennis

S. M. Staley was born in Orangeburg Dist., S. C., Jan. 1st 1851, and died near Fort Valley, July 4th 1870. B. F. B.

Miss Louisa Rebecca Dean, eldest daughter of Charles and Abigail Dean, was born March 9th 1836 and died June 26th 1870 near Hackneyville, Tallapoosa co., Ala. Her aged father and mother and three brothers (one of whom is a member of the South Georgia Conference, Rev. A. J. Dean) and an only sister survive. L. R. Bell

Mrs Mary Ann Geiger, whose maiden name was Buff, was born in Lexington co., S. C., Feb. 26th 1838, and died Sept. 4th 1870, in Marion co., Fla., near Wacahoots, to which place with her husband Wade A. Geiger, she moved some ten years since. Jas. P. DePass

Mr. J. E. Felix Boykin died at the residence of Mr. Abe Williams (his father-in-law) near Union Springs, Ala., on 4th Aug 1870. He had but recently married. He was born in Hinds co., Miss., on 18th of July 1850. Jos. B. Cottrell

Mrs. Elizabeth Davidson, relict of John Davidson, was born in Warren co., Ga., and died on 7th Sept 1870, in Harris co, Ga., aged about 76 years. She had been a member of the Primitive Baptist Church at Sardis for many years. E. D.

Rufus M. Ledford, a son of brother Allison and sister Ruthy M. Ledford, was born April 24th 1851, and died Aug. 2d 1870. M. H. Eakes

Miss Cornelia Candace Tucker, daughter of Reuben and Patience Tucker, was born August 3d, 1852, and died in Mitchell co., Ga., Sept. 19th 1870.

Tribute of Respect to Rev. Jos. Holmes who died being nearly 82 years old at the residence of his son Dr. Holmes in Barnwell co., S. C., May 30th 1870.

Issue of October 14, 1870

Mrs. Elinor Howard died in Columbus, Ga., on 29th August, aged 72 years. She was born in Clarke co., Ga., married in 1816, and joined the Church in Milledgeville in 1823, moved to Columbus in 1830. A. M. W.

Sister A. E. Boyd of Blue Springs, Harris co., Ga., died at the residence of her mother, Mrs. E. C. McGee in Troup co., Ga., 15th July 1870. She was born in Putnam co., Ga., August 1, 1831, was married to Joseph Boyd, Nov. 5, 1850. T. S. L. Harwell

Mrs. Susan Elizabeth, wife of Daniel D. Dantzler and daughter of Rev. L. G. and Mrs. M. M. Crum, was born in Orangeburg co., S. C., Feb. 17th 1848, and died July 30th 1870. James C. Stoll

Mr. Shelton Oliver was born in Elbert co., Ga., 9th July 1801 and died in Oglethorpe co., Sept. 17th 1870.

George D. Fowler was born in S. C., July 10, 1803. His father moved to Franklin co., Ga., when he was in his 16th year. He married when he was 33, Miss Sarah Adams. He was bitten by a rattle-snake on August 26th, and died 15th September. J. H. Mashburn

Mrs. Eliza Caroline Dawkins was born 29th June 1808 in Newberry Dist., S. C., and died on 29th August 1870 in Houston co., Ga. C. W. Smith

William D. Ogletree, son of Mrs. David Ogletree of Monroe co., Ga., was born Sept. 28, 1847 and died at his father's residence, Aug. 23d 1870. F. A. Kimball

Jesse Thomas Avant, son of Ransom T. and Malinda Avant, was born in Washington co., Ga., Dec. 1839, died at his father's in Bibb co., Ga., August 18th 1870. I. L. Avant

H. M. Hogan of East Macon, aged 26, died on 20th September. He leaves a widow. E. W. W.

Mrs. Elizabeth Sledge, daughter of Tolbert and Julia Anderson, was born in Jefferson co., Fla., July 6th 1851 and Sept 25th 1870.

Mary Ella Bruner, daughter of John Evans and Harriet Bruner, of St. George's Dorchester, Colleton co., S. C., died September 2d, aged 13 years and 6 months.

Issue of October 21, 1870

Died

Lula Pauline Carswell Peacock, daughter of J. B. and S. E. Peacock, died in Jeffersonville, Twiggs co., on 28th Sept 1870, aged 10 months and 23 days.

Obituary

Mrs. Elizabeth Morris was born in Mecklenburg co., North Carolina, in 1797 from whence her parents removed and settled in Rutherford co., N. C., when she was but a child. In 1817 she was married to Mr. John Morris, who died in 1835, after whose death she resided with her daughter, Mrs. James D. Bivins, first in South Carolina, and for three years preceding her death, in Dalton, Georgia.

John Raphael Kimbrough was born 29th March 1826 and died in Talbotton on 18th September 1870. J. O. A. Cook

Mrs. Martha G. Hunt, wife of Henry Hunt, died at Liberty Hill, Heard co., Ga., on 16th Sept 1870. She was born in Putnam co., and her maiden name was Hawkins. W. J. Cotter

Mrs. H. Godwin was born in Warren co., Ga., Aug. 10th 1800 and died at her son's, W. T. Godwin, near Whitesville, Ga., Aug 8th 1870. She was married to W. H. Godwin in her 18th year, joined the M. E. Church but a few years afterwards united with the Baptist Church.... T. S. L. Harwell

Mr. Osborne M. Stone died in LaGrange, Ga., August 16th 1870, aged 60 years. He was long a resident of Hamilton and Columbus, Ga. R. W. Bigham

Miss Mattie A. Hamline, daughter of W. E. Hamline, of Monroe co., Ga., died Sept 18, 1870, in her 24th year. W. W. Oslin

Timothy Goodyear was born in Connecticut, 25th August 1818 moved to Georgia about 25 years ago, and died in Macon, Sept. 8th 1870. J. B. S.

Mrs. Sally Mathis Lindsay died in LaGrange, Ga., Sept 18th 1870, in the 73d year of her age. She was the oldest child of the Rev. A. G. Smith.

John K. Duke, son of F. M. L. and Ellen Duke, of Fairfield co., S. C., died at the residence of Mrs. Elizabeth Gill, in Newton, N. C., August 28th 1870, in his 18th year. D. M. The Christian Neighbor will please copy.

William G. Johnson died in Warren co., Ga., August 20th 1870, in his 54th year. He left a wife and four children. Amos Johnson

Issue of October 28, 1870

Died

On Sept. 30, Joseph W., only son of John W. and M. C. Evans, of Marion co., Fla., aged 3 years, 8 months and 1 day.
Also little Salla, youngest daughter of sister S. E. Swakard, aged 3 years and 23 days, of Adamsville, Fla.
Emanuel Tarrant, son of Emanuel T. and R. O. Pouser, was born Sept. 25, 1865, and died Sept. 27, 1870.
In Laurens co., Ga., on 23d August, Daniel Hiram Mason, infant son of J. M. and Susie McNeel, aged 7 months and 20 days.

Obituary

Mrs. Elizabeth Johnson Medley, relict of the late Joseph Medley, was born in Anson co., N. C., March 4th 1795 and died in the county of her birth, on the 23d of August 1870. F. M. Kennedy. N. O. Advocate please copy.

Mrs. Mary Callahan, best known as "Aunt Polly," was born in Wilkes co., Ga., June 12th 1790, and died in Jefferson, Jackson co., Sept. 23d 1870. J. W. G.

Mrs. Antoinette V. Biggers, wife of J. L. Biggers, of Muscogee co., was born June 20, 1843, and died Sept. 13, 1870. S. D. C.

Rev. E. W. Jones, M. D., was born in Columbia co., Ga. He graduated at the Medical College, Charleston. Subsequently he moved to Chattanooga, where he remained a few years. G. W. Persons

Martha E. Leake, daughter of James and Elizabeth Harris, and wife of Rev. Sanford Leake, formerly of the Georgia Conference, was born in Forsyth co., Ga., May 23d, 1831, and died in Walker co., Ga., Sept. 11, 1870, aged 29 years, 3 months and 19 days. C. M. McClure

Mrs. Nancy Byrd died at the residence of her son, William Byrd, in Lee co., Ala., Oct. 1st, 1870, aged about 74. She was born in North Carolina, moved to Georgia, and afterwards moved to Ala in 1837.

Wm. E. Carnes, son of Eli and Jane Carnes, formerly of Henry co., Ga., died in Griffin, Ga., Sept. 8, 1870, aged 30 years. L. P. Neese

Miss Mina Murray died in Watkinsville, Clarke co., Ga., on 19th day of October 1870, aged 22 years.

Mrs. Louisa Ashford, aged 45 years, died in Watkinsville, Clarke co., Ga., Sept. 2d, 1870.

Mrs. Louisa G. Murray, died in Watkinsville, Clarke co., Ga., Aug. 29, 1870, in the 63d year of her age.

Mrs. Mary D. Dawson, died in Watkinsville, Clarke co., Ga., Sept. 28, 1870, aged 48 years.

Mrs. Emily Johnson died in Warren co., August 25, 1870, aged about 48 years. Amos Johnson

Issue of November 4, 1870

Died

On the 14th Oct., little Lucios Sextus, infant son of Col. A. W. and Sue M. Persons, aged 15 months and 2 days.

In Washington co., Ga., Sep 22d, Gertrude Kendrick, infant daughter of L. B. and A. L. Kennedy, aged two years and 10 days.

In Savannah, Ga., Oct. 25th 1870, Eddie, infant son of Hon. J. R. and Mrs. Hattie S. Sausey, aged fourteen months.

Obituary

Mrs. Georgia, wife of James B. Smith and daughter of the late Rev. Dr. Sikes, was born 12th March 1820 and died in Tattnall co., Ga., Sept. 26, 1870. She married J. B. Smith in 1840. L. B. Payne

Nancy O. Rogers, wife of Henry Rogers, was born in Hancock co.,Ga., April 23d 1796 and died in Putnam co., Ga., Oct. 1st 1870. Her husband (Henry Rogers) is in his 87th year. Thos. H. Timmons

Nancy Leonora Hutchings, wife of Benj. F. Hutchings and youngest daughter of Hartwell and Mahala Lester, died in Greenville co., S. C., Aug. 30th 1870, aged 27 years. Her father died in Cassville, Ga., when she was about three years old; and the family having returned to S. C.

R. G. Beall was born in Warren co., Ga., May 1st 1817, and died in Talbot co., Ga., August 13th 1870.

Mrs. Elizabeth Parker was born Fe.b 6th 1823 in Hancock co., and died Sept. 15th, 1870 in Washington co., Ga. C. J. Toole

D. Irwin Rast was born in Orangeburg District, S. C., January 17, 1830 and died in New Orleans, La., September 29, 1870. J. B. Walker

Miss Hattie O. Phillips, only daughter of John and Sallie Phillips, was born in Campbell co., Ga., and died Sept. 23d near Powder Springs, Cobb co., Ga., in the 25th year of her age. C. J. Stipe

Oscar A. Caldwell, a citizen of Macon and a member of Mulberry st. church, died Oct. 6th, aged 38 years. J. S. K.

Mrs. Anna S. M. Patrick, wife of George Y. Patrick, died at Bamberg, S. C., on 25th September 1870, in her 54th year. She was married 21st Sept 1837.... She left a husband and seven children.

Mrs. E. G. Broome, wife of Col. Jas. A. Broome and daughter of Boling H. and Martha G. Robinson, was born Sept. 11th 1848 and died in Blakely, Ga., Oct. 14th 1870. In 1865 she married. J. W. D. Christian Index please copy.

Miss D. D., daughter of Jefferson P. and Lucy Sturkey, died at school in Long Cane, Abbeville, S. C., Oct. 6th 1870, in her 13th year. W. F. Quillian

Rev. Wm. F. Powell died 26th Sept 1870 at the residence of Henry Smith, Dade co., Ga., in his 52d year.

Miss Nanny, daughter of R. S. and Francis Halloway, of Upson co., Ga., died on 17th Oct. aged 17 years.

Benjamin Hill Marchman who died Sept. 16th 1870... Meriwether co., Ga.

Tribute of Respect to Rev. S. D. Johnson, a local preacher of Dawsonville ct., North Ga. Conference.

Issue of November 11, 1870

Died

Emma Elizabeth Platt, the only child of H. B. and Victoria Platt of Sumter co., Ga., born 16th April and died 18th Oct. 1870.

In Spartanburg, S. C., August 16, 1870, Thomas Benton, infant son of T. B. and Hattie S. Anderson, aged 19 months and 8 days.

In Walton co., Fla., Sept. 9 AD 1870, James Miley, son of J. A. and Elizabeth R. Passmore, aged 16 months and 18 days.

Obituary

Wiley W. Strother was born in Crawford co., Ga., but from early childhood has lived in Barnesville. He was the youngest son of the late Dr. John W. Strother, was 21 years of age. G. J. Pearce

Mrs. Eliza T. Duke, relict of Ferdinand Duke, was born July 15, 1808, and died Sept. 2, 1870 in Heard co., Ga. She was the youngest daughter of James Stansell, who traveled several years as an itinerant preacher.

Sister Jane Parker, wife of Rev. B. B. Parker, of Parkertown, Hart co., Ga., died Aug. 15, 1870, in her 50th year. Amicus W. Williams

Sister Mary R. Mann was born in Elbert co., Ga., February 25, 1792, married December 26, 1815, and died in Jonesboro, September 17, 1870. She has left twelve surviving children.

Mrs. Mary E. Speight, wife of J. S. Speight and daughter of Thomas and Elizabeth Williams, was born in Bibb co., Ga., Jan. 31st 1824 and died in Randolph, Aug 7th 1870. She had nine children, seven of whom are left. She was the oldest of several sisters. Her father was killed by the Indians in 1836. Chas. E. Brown

Maj. H. K. Daniel of Sumter co., Ga., died 9th Sept 1870, in the 33d year of his age. He was a graduate of the Oglethorpe University of Georgia... A. A. Robinson

Mrs. Mary E. Roberts Rears, wife of J. W. Fears, Esq., of Macon, Ga., died Oct. 12th aged 27 years. in 1861 she joined the church in Athens, Ga. J. S. K.

Capt. John Fletcher Heath died in Macon, Ga., Oct. 26th 1870, in the 48th year of her age. G. F. Wing

William Edwin Lamberth, son of Edwin and Susan Lambert, was born in Ala., on 4th July 1859 and died in Tallapoosa co., Ala., 26th Sept 1870.

Issue of November 18, 1870

Died

On the 15th October at Reidsville, S. C., Lula Presley, daughter of J. Calvin and Sarah E. Moorer, aged 3 years, 8 months, 25 days.

In Cheraw, S. C., October 11th 1870, David Hester, youngest son of N. D. and Ester A. Stricklin, aged one year, nine months and ten days.

Obituary

Samuel C. Johnson was born in N. C., Nov. 10th 1830, married July 23d 1851, licensed to preach in 1860. He died at his home in Dawsonville, Ga., September 25th 1870. H. F. Bell

Daniel Larry was born in Orangeburg co., S. C., Dec. 18th 1775, and died at Orangeburg, S. C., Sept. 18th 1870. F. Auld

Miss Laura C., daughter of the late William G. Smith, was born in Troupville, Lowndes co., Ga., on 14th April 1851 and died at Valdosta, on 22d October 1870. Her grandparents, Mr. and Mrs. William Smith, were among the earliest settlers in this county.

Sister Permelia S. Brown was born in Hancock co., Ga., Dec. 31st 1799, and in July 1818 was married to Bro. E. G. Brown, died of cancer in Dawson, Ga., Oct. 24th 1870. She left a husband and seven children. J. M. Marshall

Sister Hettie R. Heflin, wife of L. F. Heflin, was born in Oct. 20th 1828 and died Oct. 19th 1870. Her boy Larkin, died at Camp Sumter, July 20th 1864, in his 18th year. J. R. Mayson

Mrs. Catharine Elmira Corpening was born in Catawba, N. C., and died in Caldwell co., Oct. 7th 1870, in her 49th year. Her maiden name was Robeson. When young she joined the German Reformed Church, but afterwards joined the Presbyterian Church.

Sister Jane B. Sexton was born Jan. 7th 1811 in Union Dist., S. C., was married to Mr. Sexton in 1827, and moved to Spartanburg District and there lived until 1860 when she came to her friends in LaFayette co., Ark., where she died Sept. 14th 1870. A. D. Jenkins

Delia A. Edwards, daughter of the late lamented Rev. Peyton P. Smith, was born in Gwinnett co., Ga., March 12th 1835 and died in Jefferson co., Fla., at the residence of her brother-in-law, Mr. H. B. Edwards, Oct. 28th 1870. She married Mr. Jas. B. Edwards in 1858. E. S. Tyner

Issue of November 25, 1870

Died

In Twiggsville, Twiggs co., Ga., Emma V. Evans on Oct. 18, 1870, youngest daughter of John S. and Emerly M. Evans, who was born 26th March 1866.

On 7th Nov. in Camilla, Ga., James T. Ainsworth, son of Rev. J. T. Ainsworth of South Georgia Conference, aged two years, eleven months and nineteen days.

William Austin Norman, infant son of Rev. William Norman, of the North Ga. Conference, on Sept. 26th 1870, aged 1 month and 25 days.

In Fort Valley, Ga., August 25, 1870, James W., son of Newton and Frances Hightower, aged 15 months.

Obituary

Col. R. H. Ward was born in Putnam co., March 25th 1814, and died in Green co., Oct. 25th 1870, in the 57th year of his age. Thos. F. Pierce

Martha J. Jordan was born April 1833. On 11th July, twenty years ago, we were united in marriage... W. C. Holmes

Dr. C. K. Ayer was born in Barnwell District, South Carolina, July 28th 1806 and died in Floyd co., Ga., Sept. 20th 1870.

Mrs. Edna Dawkins, wife of John Dawkins, was born in Cumberland co., N. C., july 20th 1811 and died in Jefferson co., Fla., Nov. 4th 1870. Geo C. Leavel

Sister Lucy Amanda Perry, daughter of Jefferson and Julia A. E. C. Lanier, died on the 17th Oct., aged 41 years, 11 months and 7 days. C. A. Conaway

Miss Catharine Wells Wilson died at the residence of Mrs. Winniford Brooks, near Hopewell, S. C., August 20th 1870, in the 58th year of her age. Her father died when she was but a child, leaving her mother with three little children, two sons, now the Rev. Ashley Wilson of Mississippi, Samuel Wilson, deceased and the subject of this notice. S. C. W.

Sarena J. Donald, daughter of A. D. and Rebecka Donald, was born in S. C., August 23d 1843 and died in Harris co., Ga., Nov 3, 1870. Exie Dorman

Alexander Bellamy, one of the oldest citizens of Griffin, Ga., was born Sept. 3d, 1810, and died August 4th 1870. Arminius Wright

Rebecca Johnsey died in Harris co., Ga., 18th Oct 1870. She was born 13 May 1813 and was married to A. D. Donald in Chester District S. C., on Dec. 30th 1825.

Issue of December 2, 1870

Mrs. Catharine Joy, wife of Tyra Joy, died in Abbeville co., S. C., on 31st of Oct. 1870 in the 60th year of her age. R. F. Duffy

Miss Ann D. Mason died at the old family residence, Hancock co., Ga., on 27th August 1870 in the 40th year of her age.

Eliza H. Badget, wife of J. T. Badget, was born in Elbert county, Ga., in 1841. Died in Paulding co., Ga., Oct. 13th 1870.

William B. Elliott, formerly of Clarke co., Ga., died in Tuskaloosa co., Ala., aged 57 years. He was from his early manhood a consistent member of the Presbyterian Church. J. W. B.

Tribute of Respect to Rev. W. F. Powell from Summerville circuit, N. Ga. Conference.

Issue of December 9, 1870

Died

In Houston co., Ga., on the 29th of October 1870, little Robert Eugene, infant son of Mr. Oscar A. and Mrs. Addie Cliett, aged 21 months.

Obituary

Sister Virginia E. Jones, wife of J. S. Jones and daughter of John D. Stewart was born Sept 18, 1840, married June 5th 1856, and died in Columbus, Ga., Sept. 9, 1870. She was a member of the Presbyterian Church, but after her marriage transferred her membership to the M. E. Church, South.

Mr. James B. Anderson died on 19th Nov 1870, in the 53d year of his age, in Georgetown, S. C. Mr. Anderson was born in Charleston, S. C., Oct. 18, 1818, and in early manhood (1839) came to Georgetown... proprietor of a Drug store. H. A. D. Walker.

Dr. Aaron C. F. Black was born Nov. 18, 1826, in Camden co., Ga., died Oct. 19, 1870, at his residence in Leon co., Fla. Leml. G. R. Wiggins, Pastor.

Mrs. Lizzie E. Glisson, daughter of Eben Brown, Esq., of Jefferson co., Ga., and the widow of the late Rev. Dennis Glisson, of Burke co., Ga., was born 28 Aug 1837 and died 12 Nov 1870.

B. Frank McCartha, son of Rev. J. and Emily McCartha, was born in Fairfield Dist., S., C., on 21st Jan 1850 and died in Columbia, S. C., 30 Oct 1870. Wm. W. Mood

Joseph T. Baker was born near Hamburg, South Carolina, in 1795 and died at his residence near Lowndesville, Abbeville co., Oct. 4th 1870. M. B.

John Lucius Campbell died in Meriwether co., Ga., Nov. 6, 1870, nearly 21 years of age.

Sister Rebecca J. Hutchinson died in Brunswick on Oct. 9th, in the 61st year of her age. Chas. A. Fulwood

Francis Asbury Wayne, the last surviving son of Rev. William Wayne, who was the first convert of Methodism in Georgetown, S. C, died on last Friday night. My father was remarkable for independence of character... He has gone into the grave at a ripe old age (nearly 83). C. M. Chrietzberg

Mrs. Nancy Zellars was born April 8, 1816, and joined the Baptist Church in Aug. 1835, died Oct. 31st, 1870, all in Lincoln co., Ga. J. H. Baxter

Mrs. Bettie P. Black, wife of Carey A. Black, and daughter of Reuben and Sophia Holloway died at the residence of her mother in Upson co., on Aug. 17, 1870, leaving a babe five days old. She was at an early age deprived of a father's care.

Miss Casandra Mizell died on 16th Nov of typhoid fever in her 29th year at the residence of Andrew McRae in Pulaksi co., Ga.

Issue of December 16, 1870

Mrs. Delilah Gamewell, for forty-three years the widow of Rev. John Gamewell, formerly of the South Carolina Conference, died of yellow fever in Mobile, Ala., Oct. 18, 1870, in her 79th year. She was left with six young children. Three of them preceded her to the spirit land of whom the eldest, Rev. W. A. Gamewell of the S. C. Conference, died scarcely a year before his mother. Charles Taylor. North Middleton, Ky. Conf, Dec. 1, 1870.

Rev. W. F. Powell, whose death was noticed in the Advocate of Nov. 4, was born Dec. 31, 1818, and called to his rest Sept. 20, 1870, at the residence of his brother-in-law, Henry Smith of Dade county, Ga.

Mrs. Eleanor King, wife of the late Benjamin King, was born Nov. 20, 1805. Died at Americus, Nov. 19, 1870. M. E. B.

Dr. Thomas J. Crowe, a native of Oldham co., Ky., died in Macon, Ga., Nov. 26, 1870, aged twenty-nine years, five months. In 1866 he married Miss Eliza Brown of Tuscaloosa, Ala.

Issue of December 23, 1870

Dr. W. H. Underwood was born in Lowndes co., Ga., April 4th 1843, and died at his mother's home in Jasper, Hamilton co., Fla., Sept. 23d, 1870. His father, Maj. J. J. Underwood, and his only brother, Hon. J. M. Underwood.

Richard William Dudley, one of the first settlers of the village of Bennettsville, died on Monday, the 28th day of November 1870.

E. R. Barnhardt was born in the year 1822, joined the M. E. Church in 1836 in Concord, N. C., and died in Caldwell co., Oct. 21, 1870. P. L. Herman.

William G. Pritchard died on Nov. 15, 1870, at his residence, the Horse Shoe Bend, in Tallapoosa co., Ala., and was buried at Eagle Creek Church in the fifty-ninth year of his age. He moved from Meriwether co., Ga., near 25 years ago, to the place where he died. John F. Watson

Sister Sealy E. Slater, daughter of Wm. and Meky Howard, was born in Leon co., Florida, Jan. 15, 1844, and died in Thomas co., Ga., Oct. 17, 1870. W. Lane

Miss Martha Caroline, eldest daughter of Thos. D. Ousley, died in Bibb co., Ga., on the 7th Dec., in the 19th year of her age.

Rev. Hope Watts was born Jan. 11, 1791, in Greene co., Ga., and died June 24, at his son-in-law's, Stephen C. King, of Polk co., Ga. He life quite a number of children, among whom are Joseph Watts of Polk Co., and Doctor Watts of Cave Spring. John A. Reynolds

Mrs. Winneford Sessions, wife of Asa Sessions, deceased, formerly of Pike co., Ga., and mother of Judge Wm. H. Sessions, died at Blackshear, Ga., Oct. 1, 1870 in the 78th year of her age.

Issue of January 4, 1871

Died

Lula Sardenia Eloise, infant daughter of Rev. Largus R. and Victoria Bell, was born in Tallapoosa co., Ala., June 12, 1869 and died Nov. 21 1870, aged one year, five months and nine days.

In Liberty co., Ga., Sept 21st 1870, James Lee, son of Israel L. and Sarah L. Bird, aged two years, two months and two days.

Annie Lanora, daughter of Jesse and Sealy E. Slater of Thomas co., Ga., aged three years, one month and fifteen days.

Obituary

Mrs. Sarah McCain, wife of Rev. John McCain, died in Edgefield co., S. C., Nov. 25th 1870, in the 28th year of her age. She was married to Brother McCain in 1860. R. L. Duffy

William B. Tindall died of dropsy in Madison co., Fla., on 15th Nov 1870, in the 57th year of his age. He was a native Georgian, lived long in Columbia co., and for many years in Oxford and its vicinity. J. B. Payne

Mrs. Cornelia Guyton, wife of Mr. M. J. Guyton, died in Laurens co., Ga., Nov. 11th 1870 in her 20th year. She was the daughter of the late Dr. William Fisher, of Irwinton, Ga. When but a child her father was taken to his reward. She married Mr. Guyton Nov 28th 1867. W. S. Baker.

Miss Martha J. Butts, daughter of P. P. and M. G. Butts, died in Upson co., Ga., on 24th Sept 1870 in the 18th year of her age. J. B. Payne

Miss Keziah E. Riley died 9th Nov 1870 in the thirty-ninth year of her age.

Issue of January 11, 1871

Dr. Wm. L. Ledbetter, formerly of Anson, N. C., died near Thomasville, Ga., on 8th Dec., aged 39 years. [account] J. E. M.

Mrs. Lou Askins, daughter of J. D. Williams and wife of J. H. Askins, was born Jan. 6, 1848, and died in Monroe co., Ga., Nov. 5, 1870. She was married early in 1860.

Rev. Hugh Ticer was born Jan. 3, 1791, and died in Warren co., Ga., Dec. 1870.

Issue of January 18, 1871

Mrs. Harriet Ann Kirby, the wife of Hon. Francis A. Kirby, was born in Oglethorpe county, June 16th 1831, and died Dec. 26. She was the daughter of Hon. Wesley Shropshire and joined the Baptist Church. She was married in 1848 and joined the Methodist Church at Summerville. Willie Q.

Zachariah R. Jones was born in Pendleton Dist., S. C., June 4, 1804, and died in DeKalb co., Ga., Dec. 13th 1870, aged 66 years, 6 months, 9 days. In early life he was married to Mary Bradford and with her he lived more than forty-six years. Soon after his marriage he moved to DeKalb co., Ga.

Mrs. Drucilla Wood, wife of Isham Wood, of Rutherford, N. C., was born Oct. the 4th 1807 and died Oct. 22d 1870. V. A. Sharpe

Mrs. Emeline Frazier died in Schley co., Ga., Dec. 4th 1870, in her 64th year. She was born near Raleigh, N. C., and afterwards removed with her parents to Ga. where she was married to the much esteemed Daniel Frazier.

Issue of January 25, 1871

Died

Very suddenly in Oxford, Ga., Dec. 31, 1870, little Carrie, only daughter of Dr. Irby H. and Sallie V. Harrison, aged 2 years and 11 months.

Obituary

James Love McCord, son of Jesse C. and Elizabeth R. McCord, of Upson co., Ga., was brutally assassinated near his home, in the 21st year of his age. Unfortunately the assassins, John and Frank Taylor, have made their escape. P. J. L. May

Judge Edmund Palmer died in Washington, at the residence of his son-in-law, Mr. Arnold, in his 75th year. He was long a resident of Burke county, Ga., but more recently of Richmond county. In his early life he served under General Jackson in the Indian war in Florida. He left a wife and many children and grandchildren. N. B. Ousley.

Brother Armanda Lefils died in Darien, McIntosh co., Ga., on 3d Dec 1870, aged 81 years, 2 months and 11 days.

Hon. E. B. Arnold was born Nov 1st 1800 and died in Henry co., Ga., Dec. 30, 1870. In 1829 he was married to Miss Susan Ware, daughter of James Ware, of Morgan co., Ga. In 1861 he was elected to the Convention that carried the State out of the Union. B. J. Johnson

Reuben Gaines was born June 1,1794 and died in Cobb co., Ga., at his sons, Oct. 6, 1870, in his 77th year. D. D. Byars

Rev. William Hutson, local preacher in charge of Cooper River circuit, was born in Richland co., S. C., Sept. 16, 1819, and died in Charleston co., S. C., Nov. 10, 1870. his parents died while he was a child; in consequence of which he was taken by his uncle at the tender age of 9 years to Charleston co., where he spent his early days. J. F. E.

Wilbur Wightman Gramling, son of Andrew P. and Elizabeth Gramling, was born March 30, 1843, in Spartanburg District, S. C., and died Dec. 3, 1870 in Leon co., Fla. Leml. G. R. Wiggins

S. M. Bradford died in Bartow co., Ga. Sept. 27, 1870, aged 61 years, 8 months and 24 days.

Mrs. Martha Beard, wife of Bro. Henry Beard, of the 96 circuit, died Dec. 10, 1870, aged about 45 years.

Mrs. Mary E. Lord, wife of W. R. Lord, died of consumption in Heard co., Ga., Nov. 15th 1870. She was a daughter of T. J. and M. E. Latimer, born in Oglethorpe county, March 12, 1836. W. J. Cotter

Charles Strong was born in Oglethorpe co., Ga., in 1801 and died in Newton co., Ga., Dec. 10th 1870. D. J. M.

Tribute of Respect from Talbotton station, So. GA. Conf. to J. R. Kimbrough

Issue of February 1, 1871

Mr. Isaac Colt was born in New Jersey but had long been a resident in Georgia, where he died near Social Circle, aged about sixty years. S. F. T.

Sister Nancy Jane Powell, daughter of James and Lucy Ann Brooks, was born in Washington county, Ga., in 1817 and died in Leon county, Fla., Nov. 2, 1870. Sister Powell was twice married. Her first husband was Richard Burney, and her second B. J. Powell. She was left a widow with seven children. Five of them preceded her to heaven.

SOUTHERN CHRISTIAN ADVOCATE NOTICES 1867-1878

Sister Rebecca L. Strickland died of cancer Nov. 12, 1870, aged 72 years. She was the wife of A. B. Strickland. They were married March 22, 1822. She was the mother of many children, the greater number of whom are dead.

Mrs. Sarah E. Hill, wife of Mr. W. B. Hill, died at her father's residence in Lincoln co., N. C., on the 7th December 1870, in the 24th year of her age. M. A. C.

Stephen Jasper Crawford of Cotton Valley, Macon county, Ala., and son of A. J. and Mary A. Crawford died at her father's residence in Auburn, Ala., on the 3d of November 1870, aged 27 years, 10 months and 7 days. Thos. F. McGehee

Sister Susannah Reddick, wife of Jacob Reddick and daughter of Thomas Folsom, was born Feb. 7th 1837 and died Nov. 14th 1870. J. J. Giles

Joseph Athon died in Schley co., Ga., the fourth of November last, in the seventy-third year of his age. J. T. T.

Sister Martha Thompson, daughter of James and Sarah Hambleton of South Carolina, was married to James Thompson in 1817... died 3d Dec 1870, in her 76th year. Her aged husband and children and grandchildren mourn her loss....

Issue of February 8, 1871

Died

Catharine Elizabeth, eldest child of C. G. and V. A. Evans, died at Mellonville, Fla., Nov. 28, 1870, aged four years and five months.

Obituary

Mary Louise Gregory was born in Bridgeport, Conn., Aug. 15, 1825, was married to Hugh Archer of Tallahassee, Fla., in Dec. 1853, and died on 31st Dec. 1870. When sixteen years of age, she was confirmed in the Protestant E. Church. Jas. O. Branch

Mrs. Betty Jane Nichols, wife of Mr. Jackson Nichols, died in Crawford co., Ga., Dec. 28, 1870, in her 21st year. I. L. Avant

Sister Henrietta McElveen, wife of John S. McElveen, was born in Lexington Dist., S. C., Fe.b 1, 1827, and died in Decatur co., Ga., Dec. 1, 1870. Her maiden name was Rambo. W. Lane

Joseph Baxter was born March 14, 1794 and died of pneumonia, Rutherford, N. C., Nov. 21, 1870. He was three times marriage and leaves a wife, with children, great-children and many friends.... V. A. Sharpe

James A. Harris was born in 1823, joined the church in Madison co., Fla., and died at his place near Houston, Fla., November 28, 1870. God bless his wife and child and his aged father. W. Davies

Capt. Frederick Burrows was born Oct. 20, 1800, and died Nov. 25, 1870. During the year 1870, Trinity Church, Charleston, suffered greatly in the death of several old members.

Mrs. Ann S. Hodges died in Sandersville, Jan. 14, 1871, at the residence of her son-in-law, S. B. Jones. She leaves but one child, Mrs. J. behind, the others having preceded her to the better land. J. W. Simmons

Mrs. Temperance Silvey was born Nov. 14, 1795, was married Nov. 27, 1815, to Abraham Silvey, and died Nov. 2, 1870, aged 74 years 11 months and 18 days.

Mrs. Sarah E. Brandon, wife of Dr. W. C. Brandon, and daughter of Co.. Joseph Walters, late of Floyd co., Ga., was born in Newton co., Ga., May 28, 1833 and died in Floyd co., Dec. 30, 1870.

Issue of February 15, 1871

Died

Little Ham Culver, infant son of W. D. and Mittie M. Brantley, and grand-son of Rev. L. E. Culver, deceased, in Hancock co., Ga., Feb. 1st, 1871, aged nine months and seventeen days.

Obituary

Sister Mary Eliza Crook, relict of the Rev. William Crook of the S. C. Conference, was born in Wilmington, N. C., January 11, 1816, married January 7, 1830... Sister C. was brought up in the Episcopal Church. She is buried in the cemetery at Yorkville. L. A. J.

Sister M. A. Camp, wife of J. L. Camp, of Rome, Ga., was born 18th February and died 24th December 1870. W. F. C.

My dear mother--Mrs. Hattie Dunlap, fell asleep in Jesus on the 13th January. She was born in York Dist., S. C., and according to our best information was in her 69th year. She was brought up under Presbyterian influence. For the last eleven years has been a member at Mt. Pleasant Society, Merriwether county. William.

Mrs. Mary R. Davis, wife of Richard W. Davis, died Dec. 22d 1870, aged 60 years. She was for forty years a member of the M. E. Church South, and the great part of that time lived in Black Swamp circuit, Beaufort county, S. C. James B. Campbell

Zachariah Oatis died in Georgetown, Ga., Nov. 20th 1870. Many years ago he removed from North Carolina to Georgia.

Mr. John McKee was born in 1790 and died near Trinity in Merriwether co., Ga., Nov. 9th 1870. A. M. T.

Thomas J. Allen was born in Morgan co., Ga., April 5th 1808 and died in Pike co., Ga., Dec. 13th 1870. W. H. Graham.

William Sharp Mathews was born in Ga., May 28, 1844, married to Miss Sarah Cornelia Bryant, April 2d 1867, and died Nov. 14th 1870. R. P. Thompson

Issue of February 2, 1871

Died

Sarah Alberta, only child of Bro. William W. and Sister Carrie E. Jackson, departed this life Feb. 1st, aged two years, five months and fifteen days.

Obituary

Col. W. H. Stansell was born in Greenville, S. C., 27th July 1819 and died in Warrenton, Ga., Dec. 1st 1870. he came to Georgia when about 17 years of age, was identified with the Cherokee bar, having his residence at Dalton. T. A. Seals, Pastor.

W. B. Gainey was born in N. C., and died of apoplexy, in Warrenton, Ga., Dec. 24th 1870, in the 46th year of his age. He came to Warrenton about the close of the war. T. A. Seals, Pastor.

Mrs. Sarah Bunch, wife of Jno. J. Bunch and daughter of John Gay, of Randolph co., Ga., was born July 5th 1831, and died Jan. 4th 1871, in Polk co., Fla. A. S. J.

Mrs. Martha Carter, wife of John T. Carter, of Hogansville, Ga., died, aged nearly 66 years. She was raised in Burke co., where she married, then moved to Monroe, and on to Merriwether co.

Bro. John L. Smith was born in Washington co., in 1818, and died in Marion co., Ga., Jan. 10, 1871. W. W. S.

Sister Eliza Harris, wife of Mr. James J. Harris, was born in Scriven co., Ga., about 1816 and died in Decatur co., Ga., Dec. 9, 1870. W. Lane

Mrs. Mary L. White, daughter of John Bryant of Houston co., and wife of William White, died Nov. 5th 1870. W. W. W.

Esther Ann Laramore, wife of A. A. Laramore, was born in Newberry Dist., S. C., August 25th 1819, and died in Thomson, Ga., Jan. 25th 1871.

Mrs. Molly Burkitt died Dec. 28th 1870, aged 67 years. In her 17th year she was married to Wm. Baker of Sumter co., S. C. In 1835 she was left a widow and seven children; in 1870 she was married to Stephen Burkitt.

Issue of March 1, 1871

Died

Mary E., daughter of Dr. W. H. and M. E. Hollinshead, died in Fort Valley, Fa., Feb. 7th 1871, in her 4th year.

Obituary

Margaret Just of Charleston, S. C., died 16th of Jan. 1871. She was of English descent and was born in Philadelphia in 1794. Her father died in her first year, and her mother removed to Charleston when she was five, but before she had attained twelve she was deprived both of her mother and a pious aunt with whom she lived. She was married in 1811. J. T. W.

Dr. Thomas W. Moore was born in Chester co., S. C., July 14th 1809 and died Jan. 26th 1871. Twice was he married and as often was left with motherless children. J. M. Boyd

Robert Campbell, Sen., was born in Edinburgh, Scotland, A. D. 1795, and died in Newnansville, Fla., Feb. 1st 1871. He came to the United States in 1826. In 1845 he came to Florida and married in St. Augustine, where he remained till 1847, when he moved to Newnansville. He leaves a wife, a daughter and two sons. J. M. Stokes

Bird W. Wright was born in Union District, S. C., 1801, and died in Decatur, Georgia, Dec. 14th 1870. S. Woodbery

Mrs. Rebecca Flood, wife of Capt. Samuel F. Flood, dec'd, was born in Jeffersonton, Camden co., Ga., June 30th 1805 and died in St. Mary's, Jan. 11th 1871. J. W. Simmons

Perry Osier was born in Montgomery co., N. C., Jan. 4th 1810, and died in Montgomery co., Ala., on 12th Dec 1870. W. F. Norton, P. C.

Miss Jane Simpson was born near Charlotte, N. C., came to Green co., Ga., in 1829 and died there Jan. 12th aged, nearly 60 years.

Mary Matilda Watkins, wife of B. W. Watkins, died Dec. 10th 1870, in her 40th year. Wm. M. Duncan

Mrs. Mary Jane Cornley died Dec. 20th 1870, at Bluff Springs, Fla. James E. Waller

Issue of March 8, 1871

James Calhoun Love, only son of Mrs. Caroline L. Flewellen, of Columbia, Ga, and grandson of Hon. Jas. B. Calhoun, died in Montgomery, Ala., Jan. 20, aged 10 years and 6 months. His step-father, Dr. W. W. Flewellen...

Doctor T. F. Duncan died in Abbeville, S. C., Jan. 13, 1871. G. R. F. Nashville Advocate please copy.

Mrs. Susan Capers, wife of Capt. J. T. Cloud of LaPlace, Ala., died on Feb. 5th 1871. She was born in Sumter Dist., S. C., Jan 2d, 1822, and lived to be 49 years of age. Her father was the Rev. Thomas D. Glenn, a distinguished minister of the M. E. Church. Her mother was a favorite sister of Bishop Capers of South Carolina. When she was nearly grown she came to Alabama and made a permanent home in the family of Rev. Noah Laney, who was the husband of an older sister. John J. Cloud

Maj. Moses Guiton was born in S. C., Sept. 4th 1799 and died in Laurens co., Ga., Dec. 12th 1870 in the 72d year of her age. He came to Dublin in early youth. He was married to Miss Mary A. Love of this county, Oct. 1829, who still survives him. J. J. Morgan

John S. Matthews, long a citizen of Oak Bowery, Ala., was born Aug. 25, 1806 and died Feb. 4th 1871, in the city of Opelika, where he had but recently settled. Thos. J. Williams

George L. Price, son of L. Price, formerly of Oxford, Ga., was born in Newton co., July 1836. He moved with his father to East Florida. He went with the first regiment of Florida volunteers in Pensacola. Jno C. Ley

James W. Brandon was born Oct. 3d 1846 and died 24th Jan 1871. L. D. D.

Issue of March 15, 1871

Paper has black borders in memory of Bishop James Osgood Andrew. He died in Mobile on Thursday, 2d March. He was born in Wilkes co., Ga., 3d May 1794. His father John Andrew was the first native Georgian who joined the itinerant ranks, though he traveled but three years 1789-1791. [long account] In 1816 he married that excellent woman who became the mother of all his children. The first Mrs. Andrew having died in 1840, Bishop Andrew married again.

Died

In Macon, February 24th, Corrinnia Bartow, daughter of J. F. and Ida A. Malone, aged 5 years, 10 months and 5 days.

Obituary

Sister Gladys Ethridge was born in Washington co., Ga, Nov. 20th 1798, at about 16 moved to Monroe Co., in 1826 married Mr. Elijah Ethridge by whom she had five children, only one of whom -- Mrs. Cunningham Butler of Atlanta, at whose house she died -- survives her. J. J. Singleton

Mrs. A. M. Cowles, daughter of Wm. G. and Elizabeth Andrews, was born in Oglethorpe co., March 14th 1836, and died in Upson co., Ga., Jan. 26th 1871. J. P. Duncan

Mrs. Nancy Dixon, wife of Thomas Dixon and daughter of James Stubbs, was born in Columbus, N. C., July 17th 1819 and died January 31st 1871 in Macon co., Ga., in her 52d year. W. W. Tidwell

Sister Sarah M. Roberts was born at Nassau, West Indies, on 1st June 1806 and died in Brunswick, Ga., on 15th February 1871. J. O. A. Cook

Mrs. Caroline Springer, wife of Robert H. Springer and daughter of William F. and Mary C. Storey, died at Rotherwood, Carroll co., Ga., on 15th Feb. 1871, in her 32d year.

Walter Wade Mattox was born in Morgan co., July 20, 1847, and died in DeKalb co., 20th Dec 1870.

Annie Henrietta Heath, first born in Millward W. and Sarah E. Heath, formerly of S. C., died of scarlet fever, at Hackensack, N. J. Annie died on Friday, Jan. 20th 1871, aged 5 years, 3 months and 21 days. Millward Williams Heath, first son of the above parents, followed his little sister on Friday, Jan. 27th 1871, aged 3 years, 3 months and 15 days.

Also on the last named day, William Asbury Gamewell, third son of John N. and Sarah A. E. Gamewell, aged 15 years and 6 months.

Margaret Ann Hanson was born Nov. 26th 1830, was married to G. B. Smith, Nov. 24th 1850, and died Dec. 20th 1870, all in Wilkes co., Ga. She had been a member of the Baptist Church about fifteen years. J. H. Baxter

Mr. D. B. Bower died Nov. 14th 1870, aged 85 years. Last year he was elected Superintendent of the Ogechee Academy Sunday-school. Robert Dickinson

Issue of March 22, 1871

Died

Rachel--daughter of Mrs. Mahaleh Funches-- in Orangeburg co., S., C., Jan. 1st 1871, in her 11th year.

In Nashville, Ill., March 8, 1871, in the 13th year of her age, Louisa M., daughter of Rev. T. B. Harben, formerly of the Georgia Conference.

Obituary

Augustin L. Grant was born in Washington, Wilkes co., Ga., June 16, 1814, and died at Atlanta, Feb. 12, 1871, in the 57th year of his age, leaving his wife and seven children.

Mrs. Harriet Jane Bacon, wife of Mr. O. F. Bacon and daughter of John F. and Alethia Sandiford, was born in Liberty co., Ga., February 28th 1846 and died in Savannah, Feb. 12th 1871. Geo. G. N. MacD.

Mrs. Sarah Taliaferro died in Augusta, Ga., Feb. 3d, 1871, in the 61st year of her age. A native of S. C.

William J. Berrie died in Aiken, S. C., Feb. 15th 1871, in the 64th year of his age. C. C. Fishburne

Issue of March 29, 1871

Dr. S. R. Williams was born in Jefferson co., Fla., Oct. 12, 1833. He married Mrs. Murphy, the widow of the lamented Rev. W. L. Murphy of the Fla. Conference, Dec. 4, 1867. He moved to Tampa, Fla., about a year ago for his health, where he died March 7, 1871. His grandfather, father Adams.... E. S. Tyner

Sister Martha E. Witcher was born Oct. 26, 1813 and died Feb. 17, 1871. She was the daughter of Wm. and Nancy Bell, of Jackson co., Ga. She was married to Wm. T. Price, formerly of Rome, Ga., August 5, 1830, and lived with him until his death, Jan. 7, 1853. She was married to Taliaferro Witcher of Floyd co., Ga., Oct. 29th 1857. She was the mother of ten children, several of whom are now living in different parts of the country and one in Texas. W. P. Rivers

Col. E. D. Austin was born in Albemarle co., Va., Nov. 27, 1793, removed to N. C. 1814 and died at the residence of his son, Dr. D. N. Austin, in Fort Valley, Ga., Feb. 6, 1871. R. F. B.

Mrs. Mary C. Geiger was born in St. Mary's, Ga., 1845, and died at her mother's home, St. Mary's, 18 Dec 1870. Mary C. and John F. Geiger were married by the writer, 1st Dec 1859. R. R. Rushing

Miss Mary Jane Bowen was born at Cherokee Corner, Oglethorpe co., Ga., Dec. 13, 1830 and died at the residence of James Young, near Antioch, Oglethorpe co., on 6th March. J. W. B.

Mary Middleton, daughter of Thomas and Elizabeth Townsend, was born in S. C., AD 1800 and died in McIntosh co., Ga., Jan. 26, 1871. She removed with her family to Irwin co., Ga., in 1813, from thence to McIntosh co., where she was married at 15 to A. G. Middleton. A. B. Pendom

Mrs. Fannie, wife of Mr. Thomas Young, and daughter of the venerable Wm. Wilder, died near Ft. Valley, February 7th 1871, aged twenty-eight years. Wm. L. G.

Issue of April 5, 1871

Mrs. Maria Stobo Anderson, relict of Dr. Wade Anderson, of Laurens co., S. C., was born the 30th Dec. 1794, and died at the residence of her son-in-law, Dr. G. M. Gunnels, in Marion co., Fla.... 8th Jan. 1871. Jas. P. DePass

Bro. Robert Spearman was born in Wilkes co., Dec. 28th 1804 from Wilkes, he moved to Jasper co., from thence to Heard co., where he died of dropsy, Jan. 29, 1871. In 1830 he made a profession of religion and joined the M. E. Church at what was then called Sardis, afterwards Harmony. About this time he was married to a Miss King... Robt. Stripling

W. M. Coxe was born in Lancaster co., S. C., and died in Burke co., N. C., Feb. 14th 1871. He has left but one child, Mrs. T. A. Johnson of Burke co., N. C. J. W. Ivy

Mrs. Rachel Cox, wife of James Cox, died in Orangeburg co., S. C., aged about 70 years.

Francis E. Lowe, wife of Henry Lowe and daughter of John and Martha Kemp, died in Key West, March 10th 1871, aged 37.

Perry Dye of the Yorkville circuit, S. C. Conf., died Feb. 7th 1871, in his sixty-sixth year. G. M. Boyd

Mrs. Edna Dye, my dear wife, daughter of Hezekiah Harbrick of Hamilton co., Fla., died 24th Feb 1871. We were married on 28th April 1870. She was a member of the United Baptist Church. She leaves a little boy three weeks old. J. F. D.

Miss Annie Gordon died Feb. 17th 1871, in Fairfield co., S. C. She was born in Ireland. Her father, with his family, emigrated to S. C. and settled in the vicinity of Blackstocks, where he resided up to the death of the deceased. A. G. Gantt

Mrs. Cynthia G. A. Parker, wife of John H. Parker, whose maiden name was Merritt, was born in Lincoln co., Ga., Sept. 23, 1844, and died in DeKalb co., January 26, 1871. She left an infant child.

Issue of April 12, 1871

Died

In Culloden, Ga., March 28th 1871, Edwin Hebbard, son of M. F. and S. E. Malsby, aged three years, six months and fifteen days.

Obituary

Wm. Henry Gober was born May 6th 1794 in Caswell co., N. C., and died in Rehoboth Church, Morgan co., Ga., Feb. 19th 1871. He embraced religion in Franklin co., Ga., in the fall of 1809. W. R. Foote

Nathaniel S. Black was born in Virginia, April 21st 1789. He removed to Georgia and settled in Putnam co., in 1823. His death occurred at Loachapoka, Ala., 14th of Feb. 1871, in the eighty-second year of his age. Wm. B. Neal

Memorial adopted at the first quarterly conference of Fairfield ct., S. C. Conference. Adam F. Dubard was born April 21, 1797 in Richland District, S. C., joined the M. E. Church at Cedar Creek in 1819. By his efforts mainly the Mt. Pleasant Church was built about the year 1823. Adam F. Dubard was murdered and robbed on the public highway, between his residence and the city of Columbia 5 January 1871, in the seventy-fourth year of his age.

Mrs. Mary Wardlaw, wife of Rev. W. J. Wardlaw, of the North Georgia Conference, was born in South Carolina, June 30, 1820 and died in Fulton co., Ga., February 11, 1871. She was married August 4, 1836. James Boring

Issue of April 19, 1871

Died

In New York, on Tuesday morning, March 28, Edward T., eldest son of James Moore and nephew of the late John Colby of Eufaula, Ala.

Obituary

Mrs. Mary S. Turk, daughter of Burket Dean, was born in Morgan co., Ga., Oct. 21, 1814, and was married to Capt. William J. Turk, Aug. 2, 1831. She died near Villula, Russel co., Ala., Feb. 4, 1871. J. W. Solomon

William Knight, a local preacher of Ansonville circuit, N. C. Conference, died February 14th 1871, at the residence of his son, Nathaniel Knight, Esq., near Wadesboro, Anson county, N. C., in the 82d year of his age. He lost his aged companion last year. He has left several children....

Mrs. Sarah F. Spence, wife of J. R. Spence, died in Warrenton, Ga., March 10th 1871, aged 30 years. J. R. Spence

Miss Martha J. Sanders died on 23d January 1871, in her 24th year, near Twiggsville, Twiggs county, Georgia.

Sister Ann E. Knight was born 7th Dec. 1807, and died in Cypress ct., S. C., March 30th 1871. She leaves an aged companion and ten grown children, all in the church, with many grandchildren.... A. R. Danner

Sister Sarah Whitehead, wife of brother Eldridge Whitehead, died on 15th January last, in Jackson co., Ga. I. J. M. Goss. N. C. Christian Advocate, please copy.

Brother James Rigsby died on 19th February. He leaves a wife and three little children. M. F. Malsby

Tribute of Respect from Winterville circuit, N. Ga. Conference, to Wm. H. Colquitt who died 15th Jan. 1871.

SOUTHERN CHRISTIAN ADVOCATE NOTICES 1867-1878

<u>Issue of April 26, 1871</u>

Annie J., only daughter of Rev. O. R. and Ann E. Blue, died in Montgomery, Ala., on 24th March, aged 17 years and 8 months. E. H. S.

Adeline Gibson, wife of John M. Gibson, was born June 27th 1831, and died 20th March in Richmond co., N. C., leaving an affection husband and six children. C. C. Gibson

Sister Mary H. Roberts, wife of Mr. Jas. W. Roberts and daughter of Rev. Isaac N. Craven, died at Edgewood, near Atlanta, Ga., March 10, 1871, aged 43 years, 10 months and 17 days. Jas. S. Jones

Mr. Benjamin Stokes Raysor died at St. George's Colleton co., S. C., on 19th April aged 26 years, 4 months and 23 days. William Hutto

<u>Issue of May 3, 1871</u>

Died

On the 15th inst., in Warren county, Ga., Willis Hubert, son of Capt. James F. and Lizzie Fowler, aged one year, three months and twelve days.

Obituary

Mr. John A. Jordan died on 5th February at Longstreet, Ga., in his 52d year.

Mrs. Artemisia Jemison Lyle died in Chambers co., Ala., Jan. 26, 1871, in her 56th year. She joined the Methodist Church at Liberty Chapel, Upson co., Ga., in early life. E. W. A.

George Newton Bowen, eldest son of Wm. H. and Harriet Bowen, died in White co., Ga., on 23d Feb 1871, in his 23d year. He was a member of the Baptist Church.... Lamar

Susan Fleming was born in Columbia co., Ga., and died at Mr. B. Tutt's, in Lincoln co., Ga., on 10th of Feb 1871, in the eighty-third year of her age. W. F. Q.

Ms. Isabel Riley was born March 5th 1806 and died March 25th 1871. She was married to brother Isaac Riley, a class-leader of Little Saluda circuit, Dec. 23d, 1821. They reared a small family, all of whom are dead, save one daughter. J. H. Z.

Mrs. Catharine O'Cain was born 8th August 1801 and died in Columbia co., Fla., 7th March 1871. W. Davies

Miss Lucretia E., daughter of Denis and Mary Allen, was born and reared in Thomas co., Ga. On the evening of 21st March (at the house of Moses Reddicks, in Brooks co., Ga.) she died.

<u>Issue of May 10, 1871</u>

Mrs. Sarah Calhoun, wife of Dougald Calhoun, Esq., was born in Marlboro' Dist., S. C. in 1805 and died February 19th 1871. W. C. P.

Mrs. E. P. Mangham was born in Hancock co., Ga., March 3d 1808. Her maiden name was Thweatt and she was married to Henry H. Mangham, deceased, July 1825, and died in Fort Valley, Ga., March 4th 1871.
Mrs. C. C. Parker, wife of Mr. H. A. Parker and daughter of the late Mr. John B. Goodbread of Suwannee co., Fla., died in Jacksonville, on 27th March 1871, in her 19th year, leaving an infant daughter seventeen days old.

Margaret Catherine Norton, daughter of James R. and Margaret Norton, died near Clayton, Barbour co., Ala., February 20, 1871, in her 39th year. James R. Norton

Brother James Hatcher was born in Wilkinson co., Ga., March 18th 1832, where he died April 18th 1871.

Rev. Benjamin D. White died in Houston co., on 12th March last, in his 60th year. He was raised in Jones co. Ga.

Mrs. Mary E. T. Green, wife of S. B. Green, died on Black River, March 11th, aged 43 years. A. Nettles, Pastor

Issue of May 17, 1871

Died

At Bronson, Levy co., Fla., March 27th 1871, F. Corra Jackson, aged one year, nine months and six days, only child of H. P. and M. F. Jackson.

Obituary

Mrs. Sarah J. Wilson was born in Harris co., Ga., April 25th 1827. In 1833 her father removed to Chambers co., Ala. On 17th Dec 1844 she was married to Wm. L. Wilson. On 31st March 1871, her husband and children being absent, she died. Jos. T. Curry. N. O. Advocate please copy.

Bro. Asbury Cowles, well known to many in Georgia and Alabama, died at Americus, Ga., on 8th February 1871, in the 73d year of his age. S. Anthony

Sister N. J. Steed of Merriwether co., Ga., died Feb. 18th. She was born June 12th 1839.

Lot W. Johnson was born Aug. 13th 1827; married Miss Mary R. Fleming of Appling co., Ga., in 1851, moved to Lake City, Fla., in 1857, and died April 26th 1871. R. M. Tydings

Issue of May 24, 1871

Mrs. Margaret Woolley, consort of Mr. Joseph Woolley, died at Graniteville, S. C., Feb. 15th 1871, in the 68th year of her age. She was a native of Manchester, England.

Mrs. Mary H. Windsor, wife of Alfred H. Windsor and daughter of the late John Bowman, died in Bibb co., Ga., on the 7th of May in the 59th year of her age. She was born in Caswell co., N. C., and removed to Ga. in the year 1845. She was a devoted wife for 39 years. W. C. Bass

Martha J. Rawls, widow of Joseph Rawls was born in Scriven co., May 9th 1798, and died in Decatur co., Ga., April 25th 1871. R. H. R.

Calvin W. Banks, son of W. A. and M. E. Banks, was born in Monroe co., Ga., Jan. 30th 1846 and died in Macon, May 2, 1871. J. W. B.

Joel Padgett was born October 5th 1802 and died in Colleton co., S. C., February 22d 1871. He leaves a stricken wife and family. W. D. K.

Mrs. Nancy M. Arrington, wife of Levin C. Arrington, died in Brooks co., Ga., April 16th 1871, aged about 57.

Mrs. Susannah Bagwell, wife of John H. Bagwell of Polk co., Ga., was born in Rutherford county, N. C., October 27th 1797, and died in April 13th 1871.

Issue of May 31, 1871

Mrs. Amanda Thomas, daughter of Col. N. C. Barnett of Milledgeville, Ga., was a graduate of the Wesleyan Female College... S. E. H.

Curtis Hollingsworth Shockley was born in Pendleton Dist.., S. C., and died in Columbia co., Ga., April 18th 1871. His father died when he was young. [account]

Mrs. Mary Jane Giles, wife of Rev. E. H. Giles of the Florida Conference and daughter of John and Eunice S. Trantham, was born in Cheraw, S. C., Nov. 23d 1835, and died April 12th 1871. Two infants preceded her to heaven. She leaves a sweet little girl 14 months old and a husband. E. H. Giles

Nat Hunt was born in Putnam co., Ga., Nov. 23, 1831, and died in Auburn, Ala., March 29, 1871. Wm. A. McCarty

James M. Richardson was born in Edgefield co., S. C., and died near Ninety Six, S. C., March 11th 1871, aged 57 years. P. F. K.

Mrs. Louisa B. Stevens was born in Pickens co., S. C., Oct. 30th 1829, and died Feb. 25, 1871. G. T. Harmon

Brother Samuel Rice Garrison, son of Rev. N. J. Garrison, was born Jan. 2d, 1847, and died in Acworth, Ga., March 11th 1871. J. R. Mayson

Brother Jesse Engram died in Clay co., Ga., 16th March 1871, in the 65th year of his age. J. F. McKennie

Mrs. Priscilla Farr was born in Union co., S. C., June 19th 1807, and died on 7th April 1871. She was left in 1845 with a large family to provide for. Jas. F. Smith

Mrs. J. C. Meritt was born in Jackson co., Ga., 1845, she married H. C. Meritt of Greene co., Ga., in 1861, and died May 7th 1871... leaving husband and children.

Mrs. Louisa Hook died in Orangeburg co., S. C., April 12th 1871, in the 74th year of her age.

Tribute of Respect to Joseph R. Nix, who died April 24th.

Issue of June 7, 1871

Died

Near Mechanicsville, S. C., at the residence of the late Rev. Henry D. Green, on 26th April, Addie E. Dennis, aged three years and nine months, and at Bishopville on the 5th May following, 1871, Robert E. Dennis, aged one year and five months, children of Dr. Robert E. and Mrs. Mary G. Dennis, of Bishopville, Sumter county, S. C.

Obituary

Cornelius Benton Burns was born in Camden, S. C., May 22d 1835 and died May 5th 1871 among the people whom he had lived from his birth. On May 8th 1867, he was married to Miss McLaughlin of N. C. A. J. Stokes

Mrs. Mary D. Pitts, wife of Dr. J. W. Pitts of Columbus, Ga., departed this life May 9th 1871. She was the daughter of Gideon and Mary M. Johnson, formerly of Baldwin, but more recently of Monroe county, Ga., where she was raised, educated and married. She was born March 5th 1823, and married Dec. 5th 1843. She was the mother of six children, all of whom survive her.

Joseph Smyly, Esq., youngest son of the late Hon. John Smyly, of the town of Larne, Ireland, died in Colleton co., S. C., March 29th 1871, in 66th year of his age. His oldest son, Dr. Smyly, died in a Federal prison. Two younger ones, Joseph and Duncan, left their studies at Wofford College to join the army, and fell in almost the last battle of the war.

SOUTHERN CHRISTIAN ADVOCATE NOTICES 1867-1878

Mrs. Sarah Slack, wife of Uriah Slack and daughter of Wm. Glover, died in Augusta, Ga., April 19th 1871, aged 55 years. H. H. Parks

Tribute of Respect by Quarterly Conference of Hawkinsville and Longstreet station to John A. Jordan, who died on 5th February last.

Issue of June 14, 1871

Charles Samuel Oliver was born in Nottinghamshire, England, July 14, 1805, and died in Athens, Ga., April 26th 1871, having emigrated to this country in 1832 and settled in Athens about the close of 1838. C. J. O.

Rev. Henry Davis Green was born in Georgetown Dist., S. C., Oct. 5, 1791, and died in Sumter county, April 19, 1871, in the 80th year of his age. S. J. Hill

Rev. Seaborn Hickson was born in Columbia co., Ga., in the month of June 1799 and died in Schley co., Ga., May 6th 1871. George S. Johnston

Mrs. Henrietta Whitaker was a daughter of Col. Van Leonard, of Columbus, Ga. She was born near Madison, Ga., September 9, 1827. In 1852 she was married to Samuel E. Whitaker of Baldwin co. She died in Milledgeville, May 23d. A. J. Jarrell

Issue of June 21, 1871

Died

In Unionville, S. C., June 9, John Summerfield Capers, infant son of Rev. C. and Mary W. Thomason, aged 8 months.

Obituary

Mrs. Berry Rodgers, daughter of Dr. Francis and Elizabeth Mercier, old and well known citizens of Wilkes co., was born near Washington, and died in Macon on 10th May 1871.

Josie, beloved wife of Mr. J. Q. Rogers and daughter of the late Augustus Boulineau, died in the 33d year of her age in Savannah, Ga., March 31, 1871. J. E. Evans

Sister Hettie L. Reynolds, wife of the late Rev. E. W. Reynolds of the North Ga. Conf., was born March 13, 1801, and died Dec 10, 1870 in Fayette co., Ga. She only survived her husband one month. Bro. Reynolds died Nov. 10th 1870.

Sister Julia W. Willingham was born in Wrightsboro, Columbia co., Ga., Sept. 12, 1821, and died May 4, 1871. She was married to Mr. R. S. Willingham, Dec. 17, 1846.

Mrs. Martha Farabee, wife of Dr. J. M. Farabee and daughter of W. D. and Anzy Smith was born in Jackson co., Ga., Feb. 20, 1830 and died May 31, 1871. E. H. Giles

Joseph H. McDowell of Texas died the 2d April 1871. He was born in Greene co., Ga., April 5th 1871. He moved to Mississippi in 1854 and two years afterward to Texas. John M. Haisten. Texas Christian Advocate please copy.

Mrs. Ann Ashemore was born 12th Jan 1790 and died at Jas Feaster's in Liberty co., 12th May 1871. W. G. Booth.

Willie J., first born of Floyd and Kitturah Whittle, formerly of So . Ca. died near Madison, Fla., on Friday 2d June 1871, aged eight years and several months.

Issue of June 28, 1871

Mrs. E. F. Atkinson, wife of Lazarus Atkinson, was born in Hancock co., Ga., Jan. 10, 1808, and died in Cuthbert, Ga., March 31st 1871. She joined the Baptist Church in early life.

Mrs. Sarah A. Jones, wife of J. B. Jones, died in Burke co., on 1st June 1871, in the 47th year of her age. J. B. J.

Samuel W. Smith, son of Calvin G. and Ann Eliza Smith, was born in Rockingham co., N. C., Feb. 4th 1841, and died in Walker co., Ga., May 31st 1871. His mother was a daughter of Dr. Swain of N. C.

Issue of July 5, 1871

Died

June 1, 1871, in Bryan county, Sarah L. A. Downs, daughter of Emmitt and Josephine Downs, aged 7 years and 5 months.

James Hamilton, infant son of Rev. W. C. and Mrs. M. Louisa Power, died on the 30th of May, aged 7 months and 16 days.

Obituary

Mrs. Ellen J. Verstille, wife of H. W. Verstille and daughter of the late Dr. Henry Lockhart, died in Columbus, Ga., May 10th, aged 29 years.

My father, Alexander H. MacDonell, was born on Amelia Island, Florida, and died in Fernandina, Florida, with a few miles of his birth place, April 10th 1871, in the 62d year of his age. Geo. G. N. MacDonell

Miss Caroline Bryce, daughter of Dr. Whiteford and Mrs. Eliza C. Smith, died at Spartanburg, S. C., May 26, 1871.

James Kilpatrick was born Dec. 19th 1787 and died in Rutherford, N. C., April 20th 1871. V. A. Sharpe

Miss Martha V. White, daughter of Mr. W. H. H. White, of Athens, Ga., died June 11th 1871, aged 25 years.

Ransome Harwell, son of Jackson Harwell, died in Jasper co., Ga., May 27th 1871, in his 65th year. J. M. Harwell

Sister Louisa Glenn was born in Chester co., S. C., August 30th 1834 and died in York co., 7th May 1871. She leaves her husband, Dr. Glenn, and a son some thirteen year old. M. A. C.

Thomas J. Heyward, only son of Thomas J. and Margaret H. Heyward, died in Grahamville, S. C., on Sunday evening the 11th June.

Mrs. Lucy A. Carleton died in Twiggs co., May 3d 1871, in the 69th year of her age.

Tribute of Respect to Rev. Seaborn Hickson by Ellaville ct., held at Concord Church.

Issue of July 12, 1871

Died

In East Macon, on the 25th of June, William Holland, only child of Sanford D. and Charlotte A. Massey, aged 18 months.

In Palmetto, on Sunday morning, July 2d, 1871, Lilly Banks, youngest daughter of Thomas L. and Sarah E. Banks, aged 1 year and 9 months.

In Palmetto, on Monday morning, July 3d 1871, William Albert, son of A. B. and Froule B. Latham, aged 2 years and 12 days.

Obituary

James W. Meek was born in Washington co., Virginia, and died 5th April 1871, in Whitefield co., Georgia, in the 68th year of his age.

Mrs. Cornelia A. Stovall, daughter of the late Zachariah Fears, was born Jan. 13, 1841 and died May 8th 1871 in Morgan co., Ga. W. R. Foote. Christian Index please copy.

Mrs. Anna Potter, relict of Rev. Stephen Potter, died at Oxford, Ga., June 12th 1871. She was born in Spartanburg District, S. C., Nov. 16th 1797 and was married March 23d 1817. J. Lewis, Jr.

Mrs. Mary L. Fitzpatrick was born March 12th 1845 and died in Walker co., Ga., June 3d, 1871. She was the eldest daughter of Mr. Alexander and Mrs. Avis Shaw. She was educated at the LaGrange Female College--was married to Dr. W. J. Fitzpatrick, April 14th 1864. She left two little children. Nashville Christian Advocate please copy.

Sister Mary J. Bently, wife of Richard Bently and daughter of M. and Mary A. Christian, was born in Newton co., Ga., April 17th 1851 and died in Henry co., Ga., May 1, 1871.

Issue of July 19, 1871

Dr. Christopher Watkins was born 10th Oct 1796 and died at Ansonville, N. C., on 4th June 1871. M. V. Sherrill

Miss Partia A. Timmons, daughter of T. I. C. and A. A. Timmons, was born June 15th 1842 and died in Troup co., Ga., May 9, 1871. W. A. Cotter

Mrs. Elizabeth Blackwell, widow of Joseph Blackwell, died at the residence of her son Mr. Donton Blackwell, in Elbert co., Ga., 20th June 1871. She was born March 19th 1796 and married March 1813, and with her daughter Mrs. Col. Bowman, united with the M. E. Church. One of her daughters, Mrs. Florence, is the wife of an itinerant.

Dr. A. T. Henry died at his residence in Henderson, Texas, May 25th 1871. He was born in Coweta co., Ga., and moved from Henry co., in January last.

Mrs. Martha F. Creech died in Quitman, Ga., 13th June, aged 64 years.

Issue of July 26, 1871

Died

Samuel Thomas Waldron, son of Malcolm and Lucinda Waldron, was born September 19th 1860, and died July 7th 1871 in Bibb county, Georgia.

Obituary

Mrs. Mary Frances Greene was born in Decatur, Ga., Oct. 27th 1833. She was reared and educated by her grand-parents, James and Sarah McNeill, both of whom were pious Christians; her grandmother being a member of the Methodist and her grandfather a ruling elder in the Presbyterian Church. She was married to Clement C. Greene, April 25th 1850. M. J. M.

Mrs. J. Fletcher Townsend, daughter of Dr. W. C. Norwood, of Cokesbury, S. C., died at the residence of her aunt, Mrs. Jane Speer, near Hogansville, Troup co., Ga., on 29th May 1871, in the 38th year of her age. L. Wood

Margaret Elizabeth Alexander was born in Camden, S. C., Oct. 20th 1813; married to Mr. J. B. Alexander, June 28th 1834; was the mother of eleven children (six of whom preceded her to the better land); died June 4th 1871. A. J. Stokes

Sister Elizabeth Boyd, wife of Rev. Mar. M. Boyd, died in Newberry co., S. C., on 1st of June 1871, aged 58 years and 8 months. She was the mother of ten children. Eight are left behind. Two sons are probationers in the South Carolina Conference.

Mrs. Clara P., wife of Jno. J. Marable, and daughter of A. N. and M. A. Baird, died in Gwinnett co., Ga., June 1871, in her 35th year. J. J. M.

David H. Whitfield was born Sept. 5th 1812 in Anderson District, S. C., and died in Cobb co., Ga., May 3d, 1871. J. R. Mayson

Noah Gibson, Esq., died in Richmond co., N. C., on 18th April 1871, in the 55th year of his age. For many years he was a member of the M. E. Church at Boyken, S.C. C. C. G.

Sister Mary Jane Richwood was born in All Saints Parish, S. C., Aug. 18th 1802, and died May 23, 1871. Wm. Thomas

Mrs. Mary Lacy, wife of Capt. Wm. Lacy, was born Nov. 1st 1835, and died June 11th 1871. She joined the Methodist Church in Eatonton, Ga....

Issue of August 2, 1871

Died

Frank Pharr, Jr., of Macon co., Ga., aged eight years... on the 19th July.

Obituary

Major David L. Hoye was born in Rutherford co., N. C., June 2, 1814, immigrated with his parents, Nov 1822, to McMinn co., Tenn., where he grew up. He immigrated to Decatur, Ga., while a young man. Here he was married to Miss Catharine Ligon. He afterward removed to Gunter's Landing, Ala., and at a later period to Pontotoc co., Miss. He died Feb. 28, 1871. Just four days before his death, his brother Col. A. C. Hoyle died at his residence at Alverado, Texas. Feb. 24, 1871. His father, the Rev. John Hoyle was for fifty years a zealous preacher of the Methodist Church. He had lost two wives (having been thrice married) and nine children. By his first wife he had four children, only one of whom, a son, is now living. Of the others, two sons had died in the late civil war, and the other, a daughter, was murdered by a negro woman. He has left a widow and three children. G. W. Henry

139

Thomas Stewart died in Monroe co., Ga., on 14th June 1871 in the 85th year of his age. In early life he married Miss Nancy Russell. He had sons and daughters. Many grand-children, among whom is R. W. Dixon of the South Georgia Conference...

Mrs. R. A. McBryde, wife of Mr. John McBryde, of Johnson co., Texas, and daughter of Mr. Henry and Mrs. E. Freeman, was born 4th Oct 1843 in Cotton Valley, Macon co., Ala; was married 22d May 1866 and died 12 May 1871. J. C. G. R. Patton

Mrs. Ann Johnson was born in So Ca., Oct. 27, 1799 and died in Taylor co., Ga., May 31st 1871. She was married 18th of June 1835. For either years after her husband's death in Dec 1859.... J. T. Adams

Sister Sarah G. Washington was born at St. Marys, Ga., Oct. 25, 1803, and died near Kingston, Ga., May 31, 1871. She married Robt B. Washington, her surviving companion, Sept. 1, 1824. She resided in Macon from 1825 to 1861. She leaves five children behind, one in Texas, one in Alabama, and three in Georgia.

Emory Maddux was born October 11th 1810, and died May 26, 1871. He had raised a large family of sons and daughters.

Martha J. Mallory, wife of J. N. Mallory and daughter of G. B. and T. A. Candle, was born Nov. 13th 1842, and died in Troup co., Ga., June 3d, 1871. W. A. Cotter

Mrs. Francis Barnett died at her mother's residence in Butts co., Ga., July 6th 1871, aged 23 years. W. G. Hanson

Joseph Minus was born in Colleton co., So. Ca., 8th Decm 1841 and died near where he was born June 18th 1871. Thos Ryan

Issue of August 9, 1871

Died

In Floyd county, Ga., on the 3d of June, Robert Lee, infant son of Mr. and Mrs. C. W. Rush, age three months and twenty days.

In Griffin, Ga., on Sunday, July 30th 1871, Amelia Lamar Randle, infant daughter of L. C. and M. E. Randle.

Obituary

Robert Alexander Brown was born in Macon co., Ga., Sept. 1839, and died in Albany, Ga., July 16th 1871. R. J. Corley

Mrs. Malinda C. Richards was born in South Carolina, near the city of Charleston, 26 Oct 1803; died in the city of Macon, 18 June 1871. Jas. O. Branch

Hugh Winwood Proudfoot born in McIntosh co., Ga., March 16th 1795, died June 19th 1871, in Atlanta. In 1839 he united with the Presbyterian Church of Darien, and afterwards followed his pastor, Rev. N. A. Pratt to Roswell, where his body now sleeps.

Mercy Ann Wilson, daughter of John G. and Elizabeth St. John, of Newton co., Ga., and wife of W. T. Wilson, late of Lithonia, Ga., died at Langley Factory, S. C., July 17th 1871, aged nearly 34 years.

Brother John Ragin King died in Perry, Houston co., Ga., on 13th July in the 65th year of his age. J. Rufus Felder

Mrs. Harriet L. Key, wife of Dr. James B. Key and daughter of John J. and Mary Mans, was born April 24th 1822, married April 4th 1839, and died in Jonesboro, Ga., June 15th 1871. Joseph T. Smith

Benjamin A. Fussell was born in Duplin co., North Carolina, November 1st 1814, and died near Casseta, Ga., May 26th 1871. He leaves a wife and twelve children. W. M. D. Bond

Mrs. Sarah A. Turner, daughter of Wm. and Christiana D. Rawlings, was born in and reared near Sandersville, Ga; married Brother Zadock Turner, Dec. 13th 1848, and died in Putnam co., Ga., July 5th 1871, aged 50 years. W. W. Oslin

Dr. Henry Crosley Ware died in Penfield, Ga., 13th July 1871. Wm. A. Simmons

Mrs. Mary M. Johnson, widow of Gideon Johnson, was born in Washington co., Ga., in 1790 and died at the home of her son-in-law, Mr. Anderson Pittman, of Dooly co., Ga., June 21st, 1871. J. J. Singleton.

Issue of August 16, 1871

Died

Near Buford's Bridge, S. C., June 28, 1871, Elizabeth Agnes, only daughter of Col. John M. and Carrie H. Brabham, aged 2 years and five months.

In Fort Valley, Ga., July 18th, J. T., infant daughter of Dr. W. I. and E. M. Greene, aged one year.

Warren S. Tyner, son of S. I. and N. J. Tyner, in Sumter county, Ga., July 27th 1871, aged 11 years, 3 months and 1 day.

Obituary

Brother John F. Felkel was born in Orangeburg, South Carolina, January 5th 1798, and had been a Methodist for fifty years, a member of Pisgah church in Leon circuit, Florida. E. L. T. Blake

Mrs. Rachael K. Ozier, daughter of David and Barbara Kaigler, was born Feb. 18th 1816 in Lexington Dist., S. C., and died in Randolph co., Ga., May 3d 1871. She was married to Jacob Ozier Nov 10th 1840, he then being a member of the Georgia Conference.

Mrs. Lizzie S. Lewis, daughter of Samuel and Susan Pearce, was born in Columbia, S. C., and died in Augusta, Ga., July 18th 1871. H. H. Parks

Alexander Guyer was born in Mecklenburg co., North Carolina 7th Jan 1819, removed to Florida in 1849, was married to Emily J. Harriss, March 19th 1861, and died July 24th 1871, while on a visit to his native state. For twenty years he was a citizen of Jacksonville, Fla. Josephus Anderson

Col. Calvin Davis was born in North Carolina Nov. 1809 and died in Griffin, Ga., July 20th 1871. He had been a member of the Baptist church.

Sister Mary G. Core, wife of D. W. Core of the Florida Conference and daughter of Angus and Izabella Morrison, died in Waskulla co., Fla., July 4th 1871, aged 27 years. W. Williams

Georgia H., daughter of Daniel and Martha A. Guerry of Bibb co., Ga., died on 19th July 1871.

Robert B. Knox, a member of Social Circle Sunday-school died 27th July.

SOUTHERN CHRISTIAN ADVOCATE NOTICES 1867-1878

<u>Issue of August 23, 1871</u>

Died

On 12th of August, at Reynolds, Taylor co., Ga., Mary Wiliams, infant daughter of R. B. and M. L. Howard.

Obituary

Rev. John P. Dickinson died at Troy, Ala., on 30th July, at the residence of Col. E. B. Wilkerson, in the 70th year of his age. He was born in Moore co., N., C., in 1802. Wm. H. Parks

Miss Esther Dunwody, daughter of Robert and Mary Dunwody, was born at Dr. James Dunwody's in Liberty co., Ga., December 5th 1796, and died at Mr. Henry Carter's, Twiggs co., Ga., July 31st 1871, aged 84 years, 6 months and 24 days. She joined the Methodist Episcopal Church in Scriven co., Ga., in the year 1807. Samuel N. Dunwody. Nashville Christian Advocate please copy.

Mrs. Sarah M. Etchison, daughter of Charles and Mary Reagan, was born in Elbert co., Ga., December 5th 1806, was married to Allen Etchison, January 19th 1826, and died in Chambers co., Ala., June 26th 1871. S. Harwell. Nashville Christian Advocate please copy.

Mrs. Susan C. Newsome, wife of D. P. Newsome and daughter of the late Joel B. Smith, died in Micanopy, East Florida, June 27th 1871. Not quite a year before her death she was married to Mr. Newsome. Jno. C. Ley.

Sister Mary A. E. Whitfield was born in Edgefield District, S. C., married to brother B. R. Whitfield in 1855; died in Cobb co, Ga., May 9th 1871. J. R. Mayson

Susan C. B. Cannedy was born 3d March 1867 and died 7th June 1871.

<u>Issue of August 30, 1871</u>

Mrs. Mary Frances Johnson, wife of Rev. B. J. Johnson of the North Georgia Conference, died at East Point, Georgia, June 29, 1871. She was the daughter of E. V. and Susan Arnold, of Henry county, Georgia, and was born May 10, 1833. She was married October 14, 1863. Atticus G. Haygood

G. B. Riley was born in Laurens Dist., July 20, 1803, and died in Abbeville co., S. C., on 26th of July 1871. L. Wood

Mrs. Narcissa E. Murdock, third daughter of Rev. D. Roberts and N. H. Roberts, deceased, was born in Twiggs co., Ga., Feb. 20, 1841; married to Rev. C. H. Murdock of the Florida Conference, in Decatur co., Ga., June 20, 1858, and died in Welborn, Fla., July 11, 1871. Her Husband

Louisa Fletcher Jarrel, wife of Thomas Jarrel, and daughter of Denis and Mary R. Sheridan, was born Feb. 26th 1841, and died in Taylor co., Ga., May 24th 1871. She leaves behind two motherless girls.

<u>Issue of September 6, 1871</u>

Mrs. Ann Flewellen Chambers, wife of W. I. Chambers and daughter of Dr. Abner H. Flewellen, died in Oswichee, Ala., August 161, 1871. she was born May 2, 1829, and united in marriage with William L. Chambers on 19th May 1847. L. Pierce

Mr. Edmund Martin was born Nov. 4th 1796 and died in Beaufort co., S. C., August 9th 1871. J. B. Campbell

Rev. Abner Alexander was born in Darlington co., S. C., January 25th 1796 and died in Sumter co., S. C., June 13th 1871.

Rev. Thomas Hoyle died at the residence of his son, Col. L. C. Hoyle, in Dawson, Ga., on 3d August 1871, aged 69 years. He was a refugee from Tennessee to Dawson during the late war. Thus has passed away in the brief space of six months, three brothers: Col. A. C. Hoyle of Texas, Maj. D. L. Hoyle of Mississippi, and Rev. Thos Hoyle of Georgia. W. G. P.

Mrs. R. M. Hadden, daughter of Dr. Isaac Branch, died at Abbeville, S. C., on the 8th of July 1871, in the 30th year of her age. She united with the church of Christ at Castleton, Vermont, in the 15th year of her age.

Sister Mary C. Wright, wife of D. J. Wright, died in Coweta co., Ga., July 23d, 1871, in her 40th year. She was left an orphan very early in life... when she was twenty years old, she became an inmate of Rev. Hiram Camp's family.

Sister Ophelia P. Malaier was born in Newton co., Ga., May 4th 1829, and died July 21st 1871, in Spalding co., Ga., leaving three small children.

Sister Derilda Graddick died July 4th 1871, in her 51st year. her parents Robert E. and Gilla Richardson... The Hamilton church of which she was a member. W. F. Robinson.

Tribute of Respect from Clayton and Louisville station to Robert Dill, who was born at Portsmouth, N. H., 18th May 1804, and died at Clayton, Ala., 23d June 1871.

Issue of September 13, 1871

My mother, Mrs. M. M. Cook, the daughter of John Ellison, late of Talbot co., Ga., was born in Charleston and educated at Columbia, S. C. In her 20th year she was married to my father, Rev. Francis Cook, then of Camden, S. C. She died August 1, 1871, in the 63d year of her age. W. F. Cook

Col. Jack Thorington was born in Bristol, England, in 1809, and died in Montgomery, Ala., Aug. 6, 1871. His parents were natives of Ireland. They came to America and settled in Montgomery in 1828. He leaves a widow and three sons.

Sister Hessy C. Taylor, wife of David M. Taylor and daughter of Joshua and Ann Harris, was born in Cabaras [sic] co., N. C., April 1866, and died 16th July 1871. She joined the Presbyterian church and remained until her marriage in 1839. In 1840 they moved to Carrol co., Ga., and in 1844 to Paulding, Ga., where Hugh C. Taylor, their first born, joined the M. E. Church in 1868 and was killed 14 July 1869. Miles D. Norton

Mrs. Francis Martin, wife of Robert Martin of Columbia county, Ga., was a Virginian by birth,but in early life came to Georgia where she died June 10th in her 84th year. W. A. Fariss

Miss Sarah E., daughter of Rev. J. F. Dickinson, deceased, was born August 25, 1858, and died August 5, 1871, having survived her grandfather, John P. Dickinson, only five days.

Mrs. Isabella Wheeler, whose maiden name was Hamilton, widow of Paul Wheeler, who fell in defense of his country during the late war, died in Putnam co., Ga., June 5, 1871. W. W. Oslin

John B. Postell, son of James and Rebecca Postell, was born October 23, 1853, and died July 21st 1871.

M. J. Potts, a scholar in Chulafinnee (Ala.) Sunday-school, died on 1st August.

Tribute of Respect from Tuskegee ct., Ala. Conference, to Wm. E. Stewart.

SOUTHERN CHRISTIAN ADVOCATE NOTICES 1867-1878

Issue of September 20, 1871

Died

John William, son of John and Esther Ann Breanen, of Lancashire, England, died in Charleston, S. C., July 8, 1871, age eighteen months.

Obituary

Mrs. Mary Rabun Bass died at the residence of her son-in-law, Dr. Thomas Powell, in Atlanta, Ga., Aug. 31, 1871, in the 66th year of her age. She was the daughter of Gov. Wm. Rabun and the widow of Dr. Larkin Bass. Her body has been conveyed to Sparta, Hancock county....

Mrs. Sarah A. W. Maxwell, wife of James A. Maxwell, was born in Washington co., Ga., Oct. 15th 1822 and died in Griffin, Ga., July 27th 1871. She joined the Methodist Church May 3, 1839 at Wesley Chapel, Savannah, Ga.

Major John H. Hughes was born in Columbia, S. C., 5th Sept 1861, and died in Edgefield co., 16th Aug 1871. J. W. Humbert

John G. Lot was born in Fairfield Dist., S. C., April 28th 1799 and died in Forsyth co., Ga., Aug 9th 1871. in 1826 he moved to Georgia and in Hall County in 1826 or 1827, gave his hand to uncle Wm. Parks and his name to the Methodist Episcopal Church.

Moses Jenkins Potts, son of Henry Jenkins and Virginia Potts, was born Aug. 31st 1853 and died Aug. 1st 1871, in Chulafinne, Cleborn co., Ala. E. B. Norton. N. O. Christian Advocate please copy.

Mrs. Margaret Staton, relict of John R. Staton of Fort Gaines, Ga., was born April 1801 and died July 21st 1871. S. Anthony

Mrs. Mary Eliza Ruff Dubard, wife of brother Nathan Dubard, of Richland Dist., S. C., was born Nov. 19th 1839 and died June 22d 1871. She leaves three children, her husband and many friends. S. L. Shuford

Lula B. Myrick, daughter of Marcellus Myrick of Dooly co., Ga., and grand-daughter of Benj. H. and Susan F. Stroud of Crawford co., Ga., was born Sept. 2d 1859 and died Aug. 17th 1871. M. D. Stroud

Tribute of Respect to Charles J. Shelton.

Tribute of Respect by 3d Quarterly Conference of the Black Swamp circuit to Edmond Martin.

Issue of September 27, 1871

Died

At Belville, Fla., Aug. 31st 1871, Mattie Lou, only daughter of Dr. W. A. and S. M. Rowland, aged four years and fifteen days.

Mary Ida, daughter of Wm. and Mary C. Jones, was born in Gaston county, N. C., and died in Coffee county, Ga., Sept. 7th 1871, aged 1 year 7 months and 4 days.

Obituary

Sarah J. Russell, youngest daughter of Burwel and Martha Russell, was born Jan. 31, 1829 and died Aug. __ 1871, in Eatonton, Ga.

Sister Amanda Coney, wife of Bro. W. C. Coney of Cave Spring, Floyd co., Ga., was born April 1, 1837 and died June 12, 1871. She was her mother's youngest child, two years old at her mother's daughter, and was the devoted sister of Rev. W. P. Pledger of the No. Ga. Conference. Soon after her marriage (Nov. 11, 1859)....

Bro. Tyre Jay of Abbeville co., S. C., died July 17, 1871, in the 71st year of his age. R. L. Duffey. Also a tribute of Respect from the 3d Quarterly Conference of Dorn's Mine ct.

The Rev. William N. Averitt was born in No. Ca; settled in early life in Twiggs co., Ga., thence moved to Florida, then to Early co., Ga., and after a few years to Decatur co., where he died July 7, 1871, aged 70 years. He was three times married, his last wife surviving him. He left also children....

Mrs. Martha Ann Callier, wife of J. A. Callier, was born in Upson co., Ga., June 19, 1836 and died at Fort Deposit, Ala., Aug. 15, 1871. J. W. Shores

Robert M. Edwards died of yellow fever in Charleston, S. C., Sept. 2, 1871, a native of Brunswick, N. J., about 40 years old. He leaves a wife and three small children. John M. Carlisle

Miss Lucy Elizabeth Fetnam, daughter of Henry and Hannah Sophia Stipe, was born in Campbell co., Ga., July 3, 1853 and died in Palmetto, Ga., August 21, 1871. J. M. Bowden

Richard D. McIntosh, son of John T. and Margaret I. McIntosh of Carroll co., Ga., was born Dec. 26, 1853, and died July 31, 1871. Wm. Simmons

Mrs. Mary Ann Fraker, wife of George D. Fraker and daughter of Isaac N. Hair, was born in Washington co., Tenn., 1836 and died near Dalton, Ga., August 18, 1871.

Mrs. Sarah Exley was born Dec. 15, 1791, and died at the residence of her son-in-law, B. J. Morels, Effingham co., Ga., June 15, 1871. This aged servant of God was a member of the Lutheran Church for nearly 60 years.

Mrs. Sallie Jones, wife of J. Thomas Jones and daughter of A. Nichols, Esq., was born 14th June 1833 and died near Nichols' depot, Marion, S. C., 23d June 1871, aged about 38 years.

Sister Martha J. Reeves was born Feb. 20, 1837 and died at Anderson C. H., S. C., Aug. 19, 1871. W. A. Hodges

Bro. Henry Behling died at George's Station, Colleton co., on the 6th inst., in the 38th year of his age.

David Clinton Jackson, eldest son of Brother D. H. and Sister Martha Jackson, died near Land Hill P. O., Carroll co., Ga., June 29, 1871, aged 9 years, 9 months and 16 days.

Tribute of Respect from Lynchburg, S. C., Conference held at Shiloh, S. C., to Rev. Asbury M. Rush.

Issue of October 4, 1871

Died

In Morgan co., Ga., Sept 8th 1871, Margaret K. Rogers, daughter of Henry T. and Emilie K. Rogers, aged 3 years and 8 months.

In Branchville, S. C., Sept. 13th 1871, Julie E., daughter of John W. and Lavinia Fairy, aged 1 year, 9 months and 13 days.

James Britton Edward, son of Britton J. and Sarah Olive Martin, died in Orangeburg co., S. C., Sept. 14th 1871, aged six months and one week.

Obituary

Albert H. Birdsong was born 20 May 1844 and died in the city of Macon 23d September 1871.

Thos. Edward Williamson was born in Caswell co., N. C., August 29th 1797 and died August 13th 1871. He moved from North Carolina to Clark co., Ga., in 1824, where he resided for some thirty years. He moved to Floyd co., Ga., in 1854, lived in Glenville on the Coosa River about nine years. He was a resident of Floyd county about seventeen years and six months.

Mrs. Maria C. Harwell, wife of Ransom Harwell, deceased, of Jasper co., Ga., was born January 25th 1810 and died August 11, 1871. A. W. Rowland

Augustus M. Smith, son of brother Lyman Smith, was born in Leon co., Fla., October 20th 1850 and died 17th August 1871. E. L. T. Blake

Mrs. Mary Wall, wife of the late James G. Wall, died in Twiggs county, on the 17th September in the 74th year of her age. W. C. Bass

John A. McKay died in Crawford county on 23d August. He was born 10th February 1810 in Chesterfield Dist., S. C., married the daughter of the Rev. James Postell and moved to Houston co., Ga. G. W. Persons

Wilson M. Dorman died on 7th September 1871 on Maple Swamp in Horry co., S. C., in the fortieth year of his age. Mr. Dorman's ancestors were among the first settlers on the Lake Swamp in Horry County. He leaves a large family and connections.

Issue of October 11, 1871

Died

James G., oldest son of Winfield Robison, died at his father's house.

Obituary

Mr. Stephen G. Wells died in Columbus, Ga., July 30th 1871, aged seventy six years and two months. He was born in Mt. Vernon, Maine, and came to Columbus nearly forty years ago.

Major Charles Irby Shelton was born in Pittsylvania co., Va., and died on 19th July in Telfair co., Ga., in the 84th year of his age. In the last war with Great Britain, he was a faithful soldier. He was married to Miss Jane Ashley Boyd on the 2d Oct 1826. They lost three promising sons in the Southern army during the late war.

Mrs. Elizabeth M. Tyler, daughter of the late Dr. V. D. V. Jamison of S. C., died in Columbus, Ga., July 31st 1871, aged 55 years. A. M. Wynn

Capt. Jerome M. Fulton was born in York Dist., S., C., March 1st 1830, and died in Petersburg, Va., July 27th 1871. In October 1861 he married my sister... Samuel A. Weber. Petersburg Index please copy.

Sister Elizabeth Sewell, relict of J. L. Sewell, died in Meriwether co., Ga., June 29th 1871. She was born in Gwinnett co., Ga., in 1816, the daughter of Zackery and Rebecca Lee of precious memory. R. F. Jones

Alice, youngest daughter of Judge A. M. and Mrs. Mary Speer of Griffin, Ga., died in Whitefield co., during a brief summer visit, on 16th August. J. W. H.

Mrs. Margaret A. Agnew, wife of John Agnew, was born August 8th 1816 and died in Walker co., Ga., July 19th 1871. She was buried in the family cemetery with her parents. Thos H. Timmons

Sister Mary E. Fleming was born February 20th 1840 and died in Jefferson co., Ga., August 21st 1871. R. W. Flournoy

Sister Susan A. Downing, daughter of Jacob and Mary Smilie, was born in Montgomery county, Ala., Oct. 1833 and died in Alachua co., Fla., Sept 15th 1871. On 30th Jan 1853 she was married to brother Thos. W. Downing, who still lives, with their seven little girls. J. M. Stokes

Miss Sarah Wilcox, daughter of James D. Wilcox deceased, and Caroline M. Wilcox, was born in Irwin county, Ga., March 27th 1854, and died August 38th 1871 in Montgomery co., Ga. W. M. Kennedy

Issue of October 18, 1871

Died

George Towns, infant son of Mr. J. E. and L. M. Walker, near Raynolds, Ga., on 4th October, aged nine and a half months.

In Washington, Ga., on 3d October, James Vance, infants on of Jas. M. and Caroline Dubose, aged three years and five months.

Obituary

Sarah Elizabeth, wife of Dr. B. Waller Taylor, was born in Edgefield, S. C., February 1, 1815, and died in Monticello, Fla., September 21, 1871.

Susan E., beloved wife of X. H. Bagley and daughter of T. J. and Rebecca Lesley, died at her father's residence, near Silver Run, Ala., on 24th August 1871, aged 26 years. Emma Wilson

Capt. Samuel A. Hodges of Cokesbury, S. C., was born October 1st 1802, and died Sept. 11th 1871, in his 68th year. He was tax collector and sheriff of the district.

Mrs. Mildred V. Singleton, wife of Dr. F. P. Singleton, and daughter of W. H. Greer, was born Nov. 29th 1837, was married to Dr. F. P. Singleton on Nov. 6th, 1856, and died at Carsonville, Ga., August 18, 1871. J. R. Littlejohn

Mrs. Mary A. M. King, wife of L. P. Z. King, and daughter ot the late William and Mary King, died near Hartsville, Darlington co., S. C., Sept. 2d, 1871, in the 37th year of her age.

Mrs. Nancy A. Meaders, wife of C. A. Meaders, was born May 6, 1847, and died in Gainesville, Ga., Aug. 26, 1871. Geo. E. Gardner

George W. Dukes, son of Thomas E. and Susan Dukes, died in Orangeburg Dist., S. C., Sept. 1st 1871, in his 20th year. He was left early an orphan.

Mrs. Eliza M. C. Walker, daughter of Abel Nutting, of Vermont, was born Jan. 25th 1825, and died Aug. 30th 1871. Mrs. W. moved to Georgia with her brothers more than thirty years ago. She was married first to Mr. Moses A. Hirston, of Jasper co., Ga.; after his death to Mr. E. F. Walker, or

Monroe co., Ga. She was the mother of six children, one by her first marriage and five by her last, all of whom are still alive. By her second marriage she became a step-mother. J. J. Singleton

Mrs. Rebecca A. Marbut was a daughter of James J. and Nancy Diamond of DeKalb co., Ga., and the wife of Euclidus Marbut, of Polk Co., Ga., was born July 16th 1823, and died July 23d, 1871. W. P. R.

Mrs. Elizabeth H. McCulloh was born in Hancock co., Ga., Dec. 1812 and died in Walker Co., Ga., Aug. 10th 1871.

Issue of October 25, 1871

Died

Little Pearl, daughter of F. A. and M. E. Phillips, died at the residence of her father, near Perote, Alabama, on 14th Sept. 1871, aged about five years.

In Bishopville, Sumter county, S. C., Oct. 8th 1871, Lizzie Reams, infant daughter of Charles S. and Mary L. Barrett, aged 10 months and 17 days.

Obituary

My father, Moses Padgett, died 10th August in Fayette co., Ga., aged 85 years and 10 days. He came from Putnam co., Ga., and settled in Fayette co., in 1824 where he lived until a few years back. He raised fourteen children-- Rev. Moses Padgett of Alabama Conference, Rev. John R. Padgett, of Texas, are sons of his. Mrs. C. E. Glover

Mary Elizabeth, wife of Dr. Chas. A. Hentz, was born in Gadsden co., Fla., on 20th Sept 1831, and died in Quincy, Fla., on 13th Sept 1871.

H. A. Flowers died on the 3d of Sept. 1871. Much of her life was spent in Alabama, yet she returned to South Carolina, her native state, about ten years before her death. Eva Blanch

Mattie Tallulah Nolan was born June 30th 1857 and died Aug. 13th 1871 in Morgan co., Ga. W. R. Foote

Mrs. Mary E. Templeton, wife of John C. Templeton and daughter of Benjamin L. and Rosa P. Wooding, died in Burke co., Ga., 9th Oct, in her 32d year. N. B. Ousley

Miss Carrie V., daughter of Benjamin L. and Rosa P. Wooding, died in Burke co., Ga., 27th August, in her 21st year.

Mrs. Emma S. Hendrick, wife of Thos. A. Hendrick and daughter of the Rev. F. D. and M. S. Poyas of Pickens co., Ala., died near Aberdeen, Miss., Aug. 21st, 1871. Nashville Christian Advocate please copy.

Thomas S. Mood, a licensed exhorter in the Methodist Episcopal Church, South, connected with the Washington St. charge, Columbia, S. C., died on 13th September 1871. He leaves a widow and several children.

Ira Story, only son of Col. R. L. Story of Wilkinson co., died on 16th ult., aged 8 years and 7 months.

Serena Elizabeth McElmoyl, aged 31 years, died September 19th 1871. She was a member of the Methodist Church at Philadelphia Church, Yorkville ct., S. C. Conference.

Issue of November 1, 1871

Died

In Tampa, Fla., on 18th Oct., of yellow fever, Mrs. Mattie Tyner, wife of Rev. E. S. Tyner of the Florida Conference. Wm. E. Collins

Obituary

Mrs. Hibernia Lawrence Berry, wife of William B. Berry, Esq., of Newnan, Ga., was born 20th of November 1827 and died on October 4th. She leaves a husband and three children, an aged mother. J. S. B.

Mrs. Silvia Young, whose maiden name was Tarver, was born in Burke co., Ga., October 2d 1797, and with her parents moved to Hancock county, where on 20th March 1816 she was married to Rev. Enos Young, with whom she lived for more than fifty-five years--having died suddenly in Dooly county, where she had lived for twenty five years. She leaves an aged husband and children.

Mrs. Sarah Cornelia Rowland, wife of David R. Rowland and daughter of Thos. H. and Patience Smith was born June 9th 1848, and died in Green co., Ga., September 13th 1871. J. M. Louray

Maggie Amelia Mallette, eldest daughter of Dr. J. A. and Mrs. M. J. Mallette of Thomas co., Ga., died in Brooks co., Ga., at her uncle William McAllister's residence on 12th October 1871, in her 16th year.

Mr. Arra Stearns was born in Ogdensburg, N. Y., and died in Eufaula, Ala., October 5th, in the 61st year of his age. In early manhood he removed to Columbia, S. C., where he was engaged in the mercantile business. He has left a widow, two sons and three daughters.

Miss Anna Jane, eighth daughter of Stephen and Susan Boswell, formerly of Pike co., Ala., was born August 20th 1830 and died September 14th 1871. W. F. Norton, P. C.

Mrs. Malinda Beall, daughter of Edward Woodham and widow of James Beall, was born 9th of October 1795 and died in Monroe co., Ga., July 20th 1871. She joined the Methodist Church in Green county, Georgia, when fifteen or sixteen years of age. J. J. Singleton

Mrs. Smith Perry was born in Hancock co., Ga., February 1800 and died at the house of her daughter, Mrs. Georgia Ann Gardner, in Russell co., Ala., September 27th 1871. T. H. Dawson

Mrs. Ebenade Parker, wife of Wm. W. Parker and daughter of J. C. and Sarah Duck, was born September 18th 1850, was married 26th of December 1869, and died September 15th 1871. S. R. Weaver

John W. King departed this life August 17th 1871 in his 38th year. G. H. Wells

Mrs. Amy A. Matheny died on the 13th July 1871 in her 54th year. W. C. Dunlap

Helen M. Jourdan, daughter of Thomas and Hannah K. P. Early, died in Timmonsville, S. C., October 4th 1871, in her 19th year. G. H. Wells. Sumter, S. C., papers please copy.

Tribute of Respect from Hancock circuit held in Culverton, to Bro. Joseph K. Sanford.

Issue of November 8, 1871

Died

Levi Martin, son of T. J. and Zuletta Lineberger, was born at Snow Creek, Iredell co., N. C., and died in Coffee co., Ga. Oct. 2d 1871, aged 2 years, 3 months and 28 days.

Obituary

Joseph H. Hines, a citizen of Washington co., Ga., was born 30th Dec. 1820 and died on 14th Oct. 1871. He was taken away almost without a moment's warning, at No. 7, C. R. R., while on his way to Savannah. Central Georgian please copy.

Brother Samuel W. Tucker, a native of Spartanburg co., S. C., was born August 23, 1792, and died August 17th 1871.

Brother Joseph Roberts was born in West Indies, on 14th July 1806 and died in Brunswick, Ga., on 11th Oct 1871. J. O. A. Cook

Brother Israel M. Shell was born in Va., 30th March 1787 and died in Coweta county, Ga., on 5th Oct 1871.

Sister Susannah Mallard of St. George's Mission, Charleston District, S. C., died September 24th 1871, aged 78 years and 8 months. She leaves five children and many relatives. J. Hamilton Knight.

Frances J. Craig, son of W. E. and M. P. Craig, was born Sept 17th 1854, and died at Doctor James Craig's, near Cheraw, S. C., Sept. 19th 1871. J. B. Platt

Brother Wm. R. Curry was born in May 1811 in Richmond co., N. C., and died in Dodge co., Ga., June 30th 1871. L. B. Payne

Sarah A. Funches, wife of Jacob S. Funches and daughter of George and Sarah A. Bowman, was born Oct. 14th 1830 and died Sept. 17th 1871. W. Carson

Ella Johnston, daughter of Mrs. M. B. Johnston and grand daughter of the late Col. Bates of Edgefield, S. C., died on 10th Oct. near Atlanta, Ga., in the 15th year of his age. T. A. Holmes

Mrs. Rebecca H. Glass died in Newnan, Ga., Oct. 8th 1871, in the 63d year of her age. R. W. B.

Tribute of Respect from Sumter ct., S. C. Conference to Rev. H. D. Green who died 19th April 1871.

Tribute of Respect from Edgefield ct., S. C. Conference, to Maj. John H. Hughes.

Issue of November 15, 1871

Died

On Oct. 28th 1871, Robert Gage, youngest child of Rev. John and Hannah E. Finger, of the S. C. Conference, aged 4 years, 11 months and 8 days.

In Decatur co., Ga., Oct. 31st 1871, Sophia Hora, daughter of C. C. and Elizabeth Wimberly, aged 2 years and 3 months.

Obituary

Mrs. America Riggins died at her home in Bibb co., Ga., Sept. 30th 1871, in the 59th year of her age. W. C. Bass

Rev. William Franklin Harris was born in Rockingham co., N. C., on 1 May 1823 and died in Atlanta, Ga., Aug. 6th 1871. He was a graduate of Emory and Henry College in Virginia and afterwards professor in the Female College at Knoxville, Tenn.

Mrs. Mary Holt, wife of Simon Holt, deceased, died at her residence in Monroe co., Ga., Oct. 22d 1871, in the 86th year of her age. W. C. Bass

Mr. Levi Longshore died in Newberry co., S. C., August 31st 1871, in the 70th year of his age.

Malinda Jane Anderson, wife of Joseph E. Anderson and daughter of Joshua and Mary Ashley, was born Sept 20th 1812 in Abbeville Dist., S. C., and died 14th Oct 1871 in Elbert co.

Sister Amanda J. Matthews, wife of John T. Matthews and daughter of Thos. R. and Margaret McClintock, was born Feb. 28th 1827 in Chester District, and died Oct. 29th 1871 in Gainesville, East Florida. She joined the Methodist Episcopal Church, South, June 1848, two years after her marriage, at Bethesda Church, Fairfield Dist., S. C.

John M. B. Webb died at his mother's residence 29th Oct in the 21st year of his age.

Capt. Jacob E. Pooser died in Marianna, Fla., Sept. 18th 1871. To meet Capt. Pooser was at once an introduction to one of South Carolina's fairest specimens of gentility. D. C. Crook, P. C.

Mrs. Sarah Eugenie, wife of Capt. J. W. McNelly and daughter of Rev. James G. Tison, died in Glennville, Ala., Aug. 24th 1871 in the 23d year of her age. M. F. Crawford

John Bellah of Coweta co., Ga., died at the residence of his son-in-law, Mr. Jesse Rawls, on 22d Sept 1871, in the 90th year of his age. He was the father of Rev. S. J. Bellah of the North Georgia Conference. Brother B. was born in North Carolina and early in life removed to Georgia.

Temperance Selma Hayes was born in Green co., Ga., Nov. 26th 1806, was married to Josiah D. Jarrard, Oct. 16th 1833 and died in Mardesville, Talladega co., Ala., Oct. 14th 1871. David Duncan. Nashville Christian Advocate please copy.

Mrs. Elizabeth Jennings was born May 27th 1798, and died in Orangeburg co., Sept. 2d 1871. John E. Penney

Mr. Philip Lampkin died on Sept. 26th 1871, at his residence in Pike co., Ga., in his 65th year.

Margaret J. Murray, daughter of Peter A. Murray, died Oct. 12th 1871, aged 23 years. John McDonald

Tribute of Respect from Quarterly Conference, LaGrange Station to Thomas B. Greenwood.

Issue of November 22, 1871

Died

In Camden, S. C., Nov. 14th 1871, Willie, son of Rev. A. J. and M. S. Stokes of the S. C. Conference, aged 8 months and 11 days.

Obituary

My dear Mantie, the subject of this obituary, and consort of the Rev. E. S. Tyner of the Florida Conference was born in Talbot county, Georgia, January 1st 1841. She was the daughter of Mr. and Mrs. Marshall. She fell a victim to the malignant fever in Tampa, October 18th 1871. Her father died when she was an infant. A few weeks after her marriage which was on April 12th 1850, her mother died.

Mr. Wm. E. Spencer died in Tampa, Fla., Oct. 25th 1871. He was born in Savannah Ga., 1830, came to Tampa, Fla., in 1843.

Franklin C. Pinkston was born near Sparta, Georgia, December 13, 1810 and died at his own residence near Mt. Meigs, Montgomery co., Ala., Oct. 8, 1871. His father removed from Georgia to Alabama when he was only three or four years old. He had been thrice married. His last wife, who weight eight children mourns his loss, was Aurelia A. Graves.

Mrs. Eliza S. Bradford of Bartow county, Ga., was born April 15th 1833 and died Oct. 4th 1871. R. H. Jones

Lucretia E. Meritt, daughter of M. C. and S. B. Grace, was born Oct. 22d 1829 in Thomas co., Ga., where she died Oct. 14th 1871. She was first married to James Hancock, afterwards to Elijah Meritt. L. M. Sutton

Mrs. Amelia F., wife of Wm. Reaney, Esq., and step-daughter of Mr. Jas Kirkpatrick of Columbia co., Ga., was born in Richmond co., Ga., and died in Augusta, Ga., on 28th Oct last in the 54th year of her age. She resided about 35 years in Columbia co., Ga.

Mrs. Lureny Crawford, the wife of Matthew Crawford, was born Dec. 13th 1815 and died in Lowndes co., Ga., Sept. 30th 1871. Alex. P. Wright

Robert Lee Thompson, second son of S. B. and Laura Thompson and grand son of Doctor Josiah and E. B. Ashurst, of Lake City, Fla., died on 19th October, aged six years and ten months.

Tribute of Respect from Lawrenceville circuit, Eufaula Dist., Alabama Conference, at Bethel Church to Rev. Enoch Bolton, who died at his home near Abbeville, Henry co., Ala., on 20th Oct.

Tribute of Respect from Valdosta circuit to Matthew Crawford.

Issue of November 29, 1871

Died

On September 18th ult., Afton Lee, aged four years; on the 22d October last, Christopher Billups, aged ten years; and on October 27th, Henry Mortimer, aged eight years, sons of Col. S. M. and Mary E. Strong, residing near Thomasville.

November 18 at 9 o'clock, Martha C., infant daughter of Joseph N. and R. A. Hardin, died from dyphtheria, aged seven months and three days.

Obituary

Wm. Hammond, one of the oldest as he was one of the best citizens of Whitfield county, died at his residence, near Dalton, on Friday night, Oct. 20th 1871. He was the son of Job Hammond and Lucy Howard his wife, and was born in Elbert co., Ga., in 1792. In 1818 he married Frances Aker of Pendleton Dist., S. C. She only lived ten years, and in 1832 he married Lucy C. Hudson, widow of Thomas P. Carter, who survives him. After his second marriage he removed to Franklin county, and from thence to what is now Bradley co., Tenn, then a part of the Cherokee Nation. In 1836 he removed to this (then Murray) county and settled at the home now occupied by his widow. G. G. Smith

Sister Sarah A. Johnston was born in Jackson co., Ga., Dec. 23d, 1833 and died in McDuffie co., Sept. 24th 1871. T. A. Seals

Mrs. Ana M. Dickey, wife of Wm. J. Dickey and daughter of W. H. and M. A. T. Reynolds, was born Jan. 24th 1823, and died at her home in Thomas co., Oct. 13th 1871. Chas E. Brown

Mrs. Wilhelmina E. Torley, daughter of the late Robert S. Purse, of Charleston, S. C., and wife of Mr. Alfred F. Torley, died in Savannah, Ga., Nov. 2d, 1871, in the 30th year of her age. Geo G. N. MacD.

Issue of December 6, 1871

Died

Of croup in Conyers, Ga., on the 14th Nov., Little Bennie, aged four years and eleven months; son of Mr. and Mrs. Wash Clemmons.

Obituary

Georgia Ann Eliza, wife of George R. Black, was born in Scriven co., Ga., August 31st 1834, and died 25th October 1871. She was the daughter of the late Rev. Solomon Bryan, and of his wife Ann Dell Boston. Her father dying when she was a small girl, her mother afterwards was married to an estimable gentleman, the late Robert M. Williamson...

Dr. Jacob C. P. Hook, son of Jacob and Mary Hook, was born in Orangeburg Dist., S. C., March 3d 1820, removed to Ga., in 1843 and died in Milton co., Ga., Sept. 5th 1871.

My sister, Mary Jane Brown, wife of James S. Brown and daughter of Moses and Rebecca Padgett, died 8 September 1871, aged 43 years. She joined the Missionary Baptist Church with her husband. C. E. Glover

Miss Jennie Spear, daughter of the late Simon Spear, died September 16th in Griffin, Ga., aged 17 years.

Sister Margaret Alford died Sept. 27th at the residence of her son, brother H. H. D. Alford, in the 65th year of her age. Sister Alford was born and raised in Horry District, S. C. She married and became the mother of nine children, when she and her husband moved to Sampit, Georgetown District, S. C., in the year 1847 and in the year 1849 her husband died.

Mrs. Sarah Ann Edgerton, daughter of Joseph and Annie Fletcher, died at her father's residence in Gadsden co., Fla., August 30th 1871, aged 31 years, 7 months and 13 days. D. W. Core

Mary J. Fisher, wife of Harris M. Fisher and daughter of Dr. J. M. Palmer and Sarah A. A. Childers of Elbert county, died at Bay Springs, Washington county, Ga., Nov. 10th 1871.

Mrs. Mary A. Mann, wife of Samuel F. Mann and daughter of John and Nancy Means, died in Zebulon, Pike co., Ga., 4th of November 1871, in her 29th year.

Charles L. Peterson, aged 21 years, 2 months, and 20 days, the only son of his mother and she a widow, died in Greenville, South Carolina, on 24th October 1871. L. Wood

Mrs. Mary Parker died in Macon, Oct. 29, 1871, aged 50 years, 11 months, 23 days.

Mrs. Sarah W., wife of Frank S. Hearn, died in Putnam co., Ga., aged 79 years and 6 months. She passed away Nov. 17th.

Sister Milly Ivy, wife of Robert Ivy, was born in South Carolina, Aug. 8th 1798 and died in Newton co., Ga., Oct. 25th 1871. A. C. Mixon

Minnie Bell, daughter of David M. Verner, died near Thomasville, Bullock co., Ala., 28th Oct 1871, aged 12 years and 9 months.

Issue of December 13, 1871

Died

Charlie H. Walker, son of Judge Robert Walker, of Spalding co., Ga., died in Lexicon, Texas, on 17th Oct. 1871.

Obituary

Joseph Brown, one of the oldest and most influential citizens of Talbot co., Ga., died in his 70th year, near Prattsburg, Talbot co., Ga., on 22 Nov 1871. He was born in Abbeville Dist., S. C., 25th Sept. 1801. When he was quite a child, his father died and the widow mother in 1807 removed to her family to Baldwin co., Ga. He was married to Mrs. Mary Schurlock who survives him. Thos T. Christian. Baltimore Methodist please copy.

Capt. J. H. Barksdale died in Savannah, Ga., Oct. 29th 1871, in the 51st year of his age.

John C. Addison was born in Franklin co., Ga., 4th June 1820 and died in Clarksville, Ga., 11th Sept 1871.

Sister Lucinda J. Waddy, wife of Geo. E. Waddy, and daughter of Stephen and Sarah Carnes, died at her father's near Jonesboro, Ga., Sept. 15th 1871. She leaves one child and a husband. L. P. Neese

Mrs. Anna J. Barnett, wife of John E. Barnett and daughter of G. W. and Mrs. M. F. Thomas, was born March 23d 1849 and died at her father's home in Laurens co., Ga., Nov. 4th 1871. She was a member of the Baptist Church. John McCrakin

Miss Adella Ann Alexander died in Franklin co., Ga., Oct. 23d, 1871, in the 27th year of her age. She was a member of the Presbyterian church at Hebron.

Issue of December 20, 1871

Died

In Orangeburg, S. C., on the 16th Sept 1871, Julius Clarence, infant son of Benjamin and Laura M. Pooser, aged on year, 8 months and 16 days.

Obituary

Mrs. Mary S. Culler, the daughter of Hon. Howell Cobb, formerly of Houston county, Ga., and wife of Dr. B. B. D. H. Culler of Perry, died in Macon, Ga., on 28th Nov. 1871, in the 48th year of her age. W. Knox

John Tyler Adams was born in Marlboro co., S. C., August 21st 1841 and died Nov. 7th 1871.

Miss Newdygate A. Moreland, daughter of the late Dr. N. A. and Sarah A. Moreland, was born Feb. 28, 1854, and died at Corinth, Heard co., Ga., Nov. 15, 1871.

Died in Kershaw county, S. C., September 14th 1871. Emma Jane Josephine, aged 4 years and 3 months. On the 21st Sept, John Abner Weaver, aged 9 years and 3 months and 12 days. On the same day (Sept. 21), Henry Allan Tiller, aged 21 years, 1 month and 23 days. This in one week a father has lost three children.

Mrs. Eliza A. Leeman, late of Charleston, S. C., was born Sept. 1st 1801, and died at the residence of her son-in-law, Thos. H. Goodwin, Esq., at Ridgeville, S. C., Sept. 13, 1871. M. H. Pooser

Mrs. Esther Ellzey, wife of Rev. Robt. M. Ellzey and daughter of Henry and Priscilla Holman of Barnwell, S. C., died in her 31st year on 20th Nov. 1871. She was married in 1857. James A. Wiggins

Louisa Jane Stroman in Leon co., Fla., in February 1847. Less than one year ago, she was married to Mr. Judge Williamson of Leon County. She died 19th October 1871. E. L. T. Blake

Sister Nancy M. Presley, wife of W. V. Presley, died in Gainesville, Fla., Nov. 24, 1871. R. H. Barnett

Mrs. Ann Dickson, wife of William Dickson, was born 22 June 1809 and died in Houston co., Ga., 1 October 1871. W. W. Sentell

Mrs. Dora A. Beckman died Nov. 30th at Lake City, Fla., leaving a husband and two little children. She was born May 2d 1845.

Mrs. Julia A. Jernigan was born March 20th 1821 and died at Lake City, Fla., Nov. 15, 1871.

Issue of December 27, 1871

Died

On the 14th inst., at Sno Hill, Horry co., S. C., little Beulah, infant daughter of Frank and Addie Burroughs, aged five years.

Obituary

Mrs. Sarah A. Gaither, wife of Dr. Henry Gaither, died in Oxford, Ga., on 13th Oct., at the age of 60 years. A. Means

Mrs. Charlotte Hays was born in North Carolina, Nov. 20th 1790. When about two weeks old she was deprived by death of her mother. Shortly after this, her father, Capt. John Orr, removed to South Carolina and settled in Pendleton Dist. (now Anderson) near Ebenezer Church, where she on 19th Jan 1809 was married to Mr. Thomas Hays. In 1827 she came with her husband to Georgia and settled in DeKalb co., where in 1831 her husband died, leaving her in charge of a family of eight children--seven daughters and one son, and also her father-in-law and mother-in-law. While on a visit to Gordon co., at her daughter's (widow of Rev. Daniel Groover, deceased) she died. S. J. Bellah

Benjamin L. Harper, Lay-Delegate from Griffin District.. about sixty-five years of age.

William W. Tippins was born in Washington co., Ga., Sept. 2d 1796 and died in Tatnall co., Nov. 11th 1871. He leaves an aged wife and 5 children, 45 grandchildren and 18 great grandchildren.

Mrs. Elizabeth Rogers, daughter of William and Elizabeth Butler, was born in Lexington Dist., S. C., August 13th 1812 and died at the residence of her daughter in Quitman co., Ga., Oct. 10th 1871. She joined the Lutheran Church in 1850. In 1866 she joined the Methodist Church. J. R. Owen

Bro. Geo. N. A. Honnady was born in Jones co., Ga., 13th May 1840 and died 11th Oct. 1871 in Butler co., Ala. He leaves a wife and one child. B. L. Selman.

Bro. Geo. N. A. Honnady was born in Jones co., Ga., 13th May 1840 and died 11th Oct. 1871 in Butler co., Ala. He leaves a wife and one child. B. L. Selman.

Issue of January 10, 1872

Died

In Baldwin county on the 28th inst., in her eighty-second year, Elizabeth G. B., wife of Rev. Tilman Snead and daughter of the late Robert B. and Elizabeth Washington.

Lou Myles, daughter of J. C. and Elizabeth Wright, and great grand-daughter of the Rev. Myles Greene, deceased, was born 5th December 1865 and died 25th September 1871 in Chattahoochee county, Georgia.

Roberta, infant of Newton and Leudie Smith, and grand-child of A. M. and M. E. Danielly, of Hickory Grove, Crawford co., Ga., on Dec 3d, aged four months and twenty-three days.

Obituary

Elizabeth Stilwell was born in Mecklenburg county, North Carolina, November 3d, 1773, and died in Spalding county, Georgia, Dec. 14th 1871. She was the daughter of William and Margaret Houston. She married Elijah Stilwell, 17th Jan 1793, who died 6th Sept 1846. [account] John Stilwell

Mrs. Fanny Branch, wife of Dr. Isaac Branch, died at Abbeville C. H., on the morning of the 28th of November 1871, in the 66th year of her age.

B. L. Harper of McDonough, Henry county, Georgia, was born in Jasper co., Ga., in the year 1809 and died in Athens, Ga., Dec. 2d, 1871. He leaves and wife and six children. John H. Harris.

Mrs. Frances Harriet Jordan, wife of Rev. Junius Jordan, died on the 6th of Nov. 1871 in Eufaula, Ala. She was the daughter of Edward and Elizabeth Weyman, born in St. Mary's Ga., 14th Feb. 1814 and educated in Norwich, Connecticut. Removed thence in orphanage to Charleston, S. C., where she spent many years with relatives and was married in Columbus, Ga., 1st Dec 1836. She joined the Methodist Episcopal Church, South, at Glennville, Ala., in 1846.

Mrs. Mary Hanson Fletcher Stevens was born in Putnam co., Ga., March 1st 1823. Her maiden name was Burt. She was married to Milton Stevens, Nov. 16th, 1840, spent most of her married life in Tuskegee, Ala., where she died Dec. 19th 1871.

John Porter, Sen., died in Lancaster, S. C., on 7th Nov 1871, at the advanced age of 91 years, wanting a few weeks. He was a member of the Presbyterian Church for many years. His last wife was a Methodist lady. He left a widow whose maiden name was Jane Cherry, and two sons by a former marriage. W. C. Patterson

John C. Templeton died in Burke county, Ga., on 29th Oct about 30 years of age. He was called early to follow his wife, Mary Templeton, who preceded him three weeks.

Mrs. Mary Kemp departed this life on the 16th Dec 1871. She was about 95 years old.

Issue of January 17, 1872

Died

Little Forest L., son of J. B. and M. L. Young of Pine Level, Ala., was born April 21st 1866, and died December 8th 1871.

Obituary

Capt. Arnold Seals was born April 20th 1795 and died at Warrior Stand, Ala., Nov. 14th 1871. [long eulogy] Columbus Sun please copy.

My precious mother, Mrs. Margaret Jones, wife of Henry B. Jones and daughter of John Rudisill, died on Saturday night the 23d of December 1871, aged 57 years. Virginia

Mrs. Jane Rivers, wife of Joseph Rivers, formerly of August and Gainesville, Georgia, was born February 14th 1796 in Kent county, Delaware, and died on the 30th December 1871, in Cave Spring, Georgia.

Mrs. Mary W. Byrd was born in Warren co., N. C., 25th of October 1803 and died in Clarksville, Georgia, 14th of October 1871. John R. Parker

Mrs. Mary Walker died October 13th 1871, in Panola county, Texas, in the 61st year of her age. She was born in Abbeville, S. C., and resided there until __ years ago, when, to gratify the wishes of an only son, she removed to Texas. Mrs. Walker, whose maiden name was Cunningham....

Sarah Sineath, wife of Barney Sineath, died in Berrien county, Georgia, on the 27th November 1871, in the 43d year of her age. H. W. Sharpe

Martha Bradford, daughter of Buckner and Mary Harris, was born October 8th 1827 in Gwinnett county, Georgia, married to W. E. Bradford, November 1st 1858, and died November 17th 1871.

Martha A. Gentry, daughter of J. M. and M. J. Gentry, was born June 6th 1864 and died October 30th 1871, in Troup county, Georgia.

Issue of January 24, 1872

[on page two:] Death of Rev. J. M. Sherwood. We regret to learn from private advices, as well as through the Fayette Eagle, of the death of this minister, who was the editor of the North Carolina Presbyterian. Mr. Sherwood died in his 50th year.

Died in Marion, S. C., Dec. 28th 1871, Mr. Hamilton Mitchell, aged nearly seventy-four years. He was a native of Balomony, Ireland. His son, Rev. Thomas Mitchell. Christian Neighbor.

[on page four]: Susan E. J. McGehee, daughter of S. W. and Caroline E. McGehee, was born in Meriwether county, Ga., May 30, 1828 and died of lung disease in Jefferson county, Ark., Nov. 23d 1871, leaving her husband and three sons, one an infant three months old, besides her father and step-mother. S. W. McGehee

Rev. Dr. James Griffith, for many years superintendent of the Methodist and Baptist Union Sunday-school of Butler, Ga., died November 30th 1871.

Jane Caroline Moore, daughter of Hewlet and Mary Sullivan and wife of Samuel Moore, deceased was born the 21st Sept. 1798 and died 17th Nov. 1871.

Margaret Ella, wife of Samuel McInnis, of White Spring, Florida, died Nov. 8th 1871.

Mrs. Mary Johnson died in Atlanta, Nov. 26th 1871, aged 71 years. She leaves a husband, son and daughter. Wm. A. Simmons

Joseph E. Garlington, son of Thos. C. and Elizabeth Garlington, died in Chambers county, Ala., 22d December 1871, in the 23d year of her age. Christian Index please copy.

William Edwards was born in Culpepper county, Virginia, 28th of August 1799, and died 10th of December 1871 at the residence of his sister in Cherokee county, Georgia. Thomas J. Edwards

Tribute of Respect to Mrs. Mary S. Culler, who was born Nov. 17th 1828 and died Nov. 27th 1871, by Perry Union Sabbath-school.

Issue of January 31, 1872

Rev. Bryan Roberts was born in Iredell county, N. C., January 23d 1804, and died in Gilmer county, Ga., Nov. 6th 1871. He left a widow and children. J. M. Watkins

Mrs. Maggie Roberts Lester, wife of Samuel E. B. Lester and oldest daughter of George Roberts, formerly of Augusta, Georgia, was born October 3d 1847, and died in Savannah, Georgia, December 19th 1871. In 1868 she lost her mother.

William Hostler was born in Anderson county, Tennessee, January 17th 1807 and died November 3d 1871. He came to Murray county, Georgia. H. H. Porter

Mrs. Elizabeth G. B., wife of Rev. Tilman Snead and daughter of Robert D. and Elizabeth Washington, was born in Edgefield District, South Carolina, May 19th 1799 and died in Baldwin county, Georgia, on the 28th December 1871. Her father moved in 1791 to Washington, Wilkes county, Georgia, where she resided until her marriage, June 15th 1818. He husband was an itinerant Methodist preacher. Thos. H. Stewart

Dr. M. T. C. Lovelace of West Point, Ga., fell asleep in Jesus, January 8th 1871. He was born in Columbia county, October 8th 1797; moved to Troup county in 1833 and was married to Miss Eliza J. Smith, sister of the present Governor of Georgia, on January 16th 1856.

William Stripling was born in Hancock county, Georgia, February 20th 1799 and died at his residence in Bibb county, January 7th 1872. He was buried in the graveyard at Liberty Chapel.

Died near Montezuma, Macon county, Georgia, on the 5th January 1872, Dr. A. D. Smith, aged 35 years and 8 months. He was elected Mayor of Montezuma in 1871, and re-elected in 1872. He left four children.

Joshua Kennett died at his residence near Covington, Georgia, January 2d in the 78th year of his age.

Miss Loretta Chappell, daughter of Mrs. Matilda Chappell, died near West Point, Georgia, September 6th 1871, aged 22 years.

Lewis Saxon was born in Laurens District, South Carolina, on 3d August 1807 and died October 6th 1871, within a few miles of his birthplace. Jas. F. Smith. Laurensville Herald copy.

Mrs. Mary Gault was born in Essex county, Georgia, January 19th 1804 and died in Cherokee county, Georgia, September 19th 1871. Jas. F. Smith. Union Times copy.

Tribute of Respect from LaGrange Quarterly Conference to Dr. H. A. T. Ridley, who died 20th December 1871.

Issue of February 7, 1872

Miss Sallie E. Smith, daughter of the late Rev. Burgess Smith, was born in Franklin county, Ga., 9th April 1848 and died in West End, Atlanta, Ga., 5th October 1871.

Mary Eliza Jones, daughter of Capt. Lewis and Rebecca Jones, of Edgefield county, died in Spartanburg, S. C., at the residence of W. K. Blake, on Tuesday 16th January 1872.

Col. A. A. Franklin Hill was born in Oglethorpe county, Ga., Dec. 4th 1836 and died in Barbour county, Ala., Jan. 9th 1871 [sic]. He was graduated at Franklin College in 1845 and received the degree of M. D. in 1848 at Jefferson Medical School, Philadelphia. He served for six years as assistant surgeon in the United States navy, and for a short time edited the Southern Banner, at Athens, Ga. In June 1869 he was married to Miss Gazzle Williams, daughter of Maj. Gassoway Williams, of Alabama. He leaves and wife and child.

Maj. Wiley E. Jones was born in Warren county, Ga., and died in Bibb county, near Macon, 16th of January 1872. While a child his father moved to Jones county, where he was reared and educated. He married Miss Wiggins in his 24th year. Soon after, he moved to Columbus, Ga., where he lived for thirty years or more. Col. H. J. Lamar, his son-in-law.

Tribute of Respect by Quarterly Conference, Mulberry St. charge, Macon, Ga. James Williams was born in Edgecombe county, N. C., Feb. 10th 1795, was married to Catharine Arnett, Oct. 20th 1818, and died at his residence in Macon, Ga., Oct. 17th 1871.

Cornelius A. Norwood, youngest son of L. D. and C. A. Norwood, of Houston county, Ga., died November 14th 1871.

Catharine Elizabeth, daughter of A. S. and Margaret Colquitt, was born October 5th 1845, and died in Clay county, Ala., Dec. 18th 1871. L. E. Bell

Issue of February 14, 1872

Rev. Churchwell Anderson Crowell was born in Mecklenburg county, North Carolina, September 15th 1806 and died at Magnolia Springs, Sumter county, Georgia, Jan 16th 1872. He was in charge of circuits in North Carolina, South Carolina, and Georgia.

Mrs. Emma Frances Dawson, daughter of Rev. S. and E. F. Harwell was born Nov. 12th 1847. She was married to George W. Dawson, Oct. 12th 1863, and died in Opelika, Ala., Dec. 16th 1871. Mary S. Harwell. New Orleans Christian Advocate please copy.

Joseph F. C. Harley was born in Orangeburg District, South Carolina, Nov. 15th 1805, removed to Middle Georgia in early childhood, thence to Alabama in his thirteenth year, and in 1825 came to Florida, where he purchased land at the first public land sales in the State. He died 28th Nov 1871. In January 1833 he was married to Elizabeth A. Whitehurst. E. L. T. Blake

James Jackson Whitehurst was born in the State of Alabama, August 30th 1820, removed with his parents to Leon county, Florida, in 1838, was married in October 1847 to Mary E. Harley, and died 30th December 1871. His wife and all his children, save one, have gone before him to the spirit land, but his mother, still lingers. E. L. T. Blake

John D. Harley was born in Orangeburg District, South Carolina, Oct. 28th 1812, and died Nov. 27th 1871, in Leon County, Florida, where he had long resided. He had been twice married, first in 1832 to Martha D. Hall, who ten years afterwards died. In 1855, Mahala R. Stephens, his second wife, who survives him. On 7th November, his only son died. E. L. T. Blake

Brother James A. Bailey was born in Laurens District, S. C., Jan. 26th 1835 and died in Greenwood, Nov. 18th 1871. W. H. Lawton

Mrs. Elizabeth E. Gladden was born Aug. 29th 1800, and died in East Chester, S. C., Dec. 26th 1871. J. M. Boyd

Mrs. Eliza V. Clarke, daughter of Mrs. Martha Kilpatrick, died in Columbus, Georgia, Jan. 14th, aged 27 years.

Mathew Turnipseed of Coweta county, Ga., was born in Richland District, S. C., Oct. 1807, and died at the residence of his son, Z. F. Turnipseed, on 18th of December 1871. Her remains were interred at Bethel Church.

Mrs. Mary C. Q. Caisey was born in Elbert county, Georgia, 21st Oct 1847 and died Nov. 1871 in Jackson county, Georgia. John H. Parker

Issue of February 21, 1872

Mrs. Frances E. Walker, wife of William A. Walker, was born March 13th 1849 and died in Savannah, Georgia, January 7th 1872. She was united in marriage to Mr. W. A. Walker in October 1866. Geo. G. N. MacD.

George Varner died of consumption in Meltonville, Florida, 21st of Jan. 1872.

Sister Rebecca A., wife of Benjamin F. Prickett and daughter of Joel and Martha Stubbs, was born in South Carolina, March 22d 1835 and died in Douglass county, Georgia, November 22d, 1871. J. B. C. Quillian

Brother William Brown died of pneumonia at Athens, Ga., Dec. 29th 1871, in the 87th year of his age. He was a native of Italy, but emigrated to this country in comparatively early life and settled first in Charleston, South Carolina, when, shortly afterwards, he removed to Camden in the same state. He came to Athens previous to the year 1830. J. Lewis, Jr.

Mrs. Mary Ann Rhodes, wife of W. W. Rhodes, died in Richmond county, Dec. 10th 1871, in her 38th year. R. W. Flournoy

Mrs. Victoria V. Jennings, wife of J. T. Jennings and daughter of the late Col. Lewis O'Bryan, of Walterboro, S. C., was born August 27th 1838 and died Jan. 27th 1872.

Issue of February 28, 1872

Miss Anna, eldest daughter of Rev. Wm. and Mrs. V. Foster, was born in Monticello, Ga., August 16th 1845, and died of consumption at her father's residence in Harris county, Ga., January 13th 1872. W. F. Robison

Mrs. Emily I. Cauthen, consort of John T. Cauthen and daughter of William and Sarah Robertson, was born October 1st 1846 and died January 10th 1872.

Mrs. Martha Pemberton, wife of James Pemberton, died in Rome, Ga., January 14th 1872, aged seventy five years.

Mrs. S. J. Watt, wife of T. J. Watt, of Muscogee, died January 28th 1872. Her little babe was one month old.

Mrs. Sarah Green died in Macon, Ga., 12th October last, at the advanced age of 86 years. She was born in Fayetteville, N. C., removed to Georgia in early youth; was married to Dr. William Green in 1830; settled in Macon in 1832.

Charles Albert Rogers was born in Canada, March 4th 1848, and died at Macon, Ga., February 13th 1872.

Mrs. Mary DeSchamps, relict of the late Col. C. G. S. DeSchamps, died in Sumter, S. C., on 17th November 1871.

Bro. Rowland Bryant was born the 11th of February 1795 in Granville county, N. C., and died in Rome, Ga., December 19th 1871. Tribute of Respect from Quarterly Conference, Forrestville Circuit, Rome District, North Georgia Conference.

Issue of March 6, 1872

Brother James Coker was born in Jackson county, Georgia, October 3d 1793, and died in Clayton county, Ga., Jan. 31st 1872. E. R. Johnson

Mrs. Sarah Bell, the beloved wife of Jacob Bell, died in Columbia, S. C., Christmas morning 1872, in the sixty-sixth year of her age. Wm. T. Capers

Sister Mary Elizabeth Colleton Pratorius was born in St. Luke Parish, Beaufort District, S. C., Aug. 6th 1826; came to Florida in 1838, was married to brother John Pratorius of Tallahassee, Jan. 20th 1847, and died January 28th 1871 [sic]. Josephus Anderson

Moses M. Smith was born in Jasper county, Ga., October 12th 1815 and died in Douglas county, January 20th 1871. He was one of the earliest settlers of Campbell county.

Mrs. Mary Ann Warnock was born Sept. 2d, 1823, in Beaufort county, S. C., was married to Philip J. Hiers, March 21st, 1845; converted at Mt. Carmel camp-meeting in Colleton county, S. C., about 1856, and died at her home in Colleton county, S., C., Nov. 28th 1871. She left a husband and three grown sons. B. G. Jones

Mrs. Henrietta W. Baskin (whose maiden name was Harrison) was born June 6th 1800 and died January 20th 1872. Her husband, James Baskin, moved to Carroll county, Ga., then a wilderness.

N. Olin Holland, son of Rev. Dr. Holland, died at his father's residence in Abbeville county, S., C., on the 20th inst., in the 29th year of his age. W. Hutto. Christian Neighbor please copy.

Mrs. Rhoda P. Howell of Columbia county, Florida, died January 1872, aged 39 years.

Miss Jane R. Forrester died in Gadsden county, Fla., Feb. 9th 1872 in the 78th year of her age. H. E. Partridge

Issue of March 13, 1872

Anna Elizabeth, wife of Rev. A. M. Chrietzberg, of the South Carolina Conference, was born in Charleston, March 15th 1821 and died January 18th 1872.

Margaret Shand Stokes (Smith) second daughter of Rev. Whiteford Smith, D. D., was born in Augusta, Ga., October 8th 1837, was married to Rev. A. J. Stokes of the South Carolina Conference, September 8th 1859 and died in Camden, S. C., January 12th 1872.

Jacob Thomas Gill was born in Jackson county, Ga., February 4th 1828, and died in Walker county, Ga., February 13th 1872.

Sister Jane M. Pendley was born in Clark county, Ga., in 1799 and died of old age in Jonesboro, Ga., December 24th 1872. R. R. Johnson

Richard W. Sullivan, Sen., was born March 28th 1800 on the west side of Sampit Creek, Georgetown county, S. C., and died on the 9th January 1872. He left a wife, three children, two grand-children, an aged sister and many friends.

Marietta Reynolds was born June 28, 1852, and died February 25th 1872. Deceased was the daughter of W. Parks Elliott, lately deceased, of Kingston, Ga. She had been married but a few months to H. W. Reynolds, my son. Jno. A. Reynolds

Emeline Saunders died in Forsyth county, Ga., on 19th of January 1872.

R. L. Rees was born September 6th 1813 and died January 28th 1872. He died in Washington county. J. B. Culpeper

Robert D. Wyche, son of the late Jas. L. and Mrs. M. R. Wyche, died at his mother's residence near Cherry Lake, Fla., February 10th 1872, aged 8 years and 8 months. J. M. Stokes

Issue of March 20, 1872

Col. James Edmond Brown was born Oct. 25th 1799 in Wadesboro, N. C., and died in Fort Gaines, Georgia, February 15th 1872. He was a son of Rev. John Brown, D. D., who was widely and favorably known as a minister of the Presbyterian Church. Brother Brown made several moves in early life and finally went to Monticello, Georgia. Here he married Miss Susan A. Stephens in 1820. They remained in that portion of the state till 1833 when they removed to Fort Gaines. Southern Presbyterian please copy.

Hon. J. F. Johnson died at his residence in Jonesboro, Ga., ag the age of 54 years.

William Gilmer Akers, first child of J. W. and Ann Eliza Akers, was born in Chambers county, Ala., Jan. 12th 1853 and died in Adairsville, Ga., Feb. 9th 1872.

Dr. James M. Simmons, son of the late Rev. John Simmons, was born April 26, 1821, and died Jan. 11, 1872, in Atlanta, Ga.

Wilson C. Gossett was born June 28th 1817 and died Feb. 12th 1872.

James Vessels died at his father's residence near Fayettevile, Talladega county, Ala., on the 8th January last, aged about 25 years. Daniel Duncan. Nashville Christian Advocate please copy.

Brother Dennis Lester was born in Newberry District, S. C., June 10th 1793, and died in Jones county, Ga., March 1st 1872. He came to Georgia when but twelve years old. He served his country in early life as a soldier during the Indian wars.

Brother Willis Whitaker died in Washington county, Ga., Feb. 1st 1872, in the 82d year of his age. He was born and brought up in the same county in which he died.

Mrs. Anna Shackelford, wife of Robert Shackelford, died in Stewart county, Ga., December 4th 1871, in middle life.

Issue of March 27, 1872

Died

Isabella Kennedy, daughter of the late Dr. John P. Feaster, and grandchild of Rev. John A. Kennedy, was born July 14th 1869, and died February 17th 1872, in Alachua county, Fla.

At Forrest Home, Columbia county, Fla., Rosebud, infant daughter of William C. and Sarah A. Collins, aged 6 months.

Obituary

Wm. Threadgill was born in Anson county, N. C., August 18th 1823, and died at Union Springs, Ala., January 26, 1872. When he was fourteen years old, his father moved to Russell county, Ala.

Lucy, daughter of Henry E. and Caroline C. Clarke, was born in Augusta, Georgia, October 9, 1850, and died in Augusta, of typhoid fever, January 26, 1872. J. O. A. Clarke

Col. Alexander W. Persons of Macon, Georgia, died in Americus, February 21, in the 34th year of his age. He was the last remaining child of an aged father, who survives him. After the late war, in which he served as Colonel, he settled in Macon.... He leaves a wife and two children.

Dr. Robert A. Payne, son of Rev. James B. Payne, died January 10th 1872. He was a graduate of Emory College and of the Atlanta Medical College, in the class of 1860. He was married in January 1872, removed to Meltonville, Florida. He was buried in Atlanta.

Wm. P. Kendall, senior, was born on 16th February 1810 and died in Wadesboro, North Carolina, on 3d March 1872. M. V. Sherrill

Sister Julia E. Norman, daughter of Wm. B. and Mary B. Norman and wife of the late James A. Norman, died at her father's house, Dawson, Georgia, January 27, 1872. The deceased was born in Wilkes county, Georgia, October 27, 1832. In April 1837 she married James A. Norman.

Rev. Geo. W. Crymes, M. D., died suddenly at his residence in Enon, Alabama, on the night of 26th February 1872, aged 63 years and 3 days. W. K. Norton

Mrs. S. M. Redding, wife of Major Roland Redding and daughter of the late Rev. J. W. Cooper, of Wilkes county, Georgia, was born February 2d 1810 and died in Dooly county, February 20th 1872. Leaves children and grandchildren.

Mrs. Diodima Fincher, consort of Rev. William Fincher, of Tallapoosa county, Alabama, died on the 2d of February 1872. She was born in Greene county, Georgia, March 17, 1798, but removed to Jasper County, where she was married in 1868 [sic]. She leaves an aged husband and ten grown children.

Issue of April 3, 1872

Died

Little Walter Wylds, son of Thomas and Mary Wylds, of Richmond county, Ga., was born May 25th 1863, and died February 18th 1872.

Ava Eliza Crews, daughter of Mr. Paul M. and Mrs. Frances M. Crews, of Columbia county, Florida, was born July 23d 1867, and died from the effect of a most terrible burn, January 2d 1872.

Walter Scott, son of G. M. T. and Eliza D. Bower, and grandson of Rev. Allen Turner, was born 14th Feb 1867 and died 11th March 1872.

Obituary

William W. Oslin was born in Union District, S. C., Sept. 11th 1796 and died March 6th 1872, in Harris county, Ga., In his infancy his parents moved to Crocker's Neck, Greene county, Georgia.

Mrs. Dorcas Newton, wife of Rev. Cornelius Newton, died on the 9th March at her home in Marlboro' co., S. C., in the 75th year of her age.

Mrs. Annie Forehand, wife of Solomon Forehand, died Feb. 1st 1872, at the residence of her son, G. W. Forehand, of Macon county, Georgia, in the sixty-seventh year of her age.

Francis Ann Frasier was born in Columbia county, Florida, Feb. 1st 1854, and died at the residence of William Spears, in Marlboro county, S. C., March 14th 1872. L. M. Hames

Mrs. Eugenia DuBose Lomax, wife of Dr. M. G. Lomax, and daughter of Dr. E. E. DuBose, late of Glennville, Ala., died in Glennville, Jan. 12th 1872. M. F. Crawford

Mrs. Ann S. Campbell, widow of the late Archibald Campbell, was born at Round O, Colleton county, December 26th 1798, and died at the residence of her eldest son, A. L. Campbell, near Walterboro, S. C., February 6th 1872. She was reared in the Episcopal Church, but about the year 1826 united with the Methodist Church. She leaves four sons and many relatives.

Saloma Crawford, daughter of William and Julia A. Bullard was born in Franklin county, a., Aug. 25th 1821, and died in Coweta county, Ga., March 9th 1872. Jno. H. Bowden

Daniel B. Chapman was born in 1796 and died on 17th February 1872 at his residence in Sumter county, Fla. S. S. Moore

Miss Fannie H. Stokes, daughter of the late Capt. Joseph H. and Anna R. Stokes was born on the 22d of August 1850 and died ont he 15th of March 1872, at the residence of her grand-father Gen. G. W. Hodges, Abbeville County, South Carolina. L. Wood

Miss Jane Johnson died in Abbeville county, February 8, 1872. J. W. Murray.

William Mobley was born in Hartford, Connecticut, July 1817; he came South in 1839 and died in Newton county, Georgia, Feb. 5th 1872. M. F. Malsby

Issue of April 10, 1872

Died

In Clayton, Ga., December 31st 1871, Lucius E. Livingston, eldest son of W. J. and T. F. Livingston, aged about 4 years.

Obituary

Mr. J. A. Speery was born in Waterbury, Conn., and died in the 57th year of his age, at his residence in Marshallville, Ga., on 29th of December 1871. When but nineteen years old he left his native State.... His Children

James Avery died in Burke county, N. C., March 4th 1872, in the 81st year of his age. Mr. A. was born in Acomac county, Va. He emigrated to Burke county, N. C., in the year 1817 and was married to Miss Elizabeth Brown, daughter of Daniel Brown, March 6th 1833. He was brought up in the Protestant Episcopal Church. His father was a minister in that Church. Two of his daughters married Methodist preachers-- R. P. Franks and J. Finger-- of the South Carolina Conference. G. W. Ivy

Augustus G. Ware was born January 23d 1810 in Madison county, Ga., and died January 20th 1872. He lived in Madison county until he was grown up to manhood, and then moved in 1849 to Floyd county, where he lived until his death.

Mrs. Ritha Weemes, relict of Darius R. Weemes and daughter of Nicholas and Laura Sewell, was born in Franklin county, Ga., February 27th 1817, and died in Atlanta, Ga., January 14th 1872. W. C. Holbrook

Mrs. Elizabeth Nall, consort of the late John P. Nall, died in December 1871. She was a native of Georgia. S. A. Pilley

Anna L. O. Burnham, wife of Edward S. Burnham and youngest daughter of Benjamin S. D. and Louisa A. Muckenfuss, was born at Charleston, S. C., August 15th 1850 and died March 13th 1872.

Anabel Faust Howell, eldest daughter of Bishop Wightman and wife of Dr. W. H. Howell, was born in Abbeville District, S. C., June 16th 1839, married March 23d 1871, and died March 3d, 1872.

Rev. William Allgood, a local preacher in the Methodist Episcopal Church, South, was born in Elbert county, Ga., and died at his residence in Spalding county, Ga., in his 55th year. He was married to his wife in Merriwether county, Ga., and she still survives.

Mrs. Ella Jordan (whose maiden name was White) was born September 18th 1851, was married to Mr. R. J. Jordan, April 27th 1870, and died March 3d, 1871. S. Anthony

Issue of April 17, 1872

Died

Robert R., son of L. H. and Amanda Gober, died Nov. 9th 1871, aged 1 year, 7 months and 12 days.

Obituary

Rev. Leonidas R. Redding was born March 20th 1830, and died at the residence of his father, Col. A. W. Redding, in Harris county, Ga., on the 22d of March 1872. Thos. T. Christian

Kennon Couch died in Talbot county, Ga., March 23d 1872, aged fifty two years. R. W. Dixon

Benjamin Thrower was born Feb. 29th 1803 in Edgefield District, S. C., and died in Atlanta, Ga., Feb. 8, 1872, In 1824, he met and married Elizabeth Dyal, of Walton county.

Mrs. Julia T., wife of J. W. Vinson, and daughter of Col. Thos. N. and Mrs. A. C. Beall (now Mrs. Pou), died at her residence in Baldwin county, March 19th 1872, in the 32d year of her age.

Henry J. Gober was born in Franklin county, Ga., March 18th 1805 and died in Banks county, Ga., Feb. 25th 1879.

P. F. Bunch, son of Geo. and Mrs. J. M. Bunch died at Eastman, Ga., March 6th 1872. The subject of this notice was born in Charleston District, South Carolina, July 20th 1846.

Jas. W. Gober, son of Henry J. and Mary Gober, was born Sept. 15th 1849 and died in Banks county, Ga., March 5th 1872. He was married to Miss Eveline Burgess, Dec. 16th 1869.

Sister Susan Ludiwick Zoucks, wife of John H. Zoucks and daughter of George and Betsey Bartlet, was born in Poughkeepsie, New York, June 20th 1816, and died March 9th 1872, in Hinesville, Ga. Her parents died before she was old enough to recollect them; and by an older sister she was brought to Savannah when but a child. H. Andrews

Mrs. Sarah Williams was born in Greene county, Ga., April 19th 1804 and died in Meriwether county, Ga., 5th Dec. 1872 [sic]. She was married to Wilson Williams in 1820, removed to Meriwether county, in 1831.

Mrs. S. S. Dixon was born Feb. 24th 1799 and died March 4th 1872. She was the daughter of R. W. Willis and was first married to Thomas Rembert, by which marriage she leaves two sons of distinguished piety and zeal in the Methodist Episcopal Church, South. In 1852 she married Ezekiel Dixon, who yet survives.

Rev. Allen Moody was born in South Carolina, Oct. 20th 1820 and died in Whitfield county, Ga., Feb. 23d 1872. He leaves a widow and eight children.

Miss Nannie J. Smith was born in Culloden, Monroe county, Ga., July 31st 1841, and died in Pike county, Ga., February 12th 1872.

Issue of April 24, 1872

Died

Near Mountville, Troup county, Ga., on April 6th, Laura V. Hightower, aged one year, five months and six days.

In Dawson, Ga., February 25th 1872, Joseph Bartley, son of John and Ann E. Moreland, aged seven years and five months.

Obituary

Col. Benj. F. Hardeman died at Athens, Ga., March 25th 1872. He was born near Lexington, Ga., August 18, 1802; was educated partly at Franklin College and partly at Union College, New York; represented Oglethorpe county, for several years in the Legislature. May 31st 1842, he was married to Miss Arabella Harris, of Athens, Ga. This union was broken by the death of Mrs. Hardeman in the spring of 1845. J. Lewis, Jr.

Mrs. Susannah C. Evans, wife of Rev. Lucius G. Evans was born December 2d 1824, and died in Crawford county, Ga , March 8th 1872. I. L. Avant

William M. Lovejoy was born November 3d, 1851 and died at his father's the 30th March 1862 [sic, for 1872]. Pleasant P. Lovejoy was born 5th March 1853 and fell by an accidental gunshot December 18th 1872. Sons of brother W. C. and sister Laura Lovejoy of Hogansville, Troup County, Ga. Jas. T. Lowe

Sarah C. Lancaster was born in North Carolina, February 27th 1801 and died in Bibb county, Ga., March 7th 1872. She was the wife of the late Leurtis L. Lancaster. I. L. Avant

Annie Ann Stewart, daughter of Rev. F. and Drucilla Winn and wife of P. G. Stewart, all of Douglass county, Ga., was born January 23d 1823, and died February 18th 1872. N. Trimble

Robert W. Whithead was born January 14th 1847 and died in Clarendon, S. C., January 20th 1872.

Joshua C. Tennant was born January 24th 1821 and died in Clarendon, S. C., January 31st 1872.

Mrs. Susan M. Randal was born 27th January 1802 and died 26th January 1872. She was married to Capt. F. R. Randal of upper Allsaints Parish, S. C., October 26th 1835. She leaves a husband and one daughter. Charles Betts

Amarintha L. Thames died in Clarendon, S. C., January 15th 1872, in her 70th year.

Jennie Waller was born in Putnam county, Ga., November 15th 1853, died in Gordon, Ga., April 4th 1872.

Cattie, daughter of T. J. and Catherine Baisden, died in Schley county, March 18th 1872, aged twenty-three years.

Issue of May 1, 1872

Capt. Wm. Sanders died in Anderson county, S. C., March 15th 1872. The light of his eighty-fifth birthday fell upon his lifeless remains, awaiting burial. In 1811 he was married to Miss Martha Ditmor. Sister Martha Sanders, who was born in Charleston, about the year 1795, died March 29th 1872. Brother and sister Sanders died at the residence of their son-in-law, Capt. P. K. Norris. Their remains sleep in the graveyard at Bethesda Church. W. A. Hodges

Mr. Offie Sauls died in Twiggs county on March 31st 1872. He was born in North Carolina in 1792, and emigrated to this State many years ago. Mr. Sauls was married twice. His former wife preceded him years ago. His last, together with several children and grand-children survive.

Judge Leroy Singleton was born November 23d 1805 and died in Jones county, Ga., April 3d, 1872. He leaves a widow, children and grandchildren. W. G. Hanson

Adelia U. Murry, wife of W. C. Murry and daughter of Daniel and Mary Killian, was born in Habersham county, Ga., 9th October 1829, and died in Pueblo county, Colorado Territory, March 27th 1872. In 1870 she with her family and a few relatives and friends, emigrated to this Territory. A. H. Quillian. The St. Louis Christian Advocate will please copy.

Clemonds M. Quillian, son of L. M. and Eliza Quillian, was born 14th June 1858 in Dahlonega, Ga., and was killed with several others by the explosion of a steam engine, near Dalton, Ga., Feb. 21st 1872. J. B. C. Quillian

Mr. Rosalius J. Walton of Talbot county, Ga., was born Jan. 11th 1840, and died March 24th 1872. He leaves a wife and two little children. W. F. Robison.

Evans Crocker, son of Dr. W. N. L. and Louisa J. Crocker, was born April 22d, 1832, and died March 1st 1872 in Marshallville, Ga. A wife and two children survive.

J. Wesley Bigby died in Abbeville county, S. C., April 12th 1872. He joined the church in a camp-meeting in Anderson county about 1861. J. W. Murray

Robert C. Jones was born in Upson county, Ga., near Whootenville, in 1843, and died in Columbus, Ga., March 2d 1872. Arminius Wright

Ezekiel R. Hamil was born Sept. 17th 1817 in Wilkes county, Ga., and died in Barnesville, Ga., Feb. 28th 1872. He removed to Pike County with his father when a child; has lived in the community ever since. Married three times.. in 1870 joined the Baptist Church. Mrs. Hamil has long been a Methodist and is the daughter of the late Rev. Cassius Tinsley, formerly of Augusta, Ga.

Mr. Jacob R. Brooks was born in Wilkes county, Georgia, May 10th 1787, and died March 22nd 1872, at the residence of his son, W. L. Brooks in Walker county, Georgia, from the infirmities of old age. He was a regular soldier in the U. S. Army five years, in the war of 1812. He represented

DeKalb and Cobb counties, Georgia, in the legislature. He raised seven sons and five daughters, seven of whom and a wife, went to the grave before him.

Henry D. Wynn died in Abbeville county, S. C., March 27th 1872. J. W. Murray

Issue of May 8, 1872

Died

On 8th July 1871, at Temple of Health, S. C., Mary Carr, an infant of Doctor and Mrs. Cunningham, aged one year and thirteen days.

Obituary

Stephen Pace died at his residence at Creek Stand, Macon county, Ala., April 14th 1872. Brother Pace was born in Edgefield District, South Carolina, July 11th 1802. his father removed to Putnam county, Ga., when he was a child. In 1828, brother Pace moved to Harris county, Ga., where he remained until 1854, when he removed to the place where he died. John Crowell

Sister Elizabeth Wood Robinson was born in North Carolina, November 18th 1799, and died near Greenwood, Jackson county, Fla., March 10th 1872. The family moved in her early life to Baldwin county, Ga., where she grew up. Forty-six years ago she was united in marriage to Alexander Robinson.

E. Alexander Funderburk, son of Isaac C. and Martha Funderburk, of Floyd county, Ga., was born February 6th 1847, and died in Worth county, Ga., April 2d, 1872. He died away from home, being en-route for Orange county, Fla., in quest of health. Brother Funderburk was the eldest child. P. G. Reynolds

A. M. Danielly, who departed this life at Hickory Grove, March 31st 1872, was born in Monroe county, Ga., July 26th 1831; was married to Miss M. E. Blasingame in the year 1851.

John C. Waters, Esq., died at his residence near Cokesbury, S. C., on 17th April 1872 in the 76th year of his age. He was born in the State of Maryland, but came to this country with his parents while yet a boy. L. Wood

Mrs. Malissa McCoy, widow of the late Hugh McCoy, died in Opelika, Ala., at the residence of her son, Dr. A. W. McCoy, 20th March 1872, aged 80 years. She was a native of North Carolina. After her marriage, she and her husband came to Alabama and settled in Russell county near Dover. From there they moved to Salem, where her husband died. C. B. Hurt

Dr. John Cunningham died suddenly at Temple of Health, Abbeville county, S., C., on 9th April 1872. In 1850 or 1860 he connected himself with the Presbyterian Church at Little Mountain.

Wm. Montgomery was born in Jackson county, Ga., on 20th December 1808 and died in Talladega county, Ala., on 11th March 1872. Brother Montgomery came to this county in 1835; he joined the Presbyterian church when a young man. J. E. Groce

Sister Francis K. Friday, wife of Thomas W. Friday, was born June 11th 1828, and departed this life April 12th 1872. She has left a husband and six children. The Church upon the Fairfield circuit has lost one of its best members. J. L. Shuford

Brother James R. Murray died at St. John's Berkeley, April 16th 1872. He left a wife and three children.

Robert Harley was born in Colleton county, S. C., August 14th 1811, and died in a few miles of his birth-place, April 6th 1872. The deceased had been a member of the Methodist Episcopal Church, South, at Zion Church, lower St. George circuit, for many years.

Tribute of Respect from Quarterly Conference held for Cheraw Station to Oliver H. Spencer, Sr., who died 17th February 1872.

Issue of May 15, 1872

Died

Florence J. C. Leitner, only daughter of John D. and Mary A. Leitner, was born March 8th 1870, in Marion county, Florida, and died Feb. 28th 1872. Christian Neighbor please copy.

Obituary

Mrs. Lucy B. Bonner died at the residence of her husband, Judge J. Bonner of Carrol county, Ga., April 7th 1872, in the sixty-sixth year of her age. She was born in Elbert county, Ga., June 1st 1806; removed from there to Clarke county, Ga., when ten years of age; married to Zadock Bonner, Dec. 28th 1825; moved to Carroll county in 1829.

Mrs. Henrietta G. Morgan of Savannah died in Effingham county, Ga., March 23d 1872, in the 44th year of her age. Her maiden name was Warren. She was born in Effingham county in 1828-- was married to Mr. Simeon Blitch in her 20th year; left a widow with six small children during the first of the war. Remaining a widow two years, she was again married to my brother, Mr. H. J. Morgan on the 30th of January 1864. J. J. Morgan

Mrs. Armisa Thomas was born in North Carolina, January 19th 1798 and died at Mt. Pleasant, S. C., February 10th 1872.

Irwin H. Woodward was born in Hancock county, Ga., on 30th of July 1809. When a youth he moved with his father's family to Monroe county in 1822. Oren Woodward, his father, the Rev. Osburn Rogers, and Edmond Jackson, all members of the Methodist Episcopal Church, built the church known as Roger's church in Monroe county. He had married Miss Martha Lockett, who was the mother of all his children. A few years after his marriage he removed to Culloden, where she died. He married Mrs. E. Gates of Meriwether county, where he lived and died on the 23d day of January last.

Mrs. P. C. Craven, wife of Rev. T. W. Craven, was born in North Carolina, Jan. 15th 1798, and died in Polk county, Ga., March 20th 1872.

Brother Croskeys Royal of the Baptist Church, died in April last in Thomasville, Ga., at the residence of his father-in-law, Judge Hardaway, in his 31st year. He was born in James' Island, South Carolina. J. P. Duncan

John C. Craig, son of Dr. Jas. C. and Laura S. Craig, was born December 2d, 1849, and died near Cheraw, South Carolina, 3d April 1872. W. Wall

Mrs. Elizabeth Dickens was born in North Carolina, January 24th 1783. When a child her parents removed to South Carolina, where she was married, more than sixty years ago. She then came to Wilkes county, Ga., where she died March 9, 1872. P. M. Ryburn

Mrs. Milly Watson was born July 5th 1786-- converted near Cokesbury, and died in Canton, Ga., Feb. 20th 1872.

Miss Ann Holland, daughter of Rev. Dr. John Holland, died 22d Feb 1872. W. H. Lawton

John Thomas Humphries was born Dec. 7th 1853 and died April 12th 1873 at his mother's residence in Union county, S. C.

SOUTHERN CHRISTIAN ADVOCATE NOTICES 1867-1878

Issue of May 22, 1872

Died

J. C. Morgan Crosby, aged about 9 years, son of Berry and Eliza Crosby, was drowned near his father's residence, in Appling county, Ga., March 13th 1872.

Nancy Matilda, only child of W. R. and M. E. Tanner, was born October 4th 1869 and died April 1st 1872.

Obituary

William H. Ezell died at his residence in Lee county, Ala., April 20th 1872, in the 68th year of his age. Georgia was his native State. He was converted in his 29th year at a campmeeting in Monroe county, Ga. In 1847, he was united in marriage to Miss Rebecca J. Saunders, only sister of Rev. R. M. Saunders, of Norfolk, Va. S. C. Pope

Charles Powell was born in Laurens county, January 27th 1810 and died at his residence in Dooly county, February 14th 1872. He was a son of James Powell, who emigrated to this county among the first settlers.

Miss Matt Wagner, our faithful co-laborer in the Sabbath-school has died. Mrs. A. M. Speer

William Humphries was born in Chester District, S. C., March 1st 1804 and died at his residence in Marion county, April 30th 1872.

Brother Frank Hester of Salem, Watkinsville circuit, North Georgia Conference, died March 26th 1872. Jas. V. McMorris.

J. W. Jones died in Troup county, Ga., April 10th 1872, aged nearly thirty-six years. W. J. Cotter

Martha Parks died at Troup Factory, Ga., April 6th 1872, aged about 54 years. She was born in Franklin county, and was the daughter of Robert and Martha Fleming. Her husband, Oliver Parks, died years ago in Forsyth county.

Issue of May 29, 1872

Mrs. Sallie A. Neill, consort of Wm. W. Neill, died in Laurens, S. C., her native county and state, April 19th 1872, in the thirtieth year of her age. W. Bowman

Deacon B. S. Sheats died in Monroe, Walden county, Ga., May 1st 1852, aged 65 years, 8 months and 15 days. J. M. Stillwell

Mrs. Martha H. Bailey, widow of Charles C. Bailey of Troup county, Ga., died on the 16th April 1872, aged 87 years, 3 months and 18 days. Her maiden name was Rowland, and she was a native of Franklin county, Va., where she was raised. She and her husband came to Georgia in 1827. Thos J. Williamson

Margaret O. Williams was born Feb. 4th 1794 and died at her home in Johnson county, Ga., April 21st 1872.

John King was born Nov. 4th 1840 and died April 24th 1872. The thirty one years and a few months of his life were spent in Green county, Ga., except the time he was in the army. M. W. Lewis, Jr.

Mrs. Cornelia A. Nash, relict of Lorenzo D. Nash and daughter of Elisha and Maria L. Tarver, was born in Jones county, Georgia, October 5th 1824 and died at the residence of her sister, Mrs. James S. Moore, near Dover, Lee county, Ala., April 5th 1872.

Mary Cobb, daughter of J. N. B. Cobb of Dalton, Ga., died at her father's, April 27th 1872. G. G. Smith

Issue of June 5, 1872

Died

In Ellaville, Schley county, Ga., on the morning of the 21st of May, Mary Eliza, infant daughter of Rev. John M. and Mrs. A. M. Marshall, aged 13 months.

Obituary

Mrs. Elizabeth Mickler, wife of Peter T. Mickler of Suwannee county Fla., and daughter of Rev. Henry and Elizabeth Saxon, was born in Leon county, Fla., November 18th 1841 and died near Welborn, Fla., May 19th 1872. On the 27th October 1859 she was married to Mr. Mickler, who was then living near Lake City. Thomas A. Carruth

Mrs. Nancy Decker died in Columbus, Ga., April 25th 1872, in the 69th year of her life. The subject of this notice was a native of South Carolina, from which state her parents removed to Elbert county, Ga., in her early life.

Mrs. Catherine Hanson, daughter of Hugh and Margaret McCollum, was born in North Carolina, May 14th 1802 and died in Monroe county,k Ga., April 26th 1872. Her parents moved to Georgia when she was a child. From 1818 to 1822 she made her home with the family of Rev. Micajah Thomas of Hancock county, Ga. At the age of twenty two years she married the Rev. Mr. Brewer, a local minister of the Methodist Episcopal Church. After fourteen years she was left a widow with four dependent children. After living a widow for twenty two years, she married Mr. Enoch Hanson, of Monroe county, Ga. J. J. Singleton

Martha M. Rush, relict of John Rush and daughter of Rev. Hosea Camp, died in Floyd county, Ga., April 7th 1872, in the 74th year of her age.

Mrs. M. A. Davis was born in Eatonton, Ga., February 28th 1827 and died in the same place, March 7th 1872.

Bro. William E. Potts died of cancer in Monroe county, Ga., May 9th 1872, in the 83d year of his age. He was born in Oglethorpe county, Ga., May 2d 1790. In 1808 his father moved to Jasper county, Ga. On October 8th 1816 he was married to Miss Sarah Wilson. He has left an aged companion and a family of children and grand-children.
Sister Sarah Downs was born in Bryan county, Ga., where she lived until the day of her death, 18th of March 1872, in the 65th year of her age.

Mrs. Laura V. Shaw, daughter of George W. and Ann E. Shackelford, died in Augusta, Ga., April 22d, 1872, in the 22d year of her age.

Gilbert Wilson died in Harrison county, Texas, on April 25th 1872. He was born in Henry county, May 31st 1799. his parents moved t Athens, Georgia, in 1809, and subsequently died there. He settled in Madison, Georgia, in 1818. In 1829 he was married to Mary Clark, daughter of William Clark of Clarke county, Georgia, who still lives. He leaves a wife and five children.

Rev. David L. Slatton died in Dadeville, Ala., March 10th 1872, in his 54th year (just seven days after the death of his brother, Elisha Slayton [sic]). he has left a wife, a youthful son and daughter. Nashville Christian Advocate and Tallapoosa News will please copy.

Mrs. Nancy A. J. Evans died in Jeffersonville, Twiggs county, Ga., March 17th 1872, in the 30th year of her age. She left a husband and five little children.

SOUTHERN CHRISTIAN ADVOCATE NOTICES 1867-1878

Issue of June 12, 1872

Died

In Marion county, S. C., May 28th 1872, Kittie McClausen, infant daughter of Lemuel and Elizabeth A. Thompson.

Obituary

Mr. James G. Grum died at his residence in Camden county, Georgia, on 4th of May 1872, in the 57th year of his age. He was born in Jefferson county, Georgia, on the 22d of August 1815, but removed at an early age to Camden County.

Mrs. Martha C. Walker, relict of Thos. D. Walker, was born in Baldwin county, Ga., Jan. 13th 1802 and died at Longstreet, Pulaski county, March 27th 1872.

Mrs. Hannah Thompson died in Augusta, Ga., May 18th 1872, aged 83 years, lacking 10 days. She was the consort of William Thompson, who died some three years ago. He fell a victim to yellow fever in this city in 1829. C. W. Key

Col. David Shuler died at his residence in St. Matthews, S. C., on the 27th of April, in the 78th year of his age. My father was a professor of religion previous to my earliest recollection, some fifty years. My father leaves a widow and five daughters, one son, and many grand-children. W. M. S.

W. D. McCrackin died at the residence of his son-in-law, Mr. O. H. Porter, at Covington, Ga., March 24th 1872, in the 74th year of his age.

Father John Maddox was born in Hancock county, Ga., in the year 1787 and died in Jasper county, Ga., on 16th March 1872. He came to Jasper county in 1809. He leaves an aged widow. E. G. Murrah

Mrs. Anna J. Dukes, wife of R. N. Dukes and daughter of Miles M. Johnson, was born in Darlington district, S. C., Feb. 27th 1878, and died near Marrs Bluff, May 13th 1872. A. J. Stafford

William M. Thomas was born in Colleton county, S. C., Oct. 5th 1836 and died at the residence of his father in Colleton county, S., C., April 21st 1872. B. G. Jones

Matilda Moore, daughter of David and Rachel John, and wife of R. A. Moore, was born in Chesterfield district, S. C., 10th Sept. 1840, and died on 4th April 1872. She leaves four children and a loving husband. T. N. Shelton

Mrs. Margaret Tankersley, our dear mother, died at her residence in Columbia county, Ga., May 11th 1872, aged 87 years. Seven children and a great many grand-children and great grand-children survive. A. B. T.

Miss Amanda M. King died in Cherokee county, Ga., April 21st 1872, aged 42 years. She was born in South Carolina. J. N. Sullivan

Issue of June 19, 1872

Judge Asa Holt was born October 20, 1789 in North Carolina. His parents removed to Washington county, Ga., in 1798, and then to Jefferson county, Ga., in 1810. He was judge of the county court and served repeatedly in the Georgia Legislature, both from Jefferson and Chatham counties.

At sunset, on Friday the 24th of May, Samuel J. Wagner died, having attained the age of over fourscore and four years. Whiteefoord Smith

Among the losses sustained by Trinity Church, Charleston, S. C., during the present year, is Mrs. Ann M. Nelson, wife of Samuel A. Nelson, who died 13th of May, aged forty-nine years, eight months and three days. Whiteefoord Smith

Samuel Bryce, son of Robert Bryce, Esq., formerly of Columbia, S. C., died at Spartanburg, S. C., on 13th of May in the 25th year of his age. Whiteefoord Smith

Mrs. Celestia A. Davis was born in Athens, Ga., Mar. 19, 1828, and died in Griffin, Ga., May 31, 1872. She was twice married: first, to Mr. George S. Alexander of Kingston, Ga.; subsequently to Colonel Calin Davis of Jefferson county, Fla. W. A. Rogers

Archibald McCay died in the 76th year of his age, near Fayetteville, May 11, 1872.

Mrs. Rebecca Galloway of Brownsville, Marlboro' county, S. C., died May 26, 1872, in the sixty-fourth year of her age. She was born and had always lived near where she died, April 11, 1809. Her parents and grandparents were Methodists. Her married to Mr. James Galloway, 3d December 1829.

Mrs. Elizabeth Virginia Blease was born in Laurens district, S. C., in 1838, but lived mostly in Edgefield district, and died in Quitman, Ga., on 17th of May 1872. S. S. Sweet

Henry W. Page was born October 14th 1834 in Chambers county, Ala., and died May 6th 1872 in Lee county, Ala. He was married to Mrs. Sarah J. Van Brant in Leon county, Fla., on November 21st, 1860, and leaves her with four children.

Mrs. Lydia E. Burton was born May 3d 1801, and died in Columbus, Ga., May 21, 1872. J. S. Key

Issue of June 26, 1872

Died

At Hackensack, N. J., June 20th 1872, Mary Elizabeth Heath, third child of Dr. M. W. and Sarah R. Heath, and grand-child of J. M. and S. A. E. Gamewell, aged two years, seven months and fifteen days. Christian Neighbor please copy.

Obituary

The Rev. Francis Cook was born in Kershaw district, S. C., Feb. 17th 1798. His father, Wm. Cook, was a native of Virginia, but afterward removed to Anson county, N. C., and thence to Kershaw district. Francis was only a boy of ten years old when in the house of my grand-father, the Rev. Isaac Smith, in Camden. He died on May 10th 1872. He left a family of seven children. G. G. Smith

Died in Forsyth, Ga., June 6th 1872, Josephine Virginia Lewis Barnes, wife of the writer and daughter of Philip and Eliza Lampkin. She was in her 34th year. She leaves a husband, a little boy and a little girl. F. N. Barnes

Mrs. Eliza R. Oslin, wife of the late W. W. Oslin and daughter of the venerable Elijah Stevens of Putnam county, died near West Point, Ga., May 6th 1872, in the 72d year of her age.

Mrs. Amelia Holmes, relict of the venerable Josiah Holmes, died in Barnesville, Pike county, Ga., 22d of May in the 77th year of her age. John P. Duncan

Mrs. Elizabeth C. Ellerbe, the last survivor of a large family, died at her home near Cheraw, Chesterfield district, S. C., on 7th May 1872, in her 79th year. Her first marriage was with Col. Boggan Cash, then to Mr. James Ellerbe. Her only child, Col. E. Boggan C. Cash, lives, an influential citizen of his native district.

William Charles Luckey was born near Bishopville, Sumter county, S. C., 14th Dec. 1843 and died at the same place, April 14th 1872. Samuel A. Weber.

Issue of July 3, 1872

Sister Susan Anderson died in Brunswick, Ga., on 2d of June 1872, aged seventy-two years. At the early age of five years she was left a lonely orphan. J. O. A. Cook

My mother, Mrs. Harriet Delespine Munro, was born in Charleston, S. C., January 17th 1784, and died at my home in Marion county, Ga., April 20th 1872. Her father was Joseph Delespine, a French surgeon, who came with the Squadrone under County D'Estaing in the time of the Revolution. He remained in Charleston three years after the birth of my mother, and moved to Norfolk, Virginia. From thence to New York city, where he remained several years and then made a visit to his parents who lived previous to the insurrection at Cape Francois, on the Island of St. Domingo. During his absence her mother accompanied her brother, John Russel, to Nassau, New Province, and was met by her husband on his return from St. Domingo. The family remained at Nassau till 1790, and moved to St. Salvador, where her father died. In the year 1795 she was sent to New York to be educated and married Edward Munro in the year 1797. With her husband she remained on St. Salvador till 1812, and moved to Daufuskie Island and remained till 1825. During the time she lost four children. From Daufuskie island with her husband and six children, she moved to Twiggs county; remained seven years and moved to Dooly county where her husband died in 1835. Geo. W. C. Munro

Benjamin C. Cox died in Bryan county, Ga., March 27, 1872, aged seventy-three years, seven months and eight days. He was born in Effingham county, August 19, 1798. His parents moved to Bryan county when he was a boy. On 27th of March 1872, he died. W. M. C. Conley

Mrs. Mary Jane was born in Leicester, Mass., February 12, 1828. She accompanied her parents, when an infant, to Augusta, Ga. She married, on 15 January 1849, Dr. H. H. Cary, and removed to Antioch, Troup county, Ga., until 1869 when the family removed to LaGrange. She died 6th June 1872. M. W. Crumley

Mrs. Elizabeth Stivender, wife of David Stivender, died in Orangeburg county, S. C., June 11, 1872, in the eighty-fifty year of her age. J. S. Beasley

Mrs. M. E. Avinger, wife of brother Augustus J. Avinger, was born February 25, 1829, and died June 3, 1872. She was a daughter of Colonel David Shuler, of Providence circuit, S. C. Conference. (whose obituary was published in the Advocate of June 12th).

Mrs. A. R. Brown, wife of Rev. L. J. Brown, died at her residence in Hernando county, Fla., on 14th May 1872, aged 43 years and six months. E. H. Giles

Mrs. Martha E. Edmunds, wife of Dr. R. H. Edmunds, died at Ridgeway, Fairfield county, S. C., May 8, 1872, in the forty-sixth year of her age.

William Gideon Pitts, son of Dr. J. W. Pitts of Columbus, Ga., was born July 24th 1852 and died May 29th 1872.

Robert Beverly Clayton was born in New Kent county, Va., April 12th 1802, and died in Vineville, Ga., April 7th 1872.

Mrs. Margaret L. McCormick died in Brooks county, Ga., May 5, 1872, in the twenty-eighth year of her age. She was the daughter of brother Z. Price-- was born in Oxford, Ga., and was known by the name of Mittie. When about ten years of age, she removed with her father to Micanopy, Fla. About four years ago she was married to Mr. Samuel McCormick. She leaves a little daughter about one month old. John C. Ley

Issue of July 10, 1872

Rev. James M. Treadaway was born June 22d, 1813 and died June 16, 1872. He lived formerly in Troup county, Ga., moved thence to Cherokee, Ga., and settled in the upper part of Floyd county, among the Indians. W. P. Rivers

James M. Gumm was born in Baldwin county, Georgia, 11th December 1809... died the second day of this month in Baldwin county. A. J. Butts

Enoch Hanson was born in Virginia, Sept. 25th 1792 and died in Monroe county, Ga., May 29th 1872. J. B. Hanson

Arnold J. Harvey was born July 9th 1804 in St. Johns' Berkley, Charleston county, S. C., and died of measles at Bonneau's Depot, in the same county, May 16th 1872. A. G. Gantt

Rev. Wm. Henry Clarke died May 1st at his residence near Decatur, Georgia, in his 68th year. He was licensed to preach in 1833. N. B. Ousley

John W. A. Grovenstine, son of Capt. John L. and Henrietta W. Grovenstine, died in St. Mary's, Ga., May 15th 1872, lacking eleven days of being 14 years old.

Mrs. Ann J. Powell, consort of Wm. S. Powell and daughter of Richard and Susan H. Dozier, deceased, was born in Talbot county, Ga., and died at Clopton, Ala., June 4th 1872. She leaves a husband and six children.

Henry G. Slappy was born in Edgefield district, S. C., Oct. 23d 1816, was married in Fort Valley, Houston county, Ga., June 24th 1838 to Miss Ann M. Kaigler. There he lived for a number of years-- moved thence to Mobile, where he lived for several years. During the war he and family came to Macon, Ga., and two years ago came to Augusta, Ga., where he died May 22d, 1872. H. H. Parks

Maggie Ann Shelverton, daughter of Henry G. and Ann M. Slappey, was born in Fort Valley, Ga., Nov. 8th 1840, was married to Mr. Alfred Shelverton, Augusta, Ga., Sept. 7th 1870, and died in that city, 14th of May 1872, leaving a girl a few weeks old. H. H Parks

Issue of July 17, 1872

Died

In Newnan, Ga., June 24th 1872, Viola, infant daughter of Capt. John C. and Viola W. Drake, aged 3 months and 17 days.

At Marietta, Ga., June 28th, Bessie Sawrie, infant daughter of Rev. W. F. and L. A. Cook, aged 10 months

In Thomson, Ga., June 28th 1872, aged 13 months and 26 days, Thomas White, son of W. J. and Mary E. Paschal and grandson of Thomas H. White, late of Wrightsboro, Ga.

A. S. C. Herrin was born March 14th 1830, and died June 5th 1872, at Camp Hill, Tallapoosa county, Ala.

Obituary

My Grandmother, Mrs. Winfield Lane Rogers, was born in Wake county, N. C., in 1780, and died on 9th May 1872, at the residence of her daughter, Mr. L. H. Kendell, Upson county, Ga. She was left a widow near Athens, Ga., with eight little children. Her youngest son being a Judge of the Supreme Court in Texas, and a Major-general in the late war. Her uncle, Joseph Lane, presented the site of Raleigh, N. C., to the State, and assisted greatly in laying out the city. Gov. David Swain of Chapel Hill, N. C., was a nephew of hers. Another nephew, Gen. Joseph Lane (at one time Governor of Oregon) was a candidate for the Presidency of the Confederate states. Judge Colquitt married her niece, and one of her sisters married a son of Nancy Hart, a famous heroine of the Revolution. She has left a long line of descendants to mourn her loss, four children, fifty grandchildren, over forty great grandchildren, and several great great grandchildren. Loula K. Rogers

Rev. James M. Arthur was born in Virginia in 1784 and died at Fingerville, Spartanburg county, S. C., May 5th 1872, in his 88th year. C. Lee

Mrs. Dorcus L. Edwards, wife of T. D. Edwards, died in Orangeburg county, May 15th 1872, in the 52d year of her age.

Bro. John B. Berry was born in Effingham county, Ga., July 9th 1800, and resided there until his death, April 17th 1872. In 1832 he joined the Lutheran Church of Old Ebenezer... in 1840 joined the Methodist Church. T. B. Lanier

Mrs. Mary J. Fleming died in Monroe county, Ga., June 10th 1872. Wm. N. Fambrough

Mrs. Ellen Perry, relict of Dr. Perry, formerly of Telfair county, Ga., died in Grooverville, Brooks county, Ga., at her son-in-law's, Dr. Wm. R. Joiner, June 1st, aged between ninety and one hundred years. R. H. Howren

Alexander Saunders departed this life on the 8th inst., in Key West. He was a native of Harbor Island, one of the Bahamas; but came to Key West when a boy. In 1850 he was married to Miss Blanca Kemp. A. A. Robinson

Mrs. Elizabeth Ledbetter died in Montgomery county, N. C., on May 11th 1872, aged 76 years, 7 months, and 21 days. She was left a widow at the age of thirty-four with six small children. T. A. Boon

Wm. H. Parrish died at his residence in Columbia county, Fla., May 8th 1872, and was about 64 years of age. Georgia was his native state. F. Goodbread

Mrs. Phoebe Wambersin Douglass died at the residence of Dr. P. W. Douglas, in Dublin, Laurens county, Ga., June 3d, 1872, in the 64th year of her age. Her maiden name was Charlton. She was born and brought up in and near Washington, Georgia. She was the wife of the late Rev. Tilman Douglas, M. D., who was a member of the Georgia Conference. H. E. Ellis

George W. Law was born in Sumter District, S. C., Dec. 15th 1801, moved to Macon county, Ga., in 1847, where he died 2d of June 1872.
Sister Nancy Harvey departed this life at the residence of her son, Thomas Harvey, in Buena Vista, Ga., May 16th 1872. She was born January 11th 1792. For some forty-five years she was a member of the Baptist Church.

Issue of July 24, 1872

Died

At Wolfsville, Union county, N. C., June 30th, Minnie Gertrude, only daughter of G. D. and M. P. Broom, aged four years, eleven months, and fifteen days.

Paytona E. McMicheal, only child of S. W. and Sussie H. McMicheal, was born Sept. 21st 1870 and died June 7th 1872.

SOUTHERN CHRISTIAN ADVOCATE NOTICES 1867-1878

Obituary

Mrs. Julia Baxter, late widow of the Hon. Eli H. Baxter, died in Houston, Texas, at the house of her daughter, Mrs. Dr. Connell, on the 10th February 1872, in the seventy second year of her age. Mrs. Baxter was a native of Hancock county, Georgia, the daughter of Mr. Obediah Richardson, where she was married to Eli H. Baxter in 1819. In 1867 Mrs. Baxter removed to Houston with her daughter Elizabeth, son Eli, and lived with her married daughter Mrs. Connell, where in 1868 she lost her son Eli. B. T. Kavanaugh

My mother-in-law, Mrs. Ellen Perry, widow of the late doctor James Perry, of Tattnall county, died at the residence of a son-in-law, Dr. Wm. R. Irwin, of Grooverville, Ga., on Sunday the 3d inst. She was over eighty years old. H. W. Sharpe

Mrs. J. W. Pennick was born in Twiggs county, Ga., Oct. 27th 1852 and died May 28th 1872, in Cochran, Ga.

Mrs. Lavinia Taylor was born in Sullivan county, Tennessee, Nov. 16th 1840 and died in Catoosa county, near Ringgold, Ga., March 20th 1872.

Emaline, wife of J. E. Waller, was born in Coffee county, Ala., Sept 27th 1843 and died in Santa Rosa county, Fla., May 6th 1872. J. E. Waller

James Coker was one of the most eminent Christian in the region in which he lived. W. R. Stillwell

Mrs. Mary A. Barnett, daughter of Simeon and Martha Perry, was born Sept. 2d 1828, married to Mr. James Barnett, Oct. 1857, and died in Auburn, Ala., June 1st 1872. She was bereaved of her husband in a storm in December 1864, leaving two young children.

William A. Adams was born the 12th Jan. 1826, married Miss Georgia Tucker on 5th of May 1850 and died at Newnan, Ga., 8th June 1872. The deceased was reared, educated, and spent the greater portion of his life in Greenville, Meriwether county, Ga.

Mrs. Martha Russell, consort of William W. Russell, died at her residence in Key West, Fla., on the 23d June. She was born and reared on one of the Bahama Islands. Chas. A. Fulwood

Brother J. D. O'Hern was born in S. C., Oct. 28th 1825, removed to Florida in 1846, married Miss M. J. Brantly in 1853... died 23d January 1872. E. E. Rushing

Rev. G. W. Stinchcomb died in Fayette county, Georgia, July 7th 1872, in the 37th year of his age.

Tribute of Respect to Daniel Douche by Quarterly Conference, Little circuit.

Sister Millie Rutledge, wife of brother Wm. F. Rutledge and daughter of Anderson and Polly Darnel Cauthen, died June 2d 1872.

L. S. Willborn was born in Wilkes county, Ga., october 12th 1816 and removed from his native state to Eufaula, Ala., in the fall of 1829. At 9 o'clock, March 28th 1872, he was brutally murdered in his own store-house.

Louise Mary Ann Whitely, wife of Dr. J. Whitely, and daughter of Timothy Priestly was born in the city of Paris, France in 1811, and died March 3d 1872, in Glascock county, Ga. She lost her mother when quite young, and then was moved to London, England. She came to the United States in 1834 and married to Dr. J. Whitely, July 4th 1840 in Brooklyn, New York. S. N. Tucker

Brother Levi Turnipseed of Bear Creek, Henry county, Georgia, was thrown from his wagon on 10th of June last... died on 26th of June. He was born in Richland district, South Carolina, in 1811. He leaves a wife and five children. John H. Harris

SOUTHERN CHRISTIAN ADVOCATE NOTICES 1867-1878

Died

At Habersham, Burke county, Ga., July 20, 1872, Mary Elizabeth, daughter of Edward and Martha Byrd, aged eleven months and eighteen days.

In Buena Vista, Ga., July 16, 1872, Thomas, infant son of Thomas B. and Dorothy Lumpkin, aged six months.

Obituary

Thomas McLeod Smith was born in Lynchburg, Sumter county S. C., April 23d, 1852, and died in Spartanburg, S. C., June 25, 1872, at the commencement of Wofford College.

Eula G. Hurt, daughter of Nathaniel and Emily F. Hurt, was born in Russell county, Ala., May 30, 1856, and died in Auburn, Ala., July 2, 1872. E. L. Loveless

Daniel Fouche died at his residence in Wilkes county, Ga., on June 18, 1872, in his sixty-first year. N. C. Ware

Mrs. Augusta E. Ewell was born in Macon, Ga., February 19, 1839 and died in Newnan, Ga., ___ 8 [no month indicated], 1872. C. W. Smith

Mrs. Elizabeth Fields, widow of John Fields, was born near Lynch's Creek in Darlington county; lived to be eighty-two years and sixteen days old, and died June 13, 1872. Her maiden name was Mixon. She was the mother of thirteen children.

Charles L. Petty, son of Benjamin F. Petty, was born August 26, 1830 and died in Clayton, Ala., April 17, 1872. He was married May 3d, 1860 to Adelia Dill, daughter of Judge Dill.

William Henry Thornton, son of Anthony R. and Susan A. Thornton, died from a wound received at the hand of an assassin, April 14, 1872, near Chehaw, Ala., aged seventeen years and twenty-four days.

Catherine J. Ritter, daughter of Joseph E. and Ellen Ritter, was born January 8, 1855, and died June 24, 1872.

Sister C. E. Bigham, wife of Rev. R. W. Bigham, died in Newnan, Ga., June 22d. H. J. Adams

Mrs. Mary J. Manson was born in Unity Township, Maine, and died in Atlanta, Ga., at the home of her brother-in-law, J. E. Whitney, June 24, 1872, in the forty-fourth year of her age. She was married to Dr. F. E. Mason, of McDonough, Henry County in the year 1854. John H. Harris

Samuel J. McLain was born February 24, 1824[?], in Baldwin [sic] county, N. C., and came to Georgia with his parents in 1827, died in Miller county, Ga., April 8, 1872. P. L. Mize

Lewis Hutto was born in Orangeburg county, S. C., October 2d, 1824, and died in Charleston county, S. C., July 3d, 1872. He was a brother of the Rev. Wm. Hutto of the South Carolina Conference.

Mrs. Charlotte Kilpatrick was born in Screven county, Ga., and died in Fulton county, Ga., on 29th day of April, aged about eighty-six years.

Mrs. Nancy Walker was born August 27, 1819, and died in Henry county, Ga., June 17, 1872. John H. Harris

Tribute of Respect to Nathan D. Stricklin, of Cheraw Station, South Carolina Conference.

Issue of August 7, 1872

Died

Died in Clay county, on 16th of June, Eulalia F. Owen, in the 5th year of her age.

Obituary

Mrs. Frances J. Hardwick, relict of William Hardwick and daughter of Green J. Dozier, was born April 4th 1817 and died at the residence of her father in Columbia county, Ga., June 14th 1872.

Albert T. Speissegger died at Charleston, S. C., June 3d 1872, aged 34 years, 10 months and 18 days. He has left a wife and three young children.

Mary Beland was born in Jasper county, Ga., 26th of Feb 1817 and married George Malone in the same county, Jan. 14th 1836 ...her death in Hogansville, Troup county, Ga., June 13th 1872. Jas. T. Lowe.

Tribute of Respect from quarterly conference of Hancock circuit to James M. Gumm.

In Memoriam to Rev. James M. Blalock who died 18th June at his home in Carrollton, Ga.. He was born March 20th 1825; licensed to preach June 28th 1868.

Tribute of Respect by Quarterly Conference of Trinity and Cumberland station, Charleston, S. C., to Samuel J. Wagner, Esq.

Mary Hightower, wife of Elisha Hightower, was born Jan. 30th 1790, and died in Johnson county, Texas, June 25th 1872. J. W. Hightower. Texas Christian Advocate please copy.

Sarah Riley was born in Orangeburg district, South Carolina, June 12th 1801, was married to Daniel Herlong, Aug. 5th 1819, and died in Butler county, Ala., June 27th 1872, aged seventy-one years and fifteen days. B. L. Selman. New Orleans Christian Advocate please copy.

Mrs. Levada L. Weaver, daughter of brother George Wise, of Union county, Ga., died on 23d June 1872, being 24 years of age. Her first husband died during the war. Her second husband, a foreigner, deserted her, leaving her with an infant, only nine months old. Marion H. Eakes

Blackwell Kenith Murchison, son of Rev. Kenith Murchison, was born in Brunswick, N. C., and died in Greenwood, S. C., on 7th June 1872, in the 39th year of his age. W. Hutto

Brother Humphry Rogerson was born in North Carolina, June 1st 1804, and died in Georgetown county, July 14th 1872. W. D. Smith

Issue of August 14, 1872

Died

August 4th 1872, in Atlanta, little Minnie Louella Wylie, infant daughter of Capt. and Mrs. D. G. Wylie, aged 16 months and 9 days.

Near Mickosukie, Leon county, Fla., on July 20th, John, aged two years and six months. On August 3d, Susan, aged ten months, children of John A. and Annie E. Cromartie.

Charles Wilson Wolfe, son of George W. Muse, Midway, S. C., was born August 26 1782, and died July 9th 1872.

Mary Julia, youngest child of Lewis D. and Mary B. Palmer, died in Dalton, Ga., July 22d, 1872, aged eleven months.

Obituary

Miss Eliva Evans, daughter of the late John Evans of Providence, in Orangeburg county, S. C., was born December 5, 1809 and died June 29, 1872. H. A. C. Walker

Lewis Payne (my father) was born in Rockingham county, North Carolina, and died in Blount county, Ala., May 17, 1872, in his eighty-second year. While yet a child, his father moved to South Carolina, where he was brought up. He was married in Pendleton district, and soon after moved to East Tennessee. He has, since my mother's death, made his home mainly among his children, and for the last eight years with his youngest son, Rev. A. P. Payne, in Blount county, Ala. L. B. Payne

Mrs. Fannie E. Neeson, wife of Dr. Horace Neeson and daughter of Mr. and Mrs. Levi Fowler, of Warrenton, Ga., died in Crawfordville, on 14th of July 1872, in her thirty-second year.

My mother, Mary Barrett, was born in North Carolina, Feb. 17th 1789 and died at my residence in Pike county, Ga., July 24th 1872, in the 84th year of her age. She was married to my father, William Barrett, Jan. 5th 1805, and was the mother of fourteen children. T. J. Barrett

Sister Mary Dempsey, wife of Lazarus Dempsey, was born Feb. 23d, 1795, and died May 13th 1872, in her 78th year. She was the mother of eleven children, among the number left behind is our beloved brother, Rev. A. G. Dempsey, one of the most successful local preachers in North Georgia. W. R. Bell

Louisa Jane, consort of A. B. Tankersley and daughter of Mr. Milton and Mrs. Jane Paschal, was born in Lincoln county, Ga., June 6, 1836, and died in Columbia county, Ga., July 14, 1872. We were married August 26, 1852. A. B. T.

J. D. H. Whetstone died in Orangeburg county, S., C., June 28, 1872, in the fifty-second year of his age. J. S. Beasley

Sister Martha E. Peacock was born August 14th 1839; was married to D. W. Peacock in 1857... died in Clayton county, Ga., July 8th 1872.

Rebecca Ansley, wife of Rev. A. Ansley and daughter of Moses and Mary Wade, died July 19th, at her residence in Sumter county, GA., in the 67th year of her age. Y. H. Stewart

Brother Irwin W. Harberson of Colleton county, S. C., was born April 3, 1854, and died April 13, 1872. E. Byrd

Issue of August 21, 1872

Died

In Cheraw, S. C., Aug 9th, Ella Jane, infant daughter of Wm. A. and Ada M. Liles--aged 6 months and 21 days.

Wm. W. E. Murdock, son of Rev. C. P. Murdock, and N. E. Murdock, deceased, was born Sept. 2, 1868, and died Aug. 9, 1872.

Obituary

Mrs. Amanda L. Smith, wife of Wiley Smith and daughter of Coley and Elizabeth Souter, was born in Lexington district, S. C., April 9th 1849, and died near Oglethorpe, Ga., 14th July 1872. Her parents moved from S. C., in her infancy, and settled in Macon County, where at the age of twenty-two she was married to Wiley Smith of the same county.

Mrs. Irene Nuella Martin, second daughter of Dr. J. L. B. and Eliza C. Gilmore, died at Holly Hill, S. C., July 9th 1872, aged 21 years and 19 days. She was married to Mr. Henry R. Martin of Charleston, S. C., November 28th 1871. E. J. Pennington

Mr. Eble L. Funderburk died at his residence in Decatur county, Ga., July 15th 1872, in the seventy-first year of his age. He was a native of South Carolina, but moved to Monroe, N. C., in 1858, from thence to Ga., in 1870.

Daisy, the youngest daughter of Jas. K. and Floretta S. Barnum, died August 3d, aged two years and ten months.

Elizabeth Hilton was born in Charleston county, March 12th 1785 and died in the same county, July 16th 1872.

Mrs. Jessie Lee Capers, wife of Sidney W. Capers, Esq., and daughter of Mr. John I. Darby, died in Charleston, Aug. 3d, 1872.

Tribute of Respect to Rev. John H. Robinson, by Quarterly Conference of Oglethorpe circuit.

Issue of August 28, 1872

Died

In Bairdstown, Ga., July 26th, 1872, Cornelia J., infant daughter of Lee M. and Roberta Lyle, age 7 months and 26 days.

John, infant son of Brother and Sister Chasteen, died in Cherokee county, Ga., August 1st 1872.

Obituary

Mrs. Lydia Vinson was born in Laurens county, S. C., July 11th 1811, was married to Hon. Wm. G. Vinson in 1839, and died in Crawford county, Ga., July 19th 1872. I. L. Avant

Ada, only daughter of B. W. and Martha C. Williams, was born March 4th 1859 and died near Trinity, Meriwether county, Ga., July 9th 1872. A. M. Thigpen

Mrs. Mary Elizabeth Bacon died in Lexington, Oglethorpe county, Sunday, July 21st. born in this place of pious parents... in 1846, she was married to John W. Bacon.

Many hearts were made sad in the town of Union, S. C., by news from Texas, of the death of Capt. B. A. Jeter. Died on 29th June. C. Thomason

Mrs. Eliza Bird died at the residence of her son-in-law, Thomas Wicker, in Washington county, Ga., August 10th 1872, in her 61st year. She had buried two husbands, and an only son (Gen. Wilson).

Mrs. Mary Hollis White was born Nov. 8th 1851, on July 13th 1871, was married to Mr. H. V. White, of Newnan, Ga., and died July 11th 1872.

Col. John McKenzie died near Tallassee, Tallapoosa county, Ala., on May 31st 1872, aged seventy years. He was born near Camden, S. C., March 3d, 1802. He was married November 21st 1826 to a daughter of Peter L. Robeson, of Chesterfield district. He was Clerk of the Court of Common Pleas and Commissioner in Equity for Lancaster District. In 1836 he moved to Alabama.

Mrs. Virginia E. Armstrong, wife of Rev. T. K. Armstrong of the Alabama Conference, and daughter of Simeon and Martha Perry, was born Sept. 21st 1844 and died at the residence of her father in Auburn, July 2, 1872. Wm. A. McCarty

Tribute of Respect to Rev. C. R. Jewett from Sabbath-school at Thomasville.

Tribute of Respect to W. K. Wallace from Sabbath-school at Drayton Church.

SOUTHERN CHRISTIAN ADVOCATE NOTICES 1867-1878

Issue of September 4, 1872

Died

Virginia Emma, youngest child of Theodore and Mary Turnbull, was born January 27th 1868, and died near Miccosukie, Florida, August 4th 1872, aged four years, six months and eight days.

Of Cholera Infantum, on 19th Aug., Fannie Ellen, infant daughter of Dr. F. R. and Mrs. A. E. Calhoun, of Euharlee, Ga., aged four months and two days.

Tiba Green Bailey, aged 10 months and 4 days, in Monroe county, Ga., July 16th 1872.

Obituary

Dr. John B. Chatfield was born in Morgan county, Ga., the 7th of January 1806, and died near Jonesboro' in Clayton county, Ga., July 27th 1872. R. E. Johnson

Brother Andrew Shearer was born Dec. 2d 1790, and died Aug. 11th 1872. In 1826 he was married to Miss Galatin Geer. He reared a large family of children. W. A. Hodges

Mrs. Nancy Branson Hays, wife of Wm. Z. Hays and daughter of Gideon and Sanna Jackson, died in Walker county, Ga., July 21st 1872, in her 26th year. S. W. McWhorter

Wm. D. Hays, youngest son of Wm. R. and Pharibee Hays, born on 9th of January 1860, died at Ellaville, Ga., 13th August 1872.

Miss Sarah Tobitha Mathis was born Feb. 20, 1857, in Walker county, Ga., and died at the same place, May 16, 1872. She died at her father's (Wm. J. Mathis) residence on the suburbs of the noted Chickamauga battlefield. S. W. McWhorter

Miss Nebraska B. Richardson, daughter of Dr. Wm. B. and Mrs. S. A. Richardson, died in Smithville, Lee county, Georgia, 17th August, aged 15 years and 8 months.

Wm. Eli Hendry departed this life July 28, 1872, in his 28th year.

Sister Elizabeth McDerment was born 29th March 1810 and died 4th August 1872. She was married to her first husband, Wily J. Norton, 4 November 1834, and was left a widow, October 21st 1849. December 25th 1859 she married John C. McDerment, who passed away before her. E. D. Edwards. Nashville Advocate will please copy.

John Madison Sanford was born in Warrenton, Warren county, Georgia, Oct. 24th 1810, and died in Boston, Thomas county, June 9th 1872. Geo. B. Werdon

Issue of September 11, 1872

Died

In McDonough, Henry county, Ga., August 22d, 1872, infant son of brother H. C. and sister M. C. Turner, aged two years and eleven days.

On the 1st of August, 1872, Annie Catharine, daughter of Dr. W. B. and Mrs. M. B. Warren, aged six years and seven months.

On June 16th in Clay county, Ga., Ella F. Owens, daughter of J. D. and R. G. Owens, aged four years, five months and sixteen days.

Enoch Smith, son of Elizabeth Smith, and grandson of Rev. Thomas Cliff, died in Brooks county, Ga., August 25th, in the thirteen year of his age.

In Griffin, Ga., July 1st, little Willie, eldest son of D. W. and Hennie Patterson, aged three years, nine months and five days.

Mattie S. Wayne was born in Monroe, Walton county, Ga., Sept. 16th 1855 and died August 16th 1872.

Obituary

John Howard, son of Joseph and Eleanor Howard, was born February 7th 1823 and died at his residence in Monroe county, Ga., July 13th 1872. He was married to Miss Sarah C. Congleton, of Monroe county, Ga., November 7th 1844. J. J. Singleton

Elizabeth Stovall, daughter of Andrew and Mary Jeter, was born in Virginia, January 20th 1787, and died at the residence of her son-in-law, A. G. Butts, in Macon, Ga., August 17th 1872. When she was quite young her father moved to Georgia and settled in Hancock County, where she was married to George Stovall. In 1824 she moved with her husband to Macon. Richmond Advocate please copy.

Sister Nancy Fargason was born in Putnam county, Ga., in 1811, and died in McDonough, Henry county, Ga., August 19th 1872. John H. Harris, P. C.

Mrs. Harriet Crawford, relict of Rev. Hinton Crawford, died near Fork Chapel, Greene county, Ga., aged seventy-six years.

Philoclea Lavinia Sitton was born in Gainesville, Ga., January 21st 1852, and died in Greensboro, Ga., May 21st 1872.

Miss Jane Eliza Clark, daughter of James A. and Frances M. Clarke, of Elbert, Ga., died at her father's residence on the morning of the 3d of August 1872. A. G. Worley

Louisa J. Ulms, wife of Ansley Ulms, of Macon co., Ga., died July 28, 1872, in her 40th year.

Issue of September 18, 1872

Died

In Columbia county, Florida, July 1st 1872, Rosa, infant daughter of Rev. Dr. Anderson and Symmadatia Peeler.

James Henry, the infant son of D.r J. P. and Mattie E. B. Moye, died in Butler, Ga., 6th of Sept., aged 10 months and 20 days.

Obituary

Henry Clay Nickelson died in Greensboro', Ga., in the 30th year of his age. W. C. Bass

Mrs. Elizabeth Andrews died in Columbus, Ga., July 25th 1872, aged 61 years. She was a native of Rhea county, Tennessee, and moved to Columbus, in its early settlement. In 1828 she was married to Mr. Samuel R. Andrews.

Mrs. Eugenia Irvin Talley was born in Orangeburg district, South Carolina, Sept. 25th 1792, and died July 29th 1872. She was married to Mr. George Barsh in 1810. He lived but a short time. In 1813 she was married to Rev. Wm. S. Talley of the S. C. Conference. He died in 1826. T. K. Armstrong

Mrs. Julia E. Grimes died in Greensboro', Ga., on 27th of June 1872 in the 82d year of her age.

Mrs. Eliza C. McAnulty, wife of N. R. McAnulty, daughter of Henry and Mary Harden, was born in Chester District, South Carolina, September 1813, and died near Greenwood, Jackson county,

Florida, August 11th 1872. Her marriage to N. R. McAnulty in 1833; moved to this county in 1846, raised an interesting family. J. J. Cassady

Martha Holman, daughter of John and Rhoda Ligon and wife of Thornton Holman, died in Meriwether county, Ga., on 18th August 1872, aged 72 years. W. B. Smith

Rev. Isaac Pitts was born in Edgefield district, South Carolina in 1810 and died at his residence in Dooly county, Ga., 19th August. His parents removed to this state and settled in Jones county while he was a child. He was received into the Primitive Baptist Church, but was excluded from their communion on account of his more liberal views on the subject of missions.... D. Blalock. Christian Index please copy.

My mother, Mary McAfee, wife of Robert McAfee, deceased, formerly of Rutherfordton, N. C., departed this life 3d August, aged 88 years, 3 months and 23 days. Her remains were placed by the side of my father in the burying ground of the old homestead, known as the McAfee bridge plantation, on the Chattahoochee river. They moved to Georgia in 1831. My mother, who has made my house her home since 1857, was on a visit in company with her daughter Mrs. Gregory, to my brother Robert. L. A. McAffee. Rutherford papers please copy.

Mrs. Catherine R. Merritt died at her residence in Midway, Bullock county, Ala., August 16th 1872. She was born in Newton county, Ga., August 21st 1826, and was the eldest daughter of Joseph and Nancy P. Maddox. In 1849 she was married to Mr. Joel Merritt, who was killed near Richmond towards the close of the late war.

Capt. John T. Jennings departed this life at the residence of his mother in Orangeburg county, June 11th 1872.

Mrs. Mary Anderson died in Laurens county, S. C., in her 79th year.
Mrs. Lucinda Stubbs was born in Jefferson county, Ga., on December 5th 1787, and departed this life in Macon county, Ga., July 27th 1872, at the house of her daughter, Mrs. C. M. Keniday. Her husband was Peter Stubbs, Sen.

Issue of September 25, 1872

Died

Victoria, daughter of Mrs. Eliza Hawkins, was born Dec. 26th 1866, and died August 1st 1872.

Francis Asbury, son of Rev. S. E. and F. E. Bassett, died near Fort Valley, Ga., August 3d, 1872, aged four years and six months.

Obituary

Andrew Woods died at the residence of his father, S. A. Woods, in Darlington, S. C., August 7th 1872, aged 26 years and five days. A. J. Stafford

Mrs. Julia E. Allen, consort of Rufus Allen and daughter of Col. A. W. Redding, died on 17th of July 1872, at the residence of the former in Stewart county, Georgia, in the 33d year of her age. C. A. Jones

Mrs. Charles Hutcherson died July 16th in Green county, Ga., aged 32.

Frederick T. Capers Myers died in bounds of the Lower St. George circuit August 15th 1872, aged 45 years. He has left a wife and seven children. A. R. Danner

Sister R. A. Wells, wife of the Rev. J. J. Wells, was born in North Carolina, April 10, 1808 and died in Hillsboro co., Fla., July 15, 1872. E. H. Giles

SOUTHERN CHRISTIAN ADVOCATE NOTICES 1867-1878

Miss E. E. Cotter was born April 5, 1821, at Gillsville, Ga., and died July 19th 1872, near Marianna, Ark. W. J. Cotter

Matilda Trippe Cheney was born in Hancock county, Georgia, in the year 1799 and departed this life at her residence near Pleasant Hill, Georgia, July 18th 1872, aged 73 years. R. L. Honiker

Mrs. Adelaide Burn was born in Charleston, S. C., and died on the 12th of July 1872, at the residence of her son-in-law, Mr. John Bradley, St. John's Berkley, aged about 76 years. She first married Mr. McGregor, after whose death she married Captain Burn, of Charleston, S. C. A. G. Gantt

Mrs. Jane B. Camp, wife of Brother Burke Camp of Jackson county, Ga., was born August 5th 1813 and died at her home on the 6th of August last, on her birthday. J. H. Mashburn

Mrs. Margaret A. Dent was born in Charles county, Md., August 16th 1798, was married to John T. Dent March 26th 1815, jointed the Methodist Episcopal Church at New Hope, Lincoln county, Ga. She died August 20th 1872.

Henry H. Key, brother of Rev. C. W. Key of the North Georgia Conference, was born in Green county, Ga., Nov. 14, 1798. Removed from Green to Jasper, from Jasper to Henry, and from there to Harris county, near King's Gap, where he died August 7th 1872. He was married to Miss Anna West April 15th 1821. T. S. L. Harwell

William Weeks was born in Hancock county, Ga., and died at Whitesville, Harris county, Aug. 27th 1872, in his 84th year. T. S. L. Harwell

Died at the residence of her brother, Norman Campbell, Esq., in Burke co., Ga., July 7th, Sister Catharine Campbell in her 49th year. H. W. Sharpe

Wm. Eli Hendry died near Deadman's Bay, Fla., July 28th 1872, in his 28th year. He leaves a wife and little daughter.

Erastus M. Young died July 1872, in Jefferson county, in the 60th year of his age. He leaves an aged companion and two children. N. B. Ousley

Samuel S. Bell died in the bounds of Lower St. George circuit, South Carolina, aged 62 years. He has left a wife and several children. A. B. Danner

Issue of October 2, 1872

Died

George Dawson, infant son of Dr. W. A. and Sallie E. Russell, died in Tuskegee, Ala., August 31st, aged 1 year, 4 months and 6 days.

Lelia V. Brown, infant daughter of Allen W. and Susan T. Brown was born December 29, 1869, and died July 4th 1872.

Obituary

Ardella Smith died in Houston county, Ga., June 20th 1872, in the 69th year of her age. She was born in Washington county, Ga., November 1st 1803, was married to Needham Smith in her eighteenth year, and soon after moved to Houston county, Ga.

Samuel S. Brown of Opelika, Ala., son of L. M. Brown, of Newton county, Ga., and grand-son of Samuel Starr (deceased) of Oxford, Ga., died August 30th 1872, in the 32d year of his age. His wife, Miss Lizzie Hill, was the step-daughter of sister Vincent R. Rommey, of Decatur, Ga. Albert Gray

William K. Wallace died in Drayton, Dooly county, Ga., August 1st 1872, in the 33d year of his age.

Cinther Mary Jane Register was born April 19th 1840, and died at her mother's house in Darlington county, S. C., July 15th 1872. She leaves an aged mother, a husband and three small children.

Mrs. Elizabeth Oxner, wife of George Oxner, died July 30th 1872, aged seventy four years. Wm. Strobel Dickert

Mrs. Mary Bowman, daughter of Jas. and Mary Kilpatrick, formerly of Rutherfordton, N. C., and wife of Rev. Wm. Bowman, of the South Carolina Conference, died in Crawfordsville, S. C., September 11, 1872, in the 46th year of her age.

Mrs. Sarah A. Reed, wife of John M. C. Reed, residing near Atlanta, Ga., was born in Upson county, December 12th 1832, and died September 4th 1872.

Emma M. Phillips died August 22, 1872. E. A. Austin

Sister Mary Cook was born October 8th 1805 and died July 13th 1872.
Annie Smith, daughter of the Rev. Wesley F. Smith, died September 11th 1872. She was nearly eleven years old.

Tribute of Respect to P. M. Butler from Sunday-school at Springvale, Ga.

Issue of October 9, 1872

Died

Ramsay Reneau, son of Mr. S. L. and Mrs. Julia S. Reneau, died at the residence of his father near Memphis, Tennessee, Sept. 12th 1872, aged 7 years, 1 month, and 10 days.

Thomas Robert, son of Mrs. J. C. Edgerton, died near Quincy, Fla., Aug. 7th 1872, aged seven years and ten months.

On Friday the 6th Sept., Green Berry, youngest son of Green B. and Izora D. Rogers, of Herrin county, Ga., aged 4 years, 1 month, and 7 days.

Obituary

My father, Capt. James H. Boyd, died at his home in Laurens county, S. C., September 13th 1872, in the 62d year of his age. J. W. B. Laurensville Herald please copy.

Mrs. Christian Love, wife of Alexander Love, died in Quincy, Fla., Aug. 2, 1872, aged 67 years. Her maiden name was McRae, and her birth place was Marion or Marlboro county, South Carolina. H. E. Partridge

Nathan Truman Land, third son of Judge Nathan and Mourning R. Land, departed this life on August 5th 1872, at Cassville, Ga., aged 20 years, 5 months and 20 days.

David Pravy died in his seventy-sixth year, at his residence in Merriwether county, Georgia, July 23d, 1872. J. T. Lowe

Rev. John M. Richardson was born August 30th [year not given] in Rutherford county, North Carolina and died at his residence near Dalton, Ga., on the 21st of Sept. 1872. He was a brother of the Rev. Alfred Richardson, who died a member of the South Carolina Conference many years ago. Levi Brotherton

Mrs. Indianna Cotton, daughter of W. W. and H. E. Carlisle, was born Aug. 14th 1845, and died Aug. 2d 1872. She was married to Wm. Hardentt in 1860 who died about one year after their marriage. She was afterward married to P. G. Cotton in 1864, and was a step-mother above reproach. W. M. Crumley

Rev. John Sewell Thomason died at his residence in Greenville county, S. C., September 1st, in the 58th year of his age.

Sister Phebe Ellis was born Jan. 7th 1793 in Pickens district, S. C., and died in Bartow county, Ga., July 17th 1872. She was the relict of the late Rev. Stephen Ellis. She married July 11th 1813. She was the mother of a large family of children. John A. Reynolds

Miss Ann M. Bowman died Sept. 25th 1872 at Rev. C. Austins, Ball's Gap, East Tennessee. She was born Sept. 30th 1827. D. R. Carter. Nashville Christian Advocate please copy.

Mrs. Eliza Dixon was born Feb. 14, 1814, and died in Greensboro', Ga., Sept. 14, 1872.

Wm. G. Carlisle died on the 9th of August 1872 in Jefferson county, Fla. He was born in Abbeville county, S. C., Feb. 23d, 1823, moved to Meriwether county with his parents when quite young. In 1845, he married Miss Elizabeth Elliott. In 1862 he went to Florida where he died.

Mrs. Nancy A. Langford was born in Putnam county, Ga., Oct. 20th 1803, and died in Lee county, Ala., Sept. 8th 1872. Within a few years she had suffered the loss of her husband, several children and most of her property.

Issue of October 16, 1872

Died

Jesse T., infant son of J. O. A. and Anna M. Houser, died in Houston county, Ga., July 6th 1872, aged five months.

Mary Estelle Kennon, infant daughter of H. T. and M. R. Kennon, died on the 26th of Sept. 1872, aged one year and nine days.

Obituary

Gabriella Early Evans, relict of Rev. W. H. Evans, late of the North Georgia Conference, died in Oxford, Ga., September 9th 1872, in the fifty-second year of her age. W. R. Branham

Mrs. Martha G. Purvis died in Brunswick, Ga., on the 25th of June 1872, in the seventy-fourth year of her age... resided in Middletown, Connecticut. In 1819 her parents, Jonathan and Lucy Bill, with their family removed to Brunswick.

Russel W. Johnson, son of Rev. R. W. Johnson, died at Bartow, Ga., on Friday morning, the 20th September 1872, in the 17th year of his age.

Mrs. M. J. Mallory, wife of R. W. Mallory, died in Troup county, Ga., Aug. 20th 1872, aged about forty-nine years. Her maiden name was Hogue; one of her brothers, Rev. Robt. J. Hogue, is a Baptist minister among the Choctaw Indians.

Persons Bass was born 9th April 1786 and died 23d of Sept 1872. He was born in North Carolina, but raised from a child in Warren county, Ga. W. C. Dunlap

Mrs. Matilda Bell, wife of the late Col. Jas. S. Bell of Bellville, Fla., and daughter of Allen and Elizabeth Johnson of Tatnall county, Ga., was born October 29th 1806 and died August 11th 1872.

Mrs. A. E. Pressley, daughter of J. N. and Mrs. Ellen Latimer, was born April 8th 1851, and died in Abbeville county, S. C., Sept. 3d 1872. She was married to W. c. Pressley, Oct. 19th 1869. A. J. Cauthen

Pierce M. Butler died in Randolph county, Ga., September 7th 1872, aged twenty-four years and ten months. N. D. Morehouse

Miss Mary M. McEwen, daughter of A. D. and Rhoda McEwen, was born Oct. 22d, 1844, and died in Douglas county, Ga., July 16th 1872.

William N. Turner died in Stewart county, Ga., Aug. 12th 1872, in the forth-third year of his age.

James F., son of Daniel and Martha Moore, was born November 11th 1853, and died in Bullock county, Ala., July 29th 1872. J. W. Hightower

Tribute of Respect to Rev. Tillman D. Peurifoy from third quarterly Conference of Little Saluda circuit, South Carolina Conference.

Rev. A. McCorkle was born June 16th 1796 and died at his residence in Lincoln county, Ga., Aug. 29th 1872. He was a soldier in the war of 1812. A. McCorkle

John B. Lindley died at his home in Cobb county, Georgia, Sept. 21st 1872. As a soldier in the Mexican war, and an officer in the "lost cause." He left a widow and only child.   J. F. Cotter

Issue of October 23, 1872

Died

In Unionville, S. C., October 6th, Mary Capers, daughter of Rev. C. and Mary C. Thomason, aged about three years.

On August 16th 1872, little Ruth, infant daughter of R. W. and Jane A. Gable, aged 1 year, 10 months and 14 days.

Obituary

Rev. T. D. Peurifoy was born in Putnam county ,Ga., Jan. 21st 1809, and died at his residence in Edgefield county, S. C., June 3d, 1872. He married Miss Louisa Bird, daughter of Capt. Daniel Bird, of Edgefield county, South Carolina.

Mrs. Frances Jones departed this life in Russell county ,Ala., on the 30th of July 1872, aged seventy years. For her support she had been dependent upon the efforts of a widowed daughter, that daughter an invalid with two children. Chas. A. Peabody

Robert Edwin, son of James and M. J. Bruce, was born in Fleming county, Kentucky, July 6th 1850, and died in Abbeville county, South Carolina, September 2, 1872. A. J. Cauthen

Col. J. T. Montgomery was born in Georgia in 1819 and died in Marshall, Texas in August 1872, aged about fifty-three years. He was the son of J. M. C. and Nancy F. Montgomery, the former was long connected with the United States Government as Agent for the Cherokee Nation. The father of Joseph was a strict member of the Presbyterian Church and his mother was a Methodist.

Miss Malissa A. C. Webster died in Chester county, S. C., September 2d 1872. J. M. Boyd

Mrs. E. A. Reeves, daughter of the late U. T. and Amelia L. Lockett, of Culloden, Georgia, and wife of Wm. Reeves, died in Griffin, Ga., September 27th. She had just passed the thirty-first year of her life.

Catherine Elizabeth, daughter of Columbus and Mary L. Nelson, was born January 23d 1861, and died in Camden, S. C., September 3d, 1872. A. J. Stokes

Brother Thomas Johnson died at the residence of F. C. Johnson, Newnan, Ga., July 24th 1872. R. F. Jones

Green Moore departed this life at his home in Greene county, Ga., July 9th 1872.

Issue of October 30, 1872

Died

At Smyrna, Cobb county, Ga., Sept. 30th, Ishmael G. Dunn, infant son of J. J. and Carrie Dunn, aged 11 months and 12 days.

Margery Lily, infant daughter of Capt. J. E. and Kate M. Steed, near Palmetto, Ga., on the 16th of August, aged 11 months and 14 days.

On 12th October in Darlington county, S. C., Thomas eldest son of James and Mary Howel, aged 5 years, 9 months and 15 days.

In Boston, Georgia, Oct. 17th, Walter Winston, youngest child of Rev. Capel and Ann Rebecca Raiford, aged 5 years, 5 months, and 20 days.

In Webster county, Ga., Sarah Amelia, born Nov. 13th 1870, and died Oct. 2d 1872, only child of Zach. B. and Ella V. Johnson.

Obituary

Louisa H. Collins, wife of Stephen Collins, was born May 13th 1827 in Franklin county, Ga., and died in Macon, Ga., Sept. 19th 1872.

Rev. Thomas Gibson departed this life at his residence near Springfield, Richmond county, North carolina, 24th July 1872, in the 67th year of his age. He was born April 27th 1805. His funeral was preached on the first of October by the Rev. Mr. Black in the new church at Saint John's.

Sister Mary Jones died Sept. 20th at the residence of her son-in-law in Morgan county, Ga., aged 75 years. A. W. Rowland

Mrs. Susan Calhoun died in Abbeville county, S. C., Aug. 24th 1872. J. W. Murray

My father, William Barrett, was born June 21st 1785 and died at my residence in Pike county, Ga., Sept. 29th 1872, in the 87th year of his age. He removed from North Carolina to Walton county, Georgia, where he remained two or three years, and removed thence to Pike county. T. J. Barrett

Sister Nancy E. O'Pry was born in Jones county, Ga., Nov. 29th 1810 and died Sept. 14th 1872, at the residence of her son-in-law, brother D. H. Riley in Houston county, Ga. She leaves a brother, Rev. A. A. Robison, preaching at Key West, Florida, and another brother, W. H. Robison, of Oglethorpe, Georgia, with several children. A. J. Dean

Mrs. M. A. Croft, consort of Mr. Alston Croft, died in Georgetown, S. C., Sept. 7th 1872, in the 61st year of her age. She was the daughter of Capt. Charles LeHue, who for many years was engaged in the coast trade between Georgetown and Charleston. In early life the daughter-- Mary Anna-- was placed in the family of a Mr. Walker, of Charleston. Wm. C. Power

Sister Elizabeth Clonts, wife of Jacob Clonts, was born in 1794 and in Paulding county, Ga., Sept. 10th 1872. She united with the church in the sixteenth year of her age within the bounds of the Charlotte circuit, South Carolina Conference and removed to Georgia in 1836. J. B. C. Quillian

Miss Alice A. Featherstone was born Sept. 9th 1847 and died at Anderson, S. C., Aug. 24th 1872. E. L. Harper

Mrs. Catharine A. Wade died in Lee county ,Ala., July 25th 1872. She was in her seventieth year.

Mrs. Margaret Roper, wife of brother Caswell Roper, was born in Marlboro county, S. C., Nov. 14, 1831 and departed this life Aug. 16, 1872. Jas. C. Stoll

Joseph Hubert was born in Barnwell district, S. C., April 20th 1799, whence in early life he moved to Georgia and settled in Telfair county, where he died August 21st 1872.

Mrs. Elizabeth Grady died in Chambers county, Alabama, Sept. 20, 1872, aged about seventy-five years. R. E. Oslin

Mrs. Mary Askew was born in Greene county,Ga., in 1794 and died in
Jones county, Ga., September 29th 1872, in the 78th year of her age. Wm. J. Greene

Rev. George E. Herbert died in Putnam county, Ga., Sept. 6th 1872. He came to this state from Michigan in 1869 and engaged in teaching school. He married on the 9th November, Miss Fannie J., daughter of the late John C. Beardin, of this county. He was about 29 years of age. W. W. Oslin

Fannie J., wife of Rev. Geo. E. Herbert, died Sept. 15th 1872, in the 23d year of her age. W. W. Oslin

Issue of November 6, 1872

Rev. Benjamin C. Franklin was born on the 21st of January 1830 in Glynn county, Ga., and died in Brunswick, Ga., on the 7th October 1872. J. O. A. Cook

Rev. Daniel D. Sturgis was born in Montgomery county, Ga., Dec. 11th 1804, educated in part, at the University of Georgia, came to Florida and joined the Methodist Church in 1840, and died in Jefferson county, Oct. 4th 1872. Josephus Anderson

Leonora S. McLeod, wife of D. O. McLeod, and daughter of the Rev. Smith and sister A. H. Davenport, was born in Ga., June 20th 1852 and died in Hamilton county, Fla., Sept. 20th 1872. She was the wife of a year, having died on the anniversary of her marriage. Jas. P. DePass

Mrs. Nancy Myrick died at her residence in Bibb county, Ga., Oct. 19th 1872, in the 75th year of her age. Her maiden name was Flewellyn and she was the last of her generation. In her 20th year she became the wife of Dr. James Myrick, and with her husband, left her father's house in Baldwin county for the house where she ended her useful life.

Col. A. J. Liles was born March 13th 1830 in Wayne county,Ga., and died in Valdosta, Ga., September 11th 1874. He married first Miss Carroll of Milltown, Ga., she lived a few years and died leaving one song. His second wife was Miss Lou Ellis, daughter of Dr. Ellis, of Troupville, Lowndes county, Ga. He left a wife and a son by his first wife. W. M. Kennedy

Mrs. Mary P. Adair was born in Union District, South Carolina, 11th October 1813, and died 19th September 1872, having nearly completed her 59th year. She belonged to the Rochett family, consisting of three sisters and an only brother, all of whom have preceded her to the spirit land. Mrs. Tripp of Midway, Ga., was the oldest of the three sisters. The youngest of the three sisters was my former wife, the wife of my youth, long since dead by not forgotten. In the year 1831 the subject of this notice was married to Mr. John D. Adair of Gwinnette county, Ga. A. H. Mitchell

Mrs. Allurah C., wife of Mr. J. C. Bonds and daughter of Rev. Nathaniel C. and Mrs. Elizabeth W. Barber, was born Aug. 19th 1836... married nearly three years and left a devoted husband. died October 2d, 1872.

Mrs. Mattie Fort Anthony, wife of Mark Anthony, son of Rev. Bennet Anthony, died in Americus, Ga., Sept. 23d, 1872, aged 31 years.

Mrs. Fannie C. Hall, relict of brother Daniel Hall, the daughter of David and Jane McLaughlin, was born in Oglethorpe county, Ga., March 1800, was married to Daniel Hall in 1821 or 1822, and died at her residence in the same county October 18th 1872. She reared a family of ten children, five of whom with her husband, preceded her to the grave. H. H. Parks

Mrs. Mary McLaughlin, whose maiden name was Mary Pharr, was born March 8th 1792. She with her husband John C. McLaughlin, gave her heart to God in 1827. In 1838 God took her husband and left her to rear the children. She passed from earth at the residence of her son-in-law, Robert Livingston, in Covington, Ga., Oct. 5th 1872, in the 81st year of her age.

Mrs. Kesiah Spell died at the residence of her son-in-law, Mr. F. B. Risher on 29th September in the 82d year of her age.

Mr. John Gramlin was born in Orangeburgh county, December 31st 1804 and died September 28th 1872.

Mrs. A. M. Clark, wife of Albert Clark of Marion county, Fla., was born in Charleston district, S. C., June 23d 1805 and died September 2d 1872. W. K. Turner

Issue of November 13, 1872

Mrs. Martha F. Vaughn was born in Columbia county, Ga., April 14th 1834. She was raised in Lincoln county, Georgia, was married to Mr. John P. Vaughn of Talbot county, October 22d, 1853, and lived there until the 21st ult., when she was brought to the Asylum at Milledgeville. She died September 20.

Tribute of Respect from St. John's Church, Augusta, to John H. Mann, who was born in Charlotte county, Virginia, 8th January 1878. he came with his parents to Augusta in 1795 and continued to reside here until his death, 4th October 1872.

Eliza Susan Coles, daughter of John P. and Margaret Coles of this place, was born May 7th 1845 and died October 24th 1872. Josephus Anderson

Mrs. Elizabeth Stephens, wife of Dr. J. H. Stephens, died on September 21st 1872 at Warrenton, Va. W. J. Wooten

Matthew Winfield was born October 30th 1794 and died in Greene county, Ga., June 28th 1872.

Miss Rebecca Montgomery died in Greenville, Ga., on the night of the 15th of October aged sixty-four years.

William Columbus Campbell died at Greenville, Meriwether county, Ga., 22d August 1872, in the 47th year of his age. he leaves a wife and three children, two sisters and two brothers.

Samuel Neidlinger was born in Effingham county, Ga., January 30th 1793 and died September 12th 1872. He left a wife and three sons. Thos B. Lanier.

Sister A. S. Key, wife of Wesley Key, and mother of Rev. B. S. Key of the South Georgia Conference, was born in Robinson county, N. C., January 10th 1825 and died October 1st 1872, in Emanuel county, Ga. C. A. Moore. Sandersville Herald please copy.

Mrs. Elizabeth Ann Brazington was born in Williamsburg county, S. C., May 20th 1836. She was married to Mr. J. W. Brazington, March 24th 1857, was left a widow with four children September 1867 and died October 4th 1872. A. Nettles

Ann D. Hart, wife of Hamilton S. Hart was born October 1st 1815, and departed this life September 12th 1872, in Providence circuit, South Carolina Conference. She left a husband, one son and three daughters. T. J. Mellard

Mrs. Margaret C. Jones, wife of Duncan Jones and daughter of Robert and Lucy Hasty, died in Richmond county, North Carolina, September 19th 1872.

Rev. A. M. Corkle died at his residence in Lincoln county, 19th August 1872, in the seventy-fifth year of his age. Clay Hill.

On the 2d of October, Mary Leila Godard, passed away.

Issue of November 20, 1872

Died

On the seventh of October in Charleston, Jesse Sidney, infant son of Jessie Lee and Sidney W. Capers, aged two months and four days.

Obituary

Brother Archibald M. Nall was born in Eatonton, Ga., Oct. 10th 1810. During his residence in Forsyth, Ga., about 1840, he joined the Methodist Church. He moved to Griffin, Ga., where he lived until Oct. 8th when he became ill and died.

Mrs. Rebecca Jane Bevan was born in Florida, April 6, 1833, married to Richard J. Bevan, Dec. 25th 1863, and died Sept. 22d 1872. She leaves a husband and mother.

Sister Sarah L. Powers died in Blakely, Early county, Ga., Oct. 12th 1872, aged 67 years and 8 months. She leaves two single daughters and several married children.

Mrs. Isabella Elizabeth Tenhet, whose maiden name was Nesbitt, was a native of New castle-upon-Tyne, England, and was born in the year 1795. She arrived in Charleston, South Carolina, from Liverpool on the last day of the year 1814. In 1814 she was married to John Constable Tenhet. She was reared in the Church of England... died on the 17th September last. Whitefoord Smith

The Rev. Alexander L. Smith was born in Marlboro' district, S. C., Dec. 5, 1823. He was married to Miss McCants of Abbeville district, in January 1851. He passed away on the 25th of August. Whitefoord Smith

George H. Gruber died in Charleston, S. C., Sept. 30th 1872, in the forty-eighth year of his age.

Mrs. Elizabeth J. Boyd, wife of John B. Boyd and eldest daughter of Benjamin J. and Susan M. Rice, died at Sonora, Gordon county, Ga., Sept. 8, 1872, in the 31st year of her age.

Mrs. Sarah J. Gilbert died in Houston county, Ga., Sept. 9th 1872, aged about 56 years. She was born in Wilkinson county, Georgia, was married to Nathan W. H. Gilbert in 1841.

Mr. Tyler Harrison was born in Virginia, April 20th 1792, and died in Talbot county, Georgia, on Sept 29th 1872. his father moved to South Carolina when he was quite young. There he remained till he was forty years old, when he moved to Talbot county, where he died.

Miss Janie Beard, daughter of Brother Henry Beard, of Ninety-six, Abbeville county, S.C., died on the 10th of August 1872. Thos. G. Herbert

John Emory Beard, brother of Janie, was born 1st August 1852, and died 24th August 1872. Thos. G. Herbert

Sometime since John Cohran, died at his residence in Leon county, Florida, aged about seventy. Wm. E. Collier

Martha L., wife of Lyman Smith, died in Leon county, Florida, on the 27th of September. Wm. E. Collier.

Tribute of Respect from Summerville circuit, North Georgia conference to Gideon P. Close, who was born in Jackson county, Georgia, March 26th 1834, married to Miss E. G. A. Morgan, Dec. 29th 1853.... left a widow and five children.

Tribute of Respect from Ocala circuit, Florida Conference to Stephen Gibson Brown.

Tribute of Respect to Robert Toomis Eheney from Emory College.

Issue of November 27, 1872

Died

Ossie Theodore Buckman, son of Wm. H. and M. F. Ballard, died Nov. 6th 1872, aged 2 years, 9 months and 26 days.

Norphlette Wright Harris, youngest son of William N. and Jane Harris, was born August 17th 1864, and died October 23d 1872.

Obituary

Newton J. E. Smith, son of Doctor D. A. and Mrs. Martha O. A. Smith, of Butler, Ga., and a student in the State University, died in Athens, October 4th 1872, aged 16 years.

Bartley J. McCants died in Taylor county, Ga., September 20th 1872, aged about 24 years.

Mr. John Knott was born June 6th 1786, in Granville county, N. C., and died September 29, 1872, in Morgan county, Georgia. He was married to Miss Charlotte Daniel, October 25th 181--- she still lives. In the year 1815 he came with his family to Georgia and settled in Clarke county. J. L. Lupo

Captain John L. Jones died on the morning of the 29th August last in the town of Cartersville, Georgia. He was 46 years and 7 months old. R. H. Jones

Mrs. Emily A. Charlton, wife of John D. Charlton, died in Savannah, Ga., October 18th 1872, in the 41st year of his age. Geo. G. N. MacD.

Mrs. Mary Lassere was born at Mole, St. Nicholas, St. Domingo, 20th September 1784 and died on the Ridge, near Darien, Ga., September 17th 1872. She emigrated to the United States about the year 1808, lived a short time in Savannah, subsequently in St. Mary's and from there she came to Danie. Was a member of the Roman Catholic Church from childhood till the 56th year of her life. E. J. Burch

Sister Ann Barr, consort of Walter Barr, Esq., was born in Lexington county, S. C., and died in Newberry, S. C., August 10th 1872, in the 82d year of her age. She was the youngest daughter of the oldest Methodist on the Lexington Circuit, and a father in the Church now in his 91st year.

Mrs. John D. Whaley was born in Stewart county, Ga., 1836, married in 1854, and died in Terrell county, Ga., in 1872.

Col. S. L. Pope died at his late residence in Crawford county, Ga., October 2d 1872. He was born in Edgefield District, S. C., in 1810, and graduated at the South Carolina College. He read law in the office of his kinsman, the late Hon. J. B. O'Neal. After admission to the bar he removed to Alabama.

William E. Craig was born at Chesterfield C. H., S. C., January 4th 1818 and died at the same place October 26th 1872. J. B. Platt

James John Andrew Collins was born 19th May 1827 and died in Columbia county, Florida, September 15th 1872. He was the son of C. H. B. and Ann M. Collins, and grandnephew of the late lamented Bishop Andrew.

Mrs. Julia C. Harris (my sister) was born June 1st 1836, was married to W. L. Harris of Clarksville, Ga., in October 1857 and died August 23d 1872. She leaves five beautiful children, four boys and one girl, and her youngest, little Walter, followed her to heave the fifth day after she left. L. B. Payne

Lizzie A. Canaday, eldest child of Wm. T. and Mary Canaday, of St. George's circuit, S. C., died September 29th 1872 in the 12th year of her age.

William James Calcutt died in Marion co., S. C., October 2d 1872, in the 27th year of his age. He leaves a wife and infant children.

Issue of December 4, 1872

Died

On November 14th in Hamilton, Ga., Mary M., infant daughter of Sallie Mobley and James M. Kimbrough, aged fifteen months and fourteen days.

Obituary

Rev. John L. Oliver died in Dale county, Ala., on September 24th; he was nearly seventy-seven years of age. He was born in Granville county, North Carolina, where he lived until his marriage with Miss Lucy Glenn in 1820. He subsequently removed to Clarke county, Georgia, where his wife and child died. In 1825 he was married to Mrs. Mary K. Watson, and was soon after received into the South Carolina Conference, then embracing Georgia in its bounds.

John S. Heath died in Talbot co., Ga., Oct. 2d 1872, in the seventy-eighth year of his age.

Sister Mary V. Hardy, wife of Rev. W. Hardy, died in Henry co., Ga., Oct. 21st in her 69th year. She leaves five children and a husband. John H. Harris.

Mrs. Abigail Arline, wife of Thos. P. Arline and daughter of Judge Alex. and Lucy Herrington, was born in Scriven county, Ga., March 23d 1834 and died at her mother's residence in Albany, Ga. She was educated in Macon, Ga., and on June 20th 1849 she married her surviving husband. She leaves a husband and two children.

Brother Kinchen Holt died in Monroe county, Ga., November 3d 1872, lacking but a few months to complete his seventy-ninth year.

Mrs. Sarah C. J. Linton, wife of Isaac M. Linton and daughter of Charles and Elizabeth Hiers, departed this life September 6th 1872 in the thirty-ninth year of her age. She was born, educated, converted, joined the Methodist Episcopal Church, South, married, lived, and died in Colleton county, S. C. She has left a husband and three children.

Mrs. Evaline S. Wilson, daughter of W. P. and D. V. Melson and consort of M. V. Wilson, was born in Monroe county, Ga., April 4th 1838. She was married to Martin V. Wilson, November 3d, 1865, and died in Talbot county, Ga., September 29th 1872.

Mrs. Mary Speer, daughter of Rev. Joseph Smith and sister of Rev. Noah Smith, deceased, was born in Tennessee, February 6th 1798, and died at the residence of her son-in-law, J. M. Greer, in Harris county, Ga., October 20th 1872. T. S. L. Harwell

Tribute of Respect from Quarterly Conference of Bennettsville, S. C., circuit, to Rev. Thomas Gibson.

Tribute of Respect from Quarterly Conference for Dalton circuit, North Georgia Conference, to Rev. J. M. Richardson.

Tribute of Respect to Mrs. Sarah Hardy, who departed this life on 26th September last.

Tribute of Respect to the memory of Geo. F. Riley by the Sunday-school in Perry, Ga.

Issue of December 11, 1872

Ella Bird, eldest daughter of the late Col. Pickens Bird, of Monticello, Florida, was born 26th September 1853 and died October 18th 1872. E. L. T. Blake

Mrs. Mary Evans Crocker of Twiggs county, Ga., was born April 25th 1783 and died at the residence of her daughter, Mrs. Fort, in Stewart county, Oct. 20th 1872.

Brother George F. Riley was born in Houston county ,Ga., July 11th 1859 and died Nov. 5th 1872. A. J. Dean

Mrs. Elizabeth Redfearn, relict of the late James Redfearn, died near White's Store, Anson county, N. C., on the 10th Nov., in the 66th year of her age. Her eldest son, James, was murdered in May 1872. She leaves three sons, six daughters and a number of grandchildren. M. V. Sherrill

Melissa E. Redfearn, daughter of the late James and Elizabeth Redfearn, was born January 31st 1841 and died November 15th 1872. M. V. Sherrill

Mrs. Susan Hall was born July 3d 1814 and died in Elberton, Ga., October 2d, 1872. F. G. Hughes

Mrs. Mary J. Leitner, wife of James D. Leitner and daughter of Gladney and Mary Neil, was born in Fairfield district, S. C., Feb. 9th 1848, and died in Marion county, Fla., Oct. 21st 1872.

My wife, Mrs. Eliza A. Broadfield, was born in Morgan county, Ga., June 24th 1814. She was the daughter of Dr. Burkett Dean and died at the residence of Dr. Wilson W. Barlow, near Americus, Ga., Oct. 27th 1872. Losing her mother when quite a child, she was taken by her aunt, Mrs. Allen, afterwards Mrs. Dr. Brown, of Milledgeville. She was married to James D. Jarratt and left a widow, and as the widow, married the Rev. Isaac Boring, of the Georgia Conference last of January 1842, and as the widow of Rev. Dr. Boring was married to the writer in Eatonton, 24th June 1852. J. M. Broadfield

Mrs. Isabella, wife of N. E. Sellers and daughter of Jacob and Mary Smilie, was born in Montgomery county, Ala., January 22d 1831, and died in the same county on 28th of Oct 1872. She has left a husband and ten children. W. F. Norton

Mrs. Lesueur whose maiden name was Martha G. Raines, was born March 1st 1824, married to Drury M. Lesueur, Dec. 28th 1838, and died in Stewart county, Oct. 24th 1872.

Mrs. Leila Grimes, was born Dec. 24th 1851 and died at her fathers, Dr. A. Jernigan's, in Greene county, Oct. 4th 1872. J. L. Pierce

Mrs. A. D. Dickinson, widow of L. D. Dickinson, was born in Hancock county, Ga., and died at the residence of her daughter, Mrs. Martha Cobb, in Suwannee county, Fla., 6th October 1872. She had been a member of the Baptist Church about fifty years. W. P. Ocain. The Christian Index will please copy.
Tribute of Respect to Persons Bass from Quarterly Conference of the Summerville circuit.

Issue of December 18, 1872

Rev. Christopher Thomason of the South Carolina Conference died at Unionville, S. C., Nov. 23d 1872, in the thirtieth year of his age.

Mrs. Mary E. Chandler died on the 4th of November 1871 in Brunswick, Ga. She was born in Fayetteville, N. C. Her maiden name was Beville. She was married to George Chandler and removed to Brunswick, Ga., about for years ago. She leaves a husband and infant. J. O. A. Cook. North Carolina Advocate please copy.

Col. John M. Brabham was born 27th April 1820, married Sept. 5th 1855, and died Nov. 21st 1872. Thos. Raysor

Dr. Charles H. Bass died on the morning of the 12th instant, near Milledgeville, in the 43d year of his age.

Mr. Daniel T. Lingo was born in Washington county, Ga., December 10th 1801, removed to Jefferson county, Fla., in 1833, and died October 10th 1872. D. H. Bryan

William B. Simkins died at his residence in Jefferson county, Florida, Nov. 29th 1872, aged 25 years, 9 months, and 2 days.

Agnes Isabel, eldest daughter of Daniel F. and Georgia N. Lefils, died in Fernandina, Fla., aged 17 years and 8 months. Born in Savannah, Feb. 16th 1855; died Oct. 25th 1872.

John C. Fudge was born Nov. 5, 1827, was married to Miss S. G. Fokes in 1853, and died at his residence in Liberty county, Ga., July 31st 1872. He leaves a widow and six children. W. M. Watts

John Dawkins was born in Washington county, Ga., in 1808, removed to Florida when quite a young man and died in Jefferson county, Fla., Oct. 23d, 1872. He leaves a wife, son and daughter. D. H. Bryan

Mr. Josiah Horton Gaulding was born in Monroe county, Ga., in 1826, and died 3d October 1830 [sic] in Pike county, Ga. He leaves a wife, seven children and many friends.

Issue of December 25, 1872

Died

On October 24th 1872, near Drayton, Ga., Charlie Jasper, son of Mary L. and Jasper M. Dickson, aged eleven months.

In Thomson, Ga., on the 11th December 1872, Mrs. Angeline Bevans, wife of Dr. T. H. Bevans, aged 59 years.

Obituary

Mrs. Eliza Yarbrough, wife of F. M. Yarbrough and daughter of the late Rev. Tilman D. and Louisa Peurifoy, was born July 19th 1849 and died July 25th 1872. G. W. M. Creighton

David A. Walton was born Feb. 2d, 1829 and died in Monroe county, Ga., Oct. 13th 1872. J. J. Singleton

Brother Wm. Johnson was born Aug. 31st 1802, in Samson county, North Carolina, and died Nov. 8th 1872, near Winterville, Georgia. W. D. Heath

Agnes Ledbetter Danner, daughter of Rev. Archibald Danner of the South Carolina Conference, died in Charleston, S. C., Nov. 3, 1872, in the twenty-fourth year of her age.

Mr. Jessee Wade died in Nov. 1872 at the residence of his son, Mr. A. P. Wade, near Blackshear, Pierce co., Ga., in his 79th year. The deceased was born in Green county, Georgia, on the 13th of May 1794.

Brother George Clayton was born Nov. 12, 1801 and died Oct. 23d, 1872. G. Pierce

Mrs. Elizabeth Welburn was born 7th April 1792 and died in Chickasawhatchee, Terrell county, Oct. 32, 1872.

Mrs. Mourning H. Hester was born in Morgan county, Ga., in 1816, married to Thomas G. Hester in 1830, and died in Stewart co., Ga., Sept. 15th 1872. E. J. Rentz

Mrs. Rebecca Bristow, widow of Thomas Bristow, died in October last, having lived to be over eighty years old. She was at the time of her death the oldest member at Beauty Spot, Bennettsville circuit, S. C. Conference. L. M. Hamer

A. H. Stewart of Camden county, Georgia, departed this life Nov. 1st 1872, in his 64th year. He has left a wife and one son. J. L. Williams

Issue of January 8, 1873

Died

In Forsyth county, Ga., December 14, 1872, Emer O. Dobbs, daughter of Joseph D. and Erline[?] Dobbs.

Obituary

Mrs. Sarah A. E. Edwards died in Cartersville, Ga., December 8, 1872, in the 53d year of her age. Geo. R. Kramer

Mrs. Mary Koger, wife of Hon. Joseph Koger, and mother of Rev. T. J. Koger, formerly of the Alabama Conference, was born in Colleton District, S. C., May 24th 1790, and died at the house of her daughter, Mrs. M. A. Dixon, near Brooksville, Miss., Oct. 18th 1872. Her only son, at the time of his death, was a member of the Alabama Conference; two of her daughters married Methodist preachers. O. P. Thomas

D. L. Switzer died at his residence in Leon county, Fla., Nov. 25th 1872. He was 46 years of age. Wm. E. Collins

Mrs. Louisia Meredith died at Helena, Newberry county, S. C., Sept. 22d, 1872, in the 65th year of her age. She was born and reared in Charleston. In 1852 she was married to William C. Meredith, and the greater part of her married life was spent at Orangeburg, S. C.

Mrs. Louisia W. Telfair, daughter of the Rev. D. S. McBride, died at her residence in Quincy, Fla., November 22d, 1872. She was born in Georgia, Sept. 10th 1834, and was married to the late Dr. D. A. Telfair, May 5th 1852. H. E. Partridge

Dr. A. C. Ware died in LaGrange about the middle of October 1872. He was just in the meridian of life. W. M. Crumley

William McKendree Turner, son of Rev. James and Nancy W. Turner, formerly of Lincoln county, Ga., died near Bryan, Texas, Nov. 19th. He was born March 1st, 1821, in Lincoln co., Ga. H. V. Philpott

Mrs. Martha A. Newton, wife of Cornelius D. Newton and daughter of Barnabas and Jane Wallace, died Oct. 16th, in the 38th year of her age. She was born and brought up in Marlboro co., S. C. She leaves a husband and little daughter.

Mrs. Indiana T. Baker, wife of John M. Baker of Fulton county, Ga., died on Nov. 15th 1872, in the 23d year of his age. She has left three young children, one of whom is but six months old. She was left an orphan when very young and was brought up by her uncle, J. J. Fain.

Mr. John K. Bedell died at the residence of his brother-in-law, Judge Samuel Pearson, near Eatonton, Ga. He died on the last day of October 1872. Sister Fannie

Issue of January 15, 1873

Brother Jas. N. D. LeSueur died at Athens, Ga., Oct. 15th 1872. He was born in Elbert county, Ga., Aug. 14th 1836. About five years afterward, his father removed to Russel county, Ala. He was married Dec. 25th, 1845 to Miss Sarah J. Haynes, and afterward removed to Athens, Ga. J. Lewis, Jr.

John Dodd died in Milton county, Fla., Nov. 28th 1872, in the 82d year of his age.

My father, David Dunlap, died at the residence of his eldest living son, E. O. Dunlap, in Early county, Ga., Dec. 2d 1872, in his 83d year. He was born and reared in Lancaster district, S. C., emigrated to Georgia in 1825 and settled in Jasper county. He lived at different times in Newton, Heard, and Meriwether counties. Two years ago, when my mother died, he was forced to break up, since which time he had lived principally with brother Robert, at whose house he died, occasionally visiting my other living brother Captain S. S. Dunlap, of Macon, Ga. W. C. Dunlap

Mrs. Martha Beckham, widow of James Beckham, Sr., deceased, died at her residence near Zebulon, Pike county, Ga., on Dec. 3, 1872. She was a daughter of Joseph Carson, was born in Wilkes or Washington County, Ga., Dec. 21st, 1791, was married to James Beckham at the home of her uncle, David Carson, in Baldwin County, June 27th 1811. J. J. Caldwell

Brother B. F. H. Linsey was born in Wilkes county, Ga., on the 11th of March 1797. He married Mrs. E. Hunter in 1819, and after her death he married Mrs. S. W. Colquitt in 1851. For many years he lived with his daughter-in-law, now Mrs. Dr. Wm. E. Murphey. He died on 11th of November 1872. W. M. Crumley

Sister Rachel Earnest, wife of Felix W. Earnest, was born June 6th 1809 and died Nov. 19th 1872 in Mellonville, Orange county, Fla. Nashville Christian Advocate please copy. James Harris

Josephine Matilda Venable was born near Adairsville, Bartow county, Sept. 5, 1849, and died at the house of W. R. Venable, Esqr., in Atlanta. John A. Reynolds

Benjamin F. Kemp was born Feb. 19th 1851, and died in Wilkinson county, Dec. 2, 1872.

A. J. Benson was born in Greene county, Tenn., Jan. 12th 1840 and died in Rome, Ga., Oct. 19th 1872. He was converted at Cave Spring, Georgia.

Sister Nancy Colly, wife of Jonathan Colly, was born in Virginia in 1797, and died in Quitman county, Georgia, October 18th 1872. Wm. B. McHan

Issue of January 22, 1873

Rev. J. A. Williams, son of Josiah and Mary Williams, was born June 23d 1830 in Graves county, Kentucky. In 1859 he joined the Arkansas Conference. Avarilla Williams

The Rev. John Davis was born in Charleston, S. C., on the 25th of May 1798. He was the son of Thomas and Mary Davis, who were both natives of Great Britain. While yet very young, he lost his father, and was placed in the Charleston Orphan House. Thence he was taken by some friend and carried to Newberry, S. C., where he was placed at Mt. Bethel Academy. In May 1871 he suffered an attack of typhoid pneumonia. Whitefoord Smith

Mrs. Rosanna B. Lee, wife of Maj. John A. Lee of Spartanburg, S. C., was born in Union district, S. C., January 12, 1836 and died December 2, 1872. Whitefoord Smith

Mrs. E. F. Reid, wife of Mr. E. A. Reid, died in Troup county, Ga., Dec. 18, 1872, in her fiftieth year. W. J. Cotter

Mrs. H. M. Medlock, wife of M. S. Medlock of Hancock county, Ga., died 29th November 1872, aged 52 years, 7 months and 7 days. The deceased was the daughter of B. F. and Elizabeth Latimer. She was a member of the Baptist Church. T. J. Veazy

John N. Calhoun was born in Jones county, Ga., Jan. 24th 1812 and died at the residence of his son-in-law, William Ball, in Gadsden county, Fla., August 22, 1872. Samuel Woodberry

Mrs. Rebecca Moore, wife of Churchhill Moore, was born in Grayson county, Virginia, May 20, 1919 and died August 13, 1872.

Mrs. M. J. Bullard a member of the Methodist Episcopal Church, South, at Franklin, Heard county, Ga., died on the 5th of Dec 1872, aged 28 years. She was born and raised in Heard county; was left a widow with an orphan boy. Jno. J. little

Brother Mathews, a local preacher of the Methodist Episcopal Church, South, died at his residence near Danburg, Wilkes county, Ga., on November 19, 1872, aged seventy-five years last July. He leaves a widow. A. J. Worley

Brother Asbury Stalvey died Nov. 5th 1872, in about the 30th year of his age, in Horry county, S. C. He leaves an aged mother, a wife and three small children. R. L. Duffie

Angus Martin died near Taylor's Creek, Liberty county, Ga., Dec. 23d, 1872, in the 77th year of his age. W. G. Boothe

Tribute of Respect to James W. Horton, who died November 30, 1872, aged forty-seven years. Augusta, Ga.

Tribute of Respect from Quarterly Conference for Geneva circuit, South Georgia Conference, to John B. Heath who was born Oct. 12th 1794, and died October 2, 1872.

Issue of January 29, 1873

Died

In Greenville county, S. C., Dec. 14th 1872, James Lawrence, son of Capt. J. W. and E. L. Austin, aged 3 years, 3 months and 28 days.

Obituary

Mrs. Elizabeth Maria Stewart was the daughter of Joseph and Catharine A. M. Rembert, and was born in Houston county, Ga., May 9th 1842. She joined the Methodist Episcopal Church, South, in Columbus, Ga., in 1857; was married to Mr. Walter Stewart 18th July 1851, moved to Montgomery, Ala., in 1856, where she died 23d Dec 1872. Thomas C. M. Golland

Mrs. Sarah Smith, wife of Capt. Charles Smith of Cokesbury, S. C., was born in Edgefield county, S. C., Sept. 15th 1818, received into the Baptist Church, married the 12th of December 1836, became the mother of eight children. She died 7th of Dec. 1872. L. Wood

Mrs. Elizabeth Anthony Corley died in Bienville Parish, Louisiana, Dec. 20th 1872, in the seventieth year of her age. She was born in Baldwin county, Ga., May 30th 1803 and was married to Owen Harvey Myrick, Oct. 15th 1820. He died, leaving her with a family of five small children. She married a second time, and leaves an one living daughter from this marriage. She now quietly sleeps at Mount Clam in Bienville Parish, Louisiana, whither she moved twenty-one years ago, with all her family except the writer of this notice. D. J. Myrick

Mrs. Agnes J. Young, wife of J. M. Young, was born Sept. 10th 1828, in Abbeville, S. C., and died Dec. 9th 1872, in Batesville, Miss. About three weeks previous to her death, sister Young left her

Carolina home to visit some friends in Mississippi. Early in life she united with the Presbyterian Church. A. J. Cauthen

Sister Emily Wallin, wife of Jesse Wallin, Jr., and daughter of Allen Williams in (who died in June, 1872) was born in Cherokee county, Ga., July 23d, 1835, and died in McLemore's Cove, Walker county, Ga., Oct. 13th 1872. She left a husband and five children. S. W. McWhorter

Mrs. Ermine Imogene Askew was born in Petersburg, Virginia, June 12th 1816 and died in Macon, Georgia, December 15th 1872. Her maiden name was Somerville. On 25th of June 1839, she was married to Rev. Josiah Fletcher Askew, a member of the North Carolina Conference. he died Nov. 7th 1848. C. W. Smith

Mrs. Fannie Rudolph, wife of Amzi Rudolph and daughter of Rev. Wier and Mrs. Sarah J. Boyd of Dahlonega, Ga., was born April 23d, 1847 and died in Gainesville, Ga., December 23d, 1872. Leaves a husband and a girl four years old, a boy five weeks old. J. H. Baxter

Margaret Covington, daughter of Elijah and Sarah Covington, was born March 23d, 1779 in Queen Ann's county, Maryland; was married to Samuel Brooks, August 31, 1797; moved to Georgia in 1804, where she buried her husband in 1853 in his eighty-fourth year; when she removed to Alabama, with one of her daughters, and remainder till her death, November 27, 1872. She raised twelve children. Her youngest child is now forty-eight years of age. C. L. McCartha

Sister Josephine E. Carroll was born in Newton county, Ga., May 4th 1836 and died in Madison, Ga., Dec. 28th 1872.

John N. Calhoun was born in Jones county, Ga., January 24th 1812 and died at the residence of his son-in-law, William Ball, in Gadsden county, Fla. Samuel Woodbery

Mrs. Mary Elizabeth Hill was born in Monroe county, Ga., July 25th 1809 and died Dec. 31st 1872.

Mr. Joseph Maddox was born in Putnam county, Ga., April 19th 1803, and died at his residence near Midway, Bullock, Ala., Nov. 30th 1872.

Tribute of Respect from Quarterly Conference Waukeenah Circuit, Florida Conference, to Rev. Daniel D. Sturges, a local deacon, who died at his residence in Jefferson county, Florida, 4th October 1872.

Issue of February 5, 1873

Died

Little Frank, son of Mr. J. A. and Mrs. Mary W. Allen, was born September 7, 1869 and died in Warrenton, Ga., Dec. 28, 1872.

Immegene, daughter of G. W. and A. E. Berry, was born November 9, 1866 and died Oct. 9, 1872.

Obituary

Mrs. Adelia L. Hand, wife of Mr. D. M. Hand of East Pascagoula, Miss., died on the 1st of January 1873, in the 39th year of her age, and the 19th year of her married life. She leaves no children, but a kind husband.

My father, John T. Carter, died at his residence in Hoganville, Troupe county, Ga., December 15th 1872, in his 71st year. He was born in Burke or Emanuel county, Ga., married my mother, Martha Wooten, in 1822, moved to Monroe county, thence on to Merriwether county, about 1829 and was among the early settlers of the county. Our mother preceded him over two years ago. They leave seven of us behind--seven preceded them. W. M. C.

Mrs. Elizabeth W. Johnson died in Thomson on 30th October 1872, in the sixty-fifth year of her age. She was born in Mt. Holley, N. J., in 1808. The only regret she seemed to have was leaving her only daughter and her little grand children behind her.

My mother, Sarah Ann Elizabeth Speir, daughter of John F. and Martha Davenport, was born in Pike county, Ga., December 20th 1834 and died in Barnesville, January 12, 1873. At eighteen she was married to Wm. H. Speir, and became the mother of four children. Wm. F. Lewis

Martha S. G. Woods, only daughter of Col. James S. and Mrs. A. D. Gibson, was born in Darlington, S. C., February 22d 1850. By the death of her father, she was left in early childhood to the sole care of a devoted mother. She died November 2d 1872. She lies beside her husband and two infant children, beneath the sod of their native village. A. J. Stafford

Mrs. Susan Smith, daughter of Dr. and Deborah Swain, was born in Guilford county, N. C., Dec. 25th 1808, married Joseph H. Smith, Feb. 7th 1833, and died Jan. 8th 1873 in Walker county, Ga. Sister Smith was reared under the Quaker influence. He little grandson, Willie, gave the alarm, and her daughter Emily was at her side. Her husband, four children, grandchildren, are left. D. J. Weems

Hugh M. Prince, Sr., died at the residence of hi son, W. L. Prince, in Williamston, S. C., Jan. 13th 1873, in his 76th year. Father Prince was born in Edgefield, but moved to Abbeville county, and there spent the greater part of his life. R. W. Barber

James D. Morrison of Camden county, Ga., died. Dec. 8th, 1872, aged about 38 years. E. Crum

Franklin E. Davidson, son of Elias and Lucretia J. Davidson, was born July 23d 1857 and died Dec. 18th 1872, in Troup county, Ga.

Major Purdie Richardson was born in Bladen county, North Carolina, in August 1801 and died at his residence near Wadesboro, N. C., December 8th 1872. Raleigh Christian Advocate please copy.

Mrs. Eliza Jane Medlock, wife of B. F. Medlock and daughter of Thos. Wahley, deceased, was born in Hancock county, Ga., November 2d, 1821; married September 13, 1838; united with the Baptist Church at Horeb, the same year, and died in Columbia county, Ark., Dec. 2d, 1872.

Mr. James Cody died in Warrenton, at the residence of Mr. J. A. Allen, on 17th January 1873. The deceased was born on the 11th October 1825. Mr. Cody was born and reared in Warren county and for nearly all of his life was a resident of Warrenton. But a few days before passed away his death little grandson, Frank Allen.

Elizabeth C. Sessions, wife of L. M. C. Sessions and daughter of Rev. J. B. and Louisa Jeffcoat, was born in Orangeburg county, S. C., March 10th 1828, immigrated with her parents to Leon county, Fla., in 1848. In 1850, May 2d, she was married to L. M. C. Sessions, and in 1870, she with her husband and family came to Orange county, Fla., settling near Lake Apopka, where she met death, December 6th 1872.

Mrs. Eliza J. Smith was born 13th November 1849 and died 7th October 1872.

Mrs. Mildred P. Williams was born 3d Sept 1848 and died in Greene county, Ga., Dec. 2d, 1872. J. L. Pierce

Mrs. Mary Ware, widow of Philip Ware, was born in Georgia, and died November 2, 1872 in the eighty-fifth year of her age, at the residence of her son, her only surviving child, Johnathan Ware, in Lafayette, Chambers county, Ala. M. A. Spratling

Died

Sallie Maude, daughter of William O. and Mary F. Nelson, at Conwayboro, S. C., January 3d, 1872, aged 6 years and 1 days.

Near Milledgeville, Jan. 20th 1873, Laura Eugenia, only daughter of John and Emma Hubbard, aged 10 years and 6 months.

On 24th Oct. 1872, Emma E., aged 3 years 10 months, second daughter of J. W. and M. C. Stephens

On the 31st Oct., Benjamin Rutledge, aged 2 years, 3 months.

Obituary

Sister E. H. Bush, wife of G. H. Bush of Monroe county, Georgia, was born June 9th 1847 an, married 12th July 1862, died 12th January 1873, leaving a husband and six children.

Mrs. Mary Ann Rumney died in Americus, Ga., Dec. 18th 1872, aged 48 years. She was raised a Presbyterian. She leaves a husband and two grown sons.

Mrs. Laura L. Tarver, daughter of Caroline and Henry S. Wimberly, was born in Twiggs county, Ga., Oct. 19th 1846. [date of death not stated]

Moses H. Adams died at his residence in Hart county, Ga., on the 23d of Nov. 1872, in the 46th year of his age. He leaves a wife and five children. Jno. W. Baker

William McKemie was born in Fairfield district, S. C., Dec. 17th 1790 and died in Troup county, Ga., Oct. 31st 1872. He grew to manhood, married and professed religion in his native State. Leaves a wife and children. W. J. Cotter

Sister Lucinda A. Smith, wife of R. W. Smith of Butts county, Georgia, was born 8th October 1811; married December 17th 1861, and died January 13th 1872.She leaves a husband and three children. F. M. Hunt

Rev. Russel Welborn Johnson of Bartow, Jefferson county, Ga., died at his residence on Saturday, Jan. 18th 1872, and was buried the next day. He was about sixty-three years and two months old at his death... left widow and children. Wm. Hauser, M. D.

R. Toomes Rheney, son of John W. and E. Rheney, was born in Burke county and died at Oxford, Ga., while at College in the nineteenth year of his age. N. B. Ousley

Mrs. Paulina America Tatum, wife of Col. Robert H. Tatum, died on the 19th day of January 1873, at her residence in Rising Fawn, Dade county, Ga. The deceased was the daughter of George and Clara Mills, was born in Jackson county, Alabama, 25th December 1833; was married to Col. Tatum, April 17th 1860 (she was his second wife); she leaves one child (Ula Kate Stanton, three years of age) and a husband with eight children by the former marriage. Nashville Christian Advocate please copy.

William T. Park died at his residence in Marion county, Ga., on 10th January 1873, in the 71st year of his age. He was raised in Hancock county, Ga., married Mazy D. Rees of Putnam county; moved to Stewart county in 1831. The first wife passed away several years since. He had been a member of the United Baptist Church. He leaves six daughters and two sons, one daughter in law by his first wife, and a second wife and three daughters. Joseph A. Park

Mary Franklin died on 2d January 1873 in Brunswick, Ga., in the 79th year of her age. J. O. A. Cook

Mrs. Isa Ann Wiley, wife of Henry Wiley (and only daughter of John and Mary Reynolds), died at the residence of her father on Lake Griffin, Sumpter county, Florida, Dec. 4th 1872, in the 17th year of her age. Left an infant a few days old.

Mrs. Eliza C. P. Vaughan was born Feb. 22d 1802, near Darien, Ga., and died Dc. 1st 1872, at Fernandina, Florida. She was a member of the Presbyterian Church.

Sister Sarah Glaze was born July 29th 1795 and died in Early county ,Ga., Nov. 18th 1872. He maiden name was Howell. She was married in 1816. B. H. Lester

Issue of February 19, 1873

Died

Died in Union county, Ark., on the 16th of December 1872, Ella Innea, daughter of Mr. J. T. and Mrs. M. E. Lockhart, aged 4 years, 10 months and 16 days.

Obituary

Mrs. Lizzie Reese, wife of Dr. John Reece and daughter of Colonel Dennis Hills, late of Floyd county, Ga., was born July 2d, 1836 near Rome, Ga., and died January 19, 1782, in Cedar Town, Polk county Ga. She was educated at Cambridge Female Seminary near Boston, Mass. She was married Oct. 21st 1856 and left five children, the eldest a daughter of 13 years.

Sister Emily H. Hopkins, wife of Rev. J. H. Hopkins, died January 4, 1873. W. R. Branham

Mrs. Martha Klugh, daughter of Thomas and Parmelia Tate, was born in Elbert county, Ga., in 1796. She was married to Pascal D. Klugh in 1831 and moved to Abbeville, S. C., where she lived until her death, which took place in January 1873, her husband having died five years previously. I married her only child, Dr. H. G. Klugh, and lived in the house with her twenty-two years. Sarah E. Klugh

Mrs. Sarah Boykin was born in Putnam county, Ga., May 30, 1818; married to Sterling R. Boykin, October 24, 1834; moved to Russell county, Ala. in 1836, where she lived until her death, December 19, 1872. Wm. A. McCarty

Mrs. Helen A. Adkins, wife of David Adkins was born in South Carolina and died in Crawford county, Ga., December 23d, 1872, aged about 27 years. She spoke to her uncle, Hon. W. G. Vinson. I. L. Avery

Mrs. Margaret Brown, consort of Asa Brown, was born March 31st 1802 and died at her home in Williamsburg county, January 12, 1873.

William Folsom died in Brooks county, Ga., on 18th of November last, in the 78th year of his age. He leaves an aged wife. H. W. Sharpe

Mrs. Elizabeth Fielding was born in Davidson county, Tenn. in the year 1795 and died November 18, 1872, in Columbia county, Fla. She was married to Thos. W. Fielding in the year 1812. In 1860 with her husband, removed to Florida, and he died in 1862. She has joined her husband, two sons and a daughter. Her remains are the first ever interred at Siloam Church, Florida. WM. H. Wilson. Nashville Advocate please copy.

Thomas Sledge was born in Jefferson county, Fla., in 1846 and died in Ellis county, Texas, December 10, 1872. D. H. Bryan

Miss Elizabeth Adamson died near Reidsville, Tatnall co., Ga., at her mother's, Nov. 1st 1872, in her 19th year. Her parents , Rev. H. W. and Mrs. Anna Adamson. W. J. Jordan

George A. Whitaker, only son of Captain Hudson Whitaker of Smithville, Ga., died at Sherman, Grayson county, Texas, 4th January, in the 24th year of his age. In December last, he left his native State for a home in Texas.

Mrs. Mary Ann Elizabeth Fuller, wife of W. T. Fuller and daughter of Dennis and Dabner E. Pascal, was born in Lincoln county, Ga., November 12, 1849, married December 17, 1868, and died December 12, 1872.

Issue of February 26, 1873

Died

Jesse Smith Newton, child of Smith and Elizabeth Ann Newton, was born March 3d 1872 and died Nov. 15th 1872.

Obituary

Juliet R. Lewis, wife of B. B. Lewis and daughter of Dr. Robert and Eliza Collins, was born in Charleston, S. C., July 4th 1840 and died in Macon, Ga., Feb. 2, 1872.

Robert Anderson Allen died in Augusta, Ga., Feb. 2d 1873, in the 66th year of his age. He was a native of Richmond county.

James W. Sappington was born in Wilkes county, Ga., July 22d, 1838 and died in Edgewood, Ga., Dec. 31st, 1872. He was a member of St. Paul's Church, Columbus, Georgia. G. H. Pattillo

Mrs. M. L. Slappy died in Sumter county, Ga., on the 10th January 1873, aged 23 years. Christian Index please copy.

Mrs. Susan M. Scruggs, daughter of Rev. L. C. and Julia Peek, was born in Telfair county, Ga., Oct. 29th 1843, married William H. Scruggs, Dec. 28th 1871, and died Nov. 25th 1872, in Brooks county, Ga. Comer L. Peek

Rev. W. C. Bryant was born in Wilkes county, Ga., Jan. 28th 1806, and died in Greene county, Dec. 23d 1872. J. L. Pierce

William Manning was born in Athloue, Ireland, in August 1769, and died at the residence of Mrs. Mary Turner, Clear Water Harbor, Hillsborough county, Fla., Jan. 4th 1873. He was reared up in the Catholic Church. He had service in Europe and America, had fought under Wellington against Bonapart, had fought against Great Britain for the United States in 1812, and had been in the U. S. Navy for years. J. D. Rogers

Brother G. W. Gibson of Fairfield county, S. C., died on the 18th of January 1873, in the forty-second year of his age. J. A. Clifton

Sister Cornelia M. Wood was the daughter of Wm. J. and Susan F. Schinholster and wife of Thos. C. Wood. She was born in Bibb county, Ga., March 29th 1853, and died Nov. 28th 1872. R. A. Cain

Sister Elvira, wife of T. J. Walser[?], died at Salado, Texas, on 25th of Nov 1872. Raised by pious parents, her father, brother Cole, of Spartanburg district, S. C. Seven children and a husband are left. J. F. Hines

Mrs. Harriet Newton, wife of Giles Newton, died in Marlboro county, S. C., Nov. 19th 1872. She leaves and husband and five children.

Tribute of Respect to James Glass.

Issue of March 5, 1873

Died

Mr. Wm. Kerr, a soldier of the war of 1812, aged eighty years and six months. He was the oldest inhabitant of Rock Hill.

Little Julia Homes Hall, daughter of Mr. W. J. and Mrs. Julia Hall, of Forrestville, Ga., was born July 24, 1870, and died February 6th 1873.

Obituary

Col. Wm. E. Adams died on 26th January in Eatonton, Ga., aged 88 years. He was born in North Carolina in 1748 [sic]; was reared in Greene county, Ga. In 1808 he settled in Putnam county where he died. He married the widow of Benj. Harris, of Hancock county, which union was blessed with a large family of children. A. M. Wynn

Mrs. Eliza Sidnor Smith, wife of Col. Wm. G. Smith, was born September 5, 1814, and died at Ansonville, N. C., January 11, 1873.

Rev. Benjamin R. Searcy was born in Cumberland county, N. C., January 16, 1797, moved to Georgia in 1818, resided in Jones county until 1826 when he became a resident of Talbot county. He died near Griffin, Ga., where he died 6th of February in the 77th year of his age. Mrs. J. T. Ansley

Mrs. Jos. Rivers, late of Cave Spring, Floyd county, Ga., son of Jos. Rivers (Reviere) was born Sept. 29th 1790 and died Jan. 27, 1873. He was a native of Savannah, Ga. He was married to his wife in May 1811, who died Dec. 31st 1871. He was a citizen of Philadelphia, Pa., for many years. He was a soldier in the war of 1812, and from the late pension act of Congress he was a beneficiary.

Monroe Butler Johnson, son of Isaac and Susan Johnson, died in Brooks county, Ga., Feb. 6th 1873, aged 25 years. When about nineteen years old, he married Miss Leanea Powell, afterwards becoming the father of three children, who are still living.

Rowland Redding died on 24th of Nov 1872, in the sixty-seventh year of his life. In the beginning of last year he removed to his old home near Drayton, in Dooly county, where he soon afterward lost his wife. W. Knox

Mrs. E. Smith, wife of Edward Smith and daughter of John Owen of Oglethorpe county, died on 13th of January 1873, in Monroe county, in the 63d year of her age. She left seven children. Wallace Lampkin

Capt. Thomas H. Wade was born in Columbia, S. C., Sept. 25, 1789 and lived almost all his life in his native place; he died in the beginning of 1873. William Martin

Issue of March 12, 1873

Died

Near St. Joseph, Louisiana, on the 20th of Feb, 1873, Clement Edwin Maddux, second and only son of Dr. Thomas H. and Lela Maddux, aged one year and nine months.

Obituary

Isaac Cheney of Talbot county was born March 1, 1812, and departed this life Dec. 1872. He was married to Miss Matilda Justice, Jan. 1833. L. Rush. Christian Index please copy.

Dr. Robert Harrlee died at his home in Marion county, S. C., November 25th 1872, aged sixty-five years. He served for a series of years in the State Legislature.

Mrs. Elizabeth McKenzie, daughter of Turner and Martha Webb, was born 6th of April 1796. She was married to John McKenzie in the year 1820, and was the mother of several children. She died 19th November 1872.

Mrs. Matilda J. Nolan, wife of Thomas L. Nolan, of Morgan county, Ga., was born 29th March 1835, and died January 1st 1873. She leaves a mother, sister, husband, and children. Geo N. Nolan

Mrs. E. Louisa Ballew, whose maiden name was James, was born in Stafford county, Va., and died in Laurens, S. C., Jan. 23d, 1873. She was married in 1829 to Rev. David L. Ballew, then a member of the South Carolina Conference. J. B. Traywick

Sister Maggie Ward, wife of Capt. P. H. Ward, died in Augusta, Ga., 9th of Feb. 1873. She was the daughter of J. B. and Margaret Stripling of Tatnall county, Ga., and the cousin of Rev. Robt. Stripling, who was for many years a member of the Georgia Conference. She leaves a husband and three little children. H. H. Parks

Sarah Ann Garrison was born in Tennessee, Nov. 13th 1838. In 1855 she married Mr. E. N. Faris of South Carolina. She died Nov. 8th 1873 [sic]. On the 10th, a grave in Ebenezerville, received her body. When a little girl she joined the Presbyterian Church. J. E. Watson.

Major William George Roberds was born July 31st 1810 and died at his residence in Beaufort county, S. C., Feb. 3d 1873. In civil life he filled many offices of trust and honor, being repeatedly returned to the Legislature.

Mrs. Martha Morgan was born in Gates county, N. C., and died near Jonesboro, Ga., Jan. 5th 1873, being 55 years of age.

Nathan Gunnin was born Aug. 1797 and died Dec. 1872. In June 1845 he was married to Miss Mary Lights. In 1859 he moved from South carolina to Columbia county, Florida.

Mrs. Mary B. Sloan, wife of T. M. Sloan, died in the 65th year of her age in Clinton, S. C.   R. N. Wells

Issue of March 19, 1873

Henrietta Clark was born in Effingham co., April 23d 1796 and died in Atlanta, Jan. 6th 1873. Mother was the youngest child of Henry Gindrat, who belonged to a French Huguenot family, which, on the revocation of the Edict of Nantes, fled to Berne in Switzerland. From thence my grand-father emigrated to South Carolina. His second wife was my grand-mother, Dorcas Williams, of Pitt county, North Carolina. He was an officer in the Revolutionary army. He was the ancestor of the Gindrats of South Carolina, Georgia and Alabama, and died in Effingham county, Ga., in 1801. Grandmother survived him three years and died in 1804. Our mother was married in 1823 to my father, Josiah Hodyn Clark. In Savannah, October 1832, father died. Her firstborn, Judge Richard H. Clark, of Atlanta. She died on January 6th. Her body was deposited in Rose Hill Cemetery in Macon, by the side of three of her grandchildren, and of her son, Rev. Josiah H. Clark who died in 1851. J. O. A. Clark

Dr. Alexander Williams was born in South Carolina, Nov. 3d, 1801, and died at his son's residence in Arkansas, Jan. 7th 1873. His nephew

James Mizell, the only son of Matthew and ___ Mizell of Brooks county, Ga., was born 1 January 1850 and died in Macon, Ga., on February 3d 1873. S. S. Sweet

William Barber, father of Rev. R. W. Barber, of the South Carolina Conference, died in Chester co., S. C., Feb. 21st 1873, in his 78th year. J. M. Boyd

Humphrey Posey Oglesby died in Rockdale county, Ga., January 9, 1873, aged 16 years and 7 months.

E. Stockbridge Florence died in Columbia county, Ga., on the 3d of December last, in the 27th year of his age. Son of Rev. Wm. A. Florence of the North Georgia Conference. Luther M. Smith

Mollie, beloved wife of W. D. Rogers and daughter of Rev. W. C. and Margaret J. Patterson, died in Lancaster co., S. C., Feb. 6th 1873, in her 29th year.

Dr. A. R. Sheppard was born in Butler county, Ala., June 15th 1832 and died in the same county, June 8th 1873. He was the only son of Francis and Sally Sheppard, and was married in 1858 to Miss Mollie Golson. He leaves and wife and children. B. L. Selman

Mrs. Mary Swindall, wife of Thomas Swindall, was born in Green county, October 1801 and died in Troup county, February 26th 1873. Her maiden name was Moore (a sister of the late Green Moore, of Green county); she was married first to George Wells-- after his death to Mr. Swindall. Her second marriage was a little more than twenty-eight years ago. W. J. Cotter

Phillip B. Pritchett was born in Hancock county, Ga., April 15th 1791 and died in Jasper county, Ga., December 29th 1872. He leaves an aged widow.

Sister Dorris, wife of Rev. John M. Dorris, was born in Jackson co., in 1806 and died in Douglas county on the 26th of Jan. 1873. H. C. Christian

J. G. Minglefort died in Effingham co., Ga., on the 10th Feb. 1873, aged 86 years and 10 months.

Issue of March 26, 1873

Died

On the 19th of Feb. 1873, Willie W. S. McHan, son of Rev. W. B. and Mrs. Julia A. McHan, aged 15 years and 3 months.

Obituary

Mrs. Lavinia Dunwody, wife of the late Rev. Samuel Dunwody of the South Carolina Conference, was born in Edgefield district, S. C., on 27th May 1788 and died in Cokesbury, S. C., on 10th Feb. 1873. Her body rests by the side of her husband at old Tabernacle.

Almira Woodwarth McLeod, daughter of the late Wm. Rogers of Bishopville, Sumter county, S. C., and the beloved wife of Dr. Robt. Y. McLeod, was born in Bishopville, S. C., Nov. 4th 1845, and died Jan. 30th 1873. Wm. W. Mood

Mrs. Mary Osiana Wilson, daughter of Mrs. Elizabeth M. Richardson of Marion, S. C., and wife of John O. Wilson, Esq., was born August 4th 1852, married April 27th 1871, and died January 19th 1873, leaving a babe born Feb. 23d 1872.

Mrs. Minerva S. Mathews, wife of the Hon. Dr. W. P. Mathews and daughter of the late Dr. Wm. Drane, died in the forty-fifth year of her age, at Prattsburg, Tolbert county, Ga. L. B. Payne

Miss Mary E. Littlejohn, daughter of John and Catharine Littlejohn, was born Sept. 10th 1844 and died at the residence of her father in Polk county, N. C., on the 23d of Feb. 1873. She has left a father and two brothers. W. W. Womack

Joseph C. Gantt died in Cleveland county, N. C., in the 26th year of his age. After the war he returned to his home in North Carolina, married, and moved to East Tennessee, and resided there two years, after which he returned to his native home. He left a wife and three children.

Mrs. Mary A. Snow, wife of A. D. Snow, died in Walker county, Ga., on the 11th Dec last, aged 38 years. She left a husband and three children. A. W. Rowland

Brother Geo. M. Smith, son of Rev. Jas. R. and Mrs. Mary A. Smith, was born in Butts county, Ga., Sept. 15th 1856 and died December 27th 1873.

Issue of April 2, 1873

Died

In Putnam county, Ga., Mar. 5, 1873, Robert Oslin, youngest son of Dr. J. Z. and Mrs. M. E. Maddux, aged 1 year, 8 months and 4 days.

Near Tallahassee, Leon county, Fla., on the 17th of March 1873, Edward James Oliver, eldest son of James and Victoria Oliver, aged 5 years, six months and 15 days.

Obituary

Mrs. Ann Barbara McCants was born in Camden, S. C., November 14, 1794, and died at Orange Hill, the residence of Rev. John P. Margaret, near Eufaula, Barbour county, Ala., February 24, 1873. Mrs. McCants was the daughter of Mr. Daniel Carpenter, formerly a merchant of New York, who removed to Camden about the year 1792. About the year 1814 she was married to Mr. John McCants, a promising young merchant of Camden. He died about 1819 and left two lovely daughters. About the year 1828 she removed to Mount Ariel, now Cokesbury, S. C. About 1834, she removed to Houston county, Ga., near the town of Fort Valley, and took her aged mother under her care. Her here younger daughter was married. In 1844, Mrs. McCants was bereft of her eldest and only surviving daughter, and in 1849 her mother, Mrs. Lydia Carpenter, in the 82d year of her age. John P. Margart

Mrs. Susan A. Budington, wife of Judge Ozier Budington, was born at Easton, Maryland, Oct. 28, 1813, and died at Whitesville, Fla., February 28, 1872.

My wife, Mrs. Martha A. Nicholson, daughter of J. A. and D. Winn, was born in Jackson co., Ga., Dec. 10, 1832 and died in Pickens county, Ala., January 20, 1873. Buried at Andrew Chapel Church. Evan. Nicholson

Mrs. Eliza Dixon Baldwin was born in Autauga county, Ala., March 20, 1844, and died in Merriwether county, Ga., February 23, 1873. In childhood, death deprived her of her parents. Her aunt, Mrs. E. B. Bell, became her foster-mother. She was married to Mr. A. M. Baldwin, whom, with four children are left to mourn.

Mrs. Mary Hightower, wife of James Hightower and daughter of Wm. H. Walker, of Culloden, Ga., was born on 22d June 1841 in Macon, Ga., and died in Upson county ,Ga., Jan. 23d, 1873. She left a husband and three little daughters. J. O. A. Cook

Mrs. Emeline Gibbs, wife of Andrew J. Gibbs, of Suwanee county, Fla., was born 28th February 1849.. Her body rests in New Hope Church yard.

Mrs. Harriet Foy died in Edgefield county, S. C., on 16th of January in the 58th year of her age. She left three grown children. W. Hutto

Henry Rogers was born in Cabarras county, N. C., June 6, 1788 and died in Putnam county, Ga., February 10, 1873. Father Rogers was one of the earliest settlers of Putnam. Seven of his sons fell int he service of their country in the late war. Two survive him with several daughters. W. W. Oslin

Rev. Miles Nash, M. D., died at the residence of his son-in-law, Judge D. W. Gwynn, near Tallahassee, Fla., January 16, 1873. He was born in Norfolk county, Va., March 15, 1797; entered the Virginia Conference about 1820, sooner after which he was married. In 1836 he came to Florida and graduated in medicine in Charleston, S. C. In 1842 he was commissioned postmaster of Tallahassee. Josephus Anderson

Mrs. Elizabeth Yarbrough, mother of Rev. John W. Yarbrough of the North Georgia Conference, was born in Spartanburg, S. C., August 4, 1786, and died in Marietta, Ga., Jan. 27, 1873. Her parents, William and Milly Edwards, were among the early Methodists of Spartanburg, S. C. W. F. Cook. Christian Neighbor please copy.

Mrs. Mary Ann Thomason, relict of Sewell Thomason, late of Greenville county, S. C., was born September 17, 1830, and died January 30, 1873. Sister Thomason was a member of the Fair View Presbyterian Church.

My eldest daughter, Susan M. Polhill, wife of Dr. John G. Polhill, died in Montezuma, Ga., on 7th March in the 43d year of her age. H. W. Sharpe

Benjamin Marion Grier, son of Benjamin and Mary Grier, was born November 15, 1810 in Georgetown county, S. C., and died February 15, 1873. J. W. Kelly

Issue of April 9, 1873

Mary E. Ward was born in Paris, Kentucky, but removed while quite young to Florida. She was married to Rev. Joseph J. Sealy of the Florida Conference, Feb. 5th 1855 and died March 10th 1872. Her conversion occurred while she was at her brother-in-law's, Dr. Braden's, in Manatee. Josephus Anderson

Mrs. Sarah Arnold was born 17th Dec. 1793 and died at the residence of her son in law, Bro. Virgil Allen, near Atlanta, on the 16th Feb 1873. She was the widow of Rev. Wm. Arnold. Married before her fourteenth birth-day... Her remains were taken to Eatonton and now rest by the side of him whom she loved. Wm. H. LaPrade

Mrs. Mary A. Magruder, daughter of Major John and Mrs. Mary Power, was born in Edgefield district, S. C., May 1st 1803; was married to Rev. William Magruder of Columbus county, Ga., in December 1827, and died at Lowndesville, Abbeville district, S. C., on the 28th of December 1872. She left three children.

Mrs. Diana Ormand was born in Montgomery county, N. C., June 10th 1790 and died near Fort Mills, S. C., March 21st 1873. In the year 1812 she was married to Mr. John Ormand. J. F. England

Dr. Henry Isaac Abbott died on the 11th of March at his residence near Lodibar, Sumter county, S. C., in the 70th year of his age.

Mrs. Amy Ann Talley, oldest daughter of Capt. Samuel and Mrs. Ann Potter, was born in Brunswick county, North Carolina, 7th December 1801. She was married to Rev. Nicholas Talley, Sept. 23d 1819. She died in Columbia, S. C., February 20th 1873. Wm. Martin

Dr. J. J. Ellis of Florence, S. C., died on the 4th of February 1873, lacking 2 days of being 89 years old. He leaves a wife and three children. L. Wood

Mrs. Nancy Allen, daughter of John and Nancy Tucker, was born June 16th 1808, in Spartanburg district, S. C., and died January 14th 1873, in a few miles of the place where she was born. She was married to Emanuel Allen when she was about twenty-two years old.

Mrs. Julia Mildred Adams, daughter of Nathaniel A. and Mary Mildred Adams, died in Petersburg, Indiana, January 15th 1873, in the thirty-eighth year of her age.

My mother, extensively known as Aunt Polly Haygood, was born in Hancock County, Ga., on 14th of June 1791. She was the daughter of Mark and Martha Stroud. Her parents moved with her to Clarke county, Georgia, when she was young. She was married to William Haygood, March 8th 1806, with whom she lived until his death, July 30th 1849. She was the mother of eleven children, five sons and six daughters. One little girl died in her sixth year; the others lived to the prime of life. Her son, Green B., died Dec. 24th 1862 and John, July 17th 1864. The other eight still live.

The oldest is sixty-four and the youngest forty-one year old. She had 56 grand-children, 21 of whom are dead. F. M. Haygood

Washington Foster was born in Spartanburg district, on the 22d February 1814, and died on 31st January 1873, at his home, Rich Hill circuit, Spartanburg county, S. C. James F. Smith

A. Houghston Foster, brother of the above, was born Oct. 11, 1818 and died Feb. 1, 1873. So lived and died two of the best men in Lebanon church, Rich Hill circuit. James F. Smith

Sister Charlotte Ann Dixon, daughter of Rev. Wm. D. and Elizabeth R. Starr and wife of W. N. Dixon, was born in Spalding county, Ga., May 15th 1831 and died in Clayton county, Ga., Dec. 23d, 1872. Joseph P. Smith.

Mrs. M. J. Ruffin, wife of J. L. Ruffin and daughter of William and Elizabeth Gordon, was born Nov. 11, 1848 and died in Macon county, Ala., February 6, 1873. She leaves one child and a husband. J. W. Solomon

Samuel Pennington was born in Warren county, Ga., March 18, 1800 and died in Madison, Ga., February 22d, 1873.

Issue of April 16, 1873

Died

Near Tallahassee, Fla., March 28, 1873, Mattie Eugenia, daughter of James and Victoria E. Olivers, aged two years and eight months.

Near Loachapoka, Lee county, Ala., on 7th of March, little Nathan J., son of H. H. and Mattie Hargrove, aged six months.

Willie Taylor, only son of Joseph H. and Mary Eugenia Taylor, was born April 9, 1862, and died in Cuthbert, Ga., Feb. 18th 1873.

Obituary

Mrs. Anna Betts Owens, wife of Dr. Owens of Atlanta, and daughter of Rev. Jas. E. Godfrey, was born February 14, 1844, and died at her father's residence, March 26th 1873.

Mrs. Harriet Walker was born in Abbeville district, S. C., July 14, 1799, and died January 3d 1873, at the residence of her son-in-law, W. W. Wills, of Bradford county, Fla. Jas. P. DePass

Mrs. Mary Eugenia Taylor, only daughter of George and Catherine Duncan and wife of Jos. H. Taylor, was born in Houston county, Ga., Jan. 6th 1845 and died in Cuthbert, Ga., February 26th 1873. J. O. A. Cook

Rev. Greenberry Garrett, son of Eli and Agatha Garrett, was born in Davidson county, Tenn., July 24th 1800 and died March 20th 1873 in Summerfield, Ala. When thirty-two years of age, he was united in wedlock to Mary W. Speer, by Rev. A. L. P. Green. One son and four daughters were the fruit of this marriage. He was bereaved of his first wife in 1850, lived a widower until 1856 when he was married to Mrs. Eliza J. Plummer, who survives him. He was buried by the side of his first wife in our Woodland Cemetery. R. H. Harris

Mrs. Josephine A. Taylor, wife of H. S. Taylor and daughter of Abraham and Lucy Miller, died at the residence of her father, near Palmetto, Ga., on the 20th of March 1873, in her 28th year. W. D. Payne

Miss Eliza E. Howe, daughter of W. J. and Lucinda Howe, was born in Monroe county, Ga., 16th July 1848. In August of 1871 her cousin Mary Susan White died. She died March 24th 1873. F. M. Hunt

SOUTHERN CHRISTIAN ADVOCATE NOTICES 1867-1878

Lola Walton Biggers died at LaVert Female College in Talbotton, Ga., on the 15th March 1873. She was fourteen years and three days old.

Edward T. McGehee, eldest son of Rev. J. B. and Mrs. L. L. McGehee, was born in Houston county, Ga., 14th of November 1853 and died in Cuthbert, Ga., 17th of February 1873.

Miss Lucy A. Turner of McDonough, Ga., a member of the Junior Class of Wesleyan Female College, departed this life in Macon, Ga., on 30th January 1873, in the 19th year of her age.

Obadiah Copelan was born July 4th 1800 and died in Greene county, Ga., December 29th 1872. J. L. Pierce

Daniel Graddock died in Harris county, Ga., March 15th, in the 85th year of his age. He was born in Richland district, S. C., and removed to Georgia about forty-three years ago. H. P. Pitchford

Mary Adelia Snow, wife of A. D. Snow, died in Walton county ,Ga., December 17, 1872, aged 38 years. A. W. Rowland

J. A. Bedanbaugh was born November 16th 1826 and died January 15, 1873. He leaves a widow and nine children.

Jonathan S. Brown was born in Monroe county, Ga., February 26, 1851, and died in the same county, March 11, 873. W. H. Graham

Issue of April 23, 1873

Died

Near Lockhart, Texas, April 3d 1873, Rosalie, infant daughter of W. A. and M. Virginia Waller, aged four months and four days.

In Troup county, Ga., April 7th 1873, Linton, aged about one year, infant son of J. M. and R. D. Lovelace.

Obituary

Mrs. Irene S. Anderson, daughter of Isaac and Martha E. Winship and wife of Louis F. Anderson, was born June 7th 1844 and died in Atlanta, Ga., April 6th 1873. She was a member of Mulberry Street M. E. Church, South, and Macon, Georgia. W. C. Bass

Mrs. Mary A. Burney died at the home of her grand-daughter, in Burke county on the 7th of March, in the 65th year of her age. J. B. Jones

Sister Lucy Loyless died in Dawson, at the home of her nephew, Rev. E. B. Loyless, on the 8th of March 1873, having attained the age of 87 years.

Rebecca A. Livingstone was born Jan. 12th 1801 and died in Orangeburg county, S. C., Jan. 14th 1873.

John W. Pitts was born in North Carolina, April 2, 1804, and died at his residence in Newborn, Newton county, Ga., January 11th 1873. A Daughter

Ambrose Hanley was born in Virginia, Sept. 17th 1806 and died in Hamilton, Harris county, Ga., Feb. 21st 1873. He was first married to Miss Elizabeth Nettles, Feb. 18th 1830. His second wife was Mrs. M. A. Reese, to whom he was married Feb. 3d, 1859. He leaves a widow, three daughters by his first and one by his last marriage. W. F. Robison

Williams D. Sineath was born in South Carolina in the year 1805, removed to Lowndes, now Berrien county, Ga., about 30 years ago, and died at his residence in Berrien county, 8 March 1873. H. W. Sharpe

Cason H. Woodham, daughter of John and Mary Riley, was born in Darlington district, S. C., about 1810, was married to Ariss Woodham in the same district, Dec. 25th 1831. In 1833 they removed to Henry county, Ala., and in 1834 to Dale county, Ala., where she lived until death March 18, 1873. A. Dowling

Charles C., son of Thomas and Sarah F. Frink, was born in Ocala, Marion county, Florida, Dec. 14th 1830 and died at the residence of his mother, March 26th 1873. Geo. C. Leavel

Gardner H. Davis was born Dec. 1803 in Jasper county, Ga., and died at his home near Glennville, Russell county, Ala., on the 4th of March 1873.

Mrs. Catharine Gregg, wife of Samuel Gregg, died near Mars Bluff, S. C., January 11th 1873, in the 23d year of her age.

W. Gordon Gregg died in Marion county, S. C., March 22d 1873, in the seventy-first year of his age. A. J. Stafford

Brother J. B. Chastain died at his residence in Anderson county, S. C., Feb. 3d, 1873. D. J. McMillan

Mrs. C. G. Lamon died in Thomas county, Ga., March 19th 1873. She was born in Robinson county, N. C., where she grew up and married. In 1834, they moved to Montgomery county, Ga., and in 1842 to Thomas county. W. M. Watts

Laura Anthony, daughter of Jonathan C. and Jane Edwards and wife of H. Thomas Anthony was born in Harris county,Ga., in 1851, and died in Muscogee county, Ga., March 24th 1873.

Tribute of Respect from Long Cane circuit, North Georgia Conference to William McKinnie, an exhorter.

Issue of April 30, 1873

Died

On the 19th of April in Calvo, Thomas county, Ga., Callie V., infant daughter of Dr. D. H. and C. V. Wilmot, aged 1 year, 7 months and 2 days.

In Oglethorpe, Ga., Sunday, April 29, in the sixty-ninth year of her age, Catharine H. Watkins, widow of the late Ansel Lee Watkins, and daughter of Robert B. and Elizabeth Washington.

Obituary

Hugh B. McMaster died at Winnsboro, S. C., on the 8th of April 1873. He was born at Winnsboro, where he spent his life and died at the age of fifty-three years. He was Commissary of the 17th Regiment, S. C. V.

Mrs. Louisa Miranda Clements, daughter of Mr. D. C. R. and Mrs. Mariah E. Lowe, was born July 17, 1842, married J. W. Clements, M. D., of Subligus, Chattooga county, Ga, August 16, 1867, and died January 23d 1873. She leaves three children of tender years. James T. Lowe

Rev. Jacob E. Danforth was born in Saratoga county, N. Y., April 23d 1816 and died in Macon, Ga., February 4th 1873.

Mrs. Margaret Livingston, wife of Captain Thos. J. Livingston and daughter of the late John S. Wynche, Esq., of Madison county, Fla., died in Quitman, Ga., on the 3d of April 1873. She was married to Capt. T. J. Livingston, 20 Dec 1855. They removed to Quitman at the close of the late war. She leaves an aged mother and an only sister, a husband and five children. S. S. Sweet

Margaret H. Innes was born in Quincy, Fla., July 10, 1851; married to Jas. Watt, April 16, 1782, and died in Bainbridge, Ga., March 2d 1873. Henry Ed. Partridge

James Brady Oliver, youngest son of J. B. and Mrs. Sarah Oliver, was born July 19, 1855, and died at Damascus, Early county, Ga., February 4th 1873. John M. Potter

Mrs. Lettia F. Star, wife of Samuel F. Star, was born in Pickens District, S. C., June 11, 1817, and died in Tallapoosa county, Ala., January 17, 1873. J. N. Dupree

Mrs. P. W. Jones, wife of Rev. R. F. Jones of the North Georgia Conference, and daughter of Hill and Mary Sandeford, was born in Burke county, Ga., June 12, 1836 and died at Newnan, Ga., April 8th 1873. A. J. Dean

Mrs. Mary Fielding was born in Stewart county, Tennessee, April 1832 and died in Columbia county, January 23, 1873. She was the daughter of Christopher and Mary Brandon of Stewart county, Tenn., where she was married to Thomas W. Fielding. In 1861 she moved to Florida. She leaves eight children, most of whom are small. Wm. H. Wilson. Nashville Advocate and Dover Record copy.

Mrs. Louisa F. Fouche, formerly of Culloden, Ga., was born October 21, 1827, and died in Barnesville, Ga., March 13, 1873. She was the wife of George W. Fouche and daughter of Alfred and Mary W. Drake.

Mrs. Jane McCutcheon, wife of Benjamin R. McCutcheon, deceased, and daughter of Wm. and Nancy Bell of Jackson county, Ga., was born January 27, 1798 and died February 4, 1873. She was married in 1821. She leaves seven children. Her remains are deposited in the cemetery at Lafayette, Walker County, Ga., by the side of her husband. A. Odom

Mrs. Martha Ann, wife of J. G. Shannon and daughter of B. H. and Susan W. Mitchell, was born in Newnan, Ga., August 14, 1834, and died in the same place March 18, 1873.

Mrs. Martha Ann E. Dickson, wife of John S. Dickson and eldest daughter of Thomas S. and Francis M. Mason, died in Macon, Ga., February 5th 1873. She was born in Laurens county, May 15th 1843. She was married September 8th 1859. She left a husband and four little children, father and mother, sisters and brothers.

Wm. C. Cambell died on the 28th March 1873 in Marion county, S. C., in the 73d year of his age. E. J. Moody

Issue of May 7, 1873

Died

Egbert Lovelace (one of the twins), son of J. M. and M. A. Lovelace, died April 22d 1873, in Troup county, Ga., aged six years.

Obituary

Mrs. Martha W. Cox, whose maiden name was Ashworth, was born in Union district, S. C., about 1808 and died in Gwinnett county, Ga., March 6th 1873. Harmony Grove Church, the neighbors, an aged companion, a son and two daughters miss her.... Robt. P. Martin

Henry T. Sheats, son of John L. and Ann E. Sheats, died in Atlanta, Ga., March 19th 1873, in the nineteenth year of her age, while attending "Moore's Business University."

Cynthia Durance, daughter of Phillip Tippins, was born September 15th 1786 and died 11th February 1873, in Tatnall county, Where she was raised and had lived to the age of 87. Mother Durance lived to see her fourth generation. W. J. Ordan

Mrs. Ann S. Sistrunk, was the daughter of Daniel Riley, of Orangeburg district, S. C. She was born Nov. 11th 1826 and died March 12th 1873. Her married to George L. S. Sistrunk, which occurred in 1845, was a very happy one. In August 1870 her husband died, leaving her one child, a son twenty-three years of age, who survived his father only about one month. In the latter part of December last, she visited her sister, Mrs. Wesley Houser, near Fort Valley, Georgia. Her remains were returned to S. C. and deposited by the side of her husband and son in the village graveyard at Orangeburg C.H. F. A. Branch

Mrs. Margaret C. Toombs, wife of Dr. R. E. Toombs, died Feb. 19th 1873, at her residence in the city of Cuthbert, aged forty-one. Her youngest daughter Eva, of seven years, died on the 17th, and another daughter, Sarah Catharine, aged ten, on the 21st of the same month.

Miss Mattie E. Newman, daughter of Judge N. W. Newman, died in Forsyth, Ga., April 11th 1873, in the twenty-second year of her age. She was born in Monroe county, Ga., Sept 26th 1850, was reared and educated in Forsyth, at the Monroe Female College. D. J. Myrick

Mrs. Mary McKinnon, wife of Archibald McKinnon and daughter of Daniel Finlayson, was born in S. C., 1809 and died in Wakulla county, near Crawfordville, Fla., March 12th 1873. D. W. Core

Sarah Jane Gordy, wife of G. M. Gordy, was born Nov. 25th 1845 and died in Harris county, Ga., Feb. 4th 1873. Jas. T. Lowe

Mrs. Anna Sybella, consort of Major M. R. Marks and daughter of Judge Eli G. and Mrs. A. V. Hill, of Terrell county, Georgia, died on the 6th April, at Lake Maitland, Orange county, Florida. Her little daughter Jessie.

Mrs. Caroline Bartlett Moore died at her home, Tuskegee, Alabama, April 20th 1873. She was the daughter of Rev. Bartlett Thomason, late of the South Carolina Conference. She was born in Orangeburg district, South Carolina, October 6th 1840; she was married in Cass county, Ga., Sept 27th 1859 to Rev. Henry D. Moore. T. F. Mangum

Thomas Rivers was born in Hancock county, May 9th 1800 and died about the 10th of February 1873 in Fayette county, Ga. New Orleans Christian Advocate please copy.

Joshua P. Shropshear was born in Oglethorpe county, Ga., February 17th 1806 and died in Fayette county, March 10th 1873. Leaves a wife and daughters.

Brother Raiford M. Floyd was born at Nunansville, Fla., Jan. 1st, 1847, and died at the residence of D. L. Stroble, his brother-in-law, in Waldo, Florida.

Mr. Edward Pennick was born in Prince Edward county, Va., the 28th of April 1835 and died at his residence in Ala., March 16th 1873.

Mrs. Amanda E. Davis was born Dec. 13th 1852, joined the Methodist E. Church, South at New Hope, 1866, and died in Union County, S. C., April 1st 1873. John B. Wilson

Tribute of Respect from Bethany circuit, South Georgia Conference to Rev. Russel W. Johnson who died 18th January 1873, in the 63d year of his age.

Issue of May 14, 1873

Died

In Washington, Ga., March 15, 1873, Mary Lucy, infant daughter of Milton P. and Sallie H. Reese, aged 14 months and 3 days.

In Hogansville, Ga., May 1, 1873, little Preston, son of Col. William and Mrs. L. J. Cain, aged 4 years and 19 days.

Laura Octavia Henderson was born May 28, 1871, and died in Fayette county, Ga., April 9, 1873.

Obituary

Mary Jane Urquhart, wife of Dr. John Urquhart, died at her home in Columbus, Ga., April 22, in the 52d year of her age. She was the eldest daughter of the late Judge Eli S. Shorter; born in Eatonton, Ga., May 20th 1821; removed to Columbus in early life; married in 1837. J. S. Key

Mrs. Amilar Kiker was born in North Carolina, 4th May 1794 and died in Gordon county, Ga., 4th of April 1873. T. J. Simmons

Mrs. Mary Craig, wife of Rev. Hugh Craig, was born June 12, 1801, and died at Chesterfield C. H., S. C., January 30, 1872. A. Ervin

John J. Chitwood was born on the 27th October 1809 and died at his residence near Clarkesville, Habersham county, Ga., April 13, 1873. Wm. Parks Smith

Mrs. Elizabeth Fort, whose maiden name was Stanford, was born in Putnam county, Ga., Feb. 7th 1810, and died in Talbot county, Ga., April 15, 1873. Her marriage to Mirando Fort took place in November 1829. R. W. Dixon

Mrs. Susan L. Truluck, wife of Bryant Truluck, was born in North Carolina, April 1808; her maiden name was Shines; she was first married to Mr. Henderson of North Carolina, who lived but a short time, and then she removed to Georgia, where she was married to Mr. Truluck, and settled near Vienna, Dooly county, where she died April 20, 1873. She leaves a husband, two daughters and many grandchildren. James R. Dickson

Mrs. Susan Emma Smith, daughter of R. P. and S. A. Laney, was born 15th August 1843 in Russel county, Ala., and died in Birmingham, Ala., March 30, 1873. In early womanhood she was married to Mr. Camden Evans. In a few short years his young life was laid upon the altar of his country. Just four weeks before his death she consigned to the tomb an only son. About five years ago she was united in marriage to Mr. Stephen L. Smith.

Mrs. Sarah A. Warnock, wife of Irwin C. Warnock, died in Terrel co., Ga., Feb. 8, 1873. She was born in Lee county, December 25, 1837. She was married February 27, 1855. She leaves a husband and five little children. E. J. Rentz

Mrs. Margaret Hardwick was born in Horry county, S.,C., and died at her home, April 21, 1873.

Mrs. Permelia E. Snell, wife of David W. Snell, was born May 29th 1829 and died at her home in Orangeburg county, S. C., March 27th 1873.

Miss Mary E. Knight, daughter of Daniel and Nancy Knight, died in Fulton county, Ga., April, 12, 1873, in the 23d year of her age. J. B. C. Quillian

James Jones, a native of North Carolina, died in Troup county, Ga., April 2d, 1873, aged nearly 93 years. He was one of the first settlers in the county, coming before the Indians left. W. J. Cotter

Tribute of Respect from Quarterly Conference, Mulberry street Charge, Macon District to Jacob R. Danford, A. R. Freeman, and B. A. Wise.

Tribute of Respect from Quarterly Conference for Georgetown, Midway and St. Paul, to Thomas Berry.

Issue of May 21, 1873

Died

Near Milledgeville, Georgia, May 4th 1873, Charles Henry, eldest son of John and Emma Hubbard, aged 8 years and 10 months.

Obituary

James Merriwether Duncan, formerly of Southwestern Georgia, died at his home near Pine Bluff, Arkansas, on March 21st, 1873.

Mrs. Elizabeth Jane McRae, daughter of John and Christianna Clements, was born May 5th 1836 in Telfair county, Ga., and died April 25th 1873 in Spring Hill, Montgomery county, Ga., within ten days of her 37th birth day. In 1859 she was married and her husband became a member of the Southern army early in the late war... he died in March 1865. She has left two little boys. H. C. Fentress

Sister Iranonah C. Smith was born Sept 5th 1833 in Coweta county, Georgia, and died March 29th 1873, near Dallas, Texas. She was the daughter of C. W. and Mary E. Arnold. She moved to Louisiana with her parents in 1856; was married to Thomas H. Smith on 9th November 1871. She leaves a husband, father, mother, sister and four brothers. H. O. White. Newnan Herald please copy.

Sister Margaret Key was born in North Carolina, April 4th 1789, and died in Monroe county, at the residence of her son-in-law, Thomas T. McMullin, on 13th April 1873. Her parents Robert and Margaret Greer, moved to Morgan county, Georgia, where the subject of this obituary was married to Mr. Joseph Key in 1811. She joined the church then known as the Seceders. J. M. Bolton. Due West Telescope please copy.

George K., the only son of Rev. Benj. F. and Mrs. S. A. Breedlove, aged 12 years, 6 months, and 28 days, died at Cuthbert, Ga., March 29th 1873. J. B. Cozby

Mrs. Elizabeth Ioove[?], wife of the late Major B. Clarke, Newnan, died Dec. 29th 1872, in Coweta county, Ga., in the 62d year of her age. The deceased was a native of South Carolina. Lillie B. Clarke

Mrs. Fannie L. Russell, wife of Mr. R. Russell, died near Carrollton, Ga. She was the daughter of Sylvanus and Elizabeth Bell-- born in Coweta county, May 8; married Oct. 4, 1857. She leaves six lovely children and a husband.

Sister Elizabeth Johnson, familiarly called "Aunt Betsey," consort of William Johnson, who preceded her to the tomb only five months, was born in Franklin county, Ga., April 18th 1813, and died in Winterville, Oglethorpe county, Ga., April 15th 1873. C. A. Conoway

Christiana Rast, nee Hunkapiller, relict of Frederic Rast, deceased, was born in Orangeburg district, S. C., about the last of June 1793 and died at her home in Autauga county, Ala., April 29th 1873. She and her husband were both of Dutch descent, their parents having come to American in early life. She was married to Mr. Rast, March 7th 1815, he being a widower and having several children by a former wife. Mother Rast was reared by Presbyterian parents. W. A. Montgomery

Mrs. Nancy H. Roberts, whose maiden name was Meridy, died at her residence in Newton county, Georgia, on the 7th of April 1873, about 70 years of age. She was married to Mr. Richard F. G. Roberts in 1816. J. J. Groves

Tribute of Respect to Rev. Charles Wilson from Orange circuit, Orangeburg District, at Ebenezer.

Issue of May 28, 1873

Died

In Savannah, Ga., on the 11th of May 1873, Emmett R. Gorman, infant son of Colonel Wm. W. and Lillie E. Holland, aged five months and twenty days.

Obituary

James Freeman was born on the 5th of September 1789 in Oglethorpe county, Ga., and died near Atlanta, at the residence of his daughter, Mrs. A. F. Hurt, on the 18th of March 1873. He left a wife, children, and grandchildren.

Mrs. Mary Ross Lewis, wife of Rev. Josiah Lewis, Jr., died in Athens, Ga., April 14, 1873. She was born June 7th 1845 in Taliaferro county. In 1858 she joined the Church at Warrenton, Ga; May 3d, 1866 she was married.

Mr. J. Sutton died in White county, April 17, 1873, aged about sixty-eight years. Eight children survive. M. L. Underwood

Major Jas. A. Miller died at his residence near Fort Valley, Ga., 24th February 1873, in the 76th year of his age. He was born in Hancock county in 1797.

Sister Groover, wife of Rev. Peter Groover, of the Georgia Conference, was the daughter of F. P. and Eliza Maulden, and was born in Elbert county, Ga., July 14, 1837, and when quite young removed to Cobb county.

Miss Sallie Partridge died in Columbia, S. C., on 16th of April 1873, aged thirty-four years and two months. She was elected to the position of Instructress in English Literature in the Columbia Female College in December last.

Mrs. Margaret A. Hughes, wife of T. C. Hughes and daughter of H. and M. Cowan, was born in Anderson district, S. C., in 1836; died in Turkeytown, Ala., March 18, 1873. Wm. Cunters

Mrs. Rebecca Baggett, wife of W. F. Baggett and daughter of Berry and Elizabeth Griffith, was born in Taylor county, Ga., November 18, 1848, and died March 24, 1873. In early childhood her parents passed into rest, leaving her under the protection of her uncle, Rev. James Griffith.

Missouri Elizabeth Hightower, daughter of Young and Mary Edwards, of Lee county, Ala., was born October 23d, 1824, married to Richard Hightower in 1853, died April 9, 1873. She leaves an aged father, husband and three children. Wm. B. Neal

Dr. James C. Avery of Decatur, Dekalb county, died April 18, 1873, in the fifty-sixth year of his age. F. B. Davies

David R. Hoskins and Sarah Evans, brother and sister, died, the former March 17, 1873, the latter March 22d 1873. D. R. Hoskins was born 7th June 1816. Sarah Evans was born 4th November 1767 [sic], was married to Rev. John Evans 7th of January 1825. They left one brother and other relatives.

Issue of June 4, 1873

Eliza Jane, wife of Gen. William M. Browne, died on May 5, at the family residence, 596 Shelby street, Memphis, Tenn. She was the daughter of the Hon. Denison Becket, of Yorkshire, England.

Mrs. Amanda Robinson, daughter of W. R. and Dorinada Townsend and wife of W. A. Robinson, was born July 22d 1843, and died near Darien, Georgia, March 1873, in the thirtieth year of her age.

My father, West Lane, was born in Burke county, Georgia, on 6th May 1806, and died in Russell county, Ala., March 26th 1873. he leaves my mother and five children to mourn his loss. He now rests in McTyeire burial ground. W. Lane

Mrs. Mary F. Crawley, whose maiden name was Dunn, wife of James A. Crawley, was born in Autauga county, Ala., March 30th 1832 and died in pike county, Ga., April 23d 1873.

Mrs. Elizabeth Blackman, whose maiden name was Young, was born in Scriven county, in 1792 and died on the 11th of May 1873. Her husband, Jas. Blackman, represented the county over twenty years in the legislature. He moved to Carroll county and died there, when his widow returned to Fulton county, and was spending some time with her youngest daughter Mrs. Dr. Mangum. She was buried at Mt. Zion church, by the side of her youngest son, who died in 1859.

Mrs. Sarah A. E. Calder, widow of James R. Calder, was born in Walton county, Ga., and died in Savannah, Ga., April 20th 1873, in her forty-fourth year. Most of her married life was spent in McIntosh county, Georgia, but in 1857, she removed to Savannah, and resided there until her death. Geo. G. N. MacD.

James Bradfield was born Dec. 20th 1808 in Rockingham county, North Carolina, and died May 3d 1873 in Troup county, Georgia. He leaves a wife (a daughter of the late Rev. J. C. Traylor), a son and two daughters (one the wife of Rev. J. Reece, of Eufaula, Ala), his aged mother-in-law, an inmate of his family. W. J. Cotter

Mrs. Sarah E. Greene, wife of the Hon. James W. Greene, was born in Jasper county, Ga., on 20th November 1825; married to James W. Greene on 17th of July 1844, by the Rev. Ivy Steagall, and died in Upson county, Ga., on 30th of March 1873.

Sister Emma Garwood, daughter of Isaac and Catharine Bowen, and wife of Robt. B. Garwood, was born in Tallahassee, Fla., Feb. 12th, 1849, was married June 1866 and died May 4th 1873. Her mother and brother, husband and two children survive her. Josephus Anderson

Watson Ashurst, son of Dr. J. and E. R. Ashurst, died in Lake city, Fla., on 24th of April 1873. He was born it Putnam county, Ga., on 30th March 1837. A. A. Robinson

Rev. John Westwood was born in the city of London, England, June 28th 1791, and died in Harris county, Ga., April 9th 1873. He left his native land and came to this country in 1818. T. S. L. Harwell. Nashville Christian Advocate, will please copy.

Martha Elizabeth Renfroe, daughter of James F. and M. R. Northington and wife of W. H. Renfroe, of Sanderville, Ga., was born Oct. 10th 1842, married June 11th 1863, and died 14th May 1873. J. F. Mixon

Fannie T., daughter of Rev. T. Alonzo and J. E. D. Harris, died in Winterville, Ga., April 28th 1873, aged 17 years, 11 months and 17 days. C. A. Conoway

Issue of June 11, 1873

Died

In Orangeburg, S. c., May 13th 1873, Eugenia Riley, daughter of A. J. and U. M. Gaskins, aged 2 years, 2 months, and 10 days.

Obituary

Mrs. Emma E. Utsey, wife of D. D. Utsey, died in Charleston, S. C., May 1st 1873 in the 26th year of her age. G. Pierce

Benjamin B. Kendrick died in Talbot, Ga., April 14, 1873, aged sixty-six years. He joined the Baptist Church in Jasper County in 1872. L. Rush

Henry Sidney Myers, son of Dr. S. S. and Mrs. M. S. Oslin was born in Knoxville, Ga., September 29. 1849, and died at his father's residence in Pleasant Hill, Talbot county, Ga., March 24, 1873. W. H. Woodall

Lawrence D. Clark was born in Orangeburg, S. C., December 10, 1847, and died April 18, 1873. In September 1871 hew as married to Miss Rosa V. Gaskin.

Mrs. Rebecca S. Coffee was born in Pulaski county, Ga., July 28, 1836, and died in Hawkinsville, Ga., May 4, 1873. The deceased was married to Captain John A. Coffee in 1854, and left three surviving children.

Wiley A. Jones died at his residence, near Rehoboth Church, Morgan circuit, Ga., April 16, 1873, aged seventy-one years. He was raised in Clarke county, four miles from Watkinsville; married Sarah M. Edwards in 1838. L. G. Anderson

Capt. Simon L. Sparkman of Columbia county, Fla., died on 18th of March last, in the sixty-seventh year of his age. He was a native of Liberty county, Ga., but was removed in his boyhood with his father to Florida. Since his death, his youngest daughter, Lavinia S. Sparkman, has also passed away. She died May 6th.

Miss Ella Ann Ansley died at her father's residence, Rev. Abel Ansley, in Upson county, Ga., May 12, 1873. She was born in Sumter county in 1842. W. H. Graham

Missouri A., wife of J. W. N. Parrott and daughter of Walton and Angelina S. Robinson, was born July 1848; was married in 1865; died near Concord, Gadsden county, Fla., May 7, 1873. J. D. Rogers

Mrs. Susan Fenley, wife of John Fenley and daughter of Thomas and Francis Hendrix, died on 9th December 1872, in the thirty-sixth year of her age.

Mrs. Elizabeth Holderness was born in North Carolina in 1808 and died April 29, 1873. She died at the residence of J. S. Montford, her son-in-law.

Miss Sarah L. Lovelace, eldest daughter of John M. and Martha Lovelace, died at her father's residence in Troup county, Ga., April 30, 1873.

Daniel Johnson was born in Sumter district, S. C., April 2, 1817, and died at his residence near Tallahassee, Leon county, Fla., May 12, 1873. J. P. Roberts

Mrs. A. E. Hawthorn died in Anderson county, S. C., May 15, 1873, aged thirty-three years. J. W. Murray

Issue of June 18, 1873

Mrs. Sarah T. Bowers, wife of L. G. Bowers, Esq., died in Wynnton, near Columbus, Ga., May 8th, in the 29th year of her age. J. S. Key

Mrs. Lottie A. Snow, wife of Wm. M. Snow and daughter of Willis and Ellen H. Skinner, was born in Muscogee county, near Columbus, Ga., July 28th 1841, and died in Opelika, Ala., March 3d 1873, aged twenty-eight years, seven months and six days. O. L. Smith

Mrs. M. H. McCorkle, my wife, and daughter of James Dougherty, Esq., of Columbia county, Ga., died in Wrightsboro, McDuffie county, Ga., April 20th 1873, in her 27th year. Left motherless at about four years old, she was taken in by a pious aunt. She leaves two little children. H. McCorkle

Sister Martha C. Gilreath, wife of W. H. Gilreath and daughter of the late William Few of Greenville co., died in Greenville co., S. C., May 21st 1873. A. B. Stephens

Wm. O. E. Reese was born in Warren county, Ga., Nov. 3d 1849 and was buried April 14th 1873.

Curtis Greene, Esq., was born in Wilkes county, Ga., December 7th 1790 and died in Forsyth county, Ga., April 6th 1873. Mrs. Sallie Greene, his wife, was born in Guilford county, North Carolina, March 5th 1788 and died March the 7th 1873. They were married in August 182. Their offspring were three sons and one daughter. The eldest son died about one year ago in Texas. Mr. Greene represented Forsyth county in the Legislature in 1838, 1849, 1840, and 1841. H. P. Bell

Jno. H. Milhouse was born June 8th 1808 and died May 19th 1873. R. B. Tarrant

Brother Benjamin Wharton was born in Culpepper county, Va., Jan 15th 1806, was married Dec. 17th 1829, died in Athens, Ga., March 28th 1872. J. Lewis, Jr.

Mrs. Sidney B. Stone, whose maiden name was Briscoe, was born in Columbia county, Ga., April 25th 1793, died at the residence of her son-in-law, April 6th 1873. W. J. Parks

Tribute of Respect from Quarterly Conference of Columbia circuit, Florida Conference, to Capt. Simmon L. Sparkman, aged sixty-six years.

Tribute of Respect from Quarterly Conference, Summerville circuit, North Georgia Conference, to James T. Mosely, twenty-three years of age.

Issue of June 25, 1873

J. J. Douglas died in Meriwether county, Ga., on 4th of April 1873. He was born in South Carolina, 28th August 1830, but removed in early childhood with his parents to Meriwether county, Ga. C. A. Stiles

James Copes was born at Smithville, N. C., in 1798. When but a boy, he was removed to Charleston, S. C., where he spent the most of his life. During the war he removed to Winnsboro, S. C., and remained there till his death, Jan. 17, 1873. Sister Eliza Harriet Copes, consort of James Copes, died November 15, 1873 [sic]. J. S. Connor

Mrs. Ann Hunt, daughter of Major Hall, late of Leon county, Fla., died at the residence of her husband, Capt. J. M. Hunter, on the 16th of April, aged 53 years. J. C. Ley

Catharine H. Watkins, relict of Ansel Lee Watkins and daughter of Robert and Elizabeth Washington, was born in Wilkes county, Ga., October 19, 1804, and died in Oglethorpe, April 20, 1873. S. H. J. Sistrunk

Mrs. Harriet L. Cleckley, wife of Dr. J. D. Cleckley, was born Sept. 13, 1828, and died in Charleston, S. C., May 7, 1873. Her body sleeps in the grave-yard at Union church. John W. McRoy

Mrs. Nancy L. Sibley died in Senoia, Ga., May 28th 1873, in the seventy-fifth year of her age. She was a native of South Carolina, and married James W. Sibley of the same state. About forty-two years ago she was left a widow, and with her children and her father (H. Shell) moved to this state and settled in Coweta county. L. Bedenbaugh

Mrs. Mary Elizabeth Hines, wife of Dr. T. P. Hines, was born Sept. 15, 1841, and died in Jefferson county, Ga., May 25, 1873. Just thirteen days after her death, her little babe, Mary Elizabeth, born Feb. 12, died also, and they are both in one grave. She left a husband and one dear little child. Thos. B. Lanier

Mrs. Mattie Petrona Roberts, only daughter of Thos. H. and Sallie A. Dozier, died in Union Springs, Ala., March 11, 1873. She was born in Talbotton, Ga., November 11, 1852. John W. Dozier, Jr.

Mrs. Mary W. Law, wife of the late James E. Law, and daughter of the late Capt. Charles Williams, and sister of Judge Thos. Williams of Alabama, and Dr. Chas Williams, of South Carolina, died in Micanopy, E. F., May 5, 1873. She was born in Williamsburg, S. C., October 3, 1804. J. C. Ley

Mrs. Lucy Steger was born January 5th 1786 and died at the residence of her son-in-law, Mr. A. Allen, Pike county, Ga., May 14th 1873. She had been a Baptist for over forty years. J. M. Wood

Mrs. M. A. Zeigler, consort of Henry M. Zeigler, deceased, and eldest daughter of Edward and Margaret Hays, deceased, died at her residence in Orangeburg county, S. C., June 4th 1873. Loula H. Zeigler

Mrs. Bethany Hudson, wife of A. C. Hudson, was born in Wayne county, N. C., Sept. 18th 1816 and died in Chattahoochee co., Ga., April 24, 1873.

Capt. Jeremiah Beckwith died in Greenville, Meriwether county, Ga., March 23d 1873. He was born in Dorchester county, Maryland, December 2d, 1803.

Mrs. Mary Ann Elizabeth, relict of Hon. Turner H. Trippe, died in Cartersville, Ga., on the 18th of May last, aged sixty-five years. She was born in Putnam county, Ga., and was married in 1824, moved to Clarkesville, Ga., in 1827, and from thence to Cassville in 1839. Her remains were interred in the Cassville Cemetery, by the side of her husband.

Mrs. Sarah Maxey died in Graniteville, S. C., May 8, 1873, aged about 75 years. L. C. Loyal

Tribute of Respect to Rev. John P. Murray.

Tribute of Respect from Quarterly Conference, Bainbridge Station, South Georgia Conference, to Hardy G. Crawford, who was born February 27, 1810 and died May 9, 1873.

Issue of July 2, 1873

Bazil A. Wise was born in Statesboro, Ga., Oct. 1st, 1827 and died in Macon, Ga., April 5th 1873. Jas. O. Branch

Miss Julia Hughes died May 14th 1873 in McDuffie county, Ga., aged 27 years. Amos Johnson

Mrs. Isabella Sweatman died May 7, 1873, at her daughter's residence in Charleston county, S. C., within a few miles of where she was born and reared, at the age of 86 years. She left children and several grandchildren.

Bryant Dixon died at the residence of his son, H. H. Dixon, in Macon county, Ga., May 31, 1873, in the eighty-ninth year of his age. He was a native of North Carolina and came to Georgia when a small boy. He resided first in Burke county, Georgia, then in Hancock, Putnam, Monroe, Sumter and Macon counties. R. W. Dixon

Miss Anna Haines, daughter of Mr. and Mrs. Nathan Haines, died in Sandersville, Ga., on the 20th of March 1873, aged twenty-one years and five months.

Mrs. Martha C., daughter of Ira and Margarette Bridges and wife of Wm. J. Spears, was born in Marlboro county, S. C., 22d Dec. 1833 and died near Hollywood, Ark., May 16th 1873. She joined the Methodist E. Church, South, at Hebron, Bennettsville circuit, S. C. Conference about twenty years ago. J. P. Holmes

Nami Ellen Wilson, wife of Henry Wilson and daughter of Anthony and Sarah McCarty, was born Oct. 20th 1833 and died in Decatur county, Ga., April 17th 1873. She leaves a husband and five children.

Mrs. Lula Cudd, daughter of Mr. and Mrs. John Austin and wife of Mr. Scott Cudd, was born in Union county, S. C., Sept. 15th 1854 and died May 25th 1873. J. S. Wilson

Mrs. Malinda Turner, wife of Riley Turner, was born July 20th 1820 and died in Meriwether county, Ga., May 19th 1873. She was married to Eliss Faribe in 1838, serving him as a dutiful wife eighteen years, where he died, leaving her with three daughters.

Mrs. Emily Palestine Wright, wife of James A. Wright of Abbeville, died June 11th 1873, aged 31 years, 3 months and 13 days. Her maiden name was Robinson. Married in 1865.

Joanah M. Bunch, wife of George Bunch, was born in Orangeburg district, S. C., January 14th 1818 and died in Macon, Ga., May 27th 1873. She left a husband and two children. One year before her deceased, she witnessed the death of her second son.

Elizabeth Conner, a resident of Charleston county, South Carolina, died in the same, being upwards of 81 years of age. She was married twice, last to the father of our beloved W. G. Conner, of Texas, several years a member of the South Carolina Conference. She spent her last days with her only living daughter, Mrs. Thompson. She was taken sick on the last day of May, and was buried at Target church the following Wednesday. J. H. Zimmerman

Miss Lavinia A. E. Sparkman, daughter of the late Captain Simeon L. Sparkman, died at Eachtucknee, Columbia co., Fla., on 6th of May 1873.

Lucinda Slaughter, wife of William Slaughter, was born Sept. 12th 1828 and died in Upson county, Ga., March 4th 1873. She left a husband and several children. W. H. Graham

Issue of July 9, 1873

Died

Arthur Glover, son of W. K. and Julia Methvin, died May 13, aged 11 months and 15 days.

Mary Edna, infant daughter of Capt. D. W. Bethea, has followed her mother to the land of spirit's blest. She died June 12, 1873.

In Orangeburg, S. C., May 4, Little Sue, infant daughter of Rev. J. L. and Mrs. Sue. F. Sifly, aged 10 months and 19 days.

Obituary

Mrs. Maria A. Sifley was born in Charleston, S. C., February 12, 1801 and died at Orangeburg, S. C., April 23d, 1873. Her companion and six children remain. Youngest son

Thomas J. Shepard, my dear father-in-law, was born in Liberty county, Ga., June 26, 1803, and died at Reidsville, Tatnall county, Ga., at the residence of his son-in-law, Dr. A. B. Daniel, May 15, 1873. At the age of two weeks, he was left without a mother, and was reared by a step-mother, the sister of Dr. Daniel Baker, until he was fifteen or sixteen years of age. In early manhood he removed to Pike county. He first married Miss Susan Leake, of Pike County, and returned to Liberty county, where he buried his wife and his first born. He then married Miss Susan Way, of Liberty county. They had born until them twelve children, five of whom were taken when almost infants. T. S. L. Harwell. Hinesville Gazette will please copy.

Mrs. Sarah Jane Bethea, wife of Capt. D. W. Bethea, was born in Marlboro county, S. C., May 29, 1837, and died May 25, 1873. James C. Stoll

Abner McGehee, son of James and Mary McGehee, was born in Oglethorpe co., Ga., April 23, 1807, and died at Indian Springs, Ga., May 14, 1873. He was a steward at Eufaula, Ala., moved to Glennville, Ala., and later to Summerfield, Ala. His wife died May 27, 1864.

James Arminius Wright was drowned on the 7th of June last, in the seventeenth year of his age. He was a son of the esteemed Rev. Arminius Wright of Columbus, Ga., and was a Sophomore in Emory College. He was born February 6th 1857. J. M. Doggett

Mrs. Sallie E. Smith died May 15, 1873, in the 31st year of her age. Left father, mother, brother and sisters. J. Q. Stockman

Joel H. Bowman was born in Mississippi, Jan. 15, 1835 and died near Subligan, Chattooga co., Ga., May 17, 1873. He left a wife and two children.

Sylvester A. Hough, A. M., M. D., Professor of Physical Science in the Southern Masonic Female College, died in Atlanta, Ga., April 13th, in the 49th year of his age. He was a native of Surry co., N. C. His venerable father still lives. Luther M. Smith

John R. Scott, Jr., was born in Cusseta, Ala., March 7, 1856, and died in West Point, Ga., May 13, 1873. D. D. Cox

Mrs. Sallie C. Branch died at Mr. Richard Bradford's, in Leon county, Fla., on the 26th of May last. Josephus Anderson

Mrs. Laudonia Heir died at her residence in Tallahassee, Fla., June 1, 1873. She leaves two sons and a daughter. Josephus Anderson

Issue of July 16, 1873

Daniel Pratt of Prattville, Ala., died in Prattville, May 13, 1873. He was born in Temple, New Hampshire, July 20, 1799. He landed at Savannah, Georgia. He changed his location to Milledgeville, Georgia. S. Mims

Jane L., youngest daughter of the late Jacob and Sarah Miller of Charleston, S. C., died at the residence of her brother, Dr. S. H. Miller, near Bishopville, S. C., on 20th June 1873.

Mrs. Anna J. Cooper, wife of Dr. W. D. Cooper and daughter of Dr. J. D. Beall, was born in Taylor county, Ga., June 3d 1856, and died in Houston county, Ga., June 2d 1873. J. E. Littlejohn

Mrs. Emeline Butts, daughter of Calvin and N. B. Harman, was born in Meriwether county, Georgia, July 7, 1837, and died in Barnesville, May 28, 1873.

Capt. Wm. A. Lee was born in Virginia, October 7, 1807, and died in Barnesville, Ga., May 39, 1873. The wife of his youth and several of his children preceded him to the spirit land. He has left a widow, one child two years old, and several grown children.

Thomas G. Frazier was born on the 28th October 1805 in Granville, N. C., and died on the 31st of May 1873, in Coffee county, Ala. J. O. A. Cook

Mrs. Elizabeth Robinson, wife of James Robinson, was born in Jones county, Dec. 1799 and died May 18th 1873, in Crawford county, Ga.

Mr. Paxton Elliot died at his residence in Cleaveland county, N. C., June 6th 1873, in his 56th year. S. M. Davis

Sister Amelia B. Askins, daughter of Isaac and Amelia Holland, was born in Hancock county, on 7th of Nov 1800 and died in Monroe county, Ga., June 24th 1873. She was married to brother Wm. Askins, April 4th 1828. J. J. Singleton

Sister Polina C. Shi, daughter of Jesse and Jane Kirby, was born in Stokes county, N. C., April 3d 1803, and died in Monroe county, Ga., May 22d 1873. She moved with her parents to Georgia in 1829, and on 24th of December of the same year was united in married to brother James H. Shi, then living in Jasper county, Ga. J. J. Singleton

William Glover was born February 10, 1792 in Edgefield district, S. C.; removed to Augusta, Ga., in 1809; was married to Susan McGill, April 1816, and died among his children in Augusta, Ga., June 4, 1873. J. E. Evans

Miss Missouri Carlisle, daughter of W. W. and R. E. Carlisle, was born in Troup county, Ga., May 11, 1849 and died in LaGrange, May 27, 1873.

William Arnold was born and raised in Oglethorpe county, Ga., died in Ouachita county, near Camden, Ark., on the 13th of June 1873, in the sixtieth year of his age. Cadesman Pope

Tribute of Respect from Glennville station to Rev. Thomas H. Dawson, M. D.

Issue of July 23, 1873

Died

Julius Lamar, aged 5 years, 1 month and 23 days; William Woodliff, aged 2 years, 4 months and 14 days; Algernon Sidney, aged 2 years and 11 months; Vernon Ludwell, aged 1 year, 2 months and 3 days; all the sons of Professor W. C. and Mrs. Mary M. Day of Marion High School, Lauderdale county, Miss., have vied within a recent date, and left their parents childless.

Obituary

Mrs. Catharine W. Thomson was born in Beaufort district, S. C., December 6, 1790, married Benjamin Thomson in 1808 and died at her residence in Beaufort county, May 1, 1873.

William Witehead died on the 24th of May 1873, in the 86th year of his age. Foster & Dozier

My brother-in-law, John Gardner Hendry, son of Neil and Margaret Hendry, died near Morven, Brooks county, Ga., July 6, 1873, aged 22 years. J. H. S.

Allen Geiger was born in Bullock county, Ga., 26th October 1802 and died 7th of June 1873. He was partly raised in Bullock county, then moved to Wayne county, Ga., with his father. There he married a Migg Abigail Briggs, and settled in Liberty county. About the year 1840 his wife died. About the year 1843 he married a Miss Buford, and moved to Duval county, Florida. He leaves a wife and fifteen children. J. N. Geiger

Mrs. Francina E. Conley, wife of Rev. Wm. F. Conley of the South Georgia Conference, and daughter of S. P. Smith, was born in Tatnall co., Ga., July 10, 1842, and died May 21, 1873. She left a husband and four children. Jas. V. M. Morris

Emanuel K. Robison was born in Lincolnton, N. C., April 19, 1806, removed to Greenville, S. C., about 1835, and died May 23, 1873. He was one of the oldest inhabitants of Greenville, S. C. Mr. Robison united with the Lutheran church in 1830 and the Methodist E. Church, South, in 1859.

Edna Caroline Keith, wife of William M. Keith and daughter of Mr. John T. Gossett of Pickens county, S. C., departed this life in Greenville, S. C., May 29, 1873, aged 38 years.

Mr. Wm. O. Halladay was born in Taliaferro county, October 1, 1844, and died in Savannah, Ga., May 14, 1873.

Mrs. Jane Harvey was born in Jefferson co., May 7, 1809, and died in Talbotton, Ga., May 4, 1873.

William Scott died near Plainville, Gordon county, Ga. June 26, 1873, at the age of 70 years. He was born in South Carolina, joined the Baptist church when about sixteen years old. He raised twelve children. J. H. McCoole

Julia C. Rhodes, daughter of Fredrick and Margaret J. Felder, was born in Orangeburg district on the 10th May 1840, and died in Barnwell county, S. C., June 12, 1873. In 1865 she was united to John Rhodes in holy wedlock. She leaves a husband and a little child.

Intelligence has reached me of the death of sister Elizabeth McConnell, wife of Isaac McConnell, formerly of Cherokee county, Ga., now living in Parker county, Texas. She was born August 22d, 1820 near Lawranceville, Ga., and died June 3, 1873. Wm. A. Simmons

Brother John McKoy was born in South Carolina and died in Cherokee county, Ga., May 3d 1873. He has left a wife, a son and a daughter. A. C. Carson

Miss Eliza Ingram died May 26, 1873, at the age of ten years. Shelton R. Weaver

Issue of July 30, 1873

Died

In Greene county, Ga., on Sunday, 20th inst., Mary Elizabeth, infant daughter of Mr Alexander S. and Mrs. S. A. Kimbrough, aged 18 months.

Obituary

Dr. William M. Jordan was born in Oglethorpe county, Ga., February 11th 1810 and died at his home in Wilkes county, Ga., May 39th, 1872.

Mrs. Mary E. Pelot, only daughter of Gen. James G. Cooper and wife of Dr. J. Crews Pelot, was born near St. Mary's, Ga., Jan. 31st 1839 and died at Manatee, Fla., June 1st 1873.

Susan T. Allen, daughter of Thomas and Mary Allen, deceased, was born in Clark county, Ga., April 13, 1827, and died in Lee county, Ala., June 18, 1873. N. W. Pattillo

Rev. Stephen H. Cooper, born in Liberty county, Ga., July 1st 1812, died at Lawton, Clinch county, Ga., June 26th 1873.

Joseph Glenn Sears was born in Newton county, Georgia, 6 August 1836, was killed in Griffin, Ga., June 16th 1873. He was a conductor on a freight train on Macon & Western Railroad. He leaves a wife and five minor children.

Mrs. Nancy G. Royal, wife of James H. Royal, was born in Burke county, Ga., and died in Savannah, Ga., June 21st 1873, in the 71st year of her age. Her body was interred in Burke county within half a mile of the place of her birth. A Husband, niece and two step-daughters survive. Geo. G. N. MacD.

Wm. M. Roberts was born in Greene county, Ga., March 8, 1806, and died in Macon, Ga., June 5th 1873. Jas. O. Branch. Christian Index and South Western Baptist, please copy.

Mr. Joshua Spence died in Appling county, Ga., on 9th June in the 79th year of his age. He has left an aged widow, and a large number of children and grand-children.

Wm. C. Meredith was born in Savannah, Ga., March 25th 1808, and died at the residence of his son, in Helena, S. C., June 11th 1873. He leaves several sons and a daughter.

Mrs. Adeline P. Harvey died at her residence in Houston county, Georgia, 4th July 1873, aged 60 years and 6 months. She was a native of Putnam county, Ga.

Mrs. Erin C. Marsh, wife of Samuel G. Marsh and daughter of Stephen Howard, late of Putnam county, Ga., was born Sept. 14th 1840 and died June 18th 1873.

Mrs. Sarah Robins died at Talbotton, Ga., June 17th 1873, in her seventy-sixth year. She was born near Petersburg, Va; removed to Greene county, Ga., in early life. She removed to Talbot county, Georgia, more than forty years ago. R. W. Dixon

Mrs. Jonathan Jordan died in Abbeville county, July 7, 1873, aged 68 years. J. W. Murray

Miss Mary Hunt died on the 21st June aged 17 years, wanting about one month. She had been a member at Prospect Church, Watkinsville circuit. L. M. Fowler

Dr. Richardson was born in Jones county, Ga., December 29th 1808, and died in Smithville, Ga., May 24th 1873. Leaves a wife and six children. W. Lane

William Bouknight died on the 30th June, at his plantation on the Saluda river, Edgefield county, S. C., in the 66th year of his age.

Mrs. Martha H. Talley, wife of Rev. Nathan Talley, daughter of Mr. and Mrs. Travis, late of Fayette county, Ga., and sister of Col. John Travis, of Atlanta, Ga., died in Clinch county, Ga., July 12th 1873. J. W. Talley

Mrs. Preston Fant died at Anderson station, S. C. Conference, July 1873. G. T. Harmon

Tribute of Respect from Black Swamp circuit, South Carolina Conference, to William G. Roberds.

Issue of August 6, 1873

Mrs. Margaret Ann Farrow, wife of Mr. Albert H. Farrow and youngest daughter of Rev. John R. and Sarah A. Joy of Camden, S. C., was born January 25th 1835 and died at Columbia, S. C., July 3, 1873. W. D. Kirkland

Miss Ella Elder died in Cuthbert, Ga., June 27, 1873. She was born August 8, 1859. J. R. Owens

While the funeral services of mother McMillan, who died on the 19th June, not quite for score years old, were attended to in the Marion Church, the spirit of mother Martha Dozier passed over also to the home of God, 21st June 84 years old last March. She married James Dozier. W. L. Pegues

Samuel Kemp was born on Green Turtle Key, one of the Bahama Islands, April 24, 1830, and died in Key West, July 7, 1783. S. Davenport

Mrs. Julia C. Vogt, wife of T. P. Vogt, of Charleston county, S. C., was born June 5, 1840 and died June 20, 1873, leaving a husband and three little boys.

Mrs. Catharine Dubard, widow of Adam F. Dubard, died July 4, 1873, in the 82d year of her age, at the residence of her son, N. J. Dubard, Esq., in Richland District, S. C.

Mrs. Margaret B., wife of Wm. B. Hill and daughter of Frances and Mary Carlisle, was born in Abbeville district, S. C., March 1819 and died near Hogansville, Ga., July 7, 1873. Her body rests in the grave at the old Midway church-yard.

Willie W. Rogers, son of Rev. W. A. Rogers, was born June 16, 1850 and died in Atlanta, Ga., June 18, 1872 [sic].

Joseph M. Black was born in Lincoln county, N. C., July 2d 1789; removed from Rutherford county, N. C., to Forsyth county, Ga., in 1843; died on April 20, 1873.

Mrs. Frances Ann Niblack, wife of John W. Niblack and daughter of Mrs. Sparkman (formerly Mrs. Fry) was born July 29, 1855, married November 20, 1872, and died May 26, 1783 in Columbia county, Fla. S. S. Phillips

Mrs. M. J. Gardner, relict of John J. Gardner, deceased and daughter of R. P. and Elizabeth Hays, was born November 27, 1832 and died May 18, 1873. W. M. D. Bond

Miss Ella Pierce McKinnon, daughter of Lauchlan McKinnon, deceased, and grand-daughter of Rev. Reddick Pierce, formerly of Milledgeville, died in Nashville, Ga., June 19, 1873, in the 23d year of her age.

Mrs. Sarah Hariston was born in 1798 and died 3d of May 1873. R. N. Wells.

Rev. Wm. Parks Jones was born in Newnan county, Ga., Nov. 10, 1826 and died June 7, 1873. Son of the Rev. James Jones of the South Georgia Conference, and a graduate of Emory College.

Mrs. Rebecca Rawls was born 6th September 1801 and died at her residence in Bullock county, July 17, 1873. She leaves four children.

Horace Shuptrine died on the 14th of June 1873, aged 15 years. W. G. Booth

John B. Goudelock, Esq., was born in Spartanburg district, S. C., October 8, 1801 and died at his residence in Union county, S. C., June 25, 1873. J. C. Crisp

Elizabeth Laurimore died on the 20th of June 1873. W. L. Pegues

Tribute of Respect from Decatur circuit to James Griffin, who departed this life 13th March, aged seventy-three years.

Issue of August 13, 1873

Dr. Edward Roswell Ware was born in Richmond county in 1804, and at a very early age by the death of his father, was left to the guardianship of his uncle, Hon. Nicholas Ware. He married Miss Margaret Elizabeth Bacon in 1830 and died in 1873. Henry Hull

Mrs. Sarah E. Landrum died June 23, 1873, in Penfield, Ga., aged 63 years. She was a faithful member of Adkins church in Oglethorpe county.

Isaac W. Early, Jr., third son of Isaac W. Early, Sr., and Elizabeth, his wife, was born Dec. 3, 1850, and died in Conyers, 11th of Jan. 1873. His education was begun near Madison near where he was born.

Joseph H. Hutson was born in Colleton county, S. C., December 23d 1849 and died in same county June 20th 1873. E. J. Benton

Mrs. Elvira Bowyer of Colleton county, S. C., died at St. George's, S. C., July 17th 1873 in the 70th year of her age. Sister Bowyer was the daughter of Captain Daniel and Elizabeth Strobel. J. S. Murray

Mrs. Mary A. Woolley was born in Abbeville dist., S. C., February 15th 1862 [sic] and died in Bartow county, Ga., June 19th 1873.

Mrs. Sarah Covington, wife of Thos. S. Covington, was born Nov. 29, 1796 and died June 9, 1873. She was the daughter of James Cook, whose name is prominent among the first members of the Methodist Church in this portion of South Carolina. L. M. Hamer

Dr. Hugh J. Ogilsby was born in Caswell co., N. C., March 28th 1803, removed to Georgia in 1818 and died in Madison, Ga., June 10th 1873. W. C. Bass

Mrs. Samantha N. Merritt was born in Walton county, Ga., Oct. 7th 1836, and died in Bibb county, July 8th 1873... leaves a husband and children. W. C. Bass

Narcissa Whitfield Ross, relict of Isaac Ross, deceased, was born in Hancock county, Georgia, on 16th of September 1810 and died at her residence in Opelika, Ala., July 19th 1873. John T. Harris. New Orleans Christian Advocate please copy.

Issue of August 20, 1873

Died

Wm. R. Fishburne, eldest son of Wm. R. and Eliza S. Fishburne, died on 18th of July 1873, aged six years, 11 months and 19 days.

Near Liberty, Greene county, Ga., on 5th inst., Mattie Josephine, infant daughter of H. P. Williams, aged 10 months and 15 days.

Hattie Ida, infant daughter of Jas. W. and Emma Herbert, was born in Newberry county, S. C., April 5th 1873 and died July 21st 1873.

Minnie Francis, a little daughter of James A. and Nancy E. Overstreet, died in Levy county, Fla., June 22, 1873, aged one year and six months.

At Waynesboro, Ga., August 13, Charles LeGrande, eldest son of Rev. George H. and Emma N. Johnson, aged nine years and eight months.

Obituary

Mrs. Georgia A. Pearce, wife of Charles H. Pearce and daughter of Major John H. and Mrs. Lavoenah Jones, of Elberton, Ga., died in Augusta, Ga., on 26th June 1873, in her twenty-second year.

Elizabeth Andrews, wife of Wm. G. Andrews and daughter of Larkin and Amy Smith, was born in Cumberland county, Va., July 5th 1797 and died in Upson county, Ga., June 30th 1873. Miller H. White

Mrs. Lazina Brooks of Talbot county, Ga., died at her grand-son's, Mr. Alford Patrick, near Pleasant Hill, May 30, 1873. I think she was born in North Carolina, but moved to Georgia in early life. She died at the advanced age of 87 years. L. B. Payne

Mrs. Sarah Taylor, wife of John S. Taylor, Esq., died at her residence in Houston county, Ga., July 29, 1873, aged 58 years and two months.

A few days since we were pained to learn that the Rev. Jackson Oliver, of Banks county, had passed away. He leaves a wife and children, one a minister.

Mrs. Gertrude A. Timberlake, eldest daughter of Mr. J. D. Ramsey and wife of Captain F. A. Timberlake, formerly of Smith county, Tenn., died at Augusta, Ga., June 26, 1873, in the 30th year of her age. Nashville Advocate please copy.

Mrs. Ann Cole Griffin, wife of Rev. W. W. Griffin of Stone Mountain, a superannuated member of the South Georgia Conference, was born in Putnam county, Ga., July 38, 1815. She left two children.

Mrs. Margaret Brown was born in Duplin county, N. C., February 23d 1796 and died in Dawson, June 20, 1873. She married Mr. Jones Brown and removed with him to Marion county, Ga.

My mother, Mrs. Sarah Miers, died at Cotton Valley, Macon county, Ala., July 27, 1873. She was the daughter of Henry and Priscilla Densler, deceased, formerly of Baldwin, Ga., and sister of the late Rev. Thos. L. Densler, of the Alabama Conference, and Dr. Henry L. Densler, of Burnsville, Ala. She was born January 14, 1813, married to my father, William Wild in 1831; and to her surviving husband, Mr. Joseph J. Miers, November 22, 1830. W. H. Wild

Mrs. Elizabeth McSwain, whose maiden name was Randle, was born in Montgomery (now Stanley) county, N. C., August 11, 1811; was married to W. A. McSwain, afterwards a member of the South Carolina Conference, January 24, 1833, and died in Laurens county, S. C., June 24, 1873. J. B. Traywick

SOUTHERN CHRISTIAN ADVOCATE NOTICES 1867-1878

Died

In Cokesbury, S. C., on the 6th July 1873, Laura, infant daughter of Charles C. and Irene Smith, aged 9 months and 23 days.

Obituary

Col. Oliver P. Anthony, son of Rev. Samuel Anthony of the South Georgia Conference, died recently in Fort Gaines, Ga., from pneumonia, aged 45 years and 2 months. He leaves a wife and daughter.

Rev. Geo. Allen died 28th of June 1873 in the city of Savannah. He left a widow and large family. He was about fifty-five years old. Thos G. Herbert

Huger Wesley Snell, son of David W. and Ann Snell, was born May 29th 1844 and died June 14th 1873.

Mrs. Sarah B. Harris, wife of John W. Harris, was born in Randolph county, Feb. 15th 1832 and died in Cuthbert, Ga., July 17th 1873.

Rev. Wm. McCall Kennedy died in Jefferson co., Ga., on 27th July 1873. He was born in Bulloch county, Ga., May 18th 1817.

Mrs. Helen G. Cary was born 31 December 35 and died in Brunswick, Ga., 9th July 1873. J. O. A. Cook. Union Springs and Sparta papers please copy.

Mrs. Adaline Stevens, of Marion county, Ga., was born in South Carolina in 1810. She was married to Hempton Stevens in 1832 and died at their plantation in Terrell county, Ga., June 29th 1873. They were blessed with thirteen children.

Mrs. Lucinda E. L. Clark, daughter of John and Nancy Killian and wife of J. A. Clark, was born in Haywood county, N. C., Aug. 13th 1840 and died June 3d 1873 in Gordon county, Ga. G. R. Rankin

Mrs. Henrietta Sutherland was born in the city of New York in 1815 and died at Camden, South Carolina, June 12, 1873. Robt. L. Harper

Mrs. Mary A. Entrekin was born in Newberry county ,S. C., and died in Pickens county, S. C., July 15th 1873, aged 74 years, 9 months and 15 days. She moved to Laurens County with her husband. Two years ago she moved to Pickens county to live with her children.

Tribute of Respect from Quarterly Conference, Homer circuit, Elberton District, North Georgia Conference to Rev. Jackson Oliver.

Issue of September 3, 1873

Died

On the 7th of August in Houston county, Ga., little Willie Ashley, infant son of D. W. and F. F. Garrison.

Walter Dickenson, son of J. P. and N. H. Dickenson, of Bainbridge, Ga., died August 12, 1873.

The 29th of May 1873, Addie, daughter of Edward R. and Mary Holman, and grand-daughter of F. H. and A. H. Kennedy. Little Addie was not quite three years old.

Obituary

Dr. Thomas J. Darling was born in Columbia county, Ga., April 23d 1826 and died in Blackshear, Pierce county, Ga., June 14, 1873. He leaves a wife and eight children. Jas. D. Mauldin

Miss Sue Marshall, daughter of William and Frances Marshall, was born April 12, 1843 in Troup county, Ga., and died in Harris county, Ga., July 6, 1873. D. J. Williams

My nephew, Millard Z. Benton, was born in Savannah, Ga., September 13, 1850 and died near Ellaville, Fla., August 5, 1873. E. J. Benton

Mrs. Sarah Chappel died at Eatonton, Ga., on 22d July 1873. She was eighty years, five months and six days old. She was a native of England, born at Mt. Pleasant, Summerset Shire, England, near Bath, on 16 February 1791. She with her husband and family removed to America in 1853, reaching Greensboro, Ga., in April of that year, where they resided until 1869 when her husband died, only lacking two days of being eighty-two years old.

Mother Cynthia Baker died June 30, 1873, aged seventy-three years. A. G. Dempsey

Mrs. Sarah McMillan, whose maiden name was Avant, was born in Marion district, S. C., September 11th 1796; was married to Mr. John Mcmillan 3d April 1818, and died at Marion, S. C., on the 21st of June 1873. Wm. C. Power

Mattie S. Motley, youngest daughter of S. K. and M. A. E. motley was born Dec. 1st 1857 and died in Tuskegee, Macon county, Ala., May 18, 1873.

Mrs. Francis M. Beasley, daughter of Thomson Harrell, of Darlington county, S. C., was born February 18, 1856 and died June 26, 1798.

Mrs. Laura Jane Roberts, daughter of George and Esterpe Russell, was born on St. George Key, July 28, 1873, just nine weeks after her married to Joseph Roberts. Smith Davenport

McCaully G. Townes died in Anderson co., S. C., August 18, 1873, aged twenty-nine years. J. W. Murray.

Rev. Thomas H. Dawson died on 18th June last in the sixty-fourth year of his age. He was born in Green co., Ga., and there grew to manhood. G. F. Pierce

Mrs. George Margaret Carter Swan, daughter of Alexander and Amelia Berryhill and wife of Thomas E. Swan, was born in Jefferson county, Ga., September 3, 1840, and died in the same county, July 31, 1873. She leaves an aged father and mother, two sisters, a husband and four little children.

Mrs. Mahala Harley, relict of the late John B. Harley, was born in Jefferson county, Fla., November 9, 1833, and died in Chappel Hill, Texas, July 13, 1873. F. A. Mood

Mrs. Louisa Alexander, wife of Daniel F. Alexander and daughter of the deceased Reuben and Mary Knight, died August 5th 1873, in the 50th year of her age. She was born and brought up in Colleton co., S.C. J. Hamilton Knight

Mrs. Louisa A. Conley, daughter of A. S. Sullenberger, was born in Pendleton, now Highland county, Va., September 23, 1838, and died at Trion Factory, Chattooga county, Ga., June 18, 1873. D. P. Bass

Jackson Austin died July 17, aged sixty years. A. G. Dempsey

Died

Inez, daughter of M. M. and Hattie A. Wolf, was born Sept. 9th 1873, and died at Cleaveland Springs, North Carolina, July 31st 1873.

Anne Poyas, eldest daughter of Stobo R. and Georgia C. Perry, died July 23d 1873, aged two years and one week.

Amanda Josephine, only surviving child of Stobo R. and Georgia C. Perry, died August 8th 1873, aged two months and ten days.

In Harris county, Ga., on 27th of Aug., James Jackson, infant son of James and Elizabeth Hines, not quite a year old.

In Harris county, Ga., on 30th of Aug., Robert Lee, only son of Thomas D. and Mary Hamby, aged 7 years and 7 months.

Samuel Huston Avinger, infant and only son of M. D. and Nancy Avinger, of Hickory Hill, Cass county, Texas, died May 30th 1873, aged 15 months.

Obituary

John Pepper Atkinson was born in Brunswick county, Virginia and died in Senoia, Coweta county, Georgia. The deceased was the son of Captain and Mrs. Elizabeth Atkinson, of Brunswick county, Virginia. Leaves widow, four sons and a daughter. W. L. C. Hunnicutt

Mrs. Sarah E. McDonald, whose maiden name was Parramore, was born in Thomas county, Ga., August 26th, 1836, and died in Jefferson county, Fla., August 5th 1873. She was married to Littleton J. McDonald in 1845; in 1855 they removed to Florida. In 1862 her husband died, leaving her with three small children. D. H. Bryan

Miss Tompie Williams, aged 16 years, a member of the Junior class of Andrew Female College, died 3d August in Stewart county, Ga. A. H. Flewellen

Brother John B. Ward was born in Clarke county, Ga., and died in Monroe, Walton county, Ga., on 27th June 1873, aged about 48 years. A. W. Rowland

Mrs. Jeanette Douglass, wife of Rev. John Douglass, was born in Harnett county, N. C., August 24, 1819 and died in Little Rock, Marion county, S. C., June 18, 1873. James C. Stoll. Raleigh Christian Advocate please copy.

W. B. Brannon died in Eufaula, Ala., July 12, 1873. He was born in Edgefield District, S. C. There he married Miss Belzer, daughter of a prominent citizen of that place. She died and he was left with five small children, only two of whom survive him. In 1858 he married his second wife, Miss Mary A. Kaigler. He was a devoted member of the Baptist Church for many years.

Mrs. Rebecca Mahan was born in Pittsylvania county, Virginia, August 2, 1830, was the daughter of Joseph D. and Elizabeth Reynolds, married D. P. Mahan, November 1, 1849. J. M. Hardin

Jesse Stanford died in Americus, Ga., recently, in the 68th year of his age. He was born in Warren county, Ga., but had lived for many years in Sumter county.

Brother J. A. Girardeau died in Hinesville, Ga., 13th August 1873, in his 36th year.

Mrs. Ann Elizabeth Barineau, consort of Mr. R. J. Barineau and daughter of the Rev. R. H. Howren of the South Georgia Conference, died in Decatur county, Ga., Aug. 6, 1873, aged twenty-five years. R. H. Howren

Mrs. Nancy Vason died June 20, 1873, at Social Circle, Walton county, Ga., in the eighty-first year of her age. She was married to Mr Joseph Vason, of Morgan county, in her nineteenth year. In 1836 she was left a widow. She was the mother of ten children, eight of whom preceded her to the grave.

Mrs. R. E. Caldwell was born in North Carolina, June 26, 1836, and died in Bainbridge, Ga., June 20th 1873.

Mrs. Judith Thornton, widow of Wm. Thornton, died May 20th 1873, in the eighty-seventh year of her age, at the residence of her son-in-law, J. N. Morgan, in Jasper county, Ga. She left one son, two daughters, and many grandchildren.

Theodora Lydia Reid was born 16th November 1851 and died at the home of her grandmother, Mrs. Caroline Turnbull, in Monticello, Florida, August 14th 1873. Her mother died nearly five years ago. E. L. T. Blake

Mrs. Mary Martindale, whose maiden name was Burgess, was born in Union district, S. C., and died Dec. 29th 1872, near Waverly station, Chambers county, Alabama. She was about ninety years of age. Her first husband was Richard Coleman, her second husband, Jesse Martindale. Her son, G. W. S. Martindale, at whose home she died.

Issue of September 17, 1873

Died

August 14, 1873, Jimmie Ellis, son of John D. and Lizzie H. Stafford, of Grantville, Ga., aged 21 months.

Paul, youngest child of W. H. and R. A. Felton, died Sept. 2d, 1873, in Bartow county, Ga., aged twenty-one months.

In Clay county, Fla., Joshua H. Santer, son of Daniel and Susan C. Santer, aged six months.

In Hogansville, Ga., Sept. 4th 1873, Rufus Wade, infant son of D. E. and M. A. Cate, aged 18 months.

Obituary

Mrs. Mary Adelaide Hilton, wife of Joshua Hilton and eldest child of Rev. Louis C. and Ann F. Loyal, was born Jan. 24, 1848, and died August 15, 1873. She was brought by baptism into the Church by Rev. W. T. Capers (then in charge of St. James' Church, Charleston). August 11th 1872, she was united in marriage to Mr Joshua Hilton of Saludaville, S. C., where she resided at the time of her death. W. D. Kirkland

Mrs. Susan W. McDaniel, wife of Ira O. MCDaniel, Jr., and daughter of Sister Owings of Atlanta, died at her mother's residence, August 19th 1873. She was born April 3d 1845. She was married March 2d, 1869. She leaves two little children, one of whom is but five months old.

William West was born in Charleston, S. C., March 5th 1801, and died August 3d, 1873. John Watts

Rufus King, son of Thomas W. and Mary Jane Christian, was born in Muscogee county, Ga., October 14th 1850, and died in Panola county, Texas., 26th of July 1873.

F. R. Pittman was born in Halifax county, N. C., Dec. 12th 1813. He removed to Marianna, Florida. Removing from Florida to California in 1868 and settled in Los Angeles, where he died July 2d 1873. A. M. Campbell

Mrs. Sophia O. Sistrunk, wife of S. Oliver Sistrunk, Esq., of the county of Colleton, S. C., died at Orangeburg, S. C., August 7, 1873, aged 41 years.

Mary B. Norman was born Oct. 12th 1806, and died in Dawson, Ga., July 18th 1873. She married W. B. Norman, July 2d 1837.

Roxalana Mims was born June 13th 1833 and died August 23d 1873. S. J. Hill

Sarah A. Smith, daughter of McDade and Pheriba Dannielly, was born in Monroe county, Ga., 5th September 1841; married John F. Passmore, 19 January 1858 who died in the army during the late war; married J. W. Smith, October 18th 1863, died in Coffee county, Ala., 6th of August 1873. She leaves a husband and five little children.

Miss Victoria Smith, daughter of Isham and C. J. Smith, was born in Coweta county, Ga., June 6th 1841, and died in Palmetto, Ga., August 25th 1873. Thomas H. Timmons

Mrs. Jane E. Gordon, wife of Rev. Thomas B. Gordon, M. D., and daughter of James and Elizabeth Tooke (formerly of Tabot county, Ga.) died in Union co., Ark., 6th of August 1873. She leaves a husband and two children (a son and a daughter, both grown).

Mr. Joseph Sessions Lee was born March 15, 1839; married to Miss Caroline Jane Vereen, May 23, 1859 and died in Horry county, S. C., Aug. 16th 1873. W. M. Kirton

Issue of September 24, 1873

Died

Near Milledgeville, Ga., August 20th 1873, little Annie Lizzie, infant daughter of Adolphus F. and Elizabeth H. Bayne, aged 1 year, 10 months and 5 days.

In Bartow county, Ga., Sept. 2d, 1873, Paul, youngest son of Rev. Wm. H. and Mrs. Rebecca A. Felton, aged 20 months.

Marianna, the only daughter of the Rev. E. G. Gage (deceased) of the S. C. Conf., died August 16, 1873, aged 3 years, 11 months and 23 days.

At the residence of her step-father, George S. Leavitt, August 8th 1873, Chrodosia Williamson, aged 10 years, 5 months and 5 days.

In Maybinton, Newberry county, S. C., on 13th Sept. 1873, Mary Eliza, infant daughter of B. H. and R. M. Maybin, aged 1 year, 7 months, 15 days.

In Conyers, Ga., on the 17th August 1873, Mary, infant daughter of A. C. and M. J. Perry, aged three months and twenty-eight days.

Obituary

Rev. Uuran Cooper Tignor, son of Philip Tignor (deceased) was born in Clarke county, Ga., Oct. 16, 1805; was married to Susanah Slaton, Dec. 23, 1830; died in Talbot county, Ga., Sept. 2, 1873. L. B. Payne

Mrs. Martha H. Parker, daughter of Archibald Turner of Greene county, Ga., was born Feb. 22d, 1807, and died in Milledgeville, Ga., Aug. 38th 1873. At the age of eighteen she was married to Lewis Parker, who afterwards became a minister in the Baptist Church.

Mrs. Emily Rebecca Boone, wife of Rev. T. A. Boone and daughter of the late Simon Beckham, Esq., of Lancaster District, died at the Methodist parsonage on Pee Dee circuit, Montgomery county, N. C., on 15th July 1873, aged about 39 years.

Charles Thomas Bayne, the first born of John and Nancy Bayne, was born in Baldwin county, Ga., January 18th 1834. In 1864, he was wedded to Miss Sophronia Smith of Washington county, Ga. He died 25th August 1873.

Mrs. Cornelia J. Burrows was born in Pulaski county, Ga., November 14th 1849 and died in Hawkinsville, Ga., August 16th 1873, a member of the Baptist church. Robert J. Corley

Thomas J. Lipscomb died in Abbeville county, S. C., August 29th 1873, aged 46 years. J. W. Murray

Our dear sister Whistenhunt, wife of A. C. Whistenhunt, died June 14th 1873, aged 31 years. W. C. Dunlap. New Orleans Advocate, please copy.

Mrs. Martha Dunn was born in Horry county, S. C., March 9, 1873 [sic]. She was married to J. J. Dunn, Oct. 5, 1811; died Aug 17, 1873. W. H. Kirton

Mrs. Virginia J. Daniel, whose maiden name was Brown, wife of T. B. Daniel, was born in Talbot county, Ga., August 7th 1840, and died in Talbot county, Ga., August 14th 1873. R. W. Dixon

Mrs. Mary M., wife of Mr. C. C. Bryan and daughter of Wm. and M. E. Hix, died in Chattooga county, Ga., August 31st, 1873, aged about twenty-eight years.

Sister Rebecca A. Ulmer was born Sept. 20th 1802, and died July 17, 1873, in Beaufort county, S. C.

A. O. Norris died in Anderson, S. C., July 3d 1873, in the 66th year of his age. He was born in Abbeville, S. C., but at an early age removed to Anderson. He was a ruling elder in the Presbyterian Church for over forty years. He leaves a wife, aged mother, eight children, twenty-four grandchildren.

Mrs. Emma Matthews, wife of Col. J. D. Matthews, of Lexington, Ga., died in Athens, Ga., August 28th 1873, in the thirtieth year of her age, leaving an infant five days old.

Mrs. Mary Ann Gassaway was born in Nassau county, Florida, October 17th 1811. In 1829 she was married to Rev. Wm. Gassaway, who died some ten years later. Her home had long been in Jefferson county, Florida. E. L. T. Black

Tribute of Respect from Louisville Circuit, Savannah District, to Rev. William McCall Kennedy.

Issue of October 1, 1873

Died

In Newberry county, S. C., July 21st 1873, Lula Gertrude, infant daughter of Mr. Thomas V. Wicker, aged 2 years, 6 months and 21 days.

Mary Eliza Callahan, daughter of Jas. H. and Mary Edna Callahan, was born Nov. 26th 1868 and died in Whitesville, Harris county, Ga., Sept. 13, 1873.

Rudy, youngest daughter of Dr. P. W. and C. C. M. Cate, was born March 2d 1871, and died at Newnansville, Fla., August 28, 1873.

Obituary

William M. Starr was born April 14, 1814, and died August 21, 1873. His first wife was Martha Doss, by whom he raised several children. His last wife was Mrs. Grissom. David Nolan

Mrs. Susannah Rosamand Tignor, consort of the late Rev. U. C. Tignor, was born in Wilkes county, Ga., November 27, 1805 and died in Talbot county, Ga., September 14, 1873. She and her husband raised nine children. L. B. Payne

Mrs. Mary E. Hardaway, wife of Robt. B. Hardaway, of Columbus, Ga., died in Lafayette, Columbus county, Ala., September 8, 1873, aged fifty-four years. She was the daughter of Dana and Rachel Hungerford and was born in Harwinton, Connecticut. Soon after her birth, her parents removed to Greensboro. Mary E. Hungerford was married to Daniel Grant, February 19, 1861. Mr. Grant died in Columbus, Ga., November 4, 1864. Mrs. Grant was married to Major Robert B. Hardaway, December 5, 1865.

Mrs. Rebecca Thomas, whose maiden name was Everett, the widow of James L. Wood, deceased, was born in North Carolina, July 13, 1798, and died July 10, 1873, at the residence of her son-in-law, James A. Pattillo, in Gwinnett county, Ga. Robt. P. Martin

Joseph M. Bond was born in Abbeville district, S. C., September 28, 1797, and died in Campbell county, Ga., June 29, 1873. Thos. R. Timmons

Mrs. A. E. Adams, daughter of Joel E. Davis, was born March 12, 1847; married to James J. Adams October 15, 1866; died in Troup county, Ga., July 6, 1873. W. J. Cotter

Issue of October 8, 1873

Died

Sallie, youngest child of W. N. and S. K. Mason, died Sept. 11th 1873, in Fairfield county, S. C., aged 1 years, 6 months and 18 days.

In Little Rock, Marion county, S. C., Sept. 15, 1873, Ervin Campbell, youngest child of Rev. James C. and Mary L. Stoll, aged one year, nine months and twenty-five days.

Aug. 5, 1873, in Lancaster county, S. C., Tommy, second son of Mr. Joseph and Mrs. Martha C. Crenshaw, aged 5 years and 9 months.

September 23d, 1873, in Lancaster county, S. C., Claude Phifer, youngest child of Dr. J. M. and Mrs. M. J. Nisbet, aged about three years.

Obituary

Mrs. Matilda Ann Daniel, wife of Mr. James L. Daniel, of Eufaula, Ala., whose maiden name was Gant, was born in North Carolina; was married in Meriwether county, Georgia, Oct. 12th 1850; died in Eufaula, Ala., Aug. 14th 1873. She raised a large family of children-- four daughters, all of whom are married to excellent gentlemen, and two sons, who are doing well in the practice of the Law. Joseph B. Cottrell

Mrs. Sarah Hanchey, widow of Daniel Hanchey, was born January 1794 and died July 21st 1873, at the residence of her daughter in Alachua county, Florida. R. H. Barnett

Mrs. N. E. Lyles died in Twiggs county, Ga., August 6th 1873, in the 26th year of her age.

Mrs. Martha Neville Maddux, wife of the late Rev. Patrick Neil Maddux, of Barnesville, Ga., was born in Charleston, S. C., on 28th August 1807 and died in Atlanta, Ga., at the residence of her niece, Mrs. Henrietta J. Barnes, 28th July 1873.

Mrs. E. M. Fale, wife of Mr. John Fale, of Hawkinsville, was born 21st October 1836 and died August 6th 1873. Robert J. Corley

James Loyless was born in Pittsylvania county, Va., in 1784 and died at Dawson, Ga., April 30th 1873. In early life he moved to Warren county, Ga., and subsequently moved to Florida, from thence t Beaufort, South Carolina. He afterwards moved to Colleton county. About the year 1829 an unpleasantness sprang up between himself and his oldest son and daughter, relative to a second marriage, which caused a separation, neither knowing the other was living, for forty-three years. Last year the recognition was brought about by the publication of a meeting held at Salkehatchie in which brother E. B. Loyless' name was mentioned. A. English Williams. The Dawson Journal please copy.

Archibald H. Danner, son of Rev. A. R. Danner of the South Carolina Conference, died in Charleston, S. C., July 2, 1873, in the 28th year of his age.

Frances J. McKennie died in Clay county, Ga., September 18th 1873, in her sixty-sixth year. She leaves an aged husband and a number of children. S. R. Weaver

John R. Helderbrand was born in DeKalb co., Ga., Aug. 1830 and died August 20th 1873.

Mrs. Levicy Jones was born in Colleton county, S. C., Dec. 15th 1796 and died near Salkehatchie at the residence of her son in law, Rev. Hugh F. Porter, formerly of the South Carolina Conference, Sept. 18th 1873. Only a few months ago, Mrs. Mary P. Allen, her only surviving sister, passed away. A. English Williams

Robert T. Green was born Dec. 3d 1802 died in Clay county, Ga., August 29th 1873. He leaves a wife, children and grandchildren. S. R. Weaver

Mrs. Anna Buxton, wife of S. Dawson Buxton and oldest daughter of Mr. James and Mrs. Joice Chandler of Burke county, Ga., died 31st August 1873, in the 21st year of her age.

Tribute of Respect from Bennettsville Circuit, South Carolina Conference to Brother William Pearson, who died 1st September 1873, in his 59th year.

Issue of October 15, 1873

Died

In Colleton county, S. C., Mary Caroline, daughter of Chas. and Narcissa Smiley, aged five years and a few months.

Lilfan J., daughter of John Winship, was born in Smith county, Texas., January 17, 1861, and died in Waco, Texas, September 21, 1873.

Francis Ernest, only child of R. Henry and Susie W. Thomas, died in Sparta, Ga., 27th September, aged one year and twenty-three days.

Obituary

Mrs. Hessie Eveline Ervin, daughter of Wm. E. and Mrs. H. E. Carpenter, was born in Clarendon county, S. C., and died at Chesterfield C. H., S. C., August 23d, 1873, aged twenty years, five months and eight days. She was married to Rev. A. Ervin 19th September 1872. J. B. Platt

J. Frank Hook, eldest son of Dr. J. H. J. Cook, deceased, was born in Orangeburgh county, S. C., October 15, 1842, and died near Perry, Houston county, Ga., September 7, 1873.

Sister Susan A. Marchman, daughter of George and Mary Wells, was born in Greene county, Ga., April 10, 1827, and died in Meriwether county, Ga., August 23, 1873. In 1844 she was married to Alfred George Marchman, who died in September 1863.

Mrs. Martha L. Bowen, wife of Dr. A. H. Bowen and daughter of Charles and A. C. Bailey, died in Kershaw county, S. C., August 11, 1873, in the 29th year of her age.

Miss Rebecca B. Moreland was born in Putnam county, Ga., and died at the residence of her brother-in-law, Mr. David Reid, September 10, 1873. Jno. M. Bowden

Death of Timothy W. M. Cox. He was at the depot in Perry, on 16th inst., but before the sun arose the next morning, he had died. He was only a few days over thirty-four years of age. W. Knox

John Grierson was born in Charleston, S. C., August 14, 1831 and died in Jacksonville, Fla., September 30, 1873. He was married in April 1861 to Miss Fannie Brown, and through her persuasion he was baptized in the Roman Catholic Church a short time after their removal to Florida. He leaves a widow and several children.

Miss Sarah Ann Bentley was born in Union county, S. C., November 17, 1843, and died in her native state and county September 13, 1873. J. B. Wilson

Joseph Patterson died August 30, 1873, in Laurens county, S. C., where he was born and in the 61st year of his age. J. B. Traywick

Miss Amanda Granger, daughter of John and Nancy Granger, was born September 9, 1851, and died near Waukeenah, Florida, September 6, 1873. W. Williams

Mrs. Mary E. Hardaway, wife of Robt. S. Hardaway of Columbus, Ga., died in Lafayette, Chambers county, Ala., September 9, 1873, aged fifty-four years. She was the daughter of Dade[?] and Rachel Hungerford, and was born in Harwinton, Connecticut. Soon after her birth, her parents removed to Greensboro, Ga., at which place and in Columbus and Thomaston, her father was engaged in the mercantile business. She was married to Daniel Grant, Feb. 29, 1861. Mr. Grant died in Columbus, Ga., Nov. 4, 1864. Mrs. Grant was married to Major Robert S. Hardaway, Dec. 5, 1865. She had no children. She united with the Baptist Church in Columbus, Ga.

Miss Isabel M. Johnston, daughter of James C. Johnston, deceased, and S. C. Johnston, was born September 15, 1841, and died in Waukeecah, Florida, September 8, 1873. W. Williams

Sister C. R. Harvey, wife of the late John P. Harvey and mother of Rev. H. J. Harvey, died in East Macon, July 23, 1873, aged sixty years, four months and nineteen days.

Mr. James Ely died at White Plains, Greene county, Ga., aged seventy-six. J. L. Pierce

Mrs. Jane M. Porter died September 19, 1873, aged fifty years and three months. She was born in Union county, N. C., and died within one mile of her birth place. W. C. Patterson

Tribute of Respect from Americus Quarterly Conference to J. Volney Price who died near Americus, Ga., September 12, 1873, being fifty-nine years of age. He was born in Burke county, Ga, August 13, 1814. In early life he removed to Houston county. He married Miss Sarah Bell, who with a large number of children, survives him.

Issue of October 22, 1873

Died

Little Bessie Jones, second daughter of Martha O. Jones, died 20th Sept., 1873, aged seven years and a few months.

Obituary

Mrs. Elizabeth C. Pearce, daughter of Ashly P. and Catharine Weeks, and consort of Thomas C. Pearce, was born in Telfair county, Ga., March 29th 1848, and died in Hillsborough county, Fla., July 15th 1873. E. H. Giles

Mrs. A. C. S. Smith, wife of M. M. Smith, was born in Union county, S. C., July 15th 1848, and died in the same county, Sept. 24th 1873. J. C. Crisp

Mrs. Rebecca Caroline Anderson was the youngest daughter of William and Sophia Hollinshead and the sister of Dr. Wm. H. Hollinshead, of Fort Valley, Ga. She was born in South Carolina, March 28th 1826; married Col. Wm. J. Anderson in Fort Valley, March 18th 1847; died Sept. 29, 1873. F. A. Branch

My brother, Levin C. Palmer, son of James and Mary C. Palmer, was born in Richmond county, Ga., Feb. 20th 1848, and died in Burke county, Sept. 7th 1873. James J. Palmer

Sister Missouri E. Foust, daughter of Miel J. and Nannie C. Horton, died in Shelby county, Ala., Sept. 27th 1873, aged 28 years, 10 months and 24 days. R. G. Ragan

Mrs. Mary S. Howe was born in North Carolina in 1800 and died at the home of her son-in-law, W. A. McMichael, of Marion county, Ga., Sept. 30, 1873. She was the daughter of Clement Bryan, late of Randolph county, Ga., and was twice married-- first to J. G. Raines in 1817, and secondly to Robert Howe, of Crawford county, Ga.

Andrew C. Bird was born in Warren county, Ga., in 1848. in his childhood his parents moved to Stewart county. F. P. Brown

Alice E. Hewitt was born in Richmond, Va., March 13, 1860 and died in Union county, S. C., Aug. 14, 1873. Her step-father was Dr. M. M. Smith. J. C. Crisp

Mrs. Mary L. Martin, relict of John C. Martin, was born in Greene county, Ga., June 10, 1820, and died in Talbotton, Ga., Aug. 18, 1873. On 20th of June 1839, she was married to John C. Martin. R. W. Dixon

Mrs. Rebecca Thomas, whose maiden name was Everett, the widow of James L. Thomas, deceased, was born in North Carolina, July 13, 1798, and died July 10, 1873, at the residence of her son-in-law, James A. Pattillo, in Gwinnett county, Ga. Robt. P. Martin

Miss Leona Black was born in 1844 and died in Ruckersville, Elbert county, Ga., Sept. 9th 18773. F. G. Hughes

Mrs. Martha Bagwell, wife of Capt. J. M. Bagwell, of Carnesville, Ga., and daughter of David and Elizabeth Murrell, of Union district, S. C., was born 15th July 1814, and died 15th of Sept 1873.

Charles Akers Harralson, eldest child of Mr. and Mrs. H. W. Harralson, died in LaGrange, Ga., 15th July 1873, in the 20th year of his age.

James Carswell King was born in Jefferson county, Ga., Jan. 29, 1843, and died in Swainsboro, Ga., Aug. 15, 1873.

Issue of October 29, 1873

Reuben Webster was born December 17, 1800 and died in Polk county, Ga., September 15, 1873. W. F. Glenn

Our dear father, Samuel Pilsbury, was born in Charleston, S. C., August 28, 1803, and died on September 28, 1873. The child of the Rev. Amos and Rebecca Axon Pilsbury. His son

Miss Willie Ross died in Eatonton, Ga., Sept. 28, 1873, in the 29th year of her age.

Mrs. Fannie M. Pitts, wife of Mr. H. S. Pitts and daughter of the late Thomas and Mary A. Whitehead, was born November 4th 1843, and died at William B. Marshall's, Talbot county, Ga., August 14th 1873. In July she left her home, Osmichee, Alabama, to improve her failing health.

Mrs. Julia Ernest, wife of the late Mr. A. E. Ernest, died in Bibb county, Ga., October 4, 1873.

Mrs. Rhoda J. Tompkins, widow of John Tompkins, Sr., and daughter of Harmon and Rhoda J. Crum, was born July 19, 1831; married in December 1845; died in Sumter county, Fla., August 31, 1873.

Issue of November 5, 1873

Died

In Hamilton county, Florida, Oct. 8th 1873, Mary Leatch, daughter of Hilliard and Eliza McInnis, aged two years and seven days.

In Stewart county, Ga., 18th Oct. 1873, Mary Lillian, only child of Mr. and Mrs. W. H. Griffis, in the fourth year of her age.

In Twiggs county, Oct. 23d, 1873, Hal. E. Plank, aged nearly four years; also on the 24th Oct. Hartwell Hill, aged eight months, sons of Dr. H. S. and E. L. Wimberly

Rommie, son of Jefferson and Mary E. Stokes, of Barnwell county, S. C., was born June 12th 1867, and died Oct. 18th 1873.

On the 22d Oct. 1873, little Mamie Louisa, eldest daughter of John H. and Mrs. Emma N. Waits, of Abbeville county, S. C., aged 3 years, 7 months and 2 days.

Obituary

Mrs. Frances Brinn was born in North Carolina and died in Macon, Ga., Sept. 27th 1873, at the age of 58 years. She was married to Richard Brinn, September 21st 1832, and removed immediately to Macon, Georgia.

Mrs. Elizabeth A. Evans died at Bartow, Jefferson county, Ga., Sept. 19th 1873, in the 68th year of her age.

Mrs. Emma R. Ryle, consort of D. M. Ryle and daughter of Spencer R. and M. A. Pennie, deceased, died in Cochran, Ga., Sept. 15th 1873, aged 24 years, 3 months and 4 days.

Sister Margaret Mehaffey, daughter of Simon and Harriet K. Hendricks and wife of John Mehaffey, was born July 5, 1836, and died in Atlanta, Ga., October 6, 1873. W. F. Robison

Mrs. Caroline V. Rhodes, wife of T. J. Rhodes, was born Feb. 12th 1841, and died in Taliaferro county, Ga., Oct. 7th 1873. She married Dec. 4th 1856, at the age of fourteen. A. C. Thomas

Mrs. Mary R. Harwell, daughter of Jonathan Lane and widow of Vines Harwell, Esq., was born in Oglethorpe county, Ga., November 25, 1799, and died in Walker county, Ga., at the residence of her son-in-law, Jefferson Coulter, July 25, 1873. After her married to Vines Harwell in 1823, they removed in the fall of 1826 or 1827 to Troup county, Ga., and were some of its earliest settlers. Two of her sons, twin brothers Theophilus S. L. and Richard J., are members of the North Georgia Conference. Two of her sons lost their lives in the service of their country.

Dr. Edward Hatcher died August 15, 1873, at McBean, Richmond county, Ga., at the early age of 32 years and 10 months. M. F. Stuart

Mrs. Elizabeth K. Stubbs, wife of J. W. Stubbs, Esq., died in Marlborough county, S. C., on the 13th of Sep. 1873, in the 65th
year of her age. She leaves a husband and ten children (all grown and married).

Mrs. Mary Sartor, daughter of Wm. and Caroline McJunkin, was born in Marion county, S. C., Aug. 13th 1851. In June 1872 she was married to Wm. Sartor. She died 16th October 1873. Thos. W. Smith

Mrs. Mary Davis, mother of Mrs. R. S. McCants and P. L. Davis, died at Bouncan's Station N. E. R. R., South Carolina, September 23d, 1873 in her 85th year. A few days before her death she reached the home of her only surviving daughter.

Issue of November 12, 1873

[paper has black borders]
page 2: Death of Bishop Early. The press telegrams announce the decease on the 5th of November of this venerable servant of the Church. Bishop Early was born of Baptist parents in Bedford county, Virginia, January 1st 1786, and lack less than two months of being 88 years old.

Rev. William J. Parks was the son of Henry and Martha Parks (named name Justice). She had only one brother, William Justice, from whom William Justice Parks received his name. His father, born in Virginia, was reared in Wilkes county, North Carolina on Yadkin river, in a rough mountainous region. His parents and most of the people about them were Baptists. His mother, also born in Virginia, was an Episcopalian, baptized in infancy and trained up in that church. About the year 1785 or '86 William J. Parks' parents removed from North Carolina and settled near the mouth of Beaverdam creek, in Elbert county, Georgia. Of these parents, William Justice Parks was the youngest of eight children, born in Franklin county, Ga., November 30, 1799. He died October 16th 1873. [this notice is nearly three columns long]

Obituary

Mrs. Susie B. Stokes, wife of Augustus W. Stokes and daughter of Capt. N. C. and Mrs. Elizabeth Bridges, died in Coweta county, Ga., September 26th 1873, aged 22 years, 9 months and 17 days. Her remains were deposited in the family burying ground of her grand-father, the late Parke E. Arnold. She had been married but little more than two years. She leaves a little daughter, not yet a year old.

Rev. Nelson Osborn, in the Carnesville circuit, was born in Lincoln county, Ga., Nov. 28, 1798; was married to Miss Liney Watson in 1819; died Sept. 3d, 1873. M. H. Eakes

Mrs. Adline Hume, wife of Rev. Benj. L. Hume, formerly of Virginia, died in Morgan co., Ga., Sept. 3, 1873. Some time during the war, brother Hume and family removed from Virginia to this state, and located in this county, where sister Hume died.

Elijah Mixon was born October 31st 1795; married to Charlotte Ortry, Sept. 4, 1823; died at Oxford, Ga., August 20, 1873. Two of his sons are in the minister-- the Rev. J. F. Mixon, of the So. Georgia Conference, and Rev. Asbury Mixon, a highly useful local minister of this county.

Mrs. Sarah Margaret Moore, daughter of W. G. Huckabee and wife of Rev. Thomas M. Moore, was born in Coweta county, Ga., Nov. 22, 1848 and died in Carrollton, Ga., August 8, 1873. W. C. Dunlap

Robert Henry Cato, eldest child of Col. Wm. W. and Mrs. Lou Cato, was born in Troup county, Ga., July 13th 1851, and died at Hogansville, Ga., October 11th 1873. John M. Bowden

Willie S. Rivers, only son of W. P. and Mary F. Rivers, was born January 15th 1859 and died in Cave Spring, Ga., October 25th 1873.

Mrs. Martha Clemmons, wife of Phillip Clemmons, died August 17, 1873, in Morgan county, Ga.

P. L. Richards, son of a Baptist minister, deceased, was born August 14th 1854, and died Oct. 17, 1873, in Shelby county, Ala. R. G. Ragan

Mrs. Bathsheba Bates, whose maiden name was Mulkey, was born May 26, 1804; was married first to Mr. Seaborn S. Royal, January 26, 1819, and after his death to her now bereaved husband, Mr. W. C. Bates, March 11, 1829. She died October 2, 1873. Jas. A. Rogers

Thomas Green was born in Brunswick county, Virginia, in 1789, and died in Upson county, Ga., October 5, 1873. He leaves distinguished children to emulated his virtues. M. H. White

Mrs. Sarah A. Booker died August 7, 1873.

SOUTHERN CHRISTIAN ADVOCATE NOTICES 1867-1878

Tribute of Respect from Quarterly Conference of the First Methodist Episcopal Church, South of Atlanta, Ga., to Rev. Wm. H. Pegg, M. D.

Tribute of Respect from Quarterly Conference, Cleveland circuit, Dahlonega District, North Georgia Conference to Samuel P. Densmore, who was born in Buncombe county, N. C., March 22, 1809, moved to Habersham county, Ga., when quite young.

Issue of November 19, 1873

Died

In Edgefield, near Nashville, Tennessee, Oct. 31st 1873, George Pierce, aged eighteen months, youngest child of Rev. Atticus G. and Mrs. Mary Yarbrough Haygood, of the North Georgia Conference.

Immogiene Hinton, infant son of W. F. and M. A. Chandler in Macon county, Ala., September 8th 1873, aged not quite one year.

Obituary

Reverend Samuel H. Smith, recently one of the proprietors of the Cartersville Standard and Express, and for many years past favorable connected with the press of Georgia, died in Cartersville, Ga., Oct. 30th, in the forty-fifth year of his age.

Mrs. Theresa McDavid died in Greenville county, S. C., on the 23d of August 1873, in the 65th year of her age, leaving a husband and large family of children. Her funeral service was at Bethesda Church, performed by Rev. John Finger.

Miss M. A. Mell, daughter of brother W. H. Mell, died Oct. 2, 1873, just one month having elapsed since the death of her father.

W. H. Mell, Esq., one of the oldest and best esteemed citizens of Georgia, died in Atlanta, Ga., Sept. 2, 1873. He was born in South Carolina, Oct. 30th 1794. When a little child, his parents removed to Liberty county, Ga. He moved from Wilkes county to Newton county in 1837, and was the second settler of Oxford.

Elijah H. Mattox was born in Tattnall county, Georgia, May 31, 1812; moved to Florida in 1844; died Aug. 14, 1873. For nearly thirty years brother Mattox was a citizen of East Florida. S. E. Phillips

William W. Gray was born in Gadsden county, Florida, August 16, 1850; died October 15, 1873 in Jefferson county, Fla., where he had gone with his father, J. H. Gray, on a visit to his uncle Abel Chester. J. D. Rogers

Mrs. Mary Wilder, daughter of David and Deborah Bowers, was born Dec. 6, 1839, and died in Crawford county, Ga., Aug. 28th 1873. On Dec 30th 1868, she was married to N. Wilder. She sleeps in the silent grave at Shiloh. J. S. Blasingame

Mrs. Mary A. E. Price, wife of Joseph Price and daughter of G. W. and Rebecca Prince, was born in Washington county, Ga., May 11th 1820, and died in Columbia county, Fla., August 31st 1873.

Mrs. Nancy Hodges whose maiden name was Robinson, was born and reared in Putnam county, Ga., and died in Merriwether county, Ga., Oct. 9th 1873, aged 60 years and 3 months. Wm. N. Fambrough

Mrs. Barbary N. Garrison, whose maiden name was Jamison, wife of J. N. Garrison, was born in Spartanburg District, S. C., and died in Acworth, Ga., Sept. 26th 1873, aged 48 years. White residing with her brother, the late James Gordon, of Canton. In 1844 she married.

Mrs. Rebecca Tolbert was born in Abbeville county, S. C., and died in Columbia county, Florida, Sept. 3d, 1873, in her seventieth year. Her only son.

David R. Garrison was born in Clarke county, Ga., Dec. 31st, 1838, and died in Houston county, Ga., Sept. 22d, 1873. He leaves a wife and several little children. J. H. Littlejohn

Richard A. Lane was born in Clarke county, Ga., Nov. 3rd 1797, and died in Acworth, Cobb county, Ga., Oct. 11th 1873. Before the war, he lived on his plantation in Walker county.

Mrs. Nancy Clements Beasley, wife of Rev. J. S. Beasley of the South Carolina Conference, was born in Darlington county, S. C., May 24, 1843, and died there while on a visit among her friends, Oct. 8, 1873. H. A. C. Walker

Thomas Ward was born in Jackson county, Ga., Feb. 14th 1801, and died near Salem, Lee county, Ala., Aug. 26th 1873; was married to Edny Pool, Feb 9th 1836. He left a widow and several children.

Mrs. Eliza McLesky, wife of Mr. James McLesky, of Anderson county, S. C., was born March 15th 1815, and died Oct. 18th 1873. She had been married about forty years. She leaves a husband and six children. D. J. McMillan

James D. Morris was born of French parents, in Kent county, England, March 25th 1813, came to this country from France in 1831, located in Jefferson county, Florida, in 1836; was married in 1838 to Catharine Mathers, who survives him, and died Sept. 30th 1873. Josephus Anderson

Tribute of Respect from Quarterly Conference for Trinity and Wesley churches at Savannah to John F. Cardell, who died Sept. 15th 1873.

Tribute of Respect from Quarterly Conference for Trinity and Wesley churches at Savannah to Rev. Geo. Allen, who died June 28th 1873.

Issue of November 26, 1873

Died

Larkin Butler was born in Culpepper county, Va., November 25th 1779 and died in LaGrange, Ga., November 15, 1873, being nearly 94 years old.

In Dahlonega, Ga., October 21, 1873, Archie Wimpy, eldest son of A. J. and Fannie Reese, aged 6 years, 2 months and 1 days.

Obituary

Mary E. Wilson was born in Morgan county, Ga., Oct. 3d 1826; married in May 1850; died in Decatur, Ga., on 24th of October 1873. In early childhood her parents removed to Chattooga county, Ga., where they died.

John Floyd Cardell died in Savannah, Ga., September 15th 1873, aged about 56 years. Geo. G. N. McDonell

John Bell Dozier died on 24th October 1873. Had he lived until the 15th of March next, he would have been 67 years of age.

John Brown was born April 20, 1846, and died in Lancasterville, S. C., Sept. 20, 1873. He was licensed to preach in Jefferson City, April 3d, 1871. J. R. Little

Mrs. J. R. Christian was born in Hancock county, Ga., May 28th 1849, and died in Thomasville, Ga., Sept. 8, 1873. J. B. McGehee

SOUTHERN CHRISTIAN ADVOCATE NOTICES 1867-1878

Mrs. Ann Webb was born in Hancock county, Ga., February 20, 1799, and died while on a visit to her youngest child, Mrs. Dr. B. F. Chapman, of Tilton, Ga., August 29, 1873. She was married to John Webb in 1815, and soon after moved with her husband to Newton county, Ga. She was buried by the side of her husband in the village graveyard at Newbern, Newton county, Ga.

John Sifley, Sr., father of the Rev. J. L. Sifley of the South Carolina Conference died in Orangeburg, S. C., Oct. 1st 1873, in the 84th year of his age. F. Auld

Oliver H. Murrow was born in Orangeburg county, S. C., and died in Atlanta, Ga., October 30th 1873. He was about fifty-four years of age. F. Auld

Rev. Wm. H. Pegg, M. D., was born Nov. 14, 1814, and died August 10, 1873. The Quarterly Conference of First Church, Atlanta, paid a merited tribute.

Thomas L. Buzbee, son-in-law of Dr. Wm. H. Pegg, was born August 12, 1845, and died in Atlanta, Ga., Sept. 8, 1873. He was married to Miss Hattie Pegg in 1868.

Milburn Green Osborn was born in Johnson county, Tennessee, July 11, 1850 and was killed on the Nashville and Chattanooga Railroad, Oct. 1st 1873. Her remains were sent to his parents, Dr. J. K. Osborn and wife at Tilton, Whitfield county, Ga. T. J. Simmons

Fannie Barton, wife of Major J. J. Salley, died October 13, 1873. She leaves husband and sisters and brothers.

Tribute of Respect from Quarterly Conference of Forsyth circuit to Wm. C. Redding who died on 6th inst.

Tribute of Respect from Church at Chicksawhathcee to Samuel Bilsburg. he was born in Charleston, S. C., August 18, 1808, and died 28th September 1873.

Issue of December 3, 1873

Died

In Hogansville, Ga., 2d Nov 1873, little Jessie L. Jones, only child of Dr. Thomas J. and V. S. Jones, aged one year, 3 months and 22 days.

Near Hogansville, Ga., 3d Nov 1873, Katie Lou, infant daughter of James T. and Elizabeth Jones, aged 9 months. Both buried at the same time and place.

Obituary

Mrs. Mary P. Guyton, wife of Col. C. S. Guyton, daughter of Judge E. J. Blackshear and grand-daughter of General David Blackshear, died in Laurens county, Ga. Oct. 25th 1873, at the age of 26 years.
Mrs. A. M. Williams was born in Greene county, Ga., June 27th 1827, and died in Union Springs, Ala., October 15th 1873. J. A. Peterson

Sister Nancy Arthur, eldest sister of Gen. Henry Arthur, died in Lexington county, S. C., October 29th 1873. She was born in 1790. She resided in the bounds of the Lexington circuit, but held membership with the Washington Street Methodist Church in Columbia. J. Claudius Miller

Atchison E. Bull of Orangeburg county, S., C., died on Sept. 11th 1873.

D. H. H. Stipe, only son of Henry and Sophia Stipe, was born in Coweta county, Ga., June 5th 1849, and died in Palmetto, Ga., September 21st 1873.

Mrs. Sarah C. Parler, wife of Arnold E. Parler was born in Orangeburg District, S. C., Dec. 26th 1825, and died in Colleton county, S. C., near George's Station, Oct. 16th 1873. She leaves a husband, five daughters and two sons. Henry Abbott

Mr. Abe M. Williams was born in Hancock county, Ga., August 25th 1826 and died in Union Springs, Ala., November 10th 1873. J. A. Peterson

Elizabeth Ellison daughter of Wm. and Mary Freeman was born June 1st 1801 in Clarke county, Ga; married to J. B. Ellison, January 29th 1824; died at the residence of her son-in-law, J. F. Thomas, October 2d 1873. She resided in Columbus, Ga., for some twenty years, from which place she removed to Lee county, Ala., in 1870, where she died. William B. Neal

Mrs. Sarah Turrentine, whose maiden name was McClendon, was born in Lincoln county, Ga., January 1st 1787; married first to Mr. Street, who fell in the was of 1812; married again to Dr. Wm. Turrentine, nov. 1st 1825; died at the residence of her son-in-law, Mr. A. Morgan, Oct. 22d 1873. William B. Neal

Mrs. Marget E. Mangum, daughter of James F. Carraway, was born in N. C., Nov. 28th 1852 and died Sept. 6th 1873, in Georgetown county, South Carolina. She was married to James Mangum in 1871. She leaves him and an infant, Annie Sue. North Carolina Christian Advocate please copy. J. C. Russell

Mrs. Huldah Norton, wife of Rev. A. H. Norton, was born September 8, 1821, and died October 4, 1873. She leaves a husband and child. David Stripling

Martha Emma Cates was born Sept. 22d, 1847; married to Jno. D. Outlaw, Feb. 1873, died Nov. 14th 1873, in Wilkinson county, Ga.

Tribute of Respect from Newberry station, South Carolina Conference to Col. Robt. Moorman who died on 5th of October.

Issue of December 10, 1873

Hon. Samuel C. Candler died near Villa Rica, Carroll county, Ga., November 13, 1873. He was born December 6, 1809. He was buried at the new cemetery of the Methodist Church in Villa Rica with Masonic honors.

Sister Agnes Godfrey, wife of J. E. Godfrey, Atlanta, Ga., was the daughter of Capt. Joseph Taylor of the U. S. Navy, and was born in Charleston, S. C., October 3d, 1813. Her parents were Episcopalians. Miss Godfrey, afterwards Mrs. Charles Betts, prayed for her. On her birth-day, 2d October 1838, she was married to Rev. J. E. Godfrey, and became the mother of several children; all of whom, except Ervin, Joseph, and Alfred, have preceded her to the spirit land. She died on 21st November last. J. E. Evans

Sister Rebecca Ann Irby, daughter of Wm. J. and Martha H. Sappington, was born February 24, 1833; was married to James H. Irby, April 29th 1863, and died in Troup county, Ga., Nov. 4, 1873. D. D. Cox

Eleanor A. Haynes, daughter of Wm. Trotter, was born in Russell county, Ala., April 11, 1823; married Wilson B. Edwards, August 10, 1843, who having died in 1862 in the war, she married John W. Haynes, her surviving husband, Dec. 4th 1867, and died October 27th 1873. She leaves several children by her first husband.

Mrs. Gladys C. Weathers (maiden name, Burge) was born in Jones county, Ga., March 5th 1821; married to Mr. Seaborn Weathers, Dec. 25, 1843; died near Pleasant Hill, Ga., October 11, 1873. W. H. Woodall

Mrs. Mary H. Clifton, wife of Jesse Clifton and mother of Rev. J. A. Clifton of the South Carolina Conference, was born in 1812, and died in Chester county, S. C., October 20, 1873. She leaves a husband and children. J. M. Boyd

Miss Mary George Edwards, daughter of George and Julia Edwards, was born May 11, 1858, and died in Lee county, Ala., Sept. 30, 1873. She only two years old, her mother died and left her to the care of her grand-mother. J. H. Lockhart

Mrs. Ann Brice, daughter of Robert and Rebecca Wood, of Spartanburg district, S. C., was born April 26, 1810; married Rev. Samuel Brice in Hall county, Ga., December 29, 1831; and died in Walker county, Ga., Oct. 28, 1873. She leaves three children and a husband. D. J. Weems

Richard Walter Kopp, second son of the late Edward Kopp of Charleston, S. C., died in Ridgeville, S. C., July 6th 1873, in the twentieth year of his age. When a small boy, he was deprived by death of his father. M. H. Pooser

Miss Alice Wilson, daughter of Mrs. Sarah Wilson, was born July 1848; died in Liberty co., Ga., near Taylor's Creek, on 27th October 1873. Wm. G. Booth

Mrs. Jane S. Davis was born in Newbern, N. C., in 1826, and died in Orange Bluff, Nassau co., Fla., Nov. 12, 1873. Wm. J. Greene

Melissa J. Enicks was born in Barnwell district, S. C., 17th of November 1838 and died in Scriven county, Ga., 22d of October 1873.
Issue of December 17, 1873

Died

In Abbeville, Ala., on the 9th Sept. 1873, and buried in Eufaula, Ala., on the 11th Sept., Nannie Tabitha, infant daughter of J. F. and Fannie E. Scafe, aged one year, eleven months and ten days.

Charlie M. Newman, son of F. J. and Harriet Newman, died in Jackson county, Georgia, 24th Sept. 1873, aged seven years, two months and two days.

Obituary

William C. Redding was born in Washington county, Ga., July 30th 1795. He moved to Baldwin county with his parents when nine or ten years of age, where he lived until grown. in the fall of 1821 he was married to Miss Margaret E. Flewellen, of Baldwin county. He moved to Monroe county in 1823. He died at his old homestead in Monroe county, 6th of Nov. 1873. J. J. Singleton

Brother Henry Holliday was born August 15, 1833 and died Nov. 12, 1873. He came from Martin county, N. C., several years since, married in this state. He lived the past season on his own new-found home, just below brother L. A. Grier's on west bank of great Pee Dee-- eighteen miles above Georgetown. J. W. Kelly

My father, Mr. Simeon Tyner, was born in Effingham county, GA., Jan. 2, 1805, and died at the residence of his son, Mr. B. J. Tyner, in Macon county, Ga., Oct. 23, 1873. his body slumbers in the old "Red Hill Church" grave yard with his two children. E. S. Tyner

Rev. John J. Cassady was born in Chesterfield district, S. C., November 6, 1827; moved to Ala. in 1832, and died October 26, 1873. He was married to Miss Sallie L. Edwards, Nov. 8, 1861. June 7, 1864, his wife died. On February 7, 1866, he was married to Miss Mary D. Edmondson. M. R. Cassady

Mrs. Rachel W. Ayers, wife of J. M. Ayers, and daughter of A. W. and C. D. Miller, died in Orangeburg county, S. C., October 1, 1873, on her 32d birth day. She leaves a husband and seven children.

N. Ella Langford, daughter of Robert W. and Margaret Langford, was born in Macon county, Ala., December 31st, 1860 and died in Johnson county, Texas, Sept. 18, 1873. Ella's father died several years ago.

John McMichael of Marion county, Ga., was born in Putnam county, June 25, 1808, and died in Eatonton, Ga., Nov. 26, 1873. W. W. Stewart

John T. Coumbe was born in Edgefield district, S. C., 15th of March 1847 and died in Warrenton, Ga., Oct. 20th 1873. He joined the M. E. Church, South in 1870; married Miss Mary E. Scruggs in 1871.

Augustus B. Moran died in Crawford county, Ga., Nov. 4th 1873, in the 52d year of his age.

Tribute of Respect to Charles Thompson, who was born Jan.13, 180, and died Sept. 17, 1873... from Sandy Springs.

Issue of December 24, 1873

Died

December 14, 1873, in Palmetto, Georgia, Ransom Mozell, son of Hattie I. and Rev. R. J. Harwell of the North Georgia Conference, aged 18 months.

On the 5th of December 1873, Clara M. Cook, daughter of E. R. Cook of Taylor county, Ga.

In Lexington county, S. C., October 8, 1873, Willie Buff, infant son of M. B. and Joanna Buff.

At Early Branch, Beaufort county, S. C., Dec. 7th 1873, Franklin Boulware, infant son of Col. Wm. and Eliza J. Stokes, aged 13 months and 18 days.

Obituary

Lilly A. Andrews, wife of R. W. Andrews, and eldest daughter of Wm. T. and M. C. Williams, was born in Clark county, Ga., January 1844, and died at her residence in Griffin, Ga., Oct. 11, 1873.

John Pattillo died in Harris county, Ga., Nov. 30, 1873, in the 82d year of his age. He was raised in Greene county, Ga., was married to Mary Winfield in 1818 who died in 1868. Six sons and four daughters still live. N. W. Pattillo

Joseph Boring, Sr., was born in Washington, Wiles county, Ga., June 30, 1867, and departed this life in Waldo, Alachua county, Fla., October 30, 1867. He was married to Miss Harriet Means of Morgan county, Ga. S. Gardner

Mrs. Matilda Barber, whose maiden name was Crawford, was born in Antrim county, Ireland, in 1811; emigrated when a child with her grandparents to South Carolina; was married February 22d, 1831 to James A. Barber; died November 3, 1873. Phil L. Henderson

Mrs. Rebecca Wimberly, wife of Dr. R. S. Wimberly, was born in DeKalb county, Ga., June 19, 1829, and died in Florence, Stewart county, Ga., Sept. 29, 1873. G. T. Embry

Brother Nathan Bodie died in Edgefield co., S. C., November 9th 1873, in his seventieth year. All of his children but one, and many of his grand-children are members of the church.

Mrs. Elizabeth Witherspoon, wife of David Witherspoon, Esq., died in Clarendon, S. C., on Oct. 23, 1873, aged about sixty-four years. The deceased, with her husband, formerly resided in Darlington.

245

SOUTHERN CHRISTIAN ADVOCATE NOTICES 1867-1878

Mrs. Caroline J. Pettus, wife of Rev. E. Pettus and daughter of L. S. Malone, was born in Union county, S., C., July 2d 1836 and died in Orangeburg county, S., C., Nov. 30th 1873, at the residence of Mr. E. Nix.

Mrs. Joanna Buff, consort of Mr. B. F. Buff and daughter of John and Margaret V. Shull, of Lexington, S. C., was born in 1842; married to Mr. M. E. Buff, December 23d, 1869, and died in Lexington county, S. C., Sept. 24, 1873. She left a husband and two little children. Her Sister M. W. S.

Tribute of Respect from Waukenah circuit, Florida Conference, to James D. Morris who died 30th September last.

Issue of January 7, 1874

Died

Walter Bailey, only son of Elijah W. and Rebecca P. Bostick, of Eufaula, Ala., was born March 17, 1873, and died Oct. 13, 1873.

On the 15th November, Elizabeth Amanda, daughter of James H. and Amanda M. Hand, aged 3 years, 8 months and 3 days.

Obituary

Mrs. Harriet Jackson was born in Columbia county, Ga., March 28, 1796; was married to Judge W. F. Jackson, January 21st 1813; died at the residence of her son, W. S. Jackson, in Tuskegee, Ala., November 20, 1873.

The church at Bishopville has been called upon to make another contribute to the church above. Sister Sue Muldrow died October 16, in the 27th year of her age. She was the youngest daughter of Rev. Henry D. and Rebecca Green, of precious memory.

Rev. P. J. Malone was born in Charleston, S. C., 20th March 1814 and died in Austin, Texas, Sept. 30th 1873. F. A. Mood. Texas Advocate please copy.

Mrs. Mary Ball died at the residence of her daughter, Mrs. Annie Pearson, in Coweta county, Ga., Nov. 3d 1873. She was born in Abbeville Dist., S. C., in 1772 and had attained the age of one hundred and one years.

Mrs. Matilda Carmichael, wife of Jas. M. Carmichael, died in McDonough, Ga., December 12, 1873. Geo. M. Nolan

Mrs. Harriet W. Crawly, wife of Mr. Lindsy L. Crawly (her maiden name was Oliver), was born in Halifax county, Virginia, about 1823, and died near Snapping Shoals, Newton county, Ga., Oct. 3, 1873. Religious Herald will please copy.

Mr. Lindsy L. Crawly, husband of Mrs. Harriet Crawly, was born in Halifax county, Virginia, about 1823, and died near Snapping Shoals, Newton county, Ga., Oct. 23, 1873. He was a deacon in the Baptist Church. Religious Herald will please copy.

Sister Sarah Emeline Sprinkles (whose maiden name was George) was born in Spartanburg district, South Carolina, December 24, 1853, and died October 11, 1873. She has left a husband and an infant. C. Lee

Mrs. Eliza Boring Butler, wife of Mr. William D. Butler, of Pike county, Ga., died Nov. 30th 1873. Mrs. Butler was born February 9th 1832 and was married to Mr. Butler, Oct. 17th 1852. She was the daughter of Mr. and Mrs. Allen of Meriwether county, Ga. J. J. Caldwell

Tribute of Respect from Quarterly Conference of Spring Vale circuit, to R. G. Green.

246

Tribute of Respect from Quarterly Conference, Bainbridge station, South Georgia Conference to three members: Geo. W. Lewis, Geo. W. Pearce, and Wm. C. Subers.

Issue of January 14, 1874

Mrs. Martha H. Drane was born in Columbia county, Ga., in 1806; was married to Dr. William Drane in 1826; and died in Talbot county, Ga., Dec. 2d, 1873. Her daughter, Mrs. Thos. Mathews, of Marion county, Ga. W. W. Stewart

Mrs. Ann Proctor, wife of Daniel R. Proctor of Camden county, was born in Beaufort, S. C., Dec. 25, 1831; died Nov. 25, 1873.

James Jackson Harris was born Nov. 1st 1815 and died in Decatur county, Ga., Nov. 23d, 1873. His mother and father died during his infancy, and he was raised by an aunt, Mrs. Mary Pitts, who at the advanced age of eighty four, still survives him. He was twice married: in 1843 to Eliza Oliver, who died in 1870-- a second time to Miss Tempe Colson in 1871.

Mrs. P. J. Graham, wife of Rev. W. H. Graham, of the North Georgia Conference, was born Aug. 19, 1819, and died in Monroe county, Ga., Nov. 23, 1873. Sh was married February 11, 1837, to Rev. W. H. Graham, and became the mother of several children. W. W. Lampkin

Mrs. Fannie Spear, wife of H. H. Spear of Bainbridge, Ga., was born Nov. 19, 1844, and died Oct. 28, 1873. She grew up in the Presbyterian Church. She was married Feb. 25, 1869, to H. H. Speak, a Methodist. S. D. Clements

Hartwell J. Swearingin was among the first victims to yellow fever in Bainbridge. He was born March 14, 1836, and died October 19, 1873. He was married to Miss Eliza Crawford, December 18, 1860, and they had four children. S. D. Clements

Miss Elizabeth Heard Tucker was born Aug. 28, 1810; was married to M. C. Upshaw, Esq., Feb. 2d 1830; after his death was married to Robt. L. Harris, Esq., Dec. 1st 1840 and died in Watkinsville, Clarke county, Ga., Nov. 28, 1873.

Mrs. Margaret Kitchen of Scotch descent, was born in Richmond county, N. C., and died in Emanuel county, Ga., October 7th 1873, aged 67 years. She belonged to the Presbyterian church until she was married.

Mrs. Elizabeth C. Usher, wife of Noah Usher, was born May 6, 1838, and died Nov. 23d, 1873.

Mrs. Mary Elizabeth Fowler, wife of Capt. James F. Fowler, died in Warren county, Ga., Dec. 14, 1873, aged 31 years. R. W. Hubert

Tribute of Respect from Seneca circuit and mission, South Carolina Conference to Rev. C. H. Spears.

Issue of January 21, 1874

Rev. Amos Johnson died at his residence in McDuffie county, Ga., Dec. 15th 1873, in the 55th year of his age. Born Nov. 3d 1819.

My father, John Williams, died near Senoia, Coweta county, Ga., Dec. 29th 1873. He was born in Edgefield district, S. C., July 19th 1796. When a child, between two and three years of age, his father moved to Jackson county, Ga. He later moved to Fayette county, then to Coweta county. W. L. Williams

John Krast died on 29th of November 1873 in the 91st year of his, age having been born in a village near Plymouth, in Cornwall, England, in January 1783. He married a respectable farmer's daughter by whom he had nine children. He moved to the United States and lived a few years in Philadelphia, Pa., from which place he removed to Charleston. Here he lost his first wife and afterwards married again. He removed to Greenville, then to Spartanburg, S. C. In this place he spent the last thirty years of his life.

Brother Henry Beard died at Ninety-six, Nov. 9th 1873, in his 62d year. He was married twice and left several children. W. H. Lawton

Mrs. Martha Sledge was born in Elbert county, Ga., June 23d 1793, married to Mr. Wiley Sledge on Sept. 27th 1827, and died at Athens, Ga., Nov. 24th 1873. She leaves one daughter and an aged husband, now in his ninety-first year. J. Lewis, Jr.

Mrs. Mary Truitt died in Troup county, Ga., on the 4th of Nov. 1873, in the 78th year of her age. She was Miss Mary Fester, born in Wilkes county, Ga., married to Thomas Truitt in 1841, joined the Presbyterian Church.

Major William E. Farley was born in Virginia, Jan. 4th 1804, and died near Hamilton, Harris county, Ga., 4th Jan. 1874, in his 70th year. Jas. M. Mobley

Issue of January 28, 1874

Died

Buna Louisa, eldest daughter of Dr. J. H. and Mrs. Mary E. Watkins, was born July 2, 1870, and died in Palmetto, Ga., Jan. 13, 1874.

Bunyan, only child of George and Ella Gault, died in Union county, S. C., Oct. 19, 1873, aged 1 year, 5 months and 15 days.

Fannie, daughter of William H. and Jane M. Gault, died December 1st 1873, aged 6 years, 5 months, and 25 days.

Obituary

The city of Montgomery, Ala., was scourged by yellow fever in the months of September, October, and November 1873. The number of cases amounted to about 500, of which about 100 were fatal. The M. E. Church, South, of this place suffered great loss in the death of two excellent women, Mrs. Eleanora Beggs and Mrs. Martha H. Beall. Mrs. Beggs was born in Richmond county, Ga., May 27, 1831. In her childhood, she removed to Columbia, S. C., and in that city grew to womanhood. She was married to Mr. Thomas Beggs, Oct. 22d, 1850. in 1865 they removed from Columbia to Mississippi, and thence in 1867 to Montgomery., where she died Oct. 19, 1873. She leaves a husband and two nephews (whom she had adopted). Mrs. Beall was the daughter of Samuel and Elizabeth Cook, and widow of J. B. Beall. She was born in Clinton, Ga., March 21, 1813. She died Dec. 16, 1873. She was married Dec. 22d, 1839 and her husband died Sept. 23d, 1863. E. Wadsworth

Mrs. Nancy Moore, wife of C. F. Moore and daughter of John and Elizabeth White, was born in Caswell county, N. C., August 5, 1796, and died in Walker county, Ga., October 13, 1873. She was married in her native state; removed thence to Campbell county, Ga., afterwards to Walker county. She was the mother of nine children, all of whom survive, except for one daughter. Three sons are Methodist preachers.

Sarah Marlor, whose maiden name was Combs, was born in Wilkes county, Ga., Feb. 7, 1798, and died in the same county, Oct. 29, 1873. In 1816 she was married to Labana Marlor. In a few years her husband died, leaving her a widow with one child. Thomas H. Gibson

Mrs. Mary A. Moore, whose maiden name was Earnest, was born in Green county, Tenn., in 1811; married Col. Wm. Moore of South Carolina in 1834; after some years, moved with her husband to Missouri; died Jan. 5th 1874. Col. Moore died about twenty years ago. W. M. Crumley

Mary Ida Pearce, eldest daughter of the late George W. and Margaret A. Pearce, died in Bainbridge, Ga., Nov. 7, 1873, aged 18 years, 11 months and 10 days.

Mrs. Elizabeth Hodnett, daughter of Phillip Tigner, and relict of Major John Hodnett, was born Nov. 25th 1789, married May 1809 and died at the residence of her son-in-law, Dr. J. P. Taylor, in Haralson, Ga., 7th of November 1873.

Mrs. Annie E. Marvin, wife of Joseph Marvin, was born March 16, 1848; married April 5th 1866 and died in Beaufort county, S. C., Dec. 24, 1873. She was the daughter of the late William B. and Rebecca Davis-- the latter still lingers. She leaves a husband and three little children. G. H. Pooser

Lewis Hunt was born in Eufaula, Ala., August 18, 18742; married to Mrs. Mary Nelms, December 13, 1866; died Oct. 11, 1874. [sic] He leaves a wife and two children. Wm. N. Clemmons

Mrs. Eliza King, wife of Dr. J. M. D. King, and daughter of G. G. Youngblood, was born in Gwinnett county, Ga., September 30, 1830; died in Chattooga county, Ga., Dec. 15, 1873.

Issue of February 4, 1874

An extract from the funeral discourse delivered by Bishop W. M. Wightman over the remains of Col. Benjamin F. Evans. He was born in Georgetown, S. C., in 1831.

Brother Jas. D. Posey was born in Abbeville district, S. C., March 22d 1828 and died in Calhoun county, Ala., Dec. 16th 1873, leaving a wife and seven children. He moved to Chattooga county, Ga., and attached himself to Subligna Church in 1849. H. N. Sneed. New Orleans Advocate please copy.

Mrs. Martha A. Lamar, consort of Harmony Lamar, deceased, died at the residence of her daughter, Mrs. C. R. Howard, Tuskegee, Ala., Dec. 30, 1873, in the 72d year of her age. In 1827 she and her mother, Mrs. Catherine E. Beal, were received into the M. E. Church.

Jacob Clements died on 17th December 1873, in the 65th year of his age.

Mrs. Susan C. Durham, whose maiden name was Webb, was born in Chapel Hill, N. C., Feb. 7, 1813; in 1838 she was married to brother John Durham; died in West Point, Ga., Jan. 6, 1874. P. M. Ryburn.

Mrs. Margaret Carlisle, wife of Joseph Carlisle and daughter of the late Mr. Allen Etchison, of Chambers county, Ala., died near LaFayette, Ala., Jan. 3d, 1874. She was born 25th July 1839.

Issue of February 11, 1874

Octavia L. Livingston of Covington, Ga., has gone. She died on 5th of November last, in the town of Conyers. A. Means

Mrs. Mary E. Amoss, wife of Beverly Amoss, was born in Hancock county, Ga., December 27, 1815, and died in the same county, Jan. 2d 1873.

Mrs. Sallie McAdams, whose maiden name was Blackman, was born March 18, 1853, died Nov. 12, 1873, and was buried at Sandy Springs, according to her own request. She leaves a husband and mother. D. J. McMillan

Brother J. G. Singer was born in Rhor, Kingdom of Wertemberg, Germany, May 7th 1811, and died in Lumpkin, Ga., Jan. 17, 1874. He emigrated to America in 1835, resided a short time in Baltimore, and then removed to Lumpkin.He was reared in the Lutheran faith, but regarded the Methodist Church as an ample substitute for the Church of his fathers. A. J. Dean

Mrs. Jane E. Boyd was born in Pickens county, S.,C., Dec. 23, 1842; was married to Jas. A. Boyd in 1861, and died in Gordon county, Ga., Dec. 26, 1873. She left a husband and four children. J. G. Boyd

My mother, Mary Mildred Adams, died in Savannah, Ga., 27th January 1874. She was born June 3, 1805. H. J. Adams

Mrs. Nancy Stewart was born in Scriven county, Ga., August 3d, 1802; died October 25, 1873. G. T. Stewart

Hampton Watts was born March 18, 1807, and died at the house of his friend, Leonard Brown, Esq., of Sumter, Dec. 25, 1873.

Mrs. Amanda E. Dodd, wife of Geo. W. Dodd, was born in Anderson county ,S. C., Feb. 14, 1831; married Aug. 12, 1849; died near Walhalla, S. C., Nov. 14, 1873. J. Walter Dickson

Issue of February 18, 1874

Died

In Telfair county, Ga., Jan. 28th 1874, Duncan D., son of A. H. and S. R. Graham, aged 11 years, 3 months and 26 days.

Obituary

Col. George Dewson, third son of Col. J. Dewson of the British army, was born on the Island of St. Kitts, and died in Fernandina, Florida, December 25th 1873, in the 50th year of his age. The military service called his father to Toronto, Canada, where his family were permanently settled, and where the deceased was raised. In 1852, he was married to Rosalie A., eldest daughter of Alexander H. and Anne E. MacDonell, of Early county, Ga. In 1854 he removed to Florida. Geo. G. N. MacD.

Miss Mary Eliza LeSueur died in Athens, Ga., Dec. 9th 1873, aged 21 years.

Mrs. Susan A. Braid, wife of Robert S. Braid and daughter of J. D. and S. J. Williamson of Beaufort county, S. C., was born Jan. 16th 1855; died Jan. 25th 1874. G. H. Pooser

Mrs. Eliza Edwards, whose maiden name was Dunlap, was born in South Carolina in 1814; first married to a Mr. Laller, and afterwards, Aug. 31st 1865, to Mr. Young Edwards; died December 26th 1873. William B. Neal

My beloved brother, H. K. Quillian, was born in Franklin county, Ga., June 27th 1828 and died in Auburn, Ala., Dec. 28th 1874. He was married when very young to Miss Alcy Hancock, who preceded him many years to the spirit land. He was married the second time to Mrs. Fannie Hall, who still survives him. J. B. C. Quillian

Mary Jane Swindall was born in North Carolina, May 14th 1808; converted in Greene county, Ga; married to George P. Holmes, Aug. 1831; died at the parsonage in Clark county, Ark., Nov. 14th 1873. Her son

Mrs. Julia Belton Richardson died in Wadesboro, N. C., Feb. 2, 1874, aged 59 years. O. J. Brent

Mrs. Isabella G. Cross, wife of Mr. L. J. Cross, died in Barnwell county, S. C., in the eighty-fourth year of her age. For many years her home was in Georgia. She died at the residence of the Rev. L. Bellinger.

Duncan McQuaig was born in North Carolina, May 20th 1812, and died in Savannah, Georgia, December 18th 1873. He leaves six children. Geo. G. N. MacD.

S. William Moss, son of Mr. and Mrs. WM. C. Moss, of Orangeburg county, S. C., was born March 17, 1857, and closed his career Jan 4, 1874, at Spartanburg, S. C., being a student in Wofford College. H. A. C. Walker.

Issue of February 25, 1874

Died

In Sumter, S. C., Feb. 3d, 1874, Ida Gamewell, daughter of J. D. and E. E. Craig, aged 11 years and 2 months.

At Laurens C. H., S. C., on the 29th of January 1874, Rutherford Pressley, infant son of Mr. and Mrs. S. R. Todd, Jr., aged one year and two days.

In Sparta, Ga., Feb. 25th 1874, Maria Gertrude, daughter of Dr. P. T. and Mrs. M. A. Pendleton, aged 2 months and 3 weeks.

Obituary

Mrs. Frances Anna Johnson, wife of Chas. H. Johnson and daughter of Willis A. and Temperance Mangham, late of Pike county, Ga., died in Griffin, Ga., Dec. 21st 1873. She was born near Eatonton in Putnam county, Ga., 19th September 1821.

Jesse W. Avant was born in Washington county, Ga., March 11th 1840 and died in Fort Valley, Ga., January 22d 1874. His first wife was the daughter of Dr. Hitchcock, to whom he was married January 10th 1861. She lived but a short time, and in August 1864 he married a daughter of Judge G. P. Culverhouse of Knoxville, Ga., who survives him with four young children.

William Parks Merritt was born in Henry county, Ga., August 9th 1833 and died in the same county January 18th 1874. He leaves an aged other, brothers and sisters and a young wife. Geo. M. Nolan

Mrs. S. F. Bell, consort of John W. Bell and daughter of D. T. White, was born in Conyers, Ga., January 26th 1846; was married to Mr. Bell, June 20th 1867; died in Conyers, November 13th 1873. S. P. Marbut

Claudius H. Pritchard, Jr., son of Rev. C. H. and Mrs. Mary B. Pritchard, was born in Fayetteville, N. C., August 23d 1850; joined the M. E. Church in Camden, S. C., in 1866; died January 20, 1874. His remains were carried by his parents to Greenville, and there interred. Sidi H. Browne

Mildred L. (Scarborough) Collinsworth, widow of the late Rev. John Collinsworth, died near Eatonton, Ga., Nov. 29th 1873, aged seventy-six years and four months. She was born in Burke county, Ga., July 20th 1797, and married in 1816. A. M. Wynn

Mrs. Martha S. M. Tippins was born in Liberty county, Ga., January 10, 1837; was married to L. A. H. Tippins, April 1st 1856; died December 29, 1873. She was raised by Major John Wells, of Liberty county, her step-grandfather. W. J. Jordan

Mrs. Sarah Kearney, whose maiden name was Eaves, was born in South Carolina 1807; was married to Mr. J. W. Kearney in 1834; moved with her husband to Bulloch county, Ga., where she died by an accident on the 12th January 1874. J. J. Morgan

Hon. Thos H. Brasher died at Fort Williams, Shelby county, Ala., Jan. 4th 1874, in the 76th year of his age. A Step Daughter

Mrs. Lucinda Leath, wife of R. L. Leath and daughter of Richard and Elizabeth Kilpatrick, was born June 14th 1842, died in Meriwether county, Ga., Feb. 6th 1874. She joined the Baptist Church in 1860. She leaves a husband and an aged widowed mother.

Robert E. McKay was born May 30th 1823, and died Dec. 29th 1873, in his 51st year. He left a widow and five children. J. W. Kelly

Issue of March 4, 1874

Died

In Crawfordville, Fla., Jan. 27th 1874, Herndon Lee Hill, only child of R. W. and Julia Hill, aged 3 years, 5 months and 21 days.

Obituary

Mrs. M. M. Latimer was born on Johnson Creek in Abbeville district, S. C., Sept. 1st 1817, and died in Lowndesville, S. C., Feb. 5th 1874. She was the daughter of William and Mrs. Sarah Young. She became the wife of J. Marion Latimer, Sen., Sept. 26th 1833. A. J. Cauthen

Mrs. Sarah Maddux was born in Maryland in 1787 and died in Jasper county, Ga., near Monticello, Jan. 4th 1874, in the eighty-seventh year of her age. Her father removed from Maryland to Hancock county, Georgia, when she was quite young. W. W. Wadsworth

Mrs. Mary L. Bean, wife of John A. Bean, was born Nov. 22d 1851; died in Forsyth, Ga., Jan. 28th 1874, leaving a husband, little step-daughter and an infant daughter only a few weeks old. D. D. Cox

Mrs. Mary Wright died at her brother's residence near Woodstock, Oglethorpe county, Ga., on the 13th February 1874, aged 75 years. Thomas J. Adams

Mrs. Cynthia Kirkland, widow of the late George Kirkland, died near Buford's Bridge, Barnwell county, S. C., Jan. 23d 1874 in the 65th year of her age. P. F. Kistler

Mrs. Margaret Costine died at the residence of her son-in-law, Mr. Henry Remley in Mishawville, Colleton county, S. C., Dec. 5th 1873. She joined the Baptist Church in early life. When left a widow, she and her daughters identified themselves with the M. E. Church, South. H. B. Green

Maj. Jesse C. Wootten, son of H. P. and Mrs. M. C. Wooten, was born in Wilkes county, Ga., October 6th 1836, and died in Newnan, Ga., Jan. 22d 1874. His devoted wife, formerly Miss Fannie Dent. He was for several years, editor of the Newnan Herald.

Mrs. Martha L. Belcher, wife of O. R. Belcher, Jr., and daughter of Nathan T. and Elizabeth T. Slaughter, died in Jasper county, Ga., Dec. 9th 1873, in the 28th year of her age. She leaves a husband and children. W. W. Wadsworth

Wilson Scarbrough (father-in-law of Rev. J. T. Lowe, of the N. G. Conference) was born in Montgomery county, N. C., July 1st 1803 and died in Palmetto, Ga., Feb. 15th 1874. He leaves an aged widow and two daughters. T. H. Timmons

Littleberry Daniel was born in Burke county, Ga., March 13th 1801 and died in Liberty county, Ga., Feb. 10th 1874. John M. Marshall

Miss Ida Adella Fudge was born in Houston county, Ga., Oct. 1853, and died in Liberty county, Ga., Nov. 30th 1873. W. G. Booth

T. O. Hill of Anderson county, S. C., was thrown from a horse January 31st and died Feb. 1st 1874, aged about 83 years. He buried three wives; two daughters died of consumption; one son fell overboard on some river in Florida and was drowned; and one fell in the late war. Only one of his family, Col. Hill of Anderson, survives him. A. J. Cauthen

Mrs. Lou Torbet, wife of Mr. R. F. Torbet and daughter of the late Rev. Richard Burt, died at Columbus, Ga., Dec. 3d 1873.

Moses E. Steedly died in Appling county, Ga., on 25th January 1874 in the 28th year of his age. He leaves a wife and seven children.

Issue of March 11, 1874

Died

In Anderson, S. C., on the 25th of February 1874, Lucia Louse, infant daughter of Wm. J. and Louisa Ligon, aged six months, within one day.

Leon Oscar, son of Mr. and Mrs. J. P. Spier, died in Hampton, Ga., February 13, 1874, aged 3 years, 2 months and 17 days.

Obituary

Chas. A. Walker was born in Jefferson county, GA., July 1st 1833 and died at Marshallville, Macon county, January 4th 1874. He was next to the youngest of thirteen children, and for years previous to his death, the only surviving member of the family. When quite young, his father, Henry Walker, removed to Sumter county, where brother Walker spent most of his life. In January 1860 he married Miss Lou Crocker. F. A. Branch

Mrs. Nancy C. Oeland, consort of Rev. P. J. Oeland and daughter of Mr. Willis and Mrs. Catharine Benson, was born in Greenville district, S. C., February 6th 1835, and died in Spartanburg district, S. C., Dec. 21st 1873. The deceased was brought up under Baptist influence; though in early life her mother was a member of the Methodist Church. She leaves a husband and eight children. N. K. Melton

My sister, Mrs. Sarah R. Knowles, daughter of Moses Padgett, was born in Putnam co., Ga., and died in Melenan co., Texas, January 15, 1874, aged 57 years and one day. When she was but a child, her father moved to Fayette co., Ga., where at the age of 14 she was married to R. P. Knowles... C. E. Glover

Mrs. Lucretia Kerlin was born March 1st 1813 and died in Walker county, Ga., January 15th 1874. She was a member of the Baptist church. G. W. Thomas

Mrs. Mary G. Spencer, wife of T. K. Spencer and daughter of Major J. B. Spencer of White Springs, Fla., died in Tampa, Fla., January 21st 1874, aged 20 years.

Rev. Jos. E. Biggs was born in Virginia, April 1792, and died in Talbot co., Ga., Jan. 5th 1874. In early life he moved to Georgia and was raised in Clark county. W. G. Boothe

Samuel Smith died in Crawford county, Ga., Feb. 12th 1874, in the 88th year of his age.

Asbury Suggs, son of Nelson and Hester Suggs, was born December 18, 1852, and died January 20, 1874. L. M. Hamer

Tribute of Respect to Richard A. Lane from Acworth circuit.

Issue of March 18, 1874

Died

Nora Ann Nease, daughter of Tropu and Sarah Jane Studstill, was born March 10th 1871, and died Feb. 10th 1874.

Obituary

Miss Kane M. Swink was born Dec. 5, 1855, joined the Church at New Hope, in Fair Forest circuit, August 1866, and died in Union county, S. C., Feb. 14th 1874. J. B. Wilson

Eliza Levy, the beloved wife of Moses Levy of Charleston, S. C., died in that city, Dec. 20, 1873, in the sixty-seventh year of her age. She was a native of New York, but early in life removed to this city.

Mr. Hardy Thurmond Sanders was born in Madison county, Ga., in 1809 and died 5th January 1874. He left a widow and children.

Mrs. Mary Lucinda Oliver, whose maiden name was Weld, was born 22d May 1849; married to Stewart L. Oliver, 14th January 1873, and died January 29th 1874.

Robert W. Tatum died in Hamilton county, Fla., Dec. 19, 1873, in the 44th year of his age. R. M. Ellzey

Mrs. Saphronia A. Darsey, wife of Rev. L. A. Darsey and only daughter of Ephraim and Axalina Ponder, was born in Burke county, Ga., Oct. 10, 1855; and died in Jasper, Hamilton county, Fla., Feb. 28th 1874. Dec. 7th 1871, she married Rev. L. A. Darsey of the South Georgia Conference.

Joseph H. Peacock, son of Nathan B. and Martha A. Peacock, was born in Macon county, Ala., January 6th 1845; moved his parents to Coffee county, Ala., Feb. 1851; was married August 19th 1868 to Miss Fannie A. Barnard; died Feb. 24th 1874, leaving a wife and three children. A. Dowling

My mother, Mrs. Armond Rutledge, relict of Robert Kay, died at the residence of her son-in-law, Rev. Fletcher Smith, near Walhalla, South Carolina, Jan. 5th 1874, aged eighty-two years. She was for many years a member of the Baptist Church. John

Miss Nettie L. Gavin, late of Charleston county, South Carolina, died at the residence of M. C. Connor, Esq., in Galveston, Texas, on 22d of February last. She was in her 32d year.

Miss Georgia V. Asbill died in Lexington county, S. C., Feb. 26th 1874, in the twentieth year of her age. She was a student at the Columbia Female College. J. A. Clifton

Issue of March 25, 1874

James Littlejohn was born in Union county, S. C., July 23d 1801 and died Jan. 25th 1874.

Mrs. Sallie S. Covington, daughter of the Rev. Lewis M. Hamer of the South Carolina Conference, was born in Marion, S. C., April 15, 1853, and died in Marlboro, January 20th 1874. She was married to Wm. J. Covington, Esq., December 23d 1863.

Mrs. Margaret B. Langford died Feb. 7th 1874, aged 37 years. Her husband was for many years superintendent of the Fulton County Alms-house.

Henry Pitman was born in Sumter co., Ga., in 1846; lost his father when he was quite a youth; moved to Burke county and married Miss Rebecca Bradley in 1867. He died Feb. 27, 1874. He lies buried beside his wife, and near by the graves of four brothers and three sisters. W. M. Watts.

Josiah Allen was born in Green county, a., July 25th 1804; was married to Miss Sarah A. Atkinson of Pike county ,Ga., Dec. 26th 1826; died in Meriwether county, Ga., February 25th 1874.

Mrs. Ann Barton, wife of Dr. W. F. Barton of Orangeburg county, S. C., was born Oct. 14th 1812 and died March 3d 1874.

Mrs. Cynthia Medora Bradford, daughter of S. A. and R. M. Harris was born in York county, S. C., Nov. 28, 1855; died at Fort Mills, S. C., Feb. 6, 1874. J. F. England

Tribute of Respect from Hartwell circuit, North Georgia Conference to Rev. Joel Ledbetter, who was born July 27th 1811 in Anderson district, S. C., and died October 25th 1873 in Franklin county, Ga.

Tribute of Respect from Warrenton circuit, North Georgia Conference, to Rev. Amos Johnson, who was born and reared in Warren county.

Tribute of Respect from Pacolet circuit, Spartanburg district, South Carolina Conference to James Littlejohn.

Tribute of Respect from Kingston circuit, North Georgia Conference, to Hawkins F. Price and Robert B. Washington.

Issue of April 1, 1874

Died

In Hogansville, Ga., March 18th 1874, little Ambrose Paul, only son of Ambrose R. and Pallie Williams, aged 6 months and 24 days.

Obituary

Miss Anna E. Reynolds was born December, 1851; died Feb. 20th 1874. R. A. Conner

Donald McDonald was born in Elbert county, Ga., Oct. 22d 1803; moved to Monroe county in 1825; to Upson county in 1855 and died there March 3d 1874. S. A. Mitchell

Mrs. Sarah C. Griffin, consort of R. W. Griffin, died on the 5th of January 1874, at the age of forty-one years and eight months. N. Miller

Mrs. Evaline Brown, wife of Rev. John Brown and daughter of John A. and D. Winn was born in Jackson county, Ga., November 1837 and died in Tuskaloosa county, Ala., Feb. 28th 1874. Evan Nicholson

Death of sister Ella Johnson, wife of Z. Johnson and daughter of M. E. and S. C. Rylander, formerly of Macon, now of Sumter county, Georgia. S. Anthony

Mrs. Nancy Bush was a native of Mecklenburg county, N. C.; was born about the year 1800 and died March 4th 1874 at Roswell, Ga. When she was quite young her parents moved to Greenville, S. C. In 1830 or 1831 she was married to William Bush, whose remains she followed to the grave about eight years thereafter. In 1860 she moved to Cobb county, Ga. She left four children. J. M. Parker

Abraham Millar was born in Stokes county, North Carolina in December 1809; was married to Lucy Stipe, Feb. 27th 1829; moved to Coweta county, Ga., where he died February 27th 1874. J. Chambers

Daniel Baxter was born in Orangeburg county, S. C., March 31st 1800 and died Jan. 18th 1874.

Mrs. Sarah Elizabeth Perry, daughter of Asa and Nancy Royal, was born April 16th 1826; married to Mark A. Perry, August 1st 1849; died in Schley county, Ga., Dec. 28th 1873.

Mrs. Permelia F. Rampley, wife of Rev. W. M. Rampley and daughter of William and Jane Rhodes, was born in Spartanburg county, S. C., May 7th 1835; died at the residence of her son-in-law, near Carnesville, Ga., January 23d 1874. She leaves a husband and nine children.

Lydia Bolton was born Nov. 5th 1788 and died Jan. 20th 1874, at the residence of her son-in-law, B. A. Willingham, in McDuffie county, Ga. She was a member of the Baptist church.

SOUTHERN CHRISTIAN ADVOCATE NOTICES 1867-1878

Issue of April 8, 1874

Jesse Proctor was born in Edgecomb county, N. C., Dec. 15, 1783 and died near Little Rock, Marion county, S. C., February 12th 1874. He was twice married; his last wife survives him. James C. Stoll. Nashville Advocate please copy.

Col. Anderson W. Redding was born January 31st 1800 in Washington county, Ga., and died February 13th 1874. He was reared in Baldwin, which was then a frontier county. He represented Monroe and Harris counties in the legislature. He was first married in 1826 and became the father of thirteen children, only four of whom survive him. His first wife died in 1850 and he married a Mrs. Smith in 1854. She died in 1864, and the same year he married Mrs. Jane Rutledge of Harris county, who still survives him. Robert L. Wiggins

My father, James F. Dozier, was born in Columbia county, Ga., October 12th 1806; married Miss Rebecca S. Wall, January 25th 1829; and died in McDuffie county, GA., January 23d 1874. he and his wife were raised a few miles apart, and each was deprived in early infancy of the loving care of a mother; they were loved and tutored by pious aunts. Mattie R. Dozier

Mrs. Martha Murray Turner, relict of the late Rev. Allen Turner, died at Senoia, Ga., February 20, 1874, in her 79th year. E. D. Bower

The Washington Street Sunday school at Columbia, S. C., had lost one of its Bible class of young ladies, Maggie Kate Miller, eldest daughter of Major and Mrs. D. B. Miller, died while on a visit to some friends in Salisbury, N. C., aged 20 years.

James O'Kelly was born March 19th 1791; married to Miss Frances Harwell, October 11th 1814; died January 12, 1874 in Walton county, Ga. M. F. Malsby

Sister Frances Coleman, wife of Rev. Thomas C. Coleman, of the South Georgia Conference, died Dec. 31st 1873, aged sixty years. P. C. Harris

Eldridge Faircloth of Spring Hill circuit, Thomas co., Ga., died March 26th 1874, aged 88 years.

Tribute of Respect from Trinity circuit, South Georgia Conference to James J. Harris.

Issue of April 15, 1874

Francis A. Lipscomb was born in Montgomery county, Ala., July 26th 1845 and died at Auburn, Ala., March 8th 1874. He entered the University of Georgia as a freshman in his fifteenth year. In Feb. 1869 he married Mary Ann, eldest daughter of Prof. William Rutherford. Wm. M. Browne

Thomas J. Mathews was born in Talbot county, Ga., Nov. 23d 1822; was married to Miss M. Julia Drane, Dec. 4th 1851; died in Marion county, Ga., Feb. 17th 1874. W. W. Stewart

Mrs. Rebecca Emma Gwinn was born Aug. 24th 1810; was married to Judge D. W. Gwynn of Tallahassee, Fla., Oct. 17th 1872; died March 5th 1874. She was the daughter of Rev. Dr. Miles Nash. Josephus Anderson

Mrs. Elizabeth Durant was born April 2d 1792; died in Conwayboro, Horry county, S. C., March 18th 1874.

John R. Easterling died in Georgetown county, S. C., January 31st 1874. This aged patriarch... L. Wood

Benjamin Davies died in Georgetown, S. C., on 28th of March 1874, aged 17 years, 9 months and 13 days. L. Wood

Joseph Kersey was born in Burke county, Ga., August 1st 1810 and died in Jefferson county, Fla., Jan. 26th 1874. He has left a widow and three children. D. H. Bryan

Father John Platt was born in North Carolina, Oct. 5th 1793, and died in Manatee county, Florida, Feb. 7th 1874. He lived in North Carolina, South Carolina, Georgia and Florida. He raised a large family of children, six of whom with their aged mother, survive. W. H. F. Robarts

Jane Mitchell, formerly Jane Ligon, was born December 23d 1813 in Spartanburg Dist., S. C., and died in Tuskegee, Alabama, February 6th 1874.

Andrew Jackson Richardson died in Georgetown, S. C., March 2d 1784, in the 55th year of his age. L. Wood

Issue of April 22, 1874

Died

In Atlanta, Ga., March 13, 1874, Weyman Porter, youngest child of Rev. W. P. and Mrs. S. W. Pledger, aged nearly 20 months.

April 2d 1874, Barbie Parramore, adopted son of S. A. and R. V. Parramore, of Madison, Fla., aged 8 years and 4 months.

Obituary

Mary Frances Cutliff, wife of Dr. Cutliff, of Shreveport, Louisiana, died in that city February 24, 1874, in the thirty-eighth year of her age. She was the daughter of the late Judge E. H. Baxter of Georgia, and was married to Dr. Cutliff in 1859.

Mrs. E. E. Porter, widow of Major Alfred Porter, of Effingham county, Ga., died in her 51st year, January 14th 1874, at the residence of her son-in-law, Mr. W. W. Smith, at Brighton, S. C. She was a member of the Baptist Church. Twice married...

Alexander H. Stephens, aged 24 years; Iberia Marchman, formerly Stephens, wife of J. H. C. Marchman, aged 32 years; N. Josiah McAndrews, formerly Stephens, wife of Wm. McAndrews, aged 28 years; and her child, Willie McAndrews, aged 2 years and 6 months, have all died within the short space of two months. The preachers on the upson circuit will remember Wm. Stephens and his interesting family. Geo. G. Smith

Mike A. Johnson, youngest son of the late Rev. Marcus D. C. Johnson, died in Griffin, Ga., on the 15th February 1874, in the 27th year of his age.

Lewis Flemister died in Griffin, Ga., on the 15th of February 1874, in the 58th year of his age.

Sister Elizabeth Moore, wife of Thomas Moore, of Fulton county, Ga., and daughter of Martin and Susan DeFoor of Franklin county, Ga., was born December 29, 1831; was married to Thomas Moore, February 13, 1849; died March 7, 1874. her grandfather was a local preacher; her father and mother--both living-- are members of the Church.

Lafayette W. Barksdale was born in Abbeville district, S. C., August 4th 1849 and died March 2d 1874. R. H. Barnett

Brother M. L. Marlin was born in Rutherford county, Tennessee in 1833; was married in 1865 to Miss M. E. whitehead of Polk county, Ga., moved to Polk county in the winter of 1872, and died Jan 21st 1874. Sister Martha E. Marlin, his wife was born in Pittsylvania county, Va., July 11, 1848. She died 31st March 1874. Wm. H. LaPrade. Nashville Christian Advocate please copy.

Joseph Tarpley Quillian, son of George T. Quillian of Atlanta, grandson of Rev. James Quillian, deceased, and a near relative of the late Rev. W. J. Parks, was born in Lumpkin county, Ga., June 27th 1849; was married to Miss Bettie Smith, daughter of Mr. A. S. Smith, November 6th 1867; died near Acworth, Ga., March 18th 1874.

Mrs. Jane Taylor, widow of the late Dr. Wesley Taylor, formerly of Leon county, Fla., died near Boston, Thomas county, Ga., March 17, 1874, in her 55th year. W. M. Watts

Mrs. Sarah A. Steele, consort of the late Dr. J. J. Steele, of Black Mingo, S. C., died March 11, 1874, in the 48th year of her age. She was the mother of two children.

Tribute of Respect from Cuthbert Station to Rev. Wm. B. McHan, a member of the South Georgia Conference.

Issue of April 29, 1874

Mrs. Mary Ann Florence, wife of Geo. W. Florence, was born in Wilkes county, Ga., August 13th 1817, and died March 26th 1874. Thos. F. Pierce

Miss Mary C. Cole, daughter of L. H. and Elizabeth A. Cole of Macon county, Ala., died Feb. 27th 1874. J. W. Solomon

Mrs. Mary E. Coward, daughter of Rev. T. L. and Susan Speight, was born in Lee county, Georgia, October 30th 1845 and died February 23d 1874 in Chattooga county, Georgia. She was married to L. G. Coward, Dec. 29th 1872, and leaves a husband and babe. G. W. Thomas

My wife was born April 8th 1830, and became a member of the M. E. Church at Henderson, Houston county, Ga., July 1853. She died 6th April 1874. My dear Rebecca.... John D. Clark

Kindred T. Hall was born Jan. 13th 1856; died in Thomas county, Ga., Feb. 3d 1874, only two months after the tragic death of his father.

Mrs. Augusta Cato, daughter of Jacob E. and Eliza Bugg, and wife of Homer Cato, was born in Russell county, Ala., February 14th 1849 and died April 6th 1874. Her Step Mother.

Mrs. Eloise Bostick, whose maiden name was Beal, was born Oct. 15th 1796; married Mr. John Bostick of Jefferson county, Ga., in 1834; died at the house of N. B. Bostick, near Buclin, Ga., March 16th 1874. Wm. Hauser, M. D. Jefferson News & Farmer please copy.

Mrs. Kezia Antoinette Phillips was born August 31st 1819, and died near Williston, Barnwell county, S. C., Feb. 4th 1874.

Alexander H. Foster died March 8th 1874 in Walker county, about ten miles from Ringgold, Catoosa county, Georgia. He leaves a wife.

Newton Bullock of Wilkinson county, Ga., died at the house Jasper Bullock, Bibb county, Ga., on 13th of April 1874 in the 47th year. His Brother

Issue of May 6, 1874

Died

In Orangeburg county, S. C., April 12, 1874, Carrie Lillian, youngest child of Benjamin and Laura M. Pooser, aged two years and nearly two months.

Obituary

Mrs. Frances Lummus, daughter of J. I. and J. A. Epperson, was born in Cherokee county, Ga., April 1850; was married to E. S. Lummus, November 24th 1864; died March 26th 1874 in Marion county, Fla. She leaves a husband and four little children.

Robert R. Washington was born in Washington, Wilkes county, Ga., and died in the 75th year of his age, while on a visit to his relatives in Macon, Ga., February 8th 1874. He was first married in 1824 to Miss Sarah Jones, and soon afterwards settled in Macon. His first wife died on 31st May

1871, and on 20th October 1873, he married Miss Mary A. Service, who still survives him. J. J. Singleton

Frances A. Johnson was born in Warren county,Ga., october 22d 1828; married to Rev. Amos Johnson, September 22d 1845; died in McDuffie county, Ga., April 19th 1874.

Mrs. Margaret Starrat died at the residence of her grandson, Mr. George S. Roux, Fernandina, Fla., February 16th 1874, in her 87th year. Wm. Davies

Tribute of Respect from Elbert circuit, North Georgia Annual Conference to Rev. W. H. Adams, who was born in Elbert county, Ga. He was ordained deacon on June 11, 1870. He left a wife and children.

Tribute of Respect from Elbert circuit, North Georgia Annual Conference to Rev. Jno. B. Wade, who was born in Bedford county, Va., April 23d, 1789, removed to Georgia with his widowed mother in 1801... well known in the counties of Franklin, Hart and Elbert, where he resided, died at the age of 84 years.

Issue of May 6, 1874

Died

In Brunswick, Ga., on the 28th of April 1874, Annie, infant daughter of Dr. L. B. and Mrs. S. A. E. Davis.

Little Julia, youngest daughter of A. W. and Mrs. Hattie Haygood, was born Sept 22d 1869 and died in Fort Gaines, Ga., ril 25th 1874.

Obituary

Miss Nannie Virginia Thompson, daughter of Jeremiah and Mary Thompson, was born in Houston county, Ga., April 16th 1839 and died in Quitman county, Ga., March 17th 1874.

Richard King died at Covington, Georgia, April 5th 1874. He was born near Centerville, Ga., Feb. 15th 1815, came to Georgia in 1837. H. J. Adams

Dr. Paul Connor was born in Abbeville county, S. C., in 1802, and died 5th April 1872 [sic]. R. N. Wells

Mrs. Mary Ann Cochran, relict of Daniel H. Cochran, was born in Abbeville county, S. C., July 17th 1809 and died at the residence of her son, R. A. Cochran, Pickens county, S. C., Feb. 2d 1874. Resided at Anderson Court House from the time of her marriage in 1837 till 1859. Removed thence to Franklin county, Ga., where her husband died in 1861. She reared nine children. Two of them preceded her to the grave. D. J. McMillan

Mary Forsyth, wife of Martin Forsyth, was born Feb. 17, 1811, in Ray county, Tennessee. Her maiden name was Owen. She came to Floyd county, Ga., in 1832. She died April 27, 1874.

Wm. E. Bouknight died in Alachua county, Fla., March 13th 1874, aged 25 years. He was a son of Elias Bouknight, long known as the first and support of the Church to the preachers of Florida. Jno. C. Ley

Mrs. S. E. Shields, wife of C. M. Shields (her maiden name was Robinson) was born in Henry county, Ga., August 9th 1836, and died April 11th 1874. She was a kind wife and stepmother.

Thomas Jefferson Dunlap, son of Hon. R. O. and Rebecca J. Dunlap, was born in Merriwether county, Ga., Jan. 17th 1856, and died March 3d 1874 in Early county, Ga. W. C. Dunlap

Mrs. Margaret A. Phipps, wife of Thomas Phipps, died near Benevolence, Randolph county, Ga., April 11, 1874, aged 26 years. J. S. West

A. F. Donald, son of John A. and May Donald, was born in Abbeville District, S. C., March 23d 1843, and died in Bartow county, Ga., March 9th 1874. W. F. Weems

Lewis Pitts, son of Dr. W. C. and N. H. Whitaker, died in Russell county, Ala., April 5th 1874, aged three years.

Issue of May 20, 1874

Died

At Carnesville, Taylor county, Ga., on 29th April 1874, Fannie Lilette, daughter of H. M. and M. V. Searcy, aged two years and twelve days.

Obituary

Sister Rawls, her maiden name was Lettie Dowling, was born Jan. 20th 1828. She was twice married, the first time to Thos. D. Owen, Feb. 29, 1843, and the second time to Thos. J. Rawls, Feb d 1849. Her death occurred on 10th April 1874. Her last husband and five children are left. Josephus Anderson

Mrs. Martha E. Brewer, wife of L. R. Brewer, died in Griffin, Ga., April 8th in her 32d year.

Mrs. Rosanna L. Odom, mother of Dr. G. J. Odom, was born in Augusta, Ga., and died March 21st 1874, in Orangeburg county, S. C., in the 66th year of her age.

Mrs. N. H. Buchanan died in Sumter county, Ga., on 9th of April. She was born in Newberry district, S. C., on 29th of March 1805. From thence she came to Georgia when quite young.

Mr. L. G. Graddy died in Griffin, Ga., May 1st 1874, in her 55th year.

Mrs. Mary M. L. Malone, wife of M. S. Malone, was born in Charleston county, S., C., March 3d 1806 and died in Orangeburg county, March 6th 1874. Two of her children had just passed to a better world, Rev. P. J. Malone of Texas, and Mrs. C. J. Pettus. Her son-in-law, Rev. E. Pettus....

Reuben L. Duffie, father of Rev. R. L. Duffie, of the South Carolina Conference, was born in Mecklenburg county, N. C., August 11, 1799, where he resided until about twenty years old, when he came to Chester, S. C., where he has lived a quiet life until his death, April 10, 1874.

Tribute of Respect from Little Rock circuit, South Carolina, Conference to Jesse Proctor.

Issue of May 27, 1874

Thornton Holman was born April 2d 1790, and died May 19th 1874. This man was a native of Virginia, born about fifty miles south of Richmond. After serving as a soldier in the war of 1812, he went to a good school in Union District, S. C., for two years. He married Miss Rhoda Ligon, near Augusta, Ga. In 1829 he settled in Meriwether county, Ga., near the line of Coweta. W. J. Cotter

Mrs. Carrie D. Jones, wife of J. D. Jones and daughter of Dr. Henry S. and Caroline Wimberly, was born in Twiggs county, Georgia, on 24th of February 1850 and died --- 21st 1874, at her residence in Jeffersonville, Ga. She leaves two little girls, one an infant.

April 23d 1873, James Jay died. Reared by the pious Tyre Jay and wife. He was buried by the side of his parents at Mt. Pleasant Church, Abbeville, S. C. G. M. Boyd

Thomas H. Marshall was born in Burlington, Conn., in 1799, and removed to Macon, Ga. He came to Graniteville, S. C., where he died March 9th 1874. L. C. Loyal

Bro. W. B. A. Ingram was born in Kershaw county, S., C., and died in Schley county, Ga., 20th April 1874. He leaves a wife and four children. W. Lane

Sister Mary K. Pace (formerly Bart) was born in Putnam county, Ga., July 17th 1832; was married to Thos. M. Pace, 9th of January 1850, and died at Cedar Town, Ga., 7th May 1874. W. H. LaPrade

Joseph T. Laurius of High Shoals, Ga., departed this life 18th April 1874, aged 30 years. For upwards of twenty years, he was a member of the M. E. Church at Rehoboth, Morgan county, Ga.

Mrs. Elizabeth Cross, daughter of ___ Hall, and wife of Richard Cross, was born in Duplin county, N. C; removed with her parents to Lowndes county, Ala., in 1825; died April 14th 1874. B. L. Selman

Robert Warren was born in South Carolina, Dec. 26th 1808 and died in Laurens county, Ga., a few days since. D. G. Pope

Issue of June 3, 1874

Died

At Gordon, Wilkinson county, Ga., May 12th 1874, Minnie Georgia, daughter of J. F. and Sarah A. Stevens, aged on year, one month and fifteen days.

In Fauquier county, Va., on the 8th inst., Alice Bayne, wife of Lewis H. Andrews, in the 31st year of her age.

At Marion, S. C., May 13, 1874, Samuel, infant son of Rev. and Mrs. W. C. Power, of the South Carolina Conference, aged two months and five days.

Albartus Charlton, infant son of Mr. L. C. and Mrs. F. W. Hawkins, aged five months and seventeen days.

Obituary

Mrs. Matilda Harrison Johnson, wife of Rev. John Calvin Johnson, died in Watkinsville, Ga., May 3d 1874.

Daniel Youngblood was born May 20th 1851 in Floyd county, Ga., and died at Rockmart, Ga., April 25th 1874. Carrie Youngblood was born June 15th 1850 in Floyd county, Ga., and died May 1st 1874, at Rockmart, Ga. W. M. Youngblood, brother to Daniel and Carrie, was born May 7th 1847 in Floyd county, Ga., and died at Rockmart, May 4th 1874. All dies of smallpox. W. B. Quillian.

Wm. Henry Butt, son of Dr. Wm. Butt, was born March 3d 1846 and died in Warrenton, April 28th 1874.

Wm. Waters, Sr., died in Scriven county, Ga., on the 4th of May 1874. He was born in Edinburg, Scotland in 1795, and when about twenty-five years of age came to Savannah. His wife (formerly Miss Mary Miller) and two sons survive him. Savannah Morning News please copy.

Mrs. Sarah A. E. Mitchell, relict of Colonel Giles Mitchell, died at Athens, Ga., on the 12th March. Born in August 1817; married in 1835.

Mrs. Mary A. Johnston, wife of Capt. J. M. Johnston, died May 10th 1874 in Colleton county, S. C., in the 65th year of her age. She was a native of South Carolina and a daughter of Capt. John

May, Sen. In early life she became the wife of Dr. Wm. Carr, by whom she leaves three sons, and was united in marriage with her surviving husband some twelve years ago.

Mrs. Carrie Fletcher, wife of Winfield Fletcher, died in Atlanta, Ga., April 23d at the residence of her grandfather, Rev. W. B. Smith, aged 19 years. Her father died when she was quite an infant, leaving a widowed mother with four small children.

Mrs. S. G. Spivey died at Columbus, Ga., April 1st 1874, aged 74 years. She was the daughter of Major Thomas McCall, late of Laurens county, who was the brother of Major Hugh McCall who wrote the first History of Georgia.

Florence Josephine Wilson, daughter of R. F. and Martha Wilson, of Putnam county, died March 17th 1874 in her 15th year.

Miss Rebecca L. Dantzler, daughter of Lewis M. and Elizabeth Dantzler, died in Orangeburg county, aged about 23 years.

Issue of June 10, 1874

Mrs. Elizabeth A. George, relict of the late James George, died in Griffin, Ga., May 17th 1874, in the 54th year of her age.

Miss Rulie A. E. Howard, daughter of P. J. and M. F. Howard, of Monroe county, Ga., was born April 4, 1853 and died April 15, 1874. Jno. A. Reynolds

Selete Perkins, wife of Alexander Perkins, Esq., of Monroe county, Ga., died May 17, 1874, being about 75 years old. She was raised in Hancock county, her father's name being Jernigan. She was married to brother Perkins on 26th December 1816. Jno. A. Reynolds

Mrs. Mattie Edmondson Dart was born in Brooks county, Ga., May 1, 1855, and died at Brunswick, Ga., April 30, 1874. She was the daughter of Col. James R. Edmondson, of Quitman, Ga., and was married to W. M. Dart, Esq., December 18, 1872. She leaves a husband and an infant boy. S. S. Sweet

Mrs. Mary W. T. Jones was born in Amherst county, Virginia, 28th December 1797 and died at the residence of her son, Dr. G. L. Jones, Atlanta, Georgia, April 10th 1874. Her parents, Wilson and Frances Penn, moved to Georgia about the year 1808 and on the 13th Oct. 1816 she was married to Rev. Dabney P. Jones, who was at the time a member of the South Carolina Conference. Ten children, of the eleven which God gave her, he took away. Her only living son and one grand-daughter are left.

Miss Louie L. LeSueur was born in Athens, Ga., Oct. 2d, 1855, and died at the same place, March 23, 1874. J. Lewis, Jr.

Mrs. Sarah C. Talley, daughter of Alexander and Rebecca E. Scott, and wife of John W. Talley, deceased, was born in Monroe county, Ga., Oct. 30th 1827 and died in Opelika, Ala., April 27th 1874. Her remains were carried to Loachapoka and there buried. W. M. Motley

George Capers Johnson was born in Abbeville county, S. C., August 19th 1847 and died April 15th 1874. He leaves a wife and two children.

Dr. James M. Hardin was born in York District, S. C., and died at the age of about 49, March 11th 1874. He has left a wife and several children. Claiborne Trussell

Mrs. Susan Lucinda McLeod, daughter of Rev. H. T. and Mrs. M. M. Bussey, was born in Wilkes county, Ga., Feb. 1847 and died in Telfair county, Ga., May 7th 1874.

Mrs. M. E. Gober, wife of C. Gober, was born in Anderson county, S. C., 1817. Her parents moved to Georgia when she was a child. She died March 14th 1874. J. R. Parker

Tribute of Respect from Villa Rica circuit, North Georgia Conference, to Rev. James Green who was born Sept. 15, 1805 and died May 11th 1874.

Issue of June 17, 1874

William Hance was born in Philadelphia, March 17th 1804; removed to Laurensville, S. C., and was married to Miss Sarah Word, December 6th 1827; continued to reside in Laurensville until his death which occurred March 27, 1874. He leaves a widow and nine grandchildren. He left no living child. He had buried them all (fourteen).

Miss Ann Eliza Boswell, daughter of Elijah Boswell, Esq., was born October 26th 1847 and died in Putnam county, Ga., April 14th 1874. W. W. Oslin

Samuel C. Neill, son of Josiah and Arispa Neill, formerly of South Carolina, was born Feb. 24th 1829 and died May 13th 1874. G. B. Neill

Rignal N. Groves died in Abbeville county, S. C., May 20th 1874 in the 68th year of his age.

Miss Mary E. Pitchford, daughter of W. G. and R. Pitchford, was born in Habersham county, Ga., december 25th 1838 and died March 28th 1874 in White county, Ga. W. B. Bell

Mrs. Martha J. Pitts, daughter of Silas M. and Martha J. Lester, was born in Pulaksi county, Ga., March 1st 1820; married to B. H. Pitts October 15th 1850, and died in Hayneville, Ga., April 1st 1874. Her parents having died when she was quite young, she was reared by her uncle, D. M. Brown, of Houston County, Ga. W. M. D. Bond

Mrs. Mary Moon was born in Laurens district, S. C., July 5th 1800. Her maiden name was Harris. She was first married to Wm. Mead, June 18th 1818. She moved to Clark county, Ga., in 1820. She lost her first husband July 2d 1828. She was married the second time in 1835 to Boler Moon. She was left a widow the second time in 1843. She moved from Clark county to Cobb county and then to Paulding county in 1838. She lived the last four years of her life with her son-in-law, Rev. Walter Lanier, in Bartow county, Ga., She died April 28th 1874. J. J. Singleton

Rebecca Mattox, whose maiden name was Smith, was born in Tatnall county, Ga., March 1820 and died near Reidsville, in the same county, March 22d 1874. Sometime after her marriage to J. J. Mattox, when the mother of several children.... Left a widow five or six years ago. W. J. Jordan

Mrs. Nancy M. Underwood, daughter of David and Mary Bradford and wife of Isaac W. Underwood, was born in South Carolina, September 28, 1823, and died near Leesburg, Gonzales county, Texas, May 21st 1874. She left a husband, grown daughter, two little sons.... A. F. Cox

Joseph T. Launius died at High Shoals, Morgan co., Ga., April 18, 1874, in the 40th year of his age.

Embery Spence Horton, son of Wiley Hill Horton, was born May 17th 1856 and died May 17th 1874.

Mrs. Elizabeth Lavinia Shepard, daughter of A. M. and Parthena Jackson, was born Nov. 1st 1827; married to Simeon Shepard, Dec. 23d 1847, and died near Monroe, Walton county, Ga., May 3d 1874. W. D. Heath

John Cutcher died in his 88th year in Union county, Ga., near Young Cane Church, where he had lived many years, April 16th 1874. His children, one of whom is a minister of the gospel in our Church, and his many grandchildren... Mother Cutcher died 28th of April 1874 and was buried at the side of her husband in the home grave-yard. Thos. J. Edwards

Mrs. Sarah A. Miley, wife of Daniel R. Miley and daughter of Randal and Sarah Folsom, was born in Irwin county, Ga., March 5th 1825 and died in Lowndes county, Ga., April 20th 1874. Her parents removed to Lowndes county in the beginning of 1827.

George Crapps was born in Lexington district, S. C., June 26th 1799 and died in Randolph co., Ga., March 24th 1874. He joined the Lutheran Church in 1811. After moving to Georgia, he found no Lutheran Church and in 1865 he and his family (with one exception) joined the Methodist Church. J. R. Owen

Miss Ella J., daughter of B. H. and D. Douthit, was born May 8th 1850 and died March 24th 1874. D. J. McMillan

Brother Birch Rickets died in Union county, Ga., May 9th 1874, in the 84th year of his age. Thos. J. Edwards

Miss Jane Osteen was born in Sumter district, S. C., February 12, 1804 and died in Taylor county, Ga., May 10, 1874.

Tribute of Respect from Allendale circuit, South Carolina Conference to J. Vincent Martin.

Issue of June 24, 1874

Mrs. Maria Louisa Magruder, wife of Dr. A. L. C. Magruder and last lineal descendant of George and Charlotte Newman, of Washington, Adams county, Mississippi, died in Macon, Ga., May 30th 1874, in the 59th year of her age.

Jesse Bernier Pye was born in Monroe county, Ga., Jan. 7th 1844 and died at Chalybeate Springs, Ga., April 27th 1874. He leaves a father, step-mother, brothers and sisters. W. H. Woodall

Mrs. Elizabeth Sessions, wife of Wm. E. Sessions and daughter of the late Judge Alexander Hendry of Randolph county, Ga., was born Nov. 2d, 1827, and died at Dover, Terrell county, Ga., May 12th 1874. her father was a member of the Presbyterian church. J. R. Littlejohn

Mrs. Jane Adaline Graham, whose maiden name was Haygood, consort of Andrew J. Graham, was born in Anderson district, S. C., Nov. 13th 1822; married to A. J. Graham, Nov. 14th 1837; and died May 26th 1874. She was the mother of fourteen children-- six of whom preceded her to the grave. She had five sons in Confederate service. D. D. Byars

Rev. Hiram Camp, a useful local preacher, died in Coweta county, Ga., May 19th 1874. he lived and died in his native state. Born in Jackson county, Dec. 23d, 1806; married 1828, Oct 5th to Miss Penina Reynolds, and moved Nov 1830 to Coweta. W. J. Cotter

Clinton Thigpen was born Oct. 20th 1812; died May 23d 1874. Wm. Davies

Death of W. H. Pegg... A. G. Dempsey

My sister-in-law, Mrs. Virginia F. Blake, died in Leon county, Florida, May 20th 1874. She was the daughter of C. B. West, of said county, and was born August 9th 1827. She was twice married-- to Mr. C. C. Moore in 1843, and to my brother, Dr. A. C. F. Blake in 1856, who died in 1870. Two children by her first marriage, three by the late, survive her. E. L. T. Blake

Mrs. Ailey (York) Simpson was born in Polk county, Ga., Jan. 5th 1832; married to Rev. W. W. Simpson, September 10th 1849; died 26th April 1874. Sam'l P. Jones

Issue of July 1, 1874

Died

Annie Featherston Fletcher died early in June, aged three months and three days, just six weeks after her mother had died.

In Orangeburg county, S. C., June 14th 1874, Joseph Edwards, eldest son of Dr. N. C. and Mrs. Elizabeth Whetstone, aged eight years and four months.

Obituary

Wm. A. Chunn was born in Meriwether county, Ga., and died at the residence of his father in the same county, April 15th 1874, aged 39 years.

Mrs. Harriet Pope was born in Pickens county, S. C., March 19th 1810, was married to Micajah Pope in 1827 and died in Walker county, Ga., April 30th 1874. She joined the Baptist church at the age of twenty years. G. W. Thomas. Christian Index please copy.

Mrs. Ann B. Rees, consort of John Rees, died at the residence of her adopted daughter, Mrs. Appy Marshall, in Clayton, Ala., May 13, 1874. The maiden name of the deceased was Brooking. She was born in Virginia, but moved to Hancock county, Ga., when a child. He marriage to John Rees, by Lovick Pierce, in 1821. S. A. Pilley

Richard Hutchings was born in Jones county, Ga., November 9th 1817, and died in Macon, Ga., June 6th 1874. Jas. O. Branch

Mrs. Maria L. Redding, wife of George A. Redding and only remaining child of Nathan Pasmore of Harris county, Ga., was born May 7th 1845; married February 1st 1870; and died at the residence of her father, June 3d 1874. C. A. Jones

Miss Mary Ella Eberhart, daughter of Robt. and Eliza Eberhart, deceased, was born in Oglethorpe county, Ga., Sept. 3d 1850, and died at the residence of Mr. P. W. Arnold in Coweta county, Ga., May 2d 1874. Her body rests in the family cemetery in Oglethorpe county, where sleeps the dust of her father and mother. T. H. Timmons

John Wesley Stinson, son of the late Rev. John Stinson, was born in Troup county, Ga., March 31st 1831; died by his own hand, April 13th 1874. Sister Nancy L. Stinson, wife of the late Rev. John Stinson, died May 28, 1874, being nearly seventy years old. She was born and reared in Green county, moved thence to Fayette, and afterwards to Troup county, Ga. She and Mr. Henry West, of Decatur, were the only surviving members that constitute Asbury Chapel Church about fifty years ago. F. M. T. Brannon

Jas. T. Harden was born January 13th 1823 and died May 30th 1874. He professed religion in Warren county and then removed to Randolph county. John S. West

Gabriella Fields was born November 10, 1855; died in Montgomery, Ala., May 17, 1874. Jos. T. Curry

Rev. Levi Pearce was born in Telfair county, Ga., April 17, 1806 and died in Hillsborough co., Fla., March 27, 1874.

Tribute of Respect from Forsyth Station, North Georgia Conference to James H. Mays, who died April 15, 1874.

Issue of July 8, 1874

[page 107, col. 2]: Death of Thos. F. Green, Jr. On our return from Southwest Georgia last week, we met the widow and three children of our old friend and brother, Thomas F. Green, Jr., of Knoxville, Ga., with his remains, which were being taken to Milledgeville for interment.

Obituary

Thomas W. Brandon was born in Virginia in 1803 and reared in Gwinnette county, Ga.; died on 11th of June. He was one of the early settlers of Bartow county, Ga. L. J. Davies

D. N. Miller was born in Wilkes county, Ga., July 1806 and died in Spalding county, Ga., May 7th 1874. He was persuaded by his brother, Jacob Miller, to attend campmeeting at Lovelace's old campground in 1829. He has left an aged widow and a number of children. Jno. D. Gray

Joseph T. West was born in Spartanburg, S. C., in 1814 and died June 9th 1874. Brother West removed from South Carolina in 1863 and spent the last seven years of his life at Trion Factory, Chattooga county, Ga. A. Y. Powell

Andrew Campbell died May 28th 1874, aged 85 years, 5 months, 15 days; his wife, Nancy Campbell, having died some time before, aged 76 years, 6 months and 25 days. W. A. Florence

Mrs. Jane P. Gresham, wife of Col. Thomas S. Gresham, died in Lexington, Ga., June 20th 1874, in the 73d year of her age.

Mrs. Mary Douglas, daughter of Elon and Mary Herrington, was born in Moore county, North Carolina, February 27th 1802; was married to Silas Douglas, Oct. 20th 1818; died June 16th 1874. Ten children were reared to maturity. One son was slain in the battle of Shiloh. Three of her sons and one grandson are now ministers of the Gospel. In 1857, sister Douglas with her husband and most of the family removed to Alabama, and settled near Orion, Pike County. She was buried in the new cemetery in the city of Troy. A. Dowling

Walter Legare Solomons, son of the late Henry E. Solomons, was born in Beaufort county, S. C., December 20th 1854 and died June 12th 1874. M. L. Banks

Mrs. Elizabeth Sewell, consort of the late Nicholas Sewell, who died in Atlanta in 1863 was born in Franklin county, Ga., January 13th 1811 and died in Harris county, Ga., June 12th 1874. She leaves several sons and daughters.

James A. Clark was born Feb. 25th 1834 and died March 18th 1874. For a number of years he had been a useful member of the Bethel Church, Sumter circuit. A widow and three little orphans mourn for him.

Mrs. Drucilla Chandler Anderson, daughter of John and Mary Lake, was born in Newberry county, S. C., and died in Laurens county, S. C., May 27th 1874. Thos. G. Herbert

Drowned on the 9th of June, near Brunswick, Ga., Charles Edward and Emma Virginia Krauss, children of Peter and Margaret Krauss, of Brunswick. J. O. A. Cook

Tribute of Respect from Putnam circuit, North Georgia Conference to Rev. Wm. Marsh, a local preacher, who was born in Virginia, August 30th 1800 and died in Putnam county, Ga., May 4th 1874.

Issue of July 15, 1874

James H. Mays was born in Lincoln county, Ga., April 12, 1800 and died in Forsyth, Ga., April 25, 1874. He was married August 15, 1820. He leaves an aged wife, two children in Georgia, seven out West. D. D. Cox

Wm. A. Grant was born in Abbeville district, S. C., May 5th 1832 and died near Wedowee, Randolph county, Ala., May 20, 1874. He was brought to Meriwether county, Ga., by his parents when an infant. When about twenty-one years old, he was married to Miss Sallie Fuller, daughter of Mr. Alsey Fuller of Meriwether county, Ga. He left a widow and ten children. R. A. Parker. The Methodist Advocate please copy.

Miss Ella Fladger, daughter of Charles J. and Jane Fladger, was born February 27, 1852 and died in Marion county, S. C., April 19, 1874. She joined the M. E. Church in Anson County, N. C. A. J. Stokes

Mrs. Elizabeth Ann Nash, whose maiden name was Strange, was born and reared in Greenville district, S. C., married Mr. Thomas Nash, July 19, 1832, and died April 30, 1874, aged sixty-one years, eight months and three days. Her husband died in the summer of 1854, leaving her with nine small children, six of whom are yet living. She came to Gwinnett county in the water after her husband died, and has lived ever since in this immediate vicinity. S. A. Hagood

William Pace was born September 28, 1788 in Kershaw district, S. C., and died at Gordon, Ga., June 9, 1874. When yet a boy, his father's family moved to Georgia. He returned to Charleston, S. C., to receive his education. C. W. Smith

Mrs. Martha G. Young, daughter of George and Rebecca Prince and consort of the late A. J. Young, was born in Washington county, Ga., December 19, 1825, and died in Lake City, Fla., May 19, 1874. Jas. P. DePass

Miss Anna L. Jones, daughter of Lawrence M. and Adelaide M. Jones, died in Calhoun, Ga., June 15th, aged 19 years. P. G. Reynolds

Mrs. Elizabeth A. Hay, daughter of John and Frances Robertson, was born June 18, 1823 and died in Randolph county, Ga., May 8th 1874. In her 16th year she became the wife of W. C. Hay. W. C. Hay, Jr.

William Dickson was born in Jones county, Ga., April 14, 1802; married Miss Nancy H. Bass, and died in Dooly county, Ga., April 7th 1874. M. C. Jordan

Issue of July 22, 1874

Died

The infant son of R. A. and Josephine McDonald, died in Griffin, Ga., June 25th 1874, aged 7 months and 22 days.

Ross Antoinette, infant daughter of Mr. and Mrs. Wm. P. Loflin, was born Dec. 14th 1873, and died in Wilkes county, Georgia, June 10th 1874.

Obituary

Wm. McRay was born in North Carolina and died in Wakulla county, Florida, June 18th 1874. His father moved to West Florida, when he was a child. His parents were Presbyterians, and his wife was a Methodist. He has left a wife who has now followed her second husband to the grave. She was, when he married her, about eight or nine years ago, a Mrs. Googe. Her first husband was Robert Googe. He also left several children and step-children. Robt. Martin

Thomas F. Green, Jr., was the only surviving son of Dr. Thos. F. and Adeline E. A. Green of Milledgeville, Ga. He was born in that city, March 3d 1843. He married Miss Ella B. Lipscomb, the only daughter of the Chancellor of the University in Athens. He located in the practice of law in Knoxville, Ga., where he died June 24th 1874. A. J. Jarrell

Benjamin Risher, Sr., was born Oct. 5th 1805 in Colleton county, South Carolina, joined the Methodist Church at Green Pond Campground, and died near Branchville in Orangeburg county, S. c., April 20th 1874.

John W. Geiger was born in Bullock county, Ga., April 25th 1805, was reared in Wayne county, Ga.; married Martha F. T. King of Darien, Ga., Jan. 9, 1829; removed to Nassau county, Florida, died April 10th 1874. R. R. Rushing

Wm. C. Carloss was born in South Carolina but removed to Georgia in 1835 and died in Bibb county, Ga., June 29th 1874, aged 62 years. C. J. Toole

Margaret M. Spicer, wife of A. Spicer, was born in Monroe county, Ga., April 24th 1829 and died June 27th 1874. S. S. Pennington

Rufus R. Heslup was born October 26th 1838, and died at Tate Springs, Tenn., May 22d 1874. Samuel P. Jones

Brother Ganaway Conner was born November 14th 1805 and died May 17th 1874. He was a member of the M. E. Church, South, at Social Circle.

Tribute of Respect to Daniel Ainsworth from Sandersville station.

Issue of July 29, 1874

Died

Norah Annah, infant daughter of Rev. Andrew J. and Rebecca M. Hughes, was born May 27th 1874 and died July 13th 1874.

On the 19th July 1874, Robt Dent Stockman, youngest child of Rev. J. Q. and Harriet L. Stockman, of the South Carolina Conference, aged 16 months and 21 days.

George Albert Watkins, infant son of James and Letitia Watkins, died June 22d 1874.

Obituary

Mrs. Mary H. Bolton, wife of James H. Bolton and daughter of Peter and Elizabeth Pelham, was born in Wilmington, N. C., March 5th 1807. Her father moved to South Carolina about the year 1817, soon after which time she was left an orphan, with two little brothers, one of whom, Mr. C. P. Pelham, is now living in Columbia, S. C. She was one of the oldest members of the Beauty Spot Church, Bennettsville. L. M. Hamer

Jacob Smith died at Wacahoota, East Florida, June 10, 1874, in the sixty-fifth year of his age. John C. Ley

Rosa Lee, daughter of W. W. and L. F. Myers, was born in Cassville, Ga., December 11, 1859, and died at the same place, June 14, 1874. J. J. Singleton

Caswell B. Black was born near Lynchburg, Va., July 5th 1811; moved to Green county, Ga., when 12 years of age; he was married twice: 1st, April 24, 1834, to Miss Sarah A. Smith, who died December 8th 1851, leaving six children; he was a citizen of Harris county, Ga., from 1834 to 1858, when he came to Russell county, Ala; united in marriage to Miss Fannie A. Johnson, of Putnam co., Ga., in October 1852, who died July 18, 1868, leaving him with five small children. his death occurred May 10th 1874.

Mrs. Sarah Slaughter, whose maiden name was Tomlinson, was born in Lancaster district, S. C., January 29th 1793; died at the house of Colonel E. M. Butt of Buena Vista, Ga., June 11, 1874. W. W. Stewart

Mrs. Martha E. Pendergrass, whose maiden name was Bryant, was born in Jackson county, Ga., July 1st 1820; May 7th 1838 she was married to Mr. N. H. Pendergrass. She died June 20th 1874. John R. Parker

Sister Sarah C. Whitlow, wife of John G. Whitlow, and daughter of George Gunby, was born in Columbia county, Ga., April 3d 1874 [sic] and died June 2d 1874.

Mrs. Henrietta McCullers, wife of Rev. J. H. McCullers and daughter of Daniel and Eliza Shiver, was born in Pulaski county, Ga., and died at Morgan, Calhoun county, Ga., May 3d 1874, aged about 49 years. She leaves a husband and ten children. J. R. Littlejohn

Miss Sallie J. Thorn died June 13 in Russell county, Ala., aged 21 years and 9 months. J. S. Key

Mr. John Callahan, a native of Jackson county, Ga., was born March 7th 1807. He died in Jefferson, May 24, 1874. John R. Parker

Mrs. N. K. Mulkey, daughter of Richmond and Elizabeth Gordon, was born in Jones county, Ga., March 27, 1823; married to J. W. Mulkey in 1844, and died near Auburn, Lee county, Ala., May 10, 1874. Leaves husband and aged father and mother.

Mrs. Caroline M. Gilbert, wife of Daniel Gilbert and daughter of George W. Kennedy, was born in Monroe county, Ga., May 6, 1836. She died June 16th.

Tribute of Respect from Fairburn circuit, North Georgia Conference, to Abram Miller.

Issue of August 5, 1874

Died

Thomas Milton McKee, infant son of John W. and Mary E. Mckee, was born 24th April 1873 and died 16th May 1874, near the White Sulphur Springs, Meriwether county, Ga.

July 24th 1874, Clifford Leonora Branch, youngest child of J. C. and M. A. Branch, of Clarksville, Ga., aged 9 months.

Obituary

Henry Cannon was born in Newberry county, S. C., July 6th 1809 and died in Abbeville county, S. C., July 8th 1874. He leaves a wife and children. Thomas A. Griffiths. Texas Advocate please copy.

Mrs. Lucy S. McGuire, wife of James M. McGuire and daughter of John B. and Nancy Marable, was born October 29th 1830 in Walton county, Georgia. While yet a child, her parents removed to Paulding county... her death occurred June 12th 1874, She was married to J. M. McGuire, March 31st 1850. C. Trussell

Brother Joseph Anthony Camp (son of J. W. Camp, and grand-son of two ministers of the gospel, Rev. Hosea Camp, a Methodist, and the Rev. Mr. Anthony, a Baptist) was born in Arkansas, April 24th 1852; joined the M. E. Church, South, at Blooming Grove, Polk county, Ga., August 1866; and died at his father's residence, June 6th 1874. Jas. W. Trawick

Judge William B. Marshall died in Talbot county, Ga., June 24th 1874, aged 78 years

Thos. W. McBride died in Union county, S. C., May 7, 1874, aged 38 years and 27 days. M. H. Pooser

Mr. Thomas A. Bradford was born in Enfield, N. C., Feb. 29th 1970 and died in Tallahassee, Fla., June 20th 1874. J. Anderson

Brother Joseph Hall died July 4th 1874, at his residence in Decatur county, Ga., aged 50 years and 2 months. J. J. Giles

Mrs. July Ann Ballard, whose maiden name was Mayfield, was born in Franklin county, Ga., April 2d 1794; was married to William Ballard in 1816; died at the residence of her son William Ballard, in Coweta county, Georgia, June 24th 1874. She had four children; two preceded her to the grave. W. F. S. Powell

Tribute of Respect from Butler circuit to Rev. Charles R. H. Hays (son of Rev. Charles Hays, deceased) who was born July 16th 1832, and died at Butler, Taylor county, Ga., June 8th 1874.

Issue of August 12, 1874

Died

Died in Burke county, Ga., on the 8th of July, Mattie Lou, eldest daughter of Hon. J. J. and Mrs. Eva Toombs Jones, aged ten years and seven months.

Mary Caroline Slaton, daughter of H. H. and Jane A. Slaton, was born in Meriwether county, Ga., and died near Prattville, Autauga county, Ala., July 23d, 1874 in her 8th year.

In Greenville, Ga., July 29, 1874, Annie Byrd Revill, infant daughter of Wm. T. and Alice A. Revill, aged one year, seven months and nine days.

Obituary

My wife, Tempy Ann Kennon, daughter of Henrietta Elizabeth and Berry Wells, died in Berden county, Ga., July 16th 1874, in the thirty-third year of her age. She leaves two little sons, an aged father and mother, several brothers and sisters. Warner L. Kennon

My father, Rev. J. W. Mills, was born April 20th 1819 in Monroe or Elbert county, Ga., and died in Shelby county, Texas, July 6th 1874. J. M. Mills

Mrs. Elizabeth Caroline Mullins, whose maiden name was Matthews, was reared in Gwinnett county, Ga., and lived most of her life in Forsyth; removed to Troup county, Ga., in 1864, where she died July 23d 1874, in the fiftieth year of her age. H. E. Ellis

Mrs. Jane Branton was born September 5th 1798 and died July 13th 1874. Eighteen children called her mother--three of them died in early childhood--fifteen of them she lived to see members of the Church, one of whom was a preacher of the gospel.

John B. Nichols was born in South Carolina, March 18th 1822 and died in Dalton, Ga., June 29th 1874. Levi Brotherton

Mrs. Sarah S. Moore was born in Washington county, Ga., August 1831, and died in Milledgeville, Ga., July 22d 1874.

Adda L. Snipes, daughter of B. F. and E. N. Snipes, died at Fort Worth, Tarrant county, Texas.

Tribute of Respect from Tampa District Conference to ministers of the Gospel, David L. White and Josiah Bullock.

Issue of August 19, 1874

Thomas Lee Penn was born in Oglethorpe county, Ga., Nov. 14th 1807 and died in Cusseta, Chambers county, Ala., May 20th 1874. He was married to Elizabeth White, June 18th 1831. R. H. Harris

Brother Thomas Simonton, a native of North Carolina, and for many years a resident of Clark county, Ga., whence he moved to Griffin, Ga., died in the latter place July 17th 1874, aged 77 years, 1 month and 5 days.

Mrs. Mary Jones, wife of Allen J. Jones, was born in Jones county, Ga., Jan. 15th 1812. She removed to Meriwether county in 1829, was married in 1832, then moved to Clayton county in 1868, and died near Jonesboro, Ga., July 4th 1874.

Mrs. Mary A. Cline, wife of Maj. Wm. M. Cline and daughter of the late Rev. Lewis Hatton, died in Griffin, Ga., July 5th 1874, in the 49th year of her age.

Mrs. Elizabeth A. (Tyson) Ferrell was born in Jones county, Ga., August 10th 1822; was married to James A. Ferrell in 1843; died in Palmetto, Ga., June 15th 1874. T. H. Timmons

Tribute of Respect from Branchville circuit, held at Cattle Creek, S. C., to William Summers who died July 22d 1874.

Mrs. Frances Elizabeth Choice, died at the residence of her son-in-law, Mr. thos. J. Perkins, of Tallahassee, Fla., August 3d, 1874. Her maiden name was Stephens and she was born in Charleston, S. C., June 5th 1800. In 1816 she became the wife of Mr. John A. Keowin, to whom she bore two daughters. In 1836 she removed to Florida in and in 1842 she was married to Rev. William Choice. Josephus Anderson

Melville S. Ledbetter was born in Atlanta, Ga., July 28, 1851; died in Polk county, Ga., July 23d 1874. He was the son of Dr. L .L. Ledbetter, deceased, who was a member of the Georgia Conference, and Mrs. Cornelia (Byrd) Ledbetter, now resident in Polk county. Wm. H. LaPrade

Rev. Nathan Baker was born in Pennsylvania in 1799 and died in Franklin county, Fla., July 25th 1874, aged 75 years, 5 months and 20 days. When but nine or ten months old, his parents removed to North Alabama, where he remained until 1830 when he removed to Florida. He was a delegate to the Baltimore Convention which nominated John C. Breckinridge, and was Collector of Customs when the late war commenced. H. G. Townsend

Mrs. Sarah Lambert, relict of the late Wm. Lambert, was born October 27th 1806 and died August 2d 1874. Richard W. Rogers

Mrs. Mary Jane Hardy, wife of Dr. W. Hardy and daughter of Judge Turner Trippe, was born in Clarksville, Ga., in 1827 and died in Cartersville, Ga., August 7th 1874. L. J. Davies

Mrs. Jane Wallace was born June 14th 1796 and died in Marlboro county, June 24th 1874. She became the wife of Barnabas Wallace, May 27th 1819, who died August 1871.

Mary Flournoy Ousley, daughter of Joseph A. and Angeline Ousley, died August 7th 1874, at the age of fifteen. J. W. Talley

Mrs. Mary McGarity was born in Virginia in 1773; moved to Elbert county, Ga., when a child, and subsequently moved to Fulton county, Ga., where she died July 24th 1874. A. G. Dempsy

Tribute of Respect to Joshua Taylor and Chas. C. Beall from Thomasville station. Joshua Taylor was born in Washington co., Ga., June 1st 1813, and died in Thomas county, Ga., in the 63rd year of his age. Charles Cotten Beall was born in Warren county, Ga., December 24th 1796 and died in Thomasville, Ga., in the seventy-eighth year of his age.

Died

At Davidson College, N. C., August 21st 1874, John Kennon, infant son of Prof. and Mrs. W. G. Richardson, of Central University, Richmond, Kentucky.

Obituary

Mrs. Jane E. Ellison, relict of James Ellison, was born in the county of Derry, Ireland, June 9th 1795, and died in Talbot county, Ga., June 30th 1874. Sister Ellison's ancestors were Irish Protestants. In 1803, her father emigrated to America and settled in Baltimore. Two years later he moved to Chester Court House, S. C. In 1812 she was married to James Ellison. She left children and grand-children. Rob't J. Corley

Rev. William Hays was born in Virginia, Oct. 8th 1795. He was licensed to preach in Morgan county, Ga. In Jan. 1839 he removed to Randolph county, Ga., and died at his home in Terrell county, Ga., July 16th 1874. J. R. Littlejohn

Mrs. S. Caroline Sims was born in Monroe, Walton county, Georgia, October 8th 1827 and died in Bainbridge, Georgia, July 11th 1874.

Mrs. A. H. Booker, wife of Mr. Oscar E. Booker, was born Dec. 13th 1836; was married Oct. 9th 1856, and died in Washington, Ga., 7th June 1874. W. P. Rivers

Mrs. Amanda Cordelia Dowling, wife of Samuel S. Dowling and daughter of Frederick and Penelope Ham, was born Nov. 27th 1835 and died July 1st 1874. L. M. Hamer

Miss Sarah G. Morel was born in Effingham county, Ga., August 20th 1850[?], and died July 15th 1874. N. D. Morehouse

Mrs. Christian E. W. Mann, wife of R. F. M. Mann of Spalding county, Ga., was born in Gwinnett county, Ga., and died near Griffin, Ga., August 12th 1874, in the 32d year of her age.

Nancy Ann Gilham, wife of Robert Gilham of Troup county, Georgia, died August 16th 1874. She was born in Oglethorpe county, Georgia, in 1811, and moved to Troup county in 1838. She joined the Presby- terian Church in 1846. H. J. Ellis

Anna Justina, eldest daughter of Edwin McTeer of Colleton county, S. C., died July 24th 1874, in her eighteenth year. A. English Williams

A. C. Morel was born in Effingham county, Ga., Oct. 18th 1851 and departed this life June 26th 1874. N. D. Morehosue

Issue of September 9, 1874

Rev. Dr. Francis E. Manson was born in Dinwiddie county, Va., March 19th 1800 and died in McDonough, Henry county, Ga., August 9, 1874. In 1822 he graduated in the University of Maryland. In 1825 he emigrated to Georgia and settled in Jasper county. His son, Z. T., and his eldest daughter Mrs. V. R. Tommey, of Decatur, Ga. Geo. M. Nolan

E. S. Carmine was born in Accomack county, Va., Dec. 15, 1815, moved to Florida in 1843, died in Leon county, Fla., August 4th 1874. He leaves a wife and six children--five sons and one daughter. R. H. Howren

Mrs. Elizabeth Maxcy, whose maiden name was McLeondon, was born in Green county, Ga., in 1789. She was married twice, and survived her last husband many years. She died at the residence of her son-in-law, R. T. Grace, in Ozark, Dale county, Ala., July 14th 1874. A. Dowling

C. Augustus Cobb died in Greenwood, Abbeville county, S. C., August 11, 1874, aged 56 years. He left a wife and eleven children. J. W. Murray

Robert Barksdale Pound, son of James and Nancy Pound, was born August 18, 1847, and died in Talbot county, Ga., June, 15, 1874. B. W. Key. The Christian Index please copy.

Mrs. Rebecca L. Lovless, wife of John Lovless of LaGrange, Ga., and daughter of Ezekiel A. and Lois T. Dozier, was born October 20, 1848, and died at her father's, Warrior Stand, Macon county, Ala., August 2, 1874. She was married to brother Lovless, Nov. 20, 1869. J. W. Solomon

Mrs. Mary E. Lane, wife of Rev. Wesley Lane of the South Georgia Conference and eldest daughter of Kenneth and Ann McKinnon, was born in Thomas county, Ga., November 28th 1843; married to Rev. W. Lane, December 23d 1869; died in Ellaville, July 7th 1874. She left two little children-- one but two days old.

James H. Taylor, late of Upson county, Ga., was born in North Carolina, October 21st 1795; was brought to Georgia by his parents when a child; was married to Charity Howard in Green county, Ga., in 1831; died July 29th 1874. He left a wife and nine children.

W. J. Taylor died at Greenwood, Abbeville county, S. C., August 2d 1874, in the sixty-fifth year of his age. J. W. Murray

John Anderson was born in North Carolina and died in Gilmer county, Ga., June 5th 1874. J. N. Sullivan

Tribute of Respect from Walterboro circuit, South Carolina Conference to Rev. Henry Bass Green, who died 30th July.

Issue of September 16, 1874

Rev. Henry Bass Green, son of Glenn and Mary Green, was born in 1846 in Colleton county, S., C., and died July 31st 1874. He was a soldier in the late war. He has left a wife, a little daughter, a mother, a sister, and two brothers. B. G. Jones

Mrs. Sarah Brannan died in Marietta, Ga., Aug. 6th 1874, in the eightieth year of her age. W. F. Glenn

Mrs. Margaret Jenkins, wife of G. F. Jenkins, deceased, died July 26th 1874, in the 78th year of her age.

Mrs. Mary A. C. Lawson, daughter of F. F. and Susan C. Jones, was born March 19th 1855 and died July 21st 1874 in Brooks county, Ga.,
Mrs. Lou Grace, wife of W. D. Grace, was born July 18th 1826 and died near Howard, Ga., July 28th 1874.

Our aged grand-father, Jesse Oslin, died May 24th. Jennie E. Wells

Mrs. Mary E. Griffin was born in Springfield, Mass., Feb. 27th 1833 and died at Atlanta, Ga., June 30th 1874. She moved to Perry, Ga., in 1859. She was married to Reuben H. Slappy, April 27th 18744, with whom she lived for three years, when he died, leaving her with two children. She was married against Aug. 23d 1860. F. A. Branch

Charles Hardy Turner, son of Jas. B. and Mary A. Turner, was born October 13th 1851; died near Villa Rica, Aug. 23d 1874. He leaves an aged father and mother, sister and brothers, a wife and little one.

Mrs. Julia Frances Heape, wife of J. Harley Heape, was born June 1856; married July 6th 1873; died July 21st 1874 in Colleton county, S. C.

Brother Hamilton died in Gilmer county, Ga., at the age of 73 years. J. N. Sullivan

Mrs. E. A. F. Bigham died at the residence of her son, W. H. Bigham, in Marion county, E. Florida, July 31st 1874, aged 51 years. She formerly lived in Jefferson county, Ga. John Penny

Tribute of Respect from Grantville and Pierce circuits to Rev. Hiram Camp and brother Thornton Holman.

Issue of September 23, 1874

Mary E. Brown, daughter of Lemon M. and Lilly B. Brown, was born June 30th 1842 and died in Newton county, Ga., August 16, 1874.

Rev. Jas. R. Middleton died in St. John's co., Fla., August 18, 1874, in the 72d year of his age. he was born in McIntosh county, Ga., and moved to Florida some twenty years ago. He leaves an aged widow and five children.

Mrs. Susan McP. Hamby, wife of David W. Hamby and daughter-in-law, of Rev. Allen Hamby, who was formerly a member of the South Carolina Conference, but is now a local preacher in the vicinity of Florence, S. C., died August 3d, 1874.

Mrs. M. M. Gooch, youngest daughter of Rev. N. C. D. Culclasure of Orangeburg, S. C., and wife of J. H. Gooch, Esq., died at Mineral Spring, Marlboro county, S., C., August 12, 1874, aged thirty-three years, seven months and seventeen days. Mrs. Gooch was first married to Rev. Daniel A. Ogburn of the South Carolina Conference on 20th October 1859, who died April 16th 1865. She then married her surviving husband, Oct. 2d 1867. She leaves behind three children, the eldest five years, the youngest sixteen months.

Mrs. Caroline Webster, wife of Major Wm. Webster, and daughter of the late Dr. William Hancock, of Union co., S. C., formerly of London England, was born June 17, 1816 died in Spartanburg co., S. C., June 12, 1874, leaving a husband and two daughters.

Rev. John Collier Carter was born in Wilkes county, Ga., in 1801; married Miss Ann H. White of Columbia County in 1822, and died near Ucone[?], Russel county, Ala., June 16, 1874. Jere S. Williams

Levin J. Smith was born in Hancock co., Aug. 15, 1805, and died in Baldwin co., Ga., Aug. 5, 1874.

Mrs. Zarilda E. Horton, daughter of Miel I. and Nannie C. Horton, died August 19th 1874, in Shelby county, Ala., aged 27 years and 6 months. C. L. Dobbs

Malcom A. Peterson was born in Montgomery county, Ga., August 14, 1849, and died in the same county, August 24, 1874. He has left a wife, two little babes, his aged parents. H. C. Fentress

Mrs. Fendorah Richardson, wife of Henry C. Richardson and daughter of David Rogers was born January 31, 1857; married October 16, 1873, and died August 17, 1874, in Morgan county Ga. our youngest sister.... B. L. Hume

Mrs. Susan E. Garlington, daughter of John J. Slaughter and wife of J. W. Garlington, died at the residence of Mr. Isaac Heard, where she was visiting in Tallapoosa county, Ala., July 7th 1874, in her 28th year. She leaves a daughter six, and a son three years old, and a husband.

Issue of September 30, 1874

Died

On the 10th of August 1874 in Decatur county, Ga., Elma, daughter of Leonidas and Helen Crowe, aged 4 years, 4 months and twenty-six days.

Obituary

Mrs. Georgia E. Mixon, wife of Rev. J. F. Mixon of the South Georgia Conference and daughter of Henry and Carrie Smith, was born in Jasper county, Ga., December 4th 1840 and died at the home of her birth-- the residence of her step-father, Dr. Wm. A. Perry, August 19th 1874. On 17 Dec. 1857 she was married to her now bereaved husband, then a practicing attorney in Covington.

Mrs. Nancy Fletcher, daughter of Capt. Byrd Ferrell of Hancock county, Ga., was born January 28th 1802; married John Fletcher, of Clinton, Jones county, Ga., whence they removed to Chambers county, now Lee county, Alabama, where she died June 14th 1874. Christian Index, Atlanta, please copy.

Samuel Malcomson Stevenson was born in Horry District, S. C., Aug. 6th 1806 and died near Marion C. H., S. C., Aug. 24th 1874. He was clerk of court of his native county. A. J. Stokes

Mrs. Maria Hull was born in Virginia in 1797 and died in Athens, Ga., June 28th 1874. Her first husband, Mr. George Cooke. After the death of her husband she became the inmate of the home of Mrs. Julia Clayton. In 1861 she was married to brother Asbury Hull. Upon his death in 1866, she resumed her old place in Sister Clayton's household, and remained there until the death of that lady in 1873. J. Lewis, Jr.

John F. Adams was born in Putnam county, Ga., in 1808; died in Hancock county, Ga., August 20th 1874.

Miss Sallie E. Shivers died at the Female Academy, Clarksville, Tenn., August 11th. J. M. Wright

Fannie Anna Dibble, elder daughter of Mr. P. V. Dibble of Orangeburg, S. C., died on Sullivan's Island, while on a visit among friends, Aug. 20th 1874. H. A. C. Walker

Mrs. Martha C. Handly was born July 25th 1842; was married to Mr. James C. Handly, Dec. 12th 1871; died Sept. 1st 1874. F. A. Kimbell

Mrs. Mary G. Bonner was born in Baldwin county, Ga., Sept. 28th 1834, and died Aug. 26th 1874.

John C. Wimbush was born in Abbeville District, S. C., Oct. 14th 1799; died July 10th 1874 in Spalding county, Ga., where he had resided for a number of years. Jno D. Gray

Miss Mary Jane Melvin, daughter of George T. and Marium Melvin was born in Bladen county, N. C., December 15th 1825 and died in Houston county, Ga., June 10th 1874.

Issue of October 7, 1874

Died

Suddenly in Sumter, S. C., on the 17th September, Edith Septima, youngest child of Anthony and Elizabeth A. White, aged three years and one month.

Obituary

Mrs. Sarah Jones died in DeKalb county, Ga., at the residence of her son, Capt. J. H. Jones, July 10, 1874. She was born in Pendleton Dist., S. C., Oct. 23, 1782. Her parents was named Roberts--pious members of the Baptist Church. She became a member of the Methodist Church, married Robt. F. Jones, who became a zealous local preacher first in South Carolina, and afterwards in Georgia. She was the mother of eight boys and four girls. This family moved in 1823 to Gwinnett county, and in a few years to DeKalb county. Two of her sons became ministers of our Church, the Rev. Jas. Jones has served the Georgia Conference since 1835 and is still effective; the other, Rev. W. F. Jones, is an acceptable local preacher in Texas. She leaves a living posterity of two or three hundred. Her son, grand-son, and great-grand-son are all members of the North Georgia Conference. R. F. Jones

Mrs. Phoebe Hodges, wife of Gabriel Hodges, was born Jan. 1, 1804, and died in Cokesbury, August 8, 1874. Mr. Gabriel Hodges was born in Abbeville, Jan. 6, 1791, and died Sept. 7, 1874. R. N. Wells

Mrs. Julia S. Felder, widow of Dr. W. L. Felder, late of Augusta, Ga., was born July 5, 1812, in Clarendon county, S. C., was confirmed in the Episcopal Church at the age of fourteen or fifteen; was married to Dr. Felder, then of Sumter district, S. C., June 21, 1832; was the mother of four children, two sons and two daughters, one each of whom still live; the daughter is the wife of Dr. W. H. Doughty, of Augusta, Ga., at whose house sister Felder died July 2d, 1874. J. E. Evans

Mrs. Attie Thomas, youngest daughter of Dr. A. C. C. Thompson, and wife of Dr. W. A. Thomas, died on the 18th Sept., at Sevens' Pottery, Baldwin county, Ga., after a short illness. She was born in Maryland, Dec. 28th 1847, moved to Georgia at five years old.

Mr. John A. Winn was born in Abbeville district, S. C., December 24, 1795. In early life he moved with his parents to Jackson county, Ga., where he spent the greater part of his life. In 1853 he moved to Tuscaloosa, Ala., where he died Aug. 10, 1874. Evan Nicholson

My mother, Mrs. Penelope Moreland, was born Oct. 30, 1796, and died Aug. 12, 1874, at the residence of her son-in-law, Wm. S. Barnett, in Grantville, Coweta county, Ga. Her maiden name was ousley. When she was quite young, her parents removed from Baldwin to Jones county, and both died early, leaving her and one brother, the late Rev. Newdaygate Ousley, orphans. She was married to the Rev. Isaac T. Moreland, a local Methodist preacher, in 1814. My father died in Jones county in 1846, soon after which time my mother removed to Coweta county, and lived as a widow for nearly twenty-eight years. She was the mother of twelve children, eight of whom survive her, and seven out of the eight were present to witness her death. John F. Moreland

Mrs. Mary Stringer, daughter of John Thalley, was born in Duplin county, N. C., August 24, 1796, and died in Tampa, Fla., August 21, 1874.

Rev. Wm. Glenn, a native of Virginia and for several years a resident of Elbert county, Ga., died at his home in Anderson county, S. C., July 1, 1874, in his 81st year. He leaves a large number of children and grand-children. J. Q. Stockman

Henry Montgomery Harris was born Sept. 5, 1852, near Bennettsville, S. C., and died June 29, 1874, of typhoid malarial fever. He removed to Prairie county, Ark., with his parents about the year 1869. R. N. Ross

Mrs. Sue M. Greene, wife of John H. Greene, and daughter of John L. and Hettie Smith, was born in Talbot county, Ga., July 5, 1836, and died in Schley county, Ga., August 24, 1874.

George W. McDonald, son of David L. and Mary A. McDonald, and grand-son of the Rev. W. H. Thomas of the South Georgia Conference, was born Jan. 16, 1864, and died in Gwinnett county, Ga., August 20, 1874.

Benjamin Cummins died in Orangeburg county, S., C., August 29, 1874, in his 73d year. T. J. Clyde

Rev. James Middleton died in St. John's county, Florida, August 18, 1874, in his 73d year. He was a native of Georgia and moved to this State about twenty years ago. W. S. Tucker

John Phillips, son of Robert and Nancy Phillips, was born in Spartanburg District, South Carolina, April 20th 1811, and died in Campbell county, Ga., July 16, 1874. His father was originally from Ireland--his mother from Scotland. T. H. Timmons

L. M. Aldridge was born in South Carolina, Sept. 3, 1836; grew to manhood in Harelson county, Ga.; married Nancy E. Bryce, of Carroll county, Jan. 17, 1866; and died in Upshur county, Texas, June 29, 1874, leaving a wife and three children to mourn his death. R. P. Thompson

Miss Susan Ann, eldest daughter of Levi and Sarah Dick, was born Nov. 28th, 1850 and died near Alcova Factory, July 31, 1874. A. C. Mixon

James B. Holman, oldest son of Major Joseph and Nancy D. Holman, was born in Barren county, Ky., June 21, 1840 and died in Pike county, Ga., August 3, 1874. Eli Smith

Sister Nancy A. Kimbell, aged 27 years, wife of John K. Kimbell, and daughter of Mrs. C. Criddle, died near McDonough, Ga., July 20, 1874. She left three little children, one of whom an infant two weeks old has since joined her in the better land. J. R. Mayson

Mrs. Maria Hill, daughter of Wm. B. S. Beard, Esq., was born in Newberry county, S. C., August 11, 1853, and graduated in 1870 at the Spartanburg Female College. She was married to Mr. Edward P. Hill of South Carolina, December 1872, who died in May last.

Franklin P. W. Thomas was born in Bartow county, Ga., Oct. 24, 1856 and died July 15, 1874 in Calhoun county, Ala.

Mr. John Rich died at Varnsville, S. C., July 4, 1874; following his wife, Mrs. Mary Rich, who died at the same place, March 25th 1874. They were formerly residents of Charleston. L. B. Varn

John M--- Harper was born in Abbeville county, S., C., 1st January 1852, and died 26th August 1874. He was the son of Col. H. H. and Ella Harper. he was educated at Wofford College, S. C. J A. H. Harper. Abbeville papers please copy.

Mrs. Margaret R. Long was born in St. Marys, Ga., and died in Columbia, S. C., July 26, 1874, aged about 75 years. W. J. Greene

Mrs. Elizabeth M. Stewart was born and spent most of her life in Laurens county, S. C., and died July 22, 1874, in Anderson county S. C., whither she had removed the previous winter. She had an only daughter.

Mrs. Cornelia Hopkins, widow of Mr. Lambeth Hopkins, long a merchant of high standing in Augusta, Ga., has passed away to her home with God. She was a Miss Smart. Her widowed mother married a Mr. Hunt of Macon, Ga; one of her sisters married Mr. Thomas A. Brown of Talbotton, Ga. She was the mother of nine children, six of whom live to mourn the loss. J. E. Evans

Hal P. Hodges, born in Cokesbury, May 20th 1848; died September 20th 1874. R. N. Wells

Mrs. Lucinda J. Rothrock, daughter of H. P. and Nancy Arnold, was born Dec. 20th 1818, and died Aug. 20th 1874. J. A. Lomax

Mrs. Margaret E. Hogan, wife of Daniel Hogan and daughter of Allen Geiger, was born in Liberty county, Ga., May 20, 1829, and died near Fort McCoy, Marion county, Fla., Sept. 13, 1874. When she was but a child, her father removed to Florida. L. J. A. Brown

Mrs. Lucy B. Heath, wife of Mr. E. P. Heath, died in Warren county, Ga., August 19th 1874, in her 29th year. R. W. Hubert

Sister Lizzie C. Dagnall, daughter of James H. Senter of Smith county, Ga., was married to H. W. Dagnall, May 4, 1871, and died at Dalton, Ga., July 5th 1874. Since her death, dear little Minnie, her babe, has gone to join the mother.

Levi Haygood, infant son of S. A. and M. A. Haygood, was born May 23, 1866[?] and died Sept. 13, 1874 in Gwinnett county, Ga. T. E. Daniel.

Issue of October 14, 1874

Died

Ella, infant daughter of W. H. and E. R. Shy, was born Aug. 14th 1873 and died Oct. 5th 1874, at Union Point, Greene county, Ga.

Obituary

Rev. Malcom Vesuvius Wood, son of Rev. Landy and Mrs. A. E. Wood, of the S. C. Conference, was born in Greenville, S. C., Feb. 18th 1846; joined the M. E. Church in Lincolnton, N. C. He was married to Miss Rebecca A. Varn, Dec. 31st 1868 and removed to Union county, Arkansas; in 1871 returned to South Carolina, and located in Beaufort county, near where the village of Varnsville now stands. He died in Conwayboro, S. C., August 27th 1874.

Mrs. Winnifred West was born near Newbern, N. C., in 1810. About 1828 she came to Baldwin county, Ga., where she died September 20th 1874. A. J. Jarrell

Martha Isabella Bruton was born Jan. 28th 1846; married Dec. 5th 1866 and died August 11th 1874 in Bainbridge, Ga.

Rev. Mozee Harp was born in Jones county, Ga., April 17th 1819; died in Fayette county, Sept. 4th 1874. Geo. E. Gardner. Texas Christian Advocate please copy.

Mrs. Mary E. Parks, wife of Capt. J. t. Parks, died in Greenwood, Abbeville county, S. C., Sept. 25th 1874, aged 45 years. J. W. Murray

Miss Mary Sison Waldrop, daughter of Robt. and Sarah Waldrop of Spartanburg county, S., C., died Sept. 2d 1874, in the 22nd year of her life.

Mrs. Mary D. Bailey, widow of James Bailey, died in Greenwood, Abbeville county, S., C., Sept. 26th 1874, aged -- years. J. W. Murray

Mrs. Elizabeth A. Fielding was born in S. C., April 7th 1790 and died in Catoosa county, Ga., Aug. 26th 1874. J. B. McFarland

Miss Mary Massey died in Greenwood, Abbeville county, S. C., Aug. 18th 1874, aged 18 years. Her aged grand-mother and aunt-- who reared her from infancy, mourn her loss. J. W. Murray

Freeman W. Riley, youngest child of Jacob and Frances Riley, died Sept. 4th 1874, at the residence of his brother, O. B. Riley, in Orangeburg county, S., C., in his 14th year. Geo. W. Gardner

Jordan C. Upton died at the residence of John upton in Thomas county, Ga., Aug. 22d 1874, aged 12 years.

Rosela Virginia, second daughter of G. Walker and E. A. Glenn, died in Greenville county, S., C., September 17th 1874, aged 6 years an 9 months.

Issue of October 21, 1874

Died

In Cheraw, S. C., October 10, 1874, Annie Jane, daughter of J. M. and F. M. Cadieu, aged 3 years, eleven months and 12 days.

In Cheraw, S. C., October 13th 1874, Jimmie Hunter, son of James and Nancy Murray, aged one year, one month and 19 days.

Ella Maude Hyer, youngest child of J. H. and E. S. Hyer, died Sept. 22d 1874, aged seven years and six months.

Georgia E. Wilson, infant daughter of T. J. and Frances E. Wilson, of Madison county, Fla., aged four years, six months and four days.

Willie P. Bryce, son of Rev. Geo. R. and E. A. Bryce, was born at Huntsville, Ark., Jan. 10, 1871, and died at Butler, Texas, Oct. 3d 1874.

Obituary

Mrs. Martha James Hamilton, daughter of James and Mary Herring of LaGrange, Ga., and wife of Rev. Dr. A. L. Hamilton of Atlanta, died in Atlanta, Ga., September 1st 1874. Her remains were conveyed to Rose Hill Cemetery, Macon.

Mrs. Evalina Zimmerman was born January 15, 1816, and died in Greensboro, Ga., August 21, 1874. She was married to John F. Zimmerman, Dec. 27, 1835. W. C. Bass

Miss Sarah Josephine Shivers was born in Webster county, Ga., and died in the same county, August 24, 1874; aged about twenty-four years. Robt. L. Wiggins

Wm. Harris was born in Warren county, Ga., April 13, 1805; and died in Fort Valley, Houston county, Ga., August 19, 1874.

Miss Nancy P. Maloney was born in Chattooga county, Ga., February 8, 1851; died September 13, 1874, in Walker county, Ga. G. W. Thomas

Minnie H. Crawford, only daughter of Rev. Robert B. and Mrs. Mattie F. Crawford, was born June 2d 1866; died in Demopolis, Ala., Sept. 5th 1874.

Thos Westbury, Sr., of St. George ct., S. C., died September 9, 1874, aged 54 years, lacking one day.

Miss Mary E. McRea, daughter of M. N. McRea, was born in Telfair county, Ga., June 1st 1857; and died July 23, 1874. J. V. M. Morris

Mrs. Rhoda Hall, daughter of James Griffin, was born in North Carolina 1872 [sic]; and died in Marion county, Fla., Sept. 3, 1874. She leaves eight children. Geo. C. Leavel

Mr. Henry Graddick died in Alachua county, Fla., August 25, 1874, in the 68th year of his age. He was a native of Richland district, S. C., moved to Florida in 1852.

Mrs. D. F. Clegg, whose maiden name was Bullock, was born in 1829, married to W. T. Clegg (who preceded her to the grave) in 1849; died July 11, 1874.

Issue of October 28, 1874

Died

Little Lovie, infant daughter of S. D. and F. C. Clements, born April 13th and died Sept. 30th 1874.

At Santuc, Union county, S. C., October 12, 1874, James Ferdinand Thomas, eldest son of Col. Mabry and Mrs. Louisa H. Thomas, aged 5 years, 10 months and 8 days.

Obituary

Mrs. Mary Ledbetter Kennedy, wife of Rev. F. M. Kennedy, D. D., was born near Wadesboro', N. C., May 24th 1836 and died in Macon, Ga., Sept. 29th 1874. We carried her remains to Wadesboro', N. C., and held funeral services. Jas. O. Branch

Rev. Isaiah L. Avant was born in Bibb county, Ga., June 27th 1840; died in Houston county, Ga., Sept. 30th 1874. W. G. Vinson

Rev. Henry Asbury died at his residence in Lincoln county, N. C., 1st Oct. 1874, in his seventy-sixth year. He was the son of Rev. Daniel Asbury, who for many years was a successful pioneer preacher in the members of the South Carolina Conference, and of Nancy L. Morris, who was a member of the first Methodist Church organized in North Carolina, West of the Catawba River. J. W. Puett

Mrs. Matilda Harris Clubb was born Nov. 3rd 1832; married James A. Clubb, 21st of June 1849; died October 1st 1874. She leaves a husband and nine children. J. O. A. Cook

Philip C. Alston, son of the late Col. Wm. J. Alston of Fairfield county, S., C., died September 14th 1874, aged twenty years.

Jacob Dantzler was born January 10th 1802 and died at his residence in lower Orangeburg county, S., C., August 18th 1874. He left a widow and four children. T. J. Mallard

Robert B. Baird was born in Winnsboro, S. C., Jan. 24th 1819, married to Miss Mary C. Allen, Nov. 24th 1840, removed shortly after to Alabama, where he and his wife joined the Methodist Church; thence they removed to Louisiana in which stated he died Sept. 28th 1874. He left a wife and ten children--five sons and five daughters.

John T. Tomlinson died near Plainville, Gordon co., Ga., August 21st 1874, in his 61st year. J. H. McCoole

Mrs. Mary Pitts was born in Johnson county, N. C., August 29th 1789, and died in Decatur county, Ga., September 20th 1874. Before she was fully grown her widowed mother moved from North Carolina to Georgia, and settled in Washington County. Of a family of ten children, she and a sister Mrs. Stafford, were the only ones for a long while still living, and they being widowed with no children, took up their abode together. J. W. Weston

Boaz Kitchings was born in Warren county, Ga., May 3d 1809; died in Sumter county, Ga., August 3d 1874. P. S. Twitty

Mrs. Elizabeth Little, daughter of Rev. Alexander Gordon, deceased, of the Georgia Conference, was born in Tatnall county, Ga., Dec. 2d 1812, and died Aug. 15th 1874. She was married to John Little, 29th of March 1831; and removed to Alachua county, Fla., in 1848, where she lost her husband. Isaac Munden

Mrs. Catharine K. Williams was born in Rutherford county, N. C., October 1801; died in Gilmer county, Ga., Sept. 20th 1874.

Issue of November 4, 1874

Mrs. Elizabeth Benton, wife of Rev. Edward J. Benton, and daughter of Francis and Elizabeth Munch, was born in Colleton district, S. C., August 27, 1844, and died at Pine Bloom Mill, Ga., October 12, 1874. She leaves a husband and nine children.

Major John Strobel died Sept. 13, 1874, in the 75th year of his age. He was born in Colleton county, S. C., and for several terms represented his native county in the Legislature. His first marriage was with Miss Barbara Dantzler, by whom he had an only daughter, who survives him. He was again married, to Miss Martha Miller, who had just preceded him to the grave. By this union he had five children, two of whom still survive.

Miss Louisiana Meriwether was born June 23d, 1847 and died October 2d 1874. W. W. Wadsworth

Henry D. Lewis died August 16, 1874, in Yorkville, S. C., aged 21 years.

Mr. Elisha Weatherford was born in Virginia, April 4th 1802, and died at High Shoals, Ga., Sept. 9th 1874. His parents moved to Spartanburg district, S. C., when he was four or five years old, where he was reared, married, and continued to reside until 1833 when he moved to Gwinnett county, Ga. He leaves a wife and several children.

Mrs. Electa Leverton, third daughter of Rev. Daniel and Mrs. Susannah Button, was born Oct. 3d 1874, and died in Spartanburg, S. C., August 11, 1874. She was married twice, first to a Mr. Patterson, next to Mr. Leverton. C. Lee

Mr. Wm. Holt was born in Hancock county, Ga., April 16, 1799; was married to Miss Frances Cox, December 1817; died in Talbot county, Ga., Sept. 15, 1874. He was left an orphan without means, at the age of twelve years. His wife died in 1870. W. H. Woodall

Nathan Haines, Sr., was born in Washington county, Ga., March 11, 1810, and died in Muscogee county, Ga., Sept. 23d, 1874. He married Miss Rebecca Dorch in 1832 and moved to Muscogee in 1837. He leaves a wife and nine children.

Mrs. Ann Elizabeth Pullin, wife of H. T. Pullin of Early county, Ga., was born September 2d 1832; died September 15th 1874, in the 43d year of her age. P. C. Harris

James H. Lamar, son of John O. and Mary A. Lamar, died in Macon county, Ala., Sept. 23d 1874, in his 19th year. N. W. Pattillo

John W. Gatlin was born in Edgecomb co., N. C., Jan. 20, 1815, and died in Houston county, Ga., August 29, 1874. He was a soldier in the last Indian war and was also in the Confederate struggle. W. M. D. Bond

Col. C. S. Edwards died in Charleston county, near Monck's Corner, Sept. 19, 1874, in the 49th year of his age. He left a widow and eight children. R. S. McCants

Miss Letty Whisnant, daughter of Adam and Susannah Whisnant, died in Greenville, S. C., Sept. 16, 1874.

Phillip Howell was born and reared in Wayne county, N. C., and died in Troup county, Ga., October 2d 1874, in his 73d year. He lived nearly fifty years in Troup county, Ga.

Tribute of Respect from Long Cane circuit, North Georgia Conference to Phillip Howell.

Issue of November 11, 1874

Died

Annie Mary, daughter of Thos. N. and Hattie M. Mims, was born Jan. 28th 1869 and died Sept. 26th 1874.

Emma Amanda Pullin, youngest daughter of H. T. Pullin of Early county, Ga., died September 11th 1874, aged 11 years, 9 months and 9 days.

Robert Lee Handley, son of J. and M. E. Handley, aged 4 years and 4 months, died in Palmetto, Ga., Oct. 20th 1874.

At Centreville, Leon county, Florida, Oct. 1st 1874, little Pearl, daughter of Dr. W. T. and M. A. Shipes, aged 3 years, 7 months and 22 days.

Obituary

Mrs. Harriet M. Robeson, wife of Rev. John H. Robeson of Holston Conference, died September 27th 1874, at the age of 45 years. She was a daughter of Rev. David B. Cumming, the first circuit preacher the Holston Conference ever appointed in Western North Carolina, and is now a member of the Indian Mission Conference. C. T. Carroll

The following was adopted by the Quarterly Conference of the Canton circuit, North Georgia Conference... Rev. Andrew Gramling, who was born on the 21st of November 1783 and died in Cherokee county, Ga.... admitted into the S. C. Conference Jan. 10th 1810 and served the Laurens circuit that year and the Rutherford circuit in 1811. Brother Gramling was married to Rebecca, daughter of John and Sidney Foster of South Carolina, Nov. 10th 1811. Mother Gramling was born Oct. 28th 1794 and survived her husband but a short time.

Mrs. Sarah E. Hubbard, daughter of Charles M. Berry of Newton county, Ga., was born May 28th 1830; married to W. L. Hubbard 24th Dec., 1848 and died in Atlanta, Ga., Oct. 19th 1874. She was of Baptist parentage.

William O. Lee was born in South Carolina, Sept. 29th 1820; was moved in infancy to Gwinnett county, Ga; married Miss L. A. Wideman of Meriwether county, Aug. 3d 1843; settled in that county in 1846 and remained there until his death, Oct. 18th 1874. W. J. Cotter

Mrs. Lucy Jane Shelnutt, wife of Hon. N. Shelnutt and daughter of Wm. and Sarah Christian, was born in Elbert county, Ga., November 2d 1819 and died in Bowdon, Carroll county, Ga., Oct. 22d 1874. W. C. Dunlap

Miss Lou Clarke Reese, daughter of Dr. J. T. and the late Mrs. C. F. Reese, was born Sept. 6th 1852; died in Newnan, Ga., Oct. 16th 1874.

Wm. E. Howard was born in Albemarle county, Va., May 9th 1804; died in Thomas county, Ga, Sept. 21st 1874. P. H. Crumpler

Miss Martha Elizabeth Crawford, daughter of William G. and Sarah B. Crawford, died in Auburn, Ala., Oct. 15th 1874, in her nineteenth year. E. F. Hurt

Father William H. Drummond of Polk county, Ga., died Aug. 19th 1874, at the advanced age of 76 years. In 1823 he joined the Presbyterian church. Jas. W. Trawick

Issue of November 18, 1874

Died

In Monroe county, Ga., Oct. 6th 1874, George Augustus Allcorn, son of G. B. and N. E. Allcorn, aged 3 years, 10 months and 24 days.

Susie Dawson, infant daughter of Americus C. Mitchell, Jr., and Susie Dawson Mitchell, of Glennville, Ala., died on the 29th of August 1874.

Obituary

Mrs. Louisa C. Jones, daughter of Col. Charles S. and Mrs. Elmina Guyton, was born March 10th 1837; married Col. Seaborn Jones, Oct. 18th 1857; died at Rockmart, Ga., August 27th 1874. Samuel P. Jones

Mrs. Sarah Ann Gordon Conley, wife of J. R. Conley, daughter of X. G. and L. A. McFarland and sister of the writer, was born in Walker county, Ga., April 22d 1819 and died Nov. 1st 1874. J. B. McFarland

Brother Israel C. Parnell was born December 28, 1805, and died August 24, 1874. At the commencement of the late war he was the father of eighteen living children. L. M. Hamer

Mr. George H. Fisher was born near White Sulphur Springs, Va., moved with his parents to Florida in boyhood, and died in Leon county, Fla., Oct. 8, 1874. He leaves a wife and three daughters. R. H. Howren

Rev. Chambers Edgar Land was born in Spartanburg, S. C., 8th of May 1833 and died in Monroe, N. C., Oct. 21st 1874. M. V. Sherrill

Robt. B. Baird, Jr., died near Alton, Richland Parish, La., Oct. 23d 1874, for eighteen years, ten months and seventeen days. he was born in Pickens county, Ala., Dec. 6th 1855, and immigrated with his parents from Monroe county, in that State, to Richland Parish, La., in January 1873.

Robert B. Fagin, son of Hon. Geo. M. Fagin of Houston co., Ga., was born May 12th 1860 and died in Macon on 29th of October 1874. S. S. Sweet

Mr. D. U. McNeil was born March 9th 1815 and died Nov. 3d 1874.

Mrs. Rebecca Brooks died at Centerville, Leon county, Fla., Oct. 21st 1874, aged 50 years. R. H. Howren

Mrs. Maggie Lenora Brockinton, daughter of Wm. G. M. and Mary Ann Quarterman was born Nov. 23d, 1839 and died at Spring Bluff, Camden county, Ga., Nov. 1st 1874. She joined the Baptist Church several years ago with her husband. In July 1873 they joined the M. E. Church, South. T. S. Armistead. Southern Presbyterian please copy.

Mrs. Martha W. Theus, daughter of J. E. and M. E. Withington, was born in 1844 and died Sept. 12, 1874. H. H. Parks

Mrs. Elizabeth Benham, wife of Major Willis Benham, died in Bartow county, Ga., Nov. 7th 1874, in the 84th year of her age. L. J. Davies

Issue of November 25, 1874

Rev. Wm. M. Fincher was born in Mecklenburg county, N. C., May 20th 1794; moved to Jasper county, Ga., in 1817; married Mrs. Diodema Graves (daughter of Isaac McClendon) in 1818; moved to Troup county, Ga; died September 28th 1874.

Mrs. Melissa Lucretia McReary was born in Twiggs county, Ga., in 1808, was married to Mr. Isaac McReary in 1829; moved to Sumter county in 1832, died in Americus, October 11th 1874.

Father Lewis Wimberly of Talbot county, Ga., died at his son's in Centreville, Oct. 22d 1874. He had nearly finished his seventy-seventh year. L. B. Payne

Miss T. Amanda Long, daughter of Nathaniel A. and Lydia Long, died in Stewart county, Ga., Nov. 4th 1874, aged near 13 years.

Dr. John Holland, a local preacher of the Methodist Episcopal Church, South, was born in Charleston, S. C., in 1810; died near Ninety-Six, Abbeville county, S. C., Oct. 3d 1874.

Mrs. Carrie H. Law, beloved wife of R. Lide Law and daughter of Dr. John Holland, died at her home in Darlington county, S. C., September 23d 1874, aged 24 years.

John M. Graham was born in Lumpkin, Ga., Jan. 4th 1849 and died Nov. 5th 1874. A. J. Dean

Mrs. Nancy J. Driggers, wife of Stephen A. Driggers and daughter of Thomas and ---- Thigpen, died Aug. 13th 1874, aged about twenty-eight years. W. H. F. Robarts

Miss Sarah A. Lowe, daughter of James and Lodisca C. Lowe, deceased, was born in Morgan county, Ga., November 18th 1842, and died in Warren county, Ga., November 6th 1874. J. M. Armstrong

Abraham Thomas was born in Georgetown, S. C., in 1805 and died in Fowlstown, Decatur county, Ga., September 29th 1874. Thomas K. Leonard

Adolphe E. Beckman of Georgetown, S. C., died Nov. 6th 1874, aged 56 years, 5 months and 7 days. He was a native of Charleston. L. Wood.

John Pasco, father of Rev. F. Pasco, Florida Conference, M. E. Church, South, was born in Lancaster, England, August 18, 1800, and died in Charlestown, Mass., Sept. 12th 1874. His Son.

Tribute of Respect to Rev. John W. McGehee from Greenville and Trinity Quarterly Conference.

Issue of December 2, 1874

Mrs. Mary Johnson, whose maiden name was Thweatt, was born in Hancock county, Ga., August 6th 1797; married General Wm. Flewellen, Nov. 3rd 1814, who died August 31st 1835; was married again, November 24th 1842, to Col. J. N. Johnson, with whom she lived until September 7th 1874, when she was left a widow the second time; died November 1st 1874, at Andrew Female College, where she had gone to spend the evening of her life with her son, A. H. Flewellen, the President of the College. L. Pierce

Mrs. Eliza A. R. Powell was born near Wilmington, N. C., in 1801, and died at the home of her youngest daughter, Mrs. L. J. Carey, near Stilesboro, Ga., Sept. 5th 1874. She was the eldest daughter of Rev. Richard Holmes, who was for many years a local preacher of the Methodist Church in Georgia. In 1818, in Monticello, Ga., she was married to Dr. Norborne B. Powell, late of Cunnenuggee, Ala., whom she survived nearly twelve years. R. H. Powell. The New Orleans and Nashville Christian Advocates will please copy.

Miss Maria Julia Gerry died in Lake City, Fla., Oct. 12, 1874, aged 28 years. She was the daughter of the late Rev. John L. Gerry, one of the pioneers of Methodism in Florida. Jas P. DePass

Mrs. Rowena Ella Hill, daughter of Samuel M. and Amanda M. V. Latimer, was born at Merry Oaks, Stewart county, Ga., March 19th 1845; died in Lumpkin, Ga., November 13th 1874. A. J. Dean

Mrs. Caroline Elenor Garrett, consort of W. J. Garrett and daughter of Col. T. A. and Mrs. C. M. Lathan, was born in Campbellton, Ga., November 13th 1838 and died in Atlanta, Ga., October 18, 1874. About two years ago she joined the Baptist Church.

Mrs. Francis E. Dean, whose maiden name was Mouchet, was born in Abbeville district, S. C., March 5th 1835, and died at Midway, Gadsden county, Fla., Oct. 14, 1874. Samuel Woodberry

Mrs. S. Goodwin, widow of James Goodwin, was born Feb. 12th 1804 and died Nov. 15th 1874. She joined the Methodist Church at Little Swamp in 1822. Thos Raysor

James R. Turner was born in Hancock county, Ga., November 8, 1807 and died near Villa Rica, Carroll county, October 14th 1874. Sanford Leake

Father F. B. Burnham was born in Connecticut in 1800 and died Oct. 11th 1874. He moved to this country when a boy and served his apprenticeship as a tailor. He leaves many children, grandchildren and friends. W. L. Mangum

Archie Brown, eldest son of T. and Flora Brown, died Sept. 7th 1874, aged fourteen years.

Mrs. Thomas McGill, formerly Mrs. C. W. Rabb, died in Fairfield county, S. C., Nov. 2, 1874, aged thirty-nine years.

Issue of December 9, 1874

Died

In Nashville, Tenn., Nov. 27th 1874, Mrs. Elizabeth Jane Loomis, wife of C. E. Loomis, in the 39th year of her age.

Obituary

Rev. Joseph Tarply Smith was born in Franklin county, Ga., May 27th 1816 and died in Clayton county, Ga., near Jonesboro, October 28th 1874.

John H. McGaughey was born Dec. 23d 1825 and died near Red Clay, Ga., Oct. 18th 1874. J. H. Huff

My father, James Gillen, died Oct. 18, 1874, in the seventy-fourth year of his age. He was born in Catholic parents in Savannah, Ga., but joined the Methodist Church in 1817. He married Margaret M. Clarke, of Liberty county, Ga., in 1827, and soon after emigrated to Florida, and settled permanently in Duval county. He leaves a wife and six children. E. W. G.

Mrs. Nancy Prickett, whose maiden name was Sewell, was born Dec. 19th 1804 and died Oct. 25th 1874. On the 8th of February 1827, she was married by her brother-in-law, the late Rev. W. J. Parks, to Jacob Prickett, who died Sept. 28th 1849. They moved from Franklin to Morgan county, where they lived about twenty years. After the death of her husband, she moved to Meriwether county, where she lived from 1850 to the close of her life. W. J. Cotter

Daniel Miller was born in Orangeburg county, South Carolina in 1790. Christian Neighbor please copy.

Mrs. Mary A. M. Blood, wife of Col. C. H. Blood, and daughter of Moses and Mildred Harris, was born in Wayne county, Ga., Sept. 19th 1821, and died in Boston, Ga., Nov. 5th 1874. She was first married to Mr. Joseph J. Oneal in 1838; left a widow with five small children in 1853. She was married to Col. Blood, June 6th 1861, by whom she leaves one daughter. W. M. Watts

Mrs. Rebecca F. Pugh, wife of Dr. W. A. Pugh, and daughter of J. G. Jordan, died in Boston, Ga., Nov. 8th 1874. She was married to her now bereaved husband, Dec. 16th 1869. W. M. Watts

Mrs. Martha Ann Cobb, relict of Mr. W. T. Cobb, died in Suwannee county, Florida, Oct. 3d 1874, aged 44 years. Wm. C. Collier

Mrs. Ann Elizabeth Harris died Oct. 6th 1874, in her 34th year.

T. W. Loyless was born in Columbia county, Ga., Sept. 12th 1844, and died in Dawson, Ga., Nov. 3d 1874. On 14th of November 1866 he was married to Miss Sue M. Alderhoff, who with two children, are left to mourn.

Issue of December 16, 1874

Died

John Wesley Tuten, infant son of Charles D. and Curtis W. Tuten, of Madison county, Ga., was born Feb. 5th 1872, and died Nov. 2d 1874.

Obituary

Mrs. Elizabeth W. Hardaway, wife of Robt. H. Hardaway, and daughter of Nathanael R. and Temperance Mitchell, of Thomas county, Ga., was born December 24th 1820; married April 10th 1839, died November 4th 1874. R. H. Hardaway

Mrs. Nancy V. McCraw was born in Brunswick county, Va., March 23d 1800 and died at the residence of her daughter, Mrs. R. I. Ezell, near Lochapoka, Ala., Oct. 13, 1874. When a child, her father, John Bass, settled near Eatonton, Ga., where he spent the remainder of his life. She was married June 8th 1820 to Shepard B. Saunders, who died in 1840, leaving her with three children. The eldest, Rev. Wm. B. Saunders, was a faithful Methodist minister. It was at the home of the second that she died. The youngest, Rev. R. M. Saunders, is a member of the Virginia Conference. After living a widow twelve years, she was married to Major W. M. McCraw. Four years ago last May, she was a second time left a widow.

Mrs. Mary Elvira Moor, wife of F. A. Moor, Esq., was born in Rutherford county, N. C., March 12th 1811; was married April 1st 1834; died in Forsyth county, Ga., while on a visit to her son, Joseph L. Moore, November 19th 1874. She leaves eight living children. H. P. Bell

Mrs. Louisa R. Moore, wife of H. G. Moore, was born in Walker county, Ga., December 20th 1846; died in the same county, October 13th 1874. G. W. Thomas

Mrs. Ann Eliza Harwell, whose maiden name was Rivers, was born in Jasper county, Ga., May 18th 1818; married Wm. S. Harwell, Oct. 10th 1839, and died in Troup county, Ga., November 22d 1874.

Brother Archey T. Harberson, of St. George's circuit, South Carolina Conference, died October 16th 1874, aged forty-five years. He leaves a widow and six children.

Marcus A. Campbell, youngest son of S. A. and M. A. Campbell of Oglethorpe county, Ga., died October 25th 1874, aged sixteen years, four months and seventeen days.

<u>Issue of December 30, 1874</u>

Died

Linton Marvin, only son of Dr. E. W. and Georgia A. Watkins, aged two years and one month, died Sunday, Dec. 13th at their home in Elijah, Ga.

In Eufaula, Ala., on 17th Sept. 1874, Pauline Elizabeth, infant daughter of J. F. and F. E. Scaife, aged two months and seven days.

Obituary

Rev. John William McGehee, son of Rev. Thos. F. and Sarah E. McGehee, was born in Meriwether county, Ga., July 31st 1833, and died at White Sulphur Springs, Ga., Oct. 7th 1874.

Mrs. Sarah Van Horn Jackson, wife of Joseph B. Jackson, was born in Bucks county, Penn., Aug. 2d, 1811, and died in Talbotton, Ga., Nov[?] 16th 1874.

Ludie Danielly Smith, eldest daughter of A. and M. E. Danielly, and wife of Newton Smith, died Nov. 10th 1874, in Crawford county, Ga., at the home of her maternal grandfather, James B. Blassengame, being twenty-two years old. J. Fletcher Weathersbee, Sen. Congregational Methodist please copy.

Oliver Danforth was born in Hancock county, Ga., Aug. 23d 1830, and died in Macon, Ga., Nov. 1st 1874. His wife and five children survive him. Jas. O. Branch

Mrs. Ann Oliver was born in Richmond county, Ga., March 10th 1801, and died in Decatur county, Ga., November 25th 1874. J. W. Weston

Mrs. Mary Maffett was born Feb. 14th 1824 and died in Gwinnett county, Ga., Oct. 24th 1874.

Mrs. Elizabeth Stapleton was born in Wayne county, Ga., March 17th 1796 and died at her daughter's, Mrs. Williams, at Suwanee Station, Florida, Nov. 28th 1874. Jas. S. Mikell

Laura Jane Hyer, daughter of Rev. Wm. and Mary Stewart of Newton county, Ga., and wife of Mr. Wm. L. Hyer of Atlanta, was born January 16th 1836 and died Oct. 18th 1874. W. R. Branham

Tribute of Respect from Washington Street Methodist Church, Columbia, S., C., to Robert Bryce.

<u>Issue of January 6, 1875</u>

[on page 1]: Memorial of Robert Bryce. Robert Bryce was born in Glasgow, Scotland, January 6th 1798. His parents, with their family, removed to this country about the year 1802, and soon after settled in Columbia, S. C. [one and one-half columns]

Obituary

Mrs. Harriet A. Strother, widow of Dr. John W. Strother, was born in Monroe county, Ga., in 1817, and died from the results of an accidental injury in Barnesville, Nov. 29, 1874. She was the oldest child of Charles T. Caldwell, one of the oldest citizens and the first Methodist in Monroe county. G. G. Smith

Mrs. Caroline Elder, widow of J. W. Elder, Esq., was born in Pike county, Ga., near Barnesville, and died in Barnesville, Nov. 8th, aged 47. She was the daughter of Isaiah and Amelia Holmes. G. G. Smith

Mrs. Sallie Brinson was born in Schley county, Ga., March 3d 1847, was married to Simeon Brinson, Nov. 13th 1867; died in Decatur county, Ga., Nov. 3d 1874. J. W. Weston

James Marvin died near Combahee Ferry, Colleton county, S. C., Nov. 30th 1874, in the fiftieth year of his age. He left a wife and children. A. English Williams

Benjamin Tutt died at his residence in Lincoln county, Ga., Sept. 30th 1874, in this eighty-third year. N. C. Ware

Jefferson Lamar Rockwell, eldest son of Geo. and Maria K. Rockwell, was born in Barnesville, Ga., March 7th 1850, and died there Sept. 16th 1874. G. G. Smith

Eleanor Wright, daughter of Dr. W. A. Wright, died in Barnesville, Sunday night the 15th November 1874, aged eighteen years. G. G. Smith

Brother Archie T. Harberson died Oct. 14th 1874, while on his way from Mt. Carmel Camp-ground. He had been a class leader at Murray's Church, St. George's circuit. A. English Williams

Mrs. Lucinda K. Strange was born Oct. 12th 1800 and died Nov. 25th 1874. She was on a visit at the house of her son-in-law, Mr. George Stewart. W. A. Hodges

Tribute of Respect from Crawford circuit, South Georgia conference, to Rev. J. L. Avant.

Issue of January 13, 1875

Died

Rachel Armida, youngest daughter of Charles and Ella Harby, died at Station 5, Florida, Nov. 30th 1874.

Obituary

Mrs. Lula Thomas, wife of Mr. W. B. Thomas and daughter of Dr. Eustace W. Speer, died in Athens, Ga., December 18th, aged twenty-four years and three months. P. A. Heard

Joseph Benson Dunwody, son of Rev. James Dunwody, of the South Georgia Conference, was born in Crawford county, Ga., July 14th 1831 and died December 24th 1874. W. M. D. Bond

Mrs. Caroline A. Wolfe died September 17th 1874 at the residence of her daughter, Mrs. N. S. Beckam in Lexington county, S. C., in the 70th year of her age. She was a daughter of the late George Kaigler of Lexington county, and relict of Joseph A. Wolfe, who died in June 1852.

Miss Ella Wright, daughter of Dr. W. A. and Mrs. Wright, was born in Barnesville, Ga., Jan. 20th 1857 and died Nov. 15th 1874. Little Duncan, a brother of Ella's, born Jan. 31st 1871 and died Nov. 26th 1874.

Issue of January 20, 1875

Died

Henry Erroll, only child of W. H. and N. E. Miller, was born Nov. 7th 1875 and died near Benton, Ala., Dec. 20th 1874.

Annie Nowlan, youngest child of J. H. and Hattie A. Sauney[?], died in Savannah, Ga., November 30th 1874, aged 17 months and 2 days.

Obituary

Mrs. Catharine M. Barnes, daughter of Thomas C. and Louisa H. McEntire, was born in Georgia, June 13, 1846; was married to Mr. Jesse Barnes in Newton, Dale county, Alabama, January 3d 1875. A. Dowling

Bro. John W. Southern died near Greenville, S. C., October 29th 1874, in the seventy-second year of his age.

Mary Amaryllis McCall, wife of George E. McCall and daughter of the late James Henkle, was born in Chester county, S. C., June 22d, 1849; was married October 15th 1872; and died in Darlington county, S. C., October 16th 1874. John O. Wilson

Mrs. Sarah N. Eans was born in Halifax co., N. C., June 22d 1792, and died in Macon, Ga., December 6th 1874. Jas. O. Branch

My mother, Mrs. Virginia Smith Lyon of Abbeville county, S. C., daughter of Robert and Mary Powell Delph, was born March 28th 1810; was married to Wm. Lyon, April 6th 1830; died December 6th 1874. Her Son. Nashville Advocate please copy.

Miss Elizabeth Zinn was born and reared in South Carolina; died in Jasper county, Ga., october 15th 1874, in her eighty-sixth year.

William Cheshure died in Hamilton county, Florida, about the middle of October last; about seventy-five years of age. He was born in North Carolina, but came to Florida near fifty years since. J. M. Hendry

Mrs. Vashti M. Phillips was born Jan. 13th 1855 and died in Alachua county, Fla., Nov. 3d, 1874. She was the daughter of John and Elizabeth Little--their youngest child. She was married to Mr. Littleton J. Phillips, January 4th 1874. Isaac Munden

Mrs. Keren H. Stewart, relict of Daniel Stewart, died in Dallas county, Ala., December 26th 1874, aged 69 years. P. R. McCrary

Bro. Marion Large died December 2d 1874. He leaves a wife and four children. J. J. Reynolds

Tribute of Respect to Rev. C. L. Gaillard from Pendleton circuit, South Carolina Conference.

Issue of January 27, 1875

Mrs. Ann Dawson Rivers, daughter of Turner and Sallie Persons, was born in Warren county, Ga., Dec. 13th 1815; married Col. Thos. H. B. Rivers, Dec. 13th 1835; died in Glennville, Ala., Dec. 14th 1874. Wm. A. McCarty

Mrs. Harriet S. Gunn, widow of Wm. S. Gunn and sister of Harris T. Wyatt, was born in Lunenburg county, Va., June 2nd 1808; died Nov. 18th 1874, near Quincy, Fla. Henry Ed. Partridge. Richmond Christian Advocate please copy.

Mrs. Mary John, consort of Daniel John, Esq., was born in Marlboro county, S., C., April 6th 1796; died near the place of her birth, Oct. 21st 1874. J. A. Mood

R. J. Gregg was born in Marion county, S. C., Aug. 10th 1800; married to Miss Zilpha Evans, April 14th 1818; died at Marion, S. C., Nov. 2d 1874. A. J. Stokes

John W. Stoy died in Augusta, Ga., on Dec. 23d 1874. He was born in that city, June 3d 1810. He was for some years employed as agent of the Methodist Book Depository in Charleston.

Mrs. Mary Shirling was born April 15th 1792 and died in Putnam county, Ga., at the home of her only son, B. B. Odom, Dec. 1st 1874. She was married twice, first to brother Winbourn Odom, and after his death to Isam Shirling, both of whom died before her. She joined the Methodist Church in North Carolina, before her first marriage. W. L. Wootten, Jr. New Orleans Advocate please copy.

Mrs. T. E. Stewart, whose maiden name was Scott, was born in Scriven county, Ga., June 11th 1842; was married March 17th 1867.

Richard Lane, only son of Rev. R. Lane, formerly of the Georgia Conference, died Dec. 7th 1874, at his father's residence near Jefferson, Texas, being nearly 19 years of age. S. G. Cotton.

Henry Lester died in Quincy, Fla., Nov. 15th 1874, aged 33 years. Henry Ed. Partridge

Tribute of Respect from South Carolina Conference at Greenville, to H. B. Green and Malcom V. Woods.

Issue of February 3, 1875

Died

Died, October 29th 1874, Lalla Sullivan, second daughter of Gen. L. Mims and Mrs. Mary V. Sullivan, of Greenville, S. C., aged four years.

John Whitfield Frazier, eldest son of Arthur and Antoinette Frazier, was born April 7th 1873 in Lee county, Ala., and died Dec. 19th 1874.

Haywood Anderson Frazier, youngest son of Arthur and Antoinette Frazier, was born Oct. 7th 1874 and died Jan. 17th 1875.

Obituary

Mrs. Isabel G. Brewer was born in Sumter District, South Carolina, August 13th 1799; married to John R. Brewer, March 28th 1816; left a widow February 18th 1822; moved to Montgomery county, Ala., in 1827 where she remained until her death, January 7th 1875. She leaves one son and four grand-children. C. S. Huey

Mary Annie Elizabeth Grainger, only daughter of H. E. and M. A. C. M. Grainger, of Charleston, S. C., died October 17, 1874, in her eighteenth year of age. Her body reposes in the grave yard of Bethel Church, in this city.

Martha Bedell, wife of Dr. Charles Bedell, died at Hamilton, Harris county, Georgia, January 8th 1875. Martha Rogers grew up a bright girl... married to Charles Bedell, a step-son of Col. William C. Osborn of Waverly Hall. Henry W. Hilliard

Mrs. Sarah Elizabeth Game, wife of R. B. Game, died October 29th 1874, near Mullins Depot, in Marion county, S. C., aged 42 years and 9 months. She was married June 28th 1854. S. Campbell

Mrs. Mary Maxley was born in Burke co., Georgia; removed to Emanuel county about thirty years ago; died December 28th 1874. She leaves an aged husband and six children. W. J. Flanders

Mrs. Mamie P. Griffin, wife of Rev. W. J. Griffin and daughter of the late Hon. Robert H. Dixon, of Talbot county, Ga., was born January 6th 1856 and died near Hampton, Ga., January 6th 1875. She had been married not quite a year. Jno. D. Gray

Mrs. Evelina Geesling, relict of James M. Geesling and daughter of Anderson and Jane Smith, died near Hickory Flat, Alabama, Nov. 28th 1874, in her 32d year. She was married on 1860 but was bereaved of her husband in about eighteen months, and returned to her parents.

Mrs. Elizabeth H. Fouche died on the 10th of December 1875, in Wilkes county, Ga., in the 62d year of her age. W. W. Lampkin

Miss Nancy J. Ross, daughter of Rev. John Ross, died near Gordon, Wilkinson county, Ga., December 19th 1874, in her fifteenth year.

Issue of February 10, 1875

Died

The only child of Rev. I. C. G. and Mrs. S. A. B. Rabun was born Sept. 4th 1874, and died Jan. 16th 1875.

Obituary

Edward Wesley Mayfield was born in Warren county, North Carolina, November 24th 1792 and died in Franklin county, Georgia, January 7th 1875. He was married December 5, 1816, to Miss Mary D. Allen, with whom he lived for fifty-eight years. Sister Mayfield still lives. J. D. Gunnels

Mrs. Caroline M. Latham, whose maiden name was Smith, was born in Clark county, Ga; and died in Campbellton, Ga., Jan. 8th 1875. In early life her father moved to Campbellton, where she grew up and was married to Col. Thomas A. Latham. Jno. M. Bowden

Brother John Rogers, son of Drura and Rhoda Rogers, was born in Jasper county, Georgia, May 1st 1802; in 1824 or 1825 he removed to Henry county; remained there until his death, Jan. 2d 1875. W. H. Speer

Mrs. E. S. Sullivan, whose maiden name was Vaughan, of Amelia Island, Fla., wife of Dr. J. M. Sullivan, died in Greenville county, S. C., Dec. 18th 1874, aged 46 years. She was married to Dr. Sullivan, June 4th 1858, and was his second wife. J. M. Carlisle

Mrs. Charlotte DuBose was born in Clarendon county, S. C., in 1788 and died in Manning, S. C., Jan. 1st 1875. If she had a surviving relative, she did not know it. She made her home with Dr. H. H. Huggins and family for many years. J. B. Platt

Hiram Scarbrough was born near Dublin, Laurens county, Ga., March 25th 1821; married Miss W. B. Newsom, Nov. 12th 1839; subsequently moved to Texas, and died near Leesburg, Camp county, Texas, January 7th 1875. He has left a wife and four grown children. M. F. Rosser. Texas Christian Advocate please copy.

Brother John C. Hodge was born in 1812; died Nov. 8th 1874. C. C. Fishburne

Thomas M. Butler died at the residence of brother John S. Andrews, Liberty county, Ga., January 12th 1875, aged 13 years and four months.

Tribute of Respect from Timmonsville circuit, Darlington county, S. C., to John Josey.

Issue of February 17, 1875

Mrs. R. M. Jones, wife of Rev. James Jones of the North Georgia Conference, my dear mother, was born in Abbeville District, S. C., February 18th 1808 and died in Senoia, Ga., December 22, 1874. She was converted in her fourteenth year, in a class-meeting at Randle's meeting-house, after her removal to Georgia. She married my father in the spring of 1828. R. F. Jones

Alfred Raysor, Esq., died in Jefferson county, Florida, November 27th 1874, in the seventy-first year of his age. He was born in Colleton county, S., C., November 22d 1801, where he lived until past the meridian of life. Daughter-in-law

Mrs. Evaline W. Leslie, wife of Rev. H. W. Leslie, died at Wytheville, Virginia, January 12th 1875, in the thirty-second year of her age. The Episcopal Methodist will please copy.

Mrs. Caroline M. King, wife of Dr. H. H. King and daughter of Thomas Greenwood and Ann Leonora Greenwood, and step-daughter of Rev. Bishop Jas. O. Andrew, died in Greensborough, Ga., December 16th 1874, in the fifty-second year of her age. My daughter-in-law... Luther M. Smith

Mrs. Phoebe Gault was born near Petersburg, Va., March 11th 1782 and died in Union county, S. C., January 23d 1875. When she was about ten years old, her father removed to Prince Edward, where she was married to Zechariah Bevis. Soon after her marriage, in 1803, she removed with her husband to Georgia. In 1806, she came to Union District, South Carolina. Soon after this, her husband died, and in 1814, she was married to Robbin Gault. After his death in 1837, she returned to Georgia where she remained until 1866. She then came back to South Carolina and lived with her son, Wm. Bevis, until her death. John B. Wilson

Mrs. Mary Octavia Terry, daughter of Benjamin F. and Elizabeth A. Jones, was born in Abbeville District, S. C., May 14th 1833; married to Wm. S. Terry, November 12th 1856; moved to Hamburg, Ashley county, Arkansas, in February 1871; died there January 17th 1875. She left a husband and eight children. A. B. Winfield. Christian Neighbor please copy.

Sister Elizabeth Roman, daughter of the late Rev. John and Elizabeth Leverman, of Augusta, Ga., was born January 2d 1808 and died at the residence of her son-in-law, Bro. Sledge, in Woodlawn, near Augusta, Ga., November 24th 1874. J. E. Evans

Joseph Henry Villeneuve was born July 6th 1835 in Charleston, S. C., and died December 28th 1874, in Cheraw, S. C., of pneumonia. He leaves a wife and six children.

Issue of February 24, 1875

Brother Wm. A. Wiggins was born Oct. 7th 1828 and died near the place of his nativity in Fort Valley, Ga., January 22d 1875.

Henry Jefferson David was born in South Carolina in 1816 and died at Mt. Pleasant, Gadsden county, Florida, January 18th 1875. Samuel Woodbery

Mrs. Cornelia Mary Grier, wife of W. K. Grier and daughter of C. B. and H. M. Sarvis, was born in Horry county, S. C., Oct. 14th 1833 and died in Georgetown county, S. C., January 20th 1875. L. A. Grier

Seth H. Hyatt was born June 17, 1838 in Macon county, N. C., and died Jan. 28, 1875 at Walhalla, S. C. J. Walter Dickson

Mrs. Mary Cherry, relict of Job. S. Cherry, was born in Williamston, Martin county, N. C., June 27th 1800; was married to J. S. Cherry in 1820; removed to Macon, Ga., in 1829, where she died January 31st 1875, at the residence of her son, Wm. A. Cherry. Arminius Wright

Mrs. Sarah J. Harrison was born in Fayette county, Ga., May 24th 1840, and died in the same county, January 15th 1875. Geo. E. Gardner

Mrs. Eliza A. Mitchell, sister of Mrs. Sarah J. Harrison, the subject of the foregoing obituary, was born in Fayette county, Ga., Sept. 14th 1855; died in the same county, Feb. 2d 1875. Geo. E. Gardner

Daniel J. Wright was born in Greene county, Ga., Aug. 8th 1825; died in Coweta county, Ga., Dec. 3d 1874. In 1852, Dec. 16th, he was married to Miss M. C. Brown, who died July 23, 1871, leaving him with six children. W. J. Cotter

Benjamin Moore was born in Marlboro county, S., C., May 25th 1812 and died January 5th 1875.

Mrs. Laura T. Dyches, consort of J. W. Dyches and daughter of H. J. and Mary Bond, formerly of Marion C. H., S. C., died at Leesburg, Fla., Nov. 21st, 1874, aged 25 years, 1 month and 15 days. She leaves a husband, two small children, a father, brothers and sisters. O. Eady

Issue of March 3, 1875

My father, Isaac Herbert, was born in Newberry county, S. C., June 19, 1801, and died in the same county, January 17th 1875. He was of Quaker parentage and was brought up in that faith and order... he, with my mother, joined the Methodist church. Thos. G. Herbert

Conrad Murph was born in South Carolina, February 6th 1786 and died at the residence of his son-in-law, B. T. Moore, in Houston county, Ga., December 26th 1874. F. A. Branch

Martha M. Rivers, wife of John Rivers and daughter of R. J. and Frances Whitaker, was born in Henry county, Ga., November 25th 1848, and died near the place of her birth, January 8th 1875.

Darling Barnes died February 12, 1875, near Bamberg, Barnwell county, S. C., in the seventy-eighth year of his age. P. F. Kistler

Mrs. Wineford A. Edwards, wife of W. P. Edwards, was born in Washington county, Ga., in 1807; was married in 1823, at Old Fort, in Jones county, Ga; moved from Jones to Talbot county (now Taylor) and was one of the original members of Rocky Mount Church, and was the last of these, save Robert Carson, now in Texas. Sister Edwards was the mother of eleven children, ten of whom survive her. She buried her husband in 1857. E. J. Rents

William G. Bell was born in Burke county, Ga., February 7th 1835 and died in Lee county, Ga., December 13th 1874. Waynesboro Expositor please copy.

Miss Ada Wilson, daughter of James W. and Martha E. Wilson, was born March 27th 1861 and died in Laurenceville, Ga., January 15th 1875.

My father, Henry Walker, was born and reared in Jasper county, Georgia, and died near the place of his birth, December 6th 1874, in his seventieth year. He leaves a widow and eight children.

Mrs. Pheraby Walker Danielly, wife of Mr. McD. Danielly, of Crawford county, Ga., was born in Warren county, Ga., in 1804; was married in 1822; died January 25th 1875.

Mrs. Amanda G. Minter, wife of L. D. Minter, deceased, died December 17, 1874, at Waverly, Lee county, Ala., aged 58. She was raised a Presbyterian but soon after her marriage, joined the Methodist Church.

Issue of March 10, 1875

Died

Maggie Smyth Ellison, infant daughter of Col. Wm. H. and Mrs. Mary C. Ellison, was born July 26th 1871 and died in Talbot Valley, Ga., Feb. 5th 1875.

In Charleston, S. C., on the 18th Jan. 1875, Bessie, aged 3 years and 11 months, and on the 25th Jan., Willie, aged 2 years and 10 months, children of William W. and Mary A. Pemberton.

Obituary

[issue torn-- first obituary notice largely obliterated]

Rev. Jno Josey was born in Sumter county, S. C., March 27th 1810, died December 30th 1875. W. L. Pegues

Sister Hattie Koger died at Round O, S. C., January 17th 1875, in her 23rd year. She leaves a husband and two children. A. E. Williams

My aunt, Mrs. Sophia Connor, wife of Jacob Connor, died in Orangeburg county, S. C., Dec. 31st 1874, in the 74th year of her age. She leaves a husband and children. W. Hutto

Ben. Hill McArthur, son of D. O. McArthur, Bibb county, Ga., died Feb. 17th 1875, in the 15th year of his age.

Charles Terry was born March 13th 1807 and died February 10th 1875. He was married to Miss Permelia McElroy in 1832. He lived near Pisgah church in Laurens circuit. John Attaway

Mr. Thomas Barron was born in Greene county, Ga., Oct. 22d 1802; was married to Miss Sabrina J. Stewart, March 1st 1829, and died in Talbot county, Ga., Jan. 15th 1875. He leaves an aged wife and children. W. H. Woodall

Sister Helen J. Porter, relict of Dr. John L. Porter, was born in Monroe county, Ga., Aug. 18th 1828; died in Lumpkin, Ga., Feb. 22nd 1875. A. J. Dean

Samuel V. Whitaker, son of R. J. and Frances Whitaker, was born in Henry county, Ga., August 15th 1837; died near his birthplace, January 11th 1875. He left a wife and seven children. M. V. Sowell

Mrs. Mary Elizabeth Fisher, daughter of Robert and Martha Sturges, and wife of Inman H. Fisher of Leon county, Florida, was born December 1834, and died February 19th 1875. E. L. T. Blake

Mrs. Catherine Blake, of St. James Santee, S. C., relict of the late John Blake, died Jan. 11th 1875, in the 80th year of her age. John S. Palmer, M. D.

Issue of March 17, 1875

Died

Bettie Kellam, daughter of S. J. and A. V. Kellam of Laurens county, Ga., was born October 17th 1866, and died in Macon, Ga., February 23d 1875.

Charles Olin Freeman, youngest son of W. C. and M. E. Freeman, died near Long Cane, Ga., February 15th 1875, aged 3 years and 6 months.

Obituary

Dr. John S. Hill of Troup county, Georgia, son of the late John Hill, and brother of the Hon. B. H. Hill, was born in Jasper county, Georgia, April 29th 1821; moved to Troup county in 1834, thence to Texas in 1840; after a few years he retired to his native state, where he died January 25th 1875. In 1848 he was married to Miss Sarah B. Cameron of Troup county. H. J. Ellis

Mrs. Elizabeth Crowder, wife of Mark H. Crowder, died in Merriwether county, Ga., January 7, 1875. She married May 12, 1840. She leaves a husband, aged father, and children. P. M. Ryburn

Mrs. Eliza Ann Clinkscales, whose maiden name was Black, relict of the late George B. Clinkscales of Abbeville county, S., C., was born in Abbeville county, April 3d, 1818, and died in Williamston, S. C., February 12th 1875. Samuel A. Weber

Thomas Singleton was born in Montgomery county, N. C., May 4th 1799 and died in Pickens county, S. C., February 8th 1875. He leaves five sons and one daughter.

Jacob M. R. Freeman was born June 15th 1858, was married December 9th 1874 to Miss Marla Haynes... died in two short months after his marriage. J. R. Mayson

William Clark Kirkland, son of the late Rev. W. C. Kirkland of the South Carolina Conference, was born in Beaufort county, S. C., September 16th 1846; married the only daughter of Rev. J. S. Burnett, in January 1869, and died in Spartanburg, S. C., January 26th 1875.

Mrs. Elizabeth W. Green, wife of Major Wm. M. Green, was born in Lancaster county, S., C., June 24th 1832; was married to Major Green, January 22d 1852; died in Sumter , S. C., January 22d 1875. W. H. Smith

Paul C. Osteen was born April 11th 1835; married Penelope Niblack, 30th May 1855; died in Columbia county, Fla., February 4th 1875. S. E. Phillips

Mrs. Lucinda Mayson, daughter of William and Mary Douglass, was born near Ninety Six, S. C., July 16th 1803; was married to J. L. Mayson, August 1822; died near Atlanta, Ga., February 3d 1875. Her son, President J. R. Mayson, wrote me "My parents moved to Georgia in January, 1827 and settled on the Chattahoochee, eight miles west of where Atlanta now stands." J. B. C. Quillian

Sallie C. Lipscomb, daughter of T. C. and S. C. Lipscomb, died at Ninety Six, Abbeville county, S., C., February 11th 1875, aged 22 years. J. W. Murray

Father Burgess Cheek died in Sumpter county, Ga., February 17th 1875, in the 81st year of his age. He lived many years in Franklin county, Georgia. T. H. Stewart

Brother Augustus M. Jenkins was born in Putnam county, Ga., December 9th 1858 and died near Eatonton, Ga., January 28th 1875. J. Lewis, Jr.

William R. Stevens, my brother, was born near Jeffersonville, Twiggs county, Ga., July 16th 1853, and died at Gordon, Ga., January 29th 1875. J. F. Stevens

Bro. D. J. Hayes, father-in-law of Bro. Freeman, was born August 18, 1825; died February 17th 1875. J. R. Mayson

Mrs. Susan V. Brabham, daughter of John and Cornelia Holly, was born February 24th 1838; was married to Dr. S. J. Brabham, November 3d 1858; died January 23d 1875, leaving a husband and three children.

Miss Leila Odeisa Watson, eldest daughter of Thomas Watson, of Merriwether county, Ga., died January 27th 1875, in her seventeenth year. William H. Watson, the next eldest, lingered until February 23d, when he died in his fifteenth year. F. M. T. Branson

Sister Dorcas Andrews was born January 1803; died in Liberty county, Ga., January 29th 1875. J. M. Marshall

Tribute of Respect to Dr. Joseph Benson Dunwoody who died Dec. 24th 1875, from Haynesville circuit.

Issue of March 24, 1875

Mrs. Frances A. Dixon, whose maiden name was Ashley, a member of St. James' Church, died in Augusta, Ga., on 12th of February 1875, in the 75th year of her age. She was a native of Lincoln county, Ga., but for many years had resided in this city. She was left a widow in 1844 with eleven children. Her husband's name was Henry Dixon.

William P. Murdock was born in Beaufort, S. C., January 17th 1809, was married to Sarah Williams of Bullock county, Ga., December 10th 1839; died near Welborn, Suwannee county, Florida, February 19th 1875. His eldest son, Rev. C. P. Murdock. Thomas A. Carruth

James Evans Wardlaw, son of Rev. W. J. Wardlaw of the North Georgia Conference, was born in Polk county, Ga., in 1867 and died in Augusta, Ga., on 1st of January 1875.

Mrs. Elizabeth W. Harmon, daughter of the late Pleasant Heath and wife of J. K. Harmon, was born in Clinton, Jones county, Georgia, May 20th 1827 and died in Macon, Georgia, February 11th 1875. Geo. G. N. MacD.

Mrs. Martha Pittman, widow of Col. J. J. Pittman, was born in Halifax county, N. C., July 31st 1801 and died in Marianna, Fla., Feb. 11th 1875. Twice she had been left a widow. She had been for many years a member of the Presbyterian Church. Southern Presbyterian please copy.

Reudolph Fowler, oldest son of James A. Fowler, died in Spartanburg, S. C., Feb. 20th 1875, aged just twenty-three years.

My wife, Mrs. Jane S. Crenshaw, was born in Scotland, April 5th 1813 and died at the residence of her son-in-law, John Sammons, in Terrell county, Ga., Feb. 24th 1875. She was left an orphan early in life. David Crenshaw

Brother Daniel J. Mann was born in Georgia, Feb. 29th 1802 and died in Baker county, Fla., March 1st 1875. He raised a large family. J. W. Barnett

Mrs. Rebecca White, whose maiden name was Pulliam, was born in Elbert county, Georgia, and died December 31st 1874, aged 87 years. Her husband, Stephen White, died only about one and a half years ago. Thos J. Adams

Miss Euanna L. Dial, daughter of Capt. W. C. and Mrs. Sarah A. Dial was born in Cherokee county, Ga., April 7th 1857 and died February 24th 1875. W. G. Hanson

J. Barber Ferguson was born May 5th 1823 and died in Chester county, S. C., Feb. 19th 1875. J. M. Boyd

J. T. M. Bentley, formerly of Henry county, Ga., died recently in Rockdale county, Ga., in the 23d year of his age.

B. C. Kirk of Kentucky, for about ten years resident in Charleston, S. C., died in this city, March 2d 1875. G. H. Wells

Mrs. Eliza Parker, relict of the late Isaac H. Parker of Newton county, Ga., died in Atlanta, Ga., January 14th 1875, in the sixty-fourth year of her age. Henry B. Parker, son of the above, died in the same city, January 16th in his twenty-sixth year. A communication from Mrs. Georgia E. Knox, daughter of sister of these persons....

Mrs. Elizabeth B. Sealy, wife of John Sealy, was born in Scottsborough, Jones county, Ga., July 22d 1800 and died at the residence of her son, P. J. Sealy, January 1st 1875. J. R. Owen

My mother, Mrs. Elizabeth Owen, was born in Haywood county, N. C., about 1804 and died in the same county January 7th 1875. She has left my dear father and eight children. J. R. Owen. Holston Christian Advocate please copy.

Sister Laura L. Felts, wife of Robert L. Felts, died January 17th 1875, in warren county, ga., aged 22 years.

Tribute of Respect to Isaac Herbert

Issue of March 31, 1875

Died

In Charleston, S. C., March 4th 1875, Eleanor Caroline Disher, only child of S. Y. and Julia O. Disher, aged 17 months.

Obituary

Elizabeth Wright died in Spartanburg, S. C., January 28th 1875, at the advanced age of ninety-three years. She was born in Brunswick county, Va., October 30th 1781, passed several years of early life in North Carolina, not far from Raleigh, and came to South Carolina about 1811. A. H. Lester

Mrs. Mary F. Lamkin, wife of Hon. S. C. Lamkin and daughter of Ebenezer and Elizabeth Williams, deceased, was born in Columbia county, Ga., January 12, 1839 and died February 12, 1875. R. A. Conner

Rev. A. J. Bryant was born February 12, 1836 and died in Chattooga county, Ga., December 21st 1874.

Mrs. Elizabeth Ronaldson was born in Twiggs county, Ga., March 23d 1815; was first married in 1832 to John B. Hodges, by whom she had six children, four of whom survive her; afterwards married to Maj. W. J. Ronaldson, who has been dead several years; died at Camilla, Ga., February 28th 1875. P. S. Twitty

Dr. John P. Smith was born January 4th 1839 and died in Miccosukia, Leon county, Fla., February 8th 1875. E. L. T. Blake

Eliza Virginia Jones, daughter of Rev. Simpson Jones of the South Carolina Conference was born in Darlington District, S. C., August 18th 1854, and died February 25th 1875. L. M. Hamer

Miss Lizzie E. Shi, daughter of James H. and P. C. Shi, was born in Morgan county, Ga., and died in Monroe county, Ga., December 8, 1874.

Miss Panola C. Price, youngest daughter of W. E. and E. M. price, was born in Glennville, Ala., March 27th 1861 and died January 17th 1875.

David L. Carn was born in Orangeburgh District, S. C., March 17th 1800; died in Centreville, Leon county, Fla., February 21st 1875. E. L. T. Blake

Wm. Jeffords died February 26th 1875, aged 87 years and 3 months. He assisted in putting up Pine Grove Church in Darlington circuit. W. L. Pegues

Mr. Sherrard Smith died near Greenwood, in Abbeville county, S. C., February 8th 1875, in the seventy-eighth year of his age. S. P. H. Elwell

Issue of April 7, 1875

Died

Talva B., only son of J. D. and E. T. Dobbs, aged 5 years, died March 22d 1875.

Randolph Woodward, son of John L. Woodward, died in Taylor county, Ga., January 21st 1875, aged 12 years.

Eliza Elon Crum, third daughter of David L. and Elizabeth Crum, died in Sumpter county, Florida, January 13th 1875, aged four years.

Obituary

My mother, Mrs. Samuel W. Tucker, of old Tabernacle Church, Belmont (formerly Union) circuit, S. C. Conference, died in the month of February 1875, at eighty-three years of age. J. Wofford Tucker

Mrs. Juliet M. Eison, whose maiden name was Brown, was born in Union county, S. C., January 8th 1823, and died near the place of her birth, January 28th 1875. She was married to Mr. James

Eison, October 16th 1842, who still survives her, and by whom she had fourteen children, all of whom are still living. On her sick bed she was admitted as a member of Sardis church. J. Claudius Miller

Mrs. Harriet Hanson, whose maiden name was Barrett, was born in Franklin county, Ga., Jan. 1st 1795, and died at the residence of her son-in-law, Col. Joe Wood, in Webster county, Ga., Jan. 25th 1875. In 1818, she was married to John Hanson of Morgan county, who preceded her some seven or eight years. W. R. Foote

Rev. David Murdock was born in South Carolina, Sept. 26th 1790, and died in DeKalb county, Ga., March 2d 1875. He joined the M. E. Church at Bush River, Anderson District, S. C., in May 1816. He moved to Newton county, Georgia in 1829. W. H. Potter

Francis Henry Kennedy was born in Sumter county, S. C., June 18th 1822; married Nov. 20th 1845, a daughter of T. M. Dick, M. D., and died at Mechanicsville, S. C., March 8th 1875. W. A. Rogers

Dr. Span Ragan was born in North Carolina, April 1st 1818; died in Terrell county, Ga., Jan. 24th 1875. In 1856 he was married to Miss Lieurany J. Speight, youngest daughter of Rev. Thos. Speight. J. R. Littlejohn

Mrs. Sarah Leonard, widow of P. L. Leonard, deceased, was born in Greene county, Ga., Sept. 22d 1800; died at the house of her son-in-law, Thos. Colwell, in Terrell county, Ga., Jan. 13th 1875. J. R. Littlejohn

Bannister A. Barksdale was born in Appling county ,Ga., April 24th 1854 and died in Orange county, Florida, Dec. 26th 1874. James Harris

Brother Latson Myers was born June 16th 1806; died in Glynn county, Georgia, Feb. 2d 1875. He leaves a wife and five children. J. W. Roberts

Mrs. Harriet Hardley Jordan was born in South Carolina, Sept. 30th 1822; was married to James M. Jordan, 28th Nov 1839; and died in Fort Valley, Georgia, March 15th 1875. S. H. J. Sistrunk

Tribute of Respect from Fort Valley and Marshallville charge, South Georgia Conference to Wm. A. Wiggins.

Tribute of Respect from Union Circuit, Tallahassee District, Florida Conference, to Alfred Raysor.

Issue of April 14, 1875

Died

Alice Boyd, daughter of R. G. and Mrs. Georgia Center, died at Graham, S. C., March 30th 1875, aged about 3 years.

Obituary

Sister Mary Francis Fort, consort of James A. Fort, whose maiden name was Harwell, was born in Hancock county, Ga., June 8th 1832; died in Stewart county, Ga., March 30th 1875. She was twice married--first to W. A. Williams, then to J. A. Fort; and leaves two families of her own, and one family of step-children. A. J. Dean

Mrs. Margaret E. Houston, whose maiden name was Roberts, was born in South Carolina, February 20th 1841; was married to Edward M. Houston, July 14th 1859; died in Wakulla county, Florida, February 17th 1875. Robert Martin

Giles G. Bonner, son of R. W. Bonner, died in Philadelphia, Pa., February 23d 1875, in the 20th year of his age.

Milton Eady, son of Rev. O. Eady, died at Adamsville, Sumter county, Fla., February 4th 1875, aged 12 years and 8 months.

Eliza J. Hartley was born in Bibb county, Ga., May 29th 1851; married to Bennett Hartley, November 7th 1872; died in Crawford county, Ga., February 19th 1875.

James Preston Richardson of Georgetown, S. C., died on the 23d of March 1875, aged 35 years, 4 months and 9 days, leaving a wife, four little girls, and an aged mother. L. Wood

Mrs. Susan R. Mathis, wife of William H. Mathis and daughter of George and Elizabeth Russell, was born in Rabun county, Ga., March 23d 1822; married January 14th 1840; died in Floyd county, Ga., January 13th 1875. B. E. L. Timmons

Issue of April 21, 1875

Died

Alice Kimbrough Pitts, daughter of H. W. and S. A. Pitts, was born January 5th 1870 and was killed by the storm, March 20th 1875, aged 5 years, 2 months and 15 days.

Mary Jones Pitts, second daughter of H. W. and S. A. Pitts, was born Dec. 25th 1867, and died from wounds inflicted by the storm, March 28th 1875, aged 7 years, 2 months and 26 days.

Obituary

Marion W. West, son of William and Sophronia E. West of Cherokee county, Ga., was born in Yancey county, N. C., Sept. 3d 1854 and died March 10th 1875.

Daniel McCormick was born in Abbeville District, S. C., and died at Berzellla, Columbia county, Ga., Sept. 29th 1875. W. A. Dodge. Long a member of Linwood S. S.

Mrs. R. Olivia Williams, wife of J. P. Williams and daughter of B. T. and P. A. C. Outland, was born in Wayne county, N. C., Jan. 13th 1856 and died in Horry county, S. C., april 4th 1875. She leaves a daughter. Wm. Thomas

Mrs. Mary A. Bigby died at her daughter's residence in Honea Path, S. C., March 13th 1875, in the seventy-sixth year of her age. S. P. H. Elwell

Lodrick Spicer was born in North Carolina and died in Houston county, Ga., March 7th 1875. He leaves a wife and five little children. S. S. Pennington

Miss Eliza M. Arthur, sister of Mrs. John Glass, died in Columbia, S. C., April 3d 1875, in the seventy-first year of her age.

Mrs. Susan Rebecca Blackman was born in Darlington District, S. C., March 8th 1837, and died in Suwanee county, Florida, March 24th 1875. Most of her early life was spent near Augusta, Georgia, until about 1852 when she removed with her father, Mr. Henry Gibbs, to Florida. On 6th of May 1854, she was married to Mr. Joab Blackman, left with eight children, one only a few weeks old, mourn the loss of a most excellent wife and mother. Thomas A. Carruth

Jacob A. Robinson, son of J. e. and M. S. Robinson, was born in Orangeburg county, South Carolina, Sept. 7th 1845 and died at the residence of J. M. Crews, his father-in-law, in Columbia county, Florida, Jan. 24th 1875. S. E. Phillips

Issue of April 28, 1875

Mrs. Clara A. Hunnicutt, whose maiden name was Atkinson, was born in Brunswick county, Va., March 12, 1812; and died in Coweta county, Ga., January 19, 1875. She had been twice married, first to Thomas Parks, the father of her children, and later to Dr. J. E. P. Hunnicutt, who survives her but advanced in years. R. F. Jones

Mrs. Ella Wyatt, wife of William R. Wyatt and daughter of Lemuel and Lucy Merrill, was born in Macon county, Alabama, January 11th 1847 and died in Chattooga county, Ga., February 12th 1875. In 1868 the family removed to North Georgia, where in 1869, February 24, she was married to Mr. W. R. Wyatt.

Mrs. Carrie Gramling, wife of Thomas A. Gramling and daughter of Col. H. C. Kellogg of Forsyth county, Ga., was born October 7th 1851; died in Atlanta, Ga., April 9th 1875. Robt. A. Eakes

Fannie E. Pitts, eldest daughter of H. W. and S. A. Pitts, was born April 7th 1861 and died March 20th 1875 in Harris county, near Hamilton, Ga. Geo. S. Johnston

Mrs. Eudocia W. Fort was born in 1792; died at the residence of Mr. John Hammond, her son-in-law, in Midway, near Milledgeville, Ga., March 31st 1875. She was the widow of Judge Fort, now about twenty years deceased.

Miss Sallie E. Gibson, second daughter of Thomas and Emily Gibson, was born in Russell county, Ala., December 18th 1858 and died in Lee county, Ala., February 7th 1875. W. W. Graham

Chesley Attaway died in Rome, Ga., March 26th 1875, in his 71st year. He left a devoted wife here; two children, one in Missouri, the other in Kansas.

Mrs. Mary Johnson died in Milledgeville, Ga., March 26th 1875.

Hiram Gillean was born May 9th 1807 and died February 7th 1875. Brother Gillean was converted and joined the Church in 1851 at Sugar Creek church, Cleveland circuit, Holston Conference.

Mrs. Mary Jane Hagin was born June 9th 1844; was married to Jas. S. Hagin, June 15th 1869; died April 10th 1875. She leaves a husband and four little children.

John Nickols was born in Lexington co., S. C., November 23d 1788 and died March 24th 1875.

Tribute of Respect from Summerville circuit, North Georgia Conference to Rev. A. J. Bryant.

Issue of May 5, 1875

Mrs. Mary R. Burke, mother of the associated editor of the Southern Christian Advocate, was born March 19, 1804, converted in Clarke county, Georgia. She was married to Richard E. Burke, January 27, 1825--died at the residence of her son-in-law, James Young, Esq., in Oglethorpe county, Georgia, 17th March 1875. Her ancestors and relatives were Presbyterians.

Martha Ann Dillon, eldest daughter of Benjamin and Elizabeth Williamson, was born in Scriven county, October 20, 1823; was married to D. James Dillon, November 10, 1846, and died April 8, 1875 in Brunswick, Georgia. J. O. A. Cook

John Harris died in Union county, South Carolina, in his seventy-seventh year, April 10, 1875. J. B. Wilson

Daniel Slade was born in Connecticut, December 3, 1800; removed to Eatonton, Ga., in 1834; was married November 30, 1836, and died February 27, 1875. J. Lewis, Jr.

John W. Hinton was born in Wake county, North Carolina, August 4, 1810 and died at Social Circle, Georgia, March 27, 1875. He came to Newton county about fort years ago. He married Miss Louisa Rogers, youngest daughter of the late Osborn Rogers. His oldest son, J. W. Hinton, Jr., of Social Circle. W. R. Branham

Mrs. Catharine R. Langston, wife of John T. Langston and daughter of Joseph Patterson, was born December 22, 1847, and died March 4, 1875. C. L. Fike

Dr. James M. Sullivan was born March 11, 1816 and died April 9, 1875. He was twice married; first to Miss Mims, and then to Miss Vaughn, who preceded him but a short time to the grave. He leaves eleven children. John Attaway

Miss Mattie C. Richardson, daughter of J. W. Richardson, Sr., was born August 16, 1852 and died in Morgan county, Georgia, March 4, 1875. S. L. Lupo

Tribute of Respect from Spartanburgh Station to Donald Fleming.

Tribute of Respect from Flowery Branch Circuit, Gainesville District, North George Conference to Rev. W. S. Williams, who died March 19, 1875.

Issue of May 12, 1875

Died

Nancy Louisa Gramling, daughter of William A. and Priscilla P. Gramling, and grand-daughter of C. W. Gramling, died from accidental burning in Madison county, Fla., April 18th, 1875, aged 5 years and 4 days.

Obituary

Mrs. Ann Saffold of Madison, Ga., died April 2d 1875, in the 83d year of her age, and in the same room which she had occupied for nearly 60 years. She was the last of the children of Maj. Oliver Porter, the sister of Mr. Anthony Porter of Savannah, Ga., and of Mr. John W. Porter of Madison, Ga., both of whom died many years ago. She was born in Greene county, Ga., January 8th 1793 and on 15 December 1813 was married to Adam G. Saffold, of Madison, Ga. She raised only two children-- a son Mr. Wm. O. Saffold, who died on the 6th of January last, and a daughter Mrs. Col. D. S. Johnson, now residing in Madison, in the old family mansion. A. Means

David Dickson was born in Hancock county, Ga., August 18, 1802 and died in Oxford, Ga., March 16th 1875. Luther M. Smith

Mrs. Lucinda J. Bates died April 4th 1875, in Cherokee county, Ga., aged fifty-two years. W. H. Sherman, M. D.

Mrs. Eliza Pace was born March 8th 1838; was married to Rev. John A. Pace in 1860 and died in Opelika, Ala., March 24th 1875. W. M. Motley

Mrs. Mary Downs, whose maiden name was Morrow, was born in 1821; was married to Joseph Pate in 1836 or '37; after his death, having lived a widow about six years, she married Isaiah Downs, with whom she lived happily until 1865 or '66 when he died; and died herself in Bryan county, Ga., March 19th 1875. W. J. Jordan

Mrs. Frances Day, whose maiden name was Hamby, was born in Pickens county, S. C., April 21st 1808; was married to Reuben Day in 1826' moved to Cherokee county, Ga., in 1852; where she remained until she died March 8th 1875. She was the mother of ten children, five of whom, with an affectionate husband, survive. W. C. Holbrook

Addie Robinson, wife of Col. S. H. Robinson and daughter of the late Dr. E. W. and Mrs. L. C. Jones of Fort Valley, died in Blakely, Early county, Ga., March 13th 1875.

Mrs. Nancy A. Elkins, whose maiden name was Sheppard, died in Washington county, Ga., February 18th 1875, in her forty-seventh year. She was first married to a Mr. Brown, by whom she had three children, and after his death, married Mr. Elkins. J. B. Culpepper

Mrs. Mariah A. Brown was born in Craven county, N. C., February 27th 1801 and died in Americus, Ga., April 22d 1875. While yet young, she removed to Florida.

William D. Lumpkin was born in Hall county, Georgia, April 23d 1810 and died in Walker county, Georgia, April 8th 1875. He leaves a widow, daughter and two sons. P. G. Reynolds

Issue of May 19, 1875

Died

At Warrenton, Ga., May 1st 1875, Addie Louise, daughter of Rev. R. W. Bigham, aged 4 years, one month and two days. She was buried at Milledgeville.

Obituary

Rev. Aaron G. Stacy, son of Rev. Jeremiah Stacy, was born near Morganton, Burke county, North Carolina, November 15, 1822; died in Austin, Texas, April 8, 1875. F. A. Mood

Rev. Edward Sessions, son of Edward and Mary Sessions, and brother of Rev. J. J. Sessions, of Terrell county, Georgia, was born near Georgetown, South Carolina, August 14, 1814, and died near Lake Butler, Florida, March 17, 1875. He leaves a wife and eight children. W. J. Morris

Thomas Kearney Cofield was born in Richland county, South Carolina, February 5, 1808 and died in Union county, South Carolina, April 14, 1875. In 1831 he married Anna Caldwell of Newberry. She has just attended him to his grave. He is buried at Ebenezer. J. E. Watson

J. W. Bradbury was born January 6, 1794 and died at Silver Creek Church, Floyd county, Georgia, March 21, 1875.

Hugh Allen Wooding was born in Burke county, Georgia, August, 26, 1849 and died March 29, 1875 in the same county. In his death a loving mother gives up the last of four sons; and of three daughters, but one remains.

Greenbury Buford was born in Scriven county, Georgia, January 1805; and died in the same county, February 16, 1875. He was married to Mary E. Ingram of Barnwell District, South Carolina, May 29th 1845, who still survives him. They had six children, four of whom are still alive. R. B. Bryan

Mrs. Martha M. Lowery, wife of W. R. Lowery, was born February 27, 1842; died at the residence of her father, Parks Hardeman, Esq., in Cobb county, Georgia, April 25, 1875. She leaves five little children. W. G. Hanson

Jonathan C. Fentress was born July 25, 1799; died near Morgan, Calhoun county, Georgia, March 25, 1875. He was left an orphan at an early age. On the 26th of December 1826 he was married to Miss Serena J. Lingo. He leaves four children. Geo. C. Clarke

Whitman Pair died in Henry county, Georgia, April 4, 1875, in the fiftieth year of his age.

Sarah E. Bagby was born September 29, 1855; died in Atlanta, Georgia, March 7, 1875.

Philemon Willhite was born in North Carolina in 1806. He spent much of his life in Union Parish, Louisiana, and moved to Florida a few years ago. R. D. Gentry. New Orleans Advocate please copy.

Tribute of Respect to Dr. J. S. Hill from Midway, Long Cane circuit.

Issue of May 26, 1875

Mrs. Sarah Eliza Kennon, wife of Capt. John Kennon of Mt. Airy, Harris county, Ga., was killed by the storm on 20th of March 1875, aged 37 years. In the same dark house and by the same fell stroke, the eldest daughter, Miss Glenara Hines Kennon, aged 20 years. By the same sad blow, the second daughter Miss Martha Elizabeth Kennon aged 18 years. Also John Elias Kennon, eldest son, aged 16 years; Sarah Bell Kennon, aged 12 years; little Ada Gertha Kennon, only two years of age. G. S. Johnston

Brother Pulaski F. Campbell was born in Butts county, Ga., November 19, 1836 and died in Augusta, Ga., May 2, 1875. The files of the Southern Christian Advocate contain obituary notices of his grand-father and grand-mother, and of his father and mother. the Grandfather, George Campbell, was a faithful soldier of the revolution of 1776. The father, Col. James H. Campbell, died in 1844. Brother Campbell was married on 6 November 1867 to Miss Sallie W. Eve, daughter of Dr. Joseph A. Eve. Clement A. Evans

Mrs. Frances S. Arrington was born in Richmond county, Ga., February 22d, 1828; married April 17, 1856; died February 24, 1875 in Augusta, Ga. She was the daughter of Rev. Alexander Averett, who was a member of the Georgia Conference at the time of his death. Clement A. Evans

Mrs. Sarah A. Wright, daughter of the late Rev. Wm. Arnold of the Georgia Conference, was born in Putnam county, Ga., January 26 1827; married Alexander H. Wright, who was a lieutenant in the 32d Georgia Regiment and died in Fort Delaware in 1864; died in Rome, Ga., May 1st 1875. Mrs. Wright was buried beside her daughter at Silver Creek church. Rome Courier.

Mrs. Lizzie Mills, wife of Capt. Frank Mills and only child of Dr. J. M. Underwood, died in Rome, Ga., April 3d 1875, in the thirty-second year of her age.

Mrs. Margaret Steele, wife of Mr. James Steele, was born at Johnston, Ranfreushire, Scotland, December 1830, and died at Graniteville, S. C., April 16, 1873. L. C. Loyal

William Hunter, Esq., was born 22 November 1808 and died on 17th of April 1875. He leaves a widow and many relatives.

William G. Andrews died March 15, 1875, in the seventy-ninth year of his age. He was born in Cumberland county, Va., but moved to Georgia when quite young and settled in Upson county. J. B. Payne

My teacher, N. A. Lewis, died in Thomson, Ga., April 12th 1875. He leaves a wife and three small children.

Miss Lucinda J. Merk, a member of the M. E. Church, South, at New Hope, Carroll county, Ga., was born in Jackson county, Ga., February 6, 1831; died March 25, 1875.

Mrs. Eugenia Boozer, wife of Rev. B. M. Boozer, local preacher of Newberry circuit, died April 18, 1875, aged 20 years, 7 months and 9 days. Mark M. Boyd

My sister-in-law, Mrs. Frances Hutto, wife of Samuel Hutto, Esq., died in Orangeburg county, S. C., April 23d, 1875, in the forty-fourth year of her age. W. Hutto

John W. Tart was born April 14, 1831; died in Marion county, S. C., April 16, 1875. R. L. Duffie

Amanda Stephens, wife of Ervin Stephens, died March 21, 1875, in the neighborhood of Walnut Grove Church, Spartanburg county, S. C. David West

Mrs. Annie Reardon, wife of Mr. Benjamin T. Reardon, was born in Edgefield District, S. C., September 8, 1802; and died at Graniteville, Aiken District, S. C., April 20th 1875. L. C. Loyal

Sister Ella Bookout died April 28, 1875, aged thirty-four years. She leaves a husband and four children, one only a few days old. John H. Harris

Mrs. Sarah M. Morgan, wife of Mr. Hardie Morgan, of Dooly county, Ga., died May 4th 1875. G. T. Embry

Tribute of Respect from Winnsboro and Ridgeway Circuit, S. C., to Joseph Lauhon, who died April 19, 1875.

Issue of June 2, 1875

Mrs. Rebecca Prince died in Charleston, S. C., March 13, 1875, in the sixty-second year of her age. She joined the Methodist Church, though she had been reared a Presbyterian. Jas. C. Stoll. Western Methodist please copy.

Mrs. Sarah K. Smith, widow of the late Rev. Isaac Smith and mother, by a previous marriage, of the late Rev. J. T. Munds, died in Columbia, S. C., May 8, 1875, in the 67th year of her age. W. D. Kirkland

Mrs. Mary Louisa Jones, wife of the late Colonel John A. Jones and daughter of the late Colonel Van Leonard, was born in Morgan county, Georgia, May 8, 1825; died in Columbus, Georgia, April 5, 1875. James O. Branch

Mrs. Mary A. C. Swaine, was born in Warren county, Georgia, November 22, 1806; was married to J. G. Swaine in 1828; joined the Baptist Church in 1832; died at the residence of her son, E. J. Swaine, April 12, 1875. She leaves two sons and three daughters. John Corley

Martha Perkins, whose maiden name was Brooks, died in Stewart county, Georgia, April 25, 1875, aged 81 years. She was married to Wright Perkins in her nineteenth year. J. W. Domingos

Joseph Hucks of Beaufort county, South Carolina, died May 9, 1875, in his 59th year. He was married to Miss Mary A. Sellers in 1845. His birth-place was Horry county, South Carolina. He leaves a widow, five sons, and one daughter. G. H. Pooser

Miss Mary A. Sexton, daughter of H. W. and Margaret J. Sexton of Gwinnett county, Georgia, was born January 23, 1849 and died May 3, 1875. M. H. Eakes

Cicero L. West, son of William and Sophronia West, was born in Fannin county, Georgia, August 29, 1856; died in Cherokee county, Ga., March 20, 1875. C. M. McClure

Mrs. Minnie O. Alfriend (late Minnie O. Houston) grand-daughter of Dr. Thomas F. Green, was born in Alabama, February 8, 1855; and died in Clayton county, Georgia, April, 27, 1875. W. W. Wadsworth

Mrs. S. L. Clark, wife of J. S. Clark and daughter of the lamented Rev. T. F. McCarthy, died at Milner, Georgia, April 24, 1875, in the 24th year of her age.

Tribute of Respect from Butler Circuit, Columbus District, South Georgia Conference, to Rev. Julius Gardner, who was born August 31, 1837; died at Butler, Georgia, March 22, 1875.

Nathan A. Lewis was born in Warren county, Georgia, August 27, 1841; was married to Miss Sicily Rogers in 1867, died in Thomson, Georgia, April 12, 1875. He leaves a wife and three children.

Joel Haley was born in Franklin county, Georgia, September 3, 1802; was married to Frances Jones of Madison county, who still survives, in 1827; died in Cherokee county, Georgia, May 6, 1875. C. M. McClure

Issue of June 9, 1875

Mrs. Frances E. Lazenby, wife of Hon. Geo. M. Lazenby and daughter of Hon. Josiah Stovall, was born October 31, 1834; died in Columbia county, Ga., May 7, 1875. She leaves a husband and four children. R. A. Conner

Mrs. Drucilla Adams was born in Elbert county, Ga., May 18th 1806; and died April 17, 1875. She was the daughter of James and Jemima Hunt and the wife of Nicholas H. Adams, who died in 1851, leaving her a widow with nine children, seven daughters and two sons. She left seven children--one son and six daughters.

Mrs. Hester Evans King, wife of the Hon. Angus M. D. King, deceased, was born in Jones county, Ga., October 25, 1806; married November 25, 1823; died at the residence of her son-in-law, Mr. Joseph Thomas in Sumter county, Ga., March 5th 1875. B. F. Breedlove

Mrs. Mary Craven, daughter of Robert Jones, was born in South Carolina, March 27th 1806; was married to Rev. Daniel Bird of the Georgia Conference, September 20, 1827; was married to Rev. I. N. Craven of the North Texas Conference, in DeKalb county, Ga., October 27th 1847; died in Whitesboro, Grayson county, Texas, April 14th 1875.

Mrs. Virginia C. Bowman died in Columbia, S. C., May 10, 1875, in the fifty-second year of her age.

Mrs. Temperance Cassady was born in North Carolina, February 4th 1804; married Alexander Cassady in Chesterfield, S. C., January 24th 1820; died in Lawrenceville, Henry county, Ala., March 1st 1875. Her husband died in 1861. M. R. Cassady

Joseph Lauhon of Ridgeway, S. C., was born January 21, 1818 and died April 19, 1875. A. J. Stafford

Dennis M. Chenault died in Lincoln county, Ga., May 9th 1875, in the 18th year of his age.

Wm. A. Cook was born in Hancock county, Ga., March 7th 1820 and died in Baldwin county, Ga., April 13th 1875. He was the son of Nathan and Lourenna Cook. W. W. Wadsworth

Mrs. Gracie Cobb, whose maiden name was Walden, was born in Hancock county, Ga., and died in Augusta, Ga., May 5th 1875, aged about 39 years. She was first married to Mr. Mote by whom she bore five children. After his death she married J. W. Cobb, Esq., by whom she had one child, a boy of some eight or ten years of age.

Willis T. Bedingfield was born in Washington county, Ga., January 15th 1806, and died in Quitman, May 15th 1875.

Abijah Willbanks was born in Pendleton county, South Carolina, in 1801 and died April 19th 1875.

Peter W. Reddick, son of Jacob and Sarah Reddick, was born in Burke county, Ga., July 29th 1823; and died in Webster county, Ga., April 29th 1875. He was married three times, first to Martha Herrington, next to Susan J. Kendrick and then to Martha E. Gregory, this last survives him, having seven children. R. L. Wiggins

Tribute of Respect from Dalton District Conference to Wilson Glenn Simmons, who died May 16, 1875, in the 54th year of his age.

Issue of June 16, 1875

Mrs. Augusta E. West, daughter of Rev. Elias Jordan, deceased, and wife of Rev. John E. West, died near Cuthbert in Randolph county, Georgia, May 21, 1875, in her forty-sixth years. R. W. Dixon

Rev. Reuben H. Lucky was born in Green county, Georgia, September 5, 1801, and died May 17, 1875, in Thomas county, Georgia. J. O. A. Cook

Mrs. Lilly Bird, the wife of Rev. U. S. Bird, South Carolina Conference, died at her mother's residence, Mount Pleasant, near Charleston, S. C., March 15, 1875, in her thirty-first year. She left two little boys. Her body rests in the family graveyard in Christ's Church Parish.

Mrs. Grissilla Fletcher Bradshaw, wife of Mr. J. M. Bradshaw, was born in Harris county, Georgia, September 29th ----; died April 24th 1875.

Mrs. Mary Eliza Garret, wife of James W. Garret of Social Circle, Georgia, died May 5th 1875, aged thirty-five years and one month.

Sarah Blitch, daughter of Solomon Zeltro, was born in Effingham county, Georgia, April 5th 1806 and died April 30th 1875. She left a husband and seven children. A. W. Harris. Savannah papers please copy.

Mrs. Mary Ann Campbell was born in Columbia county, Georgia, July 19, 1804; was married to A. H. Campbell, September 18, 1828; died in Talbot county, Georgia, April 19, 1875.

Miss Maggie R. Bailey, youngest child of the late Judge Nathaniel Bailey, died at Appling, Georgia, March 20, 1875.

Mrs. Jack Ann Merritt was born in Green county, Ga., February 20th 1797; died March 28th 1875.

Sister Hannah Bishop died near Shiloh, Newton county, Georgia, May 30th 1875, aged upward of seventy years.

Miss Fannie J. Braswell, daughter of Thomas M. Braswell, died in Jefferson county, Florida, May 7th, 1875, in the twentieth year of her age. W. G. Booth

Issue of June 23, 1875

Bro. Randal Folsom was born in Burke county, Georgia, 5th January 1799 and died at his residence in Lowndes county, Ga., 28th May 1875, aged 76 years. H. W. Sharpe

L. M. Biggers was born in York District, S. C., 17th March 1811; died 5 May 1875 at his home in Muscogee county, Georgia. Howard W. Key. Tribute of Respect from Quarterly Conference.

Mrs. F. Beulah Latimer, wife of Clement T. Latimer, died in Abbeville District, S. C., May 22d 1875, in the 54th year of her age.

Mrs. Aurelia McGehee Patton, wife of Mr. Frank Patton and daughter of the late Dr. E. J. McGehee, died in Houston county, Ga., April 28th 1875 in the 21st year of her age. W. F. Robison

Mrs. Margaret Griffith of Round O, Walterboro circuit, died April 4th 1875, in the 35th year of her age. She was the oldest daughter of Abram Willis, who preceded her some years ago to glory. She left a husband and seven children, one an infant a few days old. A. English Williams

Mrs. Mary Ann Banister was born October 8th 1838 and died May 18th 1875. She leaves a husband and several little children. C. L. Pattillo

Mrs. Theodate Carroll, whose maiden name was Kendrick, was of Rev. Daniel Carroll, of Congregation Methodist Church, was born in Columbia county, Ga., May 13th 1804; died in Meriwether county, Ga., May 26th 1875.

Mrs. Talitha E. Freeman, daughter of Rev. Jeremiah and Mrs. M. B. Freeman, was born in Meriwether county, Ga., and died in West Point, Ga., April 23, 1875. P. M. Ryburn

Dr. William C. Watkins of Clayton, Ga., was born October 1st 1844; died at the residence of his father, Robert H. Watkins, in Gainesville, Ga., May 15, 1875. J. M. Dickey

Issue of June 30, 1875

Died

On the 27th May 1875, in Orangeburg county, S. C., David Edward, infant son of Brother and Sister J. S. Funches, aged 1 year, 1 month, and 13 days.

At Fort Myers, South Florida, June 6th 1875, Julia Ellen, infant daughter of Hon. F. A. and Mrs. A. R. Hendry, aged seven months, wanting two days.

Obituary

James Tinley was born in Richmond county, Ga., December 25, 1802; died in Bibb county, Ga., June 15, 1875, in the seventy-third year of his age.

Mrs. Mary J. Ellis, wife of Myron Ellis, died in Greenville, Ga, May 31st 1875 in her 53d year. Her parents were of the pure Wesleyan type of Methodists. C. A. Simonton

Rev. Nathaniel C. Barber was born May 22d 1800 in Fairfield District, South Carolina; died May 6th 1875; married to Miss E. W. Harden, November 11, 1828; removed to Alabama and settled in Chambers county in 1845. He leaves a widow and numerous descendants. M. L. Whitten. Nashville Advocate please copy.

Mrs. Luvina H. Roberts, whose maiden name was Mead, was born in Clark county, Ga., November 13, 1827; died in Paulding county, Ga., June 12, 1875. She was married to Asa Roberts, October 31, 1849. J. W. Baker

Mr. Hardy Gaddy died at his residence in Marion county, twenty-one miles north of Marion Court House, South Carolina, on the 8th of June 1875, aged seventy-eight years, eleven months, and eighteen days.

Mrs. Francis M. Keneda died near Valley Grove, Talbot county, Ga., 1 May 1875, in the fifty-ninth year of her age. She leaves a husband and a widowed daughter with several other children and grand-children.

Mrs. Elvira Browne, consort of Dr. Jasper Browne, was born November 19, 1832 and died May 25, 1875. W. A. Hodges

Issue of July 7, 1875

Died

At Mulberry, Jackson county, Ga., June 16th 1875, Paul Lyle, aged 5 years and 12 days, youngest son of D. R. and Mary L. B. Lyle.

Obituary

Rev. Tilman Snead was born in Wilkes county, Ga., May 11th 1786; died in Baldwin county, Ga., May 3d, 1875. He served his country in the war of 1812. He joined the Methodist Episcopal Church at Bethel, Bush River circuit, South Carolina Conference. In 1818 he was married in Wilkes county, Ga., to Miss Elizabeth G. B. Washington, who preceded him to the grave in December 1871.

John W. Leverett, eldest son of Maston Leverett, was born and reared in Webster county, Ga., and died May 16th, 1875. R. S. Wiggins

Mrs. Mary Wade died at the residence of her son, Elijah Wade, at Okepilco, May 31st 1875, aged 88 years. J. H. D. McRae

Mrs. Susan E. Braswell died at her son's residence in Meriwether county, Ga., June 6th 1875, in the fifty-third year of her age. F. M. T. Branson

Mary A. C. Swaine, widow of J. G. Swaine, was born in Warren county, Ga., November 23d 1806; was married in 1823; joined the Baptist church in 1832; died April 12, 1875. She leaves two sons and three daughters. John Corley

Thomas McTeer was born in Beaufort co., S. C., Feb. 26th 1809; died June 1st 1875. He leaves a widow and large family of children. G. H. Pooser

Anna M. Hall, daughter of Morgan B. and Martha A. Hall, was born June 18th 1859 and died May 30th 1875. The Appeal and Southerner please copy.

James M. Smith, son of J. Porter Smith, of Wacohoota, East Florida, was born September 6th 1851, and died May 24th 1875. J. C. Ley

Mrs. Martha L. Preer, wife of Thomas C. Preer, was born in Harris county, Ga., June 24th 1843; died June 8th 1875.

Mrs. Jane Chambers, daughter of David Graham, was born in South Carolina--supposed to be about seventy years of age; died in Smithville, Lee county, Ga., June 17th 1875. T. S. Armistead

Miss E. M. Loveless was born October 23d 1842; died June 11th 1875. C. L. Pattillo

Mrs. Ann E. Morgan, widow of John R. Morgan, died near Mount Pleasant Church, Effingham county, Ga., June 15th 1875, in her sixty-third or sixty-fourth year.

Issue of July 14, 1875

Died

In Oglethorpe county, June 23d, 1875, Fannie L. Daniel, infant daughter of Mr. and Mrs. A. C. Daniel.

James Thomas Smith, son of J. S. and M. A. E. Smith, was born September 18th 1871 and died June 23d 1875.

In Anderson, S. C., July 2d, 1875, Clarence Gregory, infant son of Rev. Wm. W. and Mrs. M. Eugeneia Mood, of the South Carolina Conference, aged one year and six days.

Obituary

William Simmons was born in Cave Spring, Ga., May 8th 1842; died 29th May 1875. Three months before his death he lost his wife, a member of the Baptist church, leaving an infant boy only one month old.

Miss Mary Elizabeth Street was born February 17, 1855 and died June 20, 1875.

Mrs. Elizabeth Simmons (whose maiden name was Hunt) was born in Hancock county, Ga., and died in Spalding county, Ga., June 7, 1875, aged 73. She was twice married. She lived with her first husband, James Patten, seventeen years. Her youngest son, Matthew Patten, fell in Confederate service at Murfreesboro, Tenn. She was married to Wm. H. Simmons in 1856, with whom she lived happily for ten years. Left a widow again....

Mrs. Vallie Johnson, formerly Miss White, of Coweta county, Georgia, wife of J. W. Johnson, Jr., died in Oglethorpe county, Ga., June 4, 1875.

Mrs. Mary L. Hunnewell, whose maiden name was Cray, was born in Tattnall county, Georgia in 1813; died at Cairo, Georgia, June 15, 1875.

S. Hayden, son of Samuel Littlejohn, died on the 4th of April 1875. He was born in Spartanburg District, S. C., July 11, 1863.

Rev. James M. Stokes was born in Livingston Parish, La., December 23d, 1832, and died at Live Oak, Fla., April 19th 1875. Chas. A. Fulwood

Dr. H. S. Wimbish was born in Abbeville District, S. C., December 1st 1809; emigrated to Georgia when quite a young man, and lived for many years at Greenville, Merriwether county; removed from there to LaGrange, January 1st 1858; died June 24th 1875. H. H. Parks

Mrs. Caroline L. Gramling, widow of Hon. M. Gramling, late of Orangeburg, S. C., died May 8th 1875, at the age of seventy-two. She leaves an aged brother, Maj. Stroman and two daughters, Mrs. Dr. Salley and Mrs. Rev. Lawton. H. A. C. Walker

Miss Cynthia A. Barnett was born in Bradley county, Tenn., September 7th 1850; died in Whitfield county, Ga., April 20th 1875. G. W. Thomas

John B. Sweat was born in Fayette county, Georgia, January 5th 1860; died at Flat Shoals, DeKalb county, Ga., June 6th 1875. James E. England

Mrs. Eliza J. Mahoney died in Wilkes county, Ga., June 7th 1875, in the sixty-fourth year of her age. Sarah J. Snelson, her daughter, died a few months before.

Mrs. Susan Speight, whose maiden name was Bronson, was born in Houston county, Ga., in 1820; was married to Rev. T. L. Speight, February 4th 1840; died in Chattooga county, Ga., June 5th 1875. J. B. McFarland

Mrs. Robert Willis died in Wilkes county, Ga., May 6th 1875, aged sixty-eight years.

John White was born in 1801 and died in Walker county, Ga., May 23, 1875. J. B. McFarland

Died

In Swainsboro, Burke county, Ga., July 17th 1875, James Edward, infant son of John and Arladne Couse, and grandson of James H. and Mary L. Smith, of Macon Ga., aged one year, two months and a few days.

William McKemie, son of Robert J. and Mattie E. (Bailey) McKemie, died near Hackneyville, Ala., July 14, 1875, aged 1 year, 11 months, and 3 days.

At his residence near Macon, Ga., July 17th, 1875, Charles E. Stubbs, in the twenty-fifth year of his age.

July 19, 1875, Wesley Bates, aged 6 months and 7 days, son of William W. and Mary A. Pemberton, of Charleston, S. C.

Obituary

Rev. William S. Williams was born in Franklin county, Georgia, February 25, 1807; married Miss Frances Winn of Hall county, January 14, 1830. H. P. Bell

Mrs. Emily R. Stovall was born in Oglethorpe county, Georgia, October 18, 1817; was married to Isam Stovall and moved to DeKalb county, Georgia; died June 21, 1875. She leaves a husband and nine children.

Rev. James Spence died near Hawkinsville, Ga., April 23, 1875.... presume that he was beyond fifty years of age. G. T. Embry

Mrs. Elizabeth Addison, whose maiden name was Izlar, was born March 12, 1833; married to G. A. Addison, January 29, 1857; died in Orangeburg, S. C., April 19, 1875.

Hiram Mobley, about forty years old, died April 28, 1875. He left a wife and several children. D. J. McMillan

Mrs. H. Queen Davis, daughter of Mr. and Mrs. Wiley King and wife of Mr. Edward Davis, was born in Darlington county, S. C., December 1844; died near her birthplace May 5, 1875.

Mrs. M. A. Haygood, daughter of Rev. Jedidah and Mrs. Margaret Meaders, was born in Franklin county, Ga., July 22, 1835; died May 16, 1875. She was married April 24, 1859 and was the mother of eight children, two of whom preceded her to heaven. She leaves one daughter and five sons. J. N. Myers

Mrs. E. D. Flynt, whose maiden name was Duke, was born December 15, 1848 and died May 27, 1875. She embraced religion in Jackson, Butts county, Ga., in 1863. W. T. McMichael

Emily Algood, whose maiden name was Brice, was born June 23d 1811; died in Paulding county, Georgia, May 13th 1875.

Brother W. D. Smith died in Charleston, S. C., July 12, 1875. He came to this city a stranger, to educate his two daughters at the public schools. He brought his letter from his church near Georgetown, S. C.

Issue of August 4, 1875

Died

At Acworth, Ga., July 8th 1875, Bertha, infant daughter of N. J. and M. E. Garrison, aged 4 months and 3 days.

Obituary

Mariano P. Papy was born in St. Augustine, Fla., Oct. 9th 1824; came to Tallahassee when 16 years of age; was married to Fannie B. Chaires, April 27th 1854; died July 8th of the present year. Josephus Anderson

Nannie Hubert Thomas, daughter of Dr. R. W. Hubert of Warrenton and wife of Rev. Allen C. Thomas, of North Georgia Conference, died in Oxford, Ga., June 20th 1875, in the 28th year of her age.

Early Cleaveland died at his residence in Monroe county ,Ga., July 6th 1875, having completed his 69th year just one month and one day previously; was born in Elbert county, Ga; but had been a citizen of Monroe county since about the year 1827.

Caroline L. Eady was born March 1838 and was brought up in and about Columbus. She was married to Henry P. Eady, November 26th 1854. She lived at Columbus factory (where she died) for twenty-five years. She leaves a husband, two children, and an aged mother.

Mrs. Nancy A. Allen died at Trion factory, May 4th 1875, in the fortieth year of her age.

My dear mother, Mrs. Agnes Melita Adams, wife of Rev. John M. Adams and whose maiden name was Hulme, was born in Elbert county, Ga., February 24th 1814, and died in Madison county, Ga., July 5th 1875. She was the mother of fourteen children, most of whom are yet alive. Thomas J. Adams

Mrs. Marion Gibson died at the residence of her father, Dr. T. R. Center, Richland county, S. C., on the 5th of July 1875, in the thirty-second year of her age.

Miss Jennie Whitfield Lowe, daughter of David W. Lowe, died in Warren county, Ga., July 7th 1875, in her seventeenth year. E. W. Hubert

Josiah S. Allen was born in Barnwell District, S. C., in 1845; died near Quitman, Ga., June 12, 1875. Robt. D. Gentry

Mrs. Alice B. Bowdon, daughter of Mr. and Mrs. D. B. Johnson, died in Griffin, Ga., May 29th 1875, in the 29th year of her age. L. J. Davies

Issue of August 11, 1875

Died

In Sandersville, Ga., July 26th 1875, Daniel Fletcher, the infant son of J. T. and M. T. Lavingene, aged 1 year, 4 months and 9 days.

Obituary

Mrs. M. A. Smith died in Cassville, Bartow county, Ga., May 12, 1875, in her 29th year. She was the youngest daughter of Adam and C. A. Hill. Her father died when she was eight years old. She was married to Mr. R. B. Smith, November 20, 1875. A. B. Wilson

Mrs. L. J. Anderson, wife of Hon. W. D. Anderson of Marietta, Ga., was born April 12, 1845 and died July 10, 1875.

Mrs. Mary Elizabeth Johnson, whose maiden name was Rosser, wife of Lucius N. Johnson, was born in Meriwether county, Ga., and died in Griffin, Ga., July 15, 1875, in her thirty-second year. A. S. Rosser

Mrs. Maria Townsend, wife of Rev. Joel Townsend, of the South Carolina Conference, died in Cokesbury, S. C., July 24, 1873, in the seventy-first year of her age. R. W. Barber

Mrs. Harriet Duval was born in the city of New York about the year 1810 and died in Lake City, Fla., May 2, 1875. Henry Ed. Partridge

Mrs. Louisa Blakeney, daughter of Gen. J. W. and Mrs. M. V. Blakeney, was born in Chesterfield county, S. C., July 11, 1856; died in Kershaw county, S. C., July 8, 1875.

Miss Mattie E. Pennington, daughter of Rev. S. S. Pennington, was born January 21, 1856 and died in Monroe county, Ga., June 15, 1875.

Charles H. Tinsley, eldest son of Rev. E. C. Tinsley, deceased, and S. E. Johnson, and stepson of Rev. G. C. S. Johnson and grandson of Gen. B. H. Darden, deceased, of Butts county, died near Macon, on the 13th of July 1875, aged fourteen years and ten days.

Mrs. Nancy Lindsay, widow of Re.v J. W. F. Lindsay of Upson county, Ga., died at the residence of her son-in-law, F. F. Mathews, Esq., in Upson, June 23, 1875, in the eighty-second year of her age. Her girlhood was spent in Greene county. Geo. G. Smith

Garrett Morris was born in Chester District, S. C., March 21, 1792; brought up to manhood in Abbeville District, S. C; removed to Alabama in 1828, and settled near Oak Bowery, where he died June 7, 1875. Thomas J. Williamson

Issue of August 18, 1875

Died

At Centreville, Leon county, Florida, July 1st 1875, Lillie, infant daughter of Dr. W. T. and Mrs. M. A. Snipes, aged 8 months and 4 days.

In Hamilton, Ga., July 27th 1875, Lucille, infant daughter of W. S. and Mrs. Cornelia B. Robinson, aged 3 years and 9 months.

July 31st 1875, little Hattie, infant daughter of Mrs. D. J. and Thomas B. Lumpkin, aged 2 years and seven days.

Obituary

Brother Harrison Reese, of Warrenton, Ga., died June 5, 1875. He was born in Warren county, October 23d 1805, and was thrice married, first to Miss Nancy Todd, next to Miss Patsy Toler, last to Miss Eliza Norris, who survives him. By his first marriage he had four children, by the second, five, by the last three. J. Lewis, Jr.

Sister Nancy Short, daughter of B. Wallis, Sr., and wife of Rev. W. J. Short, of Marion county, Ga., was born November 12th 1840 was married to brother Short, December 25th 1860, died July 15, 1875. She leaves a husband and six children.

Charles W. Fulwood, eldest son of Rev. C. A. Fulwood, of the Florida Conference, died in Key West, Fla., July 23d 1875, in the twenty-fourth year of his age. Wm. R. Johnson

Mrs. Sarah Gillespie, wife of James C. Gillespie, was born in union county, Ga., and died July 12, 1875. She left a husband and six children. T. J. Edwards

Cyrene Inman, wife of James Inman and daughter of D. R. and Catharine McDonald, was born February 26th 1831 and died in Clinch county, Ga., May 23th 1875. J. R. Booth

William Asbury Banks was born in Elbert county, Ga., December 26th 1812 and died in Forsyth, Ga., June 19th 1875. He leaves a widow and five children.

Sister Clara Murrell of Charleston died on the 12th of July, while on a visit at the house of her brother-in-law, Major Peeples of Beaufort county, S. C.

Rev. Samuel A. McCook of the Florida Conference was born in Lee county, Ga., April 22d 1834; died July 7th 1875. O. Eady

Mrs. Laura Ann Bailey, daughter of Capt. Binion, was born in Columbia county, Ga., in 1822; died near Talbotton, Ga., July 19th 1875. W. Knox

Brother F. H. Hall was born and reared in North Carolina; moved to Florida in 1845; died in Leon county, Fla., May 12th 1875, aged sixty-three years. He leaves a wife and seven children. R. H. Howren

Issue of August 25, 1875

W. P. Mobley of Harris county, Georgia died June 24, 1875. He leaves a widow and eight children.

William C. Rice, eldest son of Spencer M. and Mary Rice, died in Union, S. C., August 2d, 1875, aged nineteen years and eight months. A. H. Lester

Mrs. Eliza J. Barnes, wife of John J. Barnes and daughter of John Anderson, was born in Monroe county, Ga., November 20th 1842 and died in the same county, July 24th 1875.

John Wesley Adams was born May 24th 1842 and died in Colleton county, S. C., June 13th 1875.

Mrs. Benetta Bingham was born in North Carolina, May 10, 1801, and died August 3, 1875, in Coweta county, Ga. J. W. Cotter

Mrs. R. F. G. Bolt, wife of Charles Bolt and daughter of Robert F. and U. M. A. Layne, deceased, died in Union, South Carolina, July 18, 1875, in the 36th year of her age. Five little children are left in charge of the bereaved husband. A. H. Lester

Mrs. Charles M. Stewart died in Key West, Fla., July 13th 1875, in the 26th year of his age. He was a native of Quincy. Chas. A. Fulwood

John James Forsyth was born in South Carolina in 1806 and died July 19th 1875. When a young man he removed to Savannah. In July 1827 he was married to Miss Mary A. Whitaker. Only one child of seven by this marriage survives him. He was buried by the I. O. O. F.

Tribute of Respect by Macon District Conference to John J. Forsyth.

Tribute of Respect by Macon District Conference to James Tinley.

Issue of September 1, 1875

Mrs. Margaret L. Lane died at the residence of her son-in-law, Luther M. Smith, Oxford, Ga., on the 21st of July ult., having but recently closed her fifty-seventh year. She was born in Madison, Ga., on 5 July 1818 and was the daughter of Mr. Ernest and Mrs. Joyce Wittich. Her brother, Rev. Lucius L. Wittich, then a professor in Emory College. Her daughter Carrie (Mrs. L. M. Smith). A. Means

My father, Col. Wm. H. Jackson, was born in Savannah, Ga., June 3d, 1786 and died at my residence in Macon, August 8th 1875. He was the eldest son of Gov. James Jackson, whose memory is almost idolized. He joined the Presbyterian Church in Athens. James Jackson

James Thomas Pattillo, youngest child of James and Sarah Pattillo of Harris county, Ga., was born August 23d 1856 and died at the house of his brother-in-law, W. A. Callaway, in West Point, Ga., July 28th 1875. W. F. Pattillo

Miss Olivia M. Curray died in Key West, Fla., July 4th 1875, in her nineteenth year. Chas. A. Fulwood

Mrs. J. W. Goodlett, late of Apalachicola, and mother-in-law to Rev. Wm. R. Johnson of the Florida Conference, died in Key West, June 27th 1875, in the fifty-eight year of her age. She was brought up in the Protestant E. Church. Chas. A. Fulwood

Charles W. Burbank died in Key West, July 4th 1875, in his eighteenth year. He was a native of New York, but reared chiefly in Manchester, N. H. He had been a resident of Key West only a few months. Chas. A. Fulwood

Miss Julia Ann C. Appleby died August 8th 1875 at the residence of Mr. R. H. Appleby in Colleton county, S. C., in the 28th year of her age. She was reared by her grand-mother, Mrs. Ann Stokes. Wm. Stokes

Elias Sinclair was born in Wilson county ,Tenn, in 1808 and died July 21st 1875. he was married in 1827 to Miss Sarah A. McDearmitt, who died several years ago, leaving five children. He removed to Georgia in 1838, and to Macon in 1852.

Brother Wm. B. Jones was born near Norfolk, Va., November 12, 1818 removed to Putnam county, Ga., in 1857 where he resided until his death in Eatonton, July 5th 1875. J. Lewis, Jr.

William C. Spear was born in Warren county, Ga., September 13th 1815; moved to Talbot county, Ga., when young, where he remained until last winter, when he moved to Upson county, Ga., where he died July 25th 1875. E. J. Rentz

Joshua Hearn was born in Franklin county, Ga., November 24th 1821; married Leah Smart in 1843, spent the greater part of his life in Campbell County, Ga., where he died June 13th 1875. He leaves a widow and eight children. Stephen Shell

Brother Thomas McMullain died in Monroe county, Ga., July 21st 1875, aged sixty-seven years.

Mrs. Sarah D. Porter, wife of John C. Porter, died July 28th 1875, in the sixtieth year of her age. She was married to her surviving partner the 3d of November 1831 by the Rev. John C. Postell. She leaves five sons--three sons and a daughter preceded her to the grave. L. Wood

Issue of September 8, 1875

Died

Near Augusta, Ga., July 21st 1875, Wm. LaPrade, infant son of Rev. W. E. and Mrs. H. C. Shackelford, aged ten months and four days.

August 27th 1875, little Hattie, infant daughter of Dr. D. S. and Harriet Brandon, aged 1 year and 3 days.

In Marion county, Ga., August 29th 1875, John T. H. Smith, son of John T. and Hattie Smith.

Obituary

Martha H. Sappington, wife of William J. Sappington and daughter of the late Rev. Joshua Storr, was born in Wilkes county, Ga., November 14, 1804; died in Troup county, Ga., July 17, 1875. She was the mother of twelve children; two died in infancy, seven of the ten that grew up preceded her to the grave. L. Rush

Dr. Cornelius O. O. Roberts was born in Columbia county, Fla., July 25, 1843 and died in Lake City, May 30, 1875. In 1867 he married Miss Mary F. Price. Henry Edw. Partride

Mrs. Goode, wife of Samuel N. Goode and daughter of J. T. Kendall, was born in Cheraw, S. C., December 25, 1852; removed with her parents to Alabama when an infant; was married October 22, 1872; died at her father's residence July 11, 1875.

Miss Georgia Holmes, daughter of J. D. and M. Holmes, died in Barnesville, Ga., June 15, 1875, aged twenty-six years.

Sarah M. Upton, wife of William R. Upton, was born April 18, 1850; was married December 2, 1869; died in Marion county, Ga., July 11, 1875 W. B. Merritt

Tribute of Respect from Troup Circuit, North Georgia Conference, to W. P. Mobley.

Issue of September 15, 1875

Mrs. Elizabeth Ellison, widow of John Ellis, was born in Londonderry, Ireland, August 13, 1791; died in Talbot county, Ga., June 19th 1875. Her parents removed to this country when she was young and settled in Chester, South Carolina. She was reared a Presbyterian, but after her marriage joined the Methodist Church.

Florence Adelle Austin, youngest child of Dr. Thomas C. and Mary T. Austin, residing near Batesville, S. C., and about twelve miles from Greenville, C. H., died July 1st 1875.

Jacob Chupp was born in Newberry District, S. C., October, 1806, and died in DeKalb county, Ga., July 17th 1875. He raised a large family. W. A. Dodge

John Cain, Jr., was born in Gwinnett county, Ga., in 1817; died in Cumming, Forsyth county, Ga., July 6th 1875.

Rufus E. Wilder, son of William A. Wilder, of Crawford county, Ga., was born in Macon near where Mulberry street church now stands. After the close of the war, he married Miss Mary Womack; was killed by a stroke of lightning, July 19th 1875.

Mrs. Nancy S. Rowland was born in Woodford county, Ky., September 29th 1801 and died in Columbus, Ga., June 18th 1875. Her husband was Allen Rowland. Jas. O. Branch

S. Fannie Miller, second daughter of J. O. and R. E. Miller, was born in Hawkins county, East Tenn., March 6th 1860 and died in Darlington county, S. C., June 12th 1875.

John D. Campbell was born September 5th 1808 in South Carolina and died July 17th 1875, at Childersburg, Ala. He was married in 1836 to Miss Charlotte McKey. He leaves a widow and four daughters.

Margaret E. Davis, daughter of Dr. Wm. Small and wife of Charles C. Davis of Georgetown, S. C., was born April 26th 1854 and died August 25th 1873. An only daughter survives her. L. Wood

Tribute of Respect to Jacob Chupp from Decatur circuit ,North Georgia Conference.

Issue of September 22, 1875

Died

September 3d 1875, Charlie Green King, youngest son of Mr. and Mrs. A. D. King, aged 14 years and two months.

Obituary

Mrs. Ann Porter was born in Putnam county, Ga., and died in Madison, Ga., July 21st 1875. Joined in marriage May 6, 1824, to Mr. John W. Porter.

Daniel Nolley was born in Hancock county, Ga., April 2, 1795, and died in Hampton, Henry county, Ga., August 5, 1875. Geo. N. Nolan

Miss Rebecca L. Martin, daughter of Ganaway and Almeda Martin, was born April 19th 1856 and died in Atlanta, Ga., August 14th 1875. She was reared by her aunt, Mrs. Winton Wood, and she and her husband loved her as her own child. T. H. Timmons

Mrs. Mary Tate Herring, whose maiden name was Stokes, was born in Wilkes county, Ga., June 27th 1808 and died near Newnan, Ga., August 11th 1875.

Miss Mary S. Lawrence was born in Whitfield county, Ga., March 17th 1852 and died in the same county, June 22d 1875. G. W. Thomas

Mrs. Martha K. Rockwell, wife of G. M. Rockwell, and youngest daughter of Josiah and Amelia Holmes, died in Barnesville, Ga., August 17, 1875, aged thirty-seven years. She was the youngest of six sisters--five of whom have crossed the river.

Rev. Wiley Horton was born in Lancaster District, S. C., February 15, 1800; died in Shelby county, Ala., August 17, 1875. He was married to Elizabeth Cauthen, January 18, 1820, who still survives him. C. L. Dobbs

Rev. H. A. Smith died in Lexington county, S. C., August the 9th 1875, in the seventy-second year of his age. J. A. Clifton

SOUTHERN CHRISTIAN ADVOCATE NOTICES 1867-1878

Issue of September 29, 1875

Died

James Leonard Collins, son of James L. and Mary E. Collins, was born December 23d 1875, died June 21st 1875.

Obituary

Mrs. Mattie E. Taylor, whose maiden name was Horton, wife of the Rev. William T. Taylor, died at Crawfordville, Fla., July 23d, 1875. Sister Taylor was born in Gwinnett county, GA., April 4th 1829. Her parents moved to Milledgeville when she was about 13 years of age, where she resided until her first marriage to a Mr. Clayton in 1852. Having removed to Valdosta during her widowhood, she was there married to the Rev. W. T. Taylor, of Thomasville, Ga. She had two brothers in Texas, ministers of the gospel, one of whom is a member of the Texas Conference. W. A. Giles. Texas Advocate please copy.

Miss Sallie E. Lipscomb, daughter of J. W. and E. Lipscomb, died in Abbeville county, S. C., September 6th 1875, aged nearly twenty-three years. J. W. Murray

Brother Obadiah E. Lewis died of consumption contracted during the late war, in Stewart county, Ga., August 12th 1875, in his 46th year. He was born in Greene county, Ga. He leaves a wife and several children. A. J. Dean

Andrew J. Booker was born October 16th 1818 in Maine, and died September 1st 1875 in Valdosta, Ga. Geo. C. Thompson

Mrs. Deborah Collins, daughter of Mr. John Calcutt, was born near Mars Bluff, Marlboro county, S. C., February 11th 1809 and died in Attapaigus, Ga., September 13th 1875. She was married to Mr. Jesse Collins in 1827 and the same year they emigrated to Decatur county, Ga. Thomas K. Leonard

Dennis Dupont Hawkins was born December 21st 1840 and died in Live Oak, Fla., July 7th 1875. He joined the M. E. Church, South, in Madison County in 1859. He leaves a wife and two children.

Thomas Jones died in Burke county, Ga., August 26, 1875, in the 44th year of his age.

Mrs. Virlinda Towns, formerly Miss Bealle, relict of the late H. L. Towns, was born in Columbia county, Ga., September 26th 1807; died at the residence of her son-in-law, Dr. M. J. Daniel in Griffin, Ga., July 24th 1875.

Uncle Ben Brewton was born in South Carolina, August 17th 1796 and died in Tatnall county, Ga., August 4th 1875. He had represented his county in the State Legislature. He has left an aged companion and six children. J. J. Giles

My mother, Mrs. Mary Hutto, died at the residence of her son-in-law, Mr. Preston P. Shuler, in Orangeburg county, S. C., September 2d, 1875, having just entered upon the 77th year of her age. Three sons and two daughters, three son-in-law, and three daughters-in-law, and a number of grandchildren survive. Wm. Hutto

Mrs. Lucy Ellen C. Hightower, formerly Miss Bass, consort of H. J. Hightower, sen., was born November 2, 1814; married February 28th 1836, died September 2d, 1875. She leaves a husband and several children. F. M. T. Brannon

Mary Jane Chipley was born in Abbeville county, S. C., March 28th 1849 and died July 10th 1875. She leaves a father, mother, brother and sister. J. W. Murray

Miss Georgia O. Garrison died August 20th 1875 in Acworth, Cobb county, Ga., in her twenty-first year. R. H. Jones

Issue of October 6, 1875

Died

At Round O, Colleton county, S. C., September 18th 1875, Robert Allen, infant son of Whitman Griffith, aged six months.

Obituary

Our venerable and much beloved father, John Brooks, died at the residence of his son, A. T. Brooks, near Hamilton, Ga., on the 31st of July 1875, in the 90th year of his age. He was born and reared in Warren county, Ga., where he married Miss Nancy Nunn, whom he survived 22 years. They had seven children, four of whom have long since closed their earthly career. J. H. L.

Wm. A. Shands was born April 5th 1830 in Spartanburg District, S. C., and died in Bronson, Fla., Sept. 3, 1875. While a young man, he moved with his father to Florida and settled near white Springs, in Hamilton county, where he was united in marriage to Miss Sallie J. Jackson. He leaves a wife and four children. S. Gardner

Mrs. Isabella Horn, whose maiden name was McLeod, was born in Marlboro District, S. C., Nov. 20, 1825, married to Daniel A. Horn, July 1855 and died in Thomas county, Ga., Sept. 7, 1875. She leaves a husband and four children.

Mrs. Catherine E. Potter was born Nov. 2, 1811, and died at Marion, S. C., Sept. 10, 1875. A. J. Stokes

Mr. J. T. Barksdale Cauthen, son of the late Dr. W. C. and Mrs. Jane Cauthen, was born January 22, 1849 in Lancaster county, S. C., and died near the old homestead, July 8, 1875. He has left a wife and four promising little children. C. J. McMillan

John F. Morton, son of Thomas R. Morton, was born July 17, 1824, and died in Chattooga county, Ga., July 1, 1875. D. J. M.

Mrs. Cynthia Morton, wife of Thomas R. Morton, of Chattooga county, Ga., died 5th September 1875, in the 63d year of her age. D. J. Myrick

Matilda C. McElroy, wife of John T. P. McElroy, and daughter of Thomas Akin, was born in DeKalb county, Ga., November 8, 1842, and died in the same county, July 7, 1875. She leaves a husband and an infant.

Issue of October 13, 1875

Died

Arthur Benettus Leigh, son of A. B. and Sarah Leigh, aged 3 years, 4 months and 24 days.

In Macon, Ga., October 23d, 1875, Nina May, infant daughter of Thos. J. and Annie E. Anderson

Obituary

George Carter Dozier, son of Ezekiel A. and Lois T. Dozier, was born in Wilkes county, Ga., October 5th 1842 and died at Warrior Stand, Macon county, Ala., August 13th 1875. When twelve years old, he came with the family to Alabama. In 1866 he married Miss Ella Adkisson, who died in 1868. By this wife he had one child. In 1870 he married Miss Mary Thomas, who with one little boy survives him. In August 1874, his sister, Rebecca L. Lovelace, of LaGrange, died at her father's house at Warrior Stand.

Mary E. Redding, wife of Capt. R. J. Redding, and daughter of Samuel and Nancy Bivins, was born March 31st 1840 and died in Ellaville, Ga., September 20th 1875. She was married May 19th 1858. From this union, eight living children were added to their earthly home.

Edwin D. Pate was born in Columbus county, N. C., October 8th 1833 and died in Suwanee county, Fla. September 27th 1875. He has left a wife and six children. Jas. S. Mikell

Mrs. Emily K. Rooker was born December 21st 1832 and died September 4th 1875.

John Whetstone, son of Absalom and Mary Whetstone, died on the Upper Orange Circuit, South Carolina, September 9th 1875, aged 33 years, 5 months and 19 days. He was a member of the Open Communion Baptist Church of Virginia, in which state he lived for a short time. He married in Virginia, but some came back to South Carolina. He leaves four little children, whom I baptized. A. R. Danner. Richmond Christian Advocate please copy.

Mrs. Elinor Fudge, wife of R. W. Fudge, near El Bethel, East Chester circuit, died July 6th 1875, aged sixty-six years. J. W. Kelly

James C. Branch, son of Armstead and Sarah Brand, of Canton, Miss., died August 30th 1875, in Volusia county, Fla., aged thirty-nine years. He leaves a wife and four children. His Widow.

Issue of October 20, 1875

Mary McCallum died on the 11th of July 1875, having attained the extreme age of ninety-two years. Up to the year 1822, she lived in Robinson county, North Carolina, when she moved to Bibb county, Georgia, and resided there until 1840. after that much of her time was spent with her only son, Archibald McCallum, of Twiggs county. In 1813 she joined the Presbyterian Church and continued in that connection until her death.

Mrs. Louisa Jeffcoat, daughter of Captain N. Riley and wife of Rev. J. B. Jeffcoat, was born in South Carolina in 1803; married May 8th 1827, and died Aug. 13th 1875. She moved with her husband to Florida near Tallahassee, where they remained until 1869 when they came to Orange County. O. W. Ransom

Mrs. Eliza C. Porter, wife of Rev. Hugh F. Porter, formerly of the South Carolina Conference, died August 31, 1875, in her forty-seventh year. A. English Williams

Mrs. Elenora Bowls was born in Jackson county, Fla., in 1853; died near Marianna, Fla., August 27, 1875.

W. Abraham Edwards died in Darlington county, S. C., July 11th 1875, aged about fifty-eight years. He leaves a wife and several children.

Luke Hendrix died in Dawson county, Ga., August 30, 1875. C. L. Pattillo

George Swilling died in Dawsonville, Ga., Sept. 14, 1875, in his eighty-fifth year. C. L. Pattillo

Isaac McGehee, one of the old settlers of Columbus and Girard, died at Porter Springs, Lumpkin county, Ga., August 13, 1875. C. L. Pattillo

Tribute of Respect from Fairburn Circuit, North George Conference, to Joshua Hearn.

Issue of October 27, 1875

Died

October 12th 1875, Wm. Metcalf Fisher, youngest son of Dr. Harris and Mrs. Julia G. Fisher, aged sixteen months.

Mary, daughter of R. R. Stone, aged five years and three months.

Obituary

Geo. J. C. Vaughn was born in Roane county, Tenn., but was early brought to Monroe county, where his youth and early manhood were passed. He died in Brooks county, Ga., September 10th 1875. He was an active captain in the war with Mexico. J. H. Brunner

Mrs. Elizabeth Trippe died at her residence near Culloden, Ga., July 1875. She was born in Mecklenburg county, Va., February 20th 1795 and her parents Captain John H. and Rebecca Bass, moving to Putnam county, Ga., during her girlhood, she was here married to Robert Trippe, with who she reared a family of eight children. T. B. Kendall

Mrs. Eliz. C. Howell, wife of Phillip Howell, was born in Rockingham, Richmond county, N. C., March 4th 1822. The family then moved to Butts county, Ga., afterwards to Henry and finally to Troup in 1828. J. R. Mayson

William Watson died in Edgefield county, S. C., October 2d 1875, in the thirty-sixth year of his age. He left a widow, an aged widowed mother, sisters and brothers. J. A. Clifton

Mrs. Elizabeth Brewer, wife of Mr. James W. Brewer, deceased, died at the residence of Mr. Johnson, her son-in-law, Fort Ogden, Manatee county, Fla., September 16th 1875, aged about fifty-five years. She was a member of the Primitive Baptist Church. Wm. H. K. Robarts

Mrs. Mary S. Bee, wife of the late Joseph Bee, of St. Andrews Parish, died in Charleston, S. C., July 23, 1875, in her seventy-third year of age. She was a member of Bethel Church. Her remains were interred in the city.

Issue of November 3, 1875

John C. Staley was born in Orangeburg District, South Carolina, Oct. 25,1825; and died in Houston county, Ga., Sept. 6, 1875. In his 21st year he was married to Miss Caroline Elley of Houston county, Ga. F. A. Branch

Mrs. Ellen F. Hutcheson, whose maiden name was Carleton, wife of Peter W. Hutcheson, died in Oglethorpe county, Ga., Oct. 6th 1875, in the 85th year of her age. Born in Mecklenburg county, Va., September 4, 1791, was married in March 19, 1818, to her aged surviving husband.

Annie Wilson Dowdle, youngest daughter of J. W. and Ann Dowdle, was born March 15, 1804; and died in Floyd county, Ga., August 28, 1875. D. J. Weems

Sherman Armstrong died in Warren county, Ga., October 1, 1875, nearly seventy-four years of age. He was the father of Rev. James M. Armstrong of the North Georgia Conference. His wife died about twenty-six year ago, but he never married again. He had ten children-- five boys and five girls-- and all of them attended his funeral. R. W. Hubert

Mrs. Mary Clifton Davis was born in Georgia in 1824; was married to Wm. Davis, Esq., in 1846, and died in Waco, Texas, August 7, 1875. She was the eldest child of T. H. Audas of Sparta, and passed most of her married life in Bartow county, Ga. She came to Texas in 1870. M. H. Wells

George Clark Bevis died near Pensacola, Fla., September 19, 1875, in the 25th year of his age. In January last he left Jackson county, where he had lived with his parents for some years past. He leaves a wife, an aged father and mother. H. M. Gillis

Mrs. Drucilla Claxton, wife of John H. Claxton, was born in Fort Valley, Ga., January 14, 1849; died August 26, 1875, and was buried near the place of her birth, by the side of her mother. She leaves two sons and one daughter. W. I. Greene

Mrs. Sarah E. Pitchford, whose maiden name was Stephens, was born in Greenville District, S. C., in 1807; and died at the residence of her son, Elijah W. Pitchford, Oct. 11, 1875. She was the wife of Eli Pitchford, who died in the Christian faith in 1855.

Laura L. Rogers, wife of L. L. Rogers, was born January 22, 1854; and died in peace at Langley, S. C., September 5, 1875. By this event, the husband and father has been bereft of all he held dear on earth, as on the 28th of June, Laura Eustacia, and on the 5th October 1875, Sudie, the lask link that bound him to earth, was broken by death.

Miss Mattie L. Hardy, died in Newton county, Ga., September 25, 1875, aged thirty years. Wm. W. Hardy.

Issue of November 10, 1875

Died

Braxton H. Kinett, son of E. T. and F. L. Kinett, was born June 24th 1866 and died August 20th 1875.

Of meningitis, in Charlotte, N. C., Mary Alieff, infant daughter of R. D. and R. E. Walsh.

Obituary

James Henry Rogers was born in Thomaston, Upson county, Ga., on the 15th of April 1840; married Miss Loula W. Kendall (Leola) 6th of January 1863; died in Thomaston, September 3, 1875. W. F. Cook

Mrs. Carrie Birdsong Caldwell, wife of the late O. A. Caldwell, Esq., was born in Oglethorpe county, Ga., October 7th 1839; and died in Macon, Ga., October 27th 1875.

Mrs. N. L. White was born in Virginia, December 31st 1814, and came to an untimely end in Stewart county, Ga., August 19th 1875. She was in rather better health than usual and in company with sister Love Kimbrough. On the way home, the horse ran away, threw her from hte buggy, and killed her instantly. From her grandson ,Mr. R. C. Black... "She moved from Greene county, Ga., when young... She moved to Stewart county, Ga., in 1845, was married three times, and lived to sell all of her husbands and children buried." Only one grandson and granddaughter survive her. A. J. Dean.

Mrs. Mary J. Respess of Eatonton, Ga., wife of William M. Respess, and daughter of the late Judge Stephen B. Marshall, of that place, died october 12th 1875, in the twenty-eighth year of her age.

Mrs. Emory C. Jones, wife of Dr. W. B. Jones, died at Birdsville, Burke county, Ga., October 13h 1875, in the thirty-second year of her age. A little over three years ago, by married with Dr. W. B. Jones, she became the step-mother of a number of children.

Mrs. Mary Drusilla Wood fell asleep in Jesus, September 1st, 1875, in Washington county, Ga. She was the daughter of Rev. Henry and Mrs. Huldah Scarborough.

Mr. R. A. Kirkpatrick was born in Abbeville District, S. C., July 30th 1814 and died in Madison county, Fla., October 13th 1875. E. S. Tyner

Robert Rives, Esq., was born in Hancock county, near Sparta, Ga., December 29th 1804; and died at Springvale, Randolph county, Ga., August 29th 1875. S. Anthony

Mrs. Catharine Kelly, daughter of Rev. Henry Cranford, died in Jackson county, Ga., October 10th 1875, aged 31 years and 6 months. Amicus W. Williams

Henry E. Clarke, died in Augusta, Ga., October 23, 1875, in the fifty-third year of age. Although brother Clarke was left an orphan when but a boy, he was kindly cared for by relatives in whose family he was reared. He was a steward of St. James Church from its foundation to the day of his death.

Mrs. Sarah P. Wimberly, relict of Rev. Frederick D. Wimberly, was born in Bladen county, N. C., and died at the residence of her nephew, Dr. W. A. Matthews, in Fort Valley, Ga., October 18, 1875, in her seventy-eighth year. She left her house in Lumpkin, in company with her daughter, for a short visit. In early life she removed to Jones county, Ga., where she was married in her nineteenth year. In 1833, removed to Stewart county, Ga., in 1847 lost her husband, and in 1848 she removed to Lumpkin, where she resided as long as she lived. She was the mother of a large family of children. A. J. Dean

Margaret M. Byrd was born October 31, 1823, was united in marriage with Mr. John P. Coles, and removed to Tallahassee in 1845; died near this city, October 4, 1875. Josephus Anderson

Mrs. M. V. Means, wife of Dr. M. H. Means, was born in Jones county, Ga., February 10, 1831; married February 9, 1845; and died very suddenly in Houston county, Ga., October 13, 1875. She leaves a husband and seven children.

Charles Reed Barrineau was born April 2, 1835; and died August 18, 1875. C. C. Fishburne

Thomas Fletcher Mims, son of Wesley and Mrs. Josephine Williams, of Charleston county, S. C., was born July 31, 1863 and died September 19, 1875. W. Hutto

Died

Caleb Linsey Sample, son of Dr. C. L. and Mrs. Rachel Sample, was born March 11th 1869, and died November 8th 1875.

Gertrude Hutchinson, youngest child of W. T. and Sarah M. Hutchinson, died in Atlanta, Ga., November 7th 1875, aged 22 months and 17 days.

Obituary

Mrs. Lizzie A. Little, wife of Mr. Willis Little and daughter of Mr. James of Marion district, S. C., was born November 16th 1839; married January 5th 1879, and died near Ellaville, Ga., October 20th 1875. Left an orphan at the age of twelve, an excellent aunt took charge of her education until she was fifteen, and then, in company with a beloved brother, she came to Lanier, Ga.

James M. Dyson died suddenly in Wilkes county, Ga., September 12th 1875 in the sixty-fourth year of her age. Most of his family were members of the Baptist Church. N. C. Ware

Mrs. Amanda Williams, whose maiden name was Wade, wife of P. R. Williams, was born in Green county, Ga., and died in Floyd county, Ga., September 15th 1875, aged about fifty years. She joined the Baptist Church in her 15th year, but a few years ago, joined the Methodist church with her husband. She leaves a husband, one daughter, Mrs. Anna Mathis, and four grandchildren, an aged and afflicted mother, Mrs. Lucy Wade... her grand-son, Mr. John Wade, who was buried in Forestville the day before. Samuel King

Moses W. Murray was born in South Carolina, February 26th 1800; removed to Georgia in 1847; died at his home in Terrell county, October 8th 1875. He leaves a family and bereaved wife. J. R. Littlejohn

Mrs. Polly Wimberly, whose maiden name was Bryan, was born in Johnson county, N. C., October 12th 1787; was married to Gen. E. Wimberly in 1809; and died in Twiggs county, Ga., October 21, 1875. Six children survive her.

Martha Iverson Lane, daughter of Rev. R. and M. H. Lane, was born in Texas, April 29th 1860; died in Jefferson, Texas, October 6, 1875. W. C. Haislip

Charles R. Seawright, a native of South Carolina, died October 25th 1875, aged seventy-four years. He was married in early manhood to Miss A. M. Kaigler. heave leaves one daughter and several grand-children. Geo. C. Clarke

Mrs. Martha P. Robertson, consort of the late John M. Robertson, died at the residence of her son, N. C. Robertson, in Fairfield county, S. C., November 6th 1875, in the seventieth year of her age. J. M. Boyd

Joseph Brabham died November 6th 1875, at the residence of his son, near Buford's Bridge, S. C. He was born March 1st 1785, consequently he was in the ninety-fifth year of his age. He was first married to Miss Sarah Kirkland, of Barnwell county, S. C. They had twelve children, some of whom, with their pious mother, preceded him to the better world. His second marriage was to Mrs. Elizabeth R. Kearse. Paul F. Kistler

John Anderson Hayes died in Allendale, S. C., October 8th 1875, in the seventy-eighth year of his age.

Peter Morrison died in Montgomery county, Ga., September 20th 1875, in the fifty-fourth year of his age. C. C. Hines

Mrs. Martha J. Harris of Hamilton county, Fla., died October 16th 1875, in the thirty-third year of her age.

Saxon Bishop, aged twenty, eldest son of James and Mary Bishop, died November 3d, 1875, in Eastman, Dodge county, Ga.

Mrs. Martha W. Wood, wife of brother Richard Wood and daughter of brother and sister Duke, of Hogansville, Ga., died in Alabama, November 2, 1875, in her thirty-third year. F. M. T. Brannon

Issue of December 1, 1875

Died

Philip Washington, son of P. W. and Elizabeth Fairey, was born April 24th 1873 and died at Branchville, S. C., September 25th 1875.

Near Oswichee, Russel county, Ala., Julia, daughter of Dr. Andrew Williams, aged nine years and four months.

Obituary

Mrs. Lucy A. Barnett was born in Houston county, Ga., April 11, 1828; married Mr. John N. Barnett, September 18, 1845; and died in Columbus, Ga., October 28, 1875. Jas. O. Branch

Mrs. Mary A. E. Pounds, eldest daughter of Shadrach and Catharine Bradford, was born in Lowndes county, Ga., February 7, 1846; married James D. Pounds, August 6, 1865; died in Berrien county, Ga., August 27, 1875. She leaves a large concourse of relatives and friends, among them an aged grand-father, and two grand-mothers. J. T. Webb

My sister, Mrs. Martha D. White, wife of James W. White, of Madison county, Ga., was born in Athens, Ga., February 9, 1849; died October 22, 1875. C. A. Mitchell

Dwight Newell, son of Reason and Margaret Newell, was born in Orangeburg county, S. C., April 1849, and died August 31, 1875.

Andrew Middleton Wicker, of Newberry, S. C., was born March 17, 1817; and died Nov. 7, 1875, in his 57th year. He was married to Miss Nancy Hayes, March 30, 1843. He left a wife and children. R. P. Franks

Thomas D. Edwards was born February 28, 1809 and died in Orangeburg county, S. C., November 12, 1875. His wife, to whom he was married in 1840, preceded him some three years to the good world. John W. McRoy

D. Martin F. Huff was born September 19, 1834 and died in Orangeburg county, S., C., October 26, 1875. J. W. McRoy

Mrs. Teresa Myers, wife of Stephen A. Myers, died in Wayne county, Ga., August 28, 1875, in the 56th year of her age.

Mrs. L. A. Dilworth was born in North Carolina; moved to Union Point, Ga., after her marriage; and died August 24, 1875, in the 55th year of her age.

William H. Dutton died in Bulloch county, Ga., November 13, 1875, aged forty-four years, seven months, and two days. He leaves a wife and a large concourse of relatives and friends.

Issue of December 8, 1875

[page 194, column 1] Death of Mrs. Duncan. Dr. Whitefoord Smith appends the following sad note to the a business communication of November 27th. Mrs. Duncan was the mother of Dr. James A. and Rev. Wallace W. Duncan... "With pain I have to announce the sudden decease this day of Mrs. Duncan, wife of the venerable professor David Duncan...."

Obituary

Mrs. Freddie Tarver Baird died in Kirkwood, Ga., November 19th 1875, in the twenty-third year of her age. Reared around the fireside of her grand-father, Rev. Henry Bunn... at the age of eleven years, she joined the Baptist church. Just eighteen months before her death she was married to Mr. John B. Baird of Atlanta.

J. T. Hood was born in North Carolina, July 18th 1840 and died in Richland county, S. C., November 1st 1875. He was reared under Baptist influences. In August last he joined the M. E. Church, South. He leaves a widow and three children.

Mrs. Sarah A. Murdock, whose maiden name was Williams, was born in Bulloch county, Ga., in 1806; married to Wm. P. Murdock, December 10th 1829, and died in Suwannee county, Fla., November 1st 1875.

Jacob Heldebrand was born December 1792, and died October 10th 1875. He left an aged wife and a large family of children and grand-children. A. R. Danner

Mrs. George Ann Florida Craig was born February 23d 1852; married February 17th 1869, and died September 16th 1875. She left a husband and three small children.

Mrs. Henrietta Wooton, whose maiden name was Tuck, wife of Wm. J. wooton, was born in Spartanburg District, S. C., February 16th 1804, and died November 2d 1875 in Valley Falls, in the same District and State. She first married a gentlemen whose by the name of Bates. Her second husband was brother W. J. Wooton, who lives to mourn her loss. C. Lee

James Sharp was born in Burke county, N. C., in 1803 and died October 30th 1875 in Gilmer county, Ga. He leaves an aged companion. J. M. Watkins

Mrs. Rebecca Clemmons, wife of G. W. Clemmons, died in Conyers, Ga., October 19th 1875.

Miss Mary Antoinette McFarland, daughter of X. G. and L. A. McFarland, was born in Walker county, Ga., August 18th 1851; and died September 15th 1873. J. B. McFarland

Mrs. Marina Bruce, wife of Elija Bruce, of Edgefield, S. C., died November 9th 1875.

Tribute of Respect from Quarterly Conference of Greenville and Trinity circuit, North Georgia Conference, to Brother John A. Simonton.

Issue of December 15, 1875

Mrs. Jane G. Gerry (formerly Miss O'Neill) widow of the late Rev. John L. Gerry of the Florida Conference, was born in Nassau county, Florida, November 16, 1806; and died October 24, 1875 at Lake City, Florida. She was married to Bro. Gerry, December 21, 1827, at a time when the Conference included South Carolina, Georgia, and Florida. Henry Edw. Partridge

Mrs. John O. Clower was born April 9, 1850, and died in her native town, Grantville, Ga., November 22, 1875. She was a daughter of Mrs. A. C. Lambert, whose husband died years ago, and a granddaughter of Rev. W. B. Smith, by whom she was principally brought up. On the 15th of October 1868, she was married to Mr. G. W. Clower. They were blessed with two interesting children; the younger was taken about two years ago. The other is six years old. W. J. Cotter

Mrs. Eliza Tappan was born in Greene county, Ga., April 30th 1836; married Mr. R. Tappan, March 22, 1865; and died at White Plains, Greene county, Ga., October 30, 1875.

William Kellard died in Orangeburg county, S. C., in the eighty-sixth year of his age. We buried him in the old family grave-yard. Thos. J. Clyde

John T. P. McElroy died on the morning of November 12th 1875. Brother McElroy was licensed to exhort only two days before he died. W. T. Laine

Mrs. Rebecca Neal, relict of A. B. Neal, deceased, was born in Pendleton District, S. C., May 18, 1808; removed to McMinn county, Tenn., with her father, John Pickens, at the age of thirteen years; joined the Methodist Episcopal Church at Cedar Springs camp meeting at the age of sixteen; was married February 12, 1829, and removed to Walker county, Ga., where she died October 21, 1875. J. B. McFarland

Ignatius J. Dozier, son of Green J. Dozier, was born April 2, 1828; and died in Barnesville, Ga., October 19, 1875. He was from one of the oldest Methodist families of the State. He came when a young man to Upson county, where he married the daughter of Rev. Jack Lindsay. He left a wife and eight children. G. G. Smith

Mrs. Mary H. Cape was born July 9, 1830; and died in Orangeburg county, S. C., Nov. 24, 1875. At the age of eighteen years she joined the Baptist Church, in which she remained until about four years ago, when she united with the M. E. Church, South. A. J. Cauthen

Thomas Spencer Potts was born in Fayetteville, N. C., june 3, 1817; married in Gadsden county, Fla., in 1843; and died in Tallahassee, Fla., Nov. 14, 1875. Josephus Anderson

Issue of December 22-29, 1875

Mrs. Rebecca Jane Bateman, the eldest daughter of C. F. and R. J. Bateman, of Charleston, S. C., died November 21st 1875, in the twentieth year of her age.

Henry R. Edwards died in Jefferson county, Fla., November 10th 1875. He was born in Duval county, Fla., in 1815. He leaves a wife and many friends. R. H. Howren

Levi Ezell was born in Lancaster District, S. C., April 27th 1801, and died in Houston county, Ga., November 20th 1875. Early in life he moved to Twiggs county, Ga., where he married his first wife, Miss Sarah Roach, in 1832. He was married the second time to Miss Pamelia Hall, of Baldwin county, Ga., in 1842. W. F. Robison

John Alonzo Tyler was born in Orangeburg, S. C., and died in Columbus, Ga., September 28th 1875, aged sixty-nine years and six months. A. M. Wynn

Capt. Jas. M. Moody died in Savannah, Ga., aged fifty-nine years. He was born in Barnwell District, S. C., but moved to Augusta in early childhood, where he was raised. He leaves a wife, daughter, and a family of grandchildren.

Mrs. Elenora McCorquodale, wife of Rev. Allan McCorquodale, died November 23d, 1875. When her sainted husband left us, she was expected hourly to follow, but did not join him for nine days. She was in her 75th year, and he his 76th. Her father Joel P. Green, was a man of large fortune on Santee. Her former husband, Capt. James J. Rembert, was also a man of fortune. S. J. Hill

Issue of January 5, 1876

Brother Francisco Diez, lay missionary to the Cubans of Key West, died at the parsonage of the First M. E. Church on the 3d inst., aged about 38 years. He was a native of the Canary Islands. When quite young his parents moved to Cuba, where he was reared. At the age of 21 he came to this country, having determined to make his home in one of the Southern states. He spent a few months in Key West, and then removed to Jacksonville. From thence he removed to Charleston, then to Augusta, Ga., and finally to Savannah. Marrying Miss Ann H. Cushman... Chas. A. Fulwood

Miss Fannie Bacon died at the residence of her nephew, W. J. Pollard, near Augusta, Ga., on the 12th of December 1875, in the sixty-fourth year of her age. She was born and brought up in Jackson county, Ga., where she spent most of her life. C. W. Key

Lucius B. Lovelace was born in Columbia county, Ga., February 1806; and died in Troup county, Ga., November 17, 1875. He was for a number of years President of the Chattahoochee Manufacturing Company, near West Point, Ga. P. M. Ryburn

Mrs. Jane M. Dozier died at her residence in Columbia county on the 18th of December, in the 56th year of her age. Left a widow with eight children, she trained them....

Capt. A. D. Way was born in 1806 and died in December, 1875. He married first in his 19th year; second in his 40th year. As to children, his quiver was full of them, having twenty in number--at his death he had thirty-seven grandchildren and one great-grandchild. J. H. Zimmerman

Issue of January 12, 1876

Mrs. Frances E. Evans, daughter of Robert and Martha Collier of Upson county, Ga., was born July 1819; married John Q. Evans, September 16th 1851; and died in Villula, Russel county, Ala., December 5th 1875. Her son-in-law was her physician. A husband, four sons, and four daughters, two son-in-law, and one daughter-in-law, and eight grandchildren compose the living family of sister Evans. John W. Solomon. New Orleans Christian Advocate please copy.

Judge John A. Simonton was born October 23d 1818; married October 23d 1843; died in Greenville, Ga., September 13th 1875.

Mrs. Mattie J. Hunt was born in Upson county, Ga., May 9th 1841; and died in Barnesville, Ga., December 2d 1875.

Mary Dowman, daughter of Charles and A. W. Dowman, was born in the County of Essex, England, June 28th 1854; and died at the home of her parents, near Mt. Gilead, Fulton county, Ga., November 23d 1875. Mary was but an infant when her parents emigrated to America and settled in Georgia. Rev. Charles Dowman, a brother of the deceased. J. Goodman

Mrs. Susan E. Crenshaw, wife of W. H. Crenshaw, died in Newton county, Ga., October 11th 1875, aged forty-one years and eight months. Her husband and six children are left. Her Uncle, G. B. C.

Mrs. Elmira Edwards, wife of Gideon Edwards of Jackson county, Ga., was born December 27, 1824; and died November 9, 1875.

Mrs. Mary Elizabeth Cothran, daughter of R. L. Mitchell, deceased, and grand-daughter of Rev. C. Trussell, of the North Georgia Conference, was born July 5th 1856 and died near Villa Rica, Ga., December 13th 1875.

Joseph H. Howell died in Orangeburg county, S. C., December 7th 1875, in the seventy-sixth year of his age. He leaves an aged widow, sons, daughters, and grandchildren. I. O. A. Connor

Robert Shields was born in Columbia county, Ga., in 1819 and died in Volusia county, Fla., October 27th 1875. He moved to Florida in 1856. Robt. D. Gentry

Mrs. Nancy J. Jenkins, a daughter of Mr. Duncan, and Mrs. A. McLeod, of Emanuel county, Ga., was born January 10th 1849; was married to Mr. C. J. Jenkins, Jr., July 14th 1874; died December 17th 1875. Louis B. Bouchelle

Issue of January 19, 1876

Died

Near Cheraw, S. C., Raiford Little Wilson, youngest son of Rev. A. J. and Fannie Wilson--aged five years and twenty-seven days.

Obituary

James H. Robinson was born in Jasper county, Ga., March 18, 1818; and died at Newborn, Newton county, Ga., December 4, 1875. J. F. Mixon

Thomas Hunt was born August 18, 1800; moved from Hancock to Jones county, Ga., in 1823; and died November 22, 1875.

Mrs. D. A. E. Pendergrass, daughter of Rufus J. and Nancy D. Hughes, was born in Walton county, Ga., December 18, 1843; married to W. N. Pendergrass on April 15, 1859; and died in Monroe, Walton county, Ga., December 19, 1875. Left a husband and six children. D. F. C. Timmons

John E. McCall was born in Bullock county, Ga., February 20, 1822; and died in Liberty county, Ga., December 21, 1875. The Church at Taylor's Creek has lost one of its strongest pillars. John M. Marshall

Mrs. Anna Elizabeth Ledbetter, wife of Col. Henry W. Ledbetter, and daughter of P. N. Stanback, Esq., was born in Richmond county, N. C., May 29, 1839; and died in Anson county, near Wadesboro, N. C., Dec. 22, 1875.

Mrs. Mary Sumner, whose maiden name was Thoby, was born of Baptist parents, October 30, 1836; married to John C. Sumner, October 15, 1857; joined the M. E. Church, South at Clemmon's Chapel, Worth Mission, South Georgia Conference; died October 23, 1875. She reared six of her own children and two of brother's Sumner's by a former wife. William N. Clemmons

Tribute of Respect from Norcross circuit, North Georgia Conference, to John T. McElroy.

Issue of January 26, 1876

Died

At Branchville, S. C., January 4th 1876, Algernon Adolphus Izlar, son of H. P. and Mamie C. Izlar, aged one year, six months and ten days.

In Irwinton, Ga., January 8th 1875, Mary L. Baker, daughter of Rev. W. S. and Mrs. M. A. Baker, aged four years, four months and thirteen days.

Obituary

Emanuel Sheftall was born October 25th 1811; and died in Savannah, Ga., November 19th 1875. Within less than a month, his youngest son, William Crumley Sheftall, died.

Mrs. Emily Mallory, wife of John Mallory and daughter of Green B. and Lucretia Caudle, died in Troup county, Georgia, November 3d, 1875, in the forty-fourth year of her age.

Mrs. Mary N. Haynes, consort of Lewis A. Haynes, was born in Troupville, Lowndes county, Ga., October 10th 1854; and died in Valdosta, Ga., at the residence of her grand-father, William Smith, Esq., November 21st 1875.   H. W. Sharpe

Lina Elrod was born May 1808 in Pickens county, S. C., and died October 26th 1875. W. A. Fariss

Alfred Sikes died near Wataula church in Russell county, Alabama, January 1st 1876, in his eighty-third year. He leaves a wife with whom he had lived forty-five years, and nine children, and grand-children.

Issue of February 2, 1876

Died

In Irwinton, Ga., January 8th 1876, Mary L. Baker, daughter of Rev. W. S. and Mrs. M. A. Baker, aged four years, four months, and thirteen days.

Obituary

Miss Texana F. Green, daughter of Jesse W. and Amanda M. Green, was born in Rabun county, Ga., November 23, 1869; and died December 25, 1875. George E. Bonner

Mrs. Sarah Patterson, wife of A. E. Patterson, was born in 1843; married May 25th 1858; died January 6th 1876, in Madison county, Fla.

Mrs. Charity Burkett, whose maiden name was Hyman, was born in Martin county, North Carolina, February 1804; and died January 10, 1876. She was first married to Randal Cain, with whom she moved to South Carolina. After his death she was married to Solomon Burkett, and in 1822 they moved to Twiggs county, Ga. They were instrument in building up the Church known as "Burkett's."

Irby Roberts was born in Columbia county, Ga., November 20th 1806; and died in Ocala, Fla., January 11, 1876. Geo C. Leavel

James D. Creighton was born September 1824 in Kershaw District, S. C., and died October 21, 1875 in Lancaster county, S. C. D. J. McMillan

Jackson Robena Bethann, youngest daughter of the late Andrew Jackson and Mary T. Askew, died in Harris county, Ga., January 13, 1876, aged 10 years 8 months and 12 days. She leaves a widowed mother and several brothers and sisters. J. T. Whitaker

Issue of February 9, 1876

Died

In Charleston, S. C., January 18th 1876, Julia Gambrill Smyth, daughter of Ellison A. and Julia G. Smyth, aged four years and five months.

Obituary

Mrs. Mary W. Deavours was born in Spartanburg District, S. C., in 1791; and died in Walton county, Ga., November 12, 1875. She was married to John Deavours, with whom she lived forty years, having a number of sons, two of whom are Methodist preachers-- one a local, the other, A. J. Deavours, a member of the North Georgia Conference. M. F. Malsby. Texas Advocate please copy.

Lemuel Johnson was born February 11th 1806; and died at the house of his father-in-law, in Cobb county, Ga., November 7, 1875. He was married twice; first to Catharine Fowler, May 15, 1825; the second time to Elizabeth Groover, November 7, 1866, whom, with four little ones, he left to mourn their loss. In the cemetery at Little River, Cherokee county, Ga., he sleeps in peace. C. M. McClure.

Willie Wallace died November 29th 1875, in the town of Butler, Ga., aged sixteen years, nine months and fourteen days. James G. Russ

Mrs. Sarah L. Henry, was born in Blount county, Tenn, December 6th 1804; was married to James W. Henry, who died four years before her, August 22d 1822; and died in Whitfield county, Ga., December 9th 1875. She has left four children. G. W. Thomas

Mrs. Mary Ann Lawson, daughter of the late William D. Sineath, and wife of John A. Lawson of Lowndes county, Ga., was born in Colleton district, S. C., February 26th 1835; and died December 26th 1875. She has left a widowed mother, husband, two daughters and many relatives. We buried her by the side of her father, at Salem Church. J. T. Webb

Mrs. Martha Crawford was a daughter of Capt. W. t. Williamson of Milledgeville. She was born at McIntosh Reserve, Coweta county, Ga., January 8, 1836. January 8, 1855, she was married to Mr. C. P. Crawford. From 1855 to 1859 she lived in Americus; from 1859 to 1863 in Lee county; from 1863 to 1871 in Florida, from 1871 to 1876 in Milledgeville. A. J. Jarrell

Rev. Henry H. Penney was born in Newberry district, S. C., April 10th 1811, and died in Oconee, January 14th 1876. He has left a widow and large family. L. C. Loyal

Francis B. Drake was born in North Carolina, October 16th 1806; and died in Johnson county, Ga., December 17th 1875. His father moved to Georgia when he was quite young ,and settled in Washington county in 1822. D. G. Pope

Miss Mary F. Snow was born January 17th 1825 and died in Walton county, Ga., November 17th 1875. M. F. Malsby

Mrs. Jane Williams, wife of R. M. Williams and daughter of John and Martha Langford, was born in Bryant county, Ga., February 16th 1834; and died in Madison county, Fla., January 25th 1876. W. W. Williams

Issue of February 16, 1876

Died

In Columbia county, Ga., February 1, 1876, Victoria Howard, infant daughter of Rev. R. A. and Mrs. E. J. Conner, aged eleven months and one days.

Obituary

At noon, January 28, 1876, Dr. Jasper Browne died at his residence on Rocky River, Anderson county, S. C., aged fifty-one years, four months and seventeen days. Less than nine months since, the six daughters and two sons were left without a mother; now they are without a father.

Rev. R. E. Oslin died at his home near Fredonia, Alabama, January 24, 1876. He was somewhat over sixty years old. He was married to Miss Mattie Randle. After her death, he married Mrs. Mattie J. Johnson, of Chambers county, Ala. J. W. Christian

Mrs. Mattie E. Brown, wife of J. M. Brown, died January 20, 1876, in Montezuma, Ga., aged 31 years. She was the daughter of Mr. and Mrs. J. H. Wallace of Drayton, Dooly county, Ga. James L. Gibson

Mrs. C. C. Nicholson was born in Oconee county, S. C., January 1828; was married to William Nicholson, of Rabun county, Ga., Jan. 12, 1847; and died Dec. 1, 1875. She was left a widow in 1865 with ten children, most of them small. George E. Bonner

Thomas Lowry Fowler died in Greenville, S. C., January 14, 1876, in the 57th year of his age. Except a few years in Hamburg, S. C., his life was passed in the neighborhood in which he died. Four children--two sons and two daughters-- and his wife are left. A. H. Lester

My son John H. Jourdan joined the Church under the ministry of Rev. Wesley Lane, on the Glascow Circuit; and died at my house November 13, 1875, in the 27th year of his age. Isaac G. Jourdan

Issue of February 23, 1876

Mrs. Eveline Dickson, consort of Mr. David Dickson, now deceased, and both of Oxford, Ga., was born September 9th 1813, and died January 13th 1876. The death of her husband... 16th of March 1875. She was a native of North Carolina, and a daughter of Mr. --- Sandefur, who removed to Georgia and was for several years a resident of Madison, Morgan county. A. Means

Peter W. Hutcheson, Sr., was born in Mecklenburg county, Va., March 17th 1794; removed thence in 1822 to Oglethorpe county, Ga., where he died December 9th 1875. Richmond Advocate please copy.

Rev. Robert Frasier Jones was born in Greene county, Ga., November 20th 1828; and died in Senoia, Ga., January 17th 1876. He graduated at Emory College in 1850. In 1854 he was married to Miss P. W. Sandeford of Burke county Ga., who preceded him to the better land near three years. A. J. Dean

Mrs. Mary B. Zipperer, daughter of Joseph E. and Sarah Law, was born December 5th 1839; married Thomas J. Zipperer, January 12th 1858; and died in Hamilton county, Florida, January 17th 1876. She was the mother of seven children, the youngest only six days old.

Mr. Wm. G. McNair was born in Pulaski county, Ga., June 8th 1812; and died in Madison county, Fla., January 30th 1876. E. S. Tyner

Mrs. Anna M. King, wife of Captain Robert N. King, and died at St. Mary's, Ga., December 25th 1875, in the 45th year of her age. She was married in December 1853.

Sallie Taylor McGregor, youngest child of Mr. and Mrs. P. G. McGregor, of Columbia, S. C., was born May 12th 1851, and died December 12th 1875.

Miss Charlotte Ann Bowen was born January 1809 and died November 18th 1875. She had but one known relative on earth, a sister living in Marietta. W. W. Oslin

Mrs. Lizzie L. Greer, whose maiden name was Chambers, was born in Cherokee county, Ga., May 15th 1845; was married to Dr. T. G. Greer, February 27th 1873; and died February 3d 1876.

Tribute of Respect from Leon circuit, Tallahassee District, Florida Conference to Richmond N. Gardner, M. D., who died 18th December last.

Issue of March 1, 1876

Mrs. Nannie Colquitt Ansley, daughter of Hon. Walter T. and Mrs. Harriet Colquitt, was born in Columbus, Ga., in 1852; married to Henry C. Ansley 18th of April 1875; and died January 5th 1876.

Thomas F. Cowlers died in Eatonton, Ga., February 11, 1876, in the 77th year of his age. D. R. Adams

Joshua Smith was born in Effingham county, Ga., November 25th 1795; and died in Bryan county, Ga., December 2d 1875.

Mrs. Amanda H. Bramhan, wife of Mr. Isaac N. Bramhan and daughter of Mr. and Mrs. James R. Green, died in Opelika, Ala., January 16th 1876, aged 32 years.

Mrs. Virginia G. Blalock was born Nov. 2d 1808; and died in Columbia county, Ga., Jan. 21st, 1876. B. F. Fariss

Mrs. Mary Virginia Evans, wife of Josiah Evans and daughter of Miles and Martha W. Greene, was born in Harris county, Ga., March 3d 1845; was married July 2d 1873; and died near Jamestown, Ga., January 25th 1876.

Barton C. Thrasher, son of Isaac Thrasher, and father-in-law of Rev. J. H. Baxter of the North Georgia Conference, was born Jan. 17th 1823; and died in Oconee county, Ga., Jan. 23d, 1876. An aged father, a brother and sister, a wife and eight children, mourn his loss. W. W. Oslin

David Solomon was born in Germany, June 13th 1792; and died at Gordon, Ga., January 23d 1876. Wm. J. Green

Mira Bedford was born in North Carolina, August 14th 1820. Her parents moved with her to East Tennessee in 1822. She was married to Jathan Gregory, February 6th 1838. She died in Murray county, Ga., December 12th 1875. D. J. Myrick

Sarah O. Baxter, wife of John F. Baxter, was born May 11th 1828; and died January 23d 1876. She leaves a husband and two children.

Tribute of Respect from Buena Vista Circuit to Bland Wallis, Sr., who died in Marion county, Ga., November 27th 1875, in the 69th year of his age.

Issue of March 8, 1876

Died

Julia Bertha Pike, infant daughter of J. C. and Mrs. Frances Pike of Orangeburg C. H., S. C., was born November 25, 1873, and died February 28, 1876.

Obituary

Rev. Gadwell Jefferson Pearce was born in Jackson county, Ga., April 10, 1813. He entered into rest on January 29th 1876. He was married June 2, 1846, to the eldest daughter of Rev. J. W. Glenn. He leaves a wife, two sons and three daughters, connected with Trinity Church, Atlanta. W. F. Cook.

Mrs. Cornelia Holly, widow of the late John Holly, died in Barnwell county, S. C., February 8, 1876, in the 77th year of her age. A. W. Walker

Mr. David Buchanan died at Princeton, near Athens, Ga., in the home of his daughter, sister Roberts, January 21, 1876 k,aged about 85 years. He was born in North Carolina, where he lived for a number of years. Moved to Georgia in 1837. He joined the Baptist Church when about sixteen years of age. After removal to Georgia, he joined the M. E. Church.

Mrs. Elizabeth A. Jack was born in Bladen county, N. C., March 2, 1804; moved to Walton county, Ga., in 1821; married in 1831, and settled in Rome, Ga., in April 1835. Near this city she died January 11, 1876.

Dr. Richmond N. Gardner died in Montgomery, Alabama, 28th December 1875. Dr. Gardner was a native of Georgia and was born January 1st 1823. His father was a Methodist minister. In 1855 he graduated, as a physician, at the University of Virginia, and settled in Florida. E. L. T. Blake

Miss Emma Hendrick, daughter of James and Lucinda Hendrick, was born March 31, 1849; died in Warren county, Ga., December 14, 1875.

Issue of March 15, 1876

Dr. W. H. Blalock was born in Randolph county, N. C., in 1813; moved to Georgia very early in life; and died in Fayette county, Feb. 19, 1876.

Mrs. Caroline Matilda Greene, daughter of Leonidas B. and Nancy Gardner, was born in Jones county, Ga., August 19, 1853. After removing with her parents to Macon county... November 7, 1871, she was married to Rev. William A. Greene, of the South Georgia Conference. She leaves a husband and two children. John M. Potter

Leila Roberta Jenkins, daughter of E. A. and Arabella Jenkins, was born Nov. 26, 1861; and died near Box Springs, Ga., Feb. 23, 1876.

William Crumley Sheftall, youngest son of Emanuel Sheftall, lately deceased, died in Savannah recently, aged twenty-three years, lacking a few days.

Mrs. Susan Brown, relict of Wm. Brown, and daughter of Rev. Stephen Shell, was born in Virginia May 26, 1788, and died at the residence of her son Lemon Brown, Esq., of Newton county, Ga., Feb. 27, 1876. She was a widow for twenty years, lacking one day. Six of sister Brown's children survive her; among them, Lemon, Stephen, Dr. William, and Rev. Thos. A. Brown. W. R. B.

Mr. Henry Pou Gessendanner was born in South Carolina, April 25, 1804; and died in Orangeburg, S. C., February 12, 1876. He has left a large family of children. A. R. Danner

Mrs. Jennett Hamilton, wife of S. C. Hamilton and daughter of Angus and Jennett Brown, was born in Cumberland county, N. C., May, 1800 and died in LaPlace, Alabama, January 23, 1876.

Tribute of Respect from M. E. Church, South in Atlanta, to Rev. John H. Harris of the North Georgia Conference.

Issue of March 22, 1876

Died

Cora Ella Quillian, infant daughter of Dr. J. Wylie and Mrs. Mary Quillian, died in Homer, Banks county, Ga., March 3, 1876.

Obituary

Mrs. Sarah Garland Eve, daughter of Sterling Combs and Mildred Wingfield, and wife of Dr. Joseph A. Eve, was born in Jackson county, Ga., June 6th 1811; and died in Augusta, Ga., March 4th 1876. Her parents were Virginians, who had quite early in life removed to Georgia. The father after residing in Jackson county many years, closed his long life of nearly eighty years at the house of Dr. Eve, June 15, 1847, the mother having died about nine years before. One of the daughters become the wife of Mr. Andrew, a young Methodist itinerant, who later became Bishop Andrew. On the first of April 1833, the daughter was joined in happy marriage to Dr. Joseph A. Even in Augusta. God blessed the union with eleven children, eight of whom survive their mother. Clement A. Evans

Mrs. Mary Rebecca Clark, wife of G. E. Clark and daughter of Burgess and Miles Cheek, was born in Henry county, Ga., June 13, 1813; and died in Sumter county, Ga., December 24, 1875. J. R. Littlejohn

Col. Joel T. Crawford was born in Greene county, Ga., October 9, 1812; married Miss S. A. Watson of Clark county, Ga., in 1832; and about twelve years afterward moved to Enon, Ala., where he resided until his death, December 18, 1875. Jere S. Williams

Angus McInnis was born in Robeson county, N., C., May 6, 1793, and died in Hamilton county, Fla., February 25, 1876. He was one of the trio of champion class-leaders, Leach, McCaskil, and McInnis-- of Fork Creek Church, S. C.

My beloved father, Wm. B. Pelot, was born near Hardeeville, Beaufort county, S. C., January 17, 1813; and died February 5, 1876. He leaves a wife, an only daughter, and son in law, with two little grand-daughters. His daughter, Annie E. Evans.

Mrs. Elizabeth Sasser was born in Screven county, Ga., July 9, 1836; and died in Terrell county, Ga., March 5, 1876.

Mrs. Mary W. (Werts) Bushart was born September 5, 1816; and died March 3, 1876, in Newberry county, S. C. Thos G. Herbert.

Mrs. Sarah Hull Neal, relict of Basil L. Neal and daughter of Mr. McKeen and Mrs. Ellen Green, was born in Augusta, Ga., January 1, 1798; was married to Basil L. Neal, July 1829; died in Thomson, Ga., December 12, 1875.

Miss Sarah Kytle was born September 13, 1794; and died in Greenville county, S., C., February 24, 1876. B. M. Boozer

Issue of March 29, 1876

Mrs. Selina Durant was born in Sumter county, S., C., January 3, 1809; was married to Elias Durant, November 9, 1826; and died in the same county, near Lynchburg, January 23, 1876. A. Coke Smith

Mrs. Martha Higgs, daughter of the late Rev. John J. Richards of the Florida Conference, was born April 21, 1846; and died in St. Marys, Ga., February 20, 1876. She was married in 1874 to Mr. Wm. Higgs, and moved to Mexico. Her health failing, she returned home to spend the few remaining days of her life with an aged mother and fond relations. B. W. Key

Christopher Columbus Cochran was born March 2, 1849, and died at his father's, a few miles above Pendleton, S. C., January 14, 1876. D. J. McMillan

Isaac H. Moreland was born January 17, 1819 in Jones county, Georgia. He was first married to Miss Mary James Dickson, April 19, 1842. She lived only about one year. He was married again June 30, 1846, to Miss Mary Jane Tooke, and the following year moved to Hayneville, Houston county, Ga., where he resided until he died, January 31, 1876. He leaves a wife and four children.

331

Miss Mary Ann Chaudoin, daughter of Rev. Lewis Chaudoin, a Baptist minister of Goochland county, Va., died January 13, 1876, in Dougherty county, Ga., at the residence of Mrs. John C. Nelms, her niece, aged 83 years in November last. W. M. Russell. Richmond Christian Advocate please copy.

William Carlton, son of John and Nancy Carlton, and husband of Harriet Carlton-- whose maiden name was Hendry-- was born in North Carolina in 1807; and died at Fort Green, Manatee county, Fla., December 16, 1876.

Susan Clark, wife of John M. Clark, formerly of newton county, Ga., was born July 15, 1806; near Dumphries, Va., and died at Buford, Ga., February 29, 1876. Her Son.

Mrs. Julia A. Bragan, wife of John W. Bragan, died in Cuthbert, Ga., March 2, 1876, in the forty-seventh year of her age. R. W. Dixon

Seaborn S. Akins, son of Thomas and Nicie Akins, was born in Jasper county, Ga., fifty or sixty years ago; and died in Texas, January 4, 1876. He moved to Texas about six years ago, and lived most of the time with Dr. P. Shi. S. S. Pennington.

Martha Ann Elizabeth Shell was born April 17, 1864, and died Dec. 27, 1875.

Tribute of Respect from Spring Vale Circuit to Robert Rives.

Issue of April 5, 1876

John B. Johnson, of the Cokesbury Circuit, South Carolina Conference, was born in Edgefield District, S. C., November 20, 1806; on the morning of March 1, 1876, died near Greenwood, S. C., leaving behind a wife and three children-- six having preceded him to the spirit world. J. B. Traywick

Mrs. W. V. Tarver, daughter of Rev. W. A. Hayles, of Jefferson county, Ga., died in Burke county, Ga., March 1, 1876, in the 28th year of her age. Her funeral services were held in the Methodist Church in Louisville, Jefferson County, Ga. Here she was born, reared, and buried.

Mrs. Sarah J. W. Pye, whose maiden name was Beckham, was born in Monroe county, Ga., September 24, 1830; and died at Forsyth, in the same county, February 16, 1876. She was twice married-- first September 22, 1850 to Dr. Josiah E. Nunnally, who died in July 1852, leaving an infant son. She afterward married B. Pye, of Forsyth, Ga., May 10, 1864. Her only child, James B. Nunnally, died in the spring of that year--April 13. D. D. Cox

Mr. Rufus Dickinson was born in Amherst, Mass., December 22, 1814; and died in Madison, Fla., March 10, 1876. He emigrated South at the age of fifteen years, and has been living in Madison county and Madison village, for the last thirty years. He left a wife, daughter and six sons. E. S. Tyner

Claude V. Wilson, son of Dr. Wm. E. Wilson, of Denver, Colorado, was born at Warsaw, near Atlanta, Ga., June 12, 1853; and died in Burke county, Ga., January 21, 1876. His mother, who was Miss Susannah Ward, died when he was about nine days old, and much of his youth was spent with his uncle, Gus Ward, near Waynesboro, Ga. He joined the M. E. Church in Decatur, Illinois, about seven years ago; and afterwards joined the same Church at Denver, whither his father removed from Illinois. He was married to miss Julia Bell of Burke county, Ga., March 4, 1875. F. A. Branch

Mrs. Martha K. Wilkes, wife of J. Wesley Wilkes, died at Baton Rouge, Chester district, S. C., March 1, 1876, aged about thirty-five years.

Miss Julia A. Pitchford died in White county, Ga., March 11, 1876, aged twenty-four years, one month and sixteen days. She was the daughter of Wm. G. and Elizabeth Pitchford. Eli Smith

Mrs. Georgia Word, wife of Dr. T. J. Word, of Columbus, Ga., died in that city, February 15, 1876 in the 45th year of her age. Mrs. Word was a daughter of Col. Daniel R. Mitchell, one of the oldest and best citizens of Rome, Ga.

Issue of April 12, 1876

Rev. John Howard Harris, son of Rev. West Harris and of Martha Harvey, his wife, was born June 7, 1830, and named for Rev. John Howard. He was converted at the old Salem Campground, Newton county, Ga. In 1852 he married Miss Martha Banks. He was permitted to enjoy this union but for a few years, when God called her and her two little ones to the home above. In 1857 he married Miss Mary E. Parks, daughter of Rev. Wm. J. Parks. By this wife he had six children, who all live with their mother. J. E. Evans

Mrs. Martha A. B. Davenport, wife of Smith Davenport, and daughter of Micajah and Nancy Hillsman, was born in Morgan county, Ga., March 7, 1817; and died in Webster county, Ga., February 9, 1876. J. R. Littlejohn

Rev. Robert S. Paden was born near Roswell, Cobb county, Ga., December 22, 1836; He died February 16, 1876. He leaves a wife (formerly Miss Elizabeth S. Tippins) and five little chidlren.

Miss Annan E. Barton, daughter of Thos. and Eliza Barton deceased, was born in Orangeburg county, S. C., July 20, 1827 and died February 2, 1876.

Mrs. Carrie Roberts Johnson was born in Macon, Ga., September 29, 1847; was married to Dr. Herschel V. Johnson, June 2, 1875; and died in Hawkinsville, Ga., February 29, 1876. James O. Branch

Mrs. H. A. Woodward, daughter of Dr. D. W. Hammond of Macon, died in Culloden, Ga., January 11, 1876. Rev. Major Speer, father of Rev. Dr. Eustace, and Judge Alexander Speer, was her maternal grand-father. On December 4, 1855, she was married to Mr. A. L. Woodward, and leaves him with three beautiful daughters and a promising son. Thos. R. Kendall

Miss Annie E. Hattaway, daughter of John B. Hattaway, was born December 6, 1854; and died in Oconee county, Ga., March 13, 1876. W. W. Oslin

Mrs. Irene Allen Waite, wife of Rev. F. C. Waite, was born in 1845; and died in Macon, Ga., February 7, 1876. M. R. Calvert

Issue of April 19, 1876

Mrs. Frances E. Weems, wife of J. B. Weems and daughter of J. C. and Mary Holbrook, was born in Franklin county, Ga., November 15, 1823. Her parents moved to Cherokee, Georgia, in 1833 and settled near the Holbrook Camp Ground. At the age of twenty-two she was married to J. B. Weems. Sister Weems died February 25, 1876. W. Manning

Mr. Henry B. Denton died in Lancaster county, S. C., March 6, 1876, aged about forty-eight years. His death was caused by a severe burn. Just before he died, he asked if his sister Mary, who now lives in Florida, was not standing by his bed. His Niece

Mrs. Sarah Ann Tatom, daughter of Stephen and Mary Curry, was born in Orangeburg district, S. C., February 19, 1819; was married to Mr. A. K. Tatom, February 3d 1841; died at Smith Station, Lee county, Ala., March 19, 1876. In 1846 she moved with her husband to Lowndes county, Miss., and from there to Macon county, Ala., in 1850 then to Lee county about 1871. She leaves a husband and five children. C. S. Hurt

Miss Nancy McIntosh died at the "old homestead," in Richmond county, N. C., January 29, 1876, aged 61 years.

Bro. A. P. Blount, son of G. Adolphus and G. Anna Blount, was born in Barnwell, S. C., July 12, 1850; and died in Augusta, Ga., March 21, 1876. He leaves a wife and child, mother and father and brothers. W. L. Wootten, Jr.

Nathan Bramlette, an exhorter in the Hall circuit, North Georgia Conference, was born May 29, 1789, and died February 10, 1876. Brother Bramlette left his second wife and a large number of children (some of the fourth generation). Chas. L. Patillo

Brother Simeon Hendrix, Jr., was born September 23, 1844, and died in Columbus, Ga., February 28, 1876. J. V. M. Morris

James E. DuTart was born in Charleston county, S. C., October 31, 1816; and died March 23, 1876. A. G. Gantt

Mr. Newton Caldwell was born in Anderson district, S. C., August 16, 1818, and died in Meriwether county, Ga., March 6, 1876. His parents moved to DeKalb county, Ga., in 1832, and thence to Meriwether in 1836, where they remained until death. They were Presbyterians. He leaves a wife and eight children.

Miss Ida B. Gray died in Columbia county, Ga., February 2, 1876, in the 15th year of her age. She joined the Church at Appling, Columbia county. B. F. Fariss

Mrs. Sophia D. Lowery, wife of Rev. John M. Lowery, of the North Georgia Conference was born in Barnwell county, S. C., and died in Norcross, Ga., March 17, 1876. She married in 1866. W. T. Laine

Issue of April 26, 1876

Mrs. Frances W. Powledge, whose maiden name was Foy, was born near Wilmington, N. C., April 4, 1810; and died in Meriwether county, Ga., March 4, 1876. When she was about ten years old her father moved to Georgia, where in 1826 on 23d of December, she was married to J. M. Powledge. She was the mother of a large family of children. One died a little boy, another a young man, and the rest, ten, all do well. Two daughters are the wives of preachers; one son, Rev. G. Powledge, is a local preacher in Texas. W. J. Cotter

Mrs. Lizzie D. Rheney, wife of Dr. Samuel C. Rheney, and daughter of Thomas and Dollie Gordon, of Opelika, Ala., was born in Dalton, Ga., March 12, 1854; and died in Burke county, Ga., March 3, 1876. F. A. Branch

Benjamin W. Barrow, Esq., son of David C. Barrow, of Oglethorpe county, Ga., died at his father's residence near Woodstock, March 22, 1876. He was a member of the Church at Milledgeville. H. J. Adams

Franklin Marshall, son of Mat. Marshall, was born in Lowndes county, Ga., February 28, 1854, and died in the same county, January 8, 1876. He was married in Nov. 1874 to Miss Esther Varn, daughter of the late Wm. T. Varn, of Berrien county, Ga. he leaves a wife, and a babe six weeks old when he died, an aged grand-father and grand-mother, a father and mother, brothers and sisters. J. T. Webb

Mrs. Elizabeth Drew, whose maiden name was Harris, wife of John J. Drew, died February 1, 1876, in Sumpter county, Ga. She had lived thirty-five years, fourteen of which she had passed as Mrs. Drew. W. B. Merritt

Mrs. M. S. Johnson was born in Jasper county, May 20, 1849; and died at Grantville, Ga., March 3, 1876. Her maiden name was Allen, and she was first married to Mr. E. D. John, of Galveston, Texas, where she lived till his death, November 21, 1871. After returning to Georgia she was married to Mr. J. C. Johnson, May 20, 1874. She left one child, a boy not quite a year old. W. J. Cotter

Mrs. Tabitha T. T. Perry, wife of Rev. Dow Perry and daughter of Turner and Martha Hunt, was born in Jasper county, Ga., July 3, 1811; was married at McDonough, Ga., October 15, 1828; and died at the house of her son, Rev. O. S. Perry, at Tallassee, Ala., March 29, 1876.

William T. Mosley, son of Thomas M. and Elizabeth D. Mosley, died March 6, 1876, at his father's residence near Macon, Ga., in his twenty-fourth year. L. G. Evans

Tribute of Respect to Rev. L. L. Strange, a member of the Georgia Conference, latterly a local Deacon in the Springfield Circuit.

Tribute of Respect from Cokesbury Station, South Carolina Conference, to General G. W. Hodges.

Tribute of Respect from Oak Bowery Circuit, Lafayette District, North Alabama Conference, to Samuel W. Harris.

Issue of May 2, 1876

Died

Rev. Llewellyn Bunch, son of Rev. John Bunch deceased, died in Charleston, S. C., April 4, 1876, in the fifty-sixth year of his age.

Annie Lowe, daughter of Rev. W. P. and Anna L. Lovejoy, died April, 21, 1876, aged two years, one month and twenty-six days.

Obituary

Green J. Dozier was born near Wrightsboro, Ga., September 7, 1793; and died near Shiloh Church, Columbia county, Ga., where he had resided more than sixty years, January 29, 1876. In 1813 he was happily married to Miss Constance Hunt, who died in 1858. They had a large and interesting family of children, all of whom, except three, preceded him to the better land. W. T. Hamilton

Mrs. Ellen Pricher Ritter, wife of Mr. Hezekiah Ritter and daughter of Mr. G. W. Broxton, died in Colleton county, S. C., January 22, 1876, aged twenty-seven years. She left a husband and tender babe of a few weeks behind her.

Jane A. A. Moore was born in Lincoln county, N. C., August 17, 1813; and died in Perry county, Ala., March 15, 1876. In early life she joined the Presbyterian Church. She was married to A. A. Moore, November 9, 1843.

Mary Atkinson was born in Virginia, August 2d, 1785; and died at the residence of Mr. Julius Baker, Fulton county, Ga., February 26, 1876. She moved to Georgia with her father when but five years old-- and after his death she went to reside with the Rev. J. M. Smith where she remained till his death, and with his daughter Mrs. Baker the remainder of her life.

Dennis Blake Baker was born in Hancock county, Ga., March 16, 1801; was married to Amanda Gresham, December 23, 1824; joined the M. E. Church at New Chapel at what is now Logansville, in Walton county, Ga., in 1831; died in Walker county, February 12, 1876. James N. Myers

Mrs. C. A. E. Singleton, wife of Rev. W. A. Singleton and daughter of Jesse and Mary A. Bryan of Scriven county, Ga., died in Buena Vista, Ga., January 31, 1876, in the forty eighth year of her age She leaves five interesting children with her faithful husband. W. B. Merritt

Mrs. M. H. Seckinger, wife of E. Seckinger and daughter of Wm. I. and C. E. Morgan, of Effingham county, Ga., died April 8, 1876, in the fortieth year of her age. She leaves a husband and eight children. D. G. Morgan

Mrs. Josephene Jordan, wife of Henry Jordan, of Sumter county, Ga., died at the residence of her brother-in-law, Thomas A. Groover, in Brooks county, Ga., March 31, 1876, aged thirty five years. H. W. Sharpe

Brother Henry Nelson, Sr., was born April 10, 1801; and died January 16, 1876. About thirty-eight years ago he was converted at Salem Church, Upson county, Ga. R. W. Rogers

Milton B. Brown, son of James and Mary E. Brown (now Jaudon), of Effingham county, Ga., died in Savannah, April 16, 1976, aged about thirty years. He was a member of the Lutheran Church.

Issue of May 9, 1876

Benj. W. Thompson was born in Butler county, Ky., November 1809; and died in Bagdad, Santa Rosa county, Fla., January 28, 1876. He moved to this county in 1830 and remained here up to the time of his death.

Mrs. Mary Strange, daughter of Mary and William Henderson, was born in Jefferson county, Tenn., June 15, 1812; and died March 22, 1876. Her parents died when she was quite small. She had several brothers and sisters older than herself. When grown up, she moved to McMinn county, Tenn. She was twice married: in 1838 to Mr. Baker, who lived only eight months; in 1841 to Mr. J. F. Strange, with whom she lived for thirty-five years. She leaves an aged husband and four children. J. B. McFarland

Joseph King Lambuth, son of the late Joseph Lambuth of Leon county, Texas, was born in Dadeville, Talapoosa county, Ala., June 6, 1852; and was killed by a stroke of lightning April 1, 1876, in Fayette co., Ga. Her father moved to Texas when he was four years of age. Upon the death of his father, he and two of his sisters returned to the house of their aged grand-father, Major Y. D. King of Fayette county. W. L. Williams. The Texas Christian Advocate please copy.

Miss Jane E. Wright, daughter of Major James Wright, deceased, died in Eatonton, Ga., at the house of Captain Berrien Rice, her brother-in-law, February 7, 1876.

Miss Emma Florina Means was born in Houston county, Ga., December 25, 1859; and died March 31, 1876.

Mrs. Eliza Ann Williams, wife of Thos. Williams, and daughter of D. M. Taylor and Hessy C. Taylor, was born May 23, 1844; married Oct. 25, 1868; and died Feb. 11, 1876.

Mrs. Mollie A. R. Dekle, consort of Lebbeus Dekle, and daughter of Col. Oliver H. Cook, was born Nov. 28, 1852; married in 1874; died March 22, 1876 in Thomasville, Ga. She left a little babe only two or three weeks of age. J. O. A. Cook

Welcome C. Lovejoy was born in Jasper county, Ga., Jan. 2, 1822; married to Catharine Parker, April 16, 1844; and died in Montezuma, Ga., April 14, 1876.

Mrs. Margaret Mood, wife of Thomas S. Mood, died in Columbia, S. C., April 14, 1876, aged 71 years, 7 months, 8 days. W. Martin

Tribute of Respect from White Plains and Oxford Station, North Alabama Conference, to Rev. A. M. LeMaster.

Issue of May 16, 1876

Died

Warren Palmer, son of Rev. W. D. and Mrs. M. Marion Kirkland, died in Greenville, S. C., May 3d, 1876, aged 8 months and 19 days.

Obituary

George W. Blackburn was born in Edgefield District, S. C., July 30, 1815, and died in Jefferson county, Fla., March 30, 1876. D. H. Bryan

Mrs. Elizabeth Abernathy, whose maiden name was Young, was born in Warren county, N. C., December 11, 1775; married in 1801 to Geo. W. Martin of Va.; married a second time in 1809 to Smith Abernathy of N. C.; and died at the residence of her son-in-law, Col. Jas. E. Rembert, in Sumter county, S. C., April 3, 1876. She attached herself to the Baptist church.

John H. Cox died in Madison, Ga., February 14, 1876, in the thirty-sixth year of his age.

Dr. Armlain Bryan Vaught died March 27, 1876, in Marion, S. C., aged about twenty-eight years. He left a wife and three children. M. A. W. LeGette

Mrs. Anna E. Skinner, wife of Mr. Benj. L. Skinner, was born in Augusta, Ga., April 26, 1844; and died at Jacksonville, Fla., April 22, 1876. She leaves a husband and three little children. H. B. Frazee

Mrs. Catharine Funches died in Orangeburg county, S. C., March 31, 1876, aged eighty-one years and seventeen days.

John Baker was born in North Carolina, December 9, 1786; and died in Broomtown Valley, Chattooga county, Ga., March 12, 1876. His parents moving to Georgia while he was young, he grew to manhood and married in this state. In each of the several counties of the State in which he lived, he held the office of Justice of the Peace. He was also a member of the Legislature and judge of the Inferior Court. A Son-in-law

George M. Venable was born in Randolph county, Ga., August 16, 1841; and died in Columbus, Ga., April 3, 1876. He left a wife and two children. J. V. M. Morris

Moses Sinquefield was born in Jefferson county, Ga., and died in Whitesville, Ga., April 11, 1876, aged fifty-five years. He was for many years a resident of Savannah.

Issue of May 23, 1876

Died

Judah Francis Strange, child of Mr. Shackleford and Mrs. Judah Francis Strange, died May 1, 1876, aged thirteen months and eleven days. Her mother, the daughter of Wm. Jeters, died April 1, 1875. All of Pulatka, Putnam City [sic], Fla.

Obituary

William Howard Jack was born in Lumpkin county, Ga., June 28, 1833; died at Rome, Ga., April 11, 1876.

Benjamin Manes was born in Columbia county, Ga., removed to Talbot county, Ga., forty-seven years ago, where he lived till his death, April 16, 1876, in the seventy-eighth year of his age. W. W. Stewart

Mrs. Emily Elizabeth Sharp, daughter of Rev. Joseph Chambers of the North Georgia Conference, and Mrs. Jane Chambers, died March 9, 1876, aged thirty-seven years and twenty days. She was left a widow with one child, by the death of her husband in the memorable battle of Gettysburg. W. C. Dunlap

Mrs. Elizabeth J. Simmons, wife of Hon. James Simmons, was born in Rutherford, N. C., March 21, 1809; was married in February 1830 and moved to Georgia the March following; died near Jasper, Ga., March 24, 1876, aged sixty-five years. John H. Mashburn, Jr.

337

Mrs. Havilla H. Risher was born March 14, 1810; and died April 9, 1870 [sic]. She was the wife of Brother Joseph K. Risher, who preceded her a few years to the better land. Thos. Raysor

Mrs. Martha Fetner, wife of William Fetner, died in Columbia, S. C., April 8, 1876, aged sixty-four years. In 1828 she joined the Washington Street Church in Columbia. When the Marion Street Church, in the same city, was organized in 1851, her name was the third on its roll of membership. J. Walter Dickson

Mrs. Rebecca Barr, whose maiden name was Emanuel, was born in Burke county, Ga., December 25, 1800; and died in Marion county, Ga., March 17, 1876. At the age of twenty she married Nathan Barr, who preceded her to the grave by many years. W. F. Lloyd

Mrs. Julia F. Williams, whose maiden name was Allen, was born in Houston county, Ga., April 1, 1832; was married to Samuel Williams in 1848; and died March 11, 1876, near Sylvan, Texas. Her husband died during the war, leaving her with five children. She removed to Lamar county, Texas, last January with her four surviving children.

Thomas Clarke Felder, son of Rev. C. W. and Mrs. J. A. J. Felder, was born in Clarendon county, S. C., December 1862; and died April 13, 1876.

Issue of May 30, 1876

Mrs. Isa Beall Erwin, daughter of Noble P. and Mrs. J. D. Beall, was born in Campbell county, Ga., July 25, 1839; was brought up in Mississippi; in 1860 was married to John A. Erwin, of Cartersville, Ga; on May 7, 1876, she died. A. J. Jarrell

Brother James M. Glass died in Griffin, Ga., April 1. 1876, aged forty-nine. He was born in Chattanooga, Tenn. A wife and eight children are left behind.

Brother Washington Allen was about sixty-five years of age; died at Buford, Gwinnett county, Ga., May 4, 1876. Marion H. Eakes

Sarah C. Hale, a worthy member of the Mt. Carmel Church in the McDonough circuit, was born October 1, 1830; died May 2, 1876. J. W. Yarbrough

Mrs. Mary Sandel died March 26, 1876, at the residence of her daughter in Orangeburg county, S. C., in the ninetieth year of her age.

Mrs. Nancy Coleman, relict of the late John Coleman, died in Edgefield county, S. C., February 28, 1876, in the eighty-second year of her age. M. H. Pooser

Mrs. Elizabeth Gramling, whose maiden name was Imboden, was born in Orangeburg District, S. C., December 13, 1789; and died in Madison county, Fla., May 7, 1876. She was married to Rev. John Gramling, deceased, October 14, 1806, with whom she lived affectionately over half a century, being left a widow February 1864. She reared ten children, all members of the Church. In 1845, she emigrated with her husband to Florida. E. S. Tyner. The N. O. Christian Advocate please copy.

Cornelia Anzolet Talley, wife of John J. Talley and daughter of the late Reuben Mobley of Harris county, Ga., died in Troup county, Ga., May 6, 1876. She was married in 1858, and was thirty-four years of age at the time of her death. H. J. Ellis

Mrs. Elmira Erwin was born in Burke county, N. C., April 23, 1812; was married to Robert H. Erwin, March 30, 1828; and died May 3, 1876 in Union county, Ga. She joined the Presbyterian Church in early life. Thos. J. Edwards. The Gainesville Eagle will please copy.

Mrs. Eliza Burke was born in Baltimore, Md., March 15, 1799; and died in Lumpkin, Stewart county, Ga., April 8, 1876. A. J. Dean

Miss Annie Reeves was born October, 23, 1857; and died April 18, 1876.

SOUTHERN CHRISTIAN ADVOCATE NOTICES 1867-1878

SOUTHERN CHRISTIAN ADVOCATE NOTICES 1867-1878

Issue of June 6, 1876

John D. Mitchell, son of Henry and Lucinda Mitchell, was born in Heard county, Ga., August 1, 1830; died of white swelling in Franklin, Ga., April 23, 1876, leaving a wife and four children. W. H. Speer

Mrs. Margaret Attaway-- formerly Griffith-- wife of Rev. John Attaway, of the South Carolina Conference, died in Williamston, S. C., April 24, 1876, aged forty-three years and two days.

Robert D. Duncan, son of the Rev. John P. Duncan, died in Dahlonega, Ga., May 11, 1876, aged twenty years and four months.

Mrs. Helen A. Wimberly, consort of Judge J. L. Wimberly and daughter of Moses and Mary Guyton, was born in Laurens county, Ga., May 7, 1841; and died in Lumpkin, Ga., March 29, 1876. She was married to Judge Wimberly in 1857. She left a husband and three children. A. J. Dean

Mrs. M. E. Hainsworth, wife of Mr. M. E. Hainsworth, was born in Lee county, Ga., Oct. 13, 1845 and died in Tampa, Fla., March 30, 1876. She leaves a husband and a little babe. J. A. Castel

Mrs. Sarah Ann Stutts was born Nov. 24, 1811; and died April 18, 1876. She leaves a sister and daughters. C. C. Fishburne

Geraldine E. Todd was born in Wilkinson county, Ga., September 29, 1850; and died May 8, 1876. Thomas A. Griffiths

Mrs. Emma E. Crum died in Orangeburg county, S. C., April 12, 1876, aged thirty-eight years. She leaves a husband and eight children.

William H. Brawner was born December 31, 1844; died in Milner, Ga., April 24, 1876.

Miss Mary J. Johnson was born in Lake City, Fla., July 12, 1857; and died in the same place, March 2, 1876. Henry Edw. Partridge

Mrs. Lazina C. Willerford, daughter of Rev. Wyatt Brooks-- a superannuated member of the Georgia Conference-- died in Eufaula, Ala., May 15, 1876. She was born in Harris county, Ga., Oct. 2, 1831, and was married to Mr. M. C. Willerford, August 2, 1859. J. Bancroft

Issue of June 13, 1876

Mrs. Sarah A. Dogan, widow of Dr. J. H. Dogan, died in Union, S. C., May 7, 1876, in the 71st year of her age. A little more than six years ago, Dr. Dogan went to his reward. Her parents, Wm. and Sarah P. Rice, were members of the M. E. Church. A. H. Lester

William B. Gill was born in Chester District, S. C., April 9, 1821; was married to Miss Mary E. Hutchings in 1855; died in Homer, La., May 8, 1879. He left an aged father, widow, and a son. Jno. A. Miller

Mrs. Esther Keen was born at Georgetown, S. C., May 30, 1795; and died at Cuthbert, Ga., May 16, 1876. She reared her children, and one of them, the wife of an itinerant Methodist preacher, Rev. W. F. Easterling. R. W. Dixon

Mrs. E. B. Brantly was born near Wilmington, N. C., in 1800; in her eighteenth year married Mr. William Vaught, of Horry District, S. C., was soon left a widow and afterwards married Mr. A. Brantly of the same district; died at Jasper, Fla., April 10, 1876. R. H. Howren

Miss Ida Gaines was born June 8, 1862; died April 23, 1876.

Henry Callier, son of Thomas and Mary Callier, was born in Greene county, Ga., December 7, 1841; removed to Talbot county, Ga., in 1831; died May 17, 1876. J. P. Wardlaw

339

Freeman W. Blount was born in Jones county, Ga., April 29, 1807; died near Greenville, Merriwether county, Ga., April 26, 1876. He was twice married, having eight living children by his first wife. He leaves a widow and six other children.

Wiley P. Warwick was born July 22, 1802; died April 22, 1876. He was the son of Wiley Warwick, one of the fathers of heroic Methodism of the South Carolina Conference, long since gone to his reward. P. F. Reynolds

Andrew J. Allen was born July 4, 1821; and died April 23, 1876.

Martha A. Brazil died February 20, 1876, aged about forty-five years.

Tribute of Respect from Senoia Circuit to Rev. Robert F. Jones.

Issue of June 20, 1876

My father, Joseph S. Bell, was born in Guilford county, North Carolina, July 22, 1794; came to Jackson county, Ga., in 1802; married Miss Rachel Phinazee, February 27, 1812; removed to Forsyth county in 1840 where he died May 10, 1876. His family, including the living and dead, and those who have intermarried with it, numbers two hundred members. H. P. Bell

George Kellogg was born in Litchfield county, Connecticut, March 3, 1803; came to Georgia and settled in Jackson county in 1819; married Miss Caroline Webster of Connecticut in August, 1826; removed to Forsyth county in 1834; where he died May 14, 1876. He was a representative and senator in the State Legislature, and Superintendent of the U. S. Branch mint at Dahlonega. H. P. Bell

Miss Elizabeth Little McCanless was born in Oglethorpe county, Ga., in 1801; and died near Pine Log, Ga., March 20, 1876, at the residence of W. K. McCanless. She was a sister-in-law of Rev. George Bright, long a member of the Georgia Conference, and at the death of her parents became a member of his family. W. W. Oslin

Mrs. Kate M. Bonner was born in Putnam county, Ga., April 29, 1840; and died in Baldwin county, Ga., May 7, 1876. W. R. Foote, Jr.

Sister Sarah McAfee, wife of John McAfee, and daughter of William and Elizabeth Smith, was born in South Carolina; removed to Tallahassee, Fla., in 1826; moved to Stark, Fla., in 1872, where she died May 7, 1876, aged seventy-six years, two months and sixteen days. R. M. Ellzey. Floridian please copy.

Mrs. Emily H. Lee, whose maiden name was Wideman, was born in Troup county, Ga., March 9, 1832; and died at the residence of her brother-in-law, J. P. Sewell, in Meriwether county, Ga., April 16, 1876. She was married December 24, 1848 to Mr. Z. Lee of Gwinnett county. Her husband died in 1865 and left her with six children. Her eldest son, Rev. J. W. Lee, of the Van Wert Circuit of the North Georgia Conference.

My son, John Fletcher Clark, died near Cuthbert, Ga., May 25, 1876, aged twenty-two years, one month and two days. John D. Clark

Miss Hester A. Bennett, daughter of George W. and Mary Bennett, died near Red Clay, Ga., March 25, 1876.

Issue of June 27, 1876

Died

Little Clyde, daughter of L. P. and M. J. Murray, died at Norcross, Ga., June 13, 1876, aged 7 months and 4 days.

Obituary

Richard Amasa Kellam was born in Laurens county, Ga., October 14, 1840; died May 29, 1876, in the same county. He leaves an aged mother, brothers and sisters. A. M. Williams

Mrs. Elizabeth W. Robson, whose maiden name was Woodward, consort of Mr. John Robson of Atlanta, died March 1876 in Culloden, Ga. Thos R. Kendall

Nathaniel R. Keeling was born in Illinois, October 10, 1827; died in Tuskegee, Ala., May 3, 1876.

George W. Dismukes was born in Davidson county, Tenn., May 11, 1845; died in Quincy, Fla., April 24, 1876. He leaves an aged mother, a wife, brothers and sisters.

Mrs. Elizabeth A. Kelsey, wife of Rev. Daniel Kelsey of the North Georgia Conference, and daughter of Lot and Sarah Townsley, was born in Sandersville, Ga., March 29, 1824; married January 16, 1848; and died in Harlem, Columbia county, Ga., May 13, 1876. She leaves a husband and three children. R. A. Conner

Mrs. Sarah Evans, wife of Judge Jesse Evans and daughter of John and Elizabeth Smith, was born in Warren county, Ga., August 9, 1795; married June 22, 1820; died April 10, 1876. R. A. Conner

Mrs. E. M. A. Mountcastle, daughter of Wm. and Frances Manning, was born in Mecklenburg county, Va., December 5, 1822; was married to Wm. R. Mountcastle in 1839; came to Georgia in 1858; died in Cartersville, Ga., May 15, 1876. A. J. Jarrell

Issue of July 4, 1876

Died

Lucie J. Irwin, daughter of Dr. J. M. and Mary F. Armstrong, died June 26, 1876, aged 1 year and 2 months.

Obituary

Robert A. Jones, son of John M. (deceased) and C. A. Jones, was born at Chunnenuggee Ridge, Ala., September 19, 1854; and died in Atlanta, Ga., June 3, 1876. W. A. Dodge

Elizabeth C. Jones, daughter of William and Sarah McKinley, was born in putnam county, Ga., in 1812; married to H. B. Jones, February 17, 1874; and died in Taliaferro county, Ga., May 26, 1876.

Mrs. A. L. Finn died at the residence of her son-in-law, Col. Willis A. Hawkins, in Americus, Ga., June 2, 1876. She was born in Athens, Ga., December 1802.

Sarah S. Sherouse was born in Effingham county, Ga., in 1797; and died in Alachua county, Fla., May 25, 1876. R. D. Gentry

Mary T. Boulware of Newberry, S. C., died June 5, 1876, at the Columbia Female College in the twenty-fourth year of her age. Samuel B. Jones

Mary Rozie Ashworth, daughter of John and Mary Reid Lockman, was born in Lincoln county, N. C., March 18, 1847; and died March 20, 1876, leaving an infant daughter four months old. She was married about five years ago to Henry Ashworth. James F. Smith

Charles E. Vance was born in Lenoir county, N. C., in 1804; died in Putnam county, Fla., June 1st, 1876. Brother Vance and his wife were members of the Presbyterian Church over twenty years; but upon coming to Florida they became members of the Methodist Church. R. D. Gentry

Miss Katie Jones, daughter of John M. Jones, deceased, and C. A. Jones, was born July 21, 1860 in Stewart county, Ga., and died in Atlanta, Ga., April 8, 1876. W. A. Dodge

Mrs. Rosa Felkel, wife of Mr. John A. Felkel, of Orangeburg county, S. C., died Monday, June 5, 1876. She was a native of Georgia, and being trained in the Presbyterian Church. When about twenty years of age, she married John A. Felkel of South Carolina... joined the Methodist Church. Southern Presbyterian will please copy.

Tribute of Respect from Appling Circuit, North Georgia Conference, to Lucius A. Luke, who died 13 May.

Tribute of Respect from Acworth Circuit, North Georgia Conference to M. L. Ruff.

Issue of July 11, 1876

John Wilson Dozier was born in Columbia county, Ga., May 29, 1801; and died near Talbotton, June 3, 1876. His father and mother, John and Fannie Dozier, were among the pioneers of Methodism in Georgia. He was married to Martha M. Haynes, July 12, 1821. Geo. C. Clarke

Mrs. Catharine Mulligan, the mother of Capt. A. B. Mulligan, of Charleston, S. C., died on June 11, 1876, at Spartanburg, S. C., in the 90th year of her age. Whiteford Smith

Mrs. Eliza L. V. Smith, daughter of Amos and Eliza Lowrey, aged twenty-seven years, died in Cherokee county, Ga., May 18, 1876. Sister smith leaves her husband, one daughter, two sons, her aged father and step-mother, brothers and sisters. James N. Myers

Levi M. Adams, Esq., died in Greenville, April 22, 1876, in the sixty-ninth year of his age. Born in Edgefield District, S. C., he passed part of his boyhood in Butts county, Ga., removed to Greenville in 1828, and organized the first Sunday-school of that place. W. A. Simmons

Mrs. Sarah E., wife of Dr. Albert W. Bivings, died in the Methodist Church in Dalton, Ga., May 16, 1876, in the fifty-second year of her age. Her maiden name was Cleveland, born in Spartanburg, S. C., September 19, 1824; married to Dr. Bivings, January 10, 1842; moved to Georgia, November 1866.

Stephen McCall was born in Bulloch county, Ga., November 29, 1802; and died in Gainesville, Fla., May 29, 1876. He was a communicant in the Baptist Church. He removed to Gainesville in 1859.

Mrs. Mattie E. Lester, whose maiden name was McCall, was born September 19, 1850 in Tatnall county, Ga., and died in Jesup, Wayne county, Ga., June 17, 1876. She was married March 29, 1871, to Dr. R. F. Lester of Reidsville, Tatnall county, Ga. She leaves a husband and one child three years old.

Mrs. Sarah M. Johnson, wife of F. A. Johnson, and daughter of B. F. and E. A. Jones, was born in Abbeville district, S. C., june 26, 1840, and died at Hamburg, Ashley county, Ark., April 15, 1876. She leaves a husband and four little children.

Mrs. Nancy Cowart, nee Middlebrook, wife of Stephen Cowart, was born in Hancock county, Ga., and died in Pike county, Ala., May 24, 1876, in the seventy-fifth year of her age. For many years she mad been a resident of Alabama. She had been married three times: first to Uriah Black, next to Mr. Ozier, and last to Stephen Cowart.

Issue of July 18, 1876

Died

Edna F., youngest child of Dr. and Mrs. H. J. Mouzon of Bennettsville, S. C., died July 5, 1876, aged nearly eleven months.

Marion, infant son of the late Rev. J. M. Parker and Laura V. Parker, died in Atlanta, Ga., June 26, 1876.

Obituary

Mrs. Sallie Porter Graves was born in Madison county, Ga., February 14, 1833; and died in the town of her birth March 31, 1876.

George Marable was born in Mecklinburg county, Va., in the year 1800; and died in Monroe, Walton County, Ga., May 22, 1876. D. F. C. Timmons. Nashville Advocate please copy.

Sister Selina A. Gaither, the wife of Augustus L. Gaither, of Newton county, Ga., and daughter of Dr. William A. and Carrie Perry of Covington, Ga., was born in Jasper county, Ga., January 6, 1847; and died May 16, 1876. A. C. Mixon

Irene P. Smith, wife of C. C. Smith and daughter of Dr. B. C. Hart of Cokesbury, S. C., was born April 7, 1850; and died June 13, 1876.

Mrs. Mary Saunders Turner, the venerable widow of Jacob P. Turner, was born near Tarboro, N. C., Sept. 8, 1794; married in Hancock county, Ga., Dec. 14, 1813; and died near Trinity, Meriwether county, May 29, 1876. A few years ago, her only child, Mrs. Dr. Fogle of Columbus, died and left her very lonely.

Mrs. Bathsheba N. Wootten, daughter of Mr. and Mrs. John Hinton and widow of Thomas L. Wootten, was born in Wilkes, and died in Chattooga county, Ga., April 5, 1876; aged about 73 years. She joined the M. E. Church at Independence. With all of her children but one, she removed to Chattooga county in the latter part of 1849.

Deacon J. F. Walker was born in Washington county, Ga., Dec. 25, 1797; and died in Mansfield, Louisiana, June 12, 1876. In 1823 he moved to Upson county, Ga., in 1859 moved to Panola county, Texas; and after the late war, to Mansfield, La. He joined the Baptist Church in Putnam county about 1821 and soon after took an active part in the constitution of Bethesda Church, one of the oldest in that county. Brother Walker's immediate descendants embraced 13 children, 78 grand-children and 11 great grand-children. He was married three times, his second wife only living a few months. His last wife, 53 grandchildren and 9 children still live. G. W. Hartsfield.

Mrs. C. P. C. Fitcher died June 11, 1876, aged 50 years. She leaves a husband and children.

Mrs. Sarah A. Smithwick, wife of Luke W. Smithwick, was born in Charleston District, S. C., August 6, 1836; and died in Leon county, Fla., June 2, 1876. Her maiden name was Fleming, and she had been married nearly twenty-two years. In her youth she joined the Presbyterian church. E. L. T. Blake

Miss Fannie K. Alston, only daughter of Col. W. J. Alston, deceased, of Fairfield county, South Carolina, died at the residence of Maj. T. W. Woodward, near Winnsboro, June 10, 1876.

Issue of July 25, 1876

Died

Robert Emmett, son of W. E. and Georgia Watley, died in Atlanta, Ga., July 2, 1876, aged sixteen months.

Clara Bernice, daughter of H. A. and Annie H. Smith, died in Atlanta, Ga., July 2, 1876, aged nine months.

Obituary

Rev. John H. Mashburn of the North Georgia Conference was born in N. C., August 20, 1803; and died in Gainesville, Ga., June 13, 1876. He had eight children by his first wife. Seven still live. He was married the second time to Mrs. Nancy M. Butler, August 27, 1869, who had one daughter, her only living child. He was buried at Ebenezer Church in Forsyth county. D. D. Cox

Mrs. Elizabeth R. Graham, wife of W. L. Graham, and daughter of the late Mrs. M. E. Baxter of Memphis, Tenn., died May 7, 1876, on her twenty-sixth birthday.

James P. Lyle died April 29, 1876, in the fifty-fifth year of his age. He leaves a large family. P. C. Harris.

Clarissa Grantham, wife of Noel Grantham, as born in Washington county, Ga., November 26, 1813; died May 26, 1876. J. P. Wardlaw

Col. Thomas J. Heard was born August 21, 1801, and died in Elberton, Ga., May 4, 1876. He was a native Georgian.

Sister Sarah W. Lowe was born about the year 1824 on Harbor Island, one of the Bahamas, and died in Manatee county, Fla. She was married to William Lowe, March 1840, moved to Key West, 1841, then to Manatee in 1873. W. H. F. Robarts

Mrs. Mary Franklin died June 16, 1876, at Starrsville, Newton county, Ga., in the seventy-seventh year of her age. Albert G. Banks

Miss Ella Tart was born February 14, 1859 and died June 28, 1876, while on a visit to her grandfather, Rev. S. J. Bethea.

Mrs. Caroline M. Felder, wife of E. D. Felder of Sumter county, S. C., died May 5, 1876. Sister Felder was sixty-three years one month and some days old. L. M. Little

Miss Addie Cate, daughter of M. A. and C. C. Brunson, and granddaughter of the Rev. J. H. Millard, died in Barbour county, Ala., June 26, 1876, in her seventeenth year. D. C. Crook

Issue of August 1, 1876

Died

Jennie Lou, daughter of Wm. T. and Jennie Ashford, died in Watkinsville, Ga., July 12, 1876, aged 16 months and 25 days.

Obituary

Sidney Toney was born in Forsyth, Monroe county, Ga., August 26 1847; and died at the same place, May 21, 1876. On 6th of February 1868 he married in Dougherty county, Ga., Miss Annie Patat, formerly of Savannah. his wife was a member of the Baptist Church. D. D. Cox

Mrs. Ann Wilder was born in Onslow county, N. C., February 6, 1794; moved to Florida in 1824; and died in Quincy, Fla., June 25, 1876.

Mrs. Matilda Lundy was born in Houston county, Ga., March 27th 1843; married Mr. Alexander Lundy, February 15th 1870; and died in Greene county, Ga., June 26, 1876.

Philip M. Boyd was born in Bradly county, Tenn., March 24, 1852; and died at the same place June 27, 1876. Toward the close of the late bloody war, his father was killed.

Mr. Jesse B. Hunter was born in Washington county, East Tennessee, September 17, 1805; married Miss M. C. Rutledge of Blacksburg, Va., November 11, 1835; moved to Mississippi in 1837; moved to Micanopy, Alachua county, Fla., in 1850 died June 8, 1876. He was a county surveyor for many years and marked out the site of Gainesville. Nashville Advocate please copy.

My son, William Archer Adams, died June 21, 1876, at the age of twenty-three years. Asbury A. Adams

Mrs. M. A. Davis was born in Camden, S. C., August 14, 1818; and died near Florence, S. C., April 27, 1876, She was at the time of her death widowed for the third time. Her maiden name was Dean. She was first married to Dr. W. S. Murphy; after his death to Mr. S. P. Cooper, and subsequently to Mr. P. F. Davis. For a number of years she was a resident of Darlington. In 1858 she removed to Jacksonville, Florida, and remained until the opening of the late war. She then returned to Charleston.

Antonia H. Mitchell, daughter of Francis and Mary B. Kirby, was born in Morgan county in 1826; married G. T. Michel in 1853; died in Floyd county near Coosa River, April 25, 1876. She leaves a husband and four children. I. N. Wilson

Rev. James Gault was born in Union county, S. C., January 7, 1810; died June 25, 1876. J. B. Wilson

Mrs. Winfred Hogan, wife of James Hogan and daughter of Rolly and Keziah Wood, was born in Chester District, S. C., in 1810; married in 1851; died in Paulding county, Ga., April 18, 1876.

Mr. C. J. Cobb died in Live Oak, Fla., June 24, 1876, aged twenty-four years. M. A. Conner

Miss Julia A. Harris, daughter of A. G. and S. J. Harris, was born August 6, 1857; and died June 26, 1876. She with three of her sisters joined the Church in 1874 at Level Creek Church. M. H. Eakes

Joseph W. Gunnin, son of Nathan and Mary Gunnin, was born August 15, 1855; died April 21, 1876, near Mikesville, Columbia county, Fla. S. E. Phillips

Tribute of Respect from Jonesville Circuit, South Carolina Conference to Rev. James Gault.

Issue of August 8, 1876

Died

Bessie, daughter of James F. and Lizzie H. Dillard, died in Oglethorpe county, Ga., July 5th 1876, aged seventeen months and twelve days.

Obituary

Rev. John S. Travis was born in Warren county, Ga., March 10, 1806, and died in Atlanta, Ga., June 4th 1876. He was twice married; first in 1836 to Miss Eldesa Parker, daughter of Rev. W. C. Parker, now of Atlanta, and sister of our lamented brother, Rev. Joshua M. Parker. The second time, to Miss Elizabeth Smith, of Griffin, Ga., September 29th 1845, who with three sons and one daughter, survive. W. F. Cook

Dr. Richard Blake Rice was born June 19th 1810 and died at his home in Colleton county, July 19th 1876. Early in life Dr. Rice joined the Baptist Church and later the Methodist Church. Thos. Rayser

Mrs. Ann Stripling, wife of Rev. David Stripling and daughter of George and Ann Butler, was born on 321 Oxford street, London, England, May 11th 1802, came to America in 1826, married November 23, 1828 and died near Carrollton, Ga., June 13, 1876. E. K. Akin

Miss Jane P. White died in Mariana, Fla., May 1st 1876, in the fifty-seventh year of her age. Elisha Phillips

Abie W. Ackerman was born April 16th 1851 and died in Colleton, S. C., June 17th 1876.

Mrs. Rebecca McBride, wife of Dr. E. H. McBride, died near Chesterfield C. H., S. C., July 9, 1876, aged eighteen years and nearly eight months. J. W. Murray

Mrs. Henrietta F. Jones, daughter of Elliott and Anna Moore, died in Bartow county, June 28th 1876, in the twenty-second year of her age.

George White, of Muscogee county, died July 11th 1876, in the sixty-ninth year of his age. He came from Virginia to Georgia, an orphan boy, embraced religion in Monroe county, raised a family of fifteen children. H. P. Pitchford

Robert Harwell Lowery was born in Hall county, Georgia, February 20, 1844; and died in Milton county, June 15, 1876. He leave a wife and three little children. J. J. Harris

David Andrews was born in Connecticut, July 19th 1805 and died in Sumter county, S. C., June 3d, 1876. He came to this state when a young man. In 1820 he professed religion in Orangeburg, S. C. L. M. Little

Tribute of Respect from Buena Vista Circuit, South Georgia Conference to Rev. C. N. Burkhalter, a local preacher, who died on the 12th of April last.

Issue of August 15, 1876

Maria Gray Rivers, daughter of Dr. W. B. Rivers and the subject of this brief memoir, was born August 22, 17862, and died at the home of her parents in Oxford, Ga., June 30, 1876. A. Means

Esther Davis, wife of Joshua Davis, was born June 1, 1788 in Laurens District, S. C., and died at Mt. Pleasant, Gadsden county, Fla., June 20, 1876. She moved to Gadsden county, Fla., in 1829 where she lived 47 years. W. F. Norton, P. C.

John A. Lucas was born February 14, 1838 in Belville, N. J., and died in Apalachicola, Fla., July 9, 1876. Isaac A. Towers

James Sanders Means, son of William and Susan Means, was born in Upson county, Ga., July 8, 1853; and died at his father's, July 22, 1876. R. L. Wiggins

Miss Mary A. Baker was born in Monroe, Walton county, Ga., October 10, 1827; died in the same county, July 10, 1876. J. W. Baker

Lucius A. Luke died in Columbia county, Ga., May 13, 1876, in the 49th year of his age. B. F. Fariss

Mrs. Excy L. Tucker, wife of Rev. Warren J. Tucker, was born February 10, 1803; died in Rockdale county, Ga., July 29, 1876. She was buried at Smyrna Presbyterian Church.

Tribute of Respect to John S. Travis, who died 4th June last in the 71st year of his age.

Issue of August 22, 1876

Sister Addie C. Cassady, daughter of Rev. John W. Norton, was born in Barbour county, Alabama, in August 1848. Her brother, Rev. W. R. Norton in Lawrenceville, Ala. In Enon, Ala., December 29, 1874, she was married to Capt. A. A. Cassady of Lawrenceville. She leaves a husband and her infant son, J. J. Cassady. A. Dowling

Our church at Garden Valley has sustained an irreparable loss. Miss Georgia A. Shirley, daughter of Ephraim and Mary Shirley, has died.

Bro. Joseph T. Wells, son of William and Sarah Wells, was born in Marion county, Ga., April 17th 1840 and departed this life at his residence near Clayton, Panola county, Texas, June the 7th 1876. He removed from Georgia with his parents in 1858. He was married to Miss N. M. Heath of Panola county, Texas, Dec. 20th 1876. J. C. A. Bridges

Mrs. Sarah S. V. Brassfield, wife of W. B. Brassfield and daughter of T. M. Parker, died near Hatchechubbee, Russell county, Ala., on the 27th of June 1876. She was born in --nes county, Ga., and came with her father of Auburn, Ala., in 1840. In June 1849 she was married to W. B. Brassfield and became the mother of seven children. W. K. Norton

Rev. William Cunyus was born in Houston county, Ga., July 21st 1828 and died in Bartow county, Ga., June 17th 1876. he was married December 12th 1850 to Miss Celestia A. Jennings of Wetumpka, Ala. He leaves a wife and children. J. J. Singleton

Mrs. Julia A. Pou, daughter of Dr. J. H. J. and Harriet N. Hook, died in Lexington county, S. C., June 27th 1876, in her thirtieth year. She graduated at Spartanburg Female College in June 1862, and was married to John B. Pou the following December. Her husband and four children survive. M. L. Banks

Milton D. Hook, son of Dr. J. H. J. Hook, deceased, was born February 7th 1849 and died in Lexington, S. C., June 28th 1876. M. L. Banks

Robert W. Disher, son of R. W. Disher, of Charleston, S. C., died in that city June 1, 1876, in the thirtieth year of his age. He soon followed a most lovely sister, Florence M. She died August 28th 1876.

Mr. W. Levis Cornog died in Hart county, Ga., June 28, 1876, in the 33th year of his age. He leaves his parents, an only sister, a wife and two children.

Issue of August 29, 1876

Died

Henry Warren Pegues, child of R. M. and S. O. Pegues, of Marlboro, S. C., Died July 18, 1876, aged about fourteen months.

Obituary

Mrs. Anna L. Owen, wife of Robert G. Owen, was born in Houston county, Ga., March 14, 1859; died in Cuthbert, Ga., July 8, 1876. Henry W. Dixon

Charles B. Zuber, a native of Oglethorpe county, Ga., died in Randolph county, Ga., July 20, 1876, in the 57th year of his age. R. W. Dixon

W. E. Kilpatrick died on the 30th of June, aged about 29 years. he was a member of the 29th Regiment of S. C. Volunteers, wounded in the heel in 1864, near Petersburg. W. L. Pegues

Brother Wm. Prather died in Lowndesville, May 19, 1876. He had nearly completed his 80th year. His wife died many years ago, leaving a family of daughters. Thus has passed another member of our Church at Lowndesville Station, South Carolina Conference. W. H. Lawton

Mrs. M. E. H. Dukes was born December 1837; died July 26, 1876. J. B. Campbell. Christian Neighbor please copy.

At her residence near Beaufort, N. C., on the morning of June 8th, died Mrs. Zilphia Marshall, aged 75 years 7 months. Her Daughter. The Raleigh, N. C., Episcopal Methodist will please copy.

Sister Sallie M. Kirkland, daughter of Edward and N. C. Blacklidge, was born in Leon county, Fla., June 16, 1850. When a little child her parents moved into Henry county, Ala., and settled in Abbeville. October 18, 1870, she married Mr. Seymore Kirkland, of Abbeville, Ala. She died July 4, 1876, and was buried in the cemetery in Abbeville, Ala. Angus Dowling.

My father, William Asprey Stubbs, was born in North Carolina, February 16, 1816; died July 9, 1876. His parents came to Randolph county, Ga., during his childhood. H. Stubbs

Miss Corinthia Patterson, daughter of John C. and Sarah Patterson, was born December 30, 1850; died in Augusta, Ga., July 11, 1867. F. A. Kimball

Miss Hattie E. Grisham, wife of Mr. Roland Grisham, and daughter of Dr. Jas. and H. E. Bivings, died July 3, 1876, in the eighteen year of her age. J. K. McCain

Died, in Thomasville, on Monday morning, July 24, Willie, youngest son of the late R. R. Evans and Mrs. Caroline Evans, in the twenty-fourth year of his age. H. W. Sharpe

Nathaniel Williams was born in Walton county, Ga., December 25, 1825; died in Fulton county, near Atlanta, Ga., June 17, 1876.

Miss Annie Julia, daughter of Col. and Mrs. John F. Treutlen, of Cokesbury, S. C., died on 23d July, in the nineteenth year of her age. Richard D. Smart.

Martha J. Man, daughter of William S. and Jane R. Man, died July 10, 1876, in Bronson, Levy county, Fla., in the twenty-sixth year of her age. E. B. Duncan

Issue of September 5, 1876

Died

In Acworth, Ga., July 19th, 1876, Luther Wightman, infant son of Geo. D. and Laura Collins, aged ten months and five days.

On August 4, 1876, Lucie Helen, daughter of J. H. and Bettie Hunter, aged eleven months and one day.

On July 31, 1876, John Isam Clements, infant son of W. L. and Emma Clements, aged one month and twenty-six days.

On the evening of the 21st of August 1876, Dannie, second child of B. D. and Ella A. Ainsworth, Thomasville, Ga.

On August 23d, 1876, little Edgar Layfield, aged one year, ten months and sixteen days.

Obituary

Gen. William Evans was born April 7th 1801, near the spot where he breathed his last; was married to Miss Sarah Ann, daughter of Gen. Thomas Godbold, June 19th 1827; died near Marion, S. C., June 6th 1873 [sic]. He served three terms in the legislature. He was buried in Marion.

Dr. John C. Lee was born May 8, 1818; converted at Rock Chapel Camp ground in DeKalb county, when in his sixteenth year; died in Walker county, Ga., July 1st 1876. He had been twice married; his first wife was the daughter of James McGuffey of Gwinnett county. his second wife was a daughter of the late W. F. Powel, who was connected with the North Georgia Conference. A. Thornburg, M. D.

Mrs. Mary Eliza Holman, of Mechanicsville, S. C., died 22d May 1876, in this thirtieth year of her age. About three years ago a little daughter went home to be with Jesus. About one year since, her sainted father, Mr. Francis H. Kennedy died. Mrs. M. had been a member of the Presbyterian church.

Rev. William R. Bell, M. D., was born in Chester District, South Carolina, October 30th 1826; was married to Miss Margaret Ryles, November 3d 1846; died in Cobb county, Ga., July 3d 1876. He leaves a widow and eight children. Three of his children had died before him. T. H. Timmons.

Mrs. Elizabeth Hardee Overstreet, whose maiden name was Goodbread, was born in Columbus, Fla., May 5th 1848; died in Live Oak, Fla., July 25th 1876. She leaves a husband, three children, a mother, sister and brother. A. Johnson

Miss Cornelia E. Mizell, daughter of Morgan and Mary F. Mizell, died at her home, in Manatee county, Florida, June 6, 1876, in the 18th year of her age.

Eleanor Jane Cottrell, daughter of the Rev. Dr. Thomas Cottrell, was born in Orange county, N. C., Sept. 25, 1818; was married to Dr. Robert L. Taggart in Mesopotamia (now Eutaw), Ala., Nov. 23, 1827 [sic]; died at Memphis, Tenn., June 5, 1876.

Rev. John D. Sharp was born in Lexington county, S., C., in what was known as the "Dutch Fork," Feb. 28th 1788; and died in Atlanta, Ga., July 11th 1876. He was married twice; first to Mrs. Mary Parish. In 1873, he became acquainted with Mrs. Elizabeth Jane Clark and they married. W. C. Dunlap. Christian Neighbor please copy.

Mr. James C. Whitaker was born in Washington county, Ga., April 30th 1815; joined the Baptist Church in Camden, S. C., in 1833; died in Baldwin County, Ga., May 31st 1876. He leaves a wife and seven grown children.

Almon Short, a native of Virginia, died in Clarke county, Ga., July 27, 1876, aged about sixty-six years.

Tribute of Respect to Henry M. Tripee who died May 21st, 1876, in the 72d year of his age. Eatonton Quarterly Conference.

Tribute of Respect from Manatee ct. Florida Conference to James G. Cooper, who died June 20th.

Issue of September 12, 1876

Died

Henry Parks, son of Rev. G. T. and Mrs. S. E. Embry, of the South Georgia Conference, died August 24, 1876, one year and thirteen days.

Obituary

Rev. Lawrence Baker was born at Covington, Ga., April 6, 1843; was married to Miss M. W. J. Smith at Atlanta, Ga., February 24, 1870; and died in Midway, Ala., July 19, 1876. D. M. Banks

John Seay was born in Columbia county, Ga., August 24, 1790; died in Jackson county, Ga., May 26, 1876. William Seay. Lumpkin Independent please copy.

Martha Ashurst, daughter of Irby Hudson and wife of John B. Harrison, was born in Eatonton, Ga., Nov. 23, 1813; and died in Monroe county, Ga., August 7, 1876. James T. Love

John P. Chase, son of Gen. J. P. and Mrs. M. E. Chase, was born in Charleston, S. C., November 21, 1846; and died at the residence of his father-in-law, Mr. P. A. Brunson near Florence, Darlington county, S. C., July 21, 1876. In October 1865 he united himself with Nazareth Presbyterian Church. On March 27, 1867, he married Maria B. Brunson, and after two years moved to Savannah, Ga., where he has been connected with the Atlantic and Gulf Railroad. W. A. Brunson. Nashville Advocate will please copy.

Absalom Baker was born in Gwinnett county, Ga., September 28, 1811; died in Cobb county, August 1, 1876. He leaves a wife and seven children. M. L. Underwood

Mrs. Sarah E. Sewell, daughter of Thomas and Elizabeth Lowe, was born in Warren county, Ga., April 6, 1813; was married to the Rev. Samuel Sewell, September 9, 1830; died in Cobb county, Ga., June 24, 1876.

Mrs. E. J. Thomas, wife of Dr. M. H. Thomas, was born in Walton county, Ga., June 8, 1833; died at Crawford, Oglethorpe county, Ga., July 15, 1876. J. F. Mixon

Mrs. Verlinda B. Coleman, whose maiden name was Caton, wife of A. J. Coleman of Enon, Ala., was born in Georgia, May 18, 1838; was married in Alabama, October 1848 [sic], and died July 7, 1876. Jere. S. William

My mother, Mrs. Mary S. Dailey, died in Henry county, Ga., August 10, 1876. She was born in Lincoln county, N. C., in 1815; where she lost both her parents when small. She came to McDonough, Ga., when she was seventeen years old, where she resided with her brother, Oliver C. Cox, until she was married to my father, John Dailey, Jr., deceased in 1825. Mrs. M. H. Turner

Mrs. Mary Partlow, daughter and only child of John and Isabella Marshall, was born in Abbeville county, S. C., March 15, 1813; was married in 1829 to Mr. J. Y. L. Partlow; died in Abbeville, August 2, 1876.

Daniel John was born in Marlboro county, S. C., July 1, 1796; died July 29, 1876.
He lived and died in the county in which he was born, and was never out of his native State but once, and than at the call of his country, in the war of 1812. Left an orphan at an early age... Two years ago he buried his excellent wife. They brought up a family of four sons and three daughters, all of whom are living. W. H. Fleming

Benjamin Hill Denninton was born March 3, 1857; died July 26, 1876. P. C. Harris

Mrs. Mildred Cook was born in Virginia, December 27, 1797; died in Talbot county, Ga., June 22, 1876. Francis Woodall

Issue of September 19, 1876

Died

Florence Shepard, daughter of Rev. T. S. L. and J. H. Harwell, of the North Georgia Conference, died September 3, 1876, aged seven years, ten months, and twenty-eight days.

Obituary

Mrs. Right Rogers was born August 25, 1804; married May 16, 1822; died in Dalton, Ga., August 6, 1876. L. Pierce

Mrs. Ann C. Baxter, relict of Daniel H. Baxter and daughter of Rev. Francis Baxter, deceased, was born in Orangeburg county, S. C., December 10, 1821; died July 26, 1876. She was connected with the New Hope Church in the Branchville circuit.

Mrs. Fannie L. Vinson, consort of Dr. J. W. Vinson of Montezuma, Ga., died at Montvale Springs, Tenn., August 7, 1876, in the thirty first year of her age.

Mrs. E. M. Spear, relict of W. C. Spear, was born in Hancock county, Ga., September 13, 1822; moved to Talbot county, Ga., with her parents, where she was married; died July 1, 1876. She leaves six children. W. C. Carter

Miss Nannie L. Spillman, daughter of Joshua and E. E. Spillman, was born February 23, 1854; died near Atlanta, Ga., August 15, 1876. T. H. Timmons

Miss Evelina E. Rockwell, daughter of Rev. and Mrs. C. S. Rockwell, died in Thomas county, Ga., August 24, 1876, aged sixteen years, seven months and nine days.

Sister Susan W. Richardson, daughter of John Simmons, Esq., was born in Rutherford county, N. C., December 29, 1795; married Rev. John L. Richardson, October 6, 1825; died in White county, Ga., July 22, 1876. W. R. Branham, Jr.

Mrs. Carrie Duncan, wife of D'Arcy P. Duncan and daughter of the late Ex-Governor Gist, died in Union county, S. C., August 19, 1876, about thirty two years of age.

The death of the Hon. Arthur Ginn on the 14th of August produced a profound sentiment of regret in this community. J. Wofford Tucker

Mrs. Belle Watters Edmundson was born in Floyd county, Ga., November 20, 1851; died at Rome, Ga., July 18, 1876.

Mrs. Mamie A. Ledingham, wife of W. J. Ledingham, Esq., and eldest daughter of Rev. C. D. Rowell, M. D., of the South Carolina Conference, was born May 12, 1856, and died July 26, 1876. Last October, she became the wife of the gentleman above named.

Mrs. Margaret Wideman, whose maiden name was McMillan, was born in 1803; was married to Samuel Wideman in 1823; died July 28, 1876. She was a member of one of the oldest families of the state, and a descendant of the earlier settlers of Jamestown, Va. She was the mother of six children, one of whom died young. S. P. H. Elwell

Tribute of Respect from Waukyenah circuit, Tallahassee District, Florida Conference, to Rev. J. C. Howren.

Issue of September 26, 1876

Died

Zacie, son of Solomon and Mary E. Hagin, died in Bullock county, Ga., September 3, 1876, aged 5 years, 4 months and 14 days.

Lora, infant daughter of Jonathan and Susan Emma McEachin, was born April 11, 1874, and died July 2, 1876, near Spring Hill, Montgomery county, Ga.

Obituary

Rev. C. C. Andrews was born in Liberty county, Ga., June 21, 1829; died in Belton, Hall county, Ga., July 26, 1876. He graduated at Trinity College, N. C., June 24, 1858, and was married to Miss Mary S. Robstean of Fayetteville, N. C., July 11, 1859. His body rests in the cemetery at Belton. He leaves a wife and six children, an aged father and mother, a sister and brothers. D. D. Cox

Mrs. Margaret J. Craig, relict of Hugh Craig, died at Chesterfield C. H., S. C., August 27, 1876, aged 42 years. She joined the Church in girlhood at Poplar Grove camp ground in Chesterfield County. She leaves a son and daughter. J. W. Murray

Brother J. L. D. Ward was born in Hancock county, Ga., May 27, 1802. He moved to Clark county, Ga., with his father in 1804 and settled near Salem, at which please he lived until 1867, when he moved to Bartow county, Ga. He was thrown from his buggy and killed in Adairsville on the 9th of July 1876. He was married November 26, 1822, to Miss Catharine Carmichael of Clark county, who still survives him. He was the father of eleven children, and seven are still living. J. J. Singleton

Rev. James C. Howren died in Jasper, Fla., July 13, 1876, in the 90th year of his age. He was married three times; first to Miss White of Georgetown, S. C.; afterwards to Miss Mitzenburg of Charleston, S. C.; and a third time to Mrs. Durant of Horry District, S. C., stepmother of the late Rev. H. H. Durant, of the South Carolina Conference. His son, Rev. R. H. Howren. St. Louis Christian Advocate please copy.

Llewellyn Nimms Norris, son of John C. and Eliza Ann Norris, died in Atlanta, Ga., August 15, 1876, aged 21 years since the 15th of January last. W. C. Dunlap

Steadman Yeaden Disher died in Charleston, S. C., August 10, 1876, in his 26th year. His little babe preceded him a little more than a year ago-- and the two await the coming of the wife and mother. G. H. Wells

Miss Bethana Forehand, second daughter of Linkfield and Marinda Forehand, was born June 15, 1858; died near Coe's Mills in Liberty county, Fla., August 26, 1876. R. F. Hosford. Hawkinsville Dispatch will please copy.

Mrs. Charlotte LeVaugh Kennedy, daughter of James and Margaret Rochelle, was born in Fairfield District, South Carolina, October 15, 1800; was married to Rev. John A. Kennedy in 1824; moved to Alachua county, Florida in 1848, where she died July 24, 1876. She was Huguenot by descent, and her ancestry on both sides were among the earliest conquests of Methodism in Virginia. John C. Ley

Hampton Stevens was born in South Carolina in 1805; moved to Marion county, Ga., in 1848; to Randolph county in 1871, and died in Harris county, while on a visit, July 25, 1876. W. W. Stewart

William Rembert Mouzon, son of L. H. and Mrs. Ann Mouzon, was born in Charleston, S. C., February 15, 1842; died at the residence of his father-in-law, Mr. Charles Richardson, in Clarendon, S. C., June 23, 1876.

Judge C. C. Carmichael was born in Marion District, S. C., September 24, 1820; died in Indianapolis, Ind., July 13, 1876. In early life he enlisted in the army to fight the Indians in Florida. While there, he filled the position of assistant clerk of the Secretary of Florida. He afterwards married, moved to Georgia...

Mrs. Georgia Oak, youngest daughter of George C. and Mary C. Powers, was born at Mayport, August 10, 1857; died August 22, 1876. She was married May 12, 1875, to Mr. Byron E. Oak, of Jacksonville.

Mrs. Sarah Binns was born in Jasper county, Ga., July 29, 1811; died in Talbot county, Ga., August 1, 1876. She joined the Baptist Church in her sixteenth year. Like her brother, B. B. Kendrick.... She leaves a sister, Mrs. Trussell. W. W. Stewart

Tribute of Respect from Berkley Circuit, South Carolina Conference, to Robert S. McCants, who died on the 10th of May in the 60th year of his age.

Issue of October 3, 1876

[page 159, first column]: Rev. Edward Howell Myers, D. D., died in Savannah, Ga., at 7 A. M., September the 26th. Dr. Myers was born in Orange county, New York in 1816. His father emigrated to Florida in his early childhood.

Died

John Curry, son of Rev. G. H. and Mrs. Amelia Wyatt, died at Manatee, Fla., August 10, 1876, aged nine years, one month, and eight days.

T. A. McC. Rogers, son of E. R. and S. E. Rogers, died September 2, 1876, aged six years, ten months, and twenty-eight days.

Obituary

Mrs. Frances G. Connor, wife of Mr. F. A. Connor of Cokesbury, S. C., was the second daughter of the late Gen. G. W. Hodges. Richard D. Smart

Vincent Nichols was born in Burke county, Ga., October 1, 1803; moved to Crawford county in 1823; died August 5, 1876. L. G. Evans

Mrs. Lucy Jones, wife of Edward Jones, Esq., of Clayton county, Ga., was born in Chesterfield District, S. C., and died September 1, 1876, aged nearly fifty-five. She was the mother of eleven children, four sons and seven daughters, all of whom except one survive her. W. A. Dodge

John M. Duffy was born in Mecklenburg county, N. C., October 19, 1799; died in Heard county, Ga., July 27, 1876. He leaves and aged wife and five children. W. H. Graham

Julius R. Clapp was born near Montague, Massachusetts, December 8, 1808; died near Columbus, Ga., September 2, 1876. For more than forty years brother Clapp has been a citizen of Columbus. J. S. Key

Mrs. Mary I. Hudson, wife of Hon. C. B. Hudson and daughter of William and Nancy Woods, was born in Lancaster District, S. C., in 1838; was married in 1850; and died near Ellaville, Ga., September 8, 1876. Her parents moved to Georgia during her girlhood.

Miss Hattie Manning Arthur was born in Columbia, S. C., November 20, 1855; died in Orangeburg county, S., C., August 27, 1876. Her father, Wm. F. Arthur died when she was an infant. M. L. Banks

Mrs. Eliza Harrell, daughter of Jonathan Miller, M. D., was born in Sumter county, S. C., October 25, 1820. her father moved to Darlington county in the year 1843 and during the same year she was married to S. W. Harrell. On the 22d June 1876, she had an attack and she survived two months longer. Lewis M. Hamer

Robert D. Gage, son of Col. R. J. and Mrs. Martha Gage of Union county, S. C., died at Sullivan's Island, September 18, 1876, in the twenty-third year of his age. In October last he came to Charleston and entered the business house of his uncle, Mr. Geo. W. Williams.

Mrs. Caroline Ellis, daughter of Edward and Rachel Lovejoy, was born in Jasper county, Ga., January 1812, was married to Henry Ellis in 1830; died July 23, 1876.

Henry B. Harbeson, of Saint George's Parish, S. C., died August 9, 1876, in the sixty-fourth year of his age. He leaves a widow and many relatives.

Mr. Mills Kelly died in Kershaw county, S. C., July 20, 1876;, aged seventy-three.

Margaret Maddox, wife of A. W. Maddox deceased, was born in Oglethorpe county, Ga., September 5, 1791; and died in Chambers county, Ala., at the residence of her son, Richard Maddox, June 7, 1876.

Mrs. Nancy E. J. Cantrell, daughter of Mrs. Adaline Craven, was born June 17, 1855; was married to Geo. Cantrell in 1874; died June 23, 1876. She joined the Baptist Church in 1874. J. D. Jarrard.

Mrs. Mary Bryan, consort of Isaac Bryan, deceased, died in Scriven county, Ga., July 4, 1876, in her seventy-first year. N. D. Morehouse.

Issue of October 10, 1876

Died

George Martin, eighth son of Jas. S. and Ella S. Hyer, died in Charleston, S. C., September 25, 1876, aged five years.

Obituary

Mrs. Lou Belle Curtiss, wife of Rev. J. T. Curtiss and daughter of Captain William Phillips of Augusta, was born on the 30th of September 1836 and died in Augusta, Ga., September 6, 1876. On January 7, 1864, she became the wife of Rev. J. T. Curtiss.

My niece, Ulrica Antoinette Philips, eldest daughter of Andrew J. and Penelope T. Phillips, was born in Clay county, Fla., May 18, 1850; died in Putnam county of the same state, August 3, 1876. E. L. T. Blake

Mrs. Anna Wylly Habersham, eldest daughter of Nathaniel Adams and relict of Dr. Joseph Clay Habersham, Sr., died at the residence of Wm. Neyle Habersham, Esq., at White Bluff, near Savannah, September 10, 1876. She had entered her 82d year. H. J. Adams

Mr. James H. Shi was born in Hancock county, Ga., March 15, 1807; died near Bolingbroke, July 8, 1876.

William D. Dansby was born in Troup county, Ga., January 11, 1839; was married to Miss Mattie B. Sappington, February 24, 1864; and died August 26, 1876. J. S. Bryan

Mr. E. A. Fretwell was born in Jefferson county, Ga., January 7, 1818; and died in Madison county, Fla., August 14, 1876. He has left a wife and several children. E. S. Tyner

Mrs. Martha Harriet Cobb, wife of J. V. W. Cobb and daughter of the late George W. Belzer, died at Simpson's Springs, in Jefferson county, Fla., August 24, 1876.

Walter F. Lewis was born in Warren county, Ga., February 9, 1817; and was killed by lightning near his lifelong residence, July 30, 1876.

Brother E. S. Sligh was born December 16, 1832; and died September 4, 1876. He leaves a widow and ten children. T. G. Herbert

Tribute of Respect from Trinity Church, Charleston, S. C., to W. W. Pemberton.

Issue of October 17, 1876

Died

Willie, son of Rev. and Mrs. T. W. Munnerlyn of the South Carolina Conference, died in Rock Hill, S. C., on Sunday, October 8, 1876, aged 5 years, 11 months and 24 days.

Obituary

Maj. Thomas H. Mitchell was born in Jackson county, Ga., June 7th 1830, and died Sept. 29th 1876. His father, Madison R. Mitchell died in 1858, leaving a wife and five minor children. Being the eldest son of his father by a former marriage.... Gustavus J. Orr

Mr. Cyrus Robinson was born September 23, 1801; and died July 18, 1876. His childhood and youth were spent in Putnam county, Ga., In 1832 he was married to Miss Malinda Brown of Talbot county, Ga.

Miss Sarah A. Green, eldest daughter of William and Jane Green, was born in Pinckneyville, Gwinnette county, Ga., July 31, 1822; died at Marietta, Ga., September 14, 1876.

Joel Lester was born in North Carolina, died near Culloden, Monroe county, Ga., July 3, 1876, in the seventy-seventh year of his age.

Dr. Samuel Marion Tucker, eldest son of J. Wofford and Emily Tucker, was born in Spartanburg, S. C., in 1847; and died near Sanford, Fla., September 18, 1876. He was educated in St. Louis, Mo., and graduated M. D., in the Belle Vue Medical College, N. Y., February 1870. After graduating, Dr. Tucker located in Texas... he sought a home in Florida. He left a wife and three little ones.

Mrs. Elizabeth W. Day, wife of the late Richard B. Day, and daughter of the late Absalom Rhodes, was born in Richmond county, Ga., February 3, 1802; died August 9, 1876.

Mrs. Rhoda Miller died at the house of her son-in-law, John Lipsey, in Pike county, Ga., August 20, 1876. Left a widow many years ago with a family of children. New Orleans Advocate please copy.

Mrs. Rebecca A. Johnson, whose maiden name was Jones, was born in Clarke county, Ga., in 1807; died in Oglethorpe county, Ga., August 8, 1876. In 1830 she was married to Mr. B. F. McRee, who less than six years afterwards, died, leaving her with three children. In 1855 she was married to Mr. Nathan Johnson.

William Wightman Pemberton died on Sullivan's Island, near Charleston, S. C., July 24, 1876. G. H. Wells

Mrs. Amanda M. Williams was born in Hancock county, Ga., June 10, 1809; died in Hancock county, Ga., August 11, 1876.

Resolutions adopted by the Faculty and Students of Wesleyan Female College on the Death of Rev. E. H. Myers, D. D.

Mrs. Sophia Glover died on the 3d August 1876, at Glenalter, near Orangeburg, S. C.

Issue of October 24, 1876

Died

George Washington and his wife Nancy S. Washington, died of Yellow Fever at No. 1 Macon and Brunswick R. R., the former on the 18th of September and the latter on the 9th of September. They leave three children.

Obituary

Two dark shadows have fallen upon the home of my brother and sister, James and Margaret M. Stokes. Harry L. Stokes, born May 10th 1866, died July 7th 1876; and Sallie M. Stokes, born September 20th 1855, died September 12th 1876. A. J. Stokes

Jeremiah Winter was born in Richmond county, Ga., June 12, 1826; married Lizzie, daughter of Dr. Thos. and Mrs. Martha Boring, formerly of the North Georgia Conference, in 1853; died in Brooks county, Ga., July 29th 1876. He removed to Gwinnett county in 1871. He left a wife and five children. J. H. D. McRae

Fannie Winter, daughter of Jeremiah and Lizzie Winter, died in Brooks county, Ga., September 26, 1876, aged seventeen years and six days. J. H. D. McRae

Mrs. F. S. Bell, whose maiden name was Davenport, died in Sumter co., Ga., July 26th 1876, in the 60th year of her age. She was first married to J. J. Hollingsworth. Both husbands preceded her many years to the better land.

Mrs. Margaret N. Rogers, daughter of George W. and Margaret Hallman, was born at Cumming, Ga., March 20th 1856; married in 1872; died September 28th 1876. He leaves a wife and two little children. M. H. Eakes

W. L. J. Reid was born in Cabarrus county, N. C., September 13, 1816; was married to Miss Ann C. Horne, of Cheraw, S. C., November 1841; died in Cheraw, S. C., September 30, 1876. D. Tiller

Mrs. Eliza Caldwell Kay, consort of B. D. Kay, was born January 16, 1809; died near Lowndesville, S. C., August 12, 1876. She was first married to Miles Hardy, and was left a widow with five children. W. H. Lawton

Jno. L. Garlington was born in Oglethorpe county, Ga., March 1st 1817. He was married twice; first to Miss Lucinda Garret, of Alabama, afterwards to Miss M. E. Oliver, of Halifax county, Va. He died July 26th, at Snapping Shoals, Henry county, Ga. W. R. Branham. Richmond Christian Advocate and Baptist paper at Raleigh, N. C., please copy.

Mr. W. L. White of Lee county, Ga., was born October 1848; died October 6th 1876. Sumter Republican please copy.

Mrs. Elizabeth C. McDaniel, wife of Benj. F. McDaniel and daughter of Williamson and Elizabeth Switzer, was born February 8th 1824 in Putnam county, Ga., and died near Hamilton, Ga., July 27th 1876.

Issue of October 31, 1876

Mrs. Sarah A. Moore, wife of Charles G. Moore, was born in Patchogue, N. Y., June 14, 1824; and died in Brunswick, Ga., October 6, 1876. She left a husband and children. J. O. A. Cook

Mrs. Elizabeth Chase, whose maiden name was Bynum, relict of the late Albon Chase of Athens, Ga., was born in Charleston, S. C., July 18, 1810; was married to Albon Chase, October 1, 1830; died at the residence of her son-in-law, Rev. W. P. Pattillo, in Atlanta, Ga., October 1, 1876. Sister Chase joined the Methodist Church in Columbia, S. C., in her girlhood. J. W. Burke

Mrs. Nancy C. Knight, wife of Daniel Knight, and daughter of Jas. L. and Lucinda Mayson, was born October 20, 1831; and died in Fulton county, Ga., July 30, 1876. P. M. Ryburn

Hampton S. Smith died at Rome, Ga., October 8, 1876, aged seventy-five years. A native of Edgefield District, S. C., he removed when about twelve years old to Putnam county, Ga. In 1828 he became one of the first settlers of Columbus, Ga.

Henry Gaines Slaughter was born in Prince Edward county, Va., May 15, 1792; died in Troup county, Ga., August 29, 1876. P. M. Ryburn

Miss Mary Elizabeth Arnold, only daughter of Wm. C. (deceased) and Mary F. Arnold of Jefferson county, Ga., was born March 23, 1859; and died September 6, 1876.

Mrs. Mariah Lee, wife of Reuben N. Lee, died in Hancock county, Ga., September 9, 1876, aged about thirty-eight years.

My niece, Miss Emma Henry, daughter of Samuel and Mary Henry, was born in Stewart county, Ga., October 21, 1849; died at the residence of her brother, Dr. J. S. Henry in Newnan, Ga., September 20, 1876. F. M. T. Brannon

Mrs. Lizell Walton, daughter of Jno. B. and Mrs. A. E. Wootten, of Wilkes county, Ga., was born November 27, 1848; married to Capt. Jno. H. Walton, July 8, 1870; died July 15, 1876.

Mrs. Jane Rakestraw was born in Kershaw county, S. C., February 3, 1815; joined the Church at Hanging Rock, S. C.; died in Cheraw, S. C., October 2, 1876. D. Tiller

Mrs. Serena Ivey died in Forsyth, Ga., October 12, 1876. She was born in February 1815; married to Travis Ivey in 1831. Geo E. Gardner. Barnesville (Ga.) Gazette please copy.

Mary Ellen Vaught, daughter of Peter Vaught, died in Horry county, S. C., September 12, 1876.

Tribute of Respect from Beaver Dam Circuit, South Georgia Conference, to Vincent Nichols.

Mrs. Mary Loudon was born February 10, 1835; died in Lumpkin county, Ga., October 2, 1876. C. L. Pattillo

SOUTHERN CHRISTIAN ADVOCATE NOTICES 1867-1878

Died

Willie A. Harris, on of Abb. G. and H. O. Harris, died in Henry co., Ga., Oct. 21, 1876, aged 5 years, 1 month and 10 days.

Carrie Lee Weaver, eldest daughter of J. B. and Mattie Weaver of Memphis, Tenn., died Oct. 4, 1876, aged 8 years and 9 months.

Mrs. Sarah E. Shaw, relict of Josias W. Shaw, died on Oct. 21, 1876, in the 82d year of her age.

Obituary

Rev. Henry Tyler was born in Elbert county, Ga., December 25, 1812, and died October 4, 1876 in Hart county, Ga. He leaves an affectionate wife (whom he married in Anderson county, S. C., January 19, 1838, Patience S. Reeves), three daughters and four grandchildren. Wm. T. Norman

Mrs. Ann B. Derrick, wife of Rev. David Derrick of the South Carolina Conference, was born July 20, 1807; died September 3, 1876. As Miss Ann B. Veach, she was a much esteemed and efficient teacher. June 11, 1846, she married Rev. David Derrick in old Bethel Church, Charleston, S. C. J. W. Kelly

E. H. Linley of Cobb county, Ga., was born in Walton county, Ga., January 25, 1816; was killed by a collision on the Western and Atlantic Railroad, six miles from Atlanta, October 12, 1876. He was first married to Miss Sarah Smith, who only lived one year. He afterwards married Miss Jane Scott, whom he left to mourn his loss.

Miss Matt. W. Mitchell, wife of Dr. P. H. Mitchell and daughter of H. H. and Mrs. E. P. Mangham, was born in Talbot county, Ga., in 1836; died at the residence of Dr. B. L. Ross in Fort Valley, Ga., August 30, 1876. At the age of seventeen she was married to Dr. Mitchell of Taylor county. She left an only sister, one brother, her husband and two children. B. L. Ross. Christian Index please copy.

Miss Mary A. L. Bevis, daughter of William Z. Bevis, Esq., was born in Union county, S. C., November 13, 1859; died at Oakland, Ga., the present home of her father, September 21, 1876. A. S. Bell

Sarah McCally Pooser, daughter of James and Elizabeth McCally, was born in St. Matthews Parish, Orangeburg District, S. C., January 28, 1813; was married to Adkinson Pooser, January 24, 1833; died in Welborn, Fla., October 12, 1876. In 1856 the family removed from South Carolina to Georgia and thence to Florida, settling near Newnansville, in Alachua county. Five children... Thomas A. Carruth

Miss Mary Ann Edwards died in Cherokee county, Ga., September 26, 1876, aged 26 years, 6 months and 19 days. J. N. Myers

Miss Ernine Cumy Rease was born July 21, 1856; died in Cherokee county, Ga., September 26, 1876. J. N. Myers

My daughter, Mrs. Mary Ann Barton, was born September 18, 1849; was happily married to Theophilus Barton, Esq., of Orangeburg, November 8, 1871; died August 23, 1876. Thos Raysor

Brother John J. Morgan was born December 8, 1801; died in Brunswick, Ga., October 15, 1876. A wife and several children are left. J. O. A. Cook

Rev. L. B. Varn died September 26, 1876, in Colleton county, S. C.

Bradford Sherman of Georgetown. S. C., died October 13, 1876, aged 67 years, 2 months and 25 days. He was a native of Rhode Island, but came South at the age of twenty-one, and first settled at Wilmington, N. C., where he married Miss Caroline Tilley in 1835. In 1851 he came to Georgetown, S. C. L. Wood

Thomas Swindall was born in North Carolina, June 30, 1806; was reared in Green county, Ga; moved to Troup county in 1837 where he died September 30, 1876. H. J. Ellis

Dr. J. L. Burney was born in Warren county, Ga., and died in Clay county, Ga., September 14, 1876, in the 68th year of his age. For many years he resided in Monroe county, Ga., where he practiced medicine. From thence he removed to Randolph county, Ga. He leaves five children, all grown, and a wife. J. S. West

George Olin Shinholser, the youngest son of Thomas J. and Amanda Shinholser, of Bibb county, Ga., died October 5, 1876, in the nineteenth year of his age. S. S. Sweet

Issue of November 14, 1876

Eleanor C. Browning, wife of J. T. Browning, was born in Charleston county, S. C., February 27, 1841; died October 4, 1876. She left a husband and five children with grandchildren. E. C. Gantt

Samuel A. Fortson was born in Wilkes county, Ga., June 30, 1860; married in 1875 Miss Mollie Barksdale, daughter of Mr. James Barksdale, of Lincoln county, Ga.; died at the home of his brother in law, Mr. R. S. Neal, in Columbia county, Ga., September 15, 1876. E. M. Whiting

Mrs. Harriet C. Gibbson, daughter of John and Jane Rison, was born in Chesterfield county, Va., January 7, 1818; died in Bartow county, Ga., October 3, 1876. She was married to George R. Gibbson, formerly of Richmond, Va., May 31, 1841. They moved from Richmond to Rockingham county, Va., in 1846 and thence to Bartow county, Ga., in 1863. J. J. Singleton

Dr. Thos. W. Carter was born in Abbeville District, S. C., April 13, 1822; died in Lake City, Fla., August 19, 1876. He married Miss L. A. Tompkins, who died a few years afterwards, leaving with him an only child, now Mrs. Hannah McNeil. He moved to Florida from Georgia in 1856. In 1873 he married Mrs. M. C. Dozier. Henry Edw. Partridge

Mrs. Jerusha H. Neilson, widow of the late Joseph Neilson of Barnwell C. H., S. C., and daughter of Mrs. Sarah A. Mixson, was born in Barnwell District, S. C., April 17, 1821; died in Lake City, Fla., August 23, 1876. In early womanhood she joined the Baptist Church. Henry Edw. Partridge. Working Christian please copy.

Sister Julia M. Adams, wife of Dr. S. S. Adams, died in Thomasville, Ga., October 10, 1876. J. O. A. Cook

Mrs. Rebecca Griffin, wife of Yancy R. Griffin, and daughter of General Mark and Mrs. Sarah A. E. Willcox, was born in Telfair county, September 28, 1834; died in the same county, September 6th 1876. J. E. Rorie

Mrs. Dellia Sappington was born July 30, 1856; died at Edgewood, Ga., October 23, 1876.

Sister Sarah Lowe, whose maiden name was Prine, was born in Missouri, in 1827, was brought by her grand parents to Houston county, Ga., where she was reared; she was married to J. W. Lowe in 1849; and at the time of her death was living in Lowndes county, Ga., near Ousley. R. L. Williams

George C. Fife was born in Monticello, Fla., April 26, 1850. He was married to Miss A. L. Jeffress of Gadsden county, Fla., December 18, 1872. He died October 5, 1876, leaving a wife and two children.

Frances P. Chambers, daughter of Josiah Chambers, was born December 20th 1806; married to Joseph B. Pledger, January 3d 1822; died in Clayton county, Ga., October 20th 1876. Rembert Smith

Mary A. Dugger, wife of William and Salome A. Dugger, was born June 17, 1845; died October 22, 1876.

Tribute of Respect from Little River Circuit ,North Georgia Conference to Matthew H. Talbot.

Issue of November 21, 1876

Died

Tallulah Susan Miller, daughter of Wm. Henry and Mary J. Miller of Troup county, Ga., died October 22, 1876, aged 2 years and 6 months.

Edward Lee Edwards was born December 13, 1867; died October 27, 1876 in Monroe county, Ga.

Obituary

Our sister Elizabeth Chupp died on the night of the 1st Sabbath in August, at her residence near Lithonia, Ga. She was a daughter of Joshua Marbut of Newberry, S. C., and born October 13, 1814. She was married to Jacob Chupp about the 1st of June 1835. Her brother-in-law, Rev. F. Haygood of Conyers. Jno. A. Reynolds

Mrs. Maria J. Stebbins, whose maiden name was Hyde, consort of Mr. M. L. Stebbins, was born in Springfield, Mass., 1811; died in Live Oak, Fla., October 29, 1876. She came to Florida with her husband some nineteen years ago. E. S. Tyner

Col. Matthew H. Talbot died in Wilkes county, Ga., September 27, 1876. He leaves a wife and little ones.

Mrs. Rebecca Davis, relict of William Davis and daughter of John and Mary Heape, was born March 6, 1811; died at the residence of her son-in-law, Joseph Marvin, in Beaufort county, S. C., September 2, 1876. She was a widow about fifteen years, having buried her husband, a son and a daughter the same year. the only remaining one of her children, sister Marvin, dying nearly three years ago, leaving three little children. G. H. Pooser

Mrs. Sallie P. Russell was born Oct. 30, 1848; was married to Mr. O. W. D. Russell of Chester county, July 16, 1874; died Oct. 20, 1876. She was the eldest daughter of Dr. and Mrs. J. C. Craig, near Cheraw, S. C. D. Tiller

Mrs. M. Callie Mitchell, formerly Swain, was born in Troup county, Ga., July 19, 1854; died near Mellonville, Fla., September 17, 1876. She had been married to Capt. L. T. Mitchell and had gone with him to their new home in Florida. G. G. Smith

Sister Sarah Harris, wife of Thomas Harris, Esq., died in Cobb county, Ga., October 16, 1876.

Brother Wyley Underwood was born Dec. 13th 1833 and died August 13th 1876. He had been a member of the Baptist Church, later of the Methodist church. H. S. Andrews

Issue of November 28, 1876

Bro. J. N. Toney was born in Franklin county, Ga., October 25th 1816; died in Forsyth, Ga., November 6th 1876. He was married October 6th 1836 by rev. Samuel Anthony to the wife who now survives him. Geo. E. Gardner

Mrs. Isabel M. Heath, wife of Alex. T. Heath and daughter of Samuel H. and Elizabeth Buxton, was born in Burke county, Ga., November 9th 1849; was married January 23d 1873; died October 27th 1876.

Mrs. Catharine A. Edwards, wife of Reuben N. Edwards, was born in Hancock county, Ga., March 21st 1816; died in Putnam county, Ga., October 5th 1876. Her parents, Thomas and Catharine Turner who moved to Putnam county,Ga., in 1823,were pioneers of Methodism. R. J. Wynn

T. H. Batton was born May 5th 1845 in Houston county, Ga., and died September 1st 1876. He left a wife and several small children. He was a member in the bounds of the Ocmulgee circuit, South Georgia Conference.

Keturah Herronton, whose maiden name was Griffen, was born in South Carolina and died August 25th 1876 in her 80th year. She was married to Mr. James Leak in 1817. In 1839 her husband died leaving her the mother of seven children. In 1840 she was married to Mr. W. S. Herronton, who still lives. Some of her children are living. A devoted daughter and son, who live in Atlanta.... J. E. Evans

Mrs. Mary C. Rawlins, daughter of Isaac and Nancy Rawlins, was born in Telfair county, Ga., in 1856; and died October 25th 1876.

Issue of December 5, 1876

Died

Little Mamie, daughter of Mr. T. W. and Mrs. Sarah Kirkpatrick, died, October 3, 1876, in Madison county, Fla., aged 9 years.

Little Bennie, son of Mr. B. F. and Mrs. Louiza Ellison of Madison county, Fla., died November 19, 1876, aged 5 years and 9 months.

Pattie, only child of Samuel and Amanda Narger, died at Homerville, Ga., November 22, 1876, aged 1 year and 1 months.

George Pierce, youngest child of J. T. and Ann E. Hill, died in Union, S. C., November 20, 1876, aged 5 years and 11 months.

Obituary

Sister Jemima Colding, daughter of Micajah Calhoun, was born March 18th 1798 in Barnwell county, S. C., and died at the residence of her youngest daughter, Mrs. Taylor, in Marion co., Fla., Nov. 5th 1876. She was baptized in childhood by Lorenzo Dow.

Mrs. Sarah E. Mell was born in Bryan county, Ga., November 12, 1799; died in Atlanta, September 13, 1876.

Died, in Monticello, Florida, on Sunday 29th October 1876, in the 80th year of his age, Brother Edward Footman. He was born 9th May 1797 in Philadelphia, Pa., but was reared and educated in Georgia, his widowed mother having removed to that state when he was but two years old. In 1825 he was married to Miss Eliza Ann Ward in Bryan county, Ga., who died in 1830, leaving three children. In 1832, he married Miss Mary Bryan Adams, of Savannah, Ga., who became the mother of seven sons, sic of whom grew to man's estate. She and six of his ten children survive him. He had had twenty-four grandchildren and one great-grandchild. In 1835 he removed to Florida, and soon transferred his membership from the Presbyterian Church to the M. E. Church. E. L. T. Blake

Mrs. M. C. Norman, daughter of Rev. Burgess and Mrs. H. W. Smith, was born April 7th 1838; died in Wilkes county, Ga., September 4th 1876. J. F. Mixon

Miss Emma F. Berry was born April 24, 1857; died September 23, 1876. John W. McRoy

Mrs. Emma J. Tarpley, daughter of Rev. Amos and Mrs. Mary E. Davis, was born in Brooks county, Ga., February 26th 1859; died in Thomasville, Ga., November 10th 1876. She married Edward Tarpley, of Dublin, Ga., a few months before her death. J. O. A. Cook

Mrs. Harriet E. Harper was born in Crawford county, Ga., November 28, 1829; moved to Putnam county, Fla., in 1870; died October 28, 1876.

Mrs. Agnes Jane Munnerlyn, consort of James K. Munnerlyn, died in Savannah, Ga., 1st of September 1876, aged 48 years and 2 months.

Issue of December 12, 1876

Died

At Magnolia, Pulaski county, Ga., on November 21, 1876, Samuel Hammond Washington, eldest son of Mrs. Mary A. and the late Col. James H. R. Washington, of Macon, Ga.

At Macon, Ga., on October 30, 1876, May Beall Washington, wife of R. Porter Washington and daughter of Dr. W. A. Gibson and daughter-in-law of Mrs. Mary A. Washington.

Obituary

Dr. P. B. D. H. Culler was born in South Carolina, December 17, 1815; died in Perry, Ga., November 7, 1876. He was married to Miss Mary Cobb, only daughter of Hon. Howell Cobb. She died nearly five years since, leaving the doctor and three daughters. He remained at the old home with his daughter, Mrs. G. White. S. Anthony

Samuel Carson Robinson was born in Anderson county, S., c., January 18, 1836; was killed on the top of an ongoing freight train on the Western and Atlantic Railroad, by coming in contact with the bridge at Oglethorpe Park-- aged 41 years. His father moved to Georgia while he was yet a child. He leaves a wife, aged parents. W. C. Dunlap

Anna Pope Glass, wife of Erastus Glass deceased, and daughter of Stephen and Mary Weston, was born in Stewart county, Ga., August 14, 1844; died at Sharpsburg, Coweta county, Ga., September 3, 1876. She was left an orphan when but eighteen months old. It was her mother's expressed wish that Harriet Williams, her niece, should rear the child. She was therefore received into the family of Dr. C. T. Williams as one of his own children. In 1871 she married E. Glass, who died in a short time afterwards.

Brother David W. Lowe died in his fifty-ninth year. The conference of Warrenton circuit passed resolutions....

John Pierce Sewell was born in Franklin county, Ga., December 20, 1810; and died in Meriwether county, November 21, 1876. He was married January 26, 1827, to Miss L. E. Wideman. They have brought up a large and respectable family. W. J. Cotter

Miss Mary Spain died at Valley Falls, Spartanburg county, S. C., November 8, 1876. She was a member of the Baptist Church at Antioch in North Carolina, near King's Mountain. She came to South Carolina about seven years ago. She leaves a little girl about two years old, one sister in North Carolina. W. J. Wooton

Mrs. Mary A. Gilstrap died in Morris county, Texas, November 12, 1876, age 27 years, 8 months and 22 days. She was born and reared in Jasper county, Ga.; in 1868 she was married to John B. Gilstrap. In the fall of 1874 her husband removed to Titus county, Texas.

Sister Penelope Williams died August 30, 1876 in Laurens county, Ga., at an advanced age.

Irene Nettie Colier, daughter of John and Mary Francis Colier, was born in Dooly county, Ga., August 12, 1865; died in the same county November 2, 1876. J. W. Domingos

SOUTHERN CHRISTIAN ADVOCATE NOTICES 1867-1878

Issue of December 16-26, 1876

Died

William Walter, infant son of W. A. and Missouri Ecord, died at Homerville, Ga., October 30, 1876, aged 7 months and 8 days.

Obituary

Clark T. Williams, M. D., was born in Clark county, Ga., in 1804; and died in Meriwether, Ga., October 29, 1876. He left a widow and one child, a son. L. Bush

Silas Foster Haywood of Atlanta, Ga., 41 years of age 13th of October last, died in Kansas City, Mo., November 19th 1876. Bro. Haywood professed religion two years ago in Nashville, Tenn., and connected himself with Elm Street Methodist Church. Being an engineer and a master machinist, he was often away from his family and home for months at a time. W. C. Dunlap. Nashville Advocate please copy.

Mrs. Sarah Griffin was born near Snow Hill, N. C., April 12, 1898 [sic]; was the daughter of Wm. and Mary Murphy; was first married to Rev. Theophilus Hardle, and subsequently to Rev. James Griffin, who died about twenty-five years ago, leaving her again a widow. She died October 27, 1876, at the home of her son-in-law, Mr. C. C. Brooks, in Stewart county, Ga. She had been a member of the Baptist Church for fifty years. Christian Index please copy.

Benjamin Crum Porter, Mizpah Church, Springfield circuit, South Georgia Conference, was born August 13, 1803; died October 28, 1876.

Brother Levie E. Young died on Calcosahatchie river, in Monroe county, Fla., November 4, 1876. he was born June 1, 1841 in South Carolina, came to Florida in 1867, spent a few years around Bartow, in Polke county, Ga. October 20, 1869, he married Miss Sallie Crawford, who is now left with three little children. Robert Martin

Mrs. Elizabeth M. Bobo was born in Spartanburg district, S. C., June 4th 1813; was married in Gwinnett county, Ga., to Mr. John Bobo, December 3d, 1835; died in Douglas county, Ga., November 1st 1876. S. Leake

Sister Uriah Williams, daughter of William R. and Nancy Cullen, was born in Florence, Ga., March 25, 1835; was married to Uriah Williams, November 16, 1852; died in Webster county, Ga., October 23, 1876. She leaves a husband and several children. A. J. Dean

Mrs. E. C. Culpepper, wife of George G. Culpepper, was born November 29, 1856; was married December 16, 1875; died in Meriwether county, Ga., November 26, 1876. W. J. Cotter

Tribute of Respect passed by St. Luke charge, Columbus, Ga., to Dr. John A. Urquhart.

Tribute of Respect from Norcross Circuit, North Georgia Conference at Mt. Calvary, to Thomas H. Mitchell, who died September 19, 1876.

Issue of January 2, 1877

Died

Of diphtheria, in Cheraw, S. C., December 13, 1876, little Willie, son of Mr. and Mrs. S. H. Reid, in the fourth year of his age.

Obituary

Benier Pye was born in Oglethorpe county, Ga., May 2, 1807. He removed to Forsyth in 1826, where he lived until his death, November 25, 1876. Geo. E. Gardner

Rev. Dr. B. E. Watkins was born in Whitley county, Ky., August 18, 1800; died in Colquitt county, Ga., November 26, 1876. After preaching six or seven years in Kentucky he moved to Alabama, where he organized several churches. In 1863 he removed to Colquitt county, Ga., where he remained until his death. C. D. Adams

Sister Rachel Bussey, wife of W. D. Bussey, died in Dodge county, Ga., October 7, 1876. J. E. Rorie

Sister Martha Eliza Carter, daughter of Joseph and Ann B. Ashmore, was born in Liberty county, Ga., April 16, 1812. She was married October 12, 1834, and became the mother of nine children, only three of whom now survive. John M. Marshall

William Perkins was born in Camden county, N. C., September 27, 1818; removed to Florida in early manhood; died at his residence near Miccosukie, Leon county, October 31, 1876. He was twice married. His second wife and one son of his first marriage survive him. E. L. T. Blake

J. H. Durant Saunders died at his home near Monticello, Fla., October 11, 1876, in the 32d year of his age. D. H. Bryan

Miss Mary E. Moore, daughter of Dr. J. R. and Mary Moore, of Lawrenceville, Ga., was born in Walton county, Ga., April 24, 1846; died in Lawrenceville, Ga., November 21, 1876.

Mrs. Matilda Sikes, whose maiden name was Vinson, died at her residence in Russel county, Ala., near Watoola church, November 13, 1876. She was born in 1809 in Muscogee county, Ga.; was married to Mr. Alfred Sikes in the year 1830, who preceded her the first of this year. W. B. Neal

Tribute of Respect from Trinity and Wesley Churches held at Savannah, to Dr. E. H. Myers.

Issue of January 9, 1877

Peter Z. Ward was born in Jackson county, Ga., November 20, 1798; died in Clayton county, Ga., November 7, 1876. In 1829 he married. Rembert Smith

My mother, Mrs. Susan M. Ware, was born in Virginia, November 19, 1791, and died in Lincoln county, Ga., December 7, 1876, in her 86th year. She was the daughter of William and Susan W. Dowling. When a child they moved to Georgia. A descendant of a Huguenot family, her great grandfather, viz., Poindexter, leaving when many others of that race fled from France on account of persecution, settled in Virginia. She was twice a widow, and orphans to care for and rear each time. Married first my father, Col. N. Bussey. The second time she married Rev. Robert Ware, a local preacher. W. D. Bussey

Uncle Wiley Roberson was born in Chesterfield District, South Carolina, February 26, 1810, removed to Georgia in 1830, was married in 1832. J. R. Mayson

Samuel Vernon Laney, son of Rev. S. D. and Mrs. Mary A. Laney, died in Russell county, Ala., December 5, 1876, aged 23 years and 6 months. Cousin Berta

Alfred H. Windsor died in Bibb county, Ga., December 15, 1876, in the 70th year of his age. He was born in Rockingham county, N. C., and moved to Georgia in 1835. W. C. Bass

Mrs. E. C. Campbell was born December 39 [sic], 1795; and died at Sumter, S. C., November 26, 1876. This woman was the mother of Rev. J. B. Campbell, of the South Carolina Conference. A. A. Gilbert

Emma E. Hudson died near Americus, Ga., November 27, 1876. She was the daughter of ____ Aycock, formerly of Floyd county, Ga., born June 2, 1851, and was next to the youngest of ten children. In 1863 her father removed to Sumter county, Ga., and in 1872 Emma was happily married to J. I. Hudson. She left two little children.

Brother James P. Newton was born September 17, 1806, and died November 28, 1876 in Horry county, S.C.   W. Carson

Issue of January 16, 1877

Died

In Macon, Ga., December 26, 1876, Edward Ferguson, infant son of Charles and Jane E. Pritchard, aged 6 months and 7 days.

In Macon, Ga., January 5, 1877, at the residence of her brother, Charles Pritchard, Mrs. Florida Bailey, late of Augusta, Ga.

Obituary

Mrs. Henrietta J. Wilkerson was born June 21, 1802; died in Wilkes county, Ga., November 26, 1876. One of her children, a daughter the wife of Rev. H. J. Adams of the North Georgia Conference.   J. F. Mixon

William Travis Timmerman was born in Edgefield District, S. C., August 30, 1816; died in Richmond county, Ga., November 27, 1876. In early manhood he left the old homestead for Augusta, Ga., where he at once embarked in mercantile business.

Mrs. Mary Gates, relict of Christian Gates, died in Orangeburg county, S. C., October 16, 1876, aged about 93 years. She was a member of St. Matthews' Evangelical Lutheran Church. She was the mother of 9 children, 40 grandchildren, 78 great grandchildren, and 13 great great grandchildren are still living.

Abner C. Dozier of Jasper county, Ga., died November 2, 1876. He leaves a widow and children.

Henry Mood, youngest son of Rev. Wright Wilson and brother of Rev. John B. Wilson of the S. C. Conference, died near Clio, Marlboro county, S. C., December 16, 1876, in his 22d year. He was married to Christiana Jernigan of Richmond county, N. C., October 12, 1873. Buried beside his brother, the late Rev. J. F. Wilson of the S. C. Conference.

Our mother, Mrs. Martha H. Baughan, wife of P. W. Baughan, and daughter of William and Elizabeth Walker, was born in Colleton county, S. C., April 23, 1827; was married in 1848; died in Savannah, Ga., October 9, 1876. She leaves a husband and several sons and daughters. Her only Daughters, Bettie and Mattie.

Mrs. Harriet C. Wagnon was born in Greene county, Ga., June 23, 1799; was married to Thomas P. Wagnon by the Rev. Dr. L. Pierce in 1818; died October 31, 1876. My father died in 1845, leaving her a widow with twelve children-- seven sons and five daughters. Three of the sons have since died. Mrs. Lumpkin, her daughter, and I left Auburns, Ala.... J. F. W.

Mary A. Gilham was born November 1, 1837 in Oglethorpe county, Ga., and died November 30, 1876. Her Brother.

Tribute of Respect from Brunswick Station, South Georgia Conference to J. J. Morgan, who died 15th October 1876, aged nearly 75 years.

Issue of January 23, 1877

Died

James Oscar, son of Mr. and Mrs. R. T. Moore, died at Ridgeville, S. C., January 4, 1877, aged four years.

In Crawford, Oglethorpe county, Ga., December 3, 1876, Lizzie Maria, second daughter of Charles S. and Almarine Hargrove, aged seven years.

Obituary

Miss Georgia Landershine, daughter of Mr. Chas. P. Landershine, of Savannah, Ga., died at the Isle of Hope, eight miles from the city, November 2, 1876, aged 24 years.

Laborn Price was born in Marion District, S. C., May 16, 1827, and died in Putnam county, Fla., December 24, 1876. Brother Price moved to Florida in 1859. He was the father of nine children. Robt. D. Gentry

Maj. Robert Allen died November 30, 1876, at his home in Pike county, Ga., aged 84 years and 7 months. Maj. Allen was born in Green county, Ga., 30th of April 1792. He removed to Pike county in the year 1822, being one of the first settlers of the county-- he located on the lot of land he drew from the State shortly before, on which he lived until his death.

Archibald Smith was born April 23, 1798; died near Jonesboro, Ga., October 21, 1876. Brother Smith lived to be nearly 79 years old, having with him at the time of his death all of his children and his wife.

Sister Delilah Ann Reaves, wife of the Rev. Rollins L. Reaves, was born 1816; married January 2, 1834; departed this life December 17, 1876. O. W. Ransom

Edward Sheftall, son of the late Emanuel Sheftall, died in Savannah, Ga., October 10, 1876.

Mrs. C. C. Gressom, whose maiden name was Willis, next Elder and then Gressom, died November 25, 1876. She leaves a husband and nine children. I. G. Parks

Issue of January 30, 1877

Died

At Lynchburg, S. C., December 18, 1876, little Frank, son of W. J. and A. M. McLeod, aged 6 months and twenty-five days.

In Macon, Ga., January 1, 1877, Mrs. Charlotte Rebecca Gibson, daughter of John and Eliza Hightower, of Lumpkin, Ga., and wife of A. W. Gibson of Macon, Ga., aged 24 years.

Obituary

Meredith Kitchens was born September 30, 1777, and died November 24, 1876, in Rome, Ga. The old man was illiterate, never having had the advantages of even a rudimentary education. W. P. Rivers

David L. Byrd was born in Wilkes county, Ga., March 22, 1822; died in Warren county, November 2, 1876. He leaves a wife and several children.

Mrs. M. W. Williams was born in Onslow county, N. C., April 26, 1791; and died in Greene county, Ga., January 1, 1877. Atticus G. Haygood

Mrs. Harriet E. Wooten, youngest daughter of Rev. Ira L. Potter, was born in Pickens District, S. C., June 2, 1835; and died in Bainbridge, Ga., January 7, 1877. W. Knox

Mrs. Sheldonia B. Salley, wife of Nathaniel Salley, Esq., of Orangeburg county, S. C., died October 30th 1876, aged 53 years. She left a husband and children.

Mrs. Ella F. Ward, daughter of Dr. A. M. Dantzler, was born April 2, 1856; married Calvin J. Ward, March 17, 1874; died in Bartow county, Ga., November 16, 1876. J. J. Singleton

Elizabeth Tankersly, wife of Rev. James Rembert Smith, M. D., and daughter of Bennett Crawford, was born in Richmond county, Ga., February 16, 1817; was married to Dr. J. Rembert Smith, in Louisiana, January 10, 1838; died January 3, 1877, in Sandersville, Ga. My aunt was one of the most amiable, unselfish women... Geo. G. Smith, Jr.

Issue of February 6, 1877

Died

Oscar B. Rivers, son of Wm. H. and Julia A. Rivers, died in Boston, Thomas county, Ga., January 20, 1877, aged 3 years, 10 months, and 14 days.

Obituary

Mr. Ferdinand Bowdre Phinizy, died in Augusta, Ga., January 15, 1877. He was born in Augusta, January 8, 1850, the eldest child of Mr. Ferdinand Phinizy, now of Clark county, Ga., His mother, the daughter of Mr. Hayes Bowdre deceased, was taken away from the family consisting of husband and eight little children, when the subject of this memoir was only 14 years old. On 31st of January 1871, he married Miss Mamie Lou, daughter of Col. B. C. Yancey of Athens, Ga. Clement A. Evans

Susan Brazil, died January 3, 1877, at the residence of Rev. P. L. Mize, Americus, Ga. She was the daughter of Wm. and Nancy Brazil, and was in her 18th year.

Mrs. Mary Hartzog, wife of Daniel Hartzog, sr., was born May 23, 1794; and died January 9, 1877. She was born in Barnwell District. She lived and died near Salem Church. She leaves an aged husband and a numerous family connection. A. J. Cauthen.

Mrs. Frances Ellen Dingle was born in Sumter, S. C., April 9, 1809; was married to J. Harvey Dingle, July 26, 1825; died December 11, 1876. R. N. Wells

Peter Shand Smith, younger brother of Dr. Whitefoord Smith, was born in Charleston, S. C., March 5, 1819; died in Spartanburg, S. C., November 27, 1876.

Tribute of Respect to the memory of Professor Albert N. Whitney from Wesleyan Female College, who died on the 23d instant.

Tribute of Respect from the Quarterly Conference of Greenville and Trinity charge to Thos. F. McGehee.

Issue of February 13, 1877

Died

William Marvin Kirton, son of W. H. and O. V. Kirton, was born in Columbus county, N. C., July 8, 1872, and died in Lancaster county, S. C., January 20, 1877.

Obituary

Sophia H. Stipe, daughter of Davis and Fetnal Whitman and beloved wife of Henry Stipe, was born in Greenville, S. C. April 23, 1825; died in Campbell county, Ga., December 27, 1876. She leaves a husband and five children. Camilla P. Stipe

Mrs. Ann E. Moody, widow of the late Captain Moody and sister of Rev. John M. Marshall, of the South Georgia Conference, died in Savannah, Ga., at the home of her son-in-law, N. C. Miller, December 18, 1876, aged 63 years.

Elizabeth Tankersly, wife of the Rev. James Rembert Smith, M. D., and daughter of Bennett Crafton, was born in Richmond county, Ga., February 16, 1817; was married to Dr. J. Rembert

Smith in Louisville, January 10, 1838; died January 3, 1877 in Sandersville, Ga. [republished in consequence of several grave errors in the former copy] George G. Smith, Jr.

Mrs. Rowena E. Sessions, wife of Rev. J. J. Sessions, of Terrell county, Ga., was born in South Carolina, September 7, 1829; died January 22, 1877. J. M. Potter

Mrs. Abigail Stanley was born in Chatham county, N. C., October 20, 1807; and died at the residence of her son in law, Robert J. Hort, in Claiborne Parish, La., January 17, 1877. December 29, 1833, she was married to Felix Stanley.. a few years ago, when he was called to his reward. J. A. Parker

Mrs. Feraby Ward was born July 23, 1802; died December 19, 1876. She joined the Methodist Church at old Pine Grove in Edgefield county over forty years ago, and at her death was a member of Spann's Church. She leaves six children, one having died before her, and has many grandchildren and great-grandchildren. Geo. F. Round

Mrs. R. Caroline Sherman, relict of the late Bradford Sherman, of Georgetown, S. C., died on the 29th of December 1876. She was a native of Wilmington, N. C., and her maiden name was Tilley. L. Wood

Mrs. Fanny A. Buckalew, daughter of James and Mary Norris, was born in 1852; died January 10, 1877. She leaves a husband and two little children, and her aged father. S. S. Pennington

Tribute of Respect from Winterville Circuit to Charles G. Hargrove, who died January 22, 1877, in the seventy-second year of his age.

Mrs. Louisa E. Sims was born in Morgan county, Ga., May 9, 1814; removed to Meriwether county when quite young, where she was married to Thomas Sims; removed to Clayton county, April 1857. She died 25th January 1877. John Oslin

Issue of February 20, 1877

Dr. William Brown, son of William and Susan Brown, was born in Newberry, S. C., June 18, 1817. His father removed thence to Newton county, Ga., in 1827. About five years since, he removed to Orange county, Fla. He died November 23, 1876. O. L. Smith

Mrs. Mary E. Wright, daughter of B. B. and Mary Fagan, was born March 9, 1849. Her father moved to Atlanta several years since. she went with the entire family connected themselves with Payne's Chapel. About one year since she married Mr. J. A. Wright and removed to DeKalb county, where she died January 30, 1877. J. C. Hendrix

John T. Partridge, son of George M. and Mary E. Partridge, was born in Alabama 1856; died in Troup county, Ga., January 27, 1876. F. M. T. Brannan

Mrs. M. C. Dawson, daughter of Joseph Ketchins, was born May 12, 1839; moved with her father to Randolph county in 1854; married Mr. Wm. Dawson, January 31, 1856; died in Clay county, Ga., January 30, 1877. S. R. Weaver

Ann D. Bennett, daughter of Wm. and Martha Appling, was born in Clark county, Ga., September 30, 1825; moved with her parents to Chickasaw county, Miss., in 1843; she married Stephen D. Bennett, December 1847 and settled in Ottibehaw county, Miss; they moved to Fresno county, Cal., in 1867, where she died December 7, 1876. She was the mother of five children, four of whom are still living, two sons and two daughters. T. L. Duke

Mrs. Susan M. Gregory, daughter of Robert and Mary McAfee, was born February 27, 1804 in Rutherford county, N. C.; married Jackson McAfee of Lunenburg county, Va., September 19, 1822; died January 4, 1877, near Cave Springs in Floyd county, Ga. Mrs. Gregory, with her husband, father and mother, moved to Cobb county, Ga., in 1833. J. R. Owen

Sister Sallie H. Breeden, daughter of Meekin Townsend deceased, was born March 11, 1839; converted when a child at Beauty Spot; was wedded to Rev. Thos. J. Breeden, September 15, 1856; died January 1, 1877. Christian Neighbor please copy.

Mrs. Emily Harris, wife of H. H. Harris of Newton county, Ga., and the daughter of Wm. Hightower, late of Greene county, Ga., was born in Putnam county, Ga., September 23, 1817; died January 9, 1877. Joined the M. E. Church, South at Mt. Zion, Russell county, Ala., in 1839.

Mrs. Irene Hart was born June 30, 1805; died at the residence of her son, Mr. D. E. Hart, in Orangeburg county, S. C., november 12, 1876.

Martha Vaughn, wife of John H. Vaughn, was born in Jones county, GA., 1808; died in Montgomery county, Ga., December 18, 1876. She leaves an aged husband, ten children.

Tribute of Respect to Harvey Wofford from Belmont Circuit, South Carolina Conference.

Issue of February 27, 1877

Died

Little Jennie, daughter of Dr. C. S. and Julia Claridy, died at Suwanee, Ga., December 13, 1876, aged 3 years, 2 months, and 13 days.

Obituary

Charles B. Muckenfuss, the oldest son of Charles H. and Rosa M. Muckenfuss of Charleston, S. C., died in that city January 13, 1877, in the sixteenth year of his age. His body reposes near the window of Bethel Church.

Mrs. Mary B. Collins, whose maiden name was McNeil, was born in Richmond county, Ga., June 16, 1794; died in Madison county, Fla., Nov. 25, 1876. She was married to Mr. Joshua Collins in Washington county, Ga., in 1810; and was left a widow with eight children in 1840. A few years after the death of her husband she moved to Florida, where she resided up to her death. She joined the Baptist Church in girlhood. E. S. Tyner. Christian Index, please copy.

Mrs. Mary R. Peeples was born in Louville, Tenn., March 28, 1845; died in Spring Place, Ga., January 27, 1877. She was married November 19, 1868 to L. F. Peeples. A. J. Hughes. Nashville Advocate, please copy.

Charles G. Hargrove was born in Oglethorpe county, Ga., June 16, 1805; died at the place of his birth, January 22, 1877. T. A. Harris

Miss Regina Rambo, daughter of Drury and Regina Rambo, died at Bluffton, Clay county, Ga., January 15, 1877, aged twenty-three years. P. S. Twitty

William B. Word was born in Laurens District, S. C., December 15, 1809; moved to Georgia and settled in Newnan in 1833; was married to Elisabeth Brown of Newton county, December 15, 1836; and died December 18, 1876. J.H. Baxter

Col. Isaac Wilkerson was born in North Carolina, February 14, 1801; died in Athens, Ga., the place of his residence for thirty years, January 10, 1877. He was reared among the Society of Friends.

William C. Martin was born August 7, 1822; died January 1, 1877. He leaves a wife and two little girls. John Attaway

Allen Lovelace died Chambers county, Ala., February 9, 1877, in the ninety-sixth year of his age. New Orleans Advocate, please copy.

Dr. J. L. B. Gilmore died in Charleston county, S. C., February 7, 1877, aged sixty years, one month, and eighteen days. He has left a wife and three children, besides two little adopted ones. Wm. Hutto

Issue of March 6, 1877

Died

Maggie Jackson Odom, daughter of Rev. Alexander and Mrs. Elizabeth M. Odom, was born in Cass county, Ga., December 24, 1868; baptized by Rev. H. J. Adams of the North Georgia Conference; and died in Wheatland, California, January 1, 1877.

Obituary

Mrs. Fannie Malone Burton was born in Richmond county, Ga., January 18, 1855; and died at Bartow, Ga., February 1, 1877. At the age of nine years she was deprived of a beloved father, and at the close of the war she was left a penniless orphan. She was married February 27, 1873, to Robt. H. Burton, of Burke county, Ga. Her Mother. Christian Index please copy.

William H. Kimbrough was born October 15, 1795; died January 7, 1877 in Atlanta, Ga. Brother Kimbrough was the last, but one, of a bright galaxy of Christians, who lived in Columbus, his former home. H. B. Ousley

Dr. J. P. Mathews was born January 8, 1818, in Wilkes county, Ga; subsequently moved to Meriwether county. In 1849 he moved to Columbia county, Ark., in which he lived until his death, December 20, 1876. He was twice married; first in Meriwether county, Ga., to Miss Mary Keith; then in Columbia, Ark., to Miss Julia F. Goode. E. N. Watson

Mrs. Mary E. Gates, wife of Mr. F. I. Gates, died February 1, 1877, in Orangeburg county, S. C., aged 28 years, 2 months and 1 day.

Brother Lewis M. Houser was born in Orangeburg District, S. C., June 24, 1823; moved to Houston county, Ga., in 1849; died near Perry, Ga., February 10, 1877. A. J. Dean

Isaiah B. Avant died in Washington county, Ga., December 30, 1876, in the 85th year of his age, leaving an aged widow, children, grand-children, and great-grand-children. He was a soldier in the war of 1812. T. L. Nease

William A. Forehand was born in Edgecombe county, N. C., October 9, 1806, came with his father to Georgia when about nine years old, removed with the family to Dooly county, Ga., in 1828-- was married January 5, 1831 to Rebecca Varnadow, and resided in the same community till he died 20th January 1877.

Issue of March 13, 1877

Died

Little Oscar Gray, son of Ab. G. and Helen O. Harris, died in Jonesboro, Ga., February 27, 1877, aged 1 year, 9 months and 7 days.

Obituary

Mrs. Victoria C. Head, wife of George W. Head and daughter of Isaac and Martha Winship, died in Macon, Ga., February 8, 1877, in the 27th year of her age. W. C. Bass

Col. Wm. W. Holland, son-in-law of Gen. G. P. Harrison, died in Savannah, Ga., January 27, 1877, aged 37 years. He was born and reared in Jasper county, where his mother and family still live. Ten years ago he married in Savannah.

Mrs. Ann E. Watts, daughter of Thomas and Barber Edwards, was born in Orangeburg, S. C., August 28, 1805; removed with her parents to Henry county, Ala., 1828, where she married Ebenezer Watts, March 38, 1830; died in Jackson county, Fla., January 19, 1877. John P. Sanders

Mrs. Mary McLain was born in North Carolina in 1790; died at the residence of her daughter, Mrs. Mary L. Bond, in Murray county, Ga., December 18, 1876. William M. Crumley of the North Georgia Conference married her daughter. A. S. Vining

Eldred J. Wills was born in Edgefield county, S. C., February 16, 1824; died December 3, 1876. M. H. Pooser

C. T. Latimer was born August 31, 1818; married Miss Beulah Young, who preceded him to the better world little over a year ago. He died December 15, 1876, and was buried in the Smyrna grave yard. W. H. Lawton

Jane Gilman Purse, daughter of Dr. J. Rembert Smith, and wife of Stephen A. Purse, was born in Sandersville, Ga., October 31, 1846; married October 4, 1869; died In Savannah, Ga., February 5, 1877. A few weeks ago it was my sad office to write an obituary notice of her mother. George G. Smith

R. W. Fogler, son of J. N. and C. R. Fogler, was born January 8, 1853; died October 31, 1876.

Materson Palmer was born in Anderson county, S. C., and died in the same county, February 15, 1877.

Issue of March 20, 1877

Died

George Pierce Embry, son of Rev. G. T. and Mrs. S. E. Embry, of the South Georgia Conference, died February 25, 1877, aged four years, eight months, and fourteen days.

Obituary

Mrs. Mary Boyd Walker, wife of Charles B. Walker, Esq., of Owensboro, Ky., and daughter of Dr. J. J. and Mrs. M. C. Boyd, was born in Spartanburg, S. C., March 25, 1857; died in Owensboro, Ky., February 3, 1877, leaving an infant son six days old. She joined the Baptist Church on March 23, 1870. She married Chas. S. Walker, January 19, 1876. Joseph B. Cottrell

Wade P. Hodges, son of Nathaniel and Martha Hodges, was born in Bullock county, Ga., December 5, 1822; was married to Miss Jennie Denmark, who survives him, April 1, 1858; died February 8, 1877. He leaves a wife and children. Samuel W. Stubbs

Mrs. Catharine Fralick, who had been a widow for several years, died January 25, 1877, in the 77th year of her age. The preachers of the old Cypress and present St. Matthews circuit will remember her hospitality.

Mrs. Phoebe H. Anderson, whose maiden name was Clarke, was born near Richmond, Va., and died in Troup county, Ga., January 13, 1877. When about sixteen or seventeen years of age her father moved to Greene county, Ga., where she married in May 1830 to Mr. Elijah Anderson. H. J. Ellis

Mr. Lemuel Burket, aged 31 years, died in Twiggs county, Ga., January 10, 1877. He leaves a wife and three small children. C. J. Toole

Mrs. Ann B. McRae was born in Wilkes county, Ga., March 31, 1832; married J. L. Sheats, May 19, 1850; and the Rev. J. H. D. McRae, April 2, 1850; died February 21, 1877 in Brooks county, Ga. Thomas Boring

Annie A. Weaver, youngest daughter of Rev. S. R. and Mrs. Rebecca Weaver, died in Clay county, near Fort Gaines, Ga., March 1, 1877, in the 15th year of her age. Jno. W. Dozier

Mrs. Nancy Bellah was born in Oglethorpe county, Ga., March 17, 1794, where she married John Bellah, Esq. In 1839 Mr. Bellah moved to Meriwether county, and thence in 1845 to Coweta county, where he died in 1871. "Aunt Nancy" resided with her daughter, Mrs. Rawls, until she died February 15, 1877. J. T. Curtis

Zachariah Franklin Turnipseed was born March 14, 1836; died in Coweta county, Ga., February 18, 1877. He leaves a wife and five children.

Issue of March 27, 1877

Mrs. Martha Heard, whose maiden name was Coffin, widow of George Heard and mother of Rev. Peter A. Heard, and Dr. Henry Heard, died in LaGrange, Ga., February 26, 1877. She was the oldest member of the Church in LaGrange. Old Thomas Stocks, her brother-in-law, had gone but a little while before. G. G. Smith

Susie, daughter of Rev. R. M. and Mrs. A. W. Ellzey of the Florida Conference, died December 14, 1876, having just entered her sixteenth year. Her Father and Mother.

Mrs. H. B. Goudelock was born October 2, 1815; was married to Dr. Hamlet Goudelock in 1835; died in Union county, S. C., February 18, 1877. She has left several children. J. B. Wilson

Mrs. A. C. Huckaby, widow of W. J. Huckaby and daughter of G. B. and Mary Hill, was born December 19, 1826; died in Spaulding county, Ga., February 7, 1877. In 1857 her husband died and left her with six small children. T. S. L. Harwell

Mrs. Edith Wyatt, wife of Rev. L. D. Wyatt, was born in East Tennessee, November 3, 1816; died in Gordon county, Ga., December 31, 1876. John Oates

My mother, Mrs. Jane M. Miller, died at the residence of her daughter in Williamsburgh county, S. C., February 15, 1877, in the 76th year of her age. She was for many years a member of the Presbyterian Church, holding her membership in the Williamsburgh Church near Kingstree, S. C. Being remote from this Church, she joined the Methodist Church, holding her membership at Union Church in the Johnsonville Circuit, South Carolina Conference. Her departed husband and six children had long gone before her. She leaves a son and daughter. J. B. Miller

Edward T. Wynn, son of R. J. Wynn, of Putnam county, Ga., February 22, 1877, in the twenty-first year of his age.

Mary C. Wright, daughter of Daniel J. and Mary C. Wright, was born March 8, 1858; died February 14, 1877. E. M. T. Brannon

Memorial Resolution by St. Johns Church, Augusta, Georgia, to William J. Blair.

Tribute of Respect from Leon Circuit, Florida Conference, to William Perkins, who died since 31st October 1876.

Issue of April 3, 1877

Died

March 17, 1877, Anna Louise, infant daughter of Dr. G. J. and Mrs. Anna Griffith.

Obituary

Ezekiel Royal was born in Burke county, Ga., January 13, 1807; died in Brooks county, February 17, 1877. In 1831 he was married to Mary A. Murray of Houston County. Sometime after his marriage he settled in Fort Valley. W. M. Hayes

Susan Elizabeth Taylor, wife of Ezekiel Taylor, was born in Sumter county, Ga., December 8, 1839; died in Americus, Ga., March 1, 1877. She was married in 1859.

Thos. Redding died in Monroe county, Ga., January 14, 1877, in his eighty-fourth year. He was born in Greene county, Ga., and married Mariah Searcy, who preceded him to the grave October 13, 1858. J. T. Lowe

Mrs. Sallie V. Land, wife of Mr. Jno. T. Land and daughter of Mr. Geo. W. and Mary Faulk, died in Twiggs county, Ga., March 6, 1877, in the 21st year of her age. W. O'Daniel

Mr. Swinton C. Warnock of Charleston county, S. C., brother of the late Rev. Joseph Warnock, of the South Carolina Conference, died January 17, 1877. He leaves a wife and stepdaughter.

John F. Collins died February 20, 1877. He was born in Marion District, S. C., January 16, 1819; removed to Florida about thirty years ago, settling seven miles southwest of Ocala. A. A. P. Neel

Sister Sarah Townsley was born in Jefferson county, Ga., February 14, 1806; died in Perry, Houston county, Ga., March 4, 1877. She was married in her 16th year. She leaves two children and several motherless grand-children. A. J. Dean

Ernest Richmond Colbert, second son of John G. and Rebecca S. Colbert, died at Stilesboro, Bartow county, Ga., March 7, 1877, in the sixteenth year of his age.

William R. Calvert was born in Liberty, Va., May 31, 1849; died in Macon, Ga., January 17, 1877. F. C. Watts

Issue of April 10, 1877

Died

In Bennettsville, S. C., March 17, 1877, Ellen Violetta, child of Dr. H. J. and Mrs. Sarah Mouzon, aged 2 years, 11 months.

On the 28th of February, George Wesley, son of Rev. B. S. and Mrs. E. C. Key, aged 3 years and 23 days.

Obituary

Thomas Jefferson Riley, son of Miles and Elizabeth Riley, died in Brighton, Beaufort county, S. C., March 30, 1877, aged fifty-one years, six months, and one day. A steward of Black Swamp Church. LeG. G. Walker

Mrs. Emeline S. Williams, whose maiden name was Campbell, wife of C. W. Williams, was born in Madison, Morgan county, Ga., January 27, 1820; died February 10, 1877, in Meriwether county, Ga. The mother of six daughters, she lived to see all of them (except Fannie, who in early life was gathered home) married... Her daughter, Mrs. Jordan, in Mississippi. James B. Hunnicutt

Mrs. Emma S. Connelly was born May 3, 1850; died at her father's near East Point, Ga., February 16, 1877.

Mrs. Sarah E. Barrett, whose maiden name was Inabnit, died in Orangeburg county, S., C., January 27, 1877, in the sixtieth year of her age. M. L. Banks

Mrs. Mary Stansel, for six years past the widow of Levi Stansel, a local minister of the M. E. Church, South, was born in Anson county, N. C., February 14, 1801; died in Conyers, Ga., February

8, 1877. She died at the house of Mr. Lewis Nash of Conyers, Rockdale county, who was the husband of one of her surviving daughters. Another daughter, Mrs. Mary Henderson, resides at Oxford, Ga., in whose quiet cemetery her remains now repose. A. Means

Greenup Arnold was born in Kentucky, February 1, 1813; died in Atlanta, Ga., February 4, 1877. In early life he settled near the lien between George and Florida, but about four years ago he moved to Orange county, Fla., and located near Orlando. O. W. Ransom

Charles C. Smith, son of Capt. Charles Smith of Cokesburg, S. C., was born July 15, 1849; killed by the falling of his horse, January 18, 1877.

Mrs. Rebecca Stoudemire died in Charleston county, S. C., February 17, 1877, aged about eighty-three years. Wm. Hutto

Mary Catharine Hunter, whose maiden name was Jones, was born in Emanuel county, Ga., May 30, 1855; died near Emanuel Church in Bradford county, Fla., February 18, 1877. J. D. Rogers

Mrs. L. S. Collier was born in Edgefield county, S. C., July 25, 1798; died December 26, 1876. S. P. H. Elwell

Issue of April 17, 1877

Died

In Spartanburg county, S. C., February 24, 1877, Woodfin Waters, son of Landon and Martha S. Waters. Aged 3 years, 2 months, and 3 days.

Obituary

Mrs. Matilda C. Smith, wife of the Rev. C. W. Smith and daughter of the Rev. Drewry and Mrs. Catherine Flowers, was born in Jasper county, Ga., November 3, 1831. She was married to c. W. Smith, son of the Rev. Noah Smith of the Georgia Conference, December 23, 1851. She leaves a husband, three children, two brothers and six sisters. S. E. Cochran

Mrs. Ann E. Mathews, wife of Mr. Frank Mathews of Monroe county, Ga., mother of Mr. J. F. West of Barnesville, Ga., died March 20, 1877, at the residence of her son in Barnesville, Pike county. Ga. She would have been 56 years of age on the 1st of May next. She was married twice and was the mother of nine children, all of them now living.

Mrs. Margaret Harvey was born in Virginia, November 27, 1783; died in Walker county, Ga., January 1877. She reared ten children to maturity. J. B. McFarland

Mrs. Nancy Lumpkin, daughter of George Lumpkin of Virginia, was born December 22, 1786; married to Robert Lumpkin, May 22, 1805; died in Walker county, Ga., February 9, 1877. J. B. McFarland

Sister Elizabeth Folsom, relict of the late William Folsom, died in Brooks county, Ga., March 16, 1877, in her 82nd year. Her husband and several children have preceded her to the better land. H. W. Sharpe

Mrs. Margaret A. Rust was born in Burke county, N. C., August 12, 1806; moved to Franklin county, Ga., in 1836, to Athens, in 1846, to Atlanta in 1865, to Bartow county in 1875; died at the residence of her son-in-law, Johnson Garwood, February 13, 1877. J. J. Singleton

Mrs. Esther S. Cogswell, daughter of Mr. Charles Mouzon, of Charleston, S. C., died February 24, 1877, at the ripe age of 72 years and 19 days. She had been married to Mr. Harvey Cogswell but a few short years, when she was left a widow with two children in 1833. Whiteford Smith

Bro. Burke Camp was born October 7, 1804; died March 21, 1877, at Flowery Branch, Ga. R. H. Rogers

Christian Mickler was born September 15, 1792; died in Lexington county, S. C., March 1, 1877. He was twice married: first to Mary Bouknight, January 12, 1813; and afterward to Caroline E. Bickley, June 13, 1867. He reared a family of 6 children, 28 grandchildren and 24 great-grandchildren. First a Lutheran, he afterwards became a Methodist. J. E. Watson

Mrs. Elizabeth Rodgers was born in Virginia, February 13, 1795; died in Walker county, Ga., February 7, 1877. When about fifteen years of age, she was married to Charles Holloway, who afterwards became a local preacher; she was married a second time, June 23, 1831, to Rev. Danswell Rodgers, who preceded her about ten years. J. B. McFarland

Mrs. Ella Tucker Stubbs, wife of Col. John M. Stubbs, died in Dublin, Ga., March 29, 1877, in the 37th year of her age. W. C. Bass

Mrs. Jane C. Dickinson died near Buford's Bridge, Barnwell county, S. C., January 23, 1877, a few days past her seventieth birthday. She was left a widow thirty-five years ago, with several children. W. L. Pegues

Sister Ellen Freeman, wife of H. P. Freeman, was born January 6 1853; died in Oglethorpe county, Ga., January 6, 1877. A. W. Williams

Wm. Speer was born May 9, 1788. He was or Irish descent; his father was born in Ireland in 1747 in the county of Antrim, near the town of Strabane; his name was Williams. He removed to this county in 1772, and after passing through the revolutionary was as a Whig, married, and settled at Cherokee Ford on Savannah river, where our deceased brother was born. He married Mary S. Gill, December 1, 1811, who still lives. They reared eight children. He was a member of the Presbyterian Church for many years. He died January 10, 1877. W. H. Lawton

David N. Duncan was born in Burke county, N. C., March 14, 1806; died in Union county, Ga., February 11, 1877. He leaves an aged widow and a large family connection. C. L. Pattillo

Mrs. Sarah Beasley died February 23, 1877, at Kinyan Terrell's, near Lawrenceville, Ga., in the 83d year of her age. J. T. Lin

Issue of April 24, 1877

Mrs. E. A. Hunt, whose maiden name was McCroan, was born in Bulloch county, Ga., June 1, 1850; married to Dr. Silas Floyd Hunt, February 1, 1877; died March 18, 1877.

Sister Gussie Badger, wife of Dr. B. M. Badger and daughter of W. J. and Elizabeth Crosswell, was born April 15, 1844; died March 2, 1877. She was the granddaughter of Rev. Jas. Jenkins of precious memory. J. L. Shuford

Brother Allen J. Webb was born September 15, 1800; died at the house of his son, W. A. Webb in Emanuel county, Ga., March 29, 1877. He was the father of nine children, five of whom preceded him to the grave.

Brother C. C. Smith was born August 12, 1840; married Miss Martha A. Stripling of Carroll county, Ga., October 12, 1865; died March 2, 1877. W. F. Quillian

Mrs. Nancy Smith, whose maiden name was Whitlow, was born in Caswell county, N. C., in 1806; moved to Clarke county, Ga., in 1824; married to Joseph Smith, December 1829; died in Walker county, Ga., February 24, 1877. She leaves a husband and eight children.

Mrs. Leonora Van Horn, daughter of Rev. John B. and Idella Elliott, was born in Leon county, Fla., in 1848; married George Van Horn, in 1874; died January 27, 1877, in Albany, Ga. R. L. Honiker

William C. Brown, son of William and Harriet M. R. Brown, was born in Twiggs county, Ga., January 15, 1834; died in Decatur county, Ga., February 4, 1877. He joined the M. E. Church in Macon county, GA., about 1853. He leaves a wife and children. W. Lane

Henry Bugg, son of the late Jackson Bugg (a Confederate soldier), and Mrs. Ella Bugg, all of Columbia County, Ga., died at Milledgeville, January 19, 1877, twenty-five years and a few months old.

Henrietta E. Pou died in Edgefield county, S. C., April 2, 1877, in the thirty-eighth year of her age. Seven of her children had preceded her to heaven. She leaves six children and a husband. J. A. Clifton.

Mrs. Ann M. Cleckley, aged eighty-one years, the last surviving grandchild of the Hon. John A. Treutlen, first Governor of Georgia under the new Constitution, leaves two sons and a daughter, also grand, and great-grandchildren.

Sister Josephine V. Dickenson, consort of brother W. D. Dickinson, died in Alachua county, Fla., March 6, 1877, aged twenty-four years. She leaves a husband and two small children. J. D. Rogers

Issue of May 1, 1877

Died

Rosa Smith, daughter of Rev. J. P. and Mrs. E. F. Smith, died in Sumter county, S. C., March 30, 1877, aged 7 years and 11 months.

Obituary

Mrs. Charlotte Exom Taylor, wife of Charles E. Taylor of Pulaski county, Ga., was born October 29, 1814; died March 1, 1877. F. D. Wimberly, Jr.

Mrs. Epsy Shields, wife of Robert Shields, originally of Warren county, Ga., was born May 14, 1803; died near Madison, Ga., January 5, 1877.

John C. Ragsdale was born March 12, 1813; died in DeKalb county, Ga., March 21, 1877. He left a large family.

T. A. D. Weaver died in Thomaston, Ga., March 26, 1877, in the 75th year of his age. J. B. Payne

Mrs. Virginia B. Harris was born in Gloucester county, Va., April 26, 1787; died at Stone Mountain, Ga., March 31, 1877. Married at the age of fifteen to the husband who died in 1820, she found herself a widow with a large family of children. Her husband, Col. Walton Harris.

Robert Jones, son of W. T. and M. T. Jones, was born November 5, 1861; died April 2, 1877, near Morgan, Calhoun county, Ga. W. D. Stewart

Mrs. Mattie C. Gaulden, wife of Mr. James W. Gaulden, daughter of Mr. and Mrs. Lawrence L. Daniel of Alabama, died in Randolph county, Ga., April 14, 1877. Her marriage to Mr. Gaulden in 1876.

Mrs. Jane Harries, wife of John D. C. Harries and sister of Rev. F. Pasco of the Florida Conference, died in Cambridge, Mass., April 10, 1877. Her Brother.

Mrs. Barcher Rucker, wife of Jacob Rucker, died March 8, 1877, on the Upper Orange Circuit, aged 51 years. She leaves a husband and many children. A. R. Danner

Mr. William J. Reid, died on the Upper Orange Circuit, April 3, 1877, aged 55 years. A. R. Danner

Tribute of Respect to Rev. Henry W. Ledbetter, an aged and esteemed local minister from Glennville Station, Alabama Conference.

Issue of May 8, 1877

Died

In Clinton, Ga., April 28, 1877, William Thomas Carvosso, son of Rev. W. T. and Mrs. A. T. McMichael, aged 4 years.

Obituary

Dr. A. C. C. Thompson was born October 12, 1821, in Dorchester county, Maryland, and died at Gordon, Ga., April 24, 1877. His son Rev. George C. Thompson of the South Georgia Conference. His mother died in his infancy and left him the only child of Dr. Absalom Thompson. Educated at St. John's College, Annapolis, Maryland. He married Miss S. A. Hadaway in his 24th year; moved to Wilmington, Del, came to Burke co., Ga., in 1852. He leaves a wife, two married daughters, a son and seven grandchildren. His remains were buried in Sandersville, Ga., April 25, 1877. J. W. Burke

Mrs. Judith W. Tindall, born in McDonough, Ga., January 19, 1820; died in Macon, Ga., April 4, 1877.

Mrs. Paulina P. Walker, daughter of the late Freeman W. Blount, was born in Meriwether county, Ga., September 11, 1838; was married by Rev. J. K. Leak, to Henry H. Walker, February 26, 1861; died in Tallapoosa county, Ala., April, 3, 1877.

Mrs. Eugenia Carlton, wife of Richard G. Carlton, died near Union Point, Green county, Ga., April, 14, 1877, aged fifty three years. Thos. F. Pierce

Bro. Jno. R. Seymore--thirty-four years old--son of William M. Seymore, of Jackson county, Ga., died April 3, 1877.

Mrs. M. A. Boggus, wife of Peter Boggus, and sister of Rev. S. R. Weaver of the South Georgia Conference, was born in Jefferson county, Ga., died near Ft. Gaines, Ga., February 23, 1877, in the sixty-second year of her age. J. W. Weston

Issue of May 15, 1877

Died

Mary Irene, daughter of Charles and Emma Meriwether of Monticello, Ga., died March 20th 1877, aged five years. Also Mattie Lou, the only surviving child, died April 1st 1877, aged two years and six months.

Thomas Moore Burtz, son of Rev. M. C. and Mrs. S. A. Burtz, died at Dahlonega, Ga., May 4th 1877, aged 2 years and 24 days.

Obituary

Alexander W. McDade was born in Washington county, Ga., Jan. 1st 1816; died at Mt. Meigs, Ala., April 13th 1877. his father moved to Alabama in 1818, when it was a territory. His devotion was to his only child, a daughter, whom he leaves fatherless and motherless.

Mary Elizabeth Berry, wife of W. H. Berry, died in Savannah, Ga., March 12, 1877.

Malcomb W. Waldron died in Bibb county, Ga., March 11th 1877, in the 44th year of his age. He left a wife and children. W. J. Jones

William Robert Williams, son of R. M. and W. A. Williams, was born October 25, 1858; was killed April 14, 1877, by a piece of timber which he was throwing from a wagon.

Miss Fannie C. Toney, eldest daughter of Mrs. C. E. Toney, died in Forsyth, Ga., April 26th 1877. L. J. Davies

Sister Hannah N. Tucker, wife of Wm. S. Tucker and daughter of the late Col. A. W. and Mrs. Mildred Appleby, was born in Colleton county, South Carolina, Sept. 19, 1845, and died in Putnam county, Florida, April 8, 1875. Thomas N. Gautier

Mrs. Elizabeth Campbell wife of William D. Campbell of Dooly county, Ga., was born March 17, 1810; died March 18, 1877.

Brother W. Y. Bates was born in Spartanburg, S. C., Nov. 9, 1827; died Bellton, Ga., April 7th 1877. He professed religion in Augusta, Ark., in 1868. J. W. Baker

Mrs. Catharine Kebler died in Orangeburg county, S. C., Feb. 22, 1877, aged about 83 years. She was a widow for many years. Two daughters, her only children, care for her.

Mrs. Frances E. Baker, widow of the late John T. Baker and daughter of Moses W. Dobbins was born December 8, 1817, in Athens, Ga., joined the Presbyterian Church at the age of 19. She died at the residence of her son in Jackson county, Georgia, April 5th 1877. M. H. Eakes

Thomas Ellis, Senior, died in Edgefield county, S. C., April 11, 1877, in the seventy-fifth year of his age. J. A. Clifton

Tribute of Respect to Allen Doucherly, a member of Notasulga M. E. Church, South, who died 26th December 1876. he was born in North Carolina, Oct. 15, 1789, joined the M. E. Church at Snow Hill Campground, N. C., from thence he moved to Ala. W. B. Neal

Brother Elihu Davis was born in Marion District, S. C., and died in Decatur county, Ga., March 19, 1877, aged 55 years. He left a widow and six children. J. M. Marshall

Issue of May 22, 1877

Mrs. Lavonia H. Neal, daughter of the late Dr. John L. Blackburn, was born in Jones county, Ga., August 3, 1821; died at the residence of her brother-in-law, Rev. T. C. Stanley, at Flat Shoals, Meriwether county, April 6, 1877. She married Mr. George V. Neal, May 1838; moved to Warrenton, Ga.; reared her nine children, seven of whom survive her.

Mrs. Rowena J. Barrett, whose maiden name was Hood, wife of R. J. Barrett, was born in Wilkes county, Ga., February 14, 1812; died in Morris county, Texas, April 27, 1877. She was married in 1830. D. F. Fuller. Texas Christian Advocate please copy.

Mrs. Zelemma Gay, wife of A. O. M. Gay, of Atlanta, Ga., and daughter of Manson and Minerva Glass, of Newborn, Ga., died February 22, 1877, in the 36th year of her age. She was the mother of four children, two of them live. J. E. Evans

Mr. Joseph T. Thomas was born in April 1823 in Anderson District, S. C.; was married April 23, 1849; died suddenly in Oglethorpe county, Ga., April 10, 1877. J. H. Echols

Mrs. Anna Lewis Merritt, daughter of Mrs. M. A. Hunt, was born in Hancock county, Ga., September 4, 1834; was married to Capt. T. M. Merritt, November 25, 1857; died at her home near Americus, Ga., February 28, 1877.

Mrs. Willie B. Birdsong, wife of Edgar E. Birdsong, died April 2, 1877, in Hancock county, Ga. She had been married about fourteen months. Her parents had been members of the M. E. Church South, both of whom had preceded her to the happy land, leaving her in early childhood an orphan.

Her education had been attended to by her eldest sister. She leaves a husband, infant son, and several brothers and sisters. her father, Rev. Levin E. Culver, died eight years ago.

Mrs. Mary Ballard, daughter of John Ballenger and wife of Jesse Ballard, was born in South Carolina; died in Campbell county, Ga., April 7, 1877, aged eighty-eight years. She was the mother of nine children, for of whom are living and five dead. Stephen Shell.

Sister Susan J. Wardlaw was born February 15, 1846, and died near East Point, Ga., April 28, 1877. Her remains were laid away in the family burying ground.

Issue of May 29, 1877

Died

Jimmie Anderson, son of E. F. and Margaret Anderson, died Saturday, May 12, 1877, aged nine years and three months.

Leonta May Stidham, daughter of B. F. and Josia Stidham of Flowry Branch, Ga., died May 1st 1877, age 11 months and 19 days.

Obituary

Martha Dixon Flournoy, relict of Josiah Flournoy deceased, was born in Dinwiddie county, Va., and died at the residence of Col. L. A. Jordan, in Lee county, Ga., in the eighty-fifth year of her age. After the decease of her husband in 1852. W. R. Branham

Mrs. Rachel Reagan Meigs was born in McMinn county, Tenn., July 4, 1810; died at Rome, Ga., April 22, 1877.

Sister Jane Jackson was born in Ireland, November 18, 1788; died near Palmetto, Ga., April 6, 1877. She was brought to America when about six years old and located in Pendleton District, S. C. She was married to Mr. Hugh Wardlaw who died in about six weeks. She remained a widow seven or eight years then was married to Mr. Robert Jackson, in 1821 they moved to Georgia and settled in Hall county and remained there two years. Then they moved to Gwinnett near Lawrenceville, lived there about ten years then moved to Campbell county and settled near where Palmetto is now located. She joined the Presbyterian Church, and later the M. E. Church, South. She leaves three children out of nine, and many grandchildren.

Mrs. A. V. Murphey, wife of M. S. Murphey and daughter of Rev. Dr. John Caston, died February 7, 1877, near Bowden, Ga. She was born October 2, 1854.

Miss Ann F. Leger died in Darlington county, S. C., April 3, 1877, aged about sixty years. She was born and reared in Georgetown county, but removed to Darlington many years previous to the beginning of the late war. John O. Willson

Robt. F. Hood, son of Eli and Mary Hood, was born in Lancaster District, S. C., was born June 3, 1822; was married to Frances Williams, February 29, 1844; died in Pike county, Ga., April 22, 1877. T. S. L. Harwell. Southern Presbyterian please copy.

Martha Theressa King, daughter of John Houston of Abbeville, S. C., was born December 3, 1828; died February 15, 1877, near Augusta, Ga.

Issue of June 5, 1877

William Davenport was born in Oglethorpe county, Ga., September 8, 1796; died in Campbell county, Ga., March 28, 1877. The subject of this notice was married to Miss Andrew (sister of our late Bishop Andrew), who still survives him. Jno. M. Bowden

Mrs. Sarah B. Hardeman, nee Sparks, was born in Putnam county, Ga., April 1, 1804; was married to Mr. Thomas Hardeman, October 16, 1821; and died in Macon, Ga., February 27, 1877. Geo. G. N. MacD.

Mrs. E. M. Williams was born in North Carolina, October 3, 1824; died near Dahlonega, Ga., May 12, 1877. She was the mother of twelve children, ten of whom are still living. Her parents both died before she was ten years of age. J. D. Hammond

Emanuel Alexander Turnipseed was born at Cedar Creek, South Carolina, September 28, 1828; died a few miles from Ocala, Fla., May 15, 1877. He leaves a wife and five children. He had been married twice. One wife and two of her children, and three children of the last wife, had preceded him to the "better land." A. A. P. Neel

Joseph Pierce Ligon, third son of Daniel and Temperance Ligon, was born August 18, 1845, in Greenville county, S. C.; married to Augusta Jane Smith, near Cokesbury, Abbeville county, November 1, 1866; died at the residence of his father-in-law, Rev. James F. Smith, Spartanburg Court-house, April 21, 1877, leaving his wife and two children.

Sister Annie C. Wilkinson was born May 1, 1852; died May 15, 1877. She was the daughter of James N. and Eliza C. Taylor, late of Sumpter county, Ga. She leaves a husband and a helpless infant. J. M. Potter

Mr. Dexter Marchant died April 28, 1877, in the 25th year of his age.

Brother George Curry was born in the Bahamas, March 12, 1806; came to Key West, Fla., in 1837; there died February 20, 1877. He was one of the oldest of the early settlers of this island. Henry Edw. Partridge

Tribute of Respect from Gordon Circuit, South Georgia Conference, to Rev. A. C. C. Thompson.

Issue of June 12, 1877

Thomas B. Howard, son of R. O. and Euphemia Howard, was born February 3, 1836; died in Russell county, Ala., April 5, 1877. He was married to Miss Fannie Anderson, April 26th 1860. He leaves a wife and children, a widowed mother, one sister and two brothers. J. W. Solomon

Mrs. Sallie Kennerly, the wife of Capt. John Kennerly, of Ridge, S. C., died May 9, 1877. Mrs. Kennerly was the daughter of Capt. Charles Smith of Cokesbury, S. C., and was born 20th February 1847.

Miss Rebecca Frances Mills was born in Sumter county, Ga., December 20, 1848; and died in Monticello, Ga., April 8, 1877. In 1872 she became a member of the Baptist Church.

Judge Robert Allen Rowland was born in Richmond county, Ga., May 17, 1819; died in Waynesboro', Ga., April 25, 1877. E. M. Whiting

Mrs. Sarah C. Crowell, widow of the late Capt. Henry Crowell, died in Russell county, Ala., at the residence of her son-in-law, Mr. John G. Abercumbie, May 16, 1877. She was buried at Fort Mitchell, Ala., by the side of her husband, who died in 1840. She was born near Camden, S. C., April 10th 1792. She was sister to my mother and to the late Maj. John and Gen. James W. Cantey, of Camden, S. C. She moved to Washington county, Ga., with her father, Maj. James Cantey, whilst a girl, and when about 17 years of age was united in marriage to Capt. Crowell. Soon after their marriage they moved to the old Agency, on Flint river, Georgia, where his brother, Col. John Crowell, was Indian Agent--living there some 15 or 20 years. They moved to Ft. Mitchell, Ala., soon after the Indian war of 1836. The leaves two sons and five daughters, and many grand and great-grandchildren. Two sons and one daughter died previous to her death. The Rev. John Crowell of Alabama is her oldest son. S. E. Whitaker

Brother Lovick Pearce died in Jackson county, Ga., May 22, 1877, aged 70 years. he was a brother of the late Rev. G. J. Pearce, who was a member of the North Georgia Conference.

Brother John S. Cauthen, son of L. M. and D. E. Cauthen, died February 5, 1877, aged about thirty-one years. He was married to Miss Emily Robertson in January 1870, who died about two years afterwards. W. H. Kirton

Issue of June 19, 1877

Died

In Blairsville, Union county, Ga., June 6, 1877, Mary Marvin, infant daughter of Charles L. and Nannie E. Pattillo, of the North Georgia Conference.

Obituary

Rev. Joshua Bradford was born in Fairfield District, South Carolina, about the year 1798 or 1799. When a young man he removed to this section of Georgia. He died May 13, 1877, the oldest member of the Conference.

Rev. John Haisten was born in Edgefield District, S. C., March 8, 1802, and died near Whitesburg, Ga., May 22, 1877. His parents removed to Greene county in this state when he was a child. He removed to Fayette county in 1827, thence to Coweta in 1834; thence to Carroll county in 1868, where he resided until his death. D. Nolan. Nashville Advocate will place copy.

Mr. John Fullerton was born in Pickens District, S. C., May 24, 1822; died in Campbell county, Ga., March 18, 1877. Born and reared by Scotch-Irish Presbyterians. When quite a youth he joined the Methodist Protestant Church at Harmony in Henry county, Ga.

George W. Davis was born in Virginia, October 21, 1812; moved to Georgia about 1832; settled in Thomaston, Ga., in 1850, where he died May 1, 1877. Richmond Christian Advocate please copy.

Mrs. Hattie C. Ruddell, whose maiden name was Turner, was born in Beaufort county, S. C., in 1840; was married to Dr. J. H. Ruddell, of Burke county, Ga., in 1866; died March 29, 1877.

Sister Cynthia Cauthen, wife of James Cauthen, died in Barnesville, Ga., May 12, 1877, in her 77th year.

Brother McGillis Helverton was born of Methodist parents in Wayne county, Ga., February 26, 1810; was reared in Camden county; died May 14, 1877. He was married to Miss Eugenia Mott, with whom he lived for forty years. Of the nine children of this union, six had preceded their father to the spirit world. Bro. Helverton was a member of the Presbyterian Church for thirty-seven years.

Captain Payton W. Sale died in Goshen, Lincoln county, Ga., May 26, 1877, in the 71st year of his age. He joined the Baptist Church in Goshen more than 40 years ago. He leaves a wife and children. J. E. Groce

Mr. Thomas N. Mims was born in Bibb county, Ga., September 13, 1834; died in the same county May 16, 1877.

Mrs. Elizabeth W. Waller, widow of John Waller deceased, was born in Putnam county, Ga., May 1, 1818; died in Gordon, Ga., May 20, 1877. F. A. Kimbell

Issue of June 26, 1877

Died

In Orangeburg, S. C., June 15, 1877, Shuford Martin Albergotti, infant son of Mr. and Mrs. T. W. Albergotti, aged 1 year, 5 months, 12 days.

SOUTHERN CHRISTIAN ADVOCATE NOTICES 1867-1878

Obituary

Mrs. Martha Mitchell Gibson was born in Warren county, Ga., August 5, 1821. Her mother's maiden name was Ellen Macfarlan, whose father settled in that portion of Old Wilkes on the east side of Little river prior to 1776. As his name would indicate, he was a Scotchman. Her father, Hon. Micajah Rogers, was for many years Judge of the County Court and represented Warren for several terms in the House of Representatives. Micajah Rogers and Ellen his wife were members of the Methodist Church at Warrenton, Ga. In 1823, Mrs. Ellen Rogers died. In her eighteenth year her father also died. On 5th March 1843, she married her present husband, William Gibson, to whom she bore four children, two sons and two daughters. Two of them preceded her to Paradise. She died 4th June 1877.

James Adams was born in Virginia, February 25, 1799; was brought to Elbert county, Ga., by his parents when about three years of age, spent the remainder of his life at and near his father's first settlement on Cold Water Creek. He was the father of six children, five of whom yet live.

Mrs. Mary Platt, daughter of Capt. Wm. Page and late consort of Rev. J. B. Platt of the South Carolina Conference, was born in Marion county, S. C., October 24, 1811; was married to Joseph Deer, June 2, 1826; and to Rev. J. B. Platt, November 3, 1843; died at Lynchburg, S. C., May 25, 1877, and was buried in the family cemetery in Marion county the following day. She left a husband and eight children-- four of her children having preceded her to the grave. A. J. Stokes

Brother William Harper Carter was born in Chester county, S. C., March 30, 1837; died March 18, 1877. M. H. Pooser

Mary Fisher Adams died at Jamestown, Ga., 1st of April 1877. This young lady was the granddaughter of brother Fisher, a Methodist preacher. R. J. Walker

Mrs. Mary Graham (formerly Johnson) was born in Lancaster county, S. C., in 1804; died in the town of Lancaster, June 1, 1877. Married in 1829, she was soon called to mourn the death of her husband. W. A. Rogers

George B. Scott was born in Gordon county, Ga., May 27, 1852; died in the same county, March 26, 1877. J. H. McCoole

Issue of July 3, 1877

Died

In Forsyth, Ga., June 19, 1877, Alexander A. Allen, son of Mr. and Mrs. Geo. D. Allen, aged 2 years.

In Atlanta, Ga., June 23, 1877, Jefferson Samuel, only child of Lorenzo S. and Ruth Brown, age 2 years and 3 months.

Obituary

Mrs. Francis R. Leonard nee Darnell, relict of the late Van Leonard, was born in Milledgeville, Ga., January 4, 1804; died near Columbus, Ga., May 29, 1877. J. S. Key

Mrs. Sarah C. Lipscomb, whose maiden name was Marshall, wife of T. C. Lipscomb, of Ninety-Six, Abbeville county, S. C., died June 10, 1877, in her fiftieth year. R. P. Franks

Mrs. Sarah Mahon died in Monroe, Walton county, Ga., May 29, 1877. She had nearly reached four score years. D. F. C. Timmons

Sister Nancy K. Eason, wife of Abram Eason, was born August 17, 1840; died April 12, 1877. She was for many years a member of the Methodist Church at Bethel, in Appling county, Ga.

381

Mrs. Mary E. Rooks, whose maiden name was Yeargin, died April 21, 1877, in her thirty-second year. R. L. Williams. Christian Index please copy.

Rev. Willis A. Jordan was born November 8, 1801; died in Spalding county, Ga., April 22, 1877. T. S. L. Harwell

Robert M. Guthrey was born in Greene county, Ga., March 24, 1811; died in Walker county, April 18, 1877.

Mary E. Oliver, wife of W. W. Oliver, died in Orangeburgh county, S. C., May 29, 1877, aged forty-one years, three months, and fourteen days. Some years ago she and her husband moved from Horry county to Orangeburgh county. She leaves three children, having two already in heavy.

Mrs. Lizzie E. Inabnet of Reevesville, S. C., died of congestion, May 21, 1877. She had been a member of the Baptist Church.

Brother Jos. L. Tiller was born October 27, 1816; died near Camden, S. C., April 24, 1877.

Mrs. A. C. Puckett, wife of Dr. W. M. Puckett of Gainesville, Ga., and daughter of the late J. J. Chitwood, died April 30, 1877, aged thirty seven years, four months and eleven days. Joined the M. E. Church, South, at Clarkesville, Ga., where she was born and lived until her marriage, October 1, 1865. She had become the mother of four children, two of whom had preceded her to the better land.

Issue of July 10, 1877

Mrs. C. J. Wilson, my beloved wife, was born in Morgan county, Ga., was twice married; died in Decatur, Ga., March 30, 1877. She was the youngest of thirteen children, of whom three only are now living. Her Bereaved Husband

John S. Riden was born in Greene county, Ga., April 23, 1801; died in Gainesville, Ga., June 12, 1877. He joined the Methodist Church in Athens, Ga., in May 1840. A wife and one child preceded him, and four children, one son and three daughters, are left behind. D. D. Cox

Greene B. Hunnicutt was born and reared in Putnam county, Ga., and died in Winterville, Ga., June 16, 1877.

Mrs. Elizabeth Ann Richardson, wife of Ervin Richardson, died in Britton's Neck, Marion county, S. C., May 7, 1877, aged 49 years. She leaves a husband and nine children.

Mrs. Elizabeth Baugh was born in Jackson county, Ga., October 21, 1807; married to William Baugh, February 15, 1838; died near Lawrenceville, Ga., June 4, 1877. J. D. Anthony

Mary W. Aycock was born in Newton county, Ga., in 1834; died May 2, 1877. She had lost a mother, two sisters, three brothers, her father.

Mrs. Annie E. Jaques, eldest daughter of Frederick Jaques of Round O, Colleton county, S. C., died May 8, 1877. A. E. Williams

Mrs. Ann E. Harbeson died in Colleton county, S. C., May 5, 1877, in the 48th year of her age.

Mrs. Mary B. Johnston, widow of the late William Johnston, Esq., of Fairfield District, S. C., died near Atlanta, Ga., June 12, 1877. F. A. Holmes

Sister Emeline Pursley died in Abbeville county, S. C., May 31, 1877, in the 45th year of her age. She leaves her only child--a young lady.

Mrs. Martha A. Brown, wife of Reuben Brown and daughter of John and R. M. Ragan, was born in Spartanburg, S. C., April 30, 1834; died May 20, 1877. She leaves her aged parents, her husband, and eight children.

Ann H. Heap, youngest daughter of John and Mary Heap, was born October 181, 184; converted at a camp meeting at Wesley chapel in Colleton county, S. C., died April 8, 1877, at the home of her nephew, Joseph Marvin, near Yemassee, Beaufort county, S. C. B. G. Jones

Issue of July 17, 1877

Died

In Atlanta, Ga., June 23, 1877, little Charlie, son of Olin F. and Sarah Claridy, aged one year, four months, and twenty days.

Obituary

Early in May fell on sleep Mrs. Harriet Isabella Middleton Harwell, wife of Rev. Richard J. Harwell, of the North Georgia Conference. She left four children.

Mrs. Sophia Weston Middlebrooks, daughter of John and Elizabeth Shell, was born in Mecklenburg county, Virginia, March 31, 1789. She joined the M. E. Church in Newberry District, S. C., whither parents had moved from Virginia. In 1808 she was married to Zera Middlebrooks, late of Newton county, Ga., and died at the house of her son, Dr. A. C. Middlebrooks, in Doraville, DeKalb county, Ga., on 10th April 1877.

Oliver P. Hott was born in Sumter, S. C., October 28, 1847; died in the town of Sumter, June 25, 1877. He leaves a wife and two small children.

Dr. W. L. Broyle was born in Monroe county, Tenn., December 3, 1826; was married to Miss Mary Ruth in September, 1858; moved to Anderson county, S. C., where he died June 3, 1877. Formerly an Episcopalian, he joined the Methodist Church. He leaves a wife and five children. T. P. Phillips

The Rev. Elijah Elmore was born in Newberry District, S. C., June 24, 1811; died in Coweta county, Ga., May 16, 1877. In early life he joined the Baptist Church, but after emigrating to Georgia, he withdrew and joined the Evangelical Lutheran Church at Mount Pilgrim, near where he lived and died.

Brother J. B. Davidson was born in South Carolina, June 10, 1819; was married to Miss Amanda D. Elliott, April 4, 1845; died in DeKalb county, Ga., June 27, 1877. W. W. Lampkin

Sister Martha Ford, relict of the late Richard Ford, was born December 1819; died at the residence of her brother, Thompson Graham, in Pike county, Ga., June 21, 1877. R. W. Rogers

Brother David Bolton died June 9, 1877. He was born in Laurens District, S. C., in 1808; moved thence and settled in Gwinnett county, Ga., in 1827. In 1844 he married Margaret Ross. W. W. Lampkin

Mrs. Selah Knight, wife of Elisha Knight, and sister of the late Rev. James B. Jackson, was born January 15, 1809; died June 10, 1877. J. H. Baxter

Dr. John O. Danforth was born December 12, 1845; died April 7, 1877. He became a member of the Church in East Macon.

Issue of July 24, 1877

Capt. George W. Stiles, the son of one of my father's sisters, departed this life in Savannah, Georgia, June 14, 1877. he was about 48 years old. Capt. Geo. W. Stiles, a gallant officer of the lost cause, and Captain of Company A., Savannah Volunteer Guards Battallion. He is a younger brother of the lamented Rev. Dr. Jos. C. Stiles. Dr. J. B. Habersham, his brother in law. H. J. Adams

My mother, Mrs. Elizabeth Ann Jones, who was the daughter of Robert L. Edwards, was born in South Carolina, July 19, 1810; married Samuel G. Jones in Elbert county, Ga., January 26, 1826; died in Bartow county, Ga., May 19, 1877. My mother's remains were deposited in the cemetery at Cartersville. R. H. Jones

Mrs. Elizabeth Hammond, daughter of John and Mary Rich, was born in Elbert county, Ga., Sept. 13th 1799, and died June 21st 1877, in her 78th year. She was married May 10th 1821 to Col. Herbert Hammond of Anderson, S. C., and raised a family of ten children, seven of whom, with many grandchildren, survive. Two of her daughters married ministers, one in the South Carolina and another in the North Carolina Conference. G. F. Round

Mrs. Sarah A. Floyd died at the residence of her son-in-law, Col. B. H. Robinson, Blakely, Early county, Ga., April 10th 1877, in the 62nd year of her age. This lady was known to the writer in Madison, Morgan county, Ga., in the days of her early girlhood. Her four surviving daughters and son. A. Means

Octavia C. Jones, daughter of Wiley A. and Sarah Jones, died near Rehoboth, Morgan county, Ga., June 7th 1877. L. G. Anderson

Mrs. Fannie Elliot was born in Wilkes county, Ga., and died near Powelton, Ga., May 31st, 1877, in the 33d year of her age. Her husband, John T. Elliot. O. C. Simmons

Mrs. Margaret Hydrick, whose maiden name was Hildebrand, wife of Maj. Jacob Hydrick, was born in Lexington county, 26th March 1819 and married March 2d 1847, died June 10th 1877, in Orangeburg county, S. C. A. R. Danner

Mrs. Mary Matilda Neese, wife of Joseph Neese, died June 10th 1877, aged 56 years. A. R. Danner

Issue of July 31, 1877

Mrs. A. A. Simmons was born November 9, 1818; died May 14, 1877. She was married to Mr. J. E. Simmons, who for many years was a pillar and stay in the Methodist Church in Cave Spring. Her husband preceded her sixteen years ago to their home in heaven, and she was left with a charge of eight children. Sister Simmons was a daughter of Major J. H. Gill of Chester, S. C., who moved to Gillsville, Hall county, Ga., and afterwards to Floyd county, and thence to Homer, La. She was educated at Athens, Ga., in the Presbyterian school. Her daughter, Mrs. W. P. Rivers. Besides several of her own children, sister Simmons leaves behind a little grandson whom she had taken to raise after the death of both father and mother.

William George Norton was born in New Britain, Conn., April 5, 1857; resided at Cahaba, Ala., and Marion, Ala., until after the late war, when he removed to Brooklyn, N. Y., where he lived five years. He joined the M. E. Church, South, at Rome, Ga., 1874. He died June 2, 1877.

Mrs. C. Elizabeth Poyas, wife of Samuel H. Poyas, of Cainhoy, S. C., and daughter of the late William F. Stone, died July 4, 1877, in the 46th year of her age.

Saraus Alexander, son of Samuel H. and Sarah A. Robeson, was born in South Carolina, October 27, 1857; died at Island Lake, Orange county, Fla., June 20, 1877. His parents moved to Florida in 1871.

Mrs. Mattie S. Cassady, wife of Wilson Cassady, was born in Sumter county, Fla., October 25, 1854; died in Gainesville, Fla., June 18, 1877. As Mattie Swicord she was known from her childhood. She has left a babe about nine months old. O. Eady

About a year and a half ago the writer attended at marriage at the residence of Col. B. F. Pegues, in Marlboro county, S. C. The bride of the occasion was the Colonel's daughter, Miss Harriet S.

J., who was married to Rev. E. T. Hodges of the South Carolina Conference. She died July 2. One Tuesday afternoon we met at New Hope Church, where sleep the remains of her grandparents.

Mrs. Sarah Prickett, wife of Rev. Prickett, of the Baptist Church, an old lady (her age not precisely known), died June 2, 1877. She joined the M. E. Church about 1821.

Albert C. Butler, son of Nancy A. and Nathan Butler was born April 9th 1857; converted at Mt. Zion Church of Little River circuit; on 29th June 1877 he was struck by lightning and killed. W. L. Yarbrough

Tribute of Respect form Perry Station, South Georgia Conference, to Lewis Myers Houser, who died 10th February 1877. He was born in Orangeburg, S. C., moved to Georgia in 1849.

Issue of August 7, 1877

Died

Little Frank, infant son of Rev. F. A. and Mrs. F. H. Kimbell, died in Eatonton, Ga., July 26, 1877, aged 25 months.

Ernest, infant son of Dr. L. S. and Mrs. Mary H. Moss, died in Forsyth, Ga., July 23, 1877, aged 6 months.

Obituary

Mrs. M. E. Massengale, eldest daughter of Rev. C. W. Key of the North Georgia Conference, died at her father's residence near Augusta, Ga., July 5, 1877, in the 44th year of her age. She was married, at the age of twenty, to Mr. A. J. Massengale, of Washington, Ga., who afterwards move t Chattanooga, Tenn. In 1856, he died, leaving two little girls--the youngest of whom in a few weeks joined her father. Her Sister

Miss Annie Catherine Moss, daughter of Mr. James E. and Mrs. Salina C. Moss, of Orangeburg county, South Carolina, was born February 5th 1840, and died June 6th 1877.

Mrs. Amanda Patterson, daughter of Capt. J. and Mrs. E. J. Leaphart, was born September 24th 1850, and died June 3d 1877, at the residence of Capt. Abraham Geiger, Lexington county, S. C. Thos. J. Clyde

Jordan F. Harvard died at his residence in Dooly county, Ga., July 2d 1877, in the 63d year of his age. He was born in Washington county, Ga., April 21st 1814, but moved with his father to Dooly county in 1822.

Rev. Benjamin Peeler was born February 5, 1793, and reared in Elbert county, Ga., and died at Jewells, July 5, 1877. In 1845 he moved to Clark county. He left several children and grandchildren.

Mrs. Sarah A. Williams, nee Wiggins, was born in Telfair county, Ga., Oct. 20th 1841, and died near Eastman, Ga., June 19th 1877. She lost her parents when she was a mere child, and was reared by her grandmother. At the age of nineteen she was married to Mr. R. F. Williams of Brunswick, Ga. She leaves a husband, two children, and a grandmother.

Mrs. Mary Rowena Marchman was born in Polk county, Ga., December 3d 1849, and died in Meriwether county, Ga., July 10, 1877. She was the daughter of the late Alfred George Marchman. She was married to Mr. W. M. Marchman, December 17th 1874. Wm. A. Simmons

Flemming McFall was born in South Carolina, July 6th 1799 and died in Monroe county, Ga., June 26th 1877. He leaves a widow and children.

Miss Mary Wright, daughter of Stephen and Sarah Wright, was born in 1828. She passed away 6th June 1877. R. M. T. Brannon

Mrs. Martha E. Rosser was born in 1812, died June 21, 1877. She was a member of old Olive Branch church, Meriwether county, Ga. Two daughters mourn her loss. F. M. T. Brannon

Issue of August 14, 1877

Died

Samuel Hodges, infant son of Geo. T. and Laura J. Reid, died July 31, 1877, at Hodges, S. C., aged 19 months.

Obituary

James L. Lovejoy was born in Clark county, Ga., February 1, 1809; died at his residence near Stockton, Clinch county, Ga., June 26, 1877, in his 68th year. He removed with his parents, John and Mary Lovejoy, to Henry county when but a child. He was married in 1839 to Eugenia I. Talley. He leaves a wife and five adult children.

Daniel H. Knoles, son of John H. and Margaret L. Knoles, was born in Clinch county, Ga., October 3, 1859; died in the same July 9, 1877. C. T. Bickley

Crawford Hancock was born in Jackson county, Ga., August 17, 1811, and died in Hall Co., July 4, 1877, aged 66 years.

Mrs. E. E. Goodwin, daughter of E. A. and A. M. Franklin, was born in Cartersville, Ga., October 15, 1856; was married to Mr. H. B. Goodwin, August 23, 1876; died at Powder Springs, Cobb county, Ga., July 10, 1877. Her remains were carried into the church in Cartersville. T. H. Timmons

Mrs. Henrietta A. Edwards, relict of L. M. Edwards, was born in Duplin county, N. C., June 21, 1851; died in Lake City, Fla., July 5, 1877. She told her widowed mother to tell her only sister, Mary, and her brother in law, to meet her in heaven.

Joel Thomas Cherry was born January 12, 1811 in South Carolina. He removed to Macon, Ga., in 1833. About two years afterwards he married Susan C. McAllum. He subsequently removed to Rutland District of Bibb county, Ga., and died July 1, 1877. C. W. Smith

Mrs. Isabel Hardy Fleming, wife of Israel W. Fleming, was born in Camden county, Ga., August 2, 1842; married J. W. Fleming, May 5, 1870; died in Camden county, Ga., July 17, 1877. T. S. Armistead

J. Dunklin Sullivan was born November 13, 1823; died in Greenville county, S. C., June 19, 1877. S. Lander

Mrs. Maria Soubray, whose maiden name was Lipsey, was born in Wilmington, N. C., July 4, 1804. Her father moved to Florida in 1818. She married in 1827. She had been on a visit to Louisiana to see a daughter and was returning to Florida, where most of her children live, and she died on the train near Live Oak, Fla., July 6, 1877. A. Peeler

L. P. Cox was born November 9, 1851; died at Williamston, S. C., May 12, 1877. S. Lander

Issue of August 21, 1877

Died

On the 8th of August 1877, near Cross Keys, Union co., S. C., Bertie Maria, daughter of William H. and Lucretia J. Norman, aged two years, nine months and five days.

In Putnam county, Ga., July 26th 1877, Barbara Elizabeth, daughter of W. H. and Amanda Miller, aged five months.

Obituary

Mrs. Phala Sanford De Bardeleben, daughter of Rev. William and Eliza W. Menefee, was born in Jackson county, Ga., July 23, 1828, and died in Tuskegee, Ala., June 15, 1877. When a child her parents moved to Chambers county, Ala. On the 8th of October 1844, she was married to John A. DeBardeleben, to whom she bore four sons and one daughter. The daughter, Mrs. Nicholson, preceded her to the better land several years ago. New Orleans Advocate please copy.

Mrs. Julia A. Jordan was born in Morgan county, Ga., September 171, 1813; was married to the late Josiah G. Jordan, and died at her residence in Monroe county, Ga., July 8, 1877.

Mrs. Callie L. Smith was born in Oxford, Georgia, August 13th 1843. Her father, Rev. George Lane, Professor in Emory College, was for many years a member of the Georgia Annual Conference. The ancestry of Mrs. Smith on the maternal side were Wittichs. Prof. Lane died in his thirty fourth year. Mrs. Harriet Lane, his widow, survived him many years. On 16th of May 1865 Callie Lane became the wife of Rev. L. M. Smith, then Professor of Greek in Emory College. To his four children, she was a watchful mother. She died July 13th 1877.

Bro. Joseph P. Roberts was born at Green Turtle Key of the Bahama Islands, September 29th 1826, and died in Key West, Fla., April 30th 1877. Henry Edward Partridge

Mrs. Winnie S. George, wife of Rev. J. W. George, and daughter of Raleigh and Elizabeth Hightower, all of Henry county, Ga., departed this life May 21, 1877. Sister George was born January 31, 1838. She leaves a husband, five children, two grandchildren. J. F. Rowan

Alice Kendall Wright, daughter of Prof. J. L. and C. K. Wright, near Thomasville, N. C., was born August 13th 1864. She died June 29th 1877.

Letitia Mouzon, daughter of Geo. L. F. and Elizabeth D. Leybt, of Cokesbury, S. C., departed this life July 21st 1877, aged 20 years, 11 months and 3 days.

Hon. Wiley G. Parks was born near Jonesville, Yadkin county, N. C., in the year 1817, and died in Dawson, Terrell county, Ga., June 15, 1877.

Mrs. Amanda R. Blakely, wife of Mr. J. M. Blakely, and daughter of Mr. John Caldwell, died in Columbia, S. C., June 26, 1877, in the 58th year of her age. She was a native of Newberry county and was married in 1846. Her body was interred in the graveyard of Washington Street Church.

William C. Pitchford was born June 30, 1849 in Habersham county, Ga., and died in White county, Ga., July 3, 1877. W. B. Bell

Died at the residence of Mr. Thomas Underhill, in Volusia county, Fla., July 16, 1877, Rev. S. J. Cosford, of the M. E. Church, South.

Mrs. Anna Mozingo, wife of Rev. McKinzie Mozingo, died July 22, 1877, in her 64th year. She has left a husband and several children. Lewis M. Hamer

Tribute of Respect from Bethel Church, Charleston, to the late pastor, Rev. W. H. Fleming, D. D., who died April 16, 1877.

Tribute of Respect from Liberty Church, Madison county, Ga., to brother A. Tabor.

<u>Issue of August 28, 1877</u>

Died

In Richmond, Va., on July 11, 1877, Albert Lawrence West, youngest child of Albert L. and Georgia C. West, aged one year and ten days.

Obituary

Mrs. Alethea Young, relict of James B. Young, and daughter of Pleasant and Mary Tydal, was born April 21st 1805 in Columbia county, Ga; died in McDuffie county, Ga., August 7th 1877. At the time of her death she had three sons and two daughters members, with a number of grandchildren. A daughter is the wife of a local preacher, Rev. E. P. Bonner. W. C. Dunlap

William Fraley was born at Germantown, Pa., August 17, 1795. He came to Sparta when he was about 21 years old. He was twice married, on the 12th of May 1825 to Demaris Ingram, and on September 21, 1843, to Martha J. Massey. He has three children, each of them the head of a family, one of them a widowed daughter, with whom he resided. He died July 18. H. J. Adams

Mrs. Sarah Wright was born in Greene county, Georgia, May 7, 1803; died within two miles of her birth place, July 14, 1877. The child of Walker Lewis. W. P. Lovejoy

Bro. Daniel W. Youngblood was born March 7th 1816; died July 1st 1877. He was born in Duval county, Fla., where he lived until about twenty years ago, when he moved to Hillsboro county.

Judge Thomas McCotry Williams, son of Charles and Elizabeth Williams, was born in Sumter county, S. C., March 25, 1806; died at his son's, Rev. Jere S. Williams, Midway, Ala., July 10, 1877. He was admitted to the bar in South Carolina as attorney, May 9, 1827. Married Mary Ann Shrewsbery, December 10, 1829. They had nine children, three of whom died early, three in the late war, and three survive. W. A. McCarty

Mrs. Elizabeth L. McLaurin, whose maiden name was Bethea, was born September 25th 1805; and died near Clio, Marlboro county, S. C., July 4th 1877.

Miss Sarah Maria Avrete, daughter of the late Alexander Avrete, was born in Richmond county, Ga., June 12, 1826; died at the residence of her sister, Mrs. J. B. Peacock, Jackson Station, S. C., July 5, 1877.

Mrs. A. W. Tweedle, consort of Rev. A. W. Tweedle, for the past for or five years has resided in Gordon county, Ga. About the 1st of May, while visiting her daughter, Mrs. Bennett, in Chattooga county, Ga., she was taken sick. She died August 3, 1877, leaving several children, grandchildren, an aged husband. J. S. Harkins

Sister Catharine Duncan, wife of Geo. Duncan, was born December 28, 1817; married November 1, 1836; spent the greater portion of her life in Georgia; died near Maitland, Orange county, Fla., July 3, 1877. She was the mother of two children, both of whom preceded her to heaven. Her father died when she was about grown, and as the eldest child, she felt it her duty to assist her mother in rearing the younger children. O. W. Ransom

Robert S. Cauthen, second son of Rev. A. J. Cauthen of the South Carolina Conference, was born in Camden, S. C., May 8, 1855; died in Lowndesville, S. C., July 26, 1877. Wm. Martin

Mrs. Emma C. Sherwood was born in Monroe county, Georgia, September 23, 1837, and died at Union Point, Georgia, August 7, 1877.

Charles Lodtman, formerly of Sparta and Augusta, Ga., died in Atlanta, Ga., May 9, 1877, aged 68. His wife, Mrs. Ann Lodtman, died July 27, aged 37. She had been married to her husband about twenty-two years, when in giving birth to her first born she died; and mother and child lie now in the same coffin. J. E. Evans

Mrs. Nancy L. Cleaveland, whose maiden name was Pittman, was born in Henry county, Georgia, September 20, 1812, and died in Troup county, Georgia, July 10, 1877.

Died

At 26 Station, S. C. R. R., Colleton county, S. C., August 12, 1877, Lula Eliza, daughter of T. C. and Ida L. Harvey, aged 2 years and 2 months.

In Washington county, Ga., August 27, 1877, Little Beulah, only child of John G. and Annie E. Harrison, aged 10 months and 12 days.

Obituary

Sister Julia F. O'Cain was born June 18th 1836; was married to John R. O'Cain, July 6th 1877. She was the daughter of Amos and Eliza Chunn of Meriwether county, Ga., in which county she was born and reared and breathed her last. J. L. Dixon

John S. Lee removed from Richland co., S. C., to Georgia in 1837, and settled in Crawford co. He died August 1, 1877, in his 76th year. G. W. Persons

Mary H. McArthur, daughter of D. P. and Mary J. McArthur, was born in Bibb county, Ga., June 30, 1853; died in the same county July 28, 1877.

Major William A. Cobb was born in Columbia county, Ga., July 12, 1798; died in Tuskegee, Ala., July 12, 1877. In early life he moved to Augusta, Ga., where he lived for several years. From there he moved to Hancock county, Ga., thence to Thomaston, Ga., which was his home the remainder of his life. He was Clerk of the Court in Thomaston several years and was Ordinary twenty five years. He died at Mr. Jackson's, his son in law's, house. He was brought to Thomaston and buried.

Brother P. Madison C. Earnest died in Ridgeville, S. C., May 22, 1877, in the forty-first year of his age. He leaves a widow and two children, an only sister.

Sarah Passmore was born in Anderson county, S. C., November 8, 1787; died at the residence of James Passmore in Harris county, Ga., June 4, 1877, in her 90th year. After her marriage to John Passmore, they followed the tide of emigration. She was left a widow about twenty years ago.

Samuel C. Cride died July 10th 1877 in his nineteenth year. A. R. Danner

Mrs. Elizabeth C. McKenzie, wife of P. H. McKenzie, was born at Chesterfield C. H., S. C., September 24, 1835; died in Tuskegee, Ala., May 19, 1877. E. L. Loveless

Mrs. Mary Ann DuPont, wife of Hon. C. H. DuPont, was born in Hancock county, Ga., April 17th 1813; died at "Cottage Home" near Quincy, Fla., July 20th 1877. She was married November 13th 1828.

Mrs. Frances Hanna, wife of Mr. C. B. Hanna, died June 25th 1877, aged about seventy-two years. She was born in Anderson county, South Carolina, about the year 1805, in which county she lived until her death. In early life she joined the Presbyterian Church.

My second sister, Indiana Eliza, wife of Mr. J. J. Griffin, of Russell co., Ala., died May 27, 1877, in the 53d year of her age. She was the mother of five children. Four of them and her husband survive. W. R. Branham

Brother John R. Glenn died August 2d 1877, in his seventieth year. He moved from Georgia, his native state, to Jacksonville, Fla., two years ago. H. B. Frazer

Mrs. Mary J. Moss, wife of brother John E. Moss and daughter of brother G. M. and sister M. H. Underwood, of Meriwether county, Ga., died June 21st 1877, in Griffin, Ga., in the thirty-ninth year of her age.

Our mother, Mrs. Frances Kinnett of Newton county, Ga., died June 17, 1877, in the 74th year of her age. She joined the M. E. Church at the early age of fourteen at old Zion Church in Spartanburg District, S. C., from which place the family moved to Georgia. V. C. Sparks

Sister Martha Taylor, whose maiden name was Flake, was born in Warren county, Ga., in 1803; died at Concord, Fla., July 9, 1877. She first married a Mr. Spivey. Afterwards she married Mr. Taylor. J. W. Reeves, M. D.

Issue of September 11, 1877

Died

August 21, 1877, Wm. Homer Morrow, infant son of Wm. C. and Laura R. Morrow, of Brooks county, Ga.

Obituary

Mrs. Margaret Harris, wife of Ezekiel C. Harris, Esq., died in Cobb county, Ga., July 30, 1877, in the 65th year of her age. W. J. Scott

Brother James R. Glenn was born in Oglethorpe co., Ga., July 22th 1808 and died in Jacksonville, Fla., August 2nd 1877. He was a brother to Rev. J. W. Glenn, formerly of the Georgia Conference, also to Rev. J. N. Glenn near Oxford, Ga. S. Anthony

Dr. William Smith Rice, son of John and Mary A. P. Rice, was born in Stewart co., Ga., Nov. 14, 1838; died in Jasper co., Ga., August 16, 1877. He was married to Eugenia C. Stewart, June 7, 1863 in Hamilton county, Florida. J. H. Johnson

My grandmother, Mrs. Alethea Young, of McDuffie co., Ga., died August 7, 1877. She had seen her husband and two of her children buried years before.

Mrs. Emeline C. Miles, wife of John J. Miles and daughter of Wm. H. and Elizabeth H. Parker, was born in DeKalb county, Ga., July 12th 1839; died near Palmetto, Ga., July 15th 1877. L. P. Neese

Mrs. Annie Heidt Jaudon, daughter of Rev. Emanuel and Mrs. Frances L. Heidt, was born in Savannah, Ga., October 14th 1843; died in Effingham county, Ga., July 19th 1877. W. C. Bass

James T. Owen, Jr., died at the residence of his father in Talbot county, Ga., July 30, 1877; aged 26 years. W. W. Stewart

Tribute of Respect from Little River Circuit, Tallahassee District, to Mr. Daniel Hinson.

Tribute of Respect from Macon circuit, South Georgia Conference to J. T. Cherry.

Issue of September 18, 1877

Died

Johnny J. Cassady, son of Capt. A. A. and Mrs. A. C. Cassady, was born May 18, 1876, and died in Lawrenceville, Ala., September 3, 1877.

Jephtha Athens Booker, son of Joseph and Riddie Booker, died July 20, 1877, aged 3 years.

Obituary

Sarah A. Broyles, daughter of Rev. Alexander N. and Edna Harris, was born near Jonesboro, Washington county, Tenn., June 2, 1847; died at Nola Chucky, in said county, June 24, 1877. She was married August 19, 1868, to W. N. Broyles, Esq., of Washington county, Tenn., and with her husband went to reside at Nola Chucky, in that State.

Mrs. Mary Barbara Cosby, wife of Mr. Wm. A. Osborn, and daughter of Mr. Thomas and Mrs. Rebecca White, died near Palmetto, Ga., August 10, 1877. She was the bride of Samuel Arnold. She was again married to Mr. Osborn of Kentucky.

David S. Ramsaur, son of L. R. and Harriet E. Ramsaur, was born January 10 1860; died August 22, 1877, at Fairmount, Gadsden county, Ga. P. G. Reynolds

Miss Mary Harden was born in Monroe county, Ga., and died July 18th 1877.

Mrs. Annie Bessent Carroll, wife of Jesse Y. Carroll, and only child of Mrs. V. F. Bessent of Edgewood, near Atlanta, Ga., died July 24th 1877.

Sidney William Capers, son of Rev. Samuel W. Capers, and Mrs. A. H. Capers, of Camden, S. C., was born Sept. 22, 1838; was married to Jessie, daughter of John T. Darby, January 18, 1859; and to Edith, daughter of Bishop W. M. Wightman, April 21, 1874; died at Camden, S. C., August 6, 1877. A. J. Stokes

Mrs. Candace Daniel, wife of Cordy Daniel and daughter of Ezekiel Akridge, was born in Washington county, Ga., April 29th 1794, and died at the residence of her son-in-law, A. Farrar, Esq., in Henry county, Ga., August 23d 1877. She leaves but three children: Mrs. L. E. Stark, wife of Rev. W. F. Stark of Jackson county, Ga., Mrs. Amanda Y. Farrar; and C. H. Daniel, of Henry county. Henry County Weekly please copy.

Rev. S. G. Gilbert, a member of the Mulberry circuit Quarterly Conference, was born in Jackson county, Ga., March 30, 1838; died in the neighborhood of his birth on July -- 1877. M. H. Eakes

David L. Tompkins was born Aug. 19, 1846; died in Alachua, Fla., June 1, 1877. He was a son of James and Mary Tompkins, of Orange Lake. He left a wife and four children. O. Eady

Mrs. Mary D. Martin, wife of John R. Martin, was born in Abbeville District, South Carolina, September 6, 1818; died in Madison county, Fla., May 26, 1877. She joined the Reformed Presbyterian Church in early life. J. M. Hendry

Miss Elizabeth Gray was born in Abbeville District, S. C., April 13, 1814 and died at her brother-in-law's, J. R. Martin's, in Madison county, Fla., July 13, 1877. J. M. Hendry.

Issue of September 25, 1877

Died

In Toccoa City, Ga., September 14, 1877, Elmore Palmer Smith, son of Rev. J. Rembert and Mrs. Carrie Palmer Smith, aged one year save two days.

Obituary

Lizzie Logan, third daughter of Col T. H. and Mrs. S. W. Logan, one of our oldest and most respected families, died August 16, 1877, in her 17th year.

Mrs. Lucy Gates Deupree was born in Brunswick county, Virginia, in May, 1807; and died at Athens, Georgia, July 3, 1877. She was the eldest daughter of Captain John Atkinson and his wife Elizabeth Lundie. Her scholastic education was complete at Salem, North Carolina, In 1833, she was married to Dudley Peebles, and soon afterward removed with him to Merriwether county, Georgia. They had three children. William and Marietta were taken, the one from Emory College at Oxford and the other from LaGrange Female College on the day of her graduation, to untimely graves. In 1860 her faithful husband died, and last of all, her dear Susan. In 1864 she was married to Lewis J. Deupree of Oglethorpe county, Georgia. In 1870 he died.

William S. Foster was born in Jasper county, Ga., September 11, 1827; moved to Carroll county in 1846; married Miss Mary E. Arnold in 1847; died near Carrollton, Ga., August 4, 1877. He leaves a wife and nine children. J. L. Perryman

Miss Mary Creamer was born in Greenville District, S. C., April 8, 1826; and died in Bartow county, Ga., July 8, 1877. For twenty-seven years she had lived with her brother-in-law, Bro. L. W. Gaines, of Euharlee. J. J. Singleton

Rev. Alvin J. Dean, beloved pastor of the M. E. Church, South, died in Perry, Ga., July 20, 1877. He was a son of Charles and Abbie Rilla Dean, and was born in Gwinnett county, Ga., February 24, 1831.

William Copeland was born in Laurens district, South Carolina, May 3, 1802; died near Bowdon, Ga., July 31, 1877. He came to this country some twenty-five years ago, where there were but few settlements in this part of Carroll county. He was reared by Presbyterian parents. He leaves a wife, nine children, and thirty-six grandchildren. J. J. Perryman

Mrs. Jane E. Lindsay, formerly Miss Pressley, was born in Abbeville District, South Carolina, in 1821. She was married in 1840 to Samuel Lindsay. She was converted at the age of sixteen and joined the Presbyterian Church. She was the mother of several children. She joined the M. E. Church after her removal to Georgia in 1851. On 1 July 1877, she was called from this life. W. B. Jones

Mrs. Catharine Winham, beloved wife of R. T. Winham, died in Sumter county, S. C., Sept. 4, 1877.

Samuel T. Houston was born in Iredell county, N. C., August 4, 1811; died in Cherokee county, Ga., August 4, 1877. C. M. McClure.

Tribute of Respect from Graham Circuit, South Carolina Conference to Robert S. Cauthen.

Issue of October 2, 1877

Died

Thomas Rabb, only child of F. C. and Nina Lupo, died September 19, 1877, aged one year, four months, and twenty-five days.

Obituary

Mrs. Theodosia McDonald, whose maiden name was Ryder, was born in Bibb county, Ga., November 1, 1862; died at Spaulding, Macon county, Ga., July 29, 1877. She leaves a husband and two little boys.

Brother William M. Meaders was born in Franklin county, Ga., July 6, 1829; died in Cherokee county, Ga., August 20, 1877. He leaves a wife and seven children. Thomas J. Edwards. Zealous Christian please copy.

Miss Clara B. Barnett was born Nov. 7, 1854; died August 17, 1877. W. L. Yarbrough

Edward Elisha McGehee, son of Wm. A. and Cynthia A. McGehee, was born in Stewart county, Ga., August 1, 1861; died in Quitman county, Ga., August 26, 1877.

Sister P. A. Smith, wife of Luke Smith, died August 12, 1877, in the 54th year of her age. She lived in Edgefield county, S. C. J. A. Clifton

My mother, Martha Long, relict of David Long and daughter of Andrew and Mary Smith, was born on Cedar Creek, Richland district, S. C., January 12, 1804; died at her son's residence, in Ocala, Marion county, Fla., August 26, 1877. She then came to Florida, July 1864. She leaves a son and daughter, and five grandchildren. H. W. Long

James W. Thornburg was born August 2, 1827; died July 19, 1877. He was converted in 1827 at or near Guntersville, Ala. He united with the Cumberland Presbyterian Church and remained in its communion until he removed to Walker county, Ga., when he joined the M. E. Church, South at Payne's Chapel. A. Thornburgh, M. D.

Thomas Littlejohn, M. D., was born in Union county, S. C., December 8, 1808, and died in his native county, July 13, 1877. Miss Medora, daughter of the above, born Dec. 27, 1845; died August 2, 1877. The family respectfully request publication in the Nashville Advocate.

Mrs. Mary D. Ormand, daughter of James McCorkle, was born in Mecklenburg (now Union) county, N. C., June 25, 1811; was married to Andrew Ormand, February 18, 1841; removed with her husband (who died a few years since) to Alachua county, Fla., sometime in 1855, where she died August 22, 1877. Her only living child, sister Jane Smith. J. D. Rogers

Edward F. Moore, son of the Rev. J. M. Moore of walker county, Ga., was born March 31, 1860; died July 15, 1877. A. Thornburgh, M. D.

Mrs. Eliza F. Holzendorf, daughter of John and Amanda Wade, and wife of W. B. Holzendorf, was born in Columbia county, Ga., December 8, 1852; died in McDuffie county, Ga., July 15, 1877. W. C. Dunlap

Issue of October 9, 1877

Died

Ira Lee Fisher, son of Inman H. and Elizabeth Fisher, was born in 1871; died September 18, 1877.

In Jefferson county, Fla., September 1, 1877, James Howren Hightower, infant son of Rev. B. Hightower, aged 6 years.

Obituary

The death of Dr. ___ Perry, of Covington, Ga., who was born November 15, 1814; and died June 23, 1877. When about 30 years old he married Mrs. N. Caroline Smith, then a widow, who still survives with two sons and one daughter. A. Means

Susan Emma Dyer, daughter of John and Missouri Dyer, was born in Bibb county, Ga., April 25, 1858; died in the same county August 22, 1877.

Rev. W. A. Hayles was born June 13th 1819 and died July 11th 1877.

Mrs. E. J. Graham was born February 8, 1831; died in the village of Graham, Barnwell county, S. C., August 6, 1877. She was the daughter of Rev. T. Mason, a Baptist minister. She was married to Captain Z. G. Graham, July 25, 1855. She leaves an aged husband and three children. A. J. Cauthen

Mrs. Rebecca M. Bunkley was born in Nash county, North Carolina, April 18, 1799; died in Talbot county, Ga., July 14, 1877. She was the daughter of James and Sarah Williams, who were among the first and most noted Methodists in that region. On the 15th of January 1818 she was married to Mr. James Bunkley of Warren county, Ga., with whom she lived till his death, July 16, 1867. In 1832 they removed to Talbot county, Ga. She died within a week after March 8, 1872.

Mrs. Elizabeth Barnes, whose maiden name was Legett, relict of Britton Barnes, was born in North Carolina, and died at Ellaville, Ga., August 14, 1877, aged 88 years. She was the mother of twelve children, eight of whom preceded her to heaven.

Mrs. Mary S. Jackson, whose maiden name was Seyle, widow of the late Rev. William J. Jackson of the South Carolina Conference, was born December 19th 1802; was married to Mr. Florence

O'Sullivan, January 18th 1824; to Rev. W. J. Jackson, February 1st 1841; died in Charleston, S. C., June 28th 1817. G. W. Walker

Martha W. Meaders died in White county, Ga., in the thirty-second year of her age. She was a daughter of Wm. G. and Elizabeth Pitchford, who within about four years past have buried four of their grown up children. Her Husband, Bro. D. A. Meaders, had five children; one of whom, Sarah Elizabeth, passed away fourteen days after the death of her mother. Geo. K. Quillian

Sister Martha Barwick, wife of William Barwick, was born in Emanuel county, Georgia, December 6th 1811; died near Lake City, Florida, September 1st 1877. She was the mother of nine children, three of whom preceded her to heaven. J. W. Barnett

Issue of October 16, 1877

Died

Dora V. Charles, daughter of J. T. and M. C. Charles, died August 18, 1877, at Williamston, S. C., aged 1 year, 1 month, and 13 days.

Homer Haygood, in Columbus, Ga., September 26, 1877, infant son of J. D. W. Ridenhour.

Obituary

Bro. David Homer Adams was a son of Rev. W. E. Adams and Mrs. Mary Adams, and was born in Putnam county, Ga., May 3d 1810; was married first to Miss Eliza Hudson, and afterward to her sister, Mrs. Sarah Trippe; died in Eatonton, Ga., August 13th 1877. J. Lewis, Jr.

Mrs. Sallie Caldwell, wife of M. J. Caldwell and daughter of Massillon and Barbary Glenn, died at the residence of Dr. G. Caldwell, at Enon, Ala., September 2d 1877, in the thirty-first year of her age. She leaves two children, the youngest about three months old, a husband, father, mother, brothers and sisters. D. M. Banks

Mrs. Kate M. Freeman, wife of B. Pope Freeman, and daughter of Nathaniel and Emma Shaw, was born in Lexington, Ky., April 16th 1837; died at Lawley, Fla., August 18th 1877.

William H. Varbracle was born in Bryan county, Ga., December 26th 1803; died in the same county, July 4th 1877. He was married three times and was the father of nineteen children--nine sons and ten daughters. W. J. Jordan

Judge Nicholas L. Howard, late of Columbus, Ga., was born in Greensboro, Ga., February 14th 1815; died near Columbus, July 22d 1877. His parents, Gen. Nicholas and Mrs. Judith Howard, were members of the Methodist Episcopal Church. He left a widow and large family of children. Jesse Boring

Milton Akin was born in York District, S. C., June 17, 180; was married to Dorinda Danill, of Morgan county, Ga., December 3, 1828; died in Henry county, Ga., July 3, 1877. Thos. R. Kendall

James T. Rast was born in Orangeburg county, S. C., February 18th 1821; died in Weakley county, West Tennessee, August 11th 1877. April 30th 1846 he married Miss Frances V. Cummings, who died soon afterward. His second marriage was to Miss Ann Shuler, who still survives him. He lived in Orangeburg county until 1856, when he moved to Charleston county in the same state, whence he emigrated to West Tennessee in the winter of 1874. He leaves a wife and four children. J. P. Sebastian

Mrs. Lucretia Copelen, wife of Rev. A. H. Copelen, was born in Greenville District, S. C., February 15, 180; died in Gwinnett county, Ga., September 19, 1877. She leaves her aged husband, two children and nine grandchildren. D. D. Cox

My father, Gen. T. H. Marone, was born in Putnam county, Ga., April 1, 1823; died in Belleview, Talbot county, Ga., July 11, 1877. HE leaves a wife and five children. Mary

Miss Nancy N. Garrison, daughter of Rev. Levi Garrison, was born in Anderson District, S. C., March 1817; died in Milton county, Ga., July 20, 1877. Her body sleeps in Alpharetta grave yard. J. J. Harris

Mary Findley, wife of James Findley, died August 27, 1877, in Henry County, Ga. She was seventy-four years old the 26th of last June. He left a husband and many children. D. L. Duffey

Issue of October 23, 1877

Died

On the 11th of October 1877, near Cuthbert, Ga., Mary Belle, daughter of Rev. J. D. and S. F. Clark, aged 2 years, 2 months and 20 days.

Irene, youngest child of Mr. and Mrs. G. W. Clemmons, died at Conyers, September 23d, 1877, aged 4 years and 9 months.

Obituary

Miss Annie Manson Gautier was born in Tuskeegee, Ala., August 24, 1856; died in that city September 21, 1877. Her paternal grandfather was Rev. Peter Gautier, and her father Dr. W. J. Gautier. R. J. Corley

Frederick A. Moor was born in Burke county, N. C., Sept. 29th 1809; was married to Miss Mary Elvira Black in April 1824; removed to Forsyth county, Ga., in 1838; died July 25th 1877. He lost his first wife some years ago and was married in 1875 to Mrs. A. J. McCarty of Gainesville, Ga., where he resided at the time of his death. H. P. Bell

Mrs. F. A. McElvaney, whose maiden name was Thompson, was born in Walton county, Ga., April 1818; died September 16, 1877. Seven years ago she married John S. McElvaney, who survives her.

Mrs. Susie C. Martin, wife of J. Robinson Martin, and daughter of Abram Eason, of Tatnall county, Ga., died near Taylor's Creek, Ga., Sept. 9th 1877.

George Branning was born in North Carolina, June 19, 1799; died August 8, 1877, at Middleburg, Fla. His father's family removed to Florida when he was a young man, and settled on Black Creek, on a donation of land from the Spanish government. He leaves his aged companion and a family of grown up children and their families.

Sister Deborah Perry, whose maiden name was Lane, was born in Houston county, Georgia, November 25, 1829; was married to Terrel Perry, November 25, 1853; died September 23, 1877. R. L. Wiggins

Miss Nannie E. Hunton died in Macon, Ga., September 13, 1877, aged 17 years, 11 months and 13 days.

Mrs. Sarah Harley, whose maiden name was Pound, died September 18, 1877, in the 83d year of her age in Leon county, Fla. She was a native of Putnam county, Ga., where she married her first husband, Pelatiah Whitehurst. Seven children were the fruit of this marriage, all of whom lived to mature age, and two a son and daughter, survive their mother. While living for some years in Alabama, in 1828 removed to Leon county, where Mr. Whitehurst died in 1834. His widow married Rev. Jos. Harley, who also died, nearly forty years ago. E. L. T. Blake

R. J. Hancock was born in Jackson county, Ga., February 9, 1839; married Miss Sallie Pendergrass in 1868; died in Jefferson, Ga., July 6, 1877. He leaves a wife and four children. John R. Parker

Mrs. Asenath Braddy was born October 6, 1800; died in Green county, Georgia, July 9, 1877. W. P. Lovejoy

Frances A. E. Chatman, daughter of W. A. and T. E. Kile, and granddaughter of Rev. James Greene, deceased, was born May 8, 1851; died in Paulding county, Georgia, August 11, 1877. She left a husband and a child three years old. Robert P. Martyn

Mrs. Jane Winter was born near Pendleton Court house, South Carolina, September 17, 1808; and died near Camp Hill, Ala., August 19, 1877. She was the youngest child of Major James and Lydda Linn, and the wife of Charles Winter who died May 19, 1860.

Issue of October 30, 1877

Mrs. Cynthia Margaret Hawkins, daughter of X. G. and L. A. McFarland, was born February 12th 1844 in Walker county, Ga.; was married September 5, 1866 to J. C. Moore of Lake City, Fla; after his death, January 22, 1860 [sic], she returned to her father's home and was again married to Wm. Hawkins, July 22, 1875. She died July 15th 1877.

Mrs. Harriet A. Hawkins, daughter of X. G. and S. A. McFarland, was born in Walker co., Ga., Jan. 20, 1854; was married to Alex. S. Hawkins, Nov. 30, 1876, died August 8, 1877.

Mrs. Lucy Ann McFarland, consort of X. G. McFarland and daughter of Robert and Cynthia Boyle, was born Oct. 16, 1819; was married Nov. 20, 1839; and died July 25, 1877. She early in life joined the Presbyterian Church.

Willie Crumley, my grandson, who was the son of Dr. M. F. and Laura Crumley, and who died on the 18th of August at the house of Col. Robinson, his maternal grandfather, though only six years old.... W. M. Crumley

Rev. L. T. Mizelle, a local minister of the M. E. Church, South, was born in Bullock county, Ga., August 29, 1803; died in Powder Springs, Ga., Sept. 8, 1877. When a young man he removed to Jones county, thence to Laurens, where he was married to a daughter of Major McCall. He subsequently settled in Russell county, Ala. J. B. S. Quillian

Mrs. Sallie N. Williams, daughter of John A. and Mary L. Hendry, and wife of F. M. Williams of Scriven county, Ga., was born in Liberty county, Ga., January 21, 1855; was married April 17, 1873; died August 23, 1877. She left a husband and two helpless children.

Mrs. Amanda H. Footman, wife of George N. Footman, and daughter of the late George H. Fisther, was born in Leon co., Fla., October 20, 1854; died in Monticello, Fla., October 9, 1877. She leaves two sisters. R. H. Howren

Johnnie Adolphus Hogan, son of Jacob L. and Martha Hogan, was born in Kershaw co., S. C., Nov. 25, 1858; died in Lee co., Ala., October 5, 1877. He was an only child. L. F. Lloyd

Mrs. Emma E. Grambling, daughter of Mr. and Mrs. B. Manning, of Leon co., Fla., was born August 16, 1856; died Oct. 6, 1877. She had been the wife of brother I. W. Grambling only three weeks and one day. W. C. Collins

Tribute of Respect from Waldo circuit, Gainesville district, Florida Conference, to Rev. O. Eady, who died at his home in Sumter county, Fla., September 5, 1877.

Issue of November 6, 1877

Rev. William Timmons was born in Hancock county, Ga., January 18, 1799; died at the residence of her son, Rev. B. E. L. Timmons, at Cave Spring, Ga., September 18th 1877. He was twice married-- first, to Mrs. P. A. Alford; the second time to Mrs. M. B. Edison. W. F. Cook. Nashville Advocate please copy.

Mrs. S. A. E. Breedlove, wife of Rev. B. F. Breedlove of the South Georgia Conference, was born in South Carolina, February 22d 1840; was married November 8th 1859; died at Bethany, Jefferson county, Georgia, September 26th 1877. L. Pierce

Mrs. Theodora E. Hudson, whose maiden name was Abbott, was born in Sumter county, S. C., June 16, 1842; died September 9, 1877. She left a husband and three small children. James C. Stoll

James McBride Witherspoon was born in Sumter District, S. C., Jan. 11, 1811; was married to Miss Sarah Thompson, of Richmond [sic] District, August 29, 1833; removed to Apalachicola, Fla., in 1857, where he died October 7, 1877. He leaves a wife and seven children with a number of grandchildren, and has rejoined seven other children who preceded him. Wm. R. Johnson

Mrs. Phoebe M. Perdue was born in Jackson county, Ga., April 1st 1821; died in Monroe county, Ga., September 12th 1877. She was a devoted wife and a kind stepmother.

Mrs. Elizabeth Hamilton Lawrence was born in Hancock county, Georgia, and died in East Tennessee, near Mossey Creek. Her husband perished in the battle of Sharpsburg. She leaves four children. G. F. Pierce

Jas. W. Langford, son of R. H. Langford (his mother went to heaven several years before him) died October 1st 1877, aged 18 years, 6 months, and 28 days. W. C. Dunlap

Issue of November 13, 1877

Died

Mary Letitia Buford, only child of R. W. and Sallie G. Buford, was born December 7, 1875, and died October 6, 1877.

Minnie Brown, daughter of Clinton and Georgia A. Brown, died October 27, 1877, aged 4 years and 11 days.

Obituary

Mrs. Sarah Virginia Simonton, daughter of H. W. and Ann M. Cozart, was born May 14, 1849; married to Mr. J. R. Simonton, October 27, 1873; died in Atlanta, Ga., September 7, 1877.

Miss Lizzie Birch, youngest daughter of the Rev. E. P. Birch, died at Fort Deposit, Ala., in the 18th year of her age, October 19th 1877. F. L. B. shaver

Mrs. Sallie Harrison, youngest daughter of the last Rev. Wm. J. Parks, was born in Franklin county, Ga., March 23, 1840; died in Monroe county, Ga., September 18, 1877.

Duncan McArthur was born in Tatnall county, Ga., January 16th 1806; died in Montgomery county, Ga., October 17th 1877. He was buried with Masonic honors in the family graveyard, and leaves an aged widow, five children.

Mrs. E. J. Wilkinson was born in Hillsborough, Ga., in 1818; died at Chiasawhatchie, Ga., September 6th 1877. She was the daughter of Mr. John and Mrs. Sally Hill of Troup county, Ga., and the wife of Robert W. Wilkinson, whom she married in 1840.

Mrs. Mary Oswald Enecks was born in Charleston, S. C., in 1818; died September 17, 1877, in Scriven county Ga. Being left an orphan at a very tender age, she was adopted and reared by a kind friend. She leaves a husband and six children.

Frances B. Smith was born in Rockingham county, N. C., October 23d 1812; was married October 29th 1835; moved to Georgia in 1839; died August 3d 1877. She leaves a husband and eight children. Her son-in-law, Mr. James Park. Sanford Leake

James R. Moorer died in Orangeburg county, S. C., October 1, 1877, in the 78th year of his age. William Hutto

Mrs. Elizabeth Green was born in Laurens District, S. C., March 6, 1805; was married to Abram Thompson, September 4, 1851; who died in February 1853; in 1858 she married Mr. Walker Green, who still survives. When quite young she joined the Presbyterian Church. Her relatives, brother John Bennett and wife in Atlanta. W. A. Dodge

Mrs. Frances M. McCleskey, relict of James R. McCleskey, Esq., late of Jackson county, Ga., deceased, died at the residence of his daughter, Mrs. Lyle, in Athens, Ga., August 14th 1877, in the eighty-sixth year of her age.

Fanny Doolittle, adopted daughter of Rev. and Mrs. F. A. Kimbell, of the North Georgia Conference, died in Eatonton, Ga., October 19, 1877, in the 18th year of her age.

Issue of November 20, 1877

Died

In Campbell county, Ga., October 13, 1877, Jimmie Mattie Harper, youngest daughter of Robert D. and Cassie Harper, aged 2 years, 3 months and 7 days.

Lilian Young, daughter of Col. Curtis C. and Mrs. Annie Faust, died at Graham, S. C., November 6, 1877. Age nearly 3 years.

Ella Wroton, twin sister, died on the 9th of November.

Obituary

Jephthah Reynolds was born in Wilkes county, Ga., December 26, 1803; died near Notasulga, Ala., Oct. 19, 1877. In 1830 he was married to Adella H. Turner, by whom he had twelve children, eleven of whom still live. M. S. Andrews

Mrs. Jane A. Malone nee Hudson, was born in Eatonton, Ga., June 15th 1819; and died in Macon, Ga., August 11th 1877. She was married in 1838 to Col. Charles J. Malone who preceded her to the grave by a few years. Her remains were taken to Americus. Geo. G. N. MacD.

Died at McClellansville, South Carolina, October 24, 1877, Warren Palmer, third son of Andrew Hibben and Esther Ann Dupre, and grandson of Rev. Daniel DuPre. The deceased was in his tenth year.

Clementine Estelle Turnley was born at Rome, Ga., December 15th 1857; died October 14th 1877. Wm. H. LaPrade

Brother R. A. Murphy died August 31st 1877 in Sumter county, Ga., aged 43 years.

Mrs. Mary Hazelton was born at Durham, England, May 2, 1774; died at Rome, Ga., Oct. 11, 1877. She was a daughter of Sir Charles Frederic Walter and sister of Sir Charles Walter. She was left an orphan in childhood, her father having died near New York city while on a visit to America. William H. LaPrade

Mr. R. A. Benson was born in Putnam county, Ga., November 13th 1821; died in Macon, Ga., October 9th 1877. Walker Lewis

Dr. Daniel S. McBean was born in Jasper county, Ga., Oct. 19, 1832; died in Loganville, Walton county, Ga., August 19, 1877. He was first married to Miss Margaret A. L. Moore, who died June 29, 1871, leaving him two sons. On 4th of February 1874 he married Miss Fannie E. Allgood, who with his two sons, is left to mourn.

Mrs. Mattie R. Hearne, wife of R. M. Hearne, died in Gainesville, Fla., September 16th 1877, in the 29th year of her age. She came into our midst in November last from Charlotte, N. C. S. B. Smitteel. The Raleigh Christian Advocate please copy.

Mrs. Eliza Gilmore, consort of the late Dr. J. B. Gilmore, died in Charleston county, S. C., October 9, 1877, aged about fifty-one years. William Hutto

Mrs. Martha Salmons died in Marlboro county, S. C., Oct. 3, 1877, aged 24 years.

Tribute of Respect from Providence Circuit, South Carolina Conference to James R. Moorer.

Issue of November 27, 1877

Charles H. DuPont was born in Beaufort district, S. C., January 27th 1805, and died at Quincy, Fla., October 14th 1837. He was educated at the University of Georgia. About 1854 he became Associate Justice of the Supreme Court, and in 1860 was chosen Chief Justice, which office he filled till 1868. C. E. Dowman

Elbert J. Driver, Jr., son of Dr. E. J. Driver, of Opelika, Ala., was born July 24, 1855; died November 9, 1877. R. B. Crawford

Mrs. Lizzie McFarlan, wife of Dr. McL. McFarlan, and daughter of James and Amma Wright, died October 7th 1877. L. M. Hamer

Miss Tallula A. Simmons died at 16 Station, S. C., Rail Road, October 2, 1877, in the eighteenth year of her age.

Dr. James Alpheus Mallette was born in Effingham county, Ga., May 5th 1829; died in Boston, Thomas county, Ga., October 14th 1877. His father was Abraham Mallette and his mother was the sister of Rev. Wm. M. Kennedy, late of the South Carolina Conference, and the aunt of Dr. Kennedy, Editor of the Southern Christian Advocate. J. T. Ainsworth

Dr. Alexander Washington Ellerbe, son of the late Thomas G. and Caroline Ellerbe, was born in Chesterfield county, S. C., December 3, 1847[?]; was married to Miss Mary E. Ellerbe, daughter of Capt. W. Ellerbe, February 13, 1873; died October 11, 1877. A. J. Stokes

Alexander S. Murphey was born in Burke county, Georgia, August 5th 1868; died in his native county, November 1st 1877.

James Lewis Mitchell, son of J. T. and Mary Mitchell, was born in Lexington county, S. C., October 19, 1850, and died October 6, 1877.

Claiborne Trussell, son of D. L. Trussell, and grandson of Claiborne Trussell, of the North Georgia Conference, died in Carrollton, Ga., September 20, 1877, aged a little more than twelve years.

Sister Mary Camp, relict of Edmund Camp, who preceded her to the grave over fifty years ago, died August 17, 1877, being about 80 years of age. F. M. T. Brannan

Mrs. Addie J. Gramling was born Dec. 13, 1857; married to Thos. A. Gramling, of Atlanta, Ga., November 16th 1876, died September 17, 1877. J. R. Parker

Tribute of Respect from Eatonton District, Augusta District, to Hon. David Rosser Adams.

Issue of December 4, 1877

[page 194] Death of Bishop Martin. On Monday the 16th inst., Enoch M. Marvin, D. D., one of the Bishops of the M. E. Church, South, died at his residence in this city. He was born in Warren county, Mo., June 12, 1823. In August, 1839, he joined the Church at Bethlehem camp ground in St. Charles county.

Dr. A. T. Bledsoe died 16th November at his home in Alexandria.

Died

Hurbert Burns Miller, youngest son of Thos. H. and Rebeckah G. Miller, died November 6, 1877, aged 3 years, 2 months, and 2 days.

Obituary

Lizzie Harllee Graham, daughter of Mrs. Ellen H. Graham, was born in 1859; died October 4th 1877. Geo. W. Walker

Willie P. Whitten, son of Barksdale A. and Mary Whitten, was born in Laurens county, S. C., July 17th 1860; died in Union county, S. C., November 13th 1877.

Mrs. Elizabeth Leonard of Talbot county, A., daughter of Henry and Sarah Crowell, died at the residence of her son, M. W. Harvey, near Society Hill, Ala., Oct. 26, 1877, in her sixty-fifth year. She was first married to Michael Harvey, who died near Society Hill; and afterwards to Alexander K. Leonard with whom she returned to Georgia, and surviving him seventeen years. W. W. Stewart

Mrs. Nannie J. Stewart, nee Dixon, wife of William J. Stewart, died November 16, 1877, in the 34th year of her age. She was born, reared, married, and died in Sumter county, Ga. R. W. Dixon

Jno. H. Green died in his eighty-fifth year in Monroe county, Georgia, August 17, 1877. He was the son of Myles Green, one of the early Methodist preachers in Georgia, who moved from Virginia and settled his family in Hancock county, Georgia, near Sparta in about 1791, there John H. Green was born March 3, 1793. There he married Elizabeth Redding and from thence in 1823 he moved to Monroe county, Georgia. He leaves a wife and five children. J. T. Lowe

Mrs. Emma Gardner, wife of Rev. Sterling Gardner of the Florida Conference, was born in Upson county, Ga., November 25, 1838, was married August 24th 1855; joined the Methodist Church at Century Nelson, in Pike county, Ga., in August 1857. She died October 30th. John C. Ley. Nashville Christian Advocate and New Orleans Christian Advocate please copy.

Mrs. R. A. Long, wife of James Long, died in Edgefield county, S. C., October 14, 1877, in the 28th year of her age. J. A. Clifton

Mrs. Caroline J. McCants was born Oct. 23, 1813; was married to the late Robert McCants in 1832; died Sept. 4, 1877.

Tribute of Respect from Hayneville circuit, Houston county, Ga., to D. M. Brown.

Issue of December 11, 1877

Died

Daisy Mouzon Baxter, child of D. H. and Emma Baxter, died at Ridgeville, S. C., November 24, 1877, aged 2 years and 5 months.

SOUTHERN CHRISTIAN ADVOCATE NOTICES 1867-1878

Obituary

Mrs. Lou Heath, daughter of James and Nancy Stewart, of York county, S. C., was born August 23, 1835; died November 24, 1877. She married Mr. J. P. Heath, March 15, 1859; joined the Presbyterian Church, moved to Georgia in 1861, and lived in Camilla, Ga., since 1863. E. J. Rentz. Southern Presbyterian please copy.

Richard Nolley Ackerman died in Colleton county, S. C., November 8th 1877, in the 68th year of his age.

Henrietta Alice McCardell, daughter of Joshua and Almira McCardell, died in Sumter county, Fla., September 22d, 1877, aged 16 years, 8 months, and 21 days. T. K. Hall

Mrs. W. H. DeBerry, wife of W. H. DeBerry, Esq., died at Timmonsville, Nov. 14, 1877.

Mrs. Mary Beasely, whose maiden name was Campbell, was born February 10, 1809; was married to Isaiah Beasely in 1832; died November 6th 1877. She leaves a husband, several children, and grandchildren. John W. Watts

Rev. Samuel J. Bethea was born in Marion district, S. C., October 22, 1808; died near where he had spent his entire life, October 24, 1877.

Mrs. Addie Lee Williams, wife of L. O. Williams and daughter of Rev. James G. and A. E. Coston[?], of Harris county, Ga., was born July 20, 1855; died October 17, 1877. John J. Little

A. C. Shockley was born May 24, 1809; died at Dahlonega, Ga., November 14th 1877. He was married December 23, 1830.

Mrs. Emeline Bryant, daughter of Wm. and Sarah Shaw, of Chester, S. C., was born June 10th 1814 and died in Harris county, Ga., September 8, 1877. She married Mr. Thos. Bryant, May 14th 1834, and the next year they moved to Georgia. We buried her remains at Bethel Church.

Mrs. Emma Dawson Price, wife of Thos. L. Kitchens, died near Irwinton, Ga., October 10th 1877, aged 22 years. She was the daughter of John V. Price, deceased. She had been married not quite one year. A little babe of an hour was buried in her arms. T. T. Christian.

Tribute of Respect from Macon, Ga., to R. A. Benson.

Issue of December 18, 1877

Bro. Joseph Russel died in Key West, Fla., December 1, 1877, in the 73d year of his age. He was a native of Green Turtle Key, but in 1846 settled in Key West. He leaves seven children, fifty-five grandchildren, and eleven great-grandchildren. C. A. Fulwood

William S. Webster was born in Washington, Ga., Nov. 10, 1818; died near Hamilton, Ga., Oct. 29, 1877.

Bro. John Whitehurst was born in Pamlico Sound, N. C., June 27, 1783; died at Clear Water Harbor, Fla., Oct. 28, 1877. He moved to Georgia about the time he was grown; to Florida about the year 1830, and has lived in various part of the state. Bro. Daniel S. Whitehurst (brother of the above) preceded him but a short time, aged 87 years, leaving an aged widow and a large family.

John Littleton Johnston was born in Jasper county, Ga., December 23, 1832; died in Hogansville, Troup county, Ga., November 19, 1877, leaving a widow and one daughter, the wife of Dr. Thos. J. Jones. Bro. Johnston lost a leg in Confederate service. John F. Moreland

November 1, 1877, we buried little Josiah C. Flowers, daughter of John C. and Laura E. Flowers, who was born in Newton county, Georgia, September 18th 1871; died October 31, 1877.

401

SOUTHERN CHRISTIAN ADVOCATE NOTICES 1867-1878

Frances R. Graham, wife of Thompson Graham, died in Pike county, Georgia, November 30th 1877, in the 58th year of her age. J. B. Payne

Tribute of Respect from Powder Springs Circuit, Rome District, North Georgia Conference to Rev. Luke F. Mizell, a local elder.

Issue of December 25, 1877

Mrs. Elizabeth Bryan, consort of Hon. Loverd Bryan of Stewart county, was born December the 9th 1809; died at the residence of her son-in-law, A. T. Newsom, in Stewart county, Georgia, November 29th 1877. She was married in Thomas county, Georgia, January 31st, 1826, it being the first white marriage in the county.

Mrs. Ann Bonner Ebon was born in Washington, N. C., August 24, 1806. Her maiden name was Floyd. In 1826 she married John B. Ebon, and in 1830, removed to Tallahassee, Fla., where her husband died in 1842. She died in Macon, Ga., at the residence of her son-in-law, Mr. R. J. Thornton, October 28, 1877. E. L. T. Blake

Mother Judith Smith was born in June 1803. She was married first to Sterling Tison, June 23, 1823, and afterward to Alexander Smith, May 8, 1832, and died September 28, 1877.

John Wesley Hickson was born in Pike county, Ga., May 11, 1852; died in Houston county, Ga., October 9, 1877.

Henry Butts was born October 26, 1783; died in Upson county, Georgia, November 24, 1877. He was a soldier in the War of 1812, reared a large and respectable family. J. B. Payne

Mrs. Harriet Sweet, wife of James L. Sweet, and daughter of the late Hon. David Kaigler, of Terrell county, Ga., died in Sabine county, Texas, November 27, 1877, aged 58 years and 9 months.

Tribute of Respect from Spring Hill and mission, South Georgia Conference to Duncan McArthur.

Issue of January 8, 1878

James Chapman Craig was born December 4th 1815, and died November 17th 1877. He married in early life and leaves behind a wife, two sons and several daughters. Wm. Thomas

Bro. M. B. Smawly died in Lincoln county, Georgia, December 7th 1877, at about forty years of age. N. C. Ware

Mrs. Sarah A. Browning, relict of W. A. Browning, died near Twenty six station, S. C. R. R., october 9, 1877, aged 73 years. G. H. Pooser

Mrs. Christiana Keller, wife of Wm. Keller deceased, died December 5, 1877, in Orangeburg county, S. C., aged about 85 years. She died at the home of Dr. T. Keller, one of her sons.

Mrs. Sophia Myers died in Orangeburg county, South Carolina, November 5th 1877, in the 68th year of her age. Wm. Hutto

Mrs. Susan J. Jessup, daughter of Matthew and Martha Mezell, was born May 6, 1851, and died in Brooks county, Ga., Nov. 23, 1877. H. W. Sharpe

Tribute of Respect from Crawford circuit, South Georgia Conference to John S. Lee.

Issue of January 15, 1878

Died

Staunton Ellsworth, infant son of Robert L. Ivie, died December 22, 1877.

Maude L., daughter of Jas. H. and Laura A. McLester, died in Lumpkin, Ga., January 6, 1878, aged 17 months.

Obituary

Mrs. Anna M. O. Jones was born in Orangeburg county, S. C., July 25, 1835; died in Columbia, S. C., November 29, 1877. Her mother dying while she was yet quite young, she was trained by her excellent father. She was married to the Rev. W. W. Jones in 1856. Samuel A. Weber

Brother Atkisson Tabor was born in Madison county, Georgia, May 6th 1818. In 1848 he was married to Miss Priscilla Landers, who still survives him. He left four sons and a daughter.

Col. Warren Akin died in Bartow county, December 27th 1877, in the 67th year of his age. He was a member of the General Assembly, as Speaker of the House of Representatives, a member of Congress. Col. Aiken was twice married, first to a daughter of Hon. John W. Hooper, who survived her marriage but a year; second to Miss Mary F. Verdere, who wish six children, survives.

Lemuel Asbury Grier was born in Georgetown, S. C., December 16th 1816; died near the same place, November 7th 1877. He leaves a widow and seven children. C. E. Wiggins

Sarah M. Vaught, whose maiden name was Brantley, was born in Columbus county, North Carolina, May 23d 1804; married Col. Joseph Vaught, of Horry district, South Carolina; moved to Florida in 1846; died at the residence of her son-in-law, B. Haynes, Esq., in Bradford county, Florida, December 12th 1877. Of fourteen children, only two remain. J. D. Rogers

Mrs. Johnnie B. Locke, relict of Col. Michael B. Locke, and daughter of Col. Homer Blackman, died at Union Springs, Ala., November 20, 1877, in the thirty fourth year of her age. The New Orleans Christian Advocate will please copy.

Mrs. Laura Bass, daughter of W. H. and Mary J. Macy and wife of William Bass, died at her father's home in Orlando, Orange county, Florida, December 3d 1877, in her eighteenth year. J. T. Duncan

Tribute of Respect to Brother A. Tabot.

Issue of January 22, 1878

William H. Goodrich died in Augusta, Ga., Dec. 2d 1877, in the 70th year of his age. He was born Aug. 4th 1808 in Rocky Hill, Connecticut, and moving to Augusta in October 1830, that city became his place of residence for life. He was married Nov. 1st 1834 to Miss Susan C. Clark, daughter of John Clark, of Augusta, who with six sons and a daughter, survives him.

Mrs. Lucy B. Cleaveland was born in Princeton, Massachusetts, July 17th 1809; died in Monroe county, Georgia, December 28th 1877. When she was about nineteen years old, a brother a few years older than herself-- Milton Wilder, came to Georgia. She came to Monroe county to be with him. In a year or two marriage a Georgia, the late Early Cleveland.

Mrs. Sarah A. Morton died near Eatonton, Ga., at the residence of R. J. Wynn, Esq., in the 70th year of her age. She was the daughter of Capt. George and Mrs. Sarah Phillips; was born in Virginia, moved with her parents to Georgia in 1818, and settled near Greensboro, Ga. She was married in 1829 to Rev. Jas. C. Talbot of Wilkes county, by whom she had six children, three of whom preceded her to the good world. After eleven years of marriage life, her husband died. In 1854 she was married to Rev. Henry Morton of Putnam county, Ga., who died in 1863. Her two daughters, Mrs I. O. Colley and Mrs. Wynn, who lived near her. She died 21st of December 1877. C. S. Credille

Dr. Waldrup of Merriwether county, Georgia, was born in Polk county, North Carolina, April 22d 1831; removed to Georgia twenty or thirty year ago; was first married to Miss M. Jones; after her death, was married to Miss Julia A. Caldwell, daughter of Rev. J. H. Caldwell, October 18th 1870; died Nov. 3d 1877. L. Rush

Mr. John Lever was born in October 1796; and died December 26, 1877. He was a native of Lexington District, S. C., and moved in early life to Richland District, where he married Miss Nancy Smith, and resided until his death. Al of his descendants, children, grandchildren, and great-grandchildren, surviving to the number of seventy-five live near the old homestead.

John Holton was born in Houston county, Ga., June 1, 1842; moved to Mitchell county in 1852; was married to Miss Andrews, of Baldwin county, September 1871; died December 3, 1877. He leaves a wife and several small children.

Tribute of Respect from St. John's Church to William H. Goodrich.

Issue of January 29, 1878

Dr. James Jarratt Hardaway, son of the late Major Robt S. and Mrs. Martha Bibb Hardaway, was born in Columbus, Ga., June 1848; died in Monroe county, Georgia, December 20th 1877. Jas. T. Flewellen, Jr.

John Henry Wynn was born March 14, 1843; and died in Green county, Georgia, November 5, 1877. W. P. Lovejoy

Mrs. Fannie B. Perry, daughter of M. B. and E. E. Freeman, was born in Meriwether county, Ga., April 16, 1853; died in Harris county, Ga., October 29th 1877. She was married November 1st 1871 to Mr. J. P. Terry [sic].

Mrs. Lizzie M. Rice was born December 21st 1823; died at the residence of her mother, Mrs. Agnes Rice in Union county, S. C., January 4th 1878. She leaves an aged mother, several brothers and sisters. R. B. Dagnall

Edmond J. Lyon died in Lincoln county, Ga., in his seventy-second year, January 3d 1878. He leaves a wife and five small children. W. H. Trammell

Issue of February 5, 1878

Died

Frances Leola, little daughter of Bro. Warren A. and sister B. R. Pace, was born January 30, 1875, and died January 11, 1878.

Obituary

Mrs. Sallie Thweatt Raines Taylor, daughter of William E. and Jane Hayes, was born in Thomas county, Georgia, November 29th 1839; was married to George W. Taylor of Jefferson county, Florida; died January 7th 1878. E. L. T. Blake

Mrs. Lucy Beard, wife of W. N. Beard and daughter of George and Elizabeth Kendall, was born in Montgomery (now Stanly) county, N. C., June 19, 1819; died in Grenada county, Miss., Sept. 23, 1877. She removed from North Carolina tin 1869 to Yallowbusha (now Grenada) county, Miss.

Mrs. Susan M. Rees was born in Maryland, October 1796; came to Georgia with her parents when eleven years of age. died at her son's, C. M. Furlow's, in Morgan county, Ga., January 8, 1878. She was twice married--first to Charles Furlow, who did not live many years, and afterwards to John C. Rees. Soon after her marriage to Mr. Rees they moved to Madison, Morgan county. She leaves five children (three sons and two daughters). James E. England

Lucy E. Bridges, daughter of Miranda and Eleanor Fort, was born in Talbotton, Ga., July 22, 1847; died in Harris county, Ga., November 9, 1877. After her marriage to Wm. Bridges, November 12, 1867, she moved to Harris county. She leaves a husband and four children.

Mrs. R. C. W. Hays, daughter of Rev. John and Mrs. C. W. Ross, was born in Upson county, Ga., December 4, 1828; died in Neshoba county, Miss., December 9, 1877. J. A. Vance. Christian Index, please copy.

Mrs. Elizabeth Morrison was born in Cumberland county, N. C., January 1, 1803; was married August 9, 1817; moved to Georgia in 1827; died in Montgomery county, Ga., December 26, 1877. She leaves over ninety children, grandchildren and great-grandchildren.

Mrs. Mary Floyd Sessions of Conwayboro, S. C., died December 4, 1877, in the 78th year of her age. L. Wood

Tribute of Respect on the death of Rev. Osborn L. Smith, D. D., by the Faculty and students of Wesleyan Female College and one from Emory College.

Tribute of Respect from the students of the University at Georgetown, to W. M. Lewis, late Professor of Mathematics in Southwestern University.

Issue of February 12, 1878

Died

Willie P. Denny, only son of R. R. and Mary G. Denny, was born December 31, 1875, and died December 26, 1877.

Obituary

Wallis W. Lewis died in Greene county, Ga., January 3, 1878, in his 25th year. W. P. Lovejoy

Rev. W. K. Mebane, aged 43 years, was born in Richmond, Va., and died in Thomasville, Ga., January 21st, 1878. In the spring of 1876 he removed from North Carolina to Thomasville, Ga. His father was a Presbyterian minister. J. O. A. Cook

Theophilus Sapp died in Chattahoochee county, Ga., November 17th 1877. He was born in Burk county, Ga., May 8th 1808 and moved in 1830 to the home where he resided until his death. He was thrice married. In 1832 to Miss Narcissa F. Clark, in 1864 to Rebecca A. Mahone; and in 1868 to Miss Hattie H. Darnell of Virginia, who still survives him. Three children were born of the first marriage, all of whom are now living. Jos. S. Key

John Huffman, son of Samuel and Elizabeth Huffman, was born in Lexington county, S. C., January 12th 1812; died in Macon county, Ga., January 8th 1878. He was a member of the Evangelical Lutheran Church. He leaves a wife and four children. S. T. Cardell

Rev. Carey Cox was born in Edgefield District, S. C., July 23, 1795; and died in Monroe county, Ga., January 12, 1878. When he was eight years old his father moved to Jones county, Ga. Texas Christian Advocate please copy.

B. F. Ellison was born in Burke county, Ga., May 22, 1816; and died in Madison county, Fla., December 10, 1877. Mary Louisa Ellison, daughter of the above, was born May 1, 1866, died December 22, 1877.

Mrs. Penelope Mimms was born August 15th 1807; died in Darlington county, S. C., October 28th 1877. E. T. Hodges

Emanuel Allen Fairy was born March 27th 1833; died January 7th 1878. He has left a wife and three sons. Thos Raysor

Mrs. Elizabeth Tomlin, wife of Jason Tomlin, died near Newnan, Ga., January 6, 1878. Geo. A. Hardy

Mrs. Elizabeth Albina Granberry, the wife of J. J. Granberry, of Americus, Ga., died January 16, 18787, in her fifty-sixth year.

Zachariah Smith was born in Lawrence county, Ga., December 22, 1810; died at Jewells, Ga., January 20, 1878. J. L. Ivey

Issue of February 19, 1878

Died

Ethelia Gertrude, infant daughter of W. P. and Almira Ocain, died in Sawanee county, Fla., Jan. 4th 1878.

Merrie Susie, only child of Americus C. Mitchell, Jr., aged 22 months, died in Glennville, Ala., February 1, 1878. Only three weeks before the mother Mrs. Susie Dawson Mitchell passed into Paradise.

Obituary

Brother Rhesee Farmer was born in Jefferson county, Ga., November 26th 1811; died near Mount Moriah church in the same county, December 2, 1877. He leaves a widow and a large family of sons and daughters. Jas. D. Mauldin

Mrs. Ann Foster Thornton, oldest daughter of Rev. Thomas F. Pierce, and wife of Joel Thornton, died in Greensboro, Ga., January 9, 1878, in the 28th year of her age. G. F. Pierce

Mrs. Susie Dawson Mitchell died in Glennville, Ala., January 6th 1878, aged 24 years. She was the youngest child of the late Rev. Dr. Thomas H. Dawson. Jos. S. Key

Mrs. Annie Houser Reed, wife of Mr. Tully Reed, died in Barnwell county, S. C., January 3, 1878, aged about 22 years. Her mother died when she was quite young; her father, Maj. Reed was killed at Secessionville. She was taken to the home of her grandfather, Mr. Houser of St. Mathews, where she was brought up. A. J. Cauthen

Mrs. Julia Ann Foxworth, whose maiden name was Felder, was born in Orangeburg county, S. C., January 8, 1842, and died in Sumter county, S. C., November 2, 1877. James C. Stoll

Mr.[sic] Angie A. Carruth, whose maiden name was Hinson, was born in Suwannee, formerly Columbia county, Fla., November 9th 1843; died at Clear Water Harbor, Fla., January 10th 1878. She was married to W. L. Carruth in September 1865. She was the mother of six children.

John Durr died near George's station, S. C., January 19th 1878.

Ezra Connor died at George's station, S. C., January 19th 1878, in the 65th year of his age.

Issue of February 26, 1878

Dr. John Fletcher Moreland was born in Putnam county, Ga., March 20, 1817; died in LaGrange, Ga., at the residence of his son-in-law, Major D. N. Speer, January 30, 1878. He was a member of the House of Representatives from Heard county in 1851 and 1852, and a member of the Senate in 1856. Dr. Moreland married Mrs. S. A. Amoss until her death the 16th of last month.

Mrs. Rebecca Powel, whose maiden name was Ousley, relict of the late Thomas Powel, deceased, was born in Putnam county ,Ga., in 1805; died at the residence of her son in law, W. K. Clay, Esq., near Pleasant Hill, Talbot county, Ga., January 12, 1878.

William F. Brown, eldest son of E. E. Brown, Esq., was born in Macon, Ga., Jan. 8th 1839; died in the city of his birth, Jan. 13th 1878. V. Burke

William R. Henry was born April 28, 1788, and died in Campbell county, Ga., January 16, 1878. He was married to Mary Thompson, May 5, 1818; was left a widower September 4, 1842; married the second time, November 29, 1843, to Mrs. Lucy G. Wright, sister of Bishop James O. Andrew. July 8, 1870, she died. W. T. Read

Percy A. Beard, the son of Mr. John Beard, died in Columbia, S. C., in his 20th year of age.

Mrs. Nancy Wade, wife of John E. Wade and daughter of Solomon and Susan Harris of Warren county, Georgia, died in Terrell county, Georgia, January 20th 1878. J. M. Potter

John M. Kirksey, son of Gideon and Caroline Kirksey, resident in Georgia, was born August 20th 1847, and died at Jefferson, Texas, February 5th 1878. M. H. Neely

Mrs. Mary M. Sessions, relict of the late Benjamin E. Sessions, died in All Saints parish, near Conwayboro, S. C., January 23, 1878, aged 63 years and 15 days. L. Wood

Tribute of Respect from Kingston Circuit, North Georgia Conference, to Warren Aiken and Hezekiah Best.

Issue of March 5, 1878

Mrs. Flora McMillan was born in Montgomery county, N. C., February 18th 1802; died at the residence of her brother, Mr. M. McCaskill, in Marshallville, Georgia, December, 3, 1877. In 1863 she lost her noble son, Capt. John McMillan, who fell at McDowell, while leading the Twelfth Georgia Regiment in a charge. This was her only child.

Sister R. M. St. John died in Darsey county, Ark., November 26th 1877, while on a visit to her children, in the 71st year of her age. Her home was near Hogansville, Ga. W. M. D. Bond

Jesse C. Marriss, son of James and Nancy Marriss, was born in Anderson county, S. C., April 25, 1811; and died February 11, 1878. His mother, 90 years old, was able to attend his burial. he also leaves his wife, two sons and four daughters. T. P. Phillips

Mrs. Mildred J. Waterman, whose maiden name was Bostwick, was born in Augusta, Ga., February 14, 1792; died in Marietta, Ga., January 18, 1878. For over fifty years she remained in the place of her nativity. There she was twice married--first to Joshua Meals, who died about 1818; the second time to Asaph Waterman, who also preceded her to the grave by many years, his death having occurred in 1846. She leaves one daughter, Mrs. Wm. Phillips, of Marietta, Ga. W. F. Cook

Tribute of Respect from Cassville, Ga., to Rev. Warren Akin.

Tribute of Respect from Cassville, Ga., to Rev. Hezekiah Best.

Mr. Isaac Barn died in Barnwell county, S. C., January 3, 1878, aged 66 years and 28 days.

Issue of March 12, 1878

Died

Minnie Harvey Rentz, infant daughter of Rev. E. J. Rentz of the South Georgia Conference, was born June 7, 1876, and died at Camilla, Ga., March 1, 1878.

Obituary

Mrs. Nellie Candler Longino died in Palmetto, Ga., January 24, 1878, aged twenty six years, three months, and thirteen days. She was born at Villa Rica, Carroll county, Ga., but while she was quite young her parents removed to Milledgeville. After the war her parents removed to Atlanta, but soon after her father died. She lived with her brothers in law, most of the time with Mr. Young Garrett in Atlanta. She was married February 13, 1873, to Dr. T. D. Longino of Palmetto, Ga.

Rev. Hezekiah Best was born at Hagerstown, Md., April 15th 1801; died at the residence of his son, A. B. Best, in Bartow county, Ga., January 12, 1878. His father and mother both died while he was an infant, and he was left under the care of his grandmother. He was married January 29, 1833, to Adaline Ball. The issues of this marriage was six children. His wife and five children survive him. He came to Georgia in November 1857 and settled near Kingston in Bartow county.

Mrs. Harriet E. Peek, wife of William Peek, was born September 5, 1805; died in Cedar Valley, Polk county, Ga., February 14, 1878. She had been twice married; her first husband was George Turner. That only child of that union became the wife of Dr. R. W. Hubert. In 1843 she became the wife of Wm. Peek, and of that union she left one child, Mrs. Jno. O. Waddel.

Mrs. Judith B. Peacock, daughter of the late Rev. Alexander Avret of the Georgia Conference, was born in Richmond county, Ga., in 1824; died at Jackson, S. C., January 14th 1878.

Mrs. Nannie Neal Dowdell, only daughter of C. H. and M. A. Davis and wife of Louis A. Dowdell, was born at Halifax C. H., Va., March 3, 1850; died in Opelika, Ala., January 9, 1878. She leaves a husband, mother, uncle, and little son of three years, four brothers and sisters. Sister Susie

Henry B. Fraker was born in Green county, Tenn., March 7, 1851; was married to the daughter of James L. Farnesworth, April 1876; died in Whitfield county, Ga., February 14, 1878. Wm. McNabb

Mr. Green Brantley Peacock was born in Washington county, Ga., October 11th 1815; died at Jackson, S. C., January 10th 1878. He left a wife and children.

Milledge Murphy, Esq., was born in Richmond county, Ga., November 20, 1808; died near Bethany, Jefferson county, Ga., February 11, 1878. His father, Rev. Nicholas Murphy. Wm. Hauser, M. D.

Miss Nancy C. Densmore of Cleveland, Ga., died at Nacoochee, Ga., January 30, 1878, aged 17 years. J. J. Methvin

Issue of March 19, 1878

Col. Charles Walker was born in Burke county, Ga., in 1800, and after spending fifty three years in his native state, moved to Faunsdale, Marengo county, Ala., where he resided until his death, January 1st 1878.

Sarah S. Ezzard, wife of Judge William Ezzard, died in Atlanta, Ga., February 8th 1878, in the 67th year of her age.

Daniel Riley of Orangeburg county, South Carolina, died January 2d 1878, in the 79th year of his age. M. L. Banks

Mrs. Sallie C. Baskin, wife of John W. Baskin and daughter of T. G. L. and Nancy L. Powell, was born June 29, 1854; and died February 20, 1878. She leaves an infant about eighteen months old, a husband, father and mother, five brothers and three sisters.

Mrs. Rebecca S. Colbert, wife of John G. Colbert, died in Bartow county, Ga., January 22, 1878. She was daughter of the late T. H. Audas, of Sparta, Ga., at which place she was born March 15, 1829. Married in 1858. A husband and four sons survive. John T. Norris. The Texas Christian Advocate will please copy.

John P. Haigler, died in Orangeburg county, S. C., December 27th 1877, aged 28 years, 3 months and 27 days.

Sister Mary J. H. Spell, whose maiden name was Rhoda, was born January 4, 1862; and died near Summerville, S. C., December 11, 1877. A sorrowing husband, father and mother mourn. G. H. Pooser

Mrs. Elizabeth Ann McPherson died February 9th 1878, in the 59th year of her age. She joined the Presbyterian church 38 years ago.

Issue of March 26, 1878

Died

In Jacksonville, Fla., March 11, 1878, Sidney Doggatt Pasco, youngest son of Rev. F. and Mrs. M. C. Pasco, of the Florida Conference, aged six months and eight days.

John English Bostick, son of John S. and Anna J. Bostick, was born February 14, 1851 and died February 1, 1878.

Near Barnett, Warren county, Ga., March 8, 1878, Edward A. Harris, son of Rev. I. C. and Mrs. M. A. Harris, aged 4 years and 19 days.

Obituary

Rev. Samuel Harwell was born near Sparta, Ga., January 17th 1805; and died at Opelika, Ala., January 1, 1878. While he was quite young, his father removed to Putnam county, Ga., where he was brought up. On the 12th of February in this year, he was married to Emily Frances Slaughter, near Milledgeville, Ga., who still survives. R. H. Crawford

Cotesworth Logan, son of Rev. Thomas A. and Mary A. Carruth, was born in Columbia county, Fla., September 7th 1855; died in Tampa, Fla., February 14th 1878. In 1867, he joined the Presbyterian Church.

Mrs. Felicia Perry Bergman Halcombe, youngest daughter of Rev. Edwin A. and Mrs. Harriet A. Bollee, was born in Charleston, S. C., July 12, 1846; died at the residence of her father in Columbia, S. C., February 11, 1878.

Mrs. Fannie Reid, consort of Alexander Reid, and daughter of Mrs. N. Whitfield, deceased, died in Atlanta, Ga., February 19, 1878, in the 48th year of her age.

Mrs. T. M. Thomason, wife of Robert Thomason, died in Greenville, S. C., February 8th 1878, aged about 60 years. She had been a member of the Baptist Church for several years, but after her marriage with Bro. Thomason, she joined the Methodist Church. Her daughter, by a previous marriage, joined the Methodist Church before her. She leaves two children, both grown and one married, and an aged husband. A. Coke Smith

Arabella H. Davenport, daughter of Willis and Lydia Hodges, was born in Twiggs county, Ga., July 24, 1825; was married in the 18th year of her age to Smith Davenport, of Houston county, Ga. They settled in Buena Vista, Ga. Removed to Mississippi, and died 6th of January last. She died in Madison county, Fla. Robt. J. Hodges

Samuel J. Higgins was born in Gwinnett county, Ga., October 24th 1851; died in Bartow county, Ga., January 24th 1878. A. C. Arnold

Tribute of Respect from East Point Circuit, Atlanta District, to William Avery who died December 19, 1877, aged 83 years.

Tribute of Respect from Crawfordville circuit, Fla., to J. S. Mooring.

Issue of April 2/3, 1878

Mr. Joseph Edwin Pinson was born in Oglethorpe county, Ga., but removed to Floyd in his early married life, in which county he died February 6, 1878, aged 59 years.

Miss Mattie E. Trussell was born November 16, 1855, and died near McDonough, Ga., March 3, 1878. Richard W. Rogers

The Rev. Francis Asbury Kimbell of the North Georgia Conference, was born in Morgan county, N. C., August 25, 1829; died in Atlanta, Ga., February 12, 1878. He was the son of Rev. Nathan Kimbell, formerly of the Virginia Conference. W. F. Cook

Mrs. Elizabeth Adams, daughter of William and Sarah Johnson, was born in Abbeville District, S. C., August 25, 1824; died in Edwardsville, Cleburne county, Ala., March 3, 1878. Her father died when she was only three years old, after which her mother married Mr. Waters, who removed to Coweta county, Ga., where she was brought up. She was married March 2, 1842 to Thomas Adams. Wm. T. Noell

Barney M. Quillian was born March 9, 1858; died January 28, 1878, in White county, Ga.

Mrs. Eliza F. Peeler, wife of David H. Peeler, died at Rutherford College, Burke county, N. C., March 1, 187, in her 57th year. J. S. Ervin

Mr. Benjamin F. Baxter died at No. 41 Station, S. C. R. R., S. C., February 3, 1878, in the thirty fifth year of his age. He leaves an aged mother, three brothers and two sisters. G. H. Pooser

Tribute of Respect from Boston, Ga., to J. A. Mallette.

Issue of April 9, 1878

Mrs. Lydia Humphreys, daughter of Jeremiah Harrison, was born in North Carolina, January 27, 1815; was married to Joab Humphreys in Carroll county, Georgia, November 24, 1836; died in Murray county, Georgia, March 11, 1878. A short time after her marriage, her father and mother, with herself and husband moved to Murray county, Georgia, where they all lived and died. Her remains were deposited beside her husband's at Mt. Zion church. John Oates

Samson J. Coleman, son of Rev. M. Coleman, was born in Marion county, S. C., and died at Nichols, S. C., March 14th 1878. He leaves a wife and many relatives. J. Thos. Pate

Dr. David S. Brandon was born in Gwinnett county ,Ga., in 1821; died in Thomasville, Ga., March 11th 1878. Thos. T. Christian

Mrs. Sarah E. Smith, daughter of Henry and Elizabeth Hardin, was born in Chester county, S. C., October 3, 1839; was married to Charles B. Smith, November 6, 1856; and died January 6, 1878. M. H. Pooser

John H. Moody died in Marion county, S. C., February 21, 1878. J. Thos Pate

Mrs. Tabitha A. Steed was born in Anderson county, Tenn., January 20th 1818; married to Henry Steed of Murray county, Ga., October 30th 1839; died December 28, 1877. Her aged husband, two sons, daughter, daughter in law were members of the Baptist Church. Joan Oatis

Mrs. Anna Malone Callaway, daughter of D. R. and Eliza Adams, of Eatonton, Georgia, was born January 5, 1853; married Mr. J. T. Callaway, October 22, 1874; died in Mitchell county, Georgia, January 21, 1878. Her mother died when she was but seventeen days old and she was taken by her aunt, Mrs. C. J. Malone, of Americus, Ga. E. J. Rentz

Samuel Wragg Capers was born in Camden, S. C., January 5th 1852; died in Columbia, S. C., March 10th 1878. W. S. Wightman

F. C. Davis, aged 67 years, died near Lumpkin, in Stewart county, Ga., January 26, 1878.

Issue of April 16, 1878

Mrs. Elizabeth Trippe, whose maiden name was McGhee, died in Eatonton, Ga., January 14, 1878, in the 74th year of her age. She was thrice married--first to Mr. Balke, then to Mr. Perry, and lastly to Mr. Henry Trippe of precious memory. She is mourned by her grandchildren.

Rev. S. J. H. Sistrunk, a local elder of the M. E. Church South, was born in Orangeburg, S. C., September 9, 1818; settled near Perry, Ga., 1843; died in Fort Valley, March 6, 1878. In the old Perry grave-yard, beside the wife of his youth. J. B. McGehee

Rev. Thomas P. Mellard was born in Charleston county, S. C., and died in the same county, March 5th 1878, in the seventy-sixth year of his age. He leaves a wife and eleven children. J. B. Platt

Mrs. Elizabeth B. Beall, whose maiden name was Mabry, was born in Jasper county, Ga., August 14, 1807; died in Thomaston, Ga., March 17, 1878. In 1824 she was married to Mr. Thomas Beall of Monticello, Ga.

Doctor Lewis Dantzler was born in Orangeburg county, S. C., August 11, 1813, and died in the same county, January 30, 1878. He leaves a wife and eight children.

Judge Joshua Harlan was born in Jackson county, Ga., April 4, 1822, and moved with his father to Walker county in its early settlement in 1837. He was married to Miss Sarah A. Haralson, May 3, 1848. He died March 26, 1878. His son, Rev. Vincent V. Harlan, of the Arkansas Conference.

Hervey M. Cleckley, son of Dr. H. M. and Mrs. Fannie Cleckley, died in Charleston, S. C., February 25, 1878, aged 21 years and 3 months. Jno. A. Porter

Sister Kate McRae, daughter of Roderick Morrison, was born near Fayetteville, N. C., about the commencement of the present century. She moved to Florida about thirty five years since; died February 22, 1878, aged about 75 years. J. D. Rogers

Issue of April 23, 1878

Eugene Aubrey Knight was born in Macon, Georgia, March 28, 1852; died in Atlanta, Ga., February 21, 1878. On 22d September 1874, he was married to Miss Julia T. Taylor, only daughter of the late Dr. J. A. Taylor of Atlanta, Ga. W. F. Cook

Mrs. Margaret Jordan, whose maiden name was Holland, wife of Rev. Wm. J. Jordan, was born in Sumter District, S. C., April 1st 1825; died near Reidsville, Tatnall County, Georgia, February 18, 1878. She was married August 15, 1844 and moved to Tattnall County, Ga., November 1851. She left her husband and eight children. W. F. Conley

Mrs. Winifred Pauline Smith Emery was born in Haywood county, N. C., July 29th 1835; died in Brunswick, Ga., January 4th 1878. She was married to Mr. D. B. Emery, January st 1867.

Mrs. Willie C. Cunningham, daughter of William and Hannah W. Watts, and wife of James S. Cunningham, was born in Fayette county, Ga., February 20, 1823; removed with her parents to Cass, now Bartow, county, in 1835; was married in 1841; died February 19, 1878.

Mrs. Lizzie Brown, wife of Dr. Walter G. Brown, daughter of Rev. Asa Chandler, of Elberton, Ga., a Baptist minister of excellent character, was born August 27, 1845; was married June 25th 1868; died at Atlanta, Ga., April 1st 1878. H. H. Parks. Christian Neighbor please copy.

Mr. Matthew C. Raiford, of Quitman, Ga., died at his father's residence, Rev. Capel Raiford, in Boston, Ga., March 14th 1878, in the 29th year of his age.

Mrs. Eliza Auldred, daughter of Henry R. and Mary Pool, was born in Warren county, Ga., October 21st 1823; died March 27th 1878. J. W. Folsom

Mrs. Martha A. Legett, wife of the Rev. David Legett, daughter of the late John Richardson, of Britton's Neck, Marion, S. C., died March 16, 1878, in the 69th year of her age. J. B. Young

Mrs. Anna C. Nabers, wife of Samuel Nabers, and youngest daughter of Dr. W. A. and Mrs. Elizabeth McSwain, late of the S. C. Conference, died March 27th 1878, in the 30th year of her age. in January 1866, the Rev. Sidi H. Browne preached the funeral sermon of her honored father. She joined the Church at Laurens C. H., S. C. She leaves a husband and five children. J. K. McCain

Mrs. Electra A. Drane died in DeSoto county, Miss., January 13, 1878. She was the daughter of Reuben and Nancy B. Haughton, and was born in Greene county, Ga., February 8, 1823. She was formerly the widow of Rev. James B. Jackson, who was a member of the Florida Conference. She was married the late time to Hiram Drane, of DeSoto county, Miss., January 7, 1875.

Mrs. Lucia Cromer Dacus was born August 30, 1854; died February 13, 1878, in Williamston, South Carolina.

Issue of April 30, 1878

Died

Wightman Meynardie DePass, son of Rev. J. P. DePass of the Florida Conference, died in Archer, Fla., April 16, 1878, aged 2 years, and six months.

Obituary

Emma Capers Nelson, daughter of the late Rev. and Mrs. S. W. Capers, was born October 19th 1850; was married to J. R. Nelson, December 30th 1875, and died in Camden, S. C., March 30th 1875. John O. Wilson

John Howard was born in Jackson county, Tenn., August 23, 1800; died in Tuskegee, Ala., February 21, 1878. He was married to Lucinda Jennings, March 24, 1824; From this union sprang twelve children. Of these, eight preceded him and four are following in his footsteps. He came to Tuskegee in 1835. E. L. Loveless

Emma E. Goss, daughter of Dr. I. J. M. Goss, of Marietta, Ga., was born October 8, 1863; died April 1, 1878.

Mrs. Martha Ware Leonard, widow of the late James P. Leonard, was born in Lincoln county, Ga., October 24, 1807; died in Talbot county, Ga., January 24, 1878. She left children and grandchildren.

Mrs. Mary Elizabeth Montfort, whose maiden name was Dugger, was born in Brunswick county, Va., August 17, 1829; died near Butler, Ga., March 10, 1878. Her father moved from Virginia in 1837; to Crawford county, Ga., where she married Joel E. Montfort, and moved to Taylor county.

Col. Richard S. Hill was born near Andersonville, S. C., December 26, 1822; died at his residence at Anderson C. H., S. C., March 23, 1878.

Burr Ragsdale was born in South Carolina, August 20th 1825; removed to Georgia in 1834; died in Hogansville, G., March 22, 1878. W. M. D. Boyd

Sampson J. Coleman was born October 29, 1824; died in Marion county, S. C., March 14, 1878. He was the son of Rev. Moses Coleman of precious memory. He leaves a widow. S. J. Hill

Mrs. Sarah E. Barnes, wife of Rev. Jos. F. Barnes, was born in North Carolina, November 15th 1828; died in Hernando county, Fla., March 7th 1878. N. Z. Glenn

Miss Ella S. Bussy, daughter of D. J. and L. C. Bussy, was born August 7th 1859; died in Senoia, Coweta county, Ga., April 1st 1878.

Mrs. Mary A. E. Cantey was born in Williamsburg District, S. C., November 7, 1805; died at the residence of her son, J. S. Cantey, in Clarendon county, S. C., February 19, 1878. Her father, Mr. Samuel Bennett, a class-leader. On February 3, 1825; she was married to Mr. William J. E. Cantey, by whom she had thirteen children, eight of whom survive her. D. J. McMillan

George W. Watters was born in Newton county, Ga., January 20th 1824; died at Rome, Ga., March 20th 1878.

Robert C. Hamer was born in Marlboro District, S. C., October 15,1801; was married t Miss Mary Bethea in 1828; died in Marion county, S. C., January 28, 1878. A few years after his marriage, Mrs. Hamer died, leaving four small children, three of whom still survive.

James Edward Mathis, son of Manning and Minerva Mathis, was born October 1, 1862; died in Camden, S. C., February 22, 1878. John O. Willson

Sister Nancy Brock was born Feburary 26, 1827; died January 12, 1878. Wm. Thomas

David Harrison Smith was born July 4, 1835; died in Camden, S. C., Feburary 21, 1878. John O. Willson

Peter Vanlandingham was born in Wilkinson county, Ga., October 21st 1821; died in Decatur county, Ga., February 26th 1878.

C. D. Oak of Jacksonville, Florida, died April 4th 1878, in the forty-fourth year of his age. He was a native of Vermont. H. B. Frazer

Issue of May 7, 1878

Mrs. Mary H. Lowman was born in Richland District, S. C., January 26, 1805; died in Cartersville, Ga., April 4, 1878. From 1833 to 1853 she was the wife of Rev. Joseph Lowman. In the latter year he died leaving her eight minor children. J. H. Baxter

Mrs. Jane Clark Smith, wife of the late Guy Smith and daughter of Hon. William Clark, of Clark county, a., was born December 25th 1800; married and removed to Morgan county, Ga., in 1817; died in Madison, Ga., January 30th 1878.

Mrs. Martha N. Hyatt, nee Satterwhite, wife of Thomas Hyatt, was born in Chester county, S. C., September 21, 1808; died Feburary 1, 1878. M. H. Pooser

Henry H. Conley was born June 4, 1796; died Feburary 28, 1878. He was a native of Burke county, N. C., was married to Nancy Brown in 1822, and in a few years after moved to Georgia and settled in what was then Habersham, but is now White county. He reared eleven children, all of whom except two survive their father--one of whom married the Rev. John M. Richardson, who died near Dalton in 1872.

Mrs. Lucy Ann Hill, maiden name Turner, daughter of Mrs. M. T. Hamilton, and step-daughter of J. T. Hamilton, died in Chattooga county, Ga., February 13, 1878, aged forty-eight years, five months, and twenty-seven days. She was married to William Hill, January 1854. During the late was her husband died and left her with five children. J. B. McFarland

Mrs. Leonora A. Martin, wife of James C. Martin, Esq., died in Cuthbert, Georgia, April 6th 1878, aged 37 years. She was the daughter of Mr. A. V. Keen, who moved with his family from Georgetown, S. C., to Decatur county, Ga. C. J. Munnerlyn

Mrs. Sarah J. Skinner, aged forty-five years, died in Macon county, Ga., April 20, 1878.

Thomas Early died in Morgan county, Ga., February 27, 1878, in the 24th year of his age. J. W. Knight

James R. Robinson was born August 15, 1834; died in Alachua county, Fla., April 21, 1878. He leaves a wife and four children. A. Peeler

Issue of May 14, 1878

Brother John D. Parker died 29th of March 1878, in the 80th year of his age.

Mr. Charles Dickinson Forbes was born in Jasper county, Ga., September 18, 1822; was married to Miss Elizabeth Winford Perry, August 12, 1845; died March 20th 1878 near Silver Spring, Marion county, Fla. He was buried in the graveyard at Fort McCoy. J. D. Rogers

Mrs. Louisa Ellen Daniel, daughter of the late Josiah and Elizabeth Wise, of Coweta county, Ga., was born August 4, 1836; married to Andrew J. Daniel, February 20, 1853; died at her home in Carrollton, Ga., February 25, 1878.

Mrs. Ella R. Norris, wife of Rev. John T. Norris, and daughter of Mr. R. R. DeJarnette, of Eatonton, Ga., died in Cartersville, Ga., April 28, 1878. She was born in Putnam county, Ga., in 1838, and married in 1860. She was blessed with five children, the eldest of whom preceded her to the better land. L. J. Davies

Sister Elizabeth Bradford was the daughter of James and Sarah Griffin; was born January 28, 1803; in Montgomery county, Ga.; was married to Mr. William Bradford of the same county, March 4, 1818; died March 2, 1878, aged seventy five years, one month and four days. She was the mother of twelve children, sixty-four grandchildren, and fifty-two great grandchildren. J. T. Webb

Mrs. Margaret A. Strange, wife of L. B. Strange, was born in Spartanburg, S. C., in 1818; died in Chatooga county, Ga., February 19, 1878. She left a husband and five children.

Mrs. Harriet Glaze, wife of William Glaze, Esq., died April 24th in the fifth-ninth year of her age. She had been a member of Washington street Methodist Episcopal Church of Columbia, South Carolina, for forty-five years.

J. Belton Long, son of H. W. and Mary A. Long, was born in Marion county, Fla., January 8th 1859 and died at his father's residence in said county, March 30th 1878. H. W. Long

Mrs. Sarah J. Cravey, daughter of Alfred and Sarah Burnham, was born in Telfair county, Georgia, June 11th 1842; died March 16. 1878, was married to Mr. John Cravey, June 12th 1870. She left three children of her own, one son and two daughters, a husband, and numerous relatives.

Issue of May 21, 1878

Bro. John D. Cook died in Burke county, Ga., February 22, 1878. Born December 22, 1805, he had just entered his 73d year. His native place was New Kent county, Va., where he was reared to manhood. In 1830 he moved to Georgia, and settled in Richmond county. Here he married Mrs. Louisa N. Holcomb, and soon after moved to Burke county. He leaves a widow, seven children (all married but one) and eighteen grandchildren.

James H. Royal died May 8, 1878, in Augusta, Georgia, at the residence of her son-in-law, Mr. John T. Miller. He was born in Burke county, Georgia, January 15, 1811, and was in the 68th year of his age. Clement A. Evans

Mrs. S. A. Pooser, daughter of D. F. and M. E. Spigner, and wife of Frank M. Pooser, was born in Orangeburg county, S. C., September 22, 1847; died April 29, 1878. S. D. Dantzler. Christian Neighbor will please copy.

Hugh, only son of Rev. Julius Gardner (deceased) and Mrs. Lou Gardner, formerly of Butler, Ga., died at Bolling, Ala., April 1st 1878, aged 11 years, 3 months, and 15 days.

Mrs. Mary F. Turnipseed, of Hampton, Ga., died April 16, 1878. She was born in Richland District, S. C., October 13, 1808; Her maiden name was Dubard. In 1826 she married Mr. Henry Turnipseed.

Mrs. Catharine Metts-maiden name Smith- was born in Lexington district, South Carolina, in 1795; died at the house of Mr. Coogler, her son in law, in Jonesboro, Georgia, Mar 4th 1878, in the 83rd year of her age. Jno. M. Bowden

Issue of May 28, 1878

Mrs. Alice E. Starr, daughter of Wm. Griffin, Sen., was born in Spalding county, Ga., on the 7th of January 1853 and died in Orange county, Fla., on the 25th of March 1878. She was married in 1875 to Dr. J. P. Starr. Their only child, little Harry.

The Rev. Isaiah Stalvey died at his residence in Socastee, Horry county, S. C., on the morning of the 3d of April 1878, in the 64th year of his age. L. Wood

Mrs. Mary Elizabeth Cantrell, daughter of Benj. and Martha E. Johnson, was born at Ellijay, Ga., November 22d, 1844; died at Americus, Ga., April 12th 1878.

W. H. Smith was born March 23, 1835; died in Orangeburg county, S. C., April 26, 1878. He leaves a widow and six children. A. J. Cauthen

Mary (--) 115
Massie (--) 96
Wm E 98
ALFORD, H H D 153
Margaret (--) 153
P A (--) 397
ALFRIEND, Benjamin C
90
Edward D 104
Minnie O (Houston)
303
ALGOOD, Emily (Brice)
309
ALLCORN, G B 282
George Augustus 282
ALLEN, -- 246
-- (--) 99, 194, 228,
246, 381
-- (Arnold) 208
-- (Kendrick) 60
-- (Steger) 220
A 220
Alexander A 381
Amanda 92
Andrew J 340
B L 35
Beverly 92
Bryan 7
Caroline (--) 35
Clarence 56
Denis 133
Eliza Boring 246
Emanuel 208
Frances (--) 37
Frank 199-200
Geo 228, 241
Geo D 381
Hugh 18
Ida F 37
J A 199-200
J R 83
John C 93
John Collinsworth 94
Joshua Soule 56
Josiah 60, 254
Josiah S 310
Julia E (Redding) 183
Julia F 338
Julian 56
L Q 56
Lucretia E 133
Luella 56
M M (--) 83
M S 334
Margaret L 37
Margaret M (Mills) 56
Mary (--) 77, 133,
224
Mary C 279
Mary D 290
Mary P (--) 235
Mary W (--) 199
Nancy (Tucker) 208

Nancy A (--) 309
Nancy H (Stanley) 7
Robert 365
Robert Anderson 203
Rufus 183
Sally (--) 92
Sarah A (Atkinson)
254
Silas D 37
Susan T 224
Thomas 224
Thomas J 127
Virgil 208
W G 6, 14
Washington 338
William C 77
William Price 83
ALLGOOD, -- (--) 164
Fannie E 399
William 164
ALLISON, Margaret 59
Margaret (--) 59
Wm 59
ALSABROOK, Asa 14
Mahala (--) 14
Mary 14
ALSTON, Fannie K 343
Philip C 279
Susannah P (Cook) 112
W J 343
William J 112
Wm J 279
AMMONS, Mary
(Alsabrook) 14
Richard 14
AMOSS, Beverly 249
Mary E (--) 249
S A (--) 406
ANDERSON, --
(Hollinshead) 6
Annie E (--) 316
Dorothea Jane 107
Drucilla Chandler
(Lake) 266
E F 378
Elijah 370
Eliza J 311
Elizabeth 106, 116
Fannie 379
George 106
Hattie S (--) 119
Irene S (Winship) 210
J 24, 57, 62, 64, 73,
269
James B 122
Jimmie 378
John 273, 311
Joseph E 151
Josephus 23, 50, 66,
141, 160, 189-90,
207-08, 217, 222,
241, 256, 260, 271,
309, 320, 323

Julia (--) 116
L G 218, 384
L J (--) 310
Louis F 210
Malinda Jane
(Ashley) 151
Margaret (--) 378
Maria Stobo (--) 131
Mary (--) 183
Mary Ella (Ezzard) 96
Nancy (--) 106
Nina May 316
Phoebe H (Clarke) 370
Rebecca Caroline
(Hollinshead) 236
Robert A 96
Susan 173
T B 119
Thomas Benton 119
Thos J 316
Tolbert 116
W D 310
W J 6
Wade 131
Wm J 236
ANDREW, -- 59, 104,
107, 193, 331, 378
-- (--) 129
-- (Wingfield) 331
Ann Leonora (--)
(Greenwood) 291
Elizabeth M 59
James O 106, 407
James Osgood 129
Jas O 291
John 129
Lucy G 107, 407
ANDREWS, -- 351, 404
-- (--) 351
A M 129
Alice Bayne (--) 261
Benjamin 100
C C 351
David 346
Dorcas 294
E E 100
Elizabeth (--) 129,
182
Elizabeth (Smith) 227
H 165
H S 359
John S 290
Lewis H 261
Lilly A (Williams)
245
M S 398
Mary S (Robstean) 351
R W 245
Samuel R 182
William G 302
Wm G 129, 227
ANSLEY, A 179
Abel 218

418

William 198-99
BALLARD, Jesse 378
July Ann (Mayfield)
269
M F (--) 192
Mary (Ballenger) 378
Ossie Theodore
Buckman 192
William 269
Wm H 192
BALLEN, Cynthia 90
BALLENGER, John 378
Mary 378
BALLEW, David L 205
E Louisa (James) 205
John G 11
Mary Ann (--) 11
BALLOUGH, Lucretia
(--) 4
BANCROFT, J 32, 339
BANISTER, -- 305
Mary Ann (--) 305
BANKS, -- (--) 311
Albert G 344
Calvin W 134
D M 349, 394
James 62
James B 56
Jane R (--) 56
Lilly 138
M E (--) 134
M Galenia 56
M L 266, 347, 353,
372, 408
Martha 333
Ruth A 37
Sallie 56
Sarah E (--) 138
Thomas L 138
Vicy (Harman) 62
W A 134
William Asbury 311
BARBER, Allurah C 189
E W (Harden) 306
Elizabeth W (--) 189
James A 245
Joseph 79
Matilda (Crawford)
245
Nathaniel C 189, 306
R W 200, 205, 310
William 205
BAREFIELD, Frederick
114
Jane (--) 114
B A R I N E A U, Ann
Elizabeth
(Howren) 230
R J 230
BARINO, Charles 71
BARKER, J H 103
Lucy 103
Mary A (--) 103

BARKSDALE, Bannister A
297
J H 154
James 358
Lafayette W 257
Mollie 358
BARLOW, Dennis 51
Rebecca Bailie
(Hill) 51
Wilsoon W 194
BARN, Isaac 407
BARNARD, Fannie A 254
BARNES, -- 25
Britton 393
Catharine M
(McEntire) 288
Darling 292
Eliza J (Anderson)
311
Elizabeth (Legett)
393
F N 172
Henrietta J (--) 234
James J 112
Jesse 288
John J 311
Jos F 412
Josephine Virginia
Lewis (Lampkin) 172
Mary (--) 112
Rebecca (Houck) 112
Sarah E (--) 412
Theresa N 115
BARNETT, -- (Moreland)
276
Amanda 134
Anna J (Thomas) 154
Clara B 392
Cynthia A 308
Fracis (--) 140
J W 295, 394
James 176
John E 154
John N 321
Lucy A (--) 321
Mary A (Perry) 176
N C 134
Patrick J 65
R H 155, 234, 257
Wm S 276
BARNETTE, Belle
(Swearingen) 62
Jno B 62
BARNHARDT, E R 123
BARNUM, Daisy 180
Floretta S (--) 180
Jas K 180
BARR, Ann (--) 192
Henry R 40
Nathan 338
Rebecca (Emanuel) 338
Walter 192
BARRET, T J 67

BARRETT, -- (Glascock)
87
Charles S 148
Harriet 297
Lizzie Reams 148
Mary (--) 179
Mary L (--) 148
R J 377
Rowena J (Hood) 377
Sarah E (Inabnit) 372
T J 179, 188
William 178, 188
BARRINEAU, Charles
Reed 320
BARRON, Sabrina J
(Stewart) 293
Thomas 293
BARROW, Benjamin W
334
David C 334
Lucy J 49
Mary A F (--) 49
William 49
BARRY, George L 59
BARSH, Eugenia Irvin
(--) 182
George 182
BART, Mary K 261
BARTLET, Betsey (--)
165
George 165
Susan Ludiwick 165
BARTLOW, Anna (--) 1
Willoughby 1
BARTON, Ann (--) 254
Anna E (--) 3
Annan E 333
Eliza (--) 333
Fannie 242
Floyd Willoughby
De Gilsie 3
Mary Ann (Raysor) 357
Theophilus 357
Thos 333
W F 354
Willoughby 3
BARTOW, Willie 1
BARWICK, Martha (--)
394
Martha Ann L 112
Sarah A M ( ) 112
William 394
Wm J 112
BASCOM, -- (Howard) 55
BASKIN, Henrietta (--)
96
Henrietta W
(Harrison) 161
James 96, 161
John W 408
M J 96
Sallie C (Powell) 408
BASS, Charles H 195

Lucy (--) 186
Martha G 186
BILLINGSLEA, Cyrus 24
Mary C (Chatfield) 24
BILSBURG, Samuel 242
BINGHAM, Benetta (--)
311
BININS, James D
(Morris) 117
BINION, -- 311
Laura Ann 311
BINNS, Sarah (Kenrick)
352
BIRCH, E P 32, 62, 72,
397
Lizzie 397
BIRD, Andrew C 237
Daniel 24, 187, 304
Eliza (--) (Wilson)
180
Elizabeth (--) 38
Ella 194
Israel L 124
James Lee 124
Lilly (--) 304
Louisa 187
Mary (Jones) 304
Mary Elizabeth (--)
69
Pickens 194
Sarah L (--) 124
U S 114, 304
BIRDSON, Robert 48
BIRDSONG, -- 378
Albert H 146
E F 24
Edgar E 377-78
Harriet Elizabeth
(Clarke) 24
Mary H (--) 28
Willie B (Culver)
377-78
BISHOP, Hannah 305
James 321
Mary (--) 321
Saxon 321
BIVINGS, Albert W 342
H E (--) 348
Hattie E 348
Jas 79, 348
Sarah E (Cleveland)
342
BIVINS, Mary E 317
Nancy (--) 317
Samuel 317
BLACK, -- 188
-- (--) 50
Aaron C F 122
Bettie P (Holloway)
123
C B 45
Carey A 123
Caswell 23

Caswell B 268
E B 50
E L T 233
Eliza Ann 293
Elizabeth A (--) 8
Ella C 114
Fannie A (Johnson)
268
Frances A (Johnson)
45
George R 153
Georgia Ann Eliza
(Bryan) 153
John B 8
Joseph 80
Joseph M 225
Joseph S 74
Lemuel 78
Leona 237
Margaret (Stillwell)
74
Mary A 78
Mary E 23
Mary Elvira 395
Mary Jane 50
Nancy (--) 104, 342
Nathaniel S 132
R C 319
S A (--) 23
Sarah A (Smith) 268
Uriah 342
W H 104
BLACKBURN, George W
337
John L 377
Lavonia H 377
BLACKLIDGE, Edward
347
N C (--) 347
Sallie M 347
BLACKMAN, -- 217
-- (--) 249
Elizabeth (Young) 217
Homer 403
Jas 217
Joab 298
Johnnie B 403
Sallie 249
Susan Rebecca
(Gibbs) 298
BLACKMON, David R 97
BLACKSHEAR, David 242
E J 242
Mary P 242
BLACKSTON, James H 93
BLACKWELL, Donton 138
Elizabeth (--) 138
Emily (--) 108
Joseph 108, 138
Linsay 108
BLAIR, William J 371
BLAKE, A C F 264
Catherine (--) 293

E L T 100, 141, 146,
154, 159, 194, 231,
264, 293, 296, 330,
343, 354, 360, 363,
395, 402, 404
John 293
Virginia F (West)
(Moore) 264
W K 158
BLAKELY, Amanda R
(Caldwell) 387
J M 387
BLAKENEY, J W 310
Louisa (Blakeney) 310
M V (--) 310
BLALOCK, D 183
James M 178
Margaret (Lewis) 45
Virginia G (--) 329
W H 45, 330
Zadock 45
BLANCH, Eva 148
BLASINGAME, J S 240
M E 167
BLASSENGAME, James B
286
M E 286
BLEASE, Elizabeth
Virginia (--) 172
BLEDSOE, A T 400
Catharine (--) 62
Jennette 62
John 62
BLITCH, -- 305
Elijah 86
Henrietta G (Warren)
168
Sarah (--) 86
Sarah (Zeltro) 305
Simeon 168
BLOOD, C H 285
Mary A M (Harris)
(Oneal) 285
BLOODWORTH, Fanizy
(--)
57
Thomas 57
BLOUNT, -- (--) 334,
340
A P 334
Freeman W 340, 376
G Adolphus 334
G Anna (--) 334
Paulina P 376
Sallie A 67
Sarah Twiggs 83
BLOW, B F 23
BLUE, Ann E (--) 133
Annie J 133
O R 133
BLUNT, Lavinia A 111
Thos 111
BLYTHE, Bethena (Ward)

424

C W 21, 115
Elizabeth (--) 139
Elizabeth J (Rice) 191
Fannie 199
G M 131, 260
Harriet (--) 48
J G 250
J J 370
J M 48, 128, 159,
187, 205, 244, 295,
321
James H 185
Jane Ashley 146
Jane E (--) 250
Jas A 250
John B 191
Joseph 116
M C (--) 370
M M 48
Mar M 139
Mark M 302
Mary 370
Mary Jane 115
Othella J (Watkins)
21
Philip M 344
Robert J 80
Sarah J (--) 199
W M D 412
Wier 199
BOYKIN, -- (Williams)
116
J E Felix 116
John T 72
Sarah (--) 202
Sterling R 202
BOYLE, Cynthia (--) 396
Lucy Ann 396
Robert 396
BOYLSTON, Fannie T
(Crum) 16
G W 16
BOYNTON, -- (Bryan) 6
Willard 6
BOZEMAN, C M 106
Hattie P (Yarborough)
106
Mary Jane 114
BRABHA, Elizabeth R
(--) (Kearse) 321
BRABHAM, Carrie H (--)
141
Elizabeth Agnes 141
John M 141, 195
Joseph 321
Minie Lee 80
S J 80, 294
S V (--) 80
Sarah (Kirkland) 321
Susan V (Holly) 294
BRADBURY, J W 301
BRADDY, Asenath (--)
396

Frances (--) 94
BRADEN, -- 208
-- (Ward) 208
James A 2
Virginia A (Ward) 2
BRADFIELD, -- 217
-- (Traylor) 217
James 217
BRADFORD, Amanda 19
B F 37
Catharine (--) 321
Cynthia Medora
(Harris) 254
David 263
Eliza S (--) 152
Elizabeth (Griffin)
414
Joshua 380
Martha (Harris) 157
Mary 124
Mary (--) 263
Mary A E 321
Nancy M 263
Rachel 14
Richard 222
S M 125
Sarah (Frederick)
(Auld) 85
Shadrach 321
Thomas A 269
W E 157
William 414
Wm 14, 19
BRADLEY, -- (--) 184
John 184
Julia Ann 93
Newman 56
R D 93
Rebecca 254
BRADSHAW, Grissilla
Fletcher (--) 304
J M 304
BRADWELL, R N R 83
BRADY, Richard H 91
BRAGAN, John W 332
Julia A (--) 332
BRAID, Robert S 250
Susan A (Williamson)
250
BRAMHAN, Amanda H
(Green) 329
Isaac N 329
BRAMLETT, Wm 114
BRAMLETTE, -- (--) 334
Nathan 334
BRANCH, -- (--) 317
Carroline T 91
Clifford Leonora 269
F A 2, 61, 80, 106,
111, 213, 236, 253,
273, 292, 318, 332,
334
Fannie (--) 156

Isaac 143, 156
J C 269
James C 72, 317
James O 303, 333
Jas O 85, 91, 101,
111, 126, 140, 220,
224, 265, 279, 286,
288, 314, 321
Louise Bond 91
M A (--) 269
R M 143
Sallie C (--) 222
BRAND, Armstead 317
Sarah (--) 317
BRANDA, Martha Rebecca
8
BRANDON, -- (Quantock)
115
Christopher 212
D S 313
David S 410
Elizabeth (--) 23
Harriet (--) 313
James Franklin 23
James W 129
John 114
Mary 212
Mary (--) 212
Sarah (--) 114
Sarah E (Walters) 127
Thomas W 265
W C 127
W N 23
BRANHAM, Indiana Eliza
389
W R 13, 113, 186,
202, 286, 299, 350,
356, 378, 389
BRANNAN, F M T 367,
399
Sarah (--) 273
BRANNING, -- (--) 395
D L 69
George 395
BRANNON, -- (Belzer) 230
E M T 371
F M T 109, 265, 315,
321, 356, 386
Mary A (Kaigler) 230
R M T 385
W B 230
BRANSON, F M T 294,
306
BRANTLEY, Anthony 14
Ham Culver 127
Mittie M (Culver) 127
Sarah M 403
W D 127
BRANTLY, -- (--) 75
A 339
E B (--) (Vaught) 339
F L 57
M J 176

426

BRANTON, Jane (--) 270
BRASHER, Thos H 251
BRASINGTON, Elizabeth 96
BRASSFIELD, Sarah S V (Parker) 346
W B 346-47
BRASWELL, -- 306
Fannie J 305
Susan E (--) 306
Thomas M 305
BRAWNER, William H 339
BRAWNING, D L 32
BRAZIL, Martha A 340
Nancy (--) 366
Susan 366
Wm 366
BRAZINGTON, Elizabeth Ann (--) 190
J W 190
BREANEN, Esther Ann (--) 144
John 144
John William 144
BRECKINRIDGE, John C 271
BREEDEN, Sallie H (Townsend) 268
Thos J 368
BREEDLOVE, B F 304, 397
B-- (--) 13
Benj F 215
George K 215
J H 94
M A (Rape) 113
S A (--) 215
S A E (--) 397
Wm M 13
BREGAN, Sarah (Ozier) 36
BRENT, O J 250
BREWER, -- 170, 289, 318
Catherine (McCollum) 170
Elizabeth (--) 318
Isabel G (--) 289
James W 318
John R 289
L R 7, 260
M E (--) 7
Martha E (--) 260
Susan H 7
BREWSTER, P H 103
BREWTON, -- (--) 315
Beb 315
BRICE, Ann (Wood) 244
Emily 3099
Samuel 110, 244
BRIDGES, Elizabeth (Arnold) 239
Ira 220

J C A 346
Lucy E (Fort) 405
Margarette (--) 220
Martha C 220
N C 239
Sarah K (--) 9
Susie B 229
Thomas 9
Wm 405
BRIGGS, A J 2, 63
Abigail 223
BRIGHT, -- (McCanless) 340
George 340
Mary J (--) 113
BRINN, Frances (--) 238
Richard 238
BRINSON, Sallie (--) 287
Simeon 287
BRISCOE, Sidney B 219
BRISTOW, Rebecca (--) 196
Thomas 196
BROADFIELD, Eliza A (Dean) (Jarratt) (Boring) 194
J M 194
BROCK, Nancy 413
BROCKINGTON, Wm 18
BROCKINTON, -- 282
Maggie Lenora (Quarterman) 282
BROCKMAN, G M T 54
BRODNAX, H P 2
BRODNEX, Mary B 2
BRONSON, Susan 308
BROOKING, Ann B 265
BROOKS, -- (--) 167, 362
A T 316
C C 362
Caledonia (--) 32
David 105
E A 32
Henry 76
Jacob 74
Jacob R 166
James 125
James Martin 30
John 316
Lazina (--) 227
Lazina C 339
Lucy Ann (--) 125
M A 74
Margaret (Covington) 199
Martha 303
Nancy (Nunn) 316
Nancy Jane 125
Rebecca (--) 282
Rebecca A 82
Samuel 199
WL 166
Winniford (--) 121

Winniford (Wilson) 105
Wyatt 46, 339
BROOM, G D 175
M P (--) 175
Minnie Gertrude 175
B R O O M E, E G (Robinson) 119
Jas A 119
BROTHERTON, Levi 106, 185, 270
BROWN, -- 300
-- (--) 194, 375
-- (Hunt) 75
-- (Smart) 277
A R (--) 173
Allen W 184
Angus 330
Archie 284
Asa 202
B B 48
Chas E 120, 152
Clinton 397
D Homer 85
D M 263, 400
D P 42
Daniel 164
E E 407
E G 120
Eben 122
Elisha 14
Elisabeth 368
Eliza 123
Elizabeth 164
Ellenor Louisa 19
Evaline (Winn) 255
F P 237
Fannie 235
Fannie E (--) 17
Flora (--) 284
Georgia A (--) 397
H T 77
Harriet M R (--) 375
Hattie (Burkhalter) 41
Hester Ann 97
J M 328
J W 41, 69
James 336
James Edmond 161
James M 44
James S 153
Jane 56
Jane (Ormand) 77
Jefferson Samuel 381
Jennett 330
Jennett (--) 330
John 161, 241, 255
Jonathan S 210
Jones 227
Joseph 154
Juliet M 296
L J 173
L J A 277

L M 184
Lelia V 184
Lemon 330
Lemon M 273
Leonard 250
Lilly B (--) 273
Lizzie (Chandler) 411
Lizzie (Hill) 184
Lizzie E 122
Lorenzo S 381
Lucretia (--) 42
M C 291
Malinda 354
Margaret (--) 202, 227
Mariah A (--) 301
Martha A (Ragan) 383
Mary (--) 48
Mary (--) (Shurlock)
154
Mary E 273
Mary E (--) 336
Mary Frances (--) 85
Mary Jane (Padgett)
153
Mattie E (Wallace) 328
Milton B 336
Minnie 397
Nancy 413
Nancy A (Sheppard) 300
Permelia S (--) 120
Priscilla 71
Reuben 383
Robert Alexander 140
Ruth (--) 381
Silas 77
Stephen 330
Stephen 'Bear' 88
Stephen Gibson 192
Susan (--) 367
Susan (Shell) 330
Susan A (Stephens) 161
Susan T (--) 184
T 284
T A 75
Thomas A 277
Thos A 330
Virginia J 233
Walter G 411
William 159, 330,
367, 375
William C 375
William F 407
Wm 330
BROWNE, -- (--) 328
Augustus T 89
Eliza Jane (Becket)
216
Elvira (--) 306
Jasper 306, 328
Jesse Irene 89
S M (--) 89
Sidi H 251, 412
William M 216

Wm M 256
BROWNING, Eleanor C
(--) 358
J T 358
Sarah A (--) 402
W A 402
BROXTON, Ellen Pricher
335
G W 335
BROYLE, Mary (Ruth) 383
W L 383
BROYLES, Sarah A
(Harris) 390
W N 390
BRUCE, Elija 323
James 187
M J (--) 187
Marina (--) 323
Robert Edwin 187
BRUNDAGE, E Moses 7
BRUNER, Harriet (--) 117
John Evans 117
Mary Ella 117
BRUNNER, J H 318
BRUNSON, Addie Cate
344
C C (Millard) 344
M A 344
Maria B 349
P A 349
W A 349
BRUTON, Martha
Isabella (--) 277
BRYAN, -- 6, 402
Ann Dell (Boston) 153
C A E 335
C C 233
Clement 237
D H 195, 202, 230,
256, 337, 363
Elizabeth (--) 402
Georgia Ann Eliza 153
Isaac 353
J S 354
Jesse 335
Loverd 402
Mary (--) 353
Mary A (--) 335
Mary M (Hix) 233
Mary S 237
R B 301
Solomon 153
Wm 16, 35, 60, 63
BRYANT, A J 296, 299
Ann (--) 82
Emeline (Shaw) 401
John 128
Martha E 268
Mary L 128
Rowland 160
Sarah Cornelia 127
Thos 401
W C 203

BRYCE, E A (--) 278
Geo R 278
John 112
Nancy E 276
Robert 172, 286
Samuel 172
Sarah F (--) 112
Willie P 278
BRYDIE, Archibald 15
BRYON, Polly 321
BUCHAN, John 34
BUCHANAN, Cartha
(Weaver) 32
David 330
N H (--) 260
R H L 49
Temperance E 32
Wm J 32
BUCKALEW, Fanny A
(Norris) 367
BUDD, Jane V (--) 23
William 23
BUDINGTON, Ozier 207
Susan A (--) 207
BUFF, B F 246
Daniel W 47
James David 47
James H 97
James Henry 84
Joanna (--) 245
Joanna (Shull) 246
M B 245
M E 246
Mary (--) 47
Mary Ann 116
S N (--) 97
Susanna Newton
(Dunwody) 84
Willie 245
BUFORD, -- 223
Greenbury 301
Mary E (Ingram) 301
Mary Letitia 397
R W 397
Sallie G (--) 397
BUGG, -- (--) 258
Augusta 258
Eliza (--) 84, 258
Ella (--) 375
Emma 84
Henry 375
Jackson 375
Jacob 84
Jacob E 258
BULL, Atchison E 242
BULLARD, Julia A (--)
163
M J (--) 198
Saloma Crawford 163
William 163
BULLOCH, Willis 46
BULLOCK, -- 258
D F 279

Nancy (--) 118
Walter T 72
William 118
C--, D L 69
 F W 30
 G B 325
 Joe H 12
 M A 126, 137
 S D 112, 118
 W F 127
 W J 68
 W M 199
CADIEU, Annie Jane 278
 F M (--) 278
 J M 278
CAIN, Charity (Hyman)
 326
 Eliza A W 45
 Elizabeth (--) 45
 James B 45
 John 313
 L J (--) 214
 Preston 214
 R A 203
 Randal 326
 William 214
CAISEY, Mary C Q (--)
 159
CALCUTT, -- (--) 193
 Deborah 315
 John 315
 William James 193
CALDER, James R 217
 Sarah A E (--) 217
CALDWELL, -- (--) 334
 Amanda R 387
 Anna 301
 Carrie Birdsong (--)
 319
 Charles T 286
 G 394
 Harriet A 286
 J H 404
 J J 197, 246
 John 108, 387
 Julia A 404
 L A 58
 M Galenia (Banks) 56
 M J 56, 394
 Newton 334
 O A 319
 Oscar A 119
 R E (--) 231
 Sallie (Glenn) 394
 Tudie (Pilsbury) 58
 W T 108
CALHOUN, A E (--) 181
 Caroline L 129
 Dougald 133
 F R 181
 Fannie Ellen 181
 James M 71
 Jas B 129

Jemima 360
John N 198-99
Micajah 360
Sarah (--) 133
Susan (--) 188
CALLAHAN, Jas H 233
 John 268
 Mary 'Aunt Polly'
 (--) 118
 Mary Edna (--) 233
 Mary Eliza 233
CALLAWAY,   Anna
Malone
 (Adams) 410
 E 3
 E J M 79
 Elisha 32
 J T 410
 Rebecca (Cockrell) 32
 W A 312
CALLIER, Henry 339
 J A 145
 James D 105
 Martha Ann (--) 145
 Mary (--) 339
 Thomas 339
CALVERT, M R 333
 William R 372
CAMBELL, Wm C 212
CAMERON, George 5
 Mary (--) 5
 Sarah B 293
CAMP, Arthur T 54
 B 50
 Burke 184, 374
 Edmund 399
 Hiram 143, 264, 273
 Hosea 170, 269
 J L 127
 J W 269
 Jane B (--) 184
 Joseph 81
 Joseph Anthony 269
 M A (--) 127
 Martha M 170
 Mary (--) 399
 Penina (Reymonds) 264
 Sarah (--) 81
 Winifred Letitia
 Delilah 81
 Winifred W (--) 50
CAMPBELL, -- (--) 128,
 190
 A H 305
 A L 163
 A M 231
 Andrew 266
 Ann Lee (--) 106
 Ann S (--) 163
 Archibald 163
 Catharine 184
 Charlotte (McKey) 314
 Charter 61

E C (--) 363
Elizabeth (--) 377
Emeline S 372
George 302
J B 142, 347, 363
J R 44
James B 34, 127
James H 302
John D 314
John Lucius 122
Lula P (--) 44
M A (--) 285
Marcus A 285
Mary 401
Mary Ann (--) 305
Nancy (--) 266
Norman 184
Pringle 44
Pulaski F 302
Robert 128
S 289
S A 285
Sallie W (Eve) 302
William Columbus 190
William D 377
William H 61
CANADAY, Lizzie A 193
 Mary (--) 193
 Wm T 193
CANDLE, G B 140
 Martha J 140
 T A (--) 140
CANDLER, Samuel C 243
CANNEDY, Susan C B 142
CANNON, -- (--) 269
 A (Dickey) 29
 Elizabeth W (--) 64
 Henry 269
 Joshua 72
CANTEY, -- 379
 J S 413
 James 379
 James W 379
 John 379
 Mary A E (Bennett) 413
 Sarah C 379
 William J E 413
CANTRELL, Geo 353
 Mary Elizabeth
 (Johnson) 415
 Nancy E J (Craven) 353
CAPE, Mary H (--) 323
CAPERS, -- 44, 58, 129
 -- (--) 412
 A H (--) 391
 Anna W 58
 Edith (Wightman) 391
 Emma 412
 Emma (--) (Jones) 105
 Jesse Sidney 191
 Jessie (Darby) 391
 Jessie Lee 191
 Jessie Lee (Darby) 180

430

431

CAULY, -- 16
CAUSEY, -- 73
  Charity Ann F (--) 75
  Julia A (--) 73
  Samuel H 75
CAUTHEN, -- (--) 316
  A J 61, 186-87, 199,
  252, 323, 366, 388,
  393, 406, 415
  Anderson 176
  Cynthia (--) 380
  D E (--) 380
  Elizabeth 314
  Emily (Robertson) 380
  Emily I (Robertson)
  160
  J T Barksdale 316
  James 380
  Jane (--) 316
  John S 380
  John T 160
  L M 380
  Millie 176
  Polly Darnel (--) 176
  Robert S 388, 392
  W D 316
CAVER, Sarah 102
CENTER, Alice Boyd 297
  E A 66
  Frances P (Thorn) 66
  Georgia (--) 297
  James T 83
  Marion 309
  R G 297
  T R 309
CHAIRES, Fannie B 309
CHAMBERLIN, Lizzie 51
CHAMBERS, Ann
  (Flewellen) 142
  Emily Elizabeth 337
  Frances P 359
  J 54, 255
  James M 64
  Jane (--) 337
  Jane (Graham) 307
  Joseph 337
  Josiah 359
  Lizzie L 329
  W I 142
  William L 142
CHAMBLESS, Ann M 102
  John 102
CHANDLER, Anna 235
  Asa 411
  George 195
  Immogiene Hinton 240
  James 235
  Joice (--) 235
  Lizzie 411
  M A (--) 240
  Mary E (Beville) 195
  W F 240
CHANEE, Florence M 101

Henry 101
Sarah (--) 101
CHAPMAN, -- (Webb) 242
  Annie M (Carleton) 53
  B F 242
  Daniel B 163
  John 53
  Milly 112
  Parsha Ann (Lifsy) 67
  Wm T 67
CHAPPEL, -- 229
  John 59
  Margaret (--)
  (Griffin) 59
  Sarah (--) 229
CHAPPELL, Ann 62
  Loretta 158
  Matilda (--) 158
CHARLES, Dora V 394
  J T 394
  M C (--) 394
CHARLTON, Eliza
  (Gugle) 76
  Emily A (--) 192
  John 76
  John D 192
  Phoebe Wambersin 175
CHASE, -- 356
  Albon 14, 356
  Elizabeth (Bynum) 356
  J P 349
  John P 349
  M E (--) 349
  Maria B (Brunson) 349
CHASTAIN, J B 211
CHASTEEN, -- 180
  -- (--) 180
  John 180
CHATFIELD, George 24
  John B 181
  Mary (--) 24
  Mary C 24
CHATMAN, -- 396
  Frances A E (Kile) 396
CHAUDOIN, Lewis 332
  Mary Ann 332
  Wm N 65
CHEATHAM, -- (--) 102
  A E (Loyless) 68
  C A 108
  John T 102
  R S 68
CHEEK, Burgess 294, 331
  Mary Rebecca 331
  Miles (--) 331
CHEESEBOROUGH,
  Charles
  27
  Georgia Alma (Doles)
  27
CHENAULT, Dennis M
304
CHENEY, Isaac 204

Matilda (Justice) 204
Matilda Trippe 184
CHERRY, Aquilla 75
  J S 291
  J T 390
  Jane 156
  Job S 291
  Joel Thomas 386
  Mary (--) 291
  Susan C (McAllum) 386
  Wm A 291
CHESHURE, William 288
CHESTER, Abel 240
CHILDERS, Sarah A A
153
CHILES, S G 49
CHIPLEY, -- 315
  -- (--) 315
  J S 7
  Martha Rebecca 7
  Mary 7
  Mary Jane 315
  William M 38
CHITTY, Julia Ann 68
CHITWOOD, A C 382
  J J 382
  John J 214
CHOICE, Frances
  Elizabeth (Stephens)
  (Keowin) 271
  William 271
CHRIETZBERG, A M 20,
161
  Anna E (--) 20
  Anna Elizabeth (--)
  161
  C M 122
  Charles Williams 20
CHRISTIAN, Ann (--) 84
  H C 206
  J B 83
  J R (--) 241
  J W 328
  Lucy E (--) 83
  Lucy Jane 281
  M 138
  Mary A (--) 138
  Mary J 138
  Mary Jane (--) 231
  Rebecca (--) 45
  Rosier Evans 83
  Rufus King 231
  Sarah (--) 281
  T T 39, 67, 401
  Thomas W 231
  Thos T 75, 154, 164,
  410
  William L 45
  Wm 281
CHRISTOPHER, Cynthia
L
  19
  Frances C (--) 19

Milton 8
Sarah (--) 8
Susan Capers (Glenn)
129
CLOWER, G W 323
John O (Lambert) 323
CLUBB, James A 279
Matilda Harris (--)
279
CLYDE, T J 9, 16, 26,
69, 276
Thos J 323, 385
CLYETT, Ann (--) 105
COBB, -- 389
-- (--) 272
C Augustus 272
C J 345
E P (--) 23
George C 75
Gracie (Walden) 304
Howell 154, 361
J N B 23, 170
J V W 354
J W 304
Martha (Dickinson)
194
Martha Ann (--) 285
Martha Harriet
(Belzer) 354
Mary 170, 361
Mary E (Smith) 75
Mary S 154
W T 285
William A 389
COCHRAN, -- 331
Catharine J (--) 53
Christopher Columbus
331
Daniel H 259
John 53
Mary Ann (--) 259
R A 259
S E 373
COCKRELL, Rebecca 32
CODY, James 200
COFER, M J 110
Mattie A (McKibben)
110
COFFEE, John A 218
Rebecca S (--) 218
COFFIN, Martha 371
COFIELD, Anna
(Caldwell) 301
Thomas Kearney 301
COGSWELL, Esther S
(Mouzon) 373
Harvey 373
COHRAN, John 191
COKER, James 160, 176
COLBERT, Ernest
Richmond 372
John G 372, 408
Rebecca S (--) 372

Rebecca S (Audas) 408
COLBY, John 132
COLCLASURE, Nathan V
103
COLDING, -- 360
Jemima (Calhoun) 360
Julia Ann (Bradley)
93
Samuel B 93
COLE, -- 203
Elizabeth A (--) 258
Elvira 203
L H 258
Mary C 258
Wm A 15
COLEMAN, -- (--) 410,
412
A E (--) 76
A J 350
Charlie Wesley 76
D L 76
Frances (--) 256
John 338
M 410
Mary (Burgess) 231
Mary E (Littlejohn)
26
Moses 412
Nancy (--) 338
Richard 231
Sampson J 412
Samson J 410
Thomas C 256
Verlinda B (Caton) 350
W S 266
COLES, Eliza Susan 190
John P 190, 320
Margaret (--) 190
Margaret M (Byrd) 320
COLIER, Irene Nettie 361
John 361
Mary Francis (--) 361
COLLEY, -- (Talbot) 403
I O 403
COLLIER, Frances E 324
L S (--) 373
Martha (--) 324
Mary M 61
Robert 324
William E 61
Wm C 285
Wm E 191-92
COLLIN, -- (Robarts) 78
COLLINS, Ann M (--) 193
Ann M (Roberts) 106
C H B 106, 193
Charles H B 102
Deborah (Calcutt) 315
Eliza (--) 203
Geo D 348
Irbin 43
Isabella J (--) 43
James John Andrew 193

James L 315
James Leonard 315
Jesse 315
John F 372
Joshua 368
Juliet R 203
Laura (--) 348
Louisa H (--) 188
Luther Wightman 348
Mary B (McNeil) 368
Mary E (--) 315
Robert 203
Rosebud 162
Sarah A (--) 162
Stephen 188
Susan E A (--) 102
W C 396
William C 162
William H B 102
Wm E 149, 196
COLLINSWORTH, John
251
Mildred L
(Scarborough) 251
COLLY, Jonathan 197
Nancy (--) 197
COLQUITT, -- 175
A S 159
Catharine Elizabeth
159
Harriet (--) 329
John H 98
Margaret (--) 159
Nannie 329
S W (--) 197
Walter T 329
Wm H 132
COLSON, Hope H 71
Martha A (--) 71
Matilda Elizabeth 71
Tempe 247
COLT, Isaac 125
COLWELL, -- (Leonard)
297
Thos 297
COMBS, Sarah 248
COMINGS, Elvirah 76
Elvirah (Comings) 76
Louisa (--) 76
Richard 76
William 76
CONAWAY, C A 121
C O N E Y, Amanda
(Pledger)
145
W C 145
CONGLETON, Sarah C
182
CONLEY, -- 413
Francina E (Smith) 223
Hannah (--) 43
Henry H 413
J R 282

Jason 52
Louisa A
   (Sullenberger) 229
Nancy (Brown) 413
Rebecca S (--) 86
Sarah Ann Gordon
   (McFarland) 282
Sarah E 52
W F 411
W M C 173
William 86
Wm F 223
CONN, -- 31
Barbary A (--) 29
Leonora A (--) 57
W T 57
CONNALLY, J H 10
CONNELL, -- (Baxter) 176
CONNELLY, Emma S (--)
   372
CONNER, E J (--) 327
Elizabeth (--) (--)
   221
Ganaway 268
M A 345
R A 16, 76, 97, 255,
   296, 303, 327, 341
Victoria Howard 327
W G 221
CONNERLY, W P H 98
CONNOR, Ezra 406
F A 352
Frances G (Hodges) 352
George D 115
I O A 325
Irene Garnett 115
J S 219
Jacob 293
M C 254
M G (--) 115
Mollie Hunter 115
Paul 259
Sophia (--) 293
CONOWAY, C A 215, 217
COOGLER, -- 415
-- (Metts) 415
COOK, -- (--) 112
Bessie Sawrie 174
Catherine (--) 70
Clara M 245
E R 245
Elizabeth (--) 248
Francis 143, 172
J H J 235
J O A 15, 36, 59, 90,
   100, 105, 117, 129,
   150, 173, 189, 195,
   201, 207, 209, 222,
   228, 266, 279, 299,
   304, 336, 356-58,
   361, 405
James 41, 226
John D 414

John J 114
John W 17
L A (--) 174
Louisa N (Holcomb) 414
Lourenna (--) 304
M M (Ellison) 143
Martha H 248
Mary 185
Mary A (--) 17
Mary A E 17
Mary W (--) 114
Mildred 350
Mollie A R 336
Nathan 304
Oliver H 336
Phillip 112
Samuel 248
Sarah 226
Susannah P 112
Thomas 41
W F 143, 174, 208,
   319, 329, 345, 397,
   407, 410-11
Wm 172
Wm A 304
COOKE, George 274
Maria (--) 274
COOPER, Anna J (Beall)
   222
J W 162
James G 224
James M 349
John 103
M A (Dean) (Murphy)
   345
Mary E 224
S M 162
S P 345
Stephen H 224
W D 222
COPELAN, A H 394
Lucretia (--) 394
Obediah 210
COPELAND, -- (--) 392
William 392
COPES, Eliza Harriet
   (--) 219
James 219
COPPAGE, Anna R 88
Lewis 88
Mary (--) 88
COPPEDGE, Elizabeth
   (--) 25
J W 25
L C 11
Mary A 11
CORBITT, Daniel E 86
CORE, D W 141, 153, 213
Mary G (Morrison) 141
CORKLE, A M 191
CORLEY, -- 77
Elizabeth Anthony
   (--) (Myrick) 198

Hugh A 100
John 38, 303, 306
Mary (Renehart) 38
R J 33, 87, 94, 140,
   395
Robert J 233-34
Robt J 271
S J 78
CORNLEY, Mary Jane
   (--) 129
CORNOG, -- (--) 347
W Levis 347
CORPENING, Catharine
   Elmira (Robeson) 121
COSBY, Mary Barbara
   (White) (Arnold) 391
COSFORD, S J 387
COSTINE, -- 252
Margaret (--) 252
COSTON?, A E (--) 401
Addie Lee 401
James G 401
COTHRAN, Mary
   Elizabeth
   (Mitchell) 325
COTTER, E E 184
J F 187
J W 311
W A 138, 140
W J 19, 29, 42, 48,
   114, 125, 169, 184,
   197, 201, 206, 214,
   217, 234, 260, 264,
   281, 284, 291, 323,
   334, 361-62
COTTINGHAM, J D 98
COTTON, A E (--) 19
Cynthia (--) 39
Indianna (Carlisle)
   (Hardentt) 185
J G 19
James E 19
P G 186
S G 289
Wm G 39
COTTRELL, Eleanor Jane
   349
Hugh B 111
J B 7, 81, 91
Jos B 116
Joseph B 27, 58, 82,
   94, 98, 111, 234, 370
Lavinia A (Blunt) 111
Mary G 81
Rachael Ellanor 94
Thomas 349
Z D 94
COUCH, Kennon 164
COULTER, -- (Harwell)
   238
Jefferson 238
COUMBE, John T 245
Mary E (Scruggs) 245

COUNTS, Louisa C 73
Mary A 73
COUSE, Arladne (Smith)
308
James Edward 308
John 308
COVINGTON, Elijah 199
Elizabeth (--) 16
Margaret 199
Nancy 16
Sarah (--) 199
Thomas 16
COVINTON, Sallie S
(Hamer) 254
Sarah (Cook) 226
Thos S 226
Wm J 254
COWAN, H 216
M (--) 216
Margaret A 216
COWARD, L G 258
Mary E (Speight) 258
COWART, Lavinia (--) 100
Margaret Minerva 100
Nancy (--) (Black)
(Ozier) 342
Stephen 100, 342
COWLERS, Thomas F 329
COWLES, A M (Andrews)
129
Asbury 134
COX, -- 212, 350
-- (--) 350
A F 263
B R 4
Benjamin C 173
Carey 405
Cary 107
Catherrine (--) 4
D D 21, 65, 108, 222,
243, 252, 266, 332,
343-44, 351, 382, 394
Emily Olivia (--) 21
Frances 280
James 131
John E (Bridges) 9
John H 337
L P 386
M E (--) 99
Martha W (Ashworth)
212
Mary S 350
Oliver C 350
Rachel (--) 131
Sarah W (--) 107
Timothy W M 235
COXE, W M 131
COXWELL, John D 6
Rachel S (English) 6
COZART, Ann M (--) 397
H W 397
Sarah Virginia 397
COZBY, J B 215

CRAFTON, Bennett 366
Elizabeth Tankersly
366
CRAIG, -- 322
-- (--) 359, 402
E E (--) 251
Frances J 150
George Ann Florida
(--) 322
H H 96
Hugh 214, 351
Ida Gamewell 251
J C 359
J D 251
J W 104
James 150
James Chapman 402
Jas C 168
John C 168
Laura S (--) 168
M P (--) 150
Margaret J (--) 351
Mary (--) 214
Sallie P 359
W E 150
William E 192
CRANFORD,   Catharine
319
Henry 319
CRAPPS, George 264
CRAPS, Ellen
(Jennings) 79
CRATON, Eliza Ann 83
Elizabeth (--) 83
Isaac 83
CRAVEN, Adaline (--) 353
Alfred 63
Cornelia (--) 63
Edward Sidney 63
I N 304
Isaac N 133
Mary (Jones) (Bird)
304
Mary H 133
Nancy E J 353
P C (--) 168
T W 168
Thomas W 80
CRAVEY, John 414
Sarah J (Burnham) 414
CRAWFORD, A J 126
Alexander 81
Amelia L 88
Augustus 88
Bennett 366
C P 52, 327
Elisha G 14
Eliza 247
Eliza E (--) 88
Elizabeth Tankersly
366
Ella Virginia 2
Fannie H 37

Hardy G 220
Harriet (--) 182
Hinton 31, 182
Joel T 331
John L 37
Lureny (--) 152
M (--) 52
M F 151, 163
Martha (Williamson)
327
Martha Elizabeth 282
Mary A (--) 126
Matilda 245
Matthew 152
Mattie F (--) 279
Minnie H 279
Nancy (--) 14
R B 15, 115, 399
R H 409
Robert B 279
S A (Watson) 331
Sallie 362
Sallie Maxwell 52
Sarah (Tatom) 14
Sarah B (--) 282
Stephen Jasper 126
William G 14, 282
William Gordon 78
CRAWLEY, James A 217
Mary F (Dunn) 217
CRAWLY, Harriet W
(Oliver) 246
Lindsy L 246
CRAY, Mary L 307
CREAMER, Mary 392
CREDILLE, C S 403
CREECH, Martha F (--)
138
CREIGHTON, G W M 195
James D 326
CRENSHAW, -- 295
David 77, 295
David K 66
Jane S (--) 295
Joseph 234
Martha C (--) 234
Susan E (--) 325
Tommy 234
W H 325
CREWS, -- 298
Ava Eliza 163
E Eugenia (Hance) 11
Frances M (--) 163
J M 298
Mary (Patterson) 108
Paul M 163
T B 11
Thos M 108
CRIDDLE, C (--) 276
Nancy A 276
CRIDE, Samuel C 389
CRISP, J C 62, 114,
226, 236-37

437

Mary E (--) 361
Mary Harriet 113
Mary R (--) 65, 127
Nannie Neal 408
Olin B 6
P F 345
P L 238
R G 105
R M 79
Rebecca (--) 249
Rebecca (Heape) 359
Richard W 65, 127
Robert 81
S A E (--) 105, 259
S E M (Beckwith) 79
S M 222
Susie 408
Thomas 197
William 51, 359
William B 249
William C 21
Wm 318
Wm C 19
Wm M 91
DAWKINS, -- (--) 195
Edna (--) 121
Eliza Caroline (--)
116
John 121, 195
DAWSON, Emma Frances
(Harwell) 159
George W 159
M C (Ketchins) 367
Mary D (--) 118
Susie 406
T H 149
Thomas H 229, 406
Thos H 91
Wm 367
DAWSSON, Thomas H 223
DAY, Algernon Sidney 223
Elizabeth W (Rhodes)
354
Frances (Hamby) 300
Joseph 7, 12
Julius Lamar 223
Mary Ann (--) 12
Mary M (--) 223
Reuben 300
Richard B 354
Vernon Ludwell 223
W D 223
William Woodliff 223
DEAN, A J 55, 83, 89,
93, 116, 188, 194,
212, 249, 283-84,
293, 297, 315,
319-20, 328, 338-9,
362, 369, 372
Abbie Rilla (--) 392
Abigail (--) 116
Alvin J 392
Burket 132

Burkett 194
Charles 116, 392
Eliza A 194
Francis E (Mouchet)
284
Louisa Rebecca 116
M A 345
Mary S 132
DEAVOURS, A J 327
John 327
Mary W (--) 327
De BARDELEBEN, Phala
Sanford (Menefee) 387
DeBARDELEBEN, -- 387
John A 387
DeBERRY, -- (--) 401
W H 401
DeBOW, -- (--) 83
John 83
DECKER, Nancy (--) 170
DEER, Joseph 381
Mary (Page) 381
DeFOOR, Elizabeth 257
Martin 257
Susan (--) 257
DeJARNETTE, Ella R 414
Mary (--) 20
R R 20, 414
DEKLE, Lebbeus 336
Mollie A R (Cook) 336
DELANE, Jane E (--) 48
Philip H 48
William H G 48
DELESPINE, -- (Russel)
173
Harriet 173
Joseph 173
DELL, Eliza Ann 90
John H 44
Maxey B 44
Miner (--) 90
Phillip 44
Simeon 90
Simeon 'Uncle Simy'
85
DELOACH, C S
(Fletcher) 26
David 26
DELPH, Mary Powell
(--) 288
Robert 288
Virginia Smith 288
DEMPSEY, A G 179, 229,
264
Lazarus 179
Mary (--) 179
DEMPSY, A G 271
DENMARK, Jennie 370
DENNINTON, Benjamin
Hill 350
DENNIS, Addie E 135
Mary G (--) 135
Robert E 135

Wesley B 100, 115
DENNY, Mary G (--) 405
R R 405
Willie P 405
DENSLER, Henry 227
Henry L 227
Priscilla (--) 227
Sarah 227
Thos L 227
DENSMORE, Nancy C 408
Samuel P 240
DENT, Fannie 252
John T 184
Margaret A (--) 184
DENTON, Henry B 333
Mary 333
DePASS, J P 412
Jacob S 79
Jas P 116, 131, 189,
209, 267, 284
Wightman Meynardie 412
Wm L 79
DERRICK, Ann B (Veach)
357
David 357
DeSCHAMPS, C G S 160
Mary (--) 160
DEUPREE, Lewis J 391
Lucy Gates (Atkinson)
(Peebles) 391
DEWSON, George 250
J 250
Rosalie A (MacDonell)
250
DIAL, Euanna L 295
Sarah A (--) 295
W C 295
DIAMOND, James J 148
Nancy (--) 148
Rebecca A 148
DIBBLE, Fannie Anna 275
P V 275
DICK, -- 297
Levi 276
Sarah (--) 276
Susan Ann 276
T M 297
DICKENS, Elizabeth
(--) 168
DICKENSON, J P 228
Josephine V (--) 375
N H (--) 228
Walter 228
DICKERSON, Ann 70
James 70
DICKERT, Mary Ann 46
Wm Strobel 185
DICKEY, A 29
Ana M (Reynolds) 152
J M 305
Lewis M 29
Mary 95
Wm J 152

DICKINSON, -- (--) 332
A D (--) 194
Elvira E (--) 97
J F 143
Jane C (--) 374
John F 97
John P 97, 142-43
L D 194
Martha 194
Martha J (Norton) 97
Robert 130
Rufus 332
Sarah E 143
W D 375
W J 85
DICKSON, Ann (--) 155
Charlie Jasper 195
David 300, 328
Eveline (Sandefur) 328
J Walter 250, 291, 338
James R 214
Jasper M 195
John S 212
Martha Ann E (Mason)
212
Mary James 331
Mary L (--) 195
Mary W Facklin
(Gregg) 82
Nancy H (Bass) 267
W J 82
William 155, 267
DIEZ, Ann H (Cushman)
324
Francisco 324
DILL, -- 177
Adelia 177
Robert 143
DILLABERRY, F J 65
Mary E (Smith) 65
DILLARD, Bessie 345
James F 345
Lizzie H (--) 345
DILLON, James 299
Martha Ann
(Williamson) 299
DILWORTH, L A (--) 322
DINGLE, Frances Ellen
(--) 366
J Harvey 366
DISHER, -- (--) 352
Eleanor Caroline 295
Florence M 347
Julia O (--) 295
R W 347
Robert W 347
S Y 295
Steadman Yeaden 352
DISMUKES, -- (--) 341
George W 341
Mary G (Wilson) 73
DITMOR, Martha 166
DIXON, -- (Lemle) 3

Abel 104
Bryant 220
Charlotte Ann (Starr)
209
Eliza 104
Eliza (--) 186
Ezekiel 165
Frances A (Ashley) 294
H H 220
Henry 294
Henry W 347
J L 389
M A (Koger) 196
Mamie P 289
Nancy (Stubbs) 129
Nannie J 400
R W 20, 32, 35, 42,
91-92, 140, 164,
214, 220, 224, 233,
237, 304, 332, 339,
347, 400
Robert H 289
Roger K 3
S S (Willis)
(Rembert) 165
Tabitha (--) 104
Thomas 129
W N 209
DOBBINS, Frances E 377
Moses W 377
DOBBS, C L 274, 314
E T (--) 296
Emer O 196
Erline(?) (--) 196
J D 296
Joseph D 196
Perry 70
Talva B 296
DODD, Amanda E (--) 250
Geo W 250
J E 52, 90
John 197
DODGE, H H (Williams)
41
W A 18, 24, 41, 298,
313, 341, 353, 398
DOGAN, J H 339
Joseph H 92
Sarah A (Rice) 339
Sarah Ann (Rice) 92
DOGGETT, J M 221
DOIG, -- (Surtis) 48
John D 48
DOLES, -- 27
Georgia Alma 27
DOMINGOS, J W 303, 361
DONALD, A D 121-22
A F 260
John A 82, 260
Malcom M 82
Mary (--) 82
May (--) 260
Rebecca (Johnsey) 122

Rebecka (--) 121
Sarena J 121
DONALDSON, Joseph 103
Melinda (--) 103
William 103
DONNAN, Hanover 89
Lucy (--) 89
DOOLITTLE, Fannie 398
DOOLY, M E (--) 102
Polly E 102
Thos 102
DORCH, Rebecca 280
DORMAN, Exie 121
Wilson M 146
DORN, Peter 105
DORRIS, -- (--) 206
John M 206
DORSEY, John 20
Wm H 5
DOSS, Martha 233
DOUCHE, Daniel 176
DOUCHERLY, Allen 377
DOUGHERTY, Ann W 52
David H 38
James 218
M H 218
DOUGHTY, -- (Felder)
275
W H 275
DOUGLAS, D S T 107
J J 219
Mary (Herrington) 266
P W 175
Silas 266
Tilman 175
DOUGLASS, Jeanette
(--) 230
John 230
Lucinda 294
Mary (--) 294
Phoebe Wambersin
(Charlton) 175
William 294
DOUTHIT, B H 264
D (--) 264
Ella J 264
DOW, Lorenzo 360
DOWDELL, J F 26, 75
James 75
Louis A 408
Louisa J D 75
Nannie Neal (Davis)
408
DOWDLE, Ann (--) 318
Annie Wilson 318
J W 318
DOWLING, A 22, 24, 46,
66, 100-01, 211, 254,
266, 272, 288, 346
Amanda Cordelia
(Ham) 272
Angus 98, 347
Lettie 260

Samuel S 272
Susan M 363
Susan W (--) 363
William 363
DOWMAN, A W (--) 324
C W 399
Charles 324
Mary 324
DOWNING, Susan A
(Smilie) 147
Thomas W 147
DOWNS, Emmitt 137
Isaiah 300
Josephine (--) 137
Mary (Morrow) (Pate)
300
Sarah 170
Sarah L A 137
DOZIER 223
-- (--) 364
-- (Lindsay) 323
Abner C 264
Ann J 174
Constance (Hunt) 335
Ella (Adkisson) 316
Ezekiel A 272, 316
Fannie (--) 342
Frances J 178
George Carter 316
Green J 178, 323, 335
Ignatius J 323
James 225
James F 256
Jane M (--) 324
Jno W 371
John 342
John Bell 241
John W 76, 219
John Wilson 342
Lois T (--) 272, 316
M C (--) 358
Martha (--) 225
Martha M (--) 76, 91
Martha M (Haynes) 342
Mary (Thomas) 316
Mattie Pettrona 219
Mattie R 256
Rebecca L 272, 316
Rebecca S (Wall) 256
Richard 174
Sallie A (--) 219
Susan H (--) 174
Thos H 91, 219
Tinie E 76
Wilson 91
DRAFFIN, J T 85
Mary Ann (--) 85
DRAIN, Wm 111
DRAKE, -- 327
Alfred 107, 212
Francis B 327
John C 174
Louisa F 212

Mary (--) 107
Mary Antoinette 107
Mary W (--) 212
Viola 174
Viola W (--) 174
DRANE, -- 247
Electra A (Haughton)
(Jackson) 412
Hiram 412
M Julia 256
Martha H (--) 247
Minerva S 206
William 247
Wm 206
DREW, Elizabeth
(Harris) 334
John J 334
DRIGGERS, Nancy J
(Thigpen) 283
Stephen A 283
DRIVER, E J 399
Elbert J 399
DRUMMOND, William H
282
DUBARD, Adam F 132,
225
Catharine (--) 225
Mary Eliza Ruff (--)
144
Mary F 415
N J 225
Nathan 144
DUBOSE, Caroline (--)
147
Elizabeth A (--) 51
James Vance 147
Jas M 147
DuBOSE, Charlotte (--)
290
E E 163
Elizabeth A (--) 44
Eugenia 163
J R 51
James R 13
Jas R 44, 87
Middleton 115
Wylie Span 87
DUCK, Ebenade 149
J C 149
Sarah (--) 149
DUDLEY, Laura O 65
Richard William 123
DUFFEY, D L 395
R L 145
DUFFIE, R L 198, 260,
302
Reuben L 260
DUFFY, -- (--) 353
John M 353
R F 122
R L 124
DUGGER, Mary A 359
Mary Elizabeth 412

Salome A (--) 359
William 359
DUKE, -- 321
-- (--) 321
Achsah (--) 25
E D 309
Eliza T (Stansell) 120
Ellen (--) 117
F M L 117
Ferdinand 120
John K 117
Lorena F 114
Margaret (--) 38
Martha W 321
Mary Catharine 38
N S 38
Nancy A (Payne) 54
T L 367
DUKES, Anna J (Johnson)
171
George W 147
M E H (--) 347
R N 171
Susan (--) 147
Thomas E 147
DUMAS, Jas H 35
DUNBAR, Emily (Pugh) 53
Thomas 53
DUNCAN, -- (--) 322, 374
Carrie (Gist) 351
Catharine 71
Catharine (--) 388
Catharine A 71
Catherine (--) 209
D'Arcy P 351
Daniel 162
David 151, 322
David N 374
E B 97, 348
Florida Caroline 50
Geo 388
George 209
Hardy 30
J P 50, 98, 114, 129,
168
J T 403
James A 322
James E 71
James Merriwether 215
John P 94, 172, 339
L 83
Mary Eugenia 209
Robert D 339
T F 129
Virginia 50
Wallace W 322
Wm M 128
DUNLAP, David 197
E O 197
Eliza 250
Hattie (--) 127
R O 259
Rebecca J (--) 259

Robert 197
S S 197
Thomas Jefferson 259
W C 34, 45, 110, 115,
149, 186, 197, 233,
239, 259, 281, 337,
349, 351, 361-62,
388, 393, 397
William 127
DUNN, -- 81
Carrie (--) 188
Ishmael G 188
J J 188, 233
Larkin 81
Martha (--) 233
Mary F 217
DUNWODY, Esther 142
James 142, 287
Jas 1
Joseph Benson 287
Lavinia (--) 206
Mary 92
Mary (--) 92, 142
Robert 92, 142
S N 55, 84, 97
Samuel 206
Samuel N 47, 142
Sarah (Sutton) 1
Susanna Newton 84
DUNWOODY, Joseph
Benson 294
DUPOIS, Seth 76
DuPONT, C H 389
Charles H 399
Mary Ann (--) 389
DUPRE, Andrew Hibben
398
Esther Ann (--) 398
Warren Palmer 398
DuPRE, Daniel 398
DUPREE, J N 212
DUPUIS, Seth Stafford 77
DURANCE, -- 213
Cynthia (Tippins)
213
DURANT, -- (--) 351
Elias 331
Elizabeth (--) 256
Matilda (--) 115
Selina (--) 331
DURDEN, -- 65
Martha 65
DURHAM, Hardy 80
John 249
Sabra (--) 80
Susan C (Webb) 249
DURR, John 406
DuTART, James E 334
DUTTON, -- (--) 322
Elizabeth (--) 93
Mann 93
William H 322
DUURANT, H H 351

DUVAL, Harriet (--) 310
W J 69
DWIGHT, Mary Ann
(Jamison) 36
Samuel B 36
DYAL, Elizabeth 164
DYCHES, J W 292
Laura T (Bond) 292
DYE, Edna (Harbrick) 131
Perry 131
DYER, John 393
Mary A (Goodall) 84
Missouri (--) 393
Otis 84
Romalie Bascom 103
Susan Emma 393
DYSON, James M 320
E--, A B 26
C A 90
J F 125
J S 72
W 96
EADDY, O 18
EADY, Caroline L (--)
309
Henry P 309
John 79
Milton 298
O 292, 298, 311, 384,
391, 396
EAKEN, Margaret M 33
Wm 33
EAKES, M H 116, 239,
303, 345, 355, 377,
391
Marion H 178, 338
Robt A 299
EANS, Sarah N (--) 288
EARLY, -- 239
Elizabeth (--) 226
Helen M 149
Isaac W 226
K P (--) 149
Thomas 149, 414
EARNEST, -- (--) 389
Felix W 197
Mary A 248
P Madison C 389
Rachel (--) 197
EASON, Abram 381, 395
Elizabeth j 77
Nancy K (--) 381
Susie C 395
Wm 77
EAST, Elizabeth 51
EASTERLING, -- (Keen)
339
John R 256
W F 339
EBERHART, Eliza (--) 265
Mary Ella 265
Robt 265
EBON, -- 402

Ann Bonner (Floyd) 402
John B 402
ECHOLS, J H 377
Lucinda A (Pat) 63
Thomas J 63
ECORD, Missouri (--) 362
W A 362
William Walter 362
EDELEN, Sallie (--) 68
EDENS, Allen 8
Anna (Thomas)
(McDaniel) 8
EDGERTON, J C (--) 185
Sarah Ann (Fletcher)
153
Thomas Robert 185
EDISON, M B (--) 397
EDMONDSON, Anna B
(--)
85
James R 262
Joseph A 85
Mary D 244
Mattie 262
Martha J (Lane) 19
EDMUNDS, Martha E (--)
173
R H 173
EDMUNDSON, Belle
Watters (--) 351
EDWARDS, -- (--) 145,
281, 317, 322-23
Ann E 370
Barber (--) 370
Bennson H 82
C S 281
Catharine A (Turner)
360
D B 82
Delia A (Smith) 121
Dorcus L (--) 175
E D 181
Edward Lee 359
Eleanor A (Trotter)
243
Eliza (Dunlap)
(Laller) 250
Elizabeth 208
Elizabeth Ann 384
Elmira (--) 325
Frances S 67
George 244
Gideon 325
H B 121
Henrietta A (--) 386
Henry R 323
Jane (--) 211
Jas B 121
Jonathan C 211
Joseph 32
Julia (--) 244
L M 386
Laura 211

443

E D 344
Fredrick 223
H R 91
Hamlin R 71
J A J (--) 338
J Rufus 71, 141
Julia Ann 406
Julia C 223
Julia S (--) 275
Lewis 72
Margaret J (--) 223
Mary C (--) 72
Thomas Clarke 338
W L 275
Wm L 28
FELKEL, Jacob L 112
Jno A 15
John A 342
John F 141
Lilla Gertrude 15
Rebecca (Houck)
(Barnes) 112
Rosa (--) 15, 342
FELTON, Paul 231-32
R A (--) 231
Rebecca A (--) 232
W H 231
Wm H 232
FELTS, Laura L (--) 295
Robert L 295
FENLEY, John 218
Susan (Hendrix) 218
FENTRESS, H C 215, 274
Jonathan C 301
Serena J (Lingo) 301
FERGUSON, F G 43
J Barber 295
Mary C 43
FERGUSSON, Martha Ann
(Stormon) 74
Thos 74
FERREE, Alexander
Joseph 21
FERRELL, Byrd 274
Elizabeth A (Tyson)
270
James A 270
Nancy 274
FESTER, Mary 248
FETNAM, Lucy Elizabeth
145
FETNER, Martha (--) 338
William 338
FEW, Martha C 218
William 218
FIELDING, Elizabeth
(--) 202
Elizabeth A (--) 278
Mary (Brandon) 212
Thomas W 212
Thos W 202
FIELDS, Elizabeth
(Mixon) 177

Gabriella 265
John 177
FIFE, A L (Jeffress) 358
George C 358
FIKE, C L 300
FINCHER, Cynthia (--) 89
Diodema (McClendon)
(Graves) 283
Diodima (--) 162
Henry H 89
William 162
Wm 89
Wm M 283
FINDLEY, Dempsy 52
James 395
Judith (--) 52
Mary (--) 395
FINGER, -- (Avery) 164
Hannah E (--) 150
J 164
John 150, 240
Robert Gage 150
FINLAYSON, Daniel 213
Mary 213
FINN, A L (--) 341
Ann S (--) 6
Jno 6
Mary E 6
FINNEY, M E (--) (Cox)
99
FISHBURNE, C C 130,
290, 320, 339
Eliza S (--) 226
Wm R 226
FISHER, -- 381
-- (--) 282
Cornelia 124
Elizabeth (--) 393
George H 282
Harris 317
Harris M 153
Inman H 293, 393
Ira Lee 393
Julia G (--) 317
Mary Elizabeth
(Sturges) 293
Mary J (Palmer) 153
William 124
William Edward 35
Wm Metcalf 317
FISTHER, Amanda H 396
George H 396
FITCHER, -- 343
C P C (--) 343
FITZGERALD, -- 31
Freeman 100
Sarah E 100
FITZPATRICK, Mary L
(Shaw) 138
W J 138
FLADGER, Charles J 266
Ella 266
Jane (--) 266

FLAKE, Martha 390
FLANDERS, Jordan 4
Rachel 4
W J 289
FLEMING, -- (--) 102
Donald 300
E Carrie (--0 47
Isabel Hardy (--) 386
Israel W 386
J W 386
James F 96
Manning Austin 47
Martha 169
Martha (--) 169
Mary E 147
Mary J (--) 175
Mary R 134
Perry H 96
Robert 169
Samantha J (--) 96
Samuel 102
Sarah A 343
W H 47, 350, 387
Wiley 96
FLEMISTER, Hattie E
(--) 67
Lewis 67, 257
Lewis E 67
FLETCHER, -- (--) 264
Annie (--) 153
Annie Featherston 264
C J 26
C S 26
Carrie (--) 262
Charles J 26
John 274
Joseph 153
Nancy (Ferrell) 274
Sarah Ann 153
Susan Ann Eliza 54
Winfield 262
FLEWELLEN, A H 230,
283
Abner H 142
Ann 142
Caroline L (Calhoun)
(Love) 129
Jas T 404
Margaret E 244
Mary (Thweatt) 283
W W 129
Wm 283
FLEWELLYN, Nancy 189
FLINN, Sarah A (--) 33
FLOOD, Rebecca (--) 128
Samuel F 128
FLORENCE, --
(Blackwell) 138
E Stockbridge 206
Geo W 258
Harriet F (--) 25
Mary Ann (--) 258
W A 25, 266

445

Samuel Ferdinand 16
Sylvanus 13
Thomas 188, 193, 299
Thomas H 248
W A 361
Wiley J 56
William 381
GILBERT, -- (Redding)
105
A A 363
Amos A 88
Caroline M (Kennedy)
269
Daniel 269
Elizabeth (--) 88
J N 105
John T 88
Margaret E (Mann) 60
Nathan W H 191
S G 391
Sarah J (--) 191
W B 60
GILES, Andrew S 113
E H 135-36, 173, 183,
236
J J 55, 126, 269, 315
John Mason 113
Mary Ann (--) 73
Mary Jane (Trantham)
135
Sue (--) 113
W A 315
W W 73
GILHAM, Mary A 364
Nancy Ann (--) 272
Robert 272
GILL, -- 339
A A 384
Elizabeth (--) 117
J H 384
Jacob Thomas 161
Josiah 26
Mary E (Hutchings) 339
Mary S 374
Richard Shelton 26
William B 339
GILLEAN, Hiram 299
GILLEN, E W 284
James 284
Margaret M (Clarke)
284
GILLESPIE, A M 43
Harriet Pegues (--) 29
James C 311
Samuel Wilds 29
Sarah (--) 311
GILLIAM, M J 97
Rebecca P 97
T T 97
GILLIS, H M 318
GILMER, -- 68
GILMORE, -- (--) 369
Cora Hart 84

Eliza 9--0 399
Eliza C (--) 180
Irene Nuella 180
J B 399
J L B 84, 180, 369
GILREATH, Martha C
(Few) 218
W H 218
GILSTRAP, John B 361
Mary A (--) 361
GINDRAT, -- (--) 205
Dorcas (Williams) 205
Henrietta 205
Henry 205
GINN, Arthur 351
GIRARDEAU, J A 230
GIST, -- 351
Carrie 351
GLADDEN, A W 29
Elizabeth E (--) 159
Minor 29
GLASCOCK, Harriet H
(--) 87
Thomas 87
GLASS, -- (--) 298, 338
Ann (Porter) 34
Anna Pope (Weston) 361
E 361
Erastus 361
James 203
James M 338
John 298
Manson 41, 377
Minerva (--) 41, 377
Rebecca H (--) 150
Sarah A 41
Thos S 34
Zelemma 377
GLAZE, -- 202
Harriet 9--) 414
Sarah (Howell) 202
William 414
GLENN, -- 129, 137, 329
-- (Capers) 129
Barbary (--) 394
E A (--) 278
Elizabeth (--) 5
G Walker 278
J N 72, 390
J W 329, 390
James R 390
Jas E 5
John B 51
John R 389
Louisa (--) 137
Lucy 193
Mandane Allen 51
Massillon 394
Milly (--) 36
N Z 412
Rosela Virginia 278
Sallie 394
Susan CaperS 129

W F 237, 273
Wm 36, 276
GLISSON, Dennis 122
Lizzie E (Brown) 122
GLOSS, Mason 38
Minerva (--) 38
Sarah A 38
GLOVER, Benjamin 86
C E 253
C E (Padgett) 148
E C 153
Sarah 136
Sophia (--) 355
Susan (McGill) 222
William 222
Wm 136
GOBER, Amanda (--) 164
C 262
Eveline (Burgess) 165
Henry J 164-65
Jas W 165
L H 164
M E (--) 262
Mary (--) 165
Robert R 164
Wm Henry 132
GODALL, Seaborn 35
GODARD, Mary Leila 191
GODBOLD, Elly 79
Olivia (--) 79
Sarah Ann 348
Thomas 348
GODFREY, -- 243
Agnes (Taylor) 243
Alfred 243
Anna Betts 209
Ervin 243
J E 243
Jas E 209
Joseph 243
GODWIN, Benjamin F 102
H (--) 117
Sarah (Caver) 102
W H 117
W T 117
GOLDEN, Sarah F 40
GOLIGHTLY, Richard B
106
GOLLAND, Thomas C M
198
GOLSAN, I H 2
Mary B (Brodnex) 2
GOLSON, Martha Malinda
P (Harden) 28
Mollie 206
W C M 28
GOOCH, J H 274
M M (Culclasure)
(Ogburn) 274
GOODALL, Mary A 84
Rebecca (--) 84
Samuel 84
GOODBREAD, -- (--) 349

C C 133
Elizabeth Hardee 349
F 175
John B 133
GOODE, -- (Kendall) 313
Julia F 369
Martha E (--) 40
S W 40
Samuel N 313
GOODIN, Antoinette
Eugenia (Butts) 27
Matthew J 27
GOODLETT, J W (--) 312
GOODMAN, -- (Frierson)
32
E R 32
J 324
GOODRICH, Susan C
(Clark) 403
William H 403-04
GOODWIN, -- (Leeman)
154
Allen 43
Caroline J (--) 14
E E (Franklin) 386
H B 386
James 284
Mary A 113
Nancy A (Hamer) 43
S (--) 284
Samuel 9, 113
Thos H 154
GOODYEAR, Timothy 117
GOOGE, -- (--) 267
Robert 267
GORDON, Alexander 280
Annie 131
B F 51
Benj F 51
D A (Palmer) 53
Dollie (--) 334
Elizabeth 111, 269,
280
Elizabeth (--) 209
James 240
Jane E (Tooke) 232
Jennie G (McGregor) 51
John M 57
Lizzie D 334
M J 209
N K 269
Richmond 269
Thomas 53, 334
Thomas B 232
William 209
GORDY, G M 213
Sarah Jane (--) 213
GORE, James W 43
Martha R (--) 43
GOSS, Emma E 412
H L 64
I J M 132, 412
Octavia (Thomson) 64

GOSSETT, Edna Caroline
223
John T 223
Wilson C 162
GOUDELOCK, D 33
H B (--) 371
Hamlet 371
John B 226
GOWAN, Martha Ann
Jennette (--) 6
R A 6
GRACE, -- (--) 272
Lou (--) 273
Lucretia E 152
M C 152
R T 272
S B (--) 152
Sarah (--) 55
W D 273
GRADDICK, Derilda
(Richardson) 143
Henry 279
GRADDOCK, Daniel 210
GRADDY, L G 260
GRADY, Elizabeth (--)
189
Marcus A 30
GRAHAM, A H 250
A J 264
Alex 110
Andrew J 264
Anna Maria 46
Charlie Gordon 3
David 307
Duncan D 250
E J (Mason) 393
Elizabeth (--) 4
Elizabeth (Ryler) 13
Elizabeth R (Baxter)
344
Ellen H (--) 400
Fannie Louse 8
Frances R (--) 402
James 46
Jane 307
Jane Adaline
(Haygood) 264
Jessee N 91
John M 283
Lee (--) 3
Lizzie Harllee 400
Martha 383
Martin 4, 13
Mary (Johnson) 381
Mary B 110
P J (--) 247
S R (--) 250
Susannah 78
Thompson 383, 402
W A 36
W H 127, 210, 218,
221, 247, 353
W P 3

W W 299
Z G 393
GRAHAMM, W L 344
GRAINGER, H E 289
M A C M (--) 289
Mary Annie Elizabeth
289
GRAMBLIN, Andrew 90
Andrew P 90
GRAMBLING, Emma E
(Manning) 396
I W 396
GRAMLIN, John 190
GRAMLING, A P 90
Addie J (--) 399
Andrew 281
Andrew P 125
C W 300
Caroline L (Stroman)
308
Carrie (Kellogg) 299
Elizabeth (--) 125
Elizabeth (Imboden)
338
John 338
M 308
Nancy Louisa 300
Priscilla P (--) 300
Rebecca (Foster) 281
Thomas A 299
Thos A 399
Wilber Wightman 125
William A 300
GRANBERRY, Elizabeth
Albina (--) 406
J J 406
GRANGER, Amanda 236
John 236
Nancy (--) 236
GRANT, -- (--) 130
Augustin L 130
Daniel 234, 236
Lydia E (Simms) 14
Mary E (Hungerford)
234, 236
Sallie (Fuller) 266
Wm A 266
GRANTHAM, Clarissa
(--) 344
Noel 344
GRAVES, Aurelia A 152
Diodema (McClendon)
283
Sallie Porter (--) 343
Yverson L 8
GRAY, -- 391
A 66
Absalom 85
Albert 184
Ambrose W 22
Caroline C (--) 51
David 95
Eliza P (--) 99

Elizabeth 391
Frances A 85
Green 51
Ida B 334
J H 240
James F 56
Jno D 265, 275, 289
Judson 90
Mary (Dickey) 95
Samuel 99
William W 240
GREEN, -- (--) 235, 265,
273, 329
A C 55
A L P 209
Adeline E A (--) 267
Amanda H 329
Amanda M (--) 326
Andrew T 57
Ann M (Chambless) 102
Elenora 324
Elizabeth (--)
(Thompson) 398
Elizabeth (Reddir ӡ)
400
Elizabeth W (--) 294
Ella B (Lipscomb) 267
Ellen (--) 331
F J 57
F P 27
Fred J 57
Glenn 273
H B 252, 289
H D 150
Henry Bass 273
Henry D 135, 246
Henry Davis 136
J A 19
James 263
James R 329
Jane (--) 354
Jesse W 326
Jno H 400
Joel P 324
John A 112
John H 400
Laura W (--) 112
Martha J (Carter) 109
Mary (--) 273
Mary A P (Hill) 57
Mary E T (--) 134
McKeen 331
Myles 400
R G 246
Rebecca (--) 246
Robert T 235
S B 134
Sallie E 27
Sallie Albert 112
Sarah (--) 160
Sarah A 354
Sarah Hull 331
Sue 246

Texana F 326
Thomas 109, 239
Thomas F 265, 267, 303
Thos F 265, 267
Walker 398
William 160, 354
Wm A M 102
Wm J 329
Wm M 294
GREENE, -- 219
Caroline Mathilda
(Gardner) 330
Clement C 138
Curtis 219
E M (--) 141
J T 141
J W 108
James 396
James W 217
John H 276
Martha W (--) 329
Mary Frances (--) 138
Mary Virginia 329
Miles 100, 329
Myles 155
Sallie (--) 219
Sallie Law 108
Sarah E (--) 108, 217
Sue M (Smith) 276
T E 396
W I 141, 318
W J 277
William A 330
Wm J 189, 244
GREENWOOD,   Ann
Leonora
(--) 291
Caroline M 291
Thomas 291
Thomas B 151
GREER, -- (Speer) 193
J M 193
Lizzie L (Chambers)
329
Margaret 215
Margaret (--) 215
Mary Jane (Rucker) 12
Mildred V 147
Robert 215
T G 329
W II 147
William H 12
GREGG, Catharine (--)
211
Mary W Fracklin 82
R J 288
Rebecca S (White)
(Keeffe) 98-99
Robert J 82
Samuel 211
W Gordon 211
William 19
Zilpha (Evans) 288

GREGORY, -- 367
-- (McAfee) 183
J T 89
J T M 89
Jathan 329
Martha E 304
Mary Louise (--)
(Archer) 126
Mira (Bedford) 329
Susan M (McAfee)
(McAfee) 367
GRESHAM, Amanda 335
Jane P (--) 266
Thomas S 266
GRESSON, -- 365
C C (Willis) (Elder)
365
GRIER, -- (--) 403
Benjamin 208
Benjamin Marion 208
Cornelia Mary
(Sarvis) 291
L A 244, 291
Lemuel Asbury 403
Mary (--) 208
W K 291
GRIERSON, Fannie
(Brown) 235
John 235
GRIFFEN, Keturah 360
GRIFFIN, Alice E 415
Ann Cole (--) 227
Elizabeth 414
Indiana Eliza
(Branham) 389
J J 389
James 226, 279, 362,
414
Jas 85
Mamie P (Dixon) 289
Margaret (--) 59
Martha 85
Mary E (--) (Slappy)
273
R W 255
Rebecca (Willcox) 358
Rhoda 279
Sarah (--) 414
Sarah (Murphy)
(Hardle) 362
Sarah C (--) 255
Silas 59
W J 289
W W 227
Wm 17, 415
Yancy R 358
GRIFFIS, -- (--) 238
Mary Lillian 238
W H 238
GRIFFITH, -- 305
Anna (--) 371
Anna Louise 371
Berry 216

Celestia A (Thrasher)
62
Elizabeth (--) 216
Francis P 62
G J 371
James 157, 216
Margaret 339
Margaret (Willis) 305
Rebecca 216
Robert Allen 316
Whitman 316
GRIFFITHS, Thomas A
269, 339
GRIMES, Julia E (--) 182
Leila (Jernigan) 194
GRINER, Natthanael G H
20
GRISHAM, Hattie E
(Bivings) 348
Roland 348
GRISSOM, -- (--) 233
GROCE, J E 47, 98, 167,
380
Mattie 98
Sarah (--) 47, 98
Susan Elizabeth 47
GROOVER, -- (Hays) 155
-- (Maulden) 216
Daniel 155
Elizabeth 327
Peter 216
Thomas A 336
G R O V E N S T I N E ,
Henrietta
W (--) 174
John L 174
John W A 174
GROVES, J J 215
Rignal NN 263
GRUBER, George H 191
GRUM, James G 171
GUERRY, Daniel 141
Georgia H 141
Martha A (--) 141
GUGLE, David 76
Eliza 76
H 76
GUITON, Mary A (Love)
129
Moses 129
GUMM, James M 174, 178
GUNBY, George 268
Sarah C 268
GUNN, Harriet (--) 49
Harriet S (Wyatt) 288
Thomas S 49
William S 49
Wm S 288
GUNNELS, -- (Anderson)
131
G M 131
J D 290
GUNNIN, Joseph W 345

Mary (--) 345
Mary (Lights) 205
Nathan 205, 345
GURLEY, J G 23
GUTHERIE, W J 108
GUTHREY, Robert M 382
GUTHRIE, Hannah (--) 66
W J 66
GUYER, Alexander 141
Emily J (Harriss) 141
GUYTON, C S 242
Charles S 282
Cornelia (Fisher) 124
Elmina (--) 282
Helen A 339
Louisa C 282
M J 124
Mary (--) 339
Mary P (Blackshear)
242
Moses 339
GWINN, Rebecca Emma
(Nash) 256
GWYNN, -- (Nash) 207
D W 207, 256
H--, J M 95
J W 147
K L 65
S E 134
W G 110
W H 109
HABERSHAM, -- (Stiles)
384
Anna Wylly (Adams) 354
J B 384
Joseph Clay 354
Wm Neyle 354
HACKETT, Morton 94
HADAWAY, S A 376
HADDEN, R M (Branch)
143
HADDOCK, -- (--) 102
Joseph 102
Mattie Udora 102
HAFER, -- (--) 85
Arabella (--) 1
Willie M 1
Wm 1
HAGIN, Jas S 299
Mary E (--) 351
Mary Jane (--) 299
Solomon 351
Zacie 351
HAGOOD, S A 266
HAIGLER, John P 408
HAINES, -- (--) 220
Anna 220
Nathan 220, 280
Rebecca (Dorch) 280
HAINSWORTH, M E (--)
339
HAIR, Isaac N 145
Jennette (Bledsoe) 62

Malcolm 62
Mary Ann 145
HAISLIP, W C 321
HAISTEN, John 380
John M 136
HALCOMBE, Felicia Perry
Bergman (Bollee) 409
HALE, Sarah C 338
HALEY, Frances (Jones)
303
Joel 303
HALL, -- 219, 258, 261
-- (--) 311
Ann 219
Anna M 307
B F 48
Daniel 190
Elizabeth 261
Elizabeth B (Mabrey)
48
F W 311
Fannie (--) 250
Fannie C (McLaughlin)
190
Hugh A 17
Isaac 64
J G M 44
Jemima 85
Jessie Alexander 17
Joseph 269
Julia (--) 204
Julia Homes 204
Kindred T 258
Lula Lee 17
Margaret E 58
Martha A (--) 307
Martha D 159
Morgan B 307
Pamelia 324
Rhoda (Griffin) 279
S A (--) 17
Susan (--) 194
T K 401
Tarpley 58
W J 204
Zilpha (--) 95
HALLADAY, Wm O 223
HALLMAN, George W 355
Margaret (--) 355
Margaret N 355
HALLOWAY, Francis (--)
119
Nanny 119
R S 119
HAM, Amanda Cordelia
272
Frederick 272
Penelope (--) 272
HAMBLETON, James 126
Martha 126
Sarah (--) 126
HAMBY, Allen 273
David W 273

Frances 300
Mary (--) 230
Robert Lee 230
Susan McP (--) 273
Thomas D 230
HAMER, Daniel H 43
Kitty (--) 43
L M 41, 43, 54, 196,
226, 253, 268, 272,
282, 296, 399
Lewis M 8, 254, 353,
387
Martha (--) 43
Mary (Bethea) 413
Nancy 54
Nancy A 43
Robert C 413
Sallie S 254
Seth 43
Wm 54
HAMES, L M 163
HAMETER, Elizabeth
(Bates) 42
Joel 42
Julia 42
HAMIL, -- (Tinsley) 166
Ezekiel R 166
HAMILL, A J 42
HAMILTON, -- 143, 273
A L 278
Isabella 143
J T 413
Jennett (Brown) 330
Joseph 65
M T (--) (Turner) 413
Martha James
(Herring) 278
Mary 65
Nancy (--) 65
S C 330
W T 335
HAMLINE, Mattie A 117
W E 117
HAMMOCK, Keziah 78
Wm H 72
HAMMOND, -- (Fort) 299
-- (Speer) 333
D W 333
Elizabeth (Rich) 384
Frances (Aker) 152
H A 333
Herbert 384
J D 379
Job 152
John 299
Lucy (Howard) 152
Lucy C (Hudson)
(Carter) 152
Wm 152
HANCE, -- (--) 11
E Eugenia 11
Sarah (Word) 263
William 11, 263

HANCHEY, -- 234
Daniel 234
Sarah (--) 234
HANCOCK, Alcy 250
Caroline 274
Crawford 286
James 152
Lucretia E (Grace) 152
R J 395
Richardson 5
Sallie (Pendergrass)
395
William 274
HAND, Adelia L (--) 199
Amanda M (--) 246
D M 199
Elizabeth Amanda 246
James H 246
HANDLEY, J 281
M E (--) 281
Robert Lee 281
HANDLY, James C 275
Martha C (--) 275
HANLEY, Ambrose 210
Elizabeth (Nettles)
210
M A (--) (Reese) 210
HANNA, C B 389
Frances (--) 389
HANNON, Elizabeth (--)
106
Elliott Cromwell 106
John 106
Mary Ann (Stubbs) 106
HANSFORD, L E 81
L I 50
Matilda (--) 81
HANSON, -- 297
Catherine (McCollum)
(Brewer) 170
Enoch 170, 174
Harriet (Barrett) 297
J B 174
John 297
John W 24
Margaret Ann 130
W G 6, 140, 166, 295,
301
HARALSON, Elizabeth
(--) (Patterson) 50
Herndon 50, 65
Sarah A 411
HARBEN, Louisa M 130
T B 130
HARBERSON, -- (--) 285
Archey T 285
Archie T 287
Irwin W 179
HARBESON, -- (--) 353
Ann E 382
Henry B 353
HARBRICK, Edna 131
Hezekiah 131

HARBY, Charles 287
Ella (--) 287
Rachel Arminda 287
HARDAWAY, -- 168
Elizabeth W
(Mitchell) 285
G W 102
James Jarratt 404
Martha Bibb (--) 404
Mary E (Hungerford)
233-34
Mary E (Hungerford)
(Grant) 236
Polly E (Dooly) 102
R H 285
Robert B 234
Robert S 236
Robt B 233
Robt H 285
Robt S 236, 404
HARDEE, Sarah C 13
Thos E (--) 13
HARDEMAN, Arabella
(Harris) 165
Benj F 165
Martha M 301
Parks 301
Sarah B (Sparks) 379
Thomas 379
HARDEN, Alexander 63
Catherine (--) 98
E W 306
Eliza C 182
George W 89
Henry 182
Ira H 45
Jas T 265
Martha Malinda P 28
Mary 391
Mary (--) 182
Neely 98
Sarah (--) 63
Stephen S 89
Surany (--) 89
HARDENTT, Indianna
(Carlisle) 185
Wm 185
HARDIN, -- (--) 262
Elizabeth (--) 410
Henry 410
J M 230
James M 262
Joseph N 152
Martha C 152
R A (--) 152
Sarah E 410
William 33
HARDLE, Sarah (Murphy)
362
Theophilus 362
HARDWICK, Frances J
(Dozier) 178
Margaret (--) 214

Lipscomb 15
M A (--) 277
M A (Meaders) 309
Mary Y (--) 15
Mary Yarbrough (--)
240
'Aunt' Polly
(Stroud) 208
S A 277
William 208
HAYLES, W A 88, 332,
393
W V 332
HAYNES, -- (Vaught) 403
B 403
Eleanor A (Trotter)
(Edwards) 243
John W 243
Lewis A 326
Marla 293
Martha M 342
Mary N (--) 326
Sarah J 197
HAYS, Charles 269
Charles R H 269
Charlotte (Orr) 155
Edward 220
Elizabeth (--) 107,
225
Elizabeth W (--) 113
Harriet A 67
M A 220
M J 225
Margaret (--) 220
Nancy Branson
(Jackson) 181
Pharibee (--) 181
R C W (Ross) 405
R P 225
Robert P 107
Thomas 155
Virginia 107
William 271
Wm D 181
Wm R 181
Wm Z 181
HAYWOOD, Silas Foster
362
HAZELTON, Mary
(Walter) 398
HEAD, Elizabeth B
(Harper) 60
George W 369
Sarah (--) 16
Victoria C (Winship)
369
Willis R 60
HEAP, Ann H 383
John 383
Mary (--) 383
HEAPE, J Harley 273
John 359
Julia Frances (--) 273

Mary (--) 359
Rebecca 359
HEARD, George 371
Henry 371
Isaac 274
Martha (Coffin) 371
P A 79, 84, 113, 287
Peter A 371
Thomas J 344
Thomas O 27
HEARN, Frank S 153
Joshua 313, 317
Leah (Smart) 313
Sarah W (--) 153
HEARNE, Mattie R (--)
399
R M 399
HEATH, Alex T 360
Annie Henrietta 130
E F (--) 111
E P 277
Elizabeth Caroline 111
Elizabeth W 295
Fanny (--) 97
Henry 97
Henry W 111
Isabel M (Buxton) 360
J P 401
John B 198
John Fletcher 120
John S 193
Lou (Stewart) 401
Lucy B (--) 277
M W 172
Mary Elizabeth 172
Mary J (Whedbee) 108
Millward W 130
Millward Williams 130
Moses Chappel 12
N M 346
Pleasant 295
Sarah E (--) 130
Sarah R (Gamewell) 172
W D 104, 195, 263
HEFLIN, Hettie R (--)
121
L F 121
Larkin 121
HEIDLE, M A M
(Whitehurst) 10
HEIDT, Christiana E 32
Emanuel 390
Frances L (--) 390
HEIR, -- 222
Laudonia (--) 222
HEISE, Ellen Victoria 20
John H 20
R S A (--) 20
HELDEBRAND, -- (--) 322
Jacob 322
HELDERBRAND, John R
235
HELVERTON, Eugenia

(Mott) 380
McGillis 380
HEMINGWAY, Martha
Eliza 21
Wm A 21
HEMMINGWAY, (--) 12
HEMPHILL, Mary
Anderson (--) 94
Sarah Lizzie 101
Wm A 101
HENDERSON, -- 214
Eliza 75
Laura Octavia 214
Mary 336
Mary (--) 336
Mary (Stansel) 373
Phil L 245
Susan L (Shines) 214
Thos 75
William 336
HENDRICK, Emma 330
Emma S (Poyas) 148
James 330
Lucinda (--) 330
Thos A 148
HENDRICKS, Harriet K
(--) 238
Margaret 238
Simon 238
HENDRIX, Francis (--)
218
J C 367
Luke 317
Simeon 334
Susan 218
Thomas 218
HENDRY, -- (--) 184
A R (--) 306
Alexander 264
Elizabeth 264
F A 306
Harriett 332
J M 17, 288, 391
John A 396
John Gardner 223
Julia Ellen 306
Margaret (--) 223
Mary L (--) 396
Neil 223
Sallie N 396
Wm Eli 181, 184
HENKLE, James 288
Mary Amaryllis 288
HENRY, A T 138
Emma 356
G W 139
J S 356
James W 327
Lucy G (Andrew) 107
Lucy G (Andrew)
(Wright) 407
Mary (--) 356
Mary (Thompson) 407

J H J 347
Jacob 153
Jacob C P 153
Julia A 347
L M 17, 91
Louisa (--) 135
Mary (--) 153
Milton D 347
Olin Coward 91
HOOPER, -- 403
John W 403
HOPKINS, Cornelia
(Smart) 277
Emily H (--) 202
J H 202
Lambeth 277
HORDAN, Wm J 411
HORN, Daniel A 316
Isabella (McLeod) 316
HORNADY, Albert
Crawford 27
Sallie E (Green) 27
HORNE, -- 12
Ann C 355
HORT, -- (Stanley) 367
Robert J 367
HORTON, -- 315
-- (McCoy) 86
Dicy 61
Elizabeth (--) 61
Elizabeth (Cauthen)
314
Embery Spence 263
Hardy 92
James 61
James W 198
M 86
Mattie E 315
Miel I 274
Miel J 237
Miley (--) 104
Milton Kennedy 104
Nancy 104
Nannie C (--) 237, 274
Polly (--) 92
T C 104
Wiley 314
Wiley Hill 263
Zarilda E (Horton) 274
HOSFORD, R F 352
HOSKINS, D R 216
David R 216
Sarah 216
HOSTLER, William 157
HOTT, -- (--) 383
Oliver P 383
HOUCK, Gaspar 112
Nancy (--) 112
Rebecca 112
HOUGH, Sylvester A 222
HOUSER, -- 406
Andrew W 34
Anna M (--) 186

Ella E 18
J O A 186
Jesse T 186
John H 113
John Hamlin 113
Lewis M 369
Lewis Myers 385
Margaret (--) 18
Mary Jane (Pooser) 113
Mary S (Whetstone) 103
103
R P 103
W 18
Wesley (Riley) 213
HOUSTON, Caroline (--)
66
Edward M 297
Elizabeth 156
John 66, 378
Margaret (--) 156
Margaret E (Roberts)
297
Martha Theressa 378
Minnie O 303
Samuel T 392
William 156
HOWARD, -- 379
-- (--) 394
-- (Lamar) 249
-- (Pollard) 61
C R 249
Caroline E 22
Charity 272
Cornelia (Lamar) 55
Eleanor (--) 182
Elinor (--) 116
Euphemia (--) 379
Fannie (Anderson) 379
James 55
John 22, 182, 333, 412
Joseph 182
Judith (--) 394
Lucinda (Jennings) 412
Lucy 152
M F (--) 262
M L (--) 142
Mary 64
Mary Williams 142
Meky (--) 123
Nicholas 394
Nicholas L 394
P J 262
R B 142
R O 379
Rebecca (Hurt) 55
Robert Henry 55
Rulie A E 262
Sarah C (Congelton)
182
Sealy E 123
Stephen 224
Tabitha (--) 55
Thomas B 379

Wm 123
Wm E 282
HOWE, Eliza E 209
Lucinda (--) 209
Mary S (Bryan)
(Raines) 237
Robert 237
W J 209
HOWEL, James 188
Mary (--) 188
Thomas 188
HOWELL, -- (--) 325
Anabel Faust
(Wightman) 164
Charlotte 69
Eliza C (--) 318
Harriet (--) (--) 104
J P 87
Joseph 104
Joseph H 325
Phillip 281, 318
Rhoda P (--) 161
Sarah 202
W H 164
HOWREN, -- (--)
(Durant) 351
-- (Mitzenburg) 351
-- (White) 351
Ann Elizabeth 230
Hannah (--) 75
J C 351
James C 351
R H 14, 65, 175,
230, 272, 282, 311,
323, 339, 351, 396
HOYE, Catharine
(Ligon) 139
David L 139
HOYLE, A C 139, 143
D L 143
John 139
L C 143
Thomas 143
Thos 143
HOYT, -- 115
-- (--) 115
HUBBARD, Charles Henry
215
Emma (--) 201, 215
John 201, 215
Laura Eugenia 201
Sarah E (Berry) 281
W L 281
HUBERT, -- (Turner) 408
E W 310
Joseph 189
Nannie 309
R W 50, 247, 277,
309, 318, 408
Robt W 50
Virginia (Duncan) 50
HUCHINGSON, S P 89
HUCKABEE, Allen 36

Sarah (--) 36
Sarah A (--) 86
Sarah Margaret 239
W G 86, 239
HUCKABY, A C (Hill) 371
W J 371
HUCKS, Joseph 303
Mary A (Sellers) 303
HUDGINS, Nancy E
(Knowles) 19
HUDSON, -- 18, 397
A C 220
Bethany (--) 220
C B 353
Charlie 8
Eliza 394
Emma E (Aycock) 363
Irby 349
J I 363
James L 72
Jane A 398
Lucy C 152
Martha Ashurst 349
Mary I (Woods) 353
Sarah 394
Theodora E (Abbott)
397
Wm 18
HUEY, C S 289
HUFF, D Martin F 322
J H 284
John Ira 28
M H (--) 52
HUFFMAN, -- (--) 405
A W 97
Elizabeth (--) 405
John 405
Samuel 405
Sarah C (Morrison) 97
HUGGINS, H H 290
HUGHES, A J 368
Andrew J 268
Andrew Paxton 108
Beatty 12
Corinne 30
D A E 325
F G 37, 40, 194, 237
F H 41
Francis G 81
G 4, 21, 40, 54
Goodman 2
Hannah 98
John H 144, 150
Julia 220
Margaret A (Cowan) 216
Mary J (--) 12
Nancy A (--) 108
Nancy D (--) 325
Norah Annah 268
Rebecca M (--) 268
Rufus J 325
T C 216
Thomas M 108

Wm 30
HUGHS, Andrew 97
Georgia C (Hines) 97
HULL, Asbury 274
Henry 226
Hope 1, 44
Maria (--) (Cooke) 274
HULME, Agnes Melita 309
HUMBERT, Hattie G 49
J W 73, 144
John G 49
M M (Kinard) 73
HUME, Adline (--) 239
B L 274
Benj L 239
HUMPHREYS, Joab 410
Lydia (Harrison) 410
HUMPHRIES, Charles 88
John Thomas 168
William 169
HUNGERFORD, Dade(?)
236
Dana 233
Mary E 233-34, 236
Rachel (--) 233, 236
HUNKAPILLER,
Christiana 215
HUNNEWELL, Mary L
(Cray) 307
HUNNICUTT, Clara A
(Atkinson) (Parks)
298
Greene B 382
J E P 299
James B 372
W L C 230
HUNT, -- 110, 277
-- (--) (Smart) 277
Ann (Hall) 219
Anna Lewis 377
Constance 335
Drucilla 303
E A (McCroan) 374
Eliza (Henderson)
(Smart) 75
Elizabeth 307
Emily J (--) (--) 16
F M 96, 114, 201, 209
James 303
Jemima (--) 303
Jno 75
Lewis 249
M A (--) 377
Martha (--) 335
Mary 224
Mary (--) (Nelms) 249
Mary H (--) 100
Mattie J (--) 324
Nat 135
Silas Floyd 374
Tabitha T T 335
Thomas 16, 325
Thos J 100

Turner 355
Wm 110
HUNTER, -- (--) 302
Annie A (Pope) 26
Bettie (--) 348
Catharine (Jones) 373
E (--) 197
Elizabeth (--) 1
H J 79
J H 348
J M 219
Jessie B 344
Lucie Helen 348
M C (Ruthledge) 344
Mary E E (--) 53
Nancy 23
Samuel 1
Sarah A 1
Thos 23
Thos T 26
William 302
HUNTON, Nannie E 395
HURT, -- 216
A F (Freeman) 216
C B 167
C S 333
E F 282
Emily F (--) 177
Eula G 177
Hallie L (Smith) 93
M Clementina (Smith)
93
Nathaniel 177
Rebecca 55
HUTCHERSON, Charles
(--) 183
HUTCHESON, Ellen F
(Carleton) 318
Peter W 318, 328
HUTCHINGS, Benj F 119
Mary E 339
Nancy Leonora
(Lester) 119
HUTCHINGSON, Julia D
(Skinner) 76
S P 52, 76
HUTCHINSON, Emily 69
Gertrude 320
Henry 54
John W 74
Rebecca J (--) 122
Sarah M (--) 320
Sarah R (--) 54
W T 320
HUTSON, Joseph H 226
William 125
HUTTO, -- 315
Frances (--) 302
Lewis 177
Mary (--) 315
Samuel 302
W 161, 178, 207,
293, 302, 320

William 10, 72, 97, 133, 398-99
Wm 36, 177, 315, 369, 373, 402
HYATT, Martha N (Satterwhite) 413
Seth H 291
Thomas 413
HYDE, Maria J 359
HYDRICK, Jacob 384
Margaret (Hildebrand) 384
HYER, E S (--) 278
Ella Maude 278
Ella S (--) 353
George Martin 353
J H 278
Jas S 353
Laura Jane (Stewart) 286
Wm L 286
HYMAN, Charity 326
IMBODEN, Elizabeth 338
INABET, Lizzie E (--) 382
INABNIT, Sarah E 372
INGRAM, -- 102
-- (--) 261
Demaris 388
Eliza 224
Florella Singleton 40
Martha (--) 40
Mary E 301
S 102
W B A 261
Wm R A 40
INMAN, Cyrene (McDonald) 311
James 311
INNES, Margaret H 212
IRBY, James H 243
Rebecca Ann (Sappington) 243
IRWIN, -- (Perry) 176
Wm R 176
IVEY, J L 406
Serena (--) 356
Travis 356
IVIE, Robert L 402
IVY, G W 164
J W 131
Milly (--) 153
Robert 153
IZLAR, Algernon Adolphus 326
Elizabeth 309
H P 326
Mamie C (--) 326
J--, A S 128
J B 137
J C 108
L A 127
JACK, -- 330

Elizabeth A (--) 330
William Howard 337
JACKSON, -- 80, 125, 389
-- (Cobb) 389
A M 263
Ada Jane (Mitchell) 29
Ada M (--) 28
Ada Mitchell 29
Benj C 20
Carrie E (--) 127
D H 145
David Clinton 145
Edmond 168
Electra A (Haughton) 412
Elizabeth Lavinia 263
F Corra 134
Gideon 181
H P 134
Harriet (--) 246
J B 33
J W 69
James 28-29, 312
James B 30, 36-37, 383, 412
Jane (--) (Wardlaw) 378
Jethro 57
John S 28
Joseph B 386
L B 34
Louisa E 28
M F (--) 134
Martha (--) 145
Mary Ann 20
Mary S (Seyle) (O'Sullivan) 393
Nancy (--) 20
Nancy Branson 181
Parthena (--) 263
Permelia F (--) 34
Robert 378
Sallie J 316
Sanna (--) 181
Sarah Alberta 127
Sarah VanHorn (--) 286
Selah 383
W F 246
W J 394
W S 246
W W (--) (Watts) 38
William J 393
William W 127
Wm H 312
JACOBS, Elizabeth (--) 22
JAMES, -- 320
E Louisa 205
Lizzie A 320
JAMISON, Barbary N 240
Elizabeth M 146
Mary Ann 36
V D V 36, 146

JAQUES, Annie E 382
Frederick 382
JARRARD, J D 353
Josiah D 151
Temperance Selma (Hayes) 151
JARRATT, Eliza A (Dean) 194
James D 194
JARREL, Louisa Fletcher (Sheridan) 142
Thomas 142
JARRELL, A J 11, 136, 267, 277, 327, 338, 341
W B 46
JAUDON, Annie (Heidt) 390
Mary E (--) (Brown) 336
JAY, -- (--) 260
James 260
Tyre 145, 260
JEFFCOAT, Elizabeth C 200
J B 200, 317
John R 78
Louisa (--) 200
Louisa (Riley) 317
JEFFORDS, S K 106
Sarah Susannah (--) 106
Wm 296
JEFFRESS, A L 358
JEMISON, Mattie (Groce) 98
S M 98
JENKINS, A D 121
Arabella (--) 330
Augustus M 294
C J 325
E A 330
Elizabeth 374
G F 273
J G 2
James 2
Jas 374
Leila Roberta 330
Margaret (--) 273
Mary J 33
Nancy J (McLeod) 325
JENNINGS, Celestia A 347
Elizabeth (--) 151
Ellen 79
J T 160
John T 183
Lucinda 421
Victoria V (O'Bryan) 160
William 79
JEPSON, Cynthia G (--) 110
William 110

461

John Elias 302
M R (--0 186
Martha Elizabeth 302
Mary Estelle 186
Sarah Bell 302
Sarah Eliza (--) 301
Tempy Ann (Wells) 270
Warner L 270
Warren L 50
KENRICK, Robert 80
KENSALL, Mary (--)
  (--) 41
KEOWIN, Frances
  Elizabeth (Stephens)
  271
John A 271
KERLIN, Lucretia (--)
  253
KERR, Wm 204
KERSEY, -- (--) 256
Joseph 256
KETCHINS, Joseph 367
M C 367
KEY, -- 215, 385
  A S (--) 190
  Ann (--) 26
  Anna (West) 184
  B S 190, 372
  B W 272, 331
  C W 29, 65-66, 96,
    171, 184, 324, 385
  E C (--) 372
  George Wesley 372
  Harriet L (Mans) 141
  Henry 26, 70
  Henry H 184
  Howard W 305
  J S 8, 14, 19, 28,
    68, 172, 214, 218,
    268, 353, 381
  James B 141
  Jos S 405-06
  Joseph 215
  M E 385
  Margaret (Greer) 215
  Mary E 70
  Sallie 26
  Susie 88
  Wesley 190
KIKER, Amilar (--) 214
KILE, Frances A E 396
  T E (Greene) 396
  W A 396
KILGO, J T 96, 100, 105
  Jas T 15
KILLIAN, Adelia U 166
  Daniel 166
  John 228
  Lucinda E L 228
  Mary (--) 166
  Nancy (--) 228
KILPATRICK, Charlotte
  (--) 177

Eliza V 159
Elizabeth (--) 251
James 137
Jas 185
Lucinda 251
Martha (--) 159
Mary 185
Mary (--) 185
Richard 251
W E 347
KIMBALL, F A 116, 348
KIMBELL, -- (--) 398
  F A 41, 63, 66, 97,
    275, 380, 385, 398
  F H (--) 385
  Fannie Doolittle 398
  Francis Asbury 410
  Frank 385
  John K 276
  Nancy A (Criddle) 276
  Nathan 410
KIMBROUGH, Alexander
  S
  224
  J R 125
  James M 193
  John Raphael 117
  Love (--) 319
  Mary Elizabeth 224
  Mary M 193
  S A (--) 224
  Sallie Mobley (--) 193
  William H 369
KINARD, F E 73
  Henry Harrison 73
  James Pinckney 73
  Jno Martin 73
  Louisa C (Counts) 73
  M M 73
  Mamie 74
  Mary A (Counts) 73
KIND, -- (Watts) 123
KINETT, Braxton H 319
  E T 319
  F L (--) 319
KING, -- 131, 304
  -- (--) 309, 314
  A D 314
  Amanda M (--) 171
  Angus M D 304
  Anna M (--) 328
  Benjamin 123
  Caroline M
    (Greenwood) 291
  Charlie Green 314
  Chas A 58
  E L 59
  Eleanor (--) 123
  Eliza (Youngblood) 249
  H H 291
  H Queen 309
  Hester Evans (--) 304
  J M D 249

James Carswell 237
Jerusha (--) 76
John 169
John Ragin 141
John W 149
L P Z 147
Martha F T 267
Martha Theressa
  (Houston) 378
Mary (--) 147
Mary A M 147
Mary A M (King) 147
Richard 259
Robert N 328
Samuel 320
Stephen C 123
Wiley 309
William 43, 147
William B 76
William G 9
William T 7
Y D 336
KINNETT, Frances (--)
  390
KIRBY, Antonia H 345
  Francis 345
  Francis A 124
  Harriet Ann
    (Shropshire) 124
  Jane (--) 222
  Jesse 222
  Mary B (--) 345
  Mary Jane 97
  Polina C 222
KIRK, B C 295
  W B 47
  W R 81
KIRKLAND, -- (Burnett)
  294
  Cynthia (--) 252
  George 252
  M Marion (--) 336
  Sallie M
    (Blacklidge) 347
  Sarah 321
  Seymore 347
  W C 294
  W D 225, 231, 303, 336
  Warren Palmer 336
  William Clark 294
KIRKPATRICK, Jas 152
  Mamie 350
  R A 319
  Sarah (--) 360
  T W 360
KIRKSEY, Caroline (--)
  407
  Gideon 407
  John M 407
KIRTON, O V (--) 366
  W H 233, 366, 380
  W M 232
  William Marvin 366

KISTLER, David 59
　Lawson H 53
　Margaret (Allison) 59
　P F 108, 252, 292
　Paul F 321
　R F 53
KITCHEN, Margaret (--)
　247
KITCHENS, Elizabeth
　(--) 78
　Emma Dawson (Price)
　401
　Meredith 78, 365
　Thos L 401
KITCHINGS, Boaz 280
KLUGH, H G 202
　Martha (Tate) 202
　Pascal D 15, 202
　Sarah E (--) 202
KNIGHT, Aaron 95
　Ann E (--) 132
　Catharine 95
　Daniel 214, 356
　E J 23, 113
　Elisha 383
　Eugene Aubrey 411
　J Hamilton 150, 229
　J W 414
　Julia T (Taylor) 411
　Louisa 229
　Mary (--) 229
　Mary E 214
　Nancy (--) 214
　Nancy C (Mayson) 356
　Nathaniel 132
　Reuben 229
　Selah (Jackson) 383
　William 132
KNOLES, Daniel H 386
　John H 386
　Margaret L (--) 386
KNOTT, Charlotte
　(Daniel) 192
　John 192
KNOWLES, -- (--) 19
　John B 19
　Nancy E 19
　R P 253
　Sarah R (Padgett) 253
KNOX, Georgia E (--) 205
　O F 86
　Robert B 141
　W 16, 113, 154, 204,
　235, 311, 365
KOGER, -- 293
　Ann A (--) 104
　Hattie (--) 293
　John 104
　Joseph 3, 196
　M A 196
　Mary (--) 196
　T J 196
KOLB, Ann (--) 72

KOPP, Edward 244
　Richard Walter 244
KORNEGAN, C 68
　Esther (--) 68
　Isaac 68
KRAMER, Geo R 196
　H P 94
　W P 36, 51, 55, 89
KRAST, -- (--) 247
　John 247
KRAUSS, Charles Edward
　266
　Emma Virginia 266
　Margaret (--) 266
　Peter 266
KYTLE, Sarah 331
L--, -- 56
　J E 115
　J H 316
　W W 111
LACY, Mary (--) 139
　Wm 139
LAINE, W T 323, 334
LAKE, Drucilla
　Chandler 266
　John 266
　Mary (--) 266
LALLER, -- 250
　Eliza (Dunlap) 250
LALLERSTEDT, L D 71
LAMAR 49
　-- 133, 249
　-- (Jones) 158
　Cornelia 55
　H J 158
　Harmony 249
　James H 280
　John O 280
　Martha A (Beal) 249
　Mary A (--) 280
LAMB, Alex 105
　Orpha Judson
　(Whitten) 105
LAMBERT, A C (Smith)
　323
　Edwin 120
　John O 323
　Sarah (--) 271
　Susan (--) 120
　Wm 271
LAMBERTH, -- (Dunn) 81
　Edwin 114
　Eugenia 114
　James 81
　Susan (--) 114
　William Edwin 120
LAMBUTH, Joseph 336
　Joseph King 336
LAMKIN, Mary F
　(Williams) 296
　S C 296
LAMON, C G (--) 211
LAMPKIN, Eliza (--) 172

Josephine Virginia
　Lewis 172
　Philip 151, 172
　W W 247, 289, 383
　Wallace 204
LAMPKINS, A (--) 63
LANCASTER, Leurtis L
　165
　Sarah C (--) 165
LAND, Chambers Edgar
　282
　Jno T 372
　Mourning R (--) 185
　Nathan 185
　Nathan Truman 185
　Sallie V (Faulk) 372
LANDER, S 386
LANDERS, Priscilla 403
LANDERSHINE, Chas P
　365
　Georgia 365
LANDRUM, Sarah E (--)
　226
LANE, -- (--) 217
　A F 15
　Ann 82
　Callie 387
　Callie L 387
　Carrie 312
　Deborah 395
　Elizabeth (--) 55
　George 387
　Harriet (Wittich) 387
　Jonathan 238
　Joseph 174-75
　Josiah J 55
　M H (--) 321
　Margaret L (Wittich)
　312
　Martha (--) 54
　Martha Iverson 321
　Martha J 19
　Mary E (McKinnon) 272
　Mary R 238
　Mary Seila 55
　Nannie J 30
　R 35, 289, 321
　Richard 289
　Richard A 241, 253
　Richard Q 19
　Thos 54
　W 6, 35, 46, 95,
　123, 126, 128, 217,
　225, 261, 272, 375
　Wesley 272, 328
　West 217
LANEY, -- (Glenn) 129
　Mary A (--) 363
　Noah 129
　R P 214
　S A (--) 214
　S D 363
　Samuel Vernon 363

467

LEGETT, David 412
Elizabeth 393
Martha A
(Richardson) 412
LEGETTE, Abner 20
Eliza Harriet 20
M A W 337
LEGG, John W 86
LEGWIN, Lot M 108
Mary (--) 108
LeHUE, Charles 188
M A 188
LeHUEM Mary Anna 188
LEIGH, A B 316
Arthus Benettus 316
Sarah (--) 316
LEITNER, Florence J C
168
George 76
James D 194
John D 168
Mary A (--) 168
Mary J (Neil) 194
Mary M (--) 24
LeMASTER, A M 336
LEMLE, Mary (--) 3
LEONARD, -- 297
Alexander K 400
Electra Fancena (--)
32
Elizabeth (Crowell)
(Harvey) 400
Francis R (Darnell)
381
Henrietta 136
James P 412
Martha Ware (--) 412
Mary Louisa 303
P L 297
R H 32
Sarah (--) 297
Thomas K 283, 315
Thos K 106
Van 136, 303, 381
LESLEY, Rebecca (--) 147
Susan E 147
T J 147
LESLIE, Evaline W (--)
290
H W 290
LESSESNE, -- (--) 96
LESTER, A H 69-70, 296,
311-12, 328, 339
B B 76
B H 202
Caroline M 19
Dennis 162
Elizabeth 69
Flora C (--) 106
Hartwell 119
Henry 289
Jno 19
Joanna 42

Joel 354
John E 69
Maggie (Roberts) 157
Mahala (--) 119
Martah J 263
Martha J (--) 263
Mattie E (McCall) 342
Nancy Leonora 119
R F 342
Samuel E B 157
Silas M 263
LESUEUR, Drury M 194
Jas N D 197
Louie L 262
Martha G (Raines) 194
LeSUEUR, Mary Eliza 250
Sarah J (Haynes) 197
LEVER, John 404
Nancy (Smith) 404
Stephen 61
Susan A (--) 61
LEVERETT, John W 306
Maston 306
LEVERMAN,   Elizabeth
291
Elizabeth (--) 291
John 291
LEVERTON, -- 280
Electa (Button)
(Patterson) 280
LEVINER, E J 113
Mary A (Goodwin) 113
LEVY, Eliza (--) 254
Moses 254
LEWIS, -- (--) 302, 315
-- (Pearse) 10
A W 10
B B 203
Geo W 247
Henry D 280
J 24, 36, 80, 138,
160, 165, 197, 219,
248, 262, 274, 294,
299, 311-12, 394
Josiah 216
Juliet R (Collins) 203
Lizzie S (Pearce) 141
M W 169
Margaret 45
Mary Ross (--) 216
N A 302
Nathan A 303
Obadiah E 315
Sarah 388
Sicily (Rogers) 303
Susannah 5
W W 405
Walker 388, 399
Wallis W 405
Walter F 354
Wm F 200
LEY, J C 219, 307
Jno C 129, 142, 259

John C 46, 173, 268,
352, 400
LEYBT, Elizabeth D
(--) 387
L F 387
Letitia Mouzon 387
LIFSEY, Benjamin 67
LIFSY, Parsha Ann 67
LIGHTS, Mary 205
LIGON, -- 58
Augusta Jane (Smith)
379
Beacham P 58
Catharine 139
Daniel 379
Jane 257
John 183
Joseph Pierce 379
Louisa (--) 253
Lucia Louse 253
Martha C (Powell) 58
Rhoda 260
Rhoda (--) 183
Temperance (--) 379
Wm J 253
Woodson L 58
LILES, -- (Carroll) 189
A J 189
Ada M (--) 179
Ella Jane 179
Lou (Ellis) 189
Wm A 179
LIN, J T 47, 69, 374
LINDLEY, -- (--) 187
John B 187
Jonathan 54
LINDSAY, -- 323
J C W 113
J W F 310
Jack 323
Jane E (Pressley) 392
John C W 104
Nancy (--) 310
Nancy (Horton) 104
Sally Mathis (Smith)
117
Samuel 392
LINEBERGER, Levi
Martin 149
T J 149
Zuletta (--) 149
LINGO, Daniel T 195
Serena J 301
LINLEY, E H 357
Jane (Scott) 357
Sarah (Smith) 357
LINN, James 396
Jane 396
Lydda (--) 396
LINSEY, -- (--) 197
B F H 197
E (--) (Hunter) 197
S W (--) 197

468

LINTON, Isaac M 193
  Sallie J 54
  Sarah C J (Hiers) 193
  Thomas J 54
LIPSCOMB, -- 267
  E (--) 315
  Ella B 267
  Francis A 256
  J W 315
  Mary Ann (Rutherford)
  256
  S C (--) 294
  Sallie C 294
  Sallie E 315
  Sarah C (Marshall) 381
  T C 294, 381
  Thomas J 233
LIPSEY, -- 386
  -- (Miller) 355
  John 355
  Maria 386
  Thomas A 45
LITTLE, -- (--) 4
  Elizabeth (--) 288
  Elizabeth (Gordon) 280
  J J 29
  J R 241
  Jno J 198
  John 280, 288
  John J 401
  L M 344, 346
  Lizzie A (James) 320
  Mary V 4
  Nancy M (Oxford) 57
  S J 29
  Vashti M 288
  Willis 57, 320
LITTLEJOHN, Abraham
17
  Agnes (--) 14
  Catharine (--) 206
  J E 222
  J H 241
  J R 147, 264, 268,
  271, 297, 320, 331,
  333
  James 254-55
  Jas 14
  John 48, 206
  Mary E 26, 206
  Medora 393
  Mollie 26
  S Hayden 307
  Sally (Richardson) 17
  Samuel 307
  Thomas 393
  Wm 26
  Wm McKendree 48
LIVINGSTON, --
  (McLaughlin) 190
  Lucius E 163
  Margaret (Wynche) 211
  Octavia L 249

  Rebecca A 210
  Robert 190
  Robt B 7
  T F (--) 163
  T J 212
  Thos J 211
  W J 163
LLOYD, L F 396
  Sarah 23
  W F 338
LOCKE, Johnnie B
  (Blackman) 403
  Michael B 403
LOCKETT, Abner 89
  Amelia L (--) 187
  E A 187
  James 89
  Martha 168
  Rebecca (--) 89
  U T 187
LOCKHART, Ella Innea
202
  Ellen J 137
  Henry 137
  J H 39, 244
  J T 202
  Jno H 105
  M E (--) 202
LOCKMAN, John 341
  Mary Reid (--) 341
  Mary Rozie 341
LODTMAN, Ann (--) 388
  Charles 388
LOFLIN, -- (--) 267
  Elizabeth (--) 114
  James T 114
  Ross Antoinette 267
  Wm P 267
LOGAN, J H 391
  Jas H 24
  Lizzie 391
  Mary Lula 24
  S W (--) 24
  William 96
LOMAX, Eugenia
  (DuBose)
  163
  J A 277
  M G 163
LONG, David 392
  H W 77, 108, 392, 414
  J Belton 414
  James 400
  Ludia (--) 283
  Margaret R (--) 277
  Martha (Smith) 392
  Mary A (--) 414
  Nathaniel A 283
  R A (--) 400
  T Amanda 283
LONGINO, Nellie
  Candler (--) 407
  T D 408

LONGSHORE, Levi 151
LOOMIS, C E 284
  Elizabeth Jane (--)
  284
LORD, Mary E (Latimer)
  125
  W R 125
LOTT, E J (--) 17
  H D 17
  John G 144
  Willie Capers 17
LOUDON, Mary (--) 356
LOURAY, J M 149
LOVE, Alexander 185
  Caroline L (Calhoun)
  129
  Christian (McRae) 185
  James Calhoun 129
  James T 349
  Mary A 129
LOVEJOY, Anna L (--)
335
  Annie Lowe 335
  Caroline 353
  Catharine (Parker) 336
  Edward 353
  Eugenia I (Talley) 386
  James L 386
  John 386
  Laura (--) 165
  Mary (--) 386
  Pleasant P 165
  Rachel (--) 353
  W C 165
  W P 335, 388, 396,
  404-05
  Welcome C 336
  William M 165
LOVELACE, Allen 368
  Egbert 212
  Eliza J (Smith) 158
  J M 210, 212
  J T 74
  John M 218
  Linton 210
  Lucius 59
  Lucius B 324
  M A (--) 212
  M A (Brooks) 74
  M T C 158
  Martha (--) 218
  Obedience (--) 59
  R D (--) 210
  Rebecca L (Dozier) 316
  Sarah L 218
LOVELADE, John M 70
  Martha A (--) 70
LOVELESS, E L 177, 389,
412
  E M 307
LOVETT, Elizabeth M
  (Andrew) 59
  Lucy Elizabeth 59

Patrick Neil 234
Robert Oslin 207
Sarah (--) 252
Thomas H 204
MAFFETT, Mary (--) 286
MAGRUDER, A L C 264
George 13
M E (--) 88
Maria Louisa (--) 264
Mary A (Power) 208
Susan (--) 13
William 208
MAHAN, D P 230
Rebecca (Reynolds) 230
MAHON, Sarah (--) 381
MAHONE, Rebecca A 405
MAHONEY, Eliza J (--)
308
Sarah J 308
MALAIER, Ophelia P
(--) 143
MALEY, Mary C (--) 88
Christianna R 88
Johnson 88
MALLARD, Susannah (--)
150
T J 279
MALLETTE, -- (Kennedy)
399
Abraham 399
J A 149, 410
James Alpheus 399
M J (--) 149
Maggie Amelia 149
MALLORY, Charles D 34
Emily (Caudle) 326
J N 140
John 326
M J (Hogue) 186
Martha J (Candle) 140
R W 186
MALONE, -- (--) 410
C J 260, 410
Caroline J 246
Charles J 398
Corrinnia Bartow 129
George 178
Ida A (--) 129
J F 129
Jane A (Hudson) 398
L S 246
M S 260
Mary Beland (--) 178
Mary M L (--) 260
P J 246, 260
MALONEY, Nancy P 279
MALSBY, Edwin Hebbard
131
M F 35, 60, 131-32,
163, 256, 327
S E (--) 131
MAN, Jane R (--) 348
Martha J 348

William S 348
MANES, Benjamin 337
MANGHAM, E P (--) 357
E P (Thweatt) 133
Frances Ann 251
H H 357
Henry H 133
Matt W 357
Temperance (--) 251
Willis A 251
MANGUM, -- (Blackman)
217
Annie Sue 243
James 243
Marget E (Carraway)
243
T F 213
W L 284
MANN, A V 97
Christian E W (--) 272
Daniel J 295
Elizabeth 67
John H 190
Margaret E 60
Marilah (--) 60
Mary A (--) 97
Mary A (Means) 153
Mary R (--) 120
R F M 272
Samuel F 153
Thomas 60
MANNING, -- (--) 396
B 396
E M A 341
Emma E 396
Frances (--) 341
W 333
William 203
Wm 341
MANNINGS 49
MANS, Harriet L 141
John J 141
Mary (--) 141
MANSHIP, Nancy (Hamer)
54
Travis 54
MANSON, Francis E 272
Mary J (--) 177
V R 272
Z T 272
MAPLES, Hettie (--) 49
Israel 49
MARABLE, Clara P
(Baird) 139
Eliza Ann (Craton) 83
George 83, 343
Jno J 139
John B 269
Lucy S 269
Nancy (--) 269
MARBUT, Elizabeth 359
Euclidus 148
Joshua 359

Rebecca A (Diamond)
148
S P 100, 251
MARCHANT, Dexter 379
MARCHMAN, Alfred
George 235, 385
Benjamin Hill 119
Iberia (Stephens) 257
J H C 257
Mary Rowena 385
Mary Rowena
(Marchman) 385
Susan A (Wells) 235
W W 385
MARCUS, Sarah E (--) 31
MARGARET, John P 207
MARGART, --
(Treadwell) 9
J P 9
John P 9, 207
MARION, -- 58, 77
MARKS, Anna Sybella
(Hill) 213
Jessie 213
M R 213
Richard S 42
MARLIN, M E
(Whitehead) 257
M L 257
Martha E (Whitehead)
257
MARLOR, Labana 248
Sarah (Combs) 248
MARONE, -- (--) 395
Mary 395
T H 395
MARRISS, -- (--) 407
James 407
Jesse C 407
Nancy (--) 407
MARSH, Erin C
(Howard) 224
Samuel G 224
Wm 266
MARSHALL, -- 151
-- (--) 151, 334
A M (--) 170
Ann E 366
Appy (--) 265
Caroline 67
Esther (Varn) 334
Frances (--) 229
Franklin 334
Isabella (--) 350
J M 67, 79, 89, 120,
294, 377
John 350
John M 46, 51, 78,
170, 252, 325, 363,
366
Mantie 151
Margaret Amanda
(Wade) 78

471

Martha 89
Mary 350
Mary Eliza 170
Mary J 319
Mat 334
Rebecca Ann (--) 95
Sarah C 381
Stephen B 319
Sue 229
Thomas H 261
William 229
William B 237, 269
Zilphia (--) 347
MARTIN, -- 400
-- (--) 368
-- (Gray) 391
-- (Smith) 7
A W 42
Almeda (--) 314
Angus 198
Anna E 42
Britton J 146
Edmond 144
Edmund 142
Elizabeth (Young) 337
Ella C 62
Exer A (--) 42
Francis (--) 143
Ganaway 314
Geo W 337
Henry R 180
Irene Nuella
(Gilmore) 180
J R 391
J Robinson 395
J Vincent 264
James Britton Edward
146
James C 413
Jemima (Hall) 85
John C 237
John R 391
Leonora A (Keen) 413
M 11
Mary C 97
Mary D (--) 391
Mary L (--) 237
Rebecca L 314
Robert 96-97, 143,
267, 297, 362
Robt P 212, 234, 237
Sarah Olive (--) 146
Susie C (Eason) 395
W 8, 336
W D 22, 41
W H 7
William 204
William C 368
Wm 108, 208, 388
MARTINDALE, G W S
231
Jesse 231
Mary (Burgess)

(Coleman) 231
MARTYN, Robert P 396
MARVIN, -- (--) 287
-- (Davis) 359
Annie E (Davis) 249
Enoch M 400
James 287
Joseph 249, 359, 383
MASHBURN, -- (--) 343
Catharine (--) 66, 69
J H 66, 69, 116, 184
John H 337, 343
Nancy M (--)
(Butler) 343
MASON, Amanda 93
Ann D 122
E J 393
Edward 56
F E 177
Francis M (--) 212
Jos B 114
Martha Ann E 212
S K (--) 234
Sallie 234
Sarah M (--) 56
T 393
Thomas S 212
W N 234
Wilbur F 81
MASSEBEAU, Augustus A
68
MASSENGALE, A J 385
A L 10
M E (Key) 385
MASSEY, Charlotte A
(--) 137
Martha J 388
Mary 278
Sanford D 137
William Holland 137
MATHENY, Amy A (--)
149
MATHERS, Catharine 241
MATHEWS, -- 198
-- (--) 198
-- (Drain) 111
-- (Drane) 247
Ann E (--) (West) 373
Aquila 16
Catharine (--) 16
Elizabeth Ann 99
F F 310
Frank 373
J P 369
Julia F (Goode) 369
M Julia (Drane) 256
Mary (Keith) 369
Mary C 16
Minerva S (Drane) 206
Sarah Cornelia
(Bryant) 127
Thomas 99
Thomas J 256

Thos 111, 247
Unity (--) 99
W P 206
William Sharp 127
MATHIS, Anna
(Williams) 320
James Edward 413
Manning 413
Minerva (--) 413
Sarah Tobitha 181
Susan R (Russell) 298
William H 298
Wm J 181
MATTHEWS, --
(Lindsay) 310
Amanda J
(McClintock) 151
Clara A E (--) 92
Elizabeth Caroline
270
Emma (--) 233
J D 233
Jane (Brown) 56
John S 92, 129
John T 151
Josiah 56
W A 320
MATTHIAS, John A 68
Sarah E E (Gardner) 68
MATTOX, Elijah H 240
J J 263
Rebecca (Smith) 263
Walter Wade 130
MAULDEN, -- 216
Eliza (--) 216
F P 216
MAULDIN, Alsy S (--) 49
Benj F 49
Jas D 61, 229, 406
MAXCY, Elizabeth
(McLeondon) (--) 272
MAXEY, Sarah (--) 220
MAXLEY, -- 289
Mary (--) 289
MAXWELL, Drucilla C
(--) 70
E A 100
James A 144
Lucy Eugenia 70
Martin B 70
Sarah A W (--) 144
MAY, John 261-62
Mary A 261-62
P J L 125
MAYBIN, B H 232
Mary Eliza 232
R M (--) 232
MAYFIELD, Edward
Wesley 290
July Ann 269
Mary D (Allen) 290
MAYS, -- (--) 266
James H 265-66

McINTIRE, -- (--)
(Wagner) 11
E (--) 94
R C 94
Robt 11
McINTOSH, John T 145
Margaret I (--) 145
Nancy 333
Richard D 145
McIVER, J W 28
McJUNKIN, Caroline
(--) 238
Mary 238
WM 238
McKALLAR, Nancy (--) 4
McKAY, -- (--) 252
-- (Postell) 146
John A 146
Mary M (Collier) 61
Robert E 252
William 50
McKEE, John 127
John W 269
Mary E (--) 269
Thomas Milton 269
McKELLAR, J W 55
John 55
Nancy 55
McKEMIE, -- (--) 201
Mattie E (Bailey) 308
Robert J 308
William 201, 308
McKENNIE, -- 235
Frances J (--0 235
J F 99, 135
McKENZIE, --
(Robeson) 180
Elizabeth (Webb) 205
Elizabeth C (--) 389
John 180, 205
P H 389
McKEY, Charlotte 314
McKIBBEN, Elizabeth
(--) 110
Mattie A 110
Thomas 110
McKINLEY, Elizabeth C
341
Sarah (--) 341
William 341
McKINNEY, Eliza J
(--) 103
J H C 12, 19, 30-31
McKINNIE, William 211
McKINNON, -- (Pierce)
225
Ann (--) 272
Archibald 213
Ella Pierce 225
Kenneth 272
Lauchlan 225
Lauchlin 96
Mary (Finlayson) 213

Mary (Pierce) 96
Mary E 272
McKINZIE, Jas 14
McKOY, -- (--) 224
John 224
McLAIN, Mary (--) 370
Mary L 370
Samuel J 177
McLARIN, Mollie 80
McLAUGHLIN, -- 135, 190
David 190
Donald 20
Ellen Victoria
(Heise) 20
Fannie C 190
J T 109
Jane (--) 190
John C 190
Mary (Pharr) 190
McLAURIN, Elizabeth L
(Bethea) 388
McLEAN, -- (Treadwell)
61
Allan 53
Mary (--) 53
Wm 53
Wm A 61
McLENDON, Dennis 115
McLENNAN, Alexander 25
Mary Ann 25
Philip 64
McLEOD, A (--) 325
A M (--) 365
Almira Woodwarth
(Rogers) 206
Angus 93
Annie (--) 93
D O 189
Duncan 325
Eugenie Marian 93
Frank 365
Isabella 316
Leonora S
(Davenport) 189
Margaret (--) 83
Nancy J 325
Robt Y 206
Susan Lucinda
(Bussey) 262
W J 365
McLEONDON, Elizabeth
272
McLERAN, Jesse T 33
McLESKY, Eliza (--) 241
James 241
McLESTER, Jas H 403
Laura A (--) 403
Maude L 403
McLIN, Annie 61
Hugh 61
Nancy (--) 61
McMANUS, Wilmeth (--)
106

McMARTIN, Jane (--) 41
Marshall 41
Sarah Kibble 41
McMASTER, Hugh B 211
McMICHAEL, -- (--) 237
-- (Bradley) 56
A T (--) (Carvosso)
376
Elizabeth 95
John 245
M J (--) 95
Seaborn 9-10
T J 95
W A 237
W T 84, 309, 376
William Thomas
Carvosso 376
Wm T 56
McMICHEAL, Paytona E
175
S W 175
Sussie H (--) 175
McMILLAN, -- (--) 225
C J 316
D J 32, 43, 99, 211,
241, 249, 259, 264,
309, 326, 331, 413
Flora (McCaskill) 407
George 40
John 229, 407
Margaret 351
Robert 27, 37
Ruth (--) 27
Ruth A (Banks) 37
Sarah (Avant) 229
Thos 25
McMORRIS, Jas V 169
McMULLAIN, Thomas 313
McMULLAN, J A 70
Lula 70
M E (--) 70
McMULLIN, -- 30-31
-- (--) 30-31
-- (Key) 215
Thomas T 215
McNABB, E (Pitman) 59
Jas G 59
Wm 408
McNAIR, Anna Kate 15
Wm G 328
McNEEL, Daniel Hiram
Mason 117
J M 117
Susie (--) 117
McNEIL, D U 282
Hannah (Carter) 358
Mary B 368
William W 15
McNEILL, James 138
Sarah (--) 138
McNELLY, J W 151
Sarah Eugenie
(Tison) 151

MICKLERR, Caroline E
(Bickley) 374
MIDDLEBROOKS, A C
383
  James H 18
  Sophia Weston
  (Shell) 383
  Zera 383
  Zere 69
MIDDLETON, -- (--) 273
  A G 131
  James 276
  Jas R 273
  Mary (Townsend) 131
MIERS, Joseph J 227
  Sarah (Densler)
  (Wild) 227
MIKELL, Jas S 286, 317
  William 57
MILES, Emeline C
  (Parker) 390
  John J 390
MILEY, Daniel R 263
  Sarah A (Folsom) 263
MILHOUSE, Jno H 219
MILLAR, Abraham 255
  Lucy (Stipe) 255
MILLARD, C C 344
  J H 344
MILLER, -- 355, 371
  -- (--) 256, 265
  -- (Moody) 366
  -- (Royal) 414
  -- (Wilson) 35
  A L (--) 65
  A W 244
  Abraham 209
  Abram 269
  Amanda (--) 386
  Barbara Elizabeth 386
  C D (--) 244
  D B 256
  D N 265
  Daniel 285
  Eliza 353
  Fannie H (--) 82
  Francis 13
  Hannah (--) 13
  Henry Erroll 287
  Hurbert Burns 400
  J B 371
  J Claudius 242, 297
  J O 314
  J W 74
  J Wesley 35
  Jacob 222, 265
  Jane L 222
  Jane M (--) 371
  Jas A 216
  Jno A 339
  John C 74
  John F 14
  John T 414

John W 45
Jonathan 353
Josephine A 209
Lucy (--) 209
Maggie Kate 256
Martha 280
Mary 261
Mary J 46
Mary J (--) 359
N 255
N C 366
N E (--) 287
N W 29
R E (--) 314
Rachel W 244
Rebeckah G (--) 400
Rhoda (--) 355
S Fannie 314
S H 222
S J (Little) 29
Sallie J (Wilson) 14
Sarah (--) 222
Tallulah Susan 359
Thos H 400
W H 287, 386
W R 82
Wm Henry 359
MILLS, Clara (--) 201
  Frank 302
  George 201
  Indiana 113
  J M 270
  J W 270
  Lizzie (Underwood) 302
  Margaret M 56
  Paulina America 201
  Rebecca Frances 379
MILNER, Robert N 87
MIMMS, Penelope (--) 405
MIMS, -- 300
  Annie Mary 281
  Hattie M (--) 281
  Josephine (--) 320
  Josie E 42
  L C 42
  Roxalana 232
  S 222
  S A (--) 42
  Thomas Fletcher 320
  Thomas N 380
  Thos N 281
MINER, -- (Eubanks) 68
MINGLEFORT, J G 206
MINTER, Amanda G (--)
292
  L D 292
MINUS, Joseph 140
MISENHIMER, J J 67
  Martha H (Shankle) 67
MITCHELL, -- (--) 339,
354
  -- (Rochett) 189
  A H 96, 189

Abram H 111
Ada Jane 29
Americus C 282, 406
Antonia H (Kirby) 345
B H 212
C A 5, 60, 321
Camilla D (--) 29
Daniel R 67, 333
E R (--) 95
Eliza A (--) 291
Elizabeth (--)
(Johnson) 99
Elizabeth (Mann) 67
Elizabeth W 77, 285
Georgia 333
Giles 62, 261
Hammilton 157
Helen Louise 111
Henry 339
Henry Matterson 83
J T 399
James Lewis 399
Jane (Ligon) 257
John D 339
Judith 84
Julia W 77
L T 359
Lizzie Persons (--)
111
Lizzie S 95
Lucinda (--) 339
M Callie (Swain) 359
Madison R 354
Martha Ann 212
Martha D 321
Mary (--) 399
Mary (Butler) 83
Mary Elizabeth 325
Matt W (Mangham) 357
Merrie Susie 406
Nathanael R 285
P H 357
R L 325
Robert 47
S A 255
Sarah A E (--) 261
Susan W (--) 212
Susie (Dawson) 406
Susie Dawson 282
Susie Dawson (--) 282,
406
Temperance (--) 285
Thomas 157
Thomas H 354, 362
Walter H 29
MITZENBURG, -- 351
MIXON, A C 69, 153, 276,
343
  Asbury 239
  Elijah 239
  Elizabeth 177
  Georgia E (Smith) 274
  I F 47

J F 34, 217, 239, 274,
325, 350, 360, 364
Jerusha H 358
Sarah A (--) 358
MIZE, P L 177, 366
MIZEL, Adaline F 115
William 115
MIZELL, -- (--) 205
Casandra 123
Cornelia E 349
James 205
Luke F 402
Mary F (--) 349
Matthew 205
Morgan 349
MIZELLE, -- (McCall) 396
L T 396
MOATE, John P 40
MOBLEY, -- (--) 309, 311
C R 63
Cornelia Anzolet 338
Hiram 309
J R 23
Jas M 248
John T 60
Reuben 338
Richard Nichols 63
S (--) 63
W P 311, 313
William 163
MOBLY, A E (--)
(Curtis?) 66
Georgia Virginia
Curtis 66
W T 66
MONCRIEF, L 75
MONROE, Charles D 103
MONTFORD, --
(Holderness) 218
J S 218
Joel E 412
Mary Elizabeth
(Dugger) 412
MONTGOMERY, Andesia
F
104
Green 24
J M C 104, 187
J T 187
Joseph 187
Mary Achsah (Turner)
67
Mary G (Cottrell) 81
Nancy F (--) 104, 187
Rebecca 190
T F 67
W A 215
W J 81
Wm 167
MOOD, -- (--) 148
Christian 11
Christian (--)
(Morgan) 10

Clarence Gregory 307
F A 229, 246, 301
J A 71, 288
James B 63
James Just 58, 63
James R 58
John 67
Lucy Jane (Rogers) 57
M Eugenia (--) 307
Margaret (--) 336
Martha K (--) 58
Mary E 67
Peter 67
Thomas S 148, 336
Wm W 67, 122, 206, 307
MOODY, -- 366
-- (--) 165, 324
Allen 165
Ann E (Marshall) 366
E J 212
Jas M 324
John H 410
W W 57
MOON, A 63
Boler 263
Mary (Harris)
(Harris) 263
MOOR, A J (--)
(McCarty) 395
F A 285
Frederick A 395
Mary Elvira (--) 285
Mary Elvira (Black)
395
MOORE, -- (--) 364
-- (Murphy 292
-- (Tarver) 169
A A 335
Anna (--) 346
B T 21, 292
Benjamin 291
C A 190
C C 264
C F 248
C R 79
Caroline Bartlett
(Thomason) 213
Charles G 356
Churchhill 198
Cornelia C (--) 91
Cynthia Margaret
(McFarland) 396
Daniel 187
Edward F 393
Edward T 132
Elizabeth (DeFoor) 257
Elliott 346
Gilly 71
Green 71, 188, 206
H D 40
H G 285
Henrietta F 346
Henry D 213

J C 396
J M 393
J R 363
J T 62
James 132
James F 187
James Oscar 364
James S 169
James Seaborn 76
Jane A A (--) 335
Jane Caroline
(Sullivan) 157
Joseph L 285
Louisa R (--) 285
Margaret A L 399
Martha (--) 187
Mary 206
Mary (--) 363
Mary A (Earnest) 248
Mary E 363
Matilda (John) 171
Nancy (White) 248
Oliver 47
R A 171
R T 364
Rebecca (--) 198
Rebecca Billing 91
S S 163
Samuel 157
Sarah A (--) 356
Sarah Margaret
(Huckabee) 239
Sarah S (--) 270
Spencer 23, 78
Susan (--) 21
Susan Turner 21
Susannah (Graham) 78
T W 86
Thomas 257
Thomas M 239
Thomas W 128
Virginia F 264
Wm 248
Wm K 91
MOORER, Ellen (--) 10
Henry 36
J Calvin 120
James R 398-99
Lula Presley 120
Mary (--) 36
S M 10
Sarah Adella 10
Sarah E (--) 120
MOORING, J S 409
MOORMAN, Robt 243
MORAN, Augustus B 245
MOREHOSUE, N D 272
MOREHOUSE, N D 16,
187,
272, 353
MOREL, A C 272
Sarah G 272
William 47

MORELAND, -- 276, 406
Ann E (--) 165
Isaac H 331
Isaac T 276
John 165
John F 276, 401
John Fletcher 406
Joseph Bartley 165
Mary James (Dickson) 331
Mary Jane (Tooke) 331
N A 154
Newdygate A 154
Penelope (Ousley) 276
Rebecca B 235
S A (--) (Amoss) 406
Sarah A (--) 154
MORELS, -- (Exley) 145
B H 145
MORGAN, -- (--) 243, 357
-- (Thornton) 231
A 243
Ann E (--) 307
C E (--) 335
C L 50
Christian (--) 10
Christiana E (Heidt) 32
D G 335
E G A 192
H J 168
Hardie 302
Henrietta G (Warren) (Blitch) 168
J J 11, 32, 129, 168, 251, 364
J N 231
Jeremiah 70
John J 357
John R 307
Lysander 88
M H 335
Martha (--) 205
S C (Watts) 26
Sarah M (--) 302
W H W 26
William 10
Wm I 32, 335
MORRIS, -- 71, 117
-- (--) 233
Agnes (--) 11
Carrie M 11
Catharine (Mathers) 241
Charles 11
Elisha 102
Eliza Ann 9
Elizabeth (--) 117
Garrett 310
J P 29
J V M 60, 279, 334, 337
J Z T 101

James D 241, 246
Jane 102
Jas V M 223
John 117
John P 30
Nancy L 279
Rachel (--) 102
W J 301
MORRISON, Andrew 97
Angus 141
Eliizabeth (--) 97, 405
Izabella (--) 141
James D 200
Kate 411
Mary G 141
Peter 321
Roderick 411
Sarah C 97
Sebbiah (--) 20
MORROW, Laura R (--) 390
Mary 300
Wm C 390
Wm Homer 390
MORSE, Anna (--) 43
Daniel Wesley 43
Oliver 43
MORTON, Cynthia (--) 316
Henry 403
John J 32, 316
Julia (--) 32
Sarah A (Phillips) (Talbot) 403
Thomas R 316
MOSELY, James T 219
Elizabeth D (--) 335
Thomas M 335
William T 335
MOSS, -- (--) 251
Annie Catherine 385
Ernest 385
James E 385
John E 389
L S 385
Mary H (--) 385
Mary J (Underwood) 389
S William 251
Salina C (--) 385
Wm C 251
MOTE, -- 304
Gracie (Walden) 304
MOTLEY, M A E (--) 229
Mattie S 229
S K 229
W M 2, 262, 300
Wm M 30
MOTT, Eugenia 380
MOUCHET, Francis E 284
MOUNTCASTLE, E M A (Manning) 341
Wm R 341
MOUZON, -- (--) 342

-- (Richardson) 352
Ann (--) 352
Charles 373
Edna F 342
Ellen Violetta 372
Esther S 373
H J 342, 372
L H 352
Lewis Henry 73
Sarah (--) 372
William Rembert 352
MOYE, J P 182
James Henry 182
Mattie E B (--) 182
MOZINGO, Anna (--) 387
McKinzie 387
MUCKENFUSS, Anna L O 164
Benjamin S D 164
Charles B 368
Charles H 368
Louisa A (--) 164
Rosa M (--) 368
MUCKINFUSS, Ann (--) 107
Elizabeth G 107
Thomas 107
MULDROW, Sue (Green) 246
MULKEY, Bathsheba 239
Homer V 32
J W 269
N K (Gordon) 269
Sarah A (--) 32
Sarah Virgin 32
MULLIGAN, A B 342
Catharine (--) 342
MULLING, -- (--) 46
J T 46
Margaret V 46
MULLINS, C (--) 50
Elizabeth Caroline (Matthews) 270
Mattie M 50
R 50
MUNCH, Elizabeth 280
Elizabeth (--) 280
Francis 280
MUNDEN, Isaac 54, 93, 103, 280, 288
MUNDS, J T 303
Sarah K (--) 303
MUNNERLYN, -- (--) 354
Agnes Jane (--) 361
C J 413
James K 361
T W 354
Thomas 77
Willie 354
MUNRO, Edward 173
Geo W C 173
Harriet (Delespine) 173

(Mixon) 358
NELMS, John C 332
  John C (--) 332
  Mary (--) 249
NELSON, Ann M (--) 172
  Catherine Elizabeth
  187
  Columbus 187
  Emma (Capers) 412
  Henry 336
  J B 98
  J R 412
  J S 91
  Mary F (--) 201
  Mary L (--) 187
  Sallie Maude 201
  Samuel A 172
  William O 201
NESBITT, Isabella
  Elizabeth 191
NETTLES, A 90, 105, 134,
  190
  Elizabeth 210
NEVILLE, Martha 109
NEWELL, Dwight 322
  Margaret (--) 322
  Reason 322
NEWMAN, Charlie M 244
  Charlotte (--) 264
  F J 244
  George 264
  Harriet (--) 244
  Mattie E 213
  N W 213
NEWSOM, -- (Bryan) 402
  A T 402
  W B 290
NEWSOME, D P 142
  Susan C (Smith) 142
NEWTON, Alexander P
106
  Ann Elizabeth 106
  Cornelius 163
  Cornelius D 196
  Dorcas (--) 163
  Elizabeth Ann (--) 203
  Giles 203
  H H 106
  Harriet (--) 203
  James P 364
  Jesse Smith 203
  Martha A (Wallace) 196
  Reuben H 35
  Sarah J (--) 106
  Smith 203
NIBLACK, Frances Ann
  (Fry) 225
  John W 225
  Penelope 294
NICHOLS, A 145
  Alonzo 28
  Betty Jane (--) 126
  Jackson 126

John B 270
Louisa E (Jackson) 28
Sallie 145
Vincent 352, 356
NICHOLSON, --
  (DeBardeleben) 387
  C C (--) 328
  E 61
  Evan 207, 255, 275
  Jane (--) 23
  Jno W 109
  Martha A (Winn) 207
  Martha M (--) 109
  Philie Allen 109
  William 328
  William R 23
NICKELSON, Jas B 95
  Julia M 95
NICKOLS, John 299
NISBET, Arabella C (--)
  12
  Claude Phifer 234
  Frank A 12
  J M 234
  Leonora 12
  M J (--) 234
NIX, E 246
  Joseph R 135
  Miles 44
  Rachael (--) 44
  Wesley 44
NIXON, Fannie A 73
  Hugh A 77
  Maria W (Walker) 66
  Wm H 77
NOBLES, H (--) 19
  Josephine E 19
  T L 19
NOELL, Wm T 410
NOLAN, D 380
  David 233
  Geo M 246, 251, 272
  Geo N 205, 314
  H (Gugle) 76
  Matilda J (--) 205
  Mattie Tallulah 148
  Q R 42
  Thomas L 205
  William Marcellus 42
NOLLEY, Daniel 314
NORMAN, Bertie Maria
386
  G G 11, 13
  James A 162
  Julia E 162
  Julia E (Norman) 162
  Lucretia J (--) 386
  M C (Smith) 360
  Mary B (--) 162, 232
  W B 232
  William 121
  William Austin 121
  William H 386

Wm B 162
Wm T 357
NORRIS, -- (Robinson) 50
  -- (Sanders) 166
  A O 50, 233
  Eliza 311
  Eliza Ann (--) 351
  Ella R (DeJarnette)
  414
  Fanny A 367
  J T 20, 28
  James 367
  John C 351
  John T 408, 414
  Llewellyn Nimms 351
  Mary (--) 367
  P K 166
NORTH, Jno W 2
NORTHCUT, Cattie 80
  Fannie J 80
  L S 80
NORTHINGTON, James F
217
  M R (--) 217
  Martha Elizabeth 217
NORTON, A H 243
  Addie C 346
  E B 15, 34, 52, 77
  Elizabeth (--) 181
  Ethelbert 27
  Huldah (--) 243
  James R 133
  John 27
  John W 97, 346
  Jonathan 109
  Margaret (--) 133
  Margaret Catherine 133
  Martha J 97
  Mary C 109
  Miles D 143
  Thos C 27
  W D 109
  W F 128, 149, 194, 346
  W K 1, 27, 36-37, 162,
  347
  W R 346
  William George 384
  Wily J 181
NORWOOD, -- 139
  C A (--) 158
  Cornelius A 158
  James M 34
  L D 158
  Sallie Margaret 85
  W C 85, 139
NUNN, Nancy 316
NUNNALLY, James B 332
  Josiah E 332
  Sarah J W (Beckham)
  332
NUTTING, Abel 147
  Eliza M C 147
O'BRYAN, Lewis 160

Victoria V 160
O'CAIN, Catharine
  (--) 133
John R 389
Julia F (Chunn) 389
Louisa M 109
O'DANIEL, W 372
O'DRISCOLL, D 94
O'HARA, F J 15
James 63
Martha (--) 15
Sarah Rebecca 15
O'HERN, J D 176
M J (Brantly) 176
O'KELLY, Frances
  (Harwell) 256
James 256
O'NEAL, J B 192
O'NEILL, Jane G 323
O'PRY, -- 188
Nancy E (Robison) 188
O'SULLIVAN, Florence
  393-94
Mary S (Seyle) 393
O--, C J 136
OAK, Byron E 352
C D 413
Georgia (Powers) 352
OATES, John 371, 410
OATIS, Joan 410
Zachariah 127
OCAIN, Almira (--) 406
Ethelia Gertrude 406
W P 194, 406
ODOM, A 97, 212
Aaron 23
Alexander 369
B B 288
Elizabeth M (--) 369
G J 260
Maggie Jackson 369
Mary (--) 288
Rosanna L (--) 260
Winbourn 288
OELAND,   Catharine
Louisa
  (Clark) (Faber) 10
John 10
Nancy C (Benson) 253
P J 253
OGBURN, Daniel A 274
J B D 47
M M (Culclasure) 274
OGILSBY, Hugh J 226
OGILVIE, Elizabeth
  (--) 105
OGLESBY, Humphrey
  Posey 205
OGLETREE, -- (--) 116
Carrie J (Stinson) 91
David 116
William D 116
OLGETREE, Jas F 91

OLIVE, Mary C
  (Mathews) 16
Thos W 16
OLIVER 49
OLIVER, -- (--) 227
Ann (--) 286
Ann (Dickerson) 70
C D 56
C S 53
Caroline M (--) 53
Charles J 47
Charles Samuel 136
Edward James 207
Eliza 247
Fernanda Jacinto
  (Hatcher) 90
Harriet W 246
J B 212
J Percival 90
Jackson 227-28
James 207
James Brady 212
James L 70
James M 52
Jessie F (Hatcher) 92
John L 193
Lucy (Glenn) 193
M E 355
Mary A (--) 52
Mary E (--) 382
Mary K (--) (Watson)
  193
Mary Lucinda (Weld)
  254
Nannie Amelia (--) 47
P J 92
R C 20, 22, 70
Sarah (--) 212
Shelton 116
Stewart L 254
Victoria (--) 207
W W 382
OLIVERS, James 209
Mattie Eugenia 209
Victoria E (--) 209
ONEAL, Joseph J 285
Mary A M (Harris) 285
ORDAN, W J 213
ORMAND, Andrew 393
Diana (--) 208
Jane 77, 393
John 208
Mary D (McCorkle) 393
ORR, Charlotte 155
Gustavus J 7, 37, 354
John 155
OSBORN, -- (--) 242
-- (--) (Bedell) 289
J K 242
Liney (Watson) 239
Mary Barbara (White)
  (Arnold) 391
Milburn Green 242

Nelson 239
William C 289
Wm A 391
OSBORNE, Leveret A 3
Pauline M (--) 93
Wm A 93
OSIER, Clarissa (--) 46
Emma F 46
Perry 46, 128
OSLIN, Eliza R (Stevens)
  172
Henry Sidney Myers 218
Jesse 273
John 367
M S (--) 218
Mattie (Randle) 328
Mattie J (--)
  (Johnson) 328
R E 189, 328
S S 218
W W 40, 82, 89, 104,
  117, 141, 143, 172,
  189, 207, 263,
  328-29, 333, 340
William W 163
OSTEEN, Jane 264
Paul C 294
Penelope (Niblack) 294
OTT, E S 21
Edward Dantzler 21
OTTO, Alexander
  Wellington 39
Anna C (--) 39
Anna G (--) 15
Anna Josephine 15
Eddie Wynn 39
Ely 15, 39
Mary Harriet 15
OUSLEY, Angeline (--)
  271
H B 369
Joseph A 271
Martha Caroline 123
Mary Flournoy 271
N B 14, 90, 125, 148,
  174, 184, 201
N F 87
N S 39
Newdaygate 276
Penelope 276
R F 65
Rebecca 406
Sarah Joanna 65
Thos D 123
OUTLAND, B T 298
P A C (--) 298
R Olivia 298
OUTLAW, Jno D 243
Martha Emma (Cates)
  243
OVERBY, William 59
OVERSTREET, -- 349
Elizabeth Hardee

284
Wiley G 387
William J 239
William Justice 239
Wm 144
Wm H 142
Wm J 58, 62, 96, 333,
397
PARLER, Arnold E 243
Sarah C (--) 243
PARMORE, Elizabeth
(Lester) 69
Nathan 69
PARNELL, Israel C 282
PARRAMORE, Barbie 257
R V (--) 257
S A 257
Sarah E 230
PARRISH, Henry C 7
Mary H (--) 7
Wm H 175
PARROTT, J W N 218
Missouri A
(Robinson) 218
PARTLOW, J Y L 350
Mary (Marshall) 350
PARTRIDE, Henry Edw
313
PARTRIDGE, George M
367
H E 161, 185, 196
Henry Ed 212, 288-89,
310
Henry Edw 323, 339,
358, 379
Henry Edward 387
Mary E (--) 367
Sallie 216
PARVY, David 185
PASCAL, Dabner E (--)
203
Dennis 203
Mary Ann Elizabeth 203
PASCHAL, Jane (--) 179
Louuisa Jane 179
Mary E (White) 174
Milton 179
Thomas White 174
W H 174
PASCHALL, A E 84
PASCO, F 283, 375, 409
Jane 375
John 283
M C (--) 409
Sidney Doggatt 409
PASMORE, Maria L 265
Nathan 265
PASSMORE, Eliza Harriet
(Legette) 20
Elizabeth R (--) 119
J A 119
James 389
James Miley 119

John 389
John F 232
Miley 20
Sarah (--) 389
Sarah A (Dannielly)
232
PATAT, Annie 344
PATE, -- (--) 317
Edwin D 317
F W 33
J Thos 410
Jesse 63
Joseph 300
Lucinda A 63
Mary (--) 63
Mary (Morrow) 300
PATILLO, Chas L 334
PATRICK, Alford 227
Anna S M (--) 119
George Y 119
William L 62
PATRIDGE, John T 367
PATTEN, Elizabeth
(Hunt) 307
Janes 307
Matthew 307
PATTERSON, -- 280
A E 326
Amanda (Leaphart) 385
Catharine R 300
Corinthia 348
D W 182
Electa (Button) 280
Elizabeth (--) 50
Hennie (--) 182
Isaac L 50
Jane A 80
John C 348
Joseph 236, 300
Margaret J (--) 206
Mary 108
Mollie 206
Sarah (--) 326, 348
W C 33, 106, 156,
206, 236
W M 37
Willie 182
PATTILLO, -- (--) 234
-- (Chase) 356
-- (Thomas) 237
Albon Chase 37
C L 305, 307, 317,
356, 374
Charles L 380
G H 28, 203
James 312
James A 234, 237
James Thomas 312
John 48, 245
Mary (Winfield) 48,
245
Mary Marvin 380
N W 224, 245, 280

Nannie E (--) 380
Sallie E (--) 37, 70
Sarah (--) 312
W F 312
W P 37, 70, 356
William Chase 70
PATTON, Aurelia
(McGehee) 305
Frank 305
J C G R 140
Jane (--) 51
Perry 51
PATTTERSON, Elizabeth
(--) 50
PAUL, Abraham 31
Sarah (--) 31
PAYNE, -- (--) 162, 179
-- (--) (Hoyt) 115
A P 179
Edwin 115
Elizabeth (--) 110
J B 124, 302, 375, 402
J T 100
James B 162
James T 110
Jeremiah 54
Julia C 193
L B 25-26, 83, 97,
118, 150, 179, 193,
206, 227, 232-33, 283
Lewis 179
Margaret (--) 54
Mary (--) (Cureton)
115
Nancy A 54
Robert A 162
Roxie E (--) 100
Theresa N (Barnes) 115
W D 209
PEABODY, Chas 57
Chas A 187
PEACH, William
Franklin 23
PEACOCK, -- (--) 408
-- (Avrete) 388
D W 179
Fannie A (Barnard) 254
Green Brantley 408
J B 117, 388
Jesse 92
Joseph H 254
Judith B (Avret) 408
Lula Pauline
Carswell 117
Martha A (--) 254
Martha E (--) 179
Nathan B 254
S E (--) 117
PEAK, Burroughs 80
Julia (--) 80
L 80
PEARCE, -- (Glenn) 329
Charles H 227

A W 118
Alexander W 162
Ann Dawson 288
Augustus A 37
G W 118, 146
Lucios Sextus 118
Mary B (Quigly) 37
Prudence 22
Sallie (--) 288
Sue M (--) 118
Turner 288
PETERS, Hannah
(Vincent) 98
W B 98
PETERSON, -- (--) 153,
274
Charles L 153
J A 142-43
Malcom A 274
PETTUS, C J (Malone) 260
Caroline J (Malone)
246
E 246, 260
PETTY, Adelia (Dill) 177
B F 104
Benjamin F 177
Benjamin Franklin 104
Charles L 177
PEURIFOY, Archibald 69
Archibald M 69
Eliza 195
Louisa (--) 195
Louisa (Bird) 187
T D 187
Tillman D 187
Tilman D 195
PHARR, Alexander 38
E M (West) 3
Frank 139
Mary 190
Permelia A (--) 38
T A 3
PHILIPS, Margarett
Ann 64
Ulrica Antoinette 354
PHILLIPS, -- (--) 407
Andrew J 354
Elisha 345
Emma M 185
F A 148
George 403
Hattie O 119
Jane C 74
John 119, 276
Kezia Antoinette
(--) 258
Lethe A B (--) 17
Littleton J 288
Lou Belle 353
M E (--) 148
Nancy (--) 276
Pearl 148
Penelope T (--) 354

Robert 276
S E 240, 294, 298, 345
S S 225
Sallie (--) 119
Sarah (--) 403
Sarah A 403
T P 383, 407
Thos H 17
Vashti M (Little) 288
William 353
Wm 407
Wm (--) 36
PHILPOTT, H V 196
PHINAZEE, Rachel 340
PHINAZER, H 100
PHINIZY, -- (Bowdre) 366
Ferdinand 366
Ferdinand Bowdre 366
Mamie Lou (Yancey) 366
PHIPPS, Andrew J 45
Elbert 45
Eliza (--) 45
Margaret A (--) 260
Thomas 260
William Henry 45
PICKENS, John 323
Rebecca 323
PICKETT, John 78
John R 96
Mollie T (--) 78
PIERCE, -- 225
A M (--) 34
Ann Foster 406
Clara Columbia 34
Elizabeth (--) 88
G 195, 217
G F 18, 25, 27, 34,
90, 229, 397, 406
J L 194, 200, 203,
210, 236
L 6, 14, 34, 97,
142, 283, 350, 364,
397
Lovick 265
Mary 96
Reddick 96, 225
Thomas F 406
Thos F 77, 90, 104,
121, 258, 376
Wm A 88
PIKE, Frances (--) 329
J C 329
Julia Bertha 329
PILCHER, Cola 95
Fanny (--) 95
John 95
PILLEY, S A 114, 164,
265
PILSBURY, -- 237
Amos 237
Antoinette (--) 58
Rebecca Axon (--) 237
Samuel 58, 237

Tudie 58
PINKERTON, Mary 49
Parazade (--) 49
W T 49
PINKSTON, Aurelia A
(Graves) 152
Franklin C 152
PINSON, Joseph Edwin 410
PITCHFORD, Eli 319
Elijah W. 319
Elizabeth
(--) 332, 394
H P 98, 210, 346
Julia A 3332
Martha W 394
Mary E 263
R (--) 263
Sarah E (Stephens) 319
W G 263
William C 387
Wm G 332, 394
PITMAN, E 59
Henry 254
Rebecca (Bradley) 254
PITNER, Annie F
(Richardson) 46
Jno C 46
PITTMAN, -- (Johnson)
141
Anderson 141
F R 231
J J 295
Jas 95
Martha (--) (--) 295
Nancy L 388
PITTS, Alice Kimbrough
298
B H 263
Elizabeth 93, 102
Fannie E 299
Fannie M (Whitehead)
237
H S 237
H W 298-99
Isaac 183
J W 135, 173
John W 210
Martha J (Lester) 263
Mary (--) 247, 280
Mary D (Johnson) 135
Mary Jones 298
S A (--) 298-99
Samuel 98
William Gideon 173
PLATT, -- (--) 257
Emma Elizabeth 119
Geo F 75
H B 119
J B 38, 71, 150, 192,
235, 290, 381, 411
John 257
Mary (Page) (Deer) 381
Mary A E (--) 75

Victoria (--) 119
PLEDGER, -- (--) 145
  Amanda 145
  Frances P (Chambers)
    359
  Joseph B 359
  S W (--) 257
  Susannah D 90
  T M 80
  Thos 90
  W P 43, 145, 257
  Weyman Porter 257
PLESS, Andrew 71
  Priscilla (Brown) 71
PLOWDEN, E Ruthvine 22
  H C (Rogers) 31
  Harriet C (Rogers) 22
PLUMMER, Eliza J (--)
  209
PLUNKET, James 83
  Mary (--) 83
POINDEXTER, -- 363
POLHILL, John G 208
  Susan M (Sharpe) 208
POLLARD, James 61
  W J 324
PONDER, Axalina (--) 254
  Ephraim 254
  John H 78
  Mary A (Black) 78
  Saphronia A 254
POOL, Edny 241
  Eliza 412
  Henry R 412
  James 106
  Mary (--) 412
POOLE, Mary C (Sibley)
  21
  W G 21
POOSER, -- (Rumph) 39
  Adkinson 357
  Annie W (--) 10
  Benjamin 154, 258
  Carrie Lillian 258
  Edward 10
  Emanuel T 113
  Frances W (--) 113
  Frank M 414
  G H 249-50, 303, 307,
    359, 402, 409-10,
  Jacob E 151
  Julius Clarence 154
  Laura M (--) 154, 258
  M H 154, 244, 269,
    338, 370, 381, 410,
    413
  Mary Jane 113
  S A (Spigner) 414
  Sarah (McCally) 357
POPE, Alexander 26
  Allen 76
  Annie A 26
  Burrel Thomas 42

Burrell 76
Cadesman 223
D G 261, 327
Fielding 7
Harriet (--) 265
Joanna (Lester) 42
John B 76
Micajah 265
S C 169
S L 192
Sarah (--) 42
Sarah (Perkins) 76
Sarah A (--) 76
Wiley 42
PORCHER, Julian H 105
  Susan B (Jones) 105
PORTER, -- (Jones) 235
  -- (McCrackin) 171
  Alfred 257
  Ann 34, 300
  Ann (--) 314
  Anthony 300
  Benj C 65
  Benjamin Crum 362
  E E (--) (--) 257
  Eliza C (--) 317
  H H 157
  Helen J (--) 293
  Hugh F 235, 317
  Jane (Cherry) 156
  Jane M (--) 236
  Jno A 411
  John 156
  John C 313
  John L 293
  John W 27-8, 300, 314
  O H 171
  Oliver 300
  Sarah (Kennedy) 65
  Sarah D (--) 313
POSEY, -- (--) 249
  Jas D 249
POSTELL, -- 146
  James 143, 146
  John B 143
  John C 313
  Rebecca (--) 143
POTTER, -- 101
  Amy Ann 208
  Ann (--) 208
  Anna (--) 138
  Catherine E (--) 316
  Frances L (--) 43
  G A 43
  Harriet E 365
  Ira L 365
  J M 367, 379, 407
  John M 212, 330
  Samuel 208
  Stephen 101, 138
  W H 101, 297
POTTLE, Johnny 86
POTTS, -- (--) 323

Henry Jenkins 144
M J 143
Moses Jenkins 144
Sarah (Wilson) 170
Thomas Spencer 323
Virginia (--) 144
William E 170
POU, -- 375
  A C (--) (Beall) 164
  Henrietta E (--) 375
  John B 347
  Julia A (Hook) 347
  Lewis 34, 38
POUCHIER, Martha (--)
  86
  William 86
POUND, James 272
  Nancy (--) 272
  Robert Barksdale 272
  Sarah 395
POUNDS, James D 321
  Mary A E (Bradford)
    321
POUSER, Emanuel T 117
  Emanuel Tarrant 117
  R O (--) 117
POWEL, -- 348, 406
  Mary (--) 5
  Rebecca (Ousley) 406
  Thomas 406
  W F 348
POWELL, -- (Bass) 144
  A Y 266
  Ann J (--) 21
  Ann J (Dozier) 174
  B J 125
  Charles 169
  Eliza A R (Holmes) 283
  Eluda 21
  James 169
  L J 283
  Leanea 204
  Martha C 58
  Nancy Jane (Brooks)
    (Burney) 125
  Nancy L (--) 408
  Norborne B 283
  R H 284
  Sallie C 408
  T G L 408
  Thomas 144
  W F 122-23
  W F S 269
  William S 21
  Wm F 119
  Wm S 174
POWER, -- (--) 261
  James Hamilton 137
  John 208
  M Louisa (--) 137
  Mary (--) 208
  Mary A 208
  Samuel 261

RAIFORD, Ann Rebecca
(--) 36, 188
Campbell 33-34
Capel 36, 188, 411
Elizabeth (Bostick) 33
Henrietta A (--)
(Wimberly) 33
Matthew C 411
Morris 33
Patience 72
Walter Winston 188
William Maurice 36
RAINES, J G 237
Martha G 194
Mary S (Bryan) 237
RAKESTRAW, Jane (--)
356
RAMBO 126
RAMBO, Drury 368
Henrietta 126
Regina 368
Regina (--) 368
RAMPLEY, Permelia F
(Rhodes) 255
W M 255
RAMSAUR, David S 391
Harriet E 391
Harriet E (Erwin) 60
L R 60, 391
RAMSEY, -- (Pollard) 61
Catharine A 39
Gertrude 227
J D 227
Jas 39
Mary E (--) 39
Roxey (--) 1
S A 1
RANDAL, F R 166
Susan M (--) 166
RANDLE, Amelia Lamar
140
Elizabeth 227
L C 140
M E (--) 140
Mattie 328
RANKIN, G R 228
RANSOM, O W 317, 365,
373, 388
RAPE, Elizabeth (--) 74
M A 13
Peter 74
Susan E 74
RAST, -- (--) 215
Ann (Shuler) 394
Christiana
(Hunkapiller) 215
D Irwin 119
Frances V (Cummings)
394
Frederic 215
James T 394
Martha (--) 81
Virginia L 86

Wm 81
RAVENS, James 54
S S 54
RAWLINGS, Christiana
D (--) 141
Sarah A 141
Wm 141
RAWLINS, Isaac 360
Mary C 360
Nancy (--) 360
RAWLS, -- (Bellah) 151,
371
Jesse 151
Joseph 134
Lettie (Dowling)
(Owen) 260
Martha J (--) 134
Rebecca (--) 226
Thos J 260
RAY, John J M 87-88
RAYSER, Thos 345
RAYSON, -- (--) 290
Alfred 297
Benjmain Stokes 133
RAYSOR, Alfred 290
Mary Ann 357
Thos 195, 284, 338,
357, 405
REA, Rhoda Maria (--) 8
William T 8
READ, W T 407
REAGAN, Charles 142
Mary (--) 142
Sarah M 142
REANEY, Amelia F (--)
152
Wm 152
REARDON, Annie (--) 302
Benjamin T 302
REARS, Mary E Roberts
(--) 120
REASE, Ernine Cumy 357
REAVES, Delilah Ann
(--) 365
Rollins L 365
REDD, James K 6
Mary L 6
REDDICK, Elisha R 98
Elizabeth M
(McCarty) 98
Jacob 126, 304
Jane (--) 98
Jonathan 98
Martha (Herrington)
304
Martha E (Gregory) 304
Peter W 304
Sarah (--) 304
Susan J (Kendrick) 304
Susannah (Folsom) 126
REDDICKS, Moses 133
REDDING, -- (--) 204,
256

-- (--) (Smith) 256
A W 164, 183
Anderson W 28, 256
Arthur 6
Augustus Berrien 28
Elizabeth 400
George A 265
Jane (--) (Rutledge)
256
John 82, 105
Julia E 183
Leonidas R 164
Margaret E
(Flewellen) 244
Maria L (Pasmore) 265
Mariah (Searcy) 372
Martha W (--) 82, 105
Mary (--) (Clemmons) 6
Mary E 82
Mary E (Bivins) 317
R J 55, 317
Roland 162
Rowland 204
S M (Cooper) 162
Thos 372
William C 244
Wm C 242
REDFEARN, Elizabeth (--)
194
James 194
Melissa E 194
REDWINE, Lewis 108
Mary (--) 108
REECE, -- (Bradfield)
217
J 217
John 202
REED, -- 406
-- (Houser) 406
Annie Houser 406
Annie Houser (Reed)
406
John M 185
Sarah A (--) 185
Tully 406
REES, Ann B (Brooking)
265
Harriet (--) 73
James W 73
John 265
John C 404
Mazy D 201
R L 161
Susan M (--)
(Furlow) 404
William L 73
REESE, A J 241
Archie Wimpy 241
C F (--) 281
Eliza (Norris) 311
Esperann (--) 20
Fannie (--) 241
Harrison 311

J T 281
Jere 20
Jordan 106
Lizzie (Hills) 202
Lou Clarke 281
M A (--) 210
Maria Saunders (--)
106
Mary Lucy 213
Milton P 213
Nancy (Todd) 311
Patsy (Toler) 311
Sallie H (--) 213
Wm O E 218
REEVES, Annie 338
E A (Lockett) 187
Florence M (Chanee)
101
J T 101
J W 390
Martha J 145
Patience S 357
Wm 187
REGISTER, -- 185
Cinther Mary Jane
(--) 185
REID, -- (--) 362
Alexander 43, 409
Ann C (Horne) 355
David 235
E A 197
E F (--) 197
Emma (--) 24
Emma T (--) 57
Fannie (Whitfield) 409
Frances T (--) 43
Geo T 386
Laura J (--) 386
Richard Turnbull 24
Richard W 57
S H 362
Samuel Hodges 386
Theodora Lydia 231
W L J 355
W R 24
William J 375
Willie 362
REMBERT, -- (--) 337
Catharine A M (--) 198
Elenora (Green) 324
Elizabeth Maria 198
James J 324
Jas E 337
Joseph 198
S S (Willis) 165
Thomas 165
REMLEY, -- (Costine) 252
Henry 252
REMSHART, Eliza 47
RENEAU, Julia S (--) 185
N 32
Norris 32
Ramsay 185

S L 185
Sally P (--) 32
RENEHART, John 38
Mary 38
Sarah (--) 38
RENFROE, H A 113
Henry Bascom 113
Martha Elizabeth
(Northington) 217
Tinnie (--) 113
W H 217
RENTS, E J 292
RENTZ, E J 40, 59, 196,
214, 312, 401, 407,
410
Minnie Harvey 407
RESPESS, Mary J
(Marshall) 319
William M 319
REVILL, Alice A (--) 270
Annie Byrd 270
Wm T 270
REYNOLDS, -- (--) 102
Adella H (Turner) 398
Ana M 152
Anna E 255
E E (Andrews) 100
E W 136
Elizabeth (--) 230
Elizabeth B
(Freeney) 85
F F 102
Freeman F 100
H W 161
Herbert 85
Hettie L (--) 136
Isa Ann 202
J J 288
Jephthah 398
Jno A 101, 115, 161,
262, 359
John 202
John A 123, 186, 197
John W 11, 94
Joseph D 230
Lorenzo Dow 65
M A T (--) 152
Marietta (Elliott)
161
Martha (Durden) 65
Mary 202
P F 340
P G 167, 267, 301, 391
Penina 264
Rebecca 230
W H 152
RHENEY, Charles 110
E (--) 201
John W 201
Lizzie D (Gordon) 334
Mary (--) 110
R Toomes 201
Samuel C 334

RHODA, -- 409
-- (--) 409
Mary J H 409
RHODES, Absalom 354
Caroline V (--) 238
Elizabeth W 354
Jane (--) 255
Jno F 82
John 223
John Wesley 82
Julia C (Felder) 223
Mary Ann (--) 160
Permelia F 255
T J 238
Temperance C (--) 82
W W 160
William 255
RICE, -- (Wright) 336
Agnes (--) 404
Benjamin J 191
Berrien 336
Elizabeth J 191
Eugenia C (Stewart)
390
John 390
Lizzie M (Rice) 404
Martha Ann 81
Mary (--) 311
Mary A P (--) 390
Richard Blake 345
Sarah A 339
Sarah Ann 92
Sarah P (--) 339
Spencer M 311
Susan M (--) 191
William C 311
William Smith 390
Wm 339
RICH, Elizabeth 384
John 276, 384
Mary (--) 276, 384
RICHARDS, -- (--) 331
A 23
John J 331
Malinda C (--) 140
Martha 331
P L 239
Wealthy Ann 94
RICHARDSON, -- 225, 352
-- (--) 225, 271, 298
-- (Conley) 413
Alfred 185
Andrew Jackson 257
Annie F 46
Charles 352
Derilda 143
Elizabeth Ann (--) 382
Elizabeth M (--) 206
Ervin 382
Fendorah (Rogers) 274
Gilla (--) 143
Henry C 274
J M 194

J W 300
James M 37, 135
James Preston 298
Jesse 17
Jno L 46
John 412
John Kennon 271
John L 350
John M 185, 413
Julia 176
Julia Belton (--) 250
Martha A 412
Mary Osiana 206
Mattie C 300
Nebraska B 181
Obediah 176
Purdie 200
Richard R 44
Robert E 143
S A (--) 181
Sally 17
Susan W (--) 46
Susan W (Simmons)
  350
W G 271
William 106
Wm B 181
RICHBOURG, Margaret
  Minerva (Cowart) 100
  William D 100
RICHWOOD, G C 18
  Geo C 31
  J J 31
  M E (--) 18
  Mary Jane 139
  Willie Murdock 18
RICKETS, Birch 264
RIDEN, -- 382
  -- (--) 382
  John S 382
RIDENHOUR, Homer
  Haygood 394
  J D W 394
RIDGILL, John 109
  Listy L 109
  Sarah (--) 109
RIDLEY, H A T 158
RIGGIN, John H 51
RIGGINS, A (--) 19
  America (--) 150
  E L D 19
  William Thomas 19
RIGGINS, E L D 19
RIGSBY, -- (--) 132
  Allen 81
  James 132
  Mary (--) 81
  Mary Ann (--)
   (Draffin) 85
  W T 85
RILEY, -- 213
  -- (O'Pry) 188
  Ann S 213

Cason H 211
D H 188
Daniel 213, 408
Elizabeth (--) 372
Frances (--) 278
Freeman W 278
G B 142
Geo F 194
George F 194
Isaac 133
Isabel (--) 133
Jacob 278
John 211
Keziah E 124
Louisa 317
Mary (--) 211
Miles 372
N 317
O B 278
S A 85
Thomas Jefferson 372
RISHER, -- (Spell) 190
  Benjamin 267
  F B 190
  Havilla H (--) 338
  Joseph K 52, 338
RISON, Harriet C 358
  Jane (--) 358
  John 358
RITTER, Catherine J 177
  Ellen (--) 177
  Ellen Pricher
   (Broxton) 335
  Hezekiah 335
  Joseph E 177
RIVERS, -- (--) 204
  -- (Simmons) 384
  Ann Dawson (Persons)
   288
  Ann Eliza 285
  Jane (--) 156
  Joel 105
  John 292
  Jos 204
  Joseph 156
  Julia A (--) 366
  Maria Gray 346
  Martha M (Whitaker)
   292
  Mary F (--) 239
  Oscar B 366
  Thomas 213
  Thos H B 288
  W B 346
  W P 130, 174, 239,
   272, 365, 384
  Willie S 239
  Wm H 366
RIVES, Robert 319, 332
ROACH, Sarah 324
ROARK, Jones W 22
ROBARTS, John W L 78
  W H F 257, 283, 344

Wm H K 318
ROBERDS, William G 225
  William George 205
ROBERSON, -- (--) 363
  Wiley 363
ROBERTS, -- (--) 157
  -- (Buchanan) 330
  A J 106
  A M L (--) 24
  Ann (--) 106
  Ann E (--) 57
  Ann M 106
  Arthur 24
  Asa 306
  Bryan 157
  Charlie A F 24
  Cornelius O O 313
  D 142
  George 57, 157
  George O E 78
  H L R 20
  H S R 24
  Irby 326
  J P 218
  J W 297
  Jas W 133
  Joseph 150, 229
  Joseph P 387
  Laura Jane
   (Russell) 229
  Luvina H (Mead) 306
  Maggie 157
  Margaret E 297
  Mary F (Price) 313
  Mary H (Craven) 133
  Mattie K 92
  Mattie Petrona
   (Dozier) 219
  N H (--) 142
  Nancy H (Meridy) 215
  Narcissa E 142
  Richard F G 215
  S A (--) 24
  S M (--) 66
  Sarah 275
  Sarah A (--) 78
  Sarah J (--) 20
  Sarah M 129
  Susan P 20, 24
  William H T 78
  Wm M 224
ROBERTSON, Elizabeth
  A 267
  Emily 380
  Emily I 160
  Frances (--) 267
  Henson J (--) 108
  J M C 84
  John 267
  John J 108
  John M 321
  Martha P (--) 321
  N C 321

R N 276
Willie 237
ROSSER, A S 310
Elizabeth Hatton
(--) 110
M F 290
Martha E (--) 386
Mary Elizabeth 310
ROTHROCK, Lucinda J
(Arnold) 277
ROUND, G F 384
Geo F 367
ROUX, George S 259
ROWAN, J F 387
ROWELL, C D 351
Mamie A 351
Robt Newton 108
ROWLAND, A W 146, 188,
206, 210, 230
Allen 314
David R 149
Martha H 169
Mattie Lou 144
Nancy S (--) 314
Robert Allen 379
S M (--) 144
Sarah Cornelia
(Smith) 149
W A 144
William 13
ROYAL, -- 414
-- (Hardaway) 168
Asa 255
Bathsheba (Mulkey) 239
Croskeys 168
Ezekiel 92, 372
James H 224, 414
John B 92
Julia Ann 46
Mary A (--) 92
Mary A (Murray) 372
Nancy (--) 255
Nancy G (--) 224
Sarah Elizabeth 255
Seaborn S 239
RUCKER, Barcher (--) 375
Jacob 375
Mary Jane 12
Richard 12
Serena (--) 12
RUDDELL, Hattie C
(Turner) 380
J H 380
RUDISILL, John 156
Margaret 156
RUDOLPH, Amzi 199
Fannie (Boyd) 199
RUFF, M L 342
RUFFIN, J L 209
M J (Gordon) 209
RUMNEY, -- 201
Mary Ann (--) 201
RUMPH, Caroline 75

Elizabeth (--) 39
Jacob 75
John 39, 56
Mary A 56
RUSH, -- 108
-- (--) 140
A B (--) 108
Asbury M 145
C W 108, 140
John 108, 170
L 96, 204, 217, 313,
404
Martha M (Camp) 170
Robert Lee 140
RUSHING, -- (Thomas) 98
E E 176
J K 98
Martha A (--) 4
R R 4, 68, 131, 267
RUSS, James G 327
RUSSEL, John 173
Joseph 401
Joseph A 58
RUSSELL, Burwel 145
Elizabeth (--) 298
Esterpe (--) 229
Fannie L (Bell--) 215
George 229, 298
George Dawson 184
J C 243
Judith L (--) 89
Laura Jane 229
Martha (--) 145, 176
Nancy 140
O W D 359
R 215
Rebecca (Furman) 58
Sallie E (--) 184
Sallie P (Craig) 359
Sarah J 145
Susan R 298
T B 64, 75
Thomas B 58
W A 184
W M 332
William W 176
RUST, Margaret A (--)
373
RUTH, Mary 383
RUTHERFORD,   Mary
Ann
256
William 256
RUTLAND, Samuel C 7
RUTLEDGE, Armond (--)
254
Benjamin 201
Jane (--) 256
John 254
M C 344
Millie (Cauthen) 176
Narcissa 95
Robert Kay 254

Wm F 176
RYAN, Thos 140
RYBURN, P M 39, 45, 84,
168, 249, 293, 305,
324, 356
RYDER, Theodosia 392
RYLANDER, Ella 255
M E 255
S C (--) 255
RYLE, D M 238
Emma R (Pennie) 238
RYLER, Elizabeth 13
RYLES, Margaret 348
S--, -- (Hendry) 223
E H 133
G B 94
J B 28-29, 100, 102,
117
J C 77
J D 29
J H 223
J L 65, 71
Jas O A 37
M W 246
S L 48
T A 97
T L 57
W 112
W H 97
W M 171
W W 128
SAFFOLD, -- 300
Adam G 300
Ann (Porter) 300
Wm O 300
SALE, -- (--) 380
Aurilla 61
Margaret Miller
(Walker) 29
Payton W 380
W W 29
SALLEY, -- (Gramling)
308
Fannie Barton (--) 242
J J 242
Nathaniel 365
Sheldonia B (--) 365
SALMONS, Martha (--)
399
SAMMONS, -- (Crenshaw)
295
John 295
SAMPEY, Mattie Eugenia
(Wilson) 100
William A 100
SAMPLE, -- (--) 101
C L 320
Caleb Linsey 320
Jesse 27
Lewis 101
Rachel (--) 320
Susannah N 101
SAMPLES, Jesse 29

Phoebe (--) 29
William V 29
SANDEFORD, Hill 212
Mary (--) 212
P W 212, 328
SANDEFUR, -- 328
Eveine 328
SANDEL, Mary (--) 338
SANDERFORD, James 28
SANDERS, -- (--) 254
Amanda (Mason) 93
B 64, 67
Hardy Thurmond 254
J B 93
John Henry 93
John P 370
Martha (Ditmor) 166
Martha J 132
Martha J (--) 46
Mary Jane 46
Saml D 46
Sarah E (--) 67
Wm 166
SANDFORD, J 112
SANDIFORD, Alethia (--)
130
Harriet Jane 130
John F 130
SANFORD, John Madison
181
Joseph K 149
SANTER, Daniel 231
Joshua H 231
Susan C (--) 231
SAPP, Hattie H
(Darnell) 405
Narcissa F (Clark) 405
Rebecca (--) 14
Rebecca A (Mahone) 405
Theophilus 14, 405
SAPPINGTON, Dellia (--)
358
James W 203
Martha H (--) 243
Martha H (Storr) 313
Mattie B 354
Rebecca Ann 243
William J 313
Wm J 243
SARTOR, Mary
(McJunkin) 238
Wm 238
SARVIS, C B 291
Cornelia Mary 291
H M (--) 291
SASSER, Elizabeth (--)
331
SATTERWHITE, Martha
N
413
SAULS, -- (--) 166
Offie 166

SAUNDERS, Alexander
175
Blanca (Kemp) 175
Emeline 161
J H Durant 363
Mary M C (Loyless) 79
Nancy V (Bas) 285
R I 285
R M 169, 285
Rebecca J 169
Shepard B 285
Wm B 285
Z F 79
SAUNEY(?), Annie
Nowlan 287
Hattie A (--) 287
J H 287
SAUSEY, Eddie 118
Hattie S (--) 118
J R 118
SAWRIE, Matthew 81
SAXON, Benjamin A 92
Elizabeth 170
Elizabeth (--) 170
Henry 170
Laura V (Johnson) 64
Lewis 158
Mary (Dunwody) 92
Susan L 12
SCAFE, Fannie E (--) 244
J F 244
Nannie Tabitha 244
SCAIFE, F E (--) 286
J F 286
Pauline Elizabeth 286
SCARBOROUGH, H G 31
H G (Rogers) 31
Henry 319
Huldah (--) 319
Mary Drucilla 319
Mildred L 251
SCARBROUGH, -- 252
Hiram 290
W B (Newsom) 290
Wilson 252
SCHINHOLSTER,
Cornelia M 203
Susan F (--) 203
Wm J 203
SCOTT, -- 29
-- (Willisson) 45
Alexander 262
Chas J 45
Elizabeth (--) 84
Emma L (--) 73
George B 381
George W 110
J E 99
Jane 357
John R 222
Lizzie Ellen 73
Mary A (--) 21
Mary J (--) 110

Nathanael 21
Nathaniel 46
Rebecca E (--) 262
Sarah C 262
T E 289
Thomas G 73
W J 390
W W 84
William 223
Wm W 110
SCRUGGS, Mary E 245
Richard H 104
Susan M (Peek) 203
William H 203
SEALE, Anna Maria
(Graham) 46
D W 8, 46
Jarvis 39
R A 39, 41
SEALS, Adele E 26
Arnold 156
Cornelius 26
Margaret (--) 26
T A 127, 152
W W 26
SEALY, Elizabeth B
(--) 295
John 295
Joseph J 208
Mary E (Ward) 208
P J 295
SEARCY, B R 9
Benjamin R 204
Fannie Lilette 260
H M 260
M V (--) 260
Margaret (--) 9
Mariah 372
SEARS, -- (--) 224
Joseph G 64, 73
Joseph G (Causey) 73
Joseph Glenn 224
Julia E 64
Mary J (--) 64
SEAWRIGHT, A M
(Kaigler) 108, 321
C R 108
Charles R 321
SEAY, John 349
William 349
SEBASTIAN, J P 394
SECKINGER, E 335
M H (Morgan) 335
SELF, N H 38
SELLERS, Isabella
(Smilie) 194
Jessee 109
Listy L (Ridgill) 109
Mary A 303
N E 194
SELMAN, B L 155, 178,
206, 261
SENTELL, E M (--) 83

SHERWOOD, Adid 25
Emma C (--) 388
J M 157
SHETTLES, Nannie E
(--) 45
SHETTLESWORTH,
Abner 88
SHEWMAKE, Jos A 104
SHI, James H 222, 296,
354
Lizzie E 296
P 332
P C (--) 296
Polina C (Kirby) 222
SHIELDS, C M 259
Epsy (--) 375
John 30
Martha Jane (Smith) 30
Robert 325, 375
S E (Robinson) 259
SHINES, Susan L 214
SHINHOLSER, Amanda
(--) 358
George Olin 358
Thomas J 358
SHIPES, M A (--) 281
Pearl 281
W T 281
SHIPP, A M 29
SHIRLEY, Ephraim 346
Georgia A 346
Mary (--) 346
SHIRLING, Isam 289
Mary (--) (Odom) 288
SHIVER, Daniel 268
Eliza (--) 268
Henrietta 268
SHIVERS, Maria E 19
Sallie E 275
Sarah Josephine 278
Sarah R (--) 10
Sarah W 19
Sarah Warren 34
Susan F (--) 34
Wm 19, 34
SHOCKLEY, A C 401
Curtis Hollingsworth
135
SHORES, J W 20, 38, 145
James W 103
SHORT, Almon 349
Nancy (Walis) 311
W J 311
SHORTER, Eli S 214
Mary Jane 214
SHOWN, Anna R
(Coppage) 88
SHREWSBERY, Mary Ann
388
SHROPSHEAR, -- (--) 213
Joshua P 213
SHROPSHIRE, C J
(Davenport) 89

Harriet Ann 124
James W 89
Olivia Rhymes 89
Wesley 124
SHUFORD, J L 167, 374
S L 144
SHULER, -- (--) 171
-- (Hutto) 315
Ann 394
David 171, 173
M E 173
Martha 79
Preston P 315
Sarah C F 97
W M 56, 97
SHULL, Joanna 246
John 105, 246
Margaret V (--) 246
SHUPTRINE, Horace 226
SHURLOCK, Mary (--) 154
SHUTTLESWORTH,
Abner 86
SHY, E R (--) 277
Ella 277
W H 277
SIBLEY, Charles S 21
James W 219
Mary C 21
Nancy L (Shell) 219
SIFLEY, -- 221
J L 242
John 242
Maria A (--) 221
SIFLY, J L 221
Sue 221
Sue F 221
SIKES, -- 118
-- (--) 326
Alfred 326, 363
Daniel 77
Elizabeth J (Eason) 77
Georgia 118
Matilda (Vinson) 363
SILBEY, Mary D G (--) 21
SILVA, Wm D 49
SILVEY, Abraham 126
Temperance (--) 126
SIMKINS, William B 195
SIMMONS, -- 384
-- (--) 307
A A (Gill) 384
Elizabeth (Hunt)
(Patten) 307
Elizabeth J 337
J C 24-25, 38, 99
J E 384
J N 94
J W 126, 128
James 337
James M 161
James W 25
John 161, 350
John C 42

Lizzie (--) 94
O C 384
Susan W 350
T J 80, 214, 242
Tallula A 399
W A 342
William 307
Wilson Glenn 304
Wm 145
Wm A 4, 141, 157,
223, 385
Wm H 307
SIMMS, Lydia E 14
Sarah (--) 14
SIMONTON, C A 306
J R 397
John A 323-324
Sarah Virginia
(Cozart) 397
Thomas 270
SIMPSON, Ailey (York)
264
Jane 128
W W 264
SIMS, John F 99
Louisa E (--) 367
Louisa M (--) 99
S Caroline (--) 271
Thomas 367
SINCLAIR, Elias 312
Sarah A (McDearmitt)
312
SINEATH, -- (--) 327
Barney 157
Mary Ann 327
Sarah (--) 1157
William D 327
Williams D 211
SINGELTON, J J 32
SINGER, J G 249
SINGLETON, -- (--) 166
C A E (Bryan) 335
F P 146
J J 129, 141, 148-49,
170, 182, 195, 222,
244, 259, 263, 268,
347, 351, 358, 365,
373, 392
Jesse Lee J J 107
Leroy 166
Mildred V (Greer) 147
Thomas 293
W A 335
W R 62
SINQUEFIELD, Jessie 102
Moses 337
SISTRUNK, -- 213
-- (--) 92
Ann S (Riley) 213
George L S 213
Gosper 92
S H J 87, 219, 297
S J H 411

497

Francina E 223
G B 130
G G 65, 152, 170, 172, 286-87, 323, 359, 371
G L 59
Geo G 65, 257, 310, 366
Geo M 207
George G 367, 370
Georgia (Sikes) 118
Georgia E 274
Guy 413
H A 314, 343
H F 57, 65
H W (--) 360
Hallie L 93
Hampton S 356
Harriot N (--) 93
Hattie (--) 313
Henry 119, 123, 274
Henry H 55
Hettie (--) 276
Iranonah C (Arnold) 215
Irene (--) 228
Irene P (Hart) 343
Isaac 172, 303
Isham 232
J A 76
J B 93, 118
J Blakely 61
J D 40
J M 34, 335
J P 375
J Porter 307
J Rembert 366-67, 370, 391
J S 307
J W 232
Jacob 268
James B 118
James F 209, 341, 379
James H 308
James M 307
James Rembert 366
James Thomas 307
Jane (--) 289
Jane (Clark) 413
Jane (Ormand) 393
Jane Gilman 370
Jas F 135, 158
Jas R 207
Jennie 86
Jeremiah 75
Jesse 100
Joel B 142
John 23, 60, 63, 341
John Boring 2
John H 36
John L 128, 276
John P 30, 296
John R 93, 95
John S 57

John T 313
John T H 313
Joseph 193, 374
Joseph Asbury 98
Joseph B 59
Joseph H 200
Joseph P 209
Joseph T 141
Joseph Tarply 284
Joshua 329
Judith (--) (Tison) 402
L M 312, 387
Larkin 227
Laura 228
Laura C 120
Lee Hampton 11
Leudie (Danielly) 156
Levin J 274
Lucinda A (--) 201
Ludie (Danielly) 286
Luke 392
Luther M 61, 96, 206, 222, 291, 300, 312
Lyman 30, 146, 192
M A (Hill) 310
M A E (--) 307
M C 360
M Clementina 93
M E (--) 76
M M 236-37
M W J 349
Margaret Ann 21
Margaret Ann (Hanson) 130
Margaret Ann Hanson 130
Margaret Shand 161
Martha 136, 392
Martha A (Stripling) 374
Martha C 114
Martha C (--) 113
Martha Jane 30
Martha L (--) 192
Martha O A (--) 192
Mary 193
Mary (--) 392
Mary (--) (Cameron) 5
Mary A (--) 207
Mary E 65, 75
Mary L (--) 308
Mary P 19
Mary W (--) 36
Matilda C (Flowers) 373
Milly (--) 60
Moses M 160
N Caroline 393
Nancy 404
Nancy (--) 45
Nancy (Whitlow) 374
Nannie J 165

Needham 184
Newton 156, 286
Newton J E 192
Noah 113, 193, 373
O L 11, 218, 367
Osborn L 405
P A (--) 392
Patience (--) 149
Peter Shand 366
Peyton P 121
R B 310
R W 201
Rachel (Flanders) 4
Rebecca 263
Rembert 359, 363
Roberta 156
Rosa 375
Roxana M (--) 110
S M (--) 108
S P 223
Sallie 379
Sallie (--) 98
Sallie E 158
Sallie E (--) 221
Sally Mathis 117
Saml Henry 86
Samuel 31, 253
Samuel H 240
Samuel Madison 101
Samuel W 137
Sarah 340-41, 357
Sarah (--) 198
Sarah A 268
Sarah A (--) 57
Sarah A (Dannielly) (Passmore) 232
Sarah Cornelia 149
Sarah E (Hardin) 410
Sarah Joanna (Ousley) 65
Sarah K (--) (Munds) 303
Sherrard 296
Sidney M 2, 27
Solomon 60
Sophronia 232
Stephen L 214
Sue M 276
Susan (Swain) 200
Susan A 102
Susan C 142
Susan Emma (Laney) (Evans) 214
Susan L (--) 22
Thomas H 215
Thomas McLeod 177
Thomas R 19
Thos H 149
Thos R 19
Thos W 238
Victoria 232
Virginia A 30
Virginia A (Smith) 30

-- (Strange) 287
A H 196
Annie Ann (Winn) 165
Carrie M (Morris) 11
Charles M 312
Daniel 288
Elizabeth M (--) 277
Elizabeth Maria
  (Rembert) 198
Eugenia C 390
G T 250
George 30, 287
Henrietta M 30
James 91, 401
John D 122
Keren H (--) 288
Laura Jane 286
Lou 401
M V (--) 44
Mary (--) 286
Nancy (--) 250, 401
Nancy (Russell) 140
Nannie J (Dixon) 400
P G 165
Sabrina J 293
Sarah Norman 44
T E (Scott) 289
T H 294
Thomas 140
Thos H 158
Virginia E 122
W D 375
W H 11
W W 40, 84-85, 245,
  247, 256, 268, 337,
  352, 390, 400
Walter 198
William J 400
Wm 286
Wm B 44
Wm E 143
Y H 179
STICKLAND, Mary Ann
  (--) 12
STIDHAM, B F 378
Josia (--) 378
Leonta May 378
STILES, -- (Adams) 383
C A 219
Geo W 383
George W 383-84
Jos C 384
STILLWELL, Elijah 74
Elizabeth (--) 74
J M 169
Margaret 74
Mollie C 29
Richard 29
Sarah A (--) 29
W R 176
STILWELL, Elijah 156
Elizabeth (Houston)
  156

John 74, 156
STINCHCOMB, G W 176
STINSON, Carrie J 91
J W 91
John 265
John Wesley 265
M L (--) 91
Nancy L (--) 265
STIPE, Arminda
  (Parker) 53
C J 119
Carmilla P 366
D H H 242
Hannah Sophia (--) 145
Henry 145, 242, 366
J W 53
Lucy 255
Sophia (--) 242
Sophia H (Whitman) 366
STIVENDER, David 173
Elizabeth (--) 173
STOCKES, John A 56
STOCKMAN, Harriet L
  (--) 268
J Q 221, 268, 276
Robt Dent 268
STOCKS, Thomas 371
STOKES, A J 25, 92, 135,
  139, 151, 161, 187,
  266, 274, 288, 316,
  355, 381, 391, 399
Ann (--) 312
Anna R (Hodges) 163
Augustus W 239
Eleanor K 57
Eliza J (--) 245
Fannie H 163
Franklin Boulware 245
Harry L 355
Ignatius 57
J M 16, 21, 128,
  147, 161
James 355
James M 308
Jefferson 238
Joseph H 163
M S (--) 151
Margaret M (--) 355
Margaret Shand
  (Smith) 161
Mary A (Rumph) 56
Mary E (--) 238
Mary Tate 314
Rebecca (--) 57
Rommie 238
Sallie M 355
Susie B (Bridges) 239
Willie 151
Wm 245, 312
STOLL, Ervin Campbell
  234
James C 87, 116,
  221, 230, 234, 256,

397, 406
Jas C 189, 303
Mary L (--) 234
STONE, -- 219
C Elizabeth 384
Charle B 2
Elizabeth Ann 74
Martha (--) 74
Mary 318
Mary H (--) 63
Octavius 63
Osborne M 117
R R 318
Sidney B (Briscoe) 219
Wallen 74
William F 384
STOREY, Caroline 130
Mary C (--) 130
William F 130
STORMON, Martha Ann
  74
STORR, Joshua 313
Martha H 313
STORY, Geo C 19
Ira 148
Josephine E (Nobles)
  19
R L 148
STOUDEMIRE 22
Lewis 22
Rebecca (--) 373
STOUDENMIRE, George
  92
Magdalene (--) 92
Samuel 92
STOVALL, -- 182
Cornelia A (Fears) 138
Elizabeth (Jeter) 182
Emily R (--) 308
Frances E 303
George 183
Isam 308
Josiah 88, 303
Mary L (--) 88
STOVER, Anna (--) 14
Jeremiah 14
Rachel A 14
STOY, John W 288
STRANGE, Elizabeth Ann
  266
J F 336
Judah Francis 337
Judah Francis
  (Jeters) 337
L B 414
L L 335
Lucinda K (--) 287
Margaret A (--) 414
Mary (Hendersson)
  (Baker) 336
Shackleford 337
STREATER, Jane (--) 73
Mary E 73

STREET, -- 243
Mary Elizabeth 307
Sarah (McClendon) 243
STRICKLAND, A B 126
John 70
Rebecca L (--) 126
Susannah (--) 70
STRICKLIN, David
Hester 120
Ester A (--) 120
N D 120
Nathan D 177
STRINGER, Mary
(Thalley) 276
STRINGFELLOW, Msrtha
14
STRIPLIN, B O 109
Elizabeth R
(Steward) 109
STRIPLING, Ann
(Butler) 345
Bryant 25
David 243, 345
E 105
J B 205
James 21
Maggie 205
Margaret (--) 205
Martha (--) 58
Martha A 374
Robert 41
Robt 58, 131, 205
William 158
STROBEL, Barbara
(Dantzler) 280
Daniel 226
Elizabeth 226
Elvira 226
John 280
Martha (Miller) 280
STROBLE, D L 213
STROMAN, -- 308
Caroline L 308
Louisa Jane 154
STRONG, Afton Lee 152
Charles 125
Christopher Billups
152
Henry Mortimer 152
Mary E (--) 152
S M 152
STROTHER, Harriet A
(Caldwell) 286
John W 103, 120, 286
Wiley W 120
STROUD, Benj H 144
M D 144
Mark 208
Martha (--) 208
Polly 208
Susan F (--) 144
STUART, Frances V
(Palmer) 76

M F 238
W D 76
STUBBLEFIELD, John C
11
STUBBS, Charles E 308
Elizabeth K (--) 238
Ella Tucker (--) 374
H 347
J W 238
James 129
Joel 159
John M 374
Lucinda (--) 183
Martha (--) 159
Mary Ann 106
Nancy 129
Peter 183
Rebecca A 159
Samuel W 370
Thos B 106
William Asprey 347
STUDSTILL, H 110
Mary B (Graham) 110
Nora Ann Nease 253
Sarah Jane (--) 253
Tropu 253
STURGES, Martha (--) 293
Mary Elizabeth 293
Robert 293
STURGESS, Daniel D 199
STURGIS, Daniel D 189
STURKEY, D D 119
Jefferson P 119
Lucy (--) 119
STUTTS, Sarah Ann (--)
339
SUBERS, Frank Perry 103
J J 103
Wm C 247
Zillah (--) 103
SUGGS, Asbury 253
Hester (--) 253
Nelson 254
SULLENBERGER, A S
229
Louisa A 229
SULLIVAN, -- (--) 161
-- (Mims) 300
-- (Vaughn) 300
E S (Vaughan) 290
Hattie G (Humbert) 49
Hewlet 157
J Dunklin 386
J M 12, 290
J N 171, 273
James M 300
Jane Caroline 157
L Mims 289
Lalla 289
Mary (--) 157
Mary V (--) 289
Richard W 161
Sallie E 12

W D 49
SUMMERHILL, Jas 16
Warren 16
SUMMERS, Elizabeth
(--) 22
John Wesley 68
William 270
SUMNER, -- (--) 325
John C 325
Mary (Thoby) 325
SUMPTER, Martha (--) 9
SUNDAY, G W 75
Martha M (--) 75
Mary Elizabeth 75
SUNDY, John 107
Sallie M (--) 107
William Douglas 107
SURTIS, Thomas 48
SUTHERLAND, Henrietta
(--) 228
SUTTON, -- (--) 57
Benjamin 1
J 216
L M 152
Sarah 1
Susannah (--) 1
SWAIN, -- 137, 200
Bettie Rhodes 78
David 175
Deborah (--) 200
Eliza 137
M Callie 359
Mary C (--) 78
W R 78
SWAINE, E J 303
J G 303, 306
Mary A C (--) 303, 306
SWAKARD, S E (--) 117
Salla 117
SWAN, George Margaret
Carter (Berryhill)
229
Thomas E 229
SWEARINGEN, Belle 62
N (--) 62
T 62
SWEARINGIN, Eliza
(Crawford) 247
Hartwell J 247
SWEAT, Georgia Cyrena
84
John B 308
Thomas 84
SWEATMAN, -- 220
Isabella (--) 220
SWEET, Harriet
(Kaigler) 402
James L 402
S S 59, 102, 172, 205,
212, 262, 282, 358
SWENNY, Eliza Jane 112
John 112
SWICORD, Joseph 43

503

Rosanna (--) 56
THWEATT, E P 133
James 6
Mary 283
TICER, Hugh 124
TIDWELL, W W 129
TIGNER, Elizabeth 249
Phillip 249
TIGNOR, Philip 232
Susanah (Slaton) 232
Susannah Rosemand
(--) 233
U C 233
Uuran Cooper 232
TILLER, D 355-56, 359
J L 115
Johnnie Manning
Brown 115
Jos L 382
Nancy (--) 115
TILLEY, Caroline 358
R Caroline 367
TIMBERLAKE, F A 227
Gertrude A (Ramsey)
227
TIMMERMAN, William
Travis 364
TIMMONS, A A (--) 138
B E L 298, 397
D F C 325, 353, 381
M B (--) (Edison) 397
P A (--) (Alford) 397
Partia A 138
T H 252, 265, 270,
276, 314, 348, 350,
386
T I C 138
Thomas H 232
Thos H 119, 147
Thos R 234
William 397
TINDALL, -- (--) 63
Annie 63
H W 63
Judith W (--) 376
William B 124
TINLEY, James 306, 312
TINSLEY, -- 166
Cassius 166
Charles H 310
E C 310
S E (Darden) 310
TIPPINS, Cynthia 213
Elizabeth S 333
L A H 251
Martha S M (--) 251
Phillip 213
William W 155
TISON, James G 151
Judith (--) 402
Sarah Eugenie 151
Sterling 402
TODD, -- (--) 251

Geraldine E 339
Nancy 311
Rutherford Pressley
251
S R 251
TOLBERT, -- 241
Rebecca (--) 241
TOLER, Patsy 311
TOLLE, C J 267
TOMLIN, Elizabeth (--)
406
Jason 406
TOMLINSON, Alice V
(--) 61
John G 61
John T 280
Sarah 268
William 61
TOMMEY, V R (Manson)
272
TOMPKINS, -- (--) 391
David L 391
James 391
John 237
L A 358
Mary 391
Rhoda J (Crum) 237
TONEY, -- (--) 359
Annie (Patat) 344
C E (--) 377
Fannie C 377
J N 359
Sidney 344
TOOKE, Elizabeth (--)
232
J J 58
James 232
Jane E 232
Joseph 54
Martha 54
Mary Jane 331
William Burt 58
TOOLE, C J 92, 119, 370
TOOLEY, George B 82
R H 82
TOOMBS, Eva 213
Margaret C (--) 213
R E 213
Sarah Catharine 213
TOOTLE, Silas 78
TORBET, Lou (Burt) 252
R F 252
TORLEY, Alfred F 152
Wilhelmina E
(Purse) 152
TOWERS, Isaac A 346
TOWNES, McCaully G 229
TOWNS, -- 315
H L 315
Virlinda (Bealle) 315
TOWNSEND, Amanda 216
Dorinada (--) 216
Elizabeth (--) 131

H G 271
J Fletcher (Norwood)
139
Joel 310
Joel W 55
Maria (--) 310
Mary 131
Meekin 368
Sallie H 368
Thomas 131
W R 216
TOWNSLEY, Elizabeth A
341
Lot 341
Sarah (--) 341, 372
TRACY, -- 103
William Rush 103
TRADER, Elender 10
TRAMMEL, Irene 98
TRAMMELL, -- 101
Eliza H (--) 94
Elizabeth (--) 101
Henry 98
Jehu 82
W H 404
W T 94, 98
TRANTHAM, Eunice S
(--) 135
John 135
Mary Jane 135
TRAVIS, -- 225
-- (--) 225
Eldesa (Parker) 345
Elizabeth (Smith) 345
John 225
John S 345-46
Martha H 225
TRAWICK, Jas W 269, 282
TRAXLER, Ann E (--) 54
TRAYLOR, -- 217
J C 217
TRAYWICK, Hiram 35
J B 62, 205, 227,
236, 332
TREADAWAY, James M
174
TREADWELL, Anna (--)
87
Benjamin F 87
C A (Pendergrass) 8
David 61, 73
Hardy 8
Mary (--) 9
Mary Ann (Bennett) 61
Samuel 9
William B 87
TREUTLEN, -- (--) 348
Annie Julia 348
John A 375
John F 348
TRICE, Jane 52
Martha Ann 52
William 52

J M 123, 302
Lizzie 302
M H (--) 389
M L 216, 349
Mary J 389
Nancy M (Bradford) 263
Sarah T (Blount) 83
W H 123
Wyley 359
UPSHAW, Elizabeth
    Heard (Tucker) 247
    M C 247
UPTON, -- (Bird) 38
    John 278
    Jordan C 278
    Sarah M (--) 313
    William R 313
URQUHART, John 214
    John A 362
    Mary Jane (Shorter)
    214
USHER, Elizabeth C
    (--) 247
    Noah 247
UTSEY, D D 217
    Emma E (--) 217
Van BRANT, Sarah J
    (--) 172
VAN HORN, George 374
    Leonora (Elliott) 374
VAN, Edward 79
    Harriet R (Skinner) 79
VANCE, -- (--) 341
    Charles E 341
    J A 405
VANLANDINGHAM,
Elizabeth
    (--) 35
    Francis 35
    Peter 413
    Wm 35
VANN, Joseph 79
    Mattie (--) 79
    Willie Seals 79
VANZANT, Elizabeth
    (--) 80
    Lewis 80
    Lou J 80
VARBRACLE, -- (--) 394
    William H 394
VARN, Aaron 16
    Adeline (--) 26
    Esther 334
    Gabriel 26
    L B 276, 357
    Rebecca A 277
    Sarah (--) 16
    Wm T 334
VARNADOW,   Rebecca
369
VARNER, David M 20
    David Mortimer 20
    George 159

L Isabella (--) 20
VARNUM, Susan L
    (Saxon) 12
    William M 12
VASON, Joseph 231
    Nancy (--) 231
VAUGHAN, E S 290
    Eliza C P (--) 202
VAUGHN, -- 300
    Geo J C 318
    John H 368
    John P 190
    Martha (--) 368
    Martha F (--) 190
VAUGHT, -- 403
    -- (--) 337
    Armlain Bryan 337
    E B (--) 339
    Joseph 403
    Mary Ellen 356
    Peter 3, 356
    Sarah M (Brantley) 403
    William 339
VEACH, Ann B 357
VEAL, Ann Eliza (--) 56
    Charlotte (--) 18
    William 18
VEAZY, T J 198
VENABLE, -- (--) 337
    George M 337
    J L 106
    John 58
    John M 12
    Josephine Matilda 197
    Martha A B (--) 12
    Matilda H (--) 106
    W R 197
VERDERE, Mary F 403
VAREEN, Caroline Jane
    232
VERNER, David M 153
    Minnie Bell 153
VERNON, -- (--) 10
VERSTILLE, Ellen J
    (Lockhart) 137
    H W 137
VESSELS, James 162
VICKERS, Amanda
    (Bradford) 19
    Matthew 19
    Robert H 3
VILLENEUVE, -- (--) 291
    Joseph Henry 291
VINCENT, Hannah 98
    Rebecca (--) 98
    Thomas 98
VINING, A S 370
VINSON, Fannie L (--)
    350
    J W 164, 350
    Julia T (Beall) 164
    Lydia (--) 180
    Matilda 363

W G 202, 279
Wm G 180
VIRDEN, Elizabeth
    (Gordon) 111
    William 111
VOGT, Julia C (--) 225
    T P 225
W--, A J 35
    A M 116
    A W 53, 56
    B E 107
    E W 116
    J A 58
    J F 364
    J H 89
    J P 96
    J T 128
    L C 110
    R F 107
    S 71
    S C 121
    W A 33
    W W 128
WADDEL, -- (Peek) 408
    Jno O 408
WADDELL, Ella Peek
    (--) 49
    John O 49
WADDY, Geo E 154
    Lucinda J (Carnes) 154
WADE, -- (--) 259
    A P 195
    Amanda 320
    Amanda (--) 393
    Catharine A (--) 189
    Catherine E (--) 78
    Daniel F 78
    Elijah 306
    Eliza F 393
    Jessee 195
    Jno B 259
    John 320, 393
    John E 407
    Lucy (--) 320
    Margaret Amanda 78
    Mary (--) 179, 306
    Moses 179
    Nancy (Harris) 407
    Peyton L 10, 18
    Rebecca 179
    Thomas H 204
WADSWORTH, E 248
    Nancy (Johnson) 18
    W W 252, 280, 303-04
    Walter 18
WAGNER, Barnard C 11
    John 11
    Matt 169
    Samuel J 172, 178
WAGNON, Harriet C
    (--) 364
    Thomas P 364
WAHLEY, Eliza Jane 200

Thos 200
WAITE, F C 333
  Irene Allen (--) 333
WAITS, Emma N (--) 238
  John H 238
  Mamie Louisa 238
WALDEN, Gracie 304
WALDRON, -- (--) 376
  Lucinda (--) 138
  Malcolm 138
  Malcomb W 376
  Samuel Thomas 138
WALDROP, Mary Sison
278
  Robt 278
  Sarah (--) 278
WALDRUP, -- 403
  Julia A (Caldwell) 404
  M (Jones) 403
WALKER, -- 188
  -- (--) 292, 343
  A W 330
  Amanda (--) 18
  Caroline E (Howard) 22
  Charles 408
  Charles B 370
  Charlie H 153
  Chas A 253
  Chas S 370
  Clara (Frederick) 102
  E F 147
  Edward B 22
  Eliza A W (Cain) 45
  Eliza Ellen 14
  Eliza M C (Nutting)
  (Hirston) 147
  Elizabeth (--) 364
  Frances E (--) 159
  G W 394
  Geo W 400
  George Towns 147
  H A C 179, 241, 251,
  275, 308
  H A D 122
  H H 10
  Harriet (--) 209
  Harriet C 24
  Henry 253, 292
  Henry H 376
  J B 119
  J E 147
  J F 343
  James F 18
  Jno G 81
  L M (--) 147
  LeG G 372
  Lou (Crocker) 253
  M J (--) 93
  Margaret Miller 29
  Maria W 66
  Martha (--) 66
  Martha C (--) 171
  Martha H 364

Mary 207
Mary (Boyd) 370
Mary (Cunningham) 157
Mary A (--) 14
Nancy (--) 177
Paulina P (Blount) 376
R J 381
Reuben Tooke 93
Robert 29, 45, 153
Samuel P 41
Sarah F 18
Thos D 171
W A 159
W B 93
William 364
William A 159
Winifred Letitia
  Delilah (Camp) 81
Wm H 14, 207
WALKLY, E Smith 22
WALL, James G 56, 146
  Mary (--) 146
  Rebecca S 256
  W 168
WALLACE, -- (--) 328
  Barnabas 196, 271
  J H 328
  Jane (--) 196, 271
  Martha A 196
  Mattie E 328
  W K 180
  William K 185
  Willie 327
WALLER, Ann A (Tatom)
52
  Elizabeth W (--) 380
  Emaline (--) 176
  J E 176
  James E 129
  Jennie 166
  John 380
  M Virginia (--) 210
  Rosalie 210
  T T 52
  W A 210
WALLIN, Emily
  (Williams) 199
  Jesse 199
WALLIS, B 311
  Bland 329
  Nancy 311
WALLS, Elizabeth S
  (Ansley) 59
  Oliver 59
WALSER(?), Elvira
  (Cole) 203
  T J 203
WALSH, Mary Alieff 319
  R D 319
  R E (--) 319
  Tracy R 26
WALTER, Charles 398
  Charles Frederic 398

Mary 398
WALTERS, Joseph 127
  Sarah E 127
WALTHALL, M L 112
WALTHOUR, Marcia
  (Slappey) 82
  Robert 82
WALTON, -- (--) 166
  David A 195
  Jno H 356
  Lizell (Wootten) 356
  M F (--) 88
  O F 88
  Rosalius J 166
WANNAMAKER, Charles
  Thornwell 101
  S A (--) 101
  T E 101
WARD, -- (--) 363
  Bethena 16
  Bethena (--) 16
  Calvin J 365
  Catharine
  (Carmichael) 351
  Edny (Pool) 241
  Eliza Ann 360
  Ella F (Dantzler) 365
  Feraby (--) 367
  George T 2
  Gus 332
  J L D 351
  John B 230
  Jonathan 16
  Maggie (Stripling)
  205
  Mary (--) 144
  Mary E 208
  P H 205
  Peter Z 363
  Philip 114
  R H 121
  R M 114
  Susannah 332
  Thomas 241
  Virginia A 2
WARDLAW, Eddie 19
  Hugh 378
  J B 90
  J P 339, 344
  James Evans 294
  Jane (--) 378
  Mary (--) 19, 132
  Susan J 378
  W J 19, 132, 294
WARE, A C 196
  Augustus G 164
  Edward Roswell 226
  Henry B 30
  Henry Crosley 141
  James 125
  Johnathan 200
  Margaret Elizabeth
  (Bacon) 226

Turner 205
W A 374
WEBER, -- 146
Samuel A 50, 54, 85,
103, 146, 173, 293,
403
WEBSTER, Caroline 340
Caroline (Hancock) 274
Malissa A C 187
Reuben 237
William S 401
Wm 274
WEEKS, Ashly P 236
Catharine (--) 236
William 184
WEEMES, Darius R 164
Ritha (Sewell) 164
WEEMS, D J 200, 244, 318
Frances E (Holbrook)
333
J B 333
W F 260
WELBORN, C G 38
WELBURN, Elizabeth
(--) 196
WELCHEL, Mary Ann
(Waters) 54
WELD, Mary Lucinda 254
WELDON, Jane C
(Phillips) 74
John W 74
WELLS, Berry 270
G H 3, 46, 79, 82,
149, 295, 352, 355
George 206, 235
Henrietta Elizabeth
(--) 270
J J 183
Jennie E 273
John 251
Joseph T 346
M H 318
Mary (--) 235
Mary (Moore) 206
N M (Heath) 346
R A (--) 183
R N 205, 225, 259,
275, 277, 366
Sarah (--) 346
Stephen G 146
Susan A 235
Tempy Ann 270
William 346
WERDON, Geo B 181
WERTS, Mary W 331
WESSON, -- (--) 85
WEST, Albert L 387
Albert Lawrence 387
Ann E (--) 373
Anna 184
Augusta E (Jordan) 304
C B 264
Cicero L 303

David 302
E M 3
Georgia C (--) 387
Harriet C (--) 67
Henry 265
J F 373
J S 260, 358
John E 304
John S 265
Joseph T 266
Marion W 298
Sophronia (--) 303
Sophronia E (--) 298
Virginia F 264
William 231, 298, 303
William Derrick 99
Winiford (--) 3
Winnifred (--) 277
Wm T 5
WESTBERRY, William T
23
WESTBURY, Thos 279
WESTER, -- (Bennett) 60
W V 60
WESTON, Anna Pope 361
J W 280, 286-87, 376
Mary (--) 361
Stephen 361
WESTWOOD, John 217
WEYMAN, Edward 156
Elizabeth (--) 156
Frances Harriet 156
WHALEY, Geo 83
John D (--) 192
WHARTON, Benjamin 219
WHEDBEE, Eliza Ansley
108
Mary J 108
Susan (--) 108
WHEELER, H 40
Isabella (Hamilton) 143
Paul 143
William H 89
WHETSTONE, Absalom
110,
317
Absolom 105
Elizabeth (--) 264
Henry 103
J D H 179
John 317
Joseph Edwards 264
Mary (--) 317
Mary S 103
N C 264
WHISNANT, Adam 281
D 32
Letty 281
Susannah (--) 281
WHISTENHUNT, -- (--)
233
A C 233
WHITAKER, -- (--) 293,

349
-- (Cantey) 379
Frances (--) 292-93
George A 203
Henrietta (Leonard)
135
Hudson 203
J T 326
James C 349
Lewis Pitts 260
Martha M 292
Mary A 312
Mary S 4
N H (--) 260
R J 292-93
S E 379
Samuel E 136
Samuel S 4
Samuel V 293
W C 260
Willis 162
WHITE, -- 351
-- (--) 58
A R 90
Ann H 274
Anthony 275
Benjamin D 134
Carrie K (--) 106
D T 251
David L 270
Edith Septima 275
Edward 114
Elizabeth 270
Elizabeth (--) 248
Elizabeth A (--) 275
Ella 164
Elvira (--) 114
Emily Celestie 44
Emma 58
G (Culler) 361
George 346
H O 215
H V 180
J 89
J M 106
James T 106
James W 321
Jane P 345
John 248, 308
Leah E (--) 40
Lucy (--) 89
M H 19, 239
Marlin 58
Martha D (Mitchell)
321
Martha V 137
Mary Barbara 391
Mary E 174
Mary Hollis (--) 180
Mary L (Bryant) 128
Mary S (--) 44
Mary Susan 114, 209
Miller H 227

510

N L (--) (--) (--) 319
Nancy 248
Rebecca (--) 391
Rebecca (Pulliam) 295
Rebecca S 98-99
Richard 98
Robert 93
Ruth (--) 98
S F 251
Sallie A 93
Stephen 295
Thomas 391
Thomas H 174
Thomas S 18
Vallie 307
W H H 137
W L 356
W T 40
Wiley M 44
William 128
WHITEFIELD, J T 85
Martha (Griffin) 85
WHITEHEAD, Charley O 2
Eldridge 132
Fannie M 237
Jane (--) 2
M E 257
Marcus J 2
Mary A (--) 237
Sarah (--) 132
Thomas 237
WHITEHURST, -- (--) 401
Daniel S 401
Elizabeth A 159
James Jackson 159
John 401
M A M 10
Mary E (Harley) 159
Pelatiah 10, 395
Sarah (--) 10
Sarah (Pound) 395
WHITELY, J 176
WHITFIELD, B R 142
David H 139
Fannie 409
Mary A E (--) 142
N (--) 409
WHITHEAD, Robert W 165
WHITING, E M 358, 379
WHITLEY, Louise Mary Ann (Priestly) 176
WHITLOW, John G 268
Nancy 374
Sarah C (Gunby) 268
WHITMAN, Davis 366
Fetnal (--) 366
Sophia H 366
WHITNEY, Albert N 366
J E 177
WHITTEN, Arfax 105

Barksdale A 400
Julia 2
M L 306
Mary (--) 400
Orpha Judson 105
Willie P 400
WHITTLE, Floyd 136
K (--) 51
Kitturah (--) 136
Leslie 51
W F 51
Willie J 136
WICHER, David L 30
Nannie J (Lane) 30
WICKER, -- (--) 180
Andrew Middleton 322
Lula Gertrude 233
Nancy (Hayes) 322
Thomas 180
Thomas V 233
WIDEMAN, Emily H 340
L A 281
L E 361
Margaret (McMillan) 351
Samuel 351
WIGGINS, -- 158, 385
-- (--) 385
C E 403
Clara Columbia (Pierce) 34
James A 154
Leml G R 77, 84, 86, 122, 125
Mary Harden (--) 103
N H 34
R L 103, 304, 346, 395
R S 306
Robert L 84, 100, 256
Robt L 278
Sarah A 385
Wm A 291, 297
WIGHTMAN, Anabel Faust 164
Edith 391
Philip D 48
W M 249, 391
W S 410
WILBURN, Mary E (Mood) 67
Wm W 67
WILCOX, -- (--) 65
Caroline M (--) 147
J M 65
James D 147
John N 101
Sarah 147
WILD, Sarah (Densler) 227
W H 227
William 227
WILDER, -- (Sherman) 39

Ann (--) 344
Eliza C (Lowry) 91
Fannie 131
Lucy B 403
Mary (Bowers) 240
Mary (Womack) 314
Milton 91, 403
N 240
Rufus E 314
William 39
William A 314
Wm 131
WILEY, Henry 202
Isa Ann (Reynolds) 202
WILKERSON, -- 364
E B 142
Henrietta J (--) 364
Isaac 368
WILKES, J Wesley 332
Martha K (--) 332
WILKINS, John 66, 95
Mary C (--) 66, 95
Sarah Matilda 66, 95
WILKINSON, -- 379
Annie C (Taylor) 379
E J (Hill) 397
Jno J 100
Robert W 397
WILL, Margaret W (--) 6
Robert W 6
WILLBANKS, Abijah 304
WILLBORN, L S 176
WILLCOX, Mark 358
Rebecca 358
Sarah A E (--) 358
WILLERFORD, Lazina C (Brooks) 339
M C 339
WILLHITE, Philemon 301
WILLIAM, Jere S 350
WILLIAMS, -- 116
-- (--) 58, 362
-- (--) (Murphy) 130
-- (Cullen) 362
-- (Stapleton) 286
A E 104, 293, 382
A English 234-35, 272, 287, 305, 317
A L (--) 41
A M 341
A M (--) 242
A W 374
Abe 116
Abe M 243
Abraham 82
Abraham McKinna 82
Ada 180
Addie Lee (Coston?) 401
Alexander 205
Alfred W 107
Allen 199
Amanda (Wade) 320

513

Harriet 387
Joyce (--) 312
Lucius L 312
Margaret L 312
WOFFORD, Harvey 368
WOLDRIDGE, A J 21, 41, 49
WOLF, Hattie A (--) 230
Inez 230
M M 230
Philip 74
Susan E (Rape) 74
WOLFE, Caroline A (Kaigler) 287
Charles Wesley 99
Charles Wilson 178
Joseph A 287
N S 287
WOLLARD, J B 85
WOMACK, Mary 314
W W 206
WOOD, -- (Hanson) 297
A E (--) 277
Ann 244
Benj J 2
C H 55
Cornelia M (Schinholster) 203
Drucilla (--) 124
Eliza (Dixon) 104
Elizabeth W (Hicklin) 92
Eva 55
Harriet P (--) 2
Igdaliah 104
Isham 124
Isham J 7
J A 29, 48, 107
J M 15, 220
James L 234
Jesse 33
Joe 297
Keziah (--) 345
L 12, 34, 52, 80, 115, 139, 142, 153, 163, 167, 198, 208, 256-57, 283, 298, 313-14, 358, 367, 405, 407, 415
Landy 102, 277
Malcom Vesuvius 277
Martha W (Duke) 321
Mary Drucilla (Scarborough) 319
Mary Jane 7
Rebecca (--) 244
Rebecca (Everett) 234
Rebecca A (Varn) 277
Richard 321
Robert 244
Rolly 345
Sarah Rebecca (O'Hara) 15

Sue Ada 55
Thos C 203
Winfred 345
Winton (--) 314
WOODALL, Francis 350
W H 218, 243, 264, 280, 293
WOODBERRY, Samuel 198, 284
WOODBERY, S 105, 128
Samuel 199, 291
WOODHAM, Ariss 211
Cason H (Riley) 211
Edward 149
Malinda 149
WOODING, -- (--) 301
Benjamin L 148
Carrie V 148
Hugh Allen 301
Mary E 148
Rosa P (--) 148
WOODRUFF, Agatha (Medlock) 8
James 8
M 99
WOODS, Andrew 183
Malcom V 289
Martha S G (Gibson) 200
Mary I 353
Nancy (--) 353
S A 183
William 353
WOODWARD, A L 333
E (--) (Gates) 168
Elizabeth W 341
H A (Hammond) 333
Irwin H 168
John L 13, 296
Martha (Lockett) 168
Oren 168
R S 8
Randolph 296
T W 343
WOODY, James 29, 39
Mary Virginia 29
Miranda 39
WOOLLEY, Joseph 134
Margaret (--) 134
Mary A (--) 226
WOOTEN, H E (--) 91
H P 252
Hattiet E (Potter) 365
J D 91
James Albert 91
M C (--) 252
Martha 199
W J 190
WOOTON, Henrietta (Tuck) (Bates) 322
W J 322, 361
Wm J 322

WOOTTEN, A E (--) 356
Bathsheba N (Hinton) 343
Fannie (Dent) 252
Jesse C 252
Jno B 356
Lizell 356
Simon 55
Thomas L 343
W L 289, 334
WORD, Elisabeth (Brown) 368
Georgia (Mitchell) 333
Sarah 263
T J 333
William B 368
WORLEY, A G 18, 79, 99, 182
A J 198
James H 69
WRIGHT, -- 336
Alex P 152
Alexander H 302
Alice Kendall 387
Amma (--) 399
Arminius 84, 94, 98, 121, 166, 221, 291
Bird W 128
C C 37
C K (--) 387
D J 143
Daniel J 291, 371
Duncan 287
Eleanor 287
Elizabeth (--) 155, 296
Ella 287
Emily Palestine (Robinson) 221
Ida F (Allen) 37
J A 367
J C 155
J L 387
J M 275
James 336, 399
James A 221
James Arminius 221
Jane E 336
Jas M 72
Jno C 5
Jno G 6
John L 14
John W 66, 95
Lizzie 399
Lou Myles 155
Lucy G (Andrew) 407
M C (Brown) 291
Mary 385
Mary (--) 42, 252
Mary C 371
Mary C (--) 143, 371
Mary E (Fagan) 367
Rachel (Bradford) 14

Heritage Books by Brent H. Holcomb:

Bute County, North Carolina, Land Grant Plats and Land Entries

*CD: Early Records of Fishing Creek Presbyterian Church,
Chester County, South Carolina, 1799–1859*

CD: Kershaw County, South Carolina, Minutes of the County Court, 1791–1799

CD: Marriage and Death Notices from The Charleston *[S.C.] Observer, 1827–1845*

CD: South Carolina, Volume 1

*CD: Winton (Barnwell) County, South Carolina Minutes of
County Court and Will Book 1, 1785–1791*

Charleston District, South Carolina, Journal of the Court of Ordinary, 1812–1830
Caroline T. Moore, Edited by Brent H. Holcomb

*Chester County, South Carolina, Deed Abstracts,
Volume I: 1785–1799 [1768–1799] Deed Books A-F*

Deaths and Obituary Notices from the
Southern Christian Advocate, *1867–1878*

*Early Records of Fishing Creek Presbyterian Church, Chester County,
South Carolina, 1799–1859, with Appendices of the Visitation List of
Rev. John Simpson, 1774–1776 and the Cemetery Roster, 1762–1979*
Brent H. Holcomb and Elmer O. Parker

Kershaw County, South Carolina, Minutes of the County Court, 1791–1799

Laurens County, South Carolina, Minutes of the County Court, 1786–1789

*Lower Fairforest Baptist Church, Union County, South Carolina:
Minutes 1809–1875, Membership Lists through 1906*

*Marriage and Death Notices from Baptist Newspapers of South Carolina,
Volume 2: 1866–1887*

*Marriage and Death Notices from Columbia, South Carolina Newspapers,
1838–1860; Including Legal Notices from Burnt Counties*

Marriage and Death Notices from The Charleston Observer, *1827–1845*

Marriage Notices from the Southern Christian Advocate, *1867–1878*

Memorialized Records of Lexington District, South Carolina, 1814–1825

*Newberry County, South Carolina Deed Abstracts,
Volume I: Deed Books A-B, 1785–1794 [1751–1794]*

*Newberry County, South Carolina Deed Abstracts,
Volume II: Deed Books C, D-2, and D, 1794–1800 [1765–1800]*

*Parish Registers of Prince George Winyah Church,
Georgetown, South Carolina, 1815–1936*

*Petitions for Land from the South Carolina Council Journals
Volume V: 1757–1765*

*Record of Deaths in Columbia, South Carolina, and
Elsewhere as Recorded by John Glass, 1859–1877*

South Carolina Deed Abstracts, 1773–1778, Books F-4 through X-4

South Carolina Deed Abstracts, 1776–1783, Books Y-4 through H-5

South Carolina Deed Abstracts, 1783–1788, Books I-5 through Z-5

*The Bedenbaugh-Betenbaugh Family:
Descendants of Johann Michael Bidenbach from
Germany to South Carolina, 1752*

Tryon County, North Carolina, Minutes of the
Court of Pleas and Quarter Sessions, 1769–1779

Union County, South Carolina Deed Abstracts,
Volume I: Deed Books A-F, 1785–1800 [1752–1800]
Volume II: Deed Books G-K, 1800–1811 [1769–1811]
Volume III: Deed Books L-P, 1811–1820 [1770–1820]

Winton (Barnwell) County, South Carolina Minutes of
County Court and Will Book 1, 1785–1791

York County, South Carolina, Will Abstracts, 1787–1862 [1770–1862]